Y0-DBS-364

SYMPOSIA OF THE

SOCIETY FOR EXPERIMENTAL BIOLOGY

NUMBER XXXX

PROCEEDINGS OF A MEETING

HELD IN DURHAM, ENGLAND

SEPTEMBER 1985

SYMPOSIA OF THE

SOCIETY FOR EXPERIMENTAL BIOLOGY

SYMPOSIA OF THE
SOCIETY FOR EXPERIMENTAL BIOLOGY

NUMBER XXXX

PLASTICITY IN PLANTS

EDITED BY
D. H. JENNINGS AND A. J. TREWAVAS

Published for the Society for Experimental Biology
by The Company of Biologists Limited, Department of Zoology,
University of Cambridge, Downing Street, Cambridge CB2 3EJ

Typeset and Printed by the Pindar Group of Companies, Scarborough, North Yorkshire

Published by The Company of Biologists Limited,
Department of Zoology, University of Cambridge,
Downing Street, Cambridge CB2 3EJ

*Typeset and Printed by the Pindar Group of Companies,
Scarborough, North Yorkshire*

ISBN 0 948601 03 5

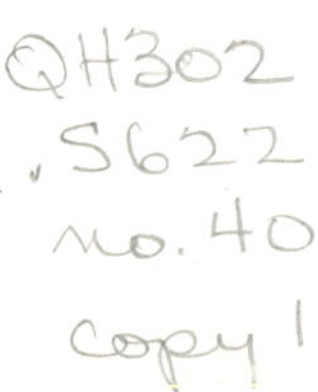

CONTENTS

PREFACE

This volume contains the written contributions of those who were invited to speak at the fortieth symposium of the Society for Experimental Biology held from 3 to 6 September 1985, at the University of Durham. As will be alluded to in the Introduction, the symposium can be considered as a sequel to the thirty-first held also in Durham in 1976.

We are most grateful to Michael Black, John Bryant, Elizabeth Cutter, Don Grierson, John Raven and Harry Smith for their advice at the early stages of planning the symposium. We are also grateful to the University of Durham for its hospitality and the help given by the Botany Department during the symposium. Our particular gratitude is extended to Alan Pearson who did a meticulous job in the administration of the symposium, thus contributing greatly to its success. We thank the British Council for meeting the expenses of some of the overseas participants.

D. H. Jennings
A. J. Trewavas

December 1985.

INTRODUCTION

A. J. TREWAVAS

Botany Department, Edinburgh University, Edinburgh EH9 3JH, UK

and D. H. JENNINGS

Botany Department, Liverpool University, Liverpool L69 3BX, UK

The expression of an individual genotype can be modified by its environment. The amount that it can be modified can be termed its plasticity. This plasticity can be either morphological or physiological; these are inter-related (Bradshaw, 1965). This volume about plasticity in plants is the fruitful consequence of our mutual interest in the phenomenon. Both of us had highlighted previously its importance; one from a more ecological viewpoint (Jennings, 1977) and the other from the developmental viewpoint (Trewavas, 1981). Indeed one of us (Jennings, 1977) had suggested that plasticity in plants should be the subject of a future Society for Experimental Biology Symposium.

This proposal has come to fruition! Though there is an important chapter by Grime on the ecological consequences for plants of plasticity and ecological aspects are often implicit *in passim*, we have focused on plasticity and stability in plant development. There is little need to argue that decision but we did feel that without a proper understanding of the physiological and molecular basis, there will be inadequate progress in understanding the ecological and evolutionary aspects of plasticity and stability. The short statement that follows represents what we feel are the salient features of this fundamental matter of plasticity and stability in plant development.

Those who study animal development and embryology are perhaps most struck by the obvious early processes of tissue specification (canalization), and the sheer complexity of visible changes all of which occur with remarkable reproducibility. Animal development is a very stable and reproducible phenomenon. This may simply result from the protection against the environment afforded to the growing embryo by the egg or uterus; the more extreme environmental variations are mitigated. But it is more probable that the stability results from the extensive and complex control circuitry built into animal development. Organisms with a very complicated distribution of labour amongst the respective parts must be very exact in the reproduction of that structure; development is stable because it is resistant to many of the internal chemical changes which inevitably follow any environmental variation. The adaptiveness of animals lies in the brain, in the almost endless number of combinations in which the different tissues can be made to work together to produce different types of behaviour. The most plastic characteristic of animals is probably their behaviour.

Even simple observation shows how different plant development can be. On individual plants of the same species, the number of branches, roots, buds, fruits, leaves can be greatly variable; the form and structure of large plants, like trees, can be visibly different, phenotypic variations in internode, leaf and petiolc size, shape and volume and an evident unusual regenerative capability all speak of different types of control. However, the pattern of change is not random. These modifications of structure occur because plants are sessile and, although they have a distinct embryonic phase ending with the formation of the seed, the embryogenetic phase continues with meristem development throughout the life cycle. The sessile plant unlike the motile animal cannot avoid environmental variation and predation. Plants respond plastically to these variations by adjusting the developing plant body to best sequester local resources. They thus help achieve desirable growth and reproductive goals by physiological and structural modification. Plants actively change their pattern and form of development in response to environmental variations rather than resist the effects of such environmental change. These plastic aspects to development must result from control structures inherently different from those operating in animal development. The molecular basis may be entirely novel. However, not all characteristics of plant development are plastic and certainly the degree of plasticity of any individual aspect of growth varies through different species and taxa. In plants, unlike animals, stable and plastic aspects to development exist side by side.

In this volume, these two aspects of development, stability and plasticity are explored. The book covers a range of intriguing plant phenomena and discusses the degree of stability (or plasticity) which can presently by assessed for many of these. One unexpected feature to emerge is that processes of apparent morphological stability might hide beneath them a great deal of plasticity at lower levels of organization.

Figure 1 summarizes this possibility for the induction of flowering. The apparently very stable and final phenomenon of flower production is preceded by very considerable plasticity in the histological and molecular events. The evidence for this view is expanded by Bernier in his chapter on flower induction. Flowering is not unique in this respect since the induction of many processes of development, abscission, sex expression, root formation or regeneration, breakage of dormancy and cell division seems equally plastic in the molecular manner in which they can be initiated. Recent work

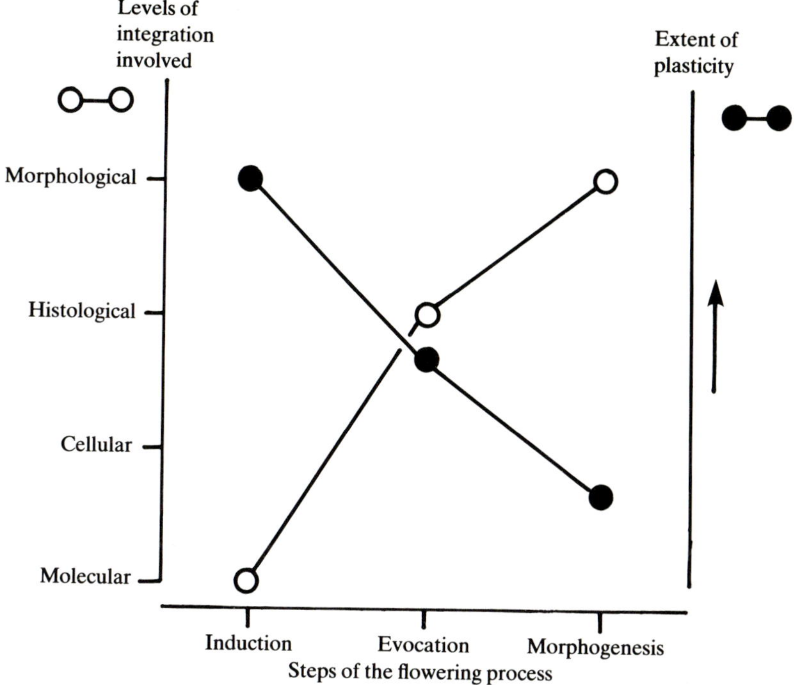

Fig. 1. The figure summarizes the levels of integration involved in recognizable stages of flower induction and the degree of plasticity in the associated events involved in these three stages. Figure kindly provided by G. Bernier.

shows that many of the metabolic events of the cell cycle previously thought to be necessary for mitosis can be simply dissociated with no ill effects on the division process (Mitchison, 1984); similarly for cell expansion (see chapter by Trewavas). Such information should caution us in the assumption of implicit seqential molecular and even histological events as necessary precedents to developmental change. Possibly the more complicated the event, the greater the possibilities for plasticity in the order, type and expression of subordinated constituents of the process.

Present information suggests that the initial changes in developmental induction may owe much more to a balance of probabilities than many experimental scientists would like to contemplate. Nevertheless, the chapter by Jennings concerning development in higher fungi indicates how an assessment of the probability of the occurrence of certain hyphal events helps model the developmental processes which can take place in a fungus. A stochastic approach to the induction of development is not an easy bed fellow with the approach via test tubes, isolated enzymes or exact measurements of growth substance levels. Nevertheless the information obtained by such an approach briefly draws aside a curtain; it provides an all-too-fleeting glimpse of the probable complexity of the control systems which must be involved in development. It suggests the presence of control systems for assessment and refinement, as well as initiation, of control systems for generating the balance between different metabolic and histological events and refining the balance when this is found wanting in certain constituents or processes, and, perhaps, of control systems for measuring the strengths of relationships between different areas of metabolism. It is in the metabolic and cellular control mechanisms that the evident difference between plasticity and stability must be sought. At the present there are only faint indications of how relevant questions may be posed but some of the difficulties may be mitigated by using the thinking and methods already available for analysing complicated systems structures.

It is 9 years since the thirty-first symposium of the Society for Experimental Biology concerned with 'Integration of Activity in the Higher Plant'. Then homeostatic control mechanisms were very much in the minds of plant physiologists. It should be clear from the above and the contents of this volume, that now the outlook is different. In another 9 years, it may be time to assess whether the newer ways of thinking and the new methodologies discussed in this book have helped improve understanding of that most complex of botanical problems, the development of form.

References

BRADSHAW, A. D (1965). Evolutionary significance of phenotypic plasticity in plants. *Adv. Genet.* **13**, 115–155.

JENNINGS, D. H. (1977). Introduction. In *Integration of Activity in the Higher Plant. 31st Symposium of the Society for Experimental Biology* (ed. D. H. Jennings), pp. 1–5. Cambridge, Cambridge University Press.

MITCHISON, J. M. (1984). Dissociation of Cell Cycle Events. In *Cell Cycle Clocks* (ed. L. N. Edmund), pp. 163–173. New York: Marcel Dekker Inc.

TREWAVAS, A. J. (1981). How do plant growth substances work? *Pl. Cell Environ.* **4**, 203–228.

THE ECOLOGICAL SIGNIFICANCE OF PLASTICITY

J. P. GRIME, J. C. CRICK AND J.E. RINCON

Unit of Comparative Plant Ecology (NERC), Department of Botany, University of Sheffield, Sheffield S10 2TN, UK

Summary

Plastic responses of plants to environmental factors may be placed in an ecological context by regarding them as components of sets of traits which are predictably related to habitat stability and productivity. In ephemeral plants of temporary habitats plasticity is a major component of the mechanisms which tend to sustain reproduction when these plants are exposed to stress. When perennials of more stable habitats are subjected to stress the most frequently observed effect of plastic changes in allocation is to defer reproduction, a mechanism which appears to safeguard survival of the parent plant.

It is suggested that plasticity is of vital importance in resource acquisition by plants. This hypothesis is supported by the results of experiments in which the roots and shoots of plants of contrasted ecology have been subjected to controlled patchiness in resource supply. We conclude that in plants of productive habitats high morphological plasticity is part of the foraging mechanisms which project new leaves and roots into the resource-rich zones of the constantly changing environmental mosaic created by the activity of competing plants. In long-lived plants of chronically unproductive habitats plasticity is expressed primarily through reversible physiological changes. These appear to maintain the viability and functional efficiency of leaves and roots over their long life spans and facilitate exploitation of the pulses of temporary and unpredictable resource supply which are characteristic of unproductive habitats.

Introduction

In previous analyses of the significance of plasticity in plants, many different examples of adjustments in the number, size, form and physiology of vegetative or reproductive structures have been documented. It is established that such changes arise not only from constraints on development imposed directly by the environment but also, and more usually, from

Table 1. *Some characteristics of competitive, stress-tolerant and ruderal plants.*

	Competitive	Stress-tolerant	Ruderal
(i) *Morphology*			
1. Life forms	Herbs, shrubs and trees	Lichens, bryophytes, herbs, shrubs and trees	Herbs, bryophytes
2. Morphology of shoot	High dense canopy of leaves. Extensive lateral spread above and below ground	Extremely wide range of growth forms	Small stature, limited lateral spread
3. Leaf form	Robust, often mesomorphic	Often small or leathery, or needle-like	Various, often mesomorphic
4. Canopy structure	Rapidly elevating monolayer	Often multilayered. If monolayer not rapidly elevating	Various
(ii) *Life history*			
5. Longevity of established phase	Long or relatively short	Long – very long	Very short
6. Longevity of leaves and roots	Relatively short	Long	Short
7. Leaf phenology	Well-defined peaks of leaf production coinciding with periods of maximum potential productivity	Evergreens, with various patterns of leaf production	Short phase of leaf production in period of high potential productivity
8. Phenology of reproduction	Occurring after (or, more rarely, before) periods of maximum potential productivity	Many different phenologies occur	Occurs early in the life history
9. Frequency of reproduction	Established plants usually reproduce each year	Intermittent over a long life history	High
10. Proportion of annual production devoted to seeds or spores	Small	Small	Large
11. Perennation	Dormant buds and seeds	Stress-tolerant leaves and roots	Dormant seeds
12. Regenerative* strategies	V, S, W, B_s	V, B_j, W	S, W, B_s

Table 1. *continued.*

	Competitive	Stress-tolerant	Ruderal
(iii) *Physiology*			
13. Maximum potential relative growth rate	Rapid	Slow	Rapid
14. Response to stress	**Rapid morphogenetic responses maximizing resource capture and vegetative growth**	**Morphogenetic responses slow and small in magnitude**	**Rapid curtailment of vegetative growth; diversion of resources into flowering**
15. Photosynthesis and uptake of mineral nutrients	Strongly seasonal, coinciding with long continuous period of vegetative growth	Opportunistic, often uncoupled from vegetative growth	Opportunistic, coinciding with vegetative growth
16. Acclimation of photosynthesis, mineral nutrition and tissue hardiness to seasonal change in temperature, light and moisture supply	**Weakly developed**	**Strongly developed**	**Weakly developed**
17. Storage of photosynthate and mineral nutrients	Most photosynthate and mineral nutrients are rapidly incorporated into vegetative structure but a proportion is stored and forms the capital for expansion of growth in the following growing season	Storage systems in leaves, stems and, or, roots	Confined to seeds
(iv) *Miscellaneous*			
18. Defence against herbivory	Relatively specialized and often ineffective	Constitutive and effective against a wide range of herbivores	Relatively specialised and often ineffective
19. Litter decay	Rapid	Slow	Rapid
20. Genome size	Usually small	Various	Small – very small

*Key to regenerative strategies (see Table 2): V, vegetative expansion; S, seasonal regeneration in vegetation gaps; W, numerous small widely-dispersed seeds or spores; B_s, persistent seed or spore bank; B_j, persistent juveniles.

the operation of sophisticated, heritable mechanisms of response activated by particular environmental cues. In the absence of a more specific theoretical framework plant ecologists have tended to draw upon this fund of information in an *ad hoc* way and our current perception of the ecological significance of plasticity is perhaps most accurately reflected in the papers of Clausen, Keck & Hiesey (1940), Bjorkman & Holmgren (1963, 1966), Bradshaw (1965, 1973) and Gutterman (1973, 1985) where plasticity is interpreted as a mechanism, replacing or supplementing genetic variation, as a buffer against spatial or temporal variability in habitat conditions. Our purpose here is not to dispute this hypothesis but to refine it. We shall suggest that variation in the form and direction of plasticity coincides with variation in other developmental features of the plant. Distinct forms of plasticity can be regarded therefore as components of sets of adaptive traits (strategies) each predictably related to habitat and ecology.

Theory

In the triangular model of primary plant strategies (Grime, 1974) it is proposed that there are three extremes of evolutionary specialization in the plant kingdom (ruderals, competitors and stress-tolerators) each characterized by a set of traits (Table 1) within which distinctive forms of plasticity are of crucial importance.

In the *ruderal strategy* which is exhibited by ephemeral herbs and bryophytes of frequently and severely disturbed habitats, it is suggested that the most common expression of plasticity is in the form of the premature development of reproductive structures in response to environmental stresses, a mechanism which in conjunction with other features of the ruderal (rapid potential growth rate, short life history) appears to increase the probability that *some* offspring will be produced in circumstances where the life span of the parent is short.

The *competitive strategy* is strongly represented among the herbaceous plants, shrubs and trees of stable productive habitats where there is a rapidly expanding biomass and success depends upon the ability to sustain high rates of resource capture above and below ground in conditions of intense competition and continuously changing spatial patterns of localized resource depletion. Here morphological plasticity in the development of shoots and roots, acting in concert with the continuous replacement of leaves and roots from year to year and in most cases within each growing season, brings about a continuous adjustment in the spatial distribution of the absorptive surfaces above and below ground. Plasticity in the competitor is thus part of an 'active foraging' mechanism whereby early successional perennials sustain high rates of resource capture through the ability to locate functional leaves and roots in the resource-rich zones of an environment which is constantly depleted by the activity of the plant and its competing neighbours.

It is clear that the dynamic root systems and leaf canopies of the competitor involve heavy costs in terms of the high rates of reinvestment of captured resources in the construction of new leaves and roots and in their rapid senescence. Moreover, as explained in Grime (1979) and Coley (1983), further costs are likely to arise from the high rates of herbivory experienced by the weakly defended ephemeral tissues of many competitors. We may expect therefore that the high degree of morphological plasticity associated with active foraging will be of selective advantage only where it allows access to large reserves of light energy, water and mineral nutrients. Accordingly a small amount of morphological plasticity may be predicted when we turn to the third avenue of adaptive specialization, that of the *stress-tolerators* which occupy habitats or niches in which productivity is chronically low and the supply of the limiting resource (usually mineral nutrients, more rarely light or water) is brief and unpredictable. In the lichens, bryophytes, herbs and small shrubs and trees of continuously harsh environments we may expect that survival will depend primarily upon the capacity to capture *and retain* scarce resources. Arising from this argument is the prediction that the leaves and roots of stress-tolerators will be comparatively long-lived structures in which plasticity is expressed primarily through reversible physiological changes (acclimation) which maintain functional integrity over the long life spans of individual organs and facilitate exploitation of temporary periods of resource availability (light as sunflecks, mineral nutrients as short pulses from decomposition processes or water as dew or occasional rain-showers). As in the case of the other two primary strategies, the full significance of the particular form of plasticity adopted by the stress-tolerator can be appreciated only by taking into account the full suite of traits listed in Table 1. Hence, physiological acclimation would be of little advantage in the conservative life style of the stress-tolerator if it was not allied to other attributes such as slow rates of growth (Bradshaw, Chadwick, Jowett & Snaydon, 1964; Higgs & James, 1969; Grime & Hunt, 1975) and strong defences against herbivory (Bryant & Kuropat, 1980; Coley, 1983; Cooper-Driver, 1985).

Already, in relation to the active foraging of competitors, reference has been made to the penalties which may be anticipated in circumstances where a form of plasticity attuned to one type of environment is invoked in another. In Table 2 this approach has been formalized as a set of predictions of the ecological consequences under different circumstances,

Table 2. *Predicted responses to stress of competitive, stress-tolerant and ruderal plants and their ecological consequences in three types of habitat (modified from Grime 1977).*

<table>
<tr><th rowspan="2">Strategy</th><th rowspan="2">Response to stress</th><th colspan="3">Consequences</th></tr>
<tr><th>Habitat 1*</th><th>Habitat 2**</th><th>Habitat 3***</th></tr>
<tr><td>Competitive</td><td>Large and rapid changes in quantity, distribution and morphology of leaves or roots</td><td>Tendency to sustain high rates of uptake of water and mineral nutrients to maintain dry-matter production under stress and to succeed in competition</td><td>Tendency to exhaust reserves of water and, or, mineral nutrients both in rhizosphere and within the plant; etiolation in response to shade increases susceptibility to fungal attack</td><td rowspan="2">Failure rapidly to reproduce reduces chance of rehabilitation after disturbance</td></tr>
<tr><td>Stress-tolerant</td><td>Changes in morphology slow and often small in magnitude</td><td rowspan="2">Overgrown by competitors</td><td>Conservative utilization of water, mineral nutrients, and photosynthate allows survival over long periods in which little dry-matter production is possible</td></tr>
<tr><td>Ruderal</td><td>Rapid curtailment of vegetative growth and diversion of resources into reproduction</td><td>Chronically low reproduction fails to compensate for high rate of mortality</td><td>Rapid production of offspring ensures rehabilitation after disturbance</td></tr>
</table>

*In the early successional stages of productive, undisturbed habitats (stresses mainly plant induced and coinciding with competition).

**In either continuously unproductive habitats (stresses more or less constant and due to unfavourable climate and/or soil) or in the late stages of succession in productive habitats.

***In severely disturbed, potentially productive habitats (stresses either a prelude to disturbance, e.g. moisture stress preceding drought fatalities or plant induced, between periods of disturbance).

of the types of plasticity associated with the three primary strategies.

In concluding this theoretical section, it must be emphasized that, for the sake of brevity, attention has been focused upon three extremes of evolutionary and ecological specialization. Comments on the role of plasticity in the wide range of plants exploiting various intermediate equilibria between stress, disturbance and competition have been attempted elsewhere (Grime, 1979). It is also necessary to point out that no reference has been made to the more specialized forms of plasticity which are peculiar to particular taxa or to specific parts of the plant. Of special interest here is the evidence that in many plant species the degree of self-fertilization in the flowers (Levins, 1972; Lord, 1981), proportion of dormant seeds produced (Cresswell & Grime, 1981; Sawhney & Naylor, 1982) and their germination requirements (Gutterman, 1973, 1978, 1980, 1982, 1985) may be strongly affected by the conditions experienced by the mother plant. These and other mechanisms undoubtedly contribute to the 'fine tuning' of plant ecologies.

Experimental evidence

Reproductive effort

There is now available a considerable volume of experimental data describing the impacts of environmental factors upon flowering and seed production. From studies such as those of Salisbury (1942), Harper & Ogden (1970), Hickman (1975), Kingsbury, Radlow, Mudie, Rutherford & Radlow (1976) and Van Andel & Vera (1977) there is support for the hypothesis (Table 2) that ephemeral species in habitats subject to frequent and severe disturbance tend to sustain a high reproductive effort (measured as percentage of the total dry weight of the plant allocated to flowers and allied structures (Thompson & Stewart, 1981)) when subjected to stress. It is inevitable that where reproduction is maintained under stress, there will be commensurate reductions in allocation to vegetative parts of the plant, a pattern which is likely to lead to reduced rates of resource capture and even premature death. This phenomenon is evident in Fig. 1 which describes the decline in allocation to leaf and root production associated with the mobilization of reserves into flowering in a nutrient-stressed population of the summer annual *Impatiens glandulifera*.

Experimental evidence suggests that it may be misleading in Table 2 to assume that all major forms of stress promote flowering in ephemeral plants. In Fig. 2 a comparison is drawn between various forms and intensities of stress in their effects upon reproductive effort in a ruderal

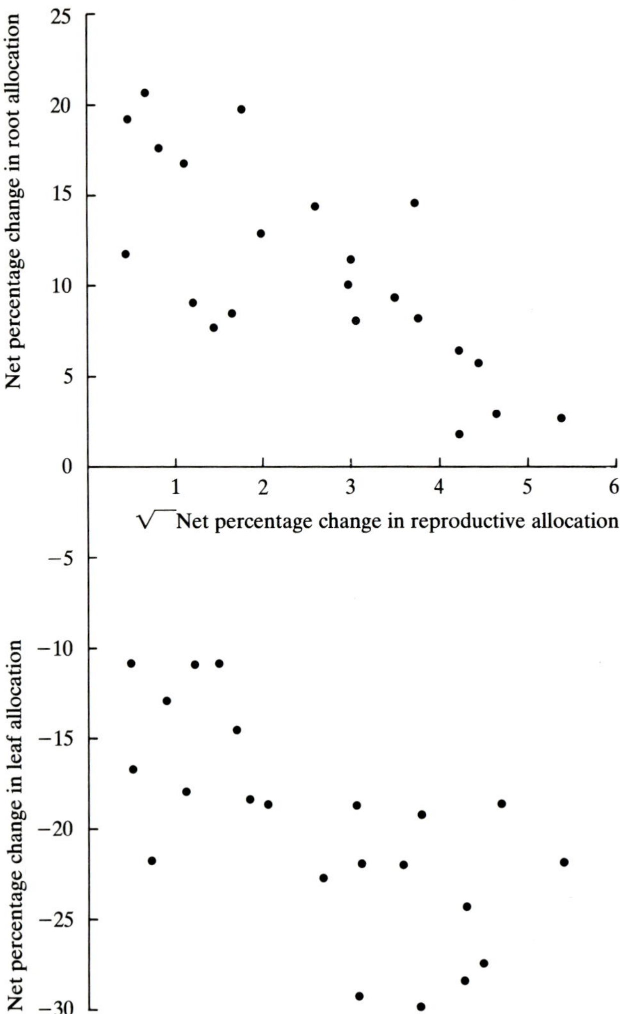

Fig. 1. Scatter diagram relating net percentage change in reproductive effort to net percentage change in allocation to leaves and roots in *Impatiens glandulifera* after 21 days exposure to a locally depleted nutrient supply. Each point refers to a calculation based upon two matched individuals, one harvested at the beginning and one at the end of the experiment. Pearson correlation coefficients for leaves $r = -0{\cdot}6628$ ($P < 0{\cdot}001$) and for roots $r = -0{\cdot}7350$ ($P < 0{\cdot}001$).

population of *Poa annua*. The results show that, at intensities comparable to those at which moisture stress and mineral nutrient stress permit considerable allocation to reproduction, shade exerted a strong inhibition on flowering. The most likely explanation for this departure from the plasticity response predicted in Table 2 appears to be that in ephemerals in a

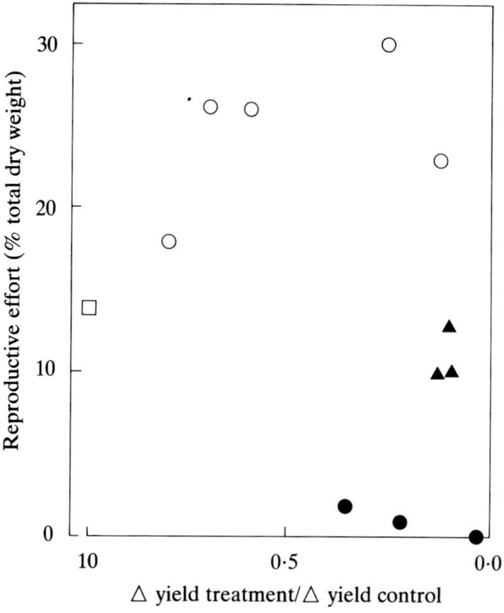

Fig. 2. Comparison of the effects of various stress treatments upon reproductive effort in *Poa annua*. The intensity of each stress treatment is characterized by comparing the growth increment of stressed plants to that of control (unstressed) plants over the same experimental period. □, control; ○, water stress (polyethylene glycol); ▲, mineral nutrient stress (dilute concentrations of Rorison solution); ●, shading by neutral filters (Smit, 1980).

disturbed habitat shade is usually experienced late in the life cycle and arises from closure of the herbaceous cover. In such circumstances the probability of effective seed production may be higher where the response to shade involves etiolation and emergence of the shoot from the shaded stratum, even though this is achieved at the cost of a temporary delay in flowering.

From a number of investigations (e.g. Lloyd & Pigott, 1967; Werner, 1975; Waite & Hutchings, 1982) there is strong evidence of the greater tendency of both monocarpic and polycarpic perennials to defer reproduction when growth is limited by the prevailing environmental conditions. An example of this phenomenon is provided in Fig. 3 which compares flowering and mortality at various intensities of moisture stress in two closely related species. From these data it is clear that flowering is strongly depressed in the perennial *Urtica dioica* by treatments in which growth and reproduction are maintained in the ephemeral *Urtica urens*. The authors of this study (Boot, Raynal & Grime, 1985) conclude that 'the drought hardening, reduction in growth and delay in flower production in *U. dioica* represents a mechanism safeguarding the survival and *eventual* reproduction of a

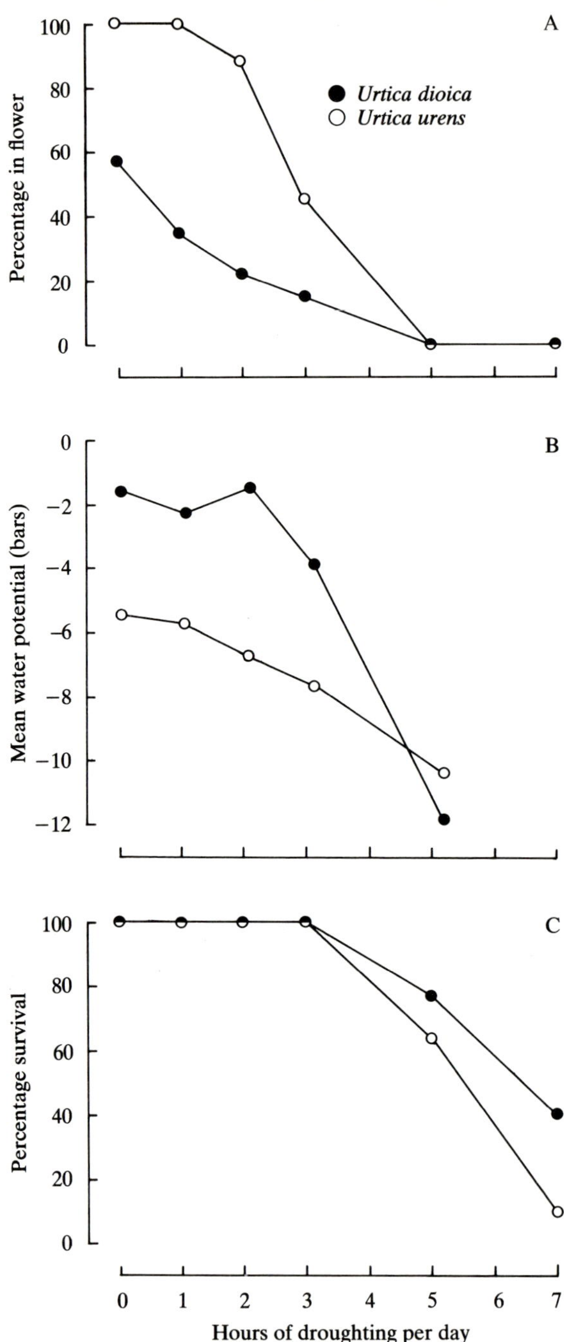
A
B
C
Urtica dioica
Urtica urens
Percentage in flower
Mean water potential (bars)
Percentage survival
Hours of droughting per day
100
80
60
40
20
0
−2
−4
−6
−8
−10
−12
1
2
3
4
5
6
7

Fig. 3

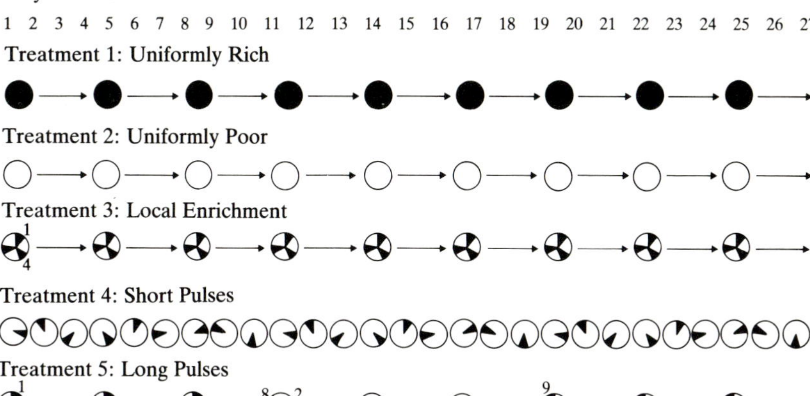

Fig. 4. Summary of treatments presenting five patterns of mineral nutrient supply over 27 days. ○ Plan view of a root growth arena with 9 compartments. ■ High nutrient solution (full Rorison solution). □ Low nutrient solution (N/100 Rorison solution).

potentially long-lived species capable of exploiting productive, relatively undisturbed habitats. The contrasted responses of *U. urens* in which growth and reproduction are maintained but at increased risk of drought mortality are not unexpected in a species restricted to temporary arable habitats and depending for its survival upon constant re-establishment by seed.'

Foraging for mineral nutrients

As early as 1954, there was recognition (Bray, 1954) of the importance of a plant's ability to 'forage' for nutrients as it grows. The concept has received little attention in terms of comparative investigation although much zoological research had been concerned with experimental studies of foraging and models have been created in an attempt to understand animal foraging tactics (MacArthur & Pianka, 1966; Schoener, 1971; Norberg, 1977; Krebs, 1978; Pianka, 1978; Cowie & Krebs, 1979). The principle that 'an optimal foraging tactic maximizes the difference between foraging profits and their costs' (Pianka 1978) appears to have been widely accepted and this approach has been extended to plants foraging for nitrogen (Sibly & Grime, 1985).

Fig. 3. Comparison of the effect of increasing severity of drought upon (A) flowering, (B) xylem water potential and (C) mortality in *Urtica dioica* (●) and *U. urens* (○). Duration of the diurnal drought treatments was manipulated using the technique of Raynal, Boot & Grime (1985).

In crop plants, root proliferation into local areas of high nutrient supply has been recorded in soil (Wiersum, 1958) and in sand and solution cultures (Drew, Saker & Ashley, 1973; Drew, 1975). Recently this approach has been developed (Crick, 1985) in an attempt to devise experimental tests of the hypotheses (Tables 1, 2) relating plasticity in root morphology to habitat and ecological strategy. Fig. 4 summarizes experimental treatments which were used to compare morphological plasticity and nitrogen capture under various nutrient regimes in individuals from populations of two ecologically contrasted species, *Agrostis stolonifera*, a species of fertile habitats, and *Scirpus sylvaticus*, a plant restricted to relatively unproductive soils. At the beginning of the 27-day experiment each plant was placed in an individual container of nutrient solution in which the root system was equally distributed between nine watertight radial sectors (Figs 5, 6). Over the course of the experiment five mineral nutrient treatments were applied. Two treatments (1 and 2) represented the maximum and minimum rates of

Fig. 5. Root growth arena of the type used in the mineral nutrient foraging experiments. Units of 10 mm are indicated on the vertical scale.

supply and involved supplying the same level (full or N/100 Rorison soluton (Hewitt, 1966) respectively) to all nine compartments. The three remaining treatments (3, 4, 5) provided the same total amount of mineral nutrients to each plant as a whole but these were presented in different spatial and temporal patterns. Constantly high nutrient compartments with low nutrient compartments interspersed (treatment 3) represented the situation which may be found in a productive environment where neighbours have encroached and depleted surrounding areas. In treatment 4 high nutrient pulses each of 24 h duration and restricted to one compartment at a time were inserted in a random sequence, thus providing a test of the species' ability to absorb nutrients from brief unpredictable and localized flushes of the kind associated with infertile soils (Davison, 1964; Gupta & Rorison, 1975). Longer pulses were provided in treatment 5 in a regime involving simultaneous enrichment of three compartments over periods of 9 days.

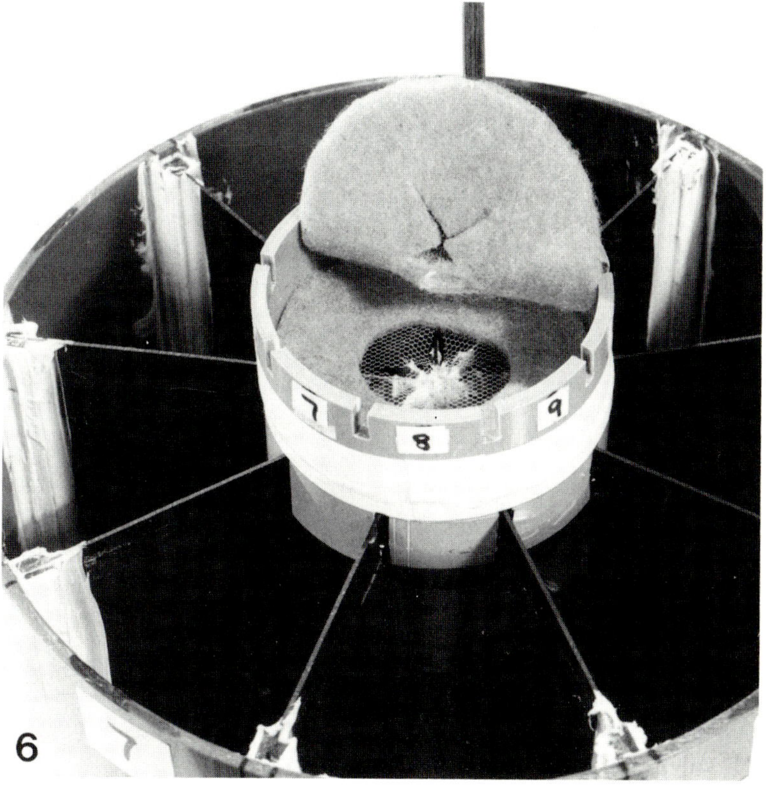

Fig. 6. Collar region of root growth arena with upper layer of moistened capillary matting displaced to show gauze through which roots enter the radial compartments via a humid air-gap of 7–10 mm.

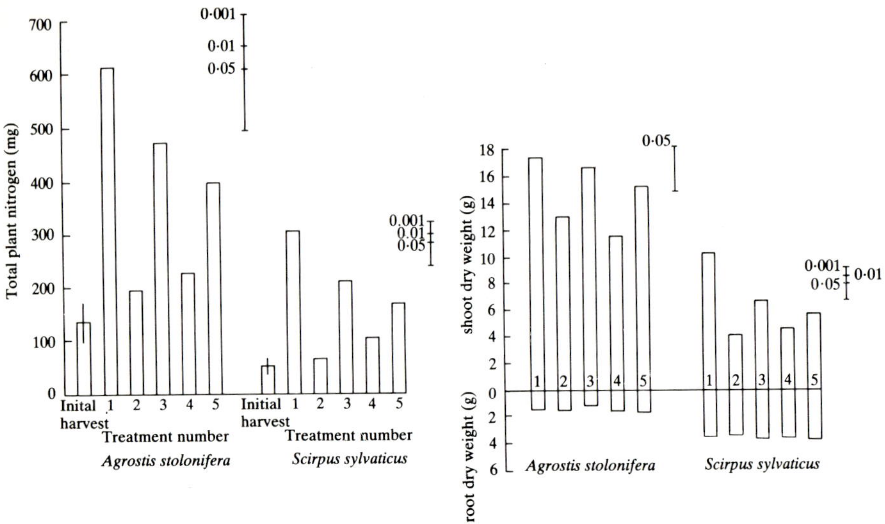

Fig. 7. (A) Total nitrogen content and (B) shoot and root dry weights of *Agrostis stolonifera* and *Scirpus sylvaticus* subjected to the five patterns of mineral nutrient supply described in Fig. 4. Vertical bars represent the LSD at $P < 0{\cdot}05$, $P < 0{\cdot}01$ and $P < 0{\cdot}001$ between treatment means. In (A) 95% confidence limits are indicated as vertical lines on the columns representing mean nitrogen content of plants harvested at the commencement of the experiment.

Fig. 7 describes the total nitrogen contents and dry weights of the two species at the beginning of the experiment and in plants exposed to each treatment. It is clear that at both high and low external concentrations nitrogen uptake in *A. stolonifera* was consistently greater than that achieved by *S. sylvaticus* although in both species the treatments could be arranged in the series 1 > 3 > 5 > 4 > 2. Reference to Fig. 7B reveals that the superior nitrogen uptake of *A. stolonifera* was achieved despite a very much lower allocation of dry matter to root development. It is also apparent that *A. stolonifera* was better able than *S. sylvaticus* to sustain nitrogen uptake and dry matter production where nutrient enrichment was in the form of spatially predictable patches (treatment 3). By calculating the increments of dry weight allocated to neighbouring high and low nutrient compartments of the treatment 3 containers over the course of the experiment it was possible to derive a 'root concentration index' (RCI) (mean increment in high nutrient compartments divided by mean increment in low nutrient compartments), reflecting the abilities of the two species rapidly to modify the spatial distribution of the root system. Paired *t* tests revealed significant differences between the species with respect to RCI. The mean root concentration index for *A. stolonifera* was 5·72 and for

S. sylvaticus was 1·42. Since *S. sylvaticus* produced significantly more root dry weight in terms of absolute and percentage increment in treatment 3 than did *A. stolonifera*, the high root concentration index in the latter could not be related to a larger amount of root production during the experiment. We may conclude therefore that the more effective capture of the spatially predictable nitrogen in treatment 3 by *A. stolonifera* was the result of higher specific absorption rates and greater morphological plasticity in root development.

Despite the generally higher rates of nitrogen uptake exhibited by *A. stolonifera*, closer examination of the data reveals a circumstance in which greater uptake was achieved by *S. sylvaticus*. In Table 3 nitrogen capture in treatments 3, 4 and 5 has been expressed as the excess over that observed in treatment 2. This allows comparison of the extent to which the two species were able to capture additional nitrogen provided in the same quantity but presented in three patterns, i.e. predictable patches maintained over the duration of the experiment (treatment 3), short localized and spatially and temporally unpredictable pulses (treatment 4) or longer and more predictable pulses (treatment 5). The results show that although *A. stolonifera* obtained considerably more of the 'relatively predictable' additional nitrogen provided in treatments 3 and 5, the species was marginally inferior to *S. sylvaticus* in its ability to capture the 'unpredictable' additional nitrogen of treatment 4. Although this result is in agreement with the theories reviewed earlier in this paper, further experimental

Table 3. *Nitrogen contents of* Agrostis stolonifera *and* Scirpus sylvaticus *plants grown for 27 days in a continuously low external concentration of nitrogen (N/100 Rorison solution) and calculations of the additional nitrogen captured by plants grown in the same nutrient solution but subjected to local nitrogen enrichment (treatments 3, 4 and 5).*

Species	N content (mg) of plants grown in low nitrogen solution culture	'Additional' nitrogen captured (mg)*		
		Treatment 3 ('Predictable patches')	Treatment 4 ('Short pulses')	Treatment 5 ('Long pulses')
Agrostis stolonifera	195·8 ± 15·9	279·1	35·1	207·0
Scirpus sylvaticus	66·8 ± 6·5	147·6	41·5	104·1

*'Additional' nitrogen captured is calculated as the excess over the nitrogen content of the plants of treatment 2. In treatments 3, 4 and 5 the quantity of 'additional' nitrogen was the same but it was presented in different spatially and temporal patterns as described in Fig. 4.

evidence is required. A more appropriate test of the relative abilities of *S. sylvaticus* and *A. stolonifera* to capture and retain nitrogen from an infertile soil would of necessity involve a longer-term study under natural climatic conditions.

Foraging for light

Numerous experiments have been conducted by physiologists and ecologists to investigate morphogenetic responses to variation in light intensity and quality. Differences of several kinds have been recorded between species and populations drawn from shaded and open habitats. These include differences in plasticity of leaf area and thickness (Blackman & Wilson, 1951; Loach, 1970; Corre, 1983*a,b*) and in petiole and internode length (Grime & Jeffrey, 1965; Morgan & Smith, 1979). More recently, in an experimental study with bryophytes, we have found that morphogenetic responses to light intensity exert a sensitive control over the angle of inclination of the shoots. In the majority of the species investigated the effect of shade was to bring about a progressive elevation of the shoot, a response which in *Thuidium tamariscinum* (Fig. 8) conforms with the tendency of the species to exploit the upper strata within pasture canopies. In marked contrast the effect of shade was to induce a more horizontal growth form in *Lophocolea bidentata*. This is consistent with the observation that *L. bidentata* is a carpet-forming species, usually restricted to areas of bare soil beneath closed canopies.

In order to examine the role of shoot plasticity in energy capture and to test the strategy concepts outlined in Tables 1 and 2, it is desirable to conduct comparative foraging experiments in environments which provide types of patchiness in irradiance analogous to those designed for mineral nutrients (Fig. 4). For flowering plants this is a technically difficult operation (Crick, 1985) in that subdivision of the shoot environment into compartments usually imposes physical barriers to the normal expansion of leaves and stems (Figs 9, 10). These problems do not apply however in bryophytes where small size and simple morphology make them more amenable subjects for enclosure in containers providing controlled spatial and temporal patchiness in irradiance. In Fig. 11 six bryophyte species are compared with respect to their ability to exploit beams of spatially predictable, unfiltered light projected into shaded containers over a period of three months. The results are expressed as a concentration index (dry weight of thallus per unit area in unfiltered light divided by dry weight of thallus per unit area in adjacent shade light) which for each species is plotted against the mean relative growth rate of control plants grown in

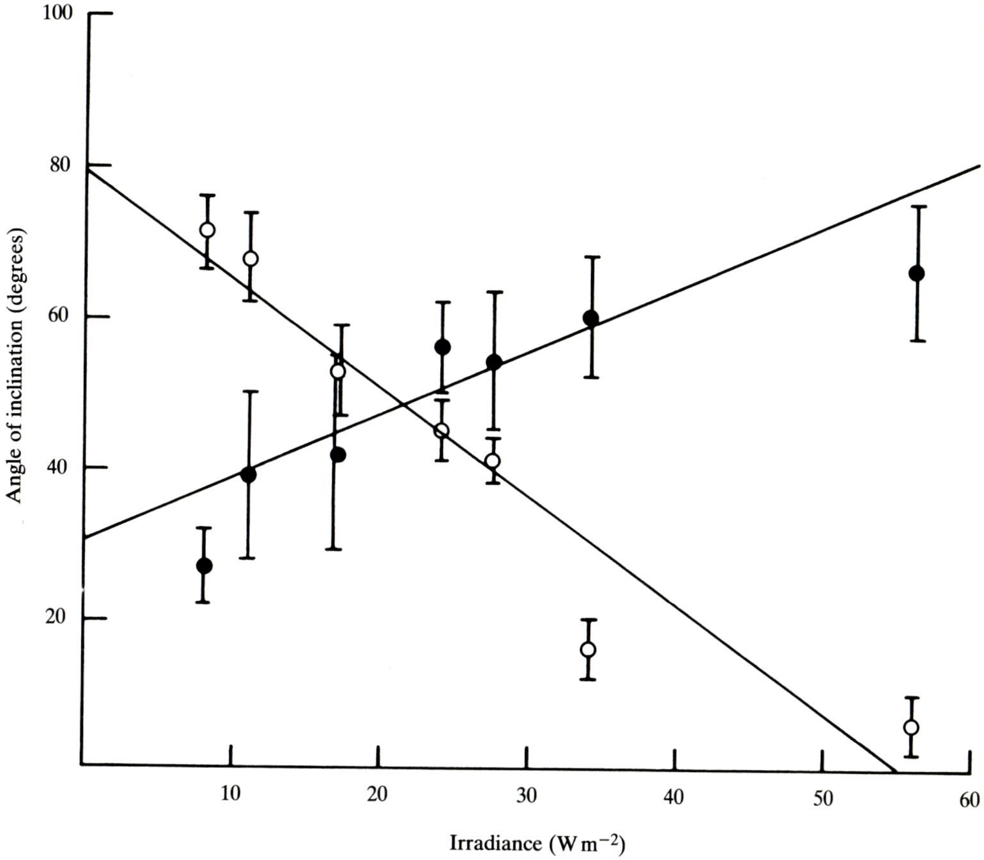

Angle of inclination (degrees)

100

80

60

40

20

10 20 30 40 50 60

Irradiance (W m^{-2})

Fig. 8. Relationships between irradiance and angle of inclination of the shoots of two bryophyte species grown for 36 days at a temperature of 16 °C and a daylength of 12 h. In *Thuidium tamariscinum* (○), r = −0·9584 (P < 0·001) and in *Lophocolea bidentata* (●), r = 0·7200 (P < 0·05).

uniformly unfiltered light of low intensity over the experimental period. Marked differences in concentration index are apparent and it is evident that the four species of higher potential relative growth rate and characteristic of mesic habitats (*Brachythecium rutabulum, Eurynchium praelongum, Pseudoscleropodium purum* and *Thuidium tamariscinum*) were more effective colonists of the local patches of unfiltered light than the two slow-growing species of shaded limestone outcrops (*Thamnium alopecurum, Fissidens cristatus*). These data are clearly consistent with the strategy predictions outlined in Tables 1 and 2 in that greater morphological plasticity was evident in the four species normally found growing in closed herbaceous vegetation, whereas the two bryophytes associated with deeply shaded conditions were relatively unresponsive. The higher

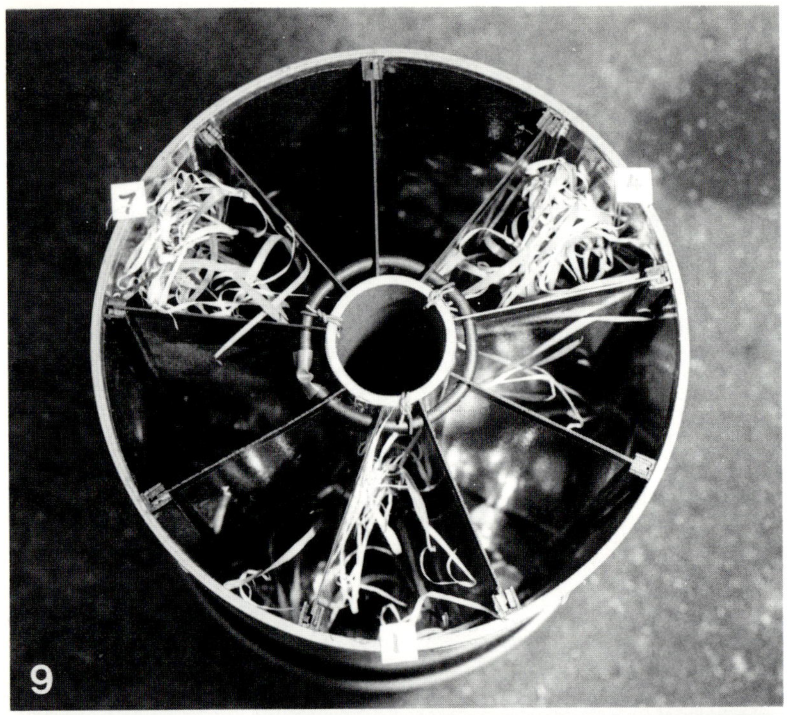

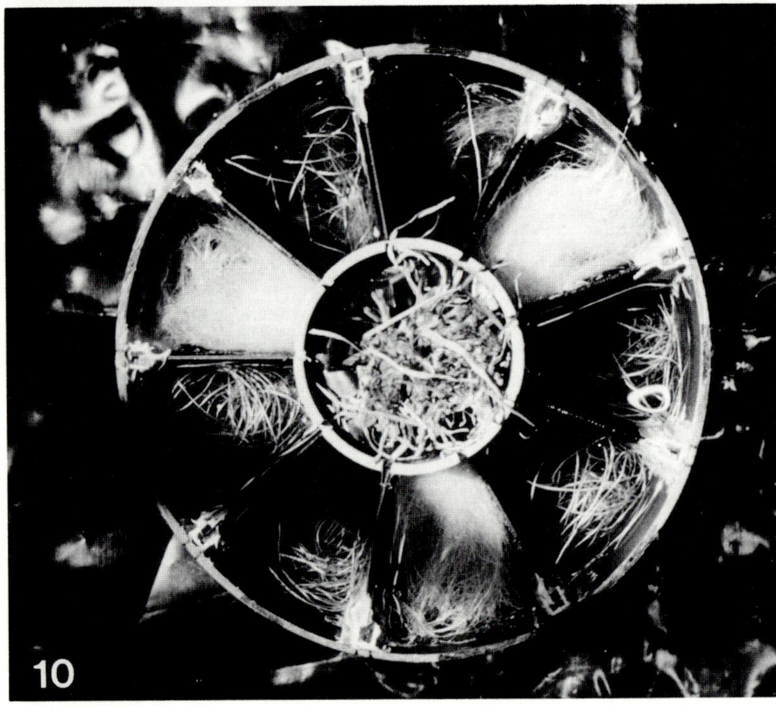

Figs 9 & 10

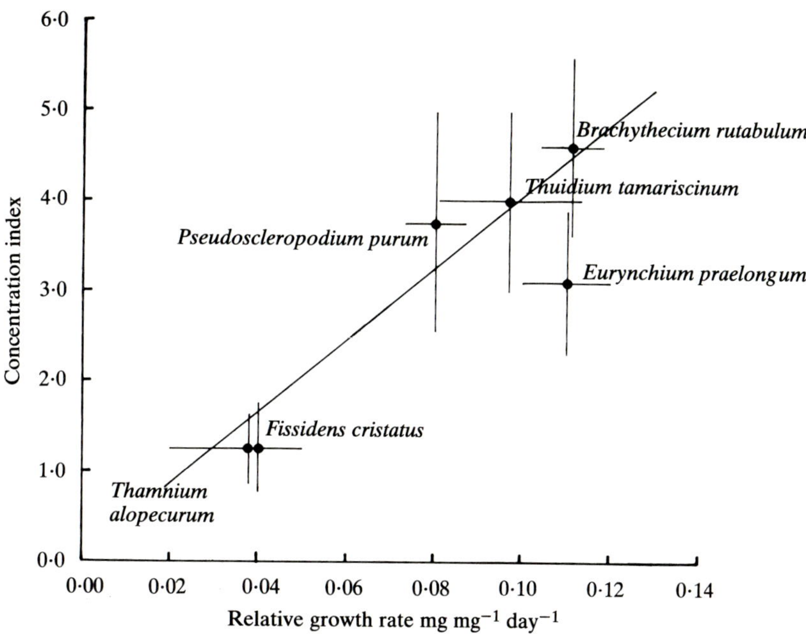

Fig. 11. Comparison of the ability of six bryophytes of contrasted ecology grown in a constant mosaic of high (48 W m^{-2}) and low (9 W m^{-2}) irradiance for 110 days to concentrate their biomass in the areas of high irradiance. The concentration indices are plotted against the relative growth rate of individuals of the same species grown concurrently at a uniformly high irradiance (48 W m^{-2}) in the same environmental conditions (temperatures 18 °C (day), 12 °C (night). Photoperiod 12 h). 95 % confidence limits are indicated by the horizontal and vertical lines. The regression equation for the fitted line is $y = 0{\cdot}057 + 39{\cdot}22x$ ($P < 0{\cdot}05$).

concentration index of species such as *B. rutabulum* could not be attributed merely to their higher potential relative growth rates; visual inspection of the bryophytes during the experiment confirmed that shoots of these species often impinged upon the light patches as a result of the lateral projection of elevated (cf. Fig. 8) and attenuated shoot tips of plants located in the shaded parts of the container.

In the same experiment the six bryophytes were compared with respect to their capacity to exploit spatially unpredictable irradiance in the form of

---

Fig. 9. Vertical view of a radially partitioned container in which the canopy of a single individual of *Agrostis stolonifera* has been allowed to expand, with equal access from below, into unfiltered natural daylight (compartments 1, 4 and 7) and into shade light (compartments 2, 3, 5, 6, 8 and 9).

Fig. 10. Vertical view of a radially partitioned container (see Figs 5, 6) in which the root system of a single individual of *Holcus lanatus* has been allowed to expand into full Rorison solution (compartments 1, 4 and 7) and into N/100 Rorison solution (compartments 2, 3, 5, 6, 8 and 9).

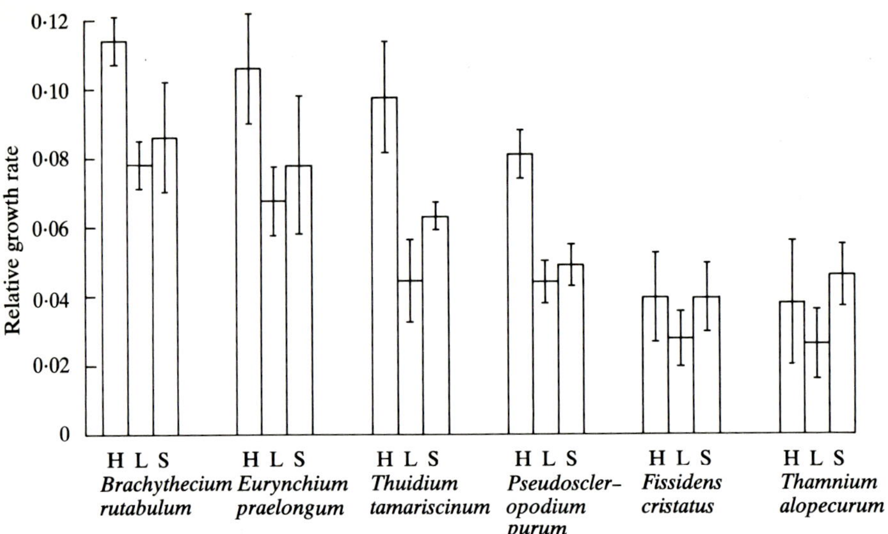

Fig. 12. Comparison of the ability of six bryophytes of contrasted ecology to exploit artificial sunflecks of 20 min duration and randomly distributed in space and time. The histograms describe the mean relative growth rate (±95%) confidence limits) over a period of 110 days exposure to high irradiance (H) (48 W m^{-2}), low irradiance (L) (9 W m^{-2}) and low irradiance + sunflecks (S). Temperatures: 18 °C (day), 12 °C (night). Photoperiod: 12 h.

artificial sunflecks each approximately 20 mm in diameter and of 20 minutes duration and located at random by intermittent rotation of a perforated disc filter over a honeycomb of short vertical reflective tubes (Rincon, 1985). The histograms in Fig. 12 compare the relative growth rates of the bryophytes in the sunfleck treatment and in two uniform levels of irradiance comparable respectively with the shade and sunfleck components of the sunfleck treatment. The data confirm the greater ability of the four grassland bryophytes to grow more rapidly at both high and continuously low irradiance. In only one of these species, *Thuidium tamariscinum*, is there any appreciable benefit from the introduction of sunflecks. In the two slow-growing bryophytes, however, there is clear evidence that sunflecks provided a major stimulus to dry matter production. These results support the hypothesis (Tables 1, 2) that morphological plasticity is of reduced importance in the mechanisms of resource acquisition of plants exploiting chronically unproductive habitats or niches.

Physiological acclimation

In the slow-growing, long-lived lichens, bryophytes, herbs and small woody plants which dominate unproductive biomes, habitats or niches, growth is intermittent and the life span of individual vegetative parts is long. In relation to the phenomenon of plasticity, this slow turnover of tissues and cells has two consequences. The first, already considered in this paper, is that for most of the time differentiating tissue forms a small proportion of the plant's biomass. This must impose a severe limitation upon the capacity of such plants to adjust to environmental fluctuations through morphogenetic plasticity. The second consequence is that during their long functional life, tissues are often exposed to severe and widely different environmental conditions. It is hardly surprising therefore to find that there is an extensive literature supporting the assertion (Table 1) that plasticity in stress-tolerant plants is usually expressed physiologically and is often both rapid and reversible. Well-documented examples are available from pioneer studies of modifications in carboxylating capacity and in the temperature optimum of photosynthesis in relation to varying light intensity and season (Miyata & Hosakawa, 1961; Mooney & West, 1964; Strain & Chase, 1966; Mooney & Shropshire, 1967; Bjorkman, 1968*a,b*; Grace & Woolhouse, 1970; Taylor & Pearcy, 1976; Kershaw, 1977*a,b*).

Conclusion

It is understandable that text-book treatments of plasticity in plants frequently use as examples spectacular switches in development such as those associated with heterophylly in aquatic plants (Schmidt & Millington, 1968; Cook & Johnson, 1968). These are observed in plants which experience gross changes in habitat conditions such as those associated with emergence from submerged to an aerial environment. Similarly much of what we have learned of plasticity from laboratory experiments has involved measurements of response to alteration of the *whole* root and, or, shoot environment. Given this emphasis in previous observation and experimentation it is hardly surprising that plasticity has come to be regarded primarily as a mechanism compensating for the lack of locomotion in plants and supplementing the role of genetic variation as a determinant of wide ecological amplitude and persistence in fluctuating conditions.

On the basis of the evidence considered in this paper we submit that plasticity has another, perhaps deeper, significance in plant biology as an integral part of the mechanisms by which plants (a) control reproductive effort and (b) capture resources from their environments. These latter phenomena are not restricted to plants; recent investigations (Savory & Gentle, 1976; Kenward & Sibly, 1977; Al-Jaborae, 1980) have shown that it is possible to induce reversible changes in the gut lengths of some vertebrates by manipulation of food quality.

We wish to thank our colleagues Mrs. J. M. L. Mackey, Mrs. N. Ruttle, Mr. P. T. Smit, Dr. D.J. Raynal, Mr. R. Boot, Dr. S.H. Hillier and Mr S.R. Band for assistance in aspects of the research described in this paper. Financial support for this research was provided by the Natural Environment Research Council.

References

AL-JABORAE, F. F. (1980). *The influence of diet on the gut morphology of the starling* (Sturnus vulgaris *L. 1758*). D.Phil. thesis, University of Oxford.

BJORKMAN, O. (1968*a*). Carboxydismutase activity in shade-adapted and sun-adapted species of higher plants. *Physiologia Pl.* **21**, 1–10.

BJORKMAN, O. (1968*b*). Further studies on differentiation of photosynthetic properties in sun and shade ecotypes of *Solidago virgaurea. Physiologia Pl.* **21**, 84–99.

BJORKMAN, O. & HOLMGREN, P. (1963). Adaptability of the photosynthetic apparatus to light intensity in ecotypes from exposed and shaded habitats. *Physiologia Pl.* **16**, 889–914.

BJORKMAN, O. & HOLMGREN, P. (1966). Photosynthetic adaptation to light intensity in plants native to shaded and exposed habitats. *Physiologia Pl.* **19**, 854–859.

BLACKMAN, G. E. & WILSON, G. L. (1951). Physiological and ecological studies in the analysis of plant environment. VII. An analysis of the differential effects of light intensity on the net assimilation rate, leaf-area ratio and relative growth rate of different species. *Ann. Bot.* **15**, 373–408.

BOOT, R., RAYNAL, D. J. & GRIME, J. P. (1985). A comparative study of the influence of moisture stress on flowering in *Urtica dioica* and *Urtica urens. J. Ecol.* (in press).

BRADSHAW, A. D. (1965). Evolutionary significance of phenotypic plasticity in plants. *Adv. Genet.* **13**, 115–155.

BRADSHAW, A. D. (1973). Environment and phenotypic plasticity. *Brookhaven Symp. Biol.* **25**, 75–94.

BRADSHAW, A. D., CHADWICK, M. J., JOWETT, D. & SNAYDON, R. W. (1964). Experimental investigations into the mineral nutrition of several grass species. IV. Nitrogen level. *J. Ecol.* 52, 665–676.

BRAY, R. H. (1954). A nutrient mobility concept of soil-plant relationships. *Soil Sci.* **78**, 9–22.

BRYANT, J. P. & KUROPAT, P. J. (1980). Selection of winter forage by subarctic browsing vertebrates: the role of plant chemistry. *A. Rev. Ecol. Systemat.* **11**, 261–285.

CHAPIN, F. S. (1980). The mineral nutrition of wild plants. *A. Rev. Ecol. Systemat.* **11**, 233–260.

CLAUSEN, J., KECK, D. D. & HIESEY, W. M. (1940). Experimental studies on the nature of species. I. Effect of varied environments on western North American plants. *Carnegie Inst. Washington Pub.* 520.

COLEY, P. D. (1983). Herbivory and defensive characteristics of tree species in a lowland Tropical forest. *Ecol. Mongr.* **53**, 209–233.

COOK, S. A. & JOHNSON, M. P. (1968). Adaptation to heterogeneous environments. I. Variation in heterophylly in *Ranunculus flammula* L. *Evol.* **22**, 496–516.

COOPER-DRIVER, G. (1985). Anti-predation strategies in pteridophytes – a biochemical approach. *Proc. R. Soc. Edinb.* **86B**, 397–402.

CORRE, W. J. (1983*a*). Growth and morphogenesis of sun and shade plants. I. The influence of light intensity. *Acta bot. neerl.* **32**, 49–62.

CORRE, W. J. (1983*b*). Growth and morphogenesis of sun and shade plants. II. The influence of light quality. *Acta bot. neerl.* **32**, 185–202.

COWIE, R. J. & KREBS, J. R. (1979). Optimal foraging in patchy environments. In *Population Dynamics* (ed. R.M. Anderson, B.D. Turner & L.R. Taylor), pp. 183–205. Blackwell Scientific Publications, Oxford.

CRESSWELL, E. & GRIME, J. P. (1981). Induction of a light requirement during seed development and its ecological consequences. *Nature* **291**, 583–585.

CRICK, J. C. (1985). *The Role of Plasticity in Resource Acquisition by Higher Plants*. Ph.D. thesis, University of Sheffield.

DAVISON, A. W. (1964). *Some Factors Affecting Seedling Establishment on Calcareous Soils*. Ph.D. thesis, University of Sheffield.

DREW, M. C. (1975). Comparison of the effects of a localized supply of phosphate, nitrate, ammonium and potassium on the growth of the seminal root system, and the shoot, in barley. *New Phytol.* **75**, 479–490.

DREW, M. C., SAKER, L. R. & ASHLEY, T. W. (1973). Nutrient supply and the growth of the seminal root system in barley. I. The effect of nitrate concentration on the growth of axes and laterals. *J. exp. Bot.* **24**, 1189–1202.

GRACE, J. & WOOLHOUSE, H. W. (1970). A physiological and mathematical study of the growth and productivity of a *Calluna-Sphagnum* community. I. Net photosynthesis of *Calluna vulgaris* (L.) Hall. *J. appl. Ecol.* **7**, 363–381.

GRIME, J. P. (1974). Vegetation classification by reference to strategies. *Nature* **250**, 26–31.

GRIME, J. P. (1977). Evidence for the existence of three primary strategies in plants and its relevance to ecological and evolutionary theory. *Amer. Nat.* **111**, 1169–1194.

GRIME, J. P. (1979). *Plant Strategies and Vegetation Processes*. John Wiley, Chichester.

GRIME, J. P. & HUNT, R. (1975). Relative growth-rate: its range and adaptive significance in a local flora. *J. Ecol.* **63**, 393–422.

GRIME, J. P. & JEFFREY, D. W. (1965). Seedling establishment in vertical gradients of sunlight. *J. Ecol.* **53**, 621–642.

GUPTA, P. L. & RORISON, I. H. (1975). Seasonal differences in the availability of nutrients down a podzolic profile. *J. Ecol.* **63**, 521–534.

GUTTERMAN, Y. (1973). Differences in the progeny due to day length and hormone treatment of the mother plant. In *Seed Ecology* (ed. W. Heydecker), pp. 59–80. Butterworths, London.

GUTTERMAN, Y. (1978). Seed coat permeability as a function of photo periodical treatments of the mother plants during seed maturation in the desert annual plant: *Trigonella arabica*, Del. *J. arid Environ.* **1**, 141–144.

GUTTERMAN, Y. (1980). Influences on seed germinability: phenotypic maternal effects during seed maturation. *Israel. J. Bot.* **29**, 105–117.

GUTTERMAN, Y. (1982). Phenotypic maternal effect of photoperiod on seed germination. In *The Physiology and Biochemistry of Seed Development, Dormancy and Germination* (ed. A. A. Khan), pp. 67–79. Elsevier Biomedical Press.

GUTTERMAN, Y. (1985). Flowering, seed development, and the influences during seed maturation on seed germination of annual weeds. In *Weed Physiology* Vol. 1 *Reproduction and Ecophysiology* (ed. S. O. Duke), pp. 2–25. CRC Press, Inc., Florida.

HARPER, J. L. & OGDEN, J. (1970). The reproductive strategy of higher plants. I. The concept of strategy with special reference to *Senecio vulgaris* L. *J. Ecol.* **58**, 681–698.

HEWITT, E. J. (1966). *Sand and Water Culture Methods used in the Study of Plant Nutrition*. Commonwealth Agricultural Bureau, Farnham Royal, Bucks., England.

HICKMAN, J. C. (1975). Environmental unpredictability and plastic energy allocation strategies in the annual *Polygonum cascadense* (Polygonaceae). *J. Ecol.* **63**, 689–701.

HIGGS, D. E. B. & JAMES, D. B. (1969). Comparative studies on the biology of upland grasses. I. Rate of dry matter production and its control in four grass species. *J. Ecol.* **57**, 553–563.

KENWARD, R. D. & SIBLY, R. M. (1977). A woodpigeon (*Columba palumbus*) feeding preference explained by a digestive bootleneck. *J. appl. Ecol.* **14**, 815–826.

KERSHAW, K. A. (1977*a*). Physiological-environmental interactions in lichens. II. The pattern of net photosynthetic acclimation in *Peltigera canina* (L.) Willd var *praetextata* (Floerke in Somm.) Hue, and *P. polydactyla* (Neck.) Hoffm. *New Phytol.* **79**, 377–390.

KERSHAW, K. A. (1977*b*). Physiological-environmental interactions in lichens. III. The rate of net photosynthetic acclimation in *Peltigera canina* (L.) Willd. var *praetextata* (Floerke in Somm.) Hue, and *P. polydactyla* (Neck.) Hoffm. *New Phytol.* **79**, 391–402.

KINGSBURY, R. W., RADLOW, A., MUDIE, P. J., RUTHERFORD, J. & RADLOW, R. (1976). Salt stress responses in *Lasthenia glabrata*, a winter annual composite endemic to saline soils. *Can. J. Bot.* **54**, 1377–1385.

KREBS, J. R. (1978). Optimal foraging: decision rules for predators. In *Behavioural Ecology: an Evolutionary Approach* (ed. J. R. Krebs & N. B. Davies), pp. 23–63. Blackwell Scientific Publications, Oxford.

LEVINS, R. (1972). Plant density, cleistogamy and self-fertilisation in natural populations of *Lithospermum caroliniense*. *Am. J. Bot.* **59**, 71–78.

LLOYD, P. S. & PIGOTT, C. D. (1967). The influence of soil conditions on the course of succession on the chalk of Southern England. *J. Ecol.* **55**, 137–146.

LOACH, K. (1970). Shade tolerance in tree seedlings. II. Growth analysis of plants raised under artificial shade. *New Phytol.* **69**, 273–286.

LORD, E. M. (1981). Cleistogamy – a tool for the study of floral morphogenesis function and evolution. *Bot. Rev.* **47**, 421–449.

MACARTHUR, R. H. & PIANKA, E. R. (1966). An optimal use of a patchy environment. *Am. Nat.* **100**, 603–609.

MIYATA, I. & HOSAKAWA, T. (1961). Seasonal variations of the photosynthetic efficiency and chlorophyll content of epiphytic mosses. *Ecology* **42**, 766–775.

MOONEY, H. A. & SHOPSHIRE, F. (1967). Population variability in temperature related photosynthetic acclimation. *Oecol. Plant.* **2**, 1–13.

MOONEY, H. A. & WEST, M. (1964). Photosynthetic acclimation of plants of diverse origin. *Am. J. Bot.* **51**, 825–827.

MORGAN, D. C. & SMITH, H. (1979). A systematic relationship between phytochrome-controlled development and species habitat, for plants grown in simulated natural radiation. *Planta* **145**, 253–258.

NORBERG, R. A. (1977). An ecological theory on foraging time and energetics and choice of optimal food searching method. *J. Anim. Ecol.* **46**, 511–529.

PIANKA, E. R. (1978). *Evolutionary Ecology*. 2nd Edition. Harper and Row.

RAYNAL, D. J., BOOT, R. & GRIME, J. P. (1985). A new method for the experimental droughting of plants. *Ann. Bot.* **55**, 893–897.

RINCON, J. E. (1985). *Experimental investigations of the ecology of pleurocarpous bryophytes in calcareous grasslands in Northern England.* Ph.D. thesis, University of Sheffield.

SALISBURY, E. J. (1942). *The Reproductive Capacity of Plants.* Bell, London.

SAVORY, C. J. & GENTLE, M. J. (1976). Changes in food intake and gut size in Japanese quail in response to manipulation of dietary fibre content. *Br. Poult. Sci.* **17**, 571–580.

SAWHNEY, R. & NAYLOR, J. M. (1982). Dormancy studies in seeds of *Avena fatua*. 13. Influence of drought stress during seed development on duration of seed dormancy. *Can. J. Bot.* **60**, 1016–1020.

SCHOENER, T. W. (1971). Theory of feeding strategies. *A. Rev. Ecol. Systemat.* **2**, 369–404.

SCHMIDT, B. L. & MILLINGTON, W. F. (1968). Regulation of leaf shape in *Proserpinaca palustris*. *Bull. Torrey bot. Club* **95**, 264–286.

SIBLY, R. & GRIME, J. P. (1985). Strategies of resource capture by plants – evidence for adversity selection. *J. theor. Biol.* **118**, 247–250.

SMIT, P. T. (1980). *Phenotypic plasticity of four grass species under water-, light- and nutrient-stress.* B.Sc. thesis, University of Groningen.

STRAIN, B. R. & CHASE, V. C. (1966). Effect of past and prevailing temperatures on the carbon dioxide exchange capacities of some woody desert perennials. *Ecology* **47**, 1043–1045.

TAYLOR, R. J. & PEARCY, R. W. (1976). Seasonal patterns in the CO_2 exchange characteristics of understorey plants from a deciduous forest. *Can. J. Bot.* **54**, 1094–1103.

THOMPSON, K. & STEWART, A. J. A. (1981). The measurement and meaning of reproductive effort in plants. *Am. Nat.* **117**, 205–211.

VAN ANDEL, J. & VERA, F. (1977). Reproductive allocation in *Senecio sylvaticus* and *Chamaenerion angustifolium* in relation to mineral nutrition. *J. Ecol.* **65**, 747–758.

WAITE, S. & HUTCHINGS, M. J. (1982). Plastic energy allocation patterns in *Plantago coronopus*. *Oikos* **38**, 333–342.

WERNER, P. A. (1975). Predictions of fate from rosette size in teasel (*Dipsacus fullonum* L.). *Oecologia (Berl.)* **20**, 197–201.

WIERSUM, L. K. (1958). Density of root branching as affected by substrate and separate ions. *Acta bot. neerl.* **7**, 174–190.

RESOURCE ALLOCATION UNDER POOR GROWTH CONDITIONS. A MAJOR ROLE FOR GROWTH SUBSTANCES IN DEVELOPMENTAL PLASTICITY

A. TREWAVAS

Botany Department, University of Edinburgh, Edinburgh EH9 3JH, UK

Summary

This article argues that the basic function for growth substance is resource allocation under poor growth conditions. The following scheme is suggested.

Plants in the wild frequently suffer a paucity of resources which result from interplant competition and ecological and local environmental variation. The strategy adopted by many plants particularly ruderals (from which crops may have evolved) to help mitigate these problems is phenotypic plasticity; the growth of the plant body is adjusted to best exploit the scarce resources and help achieve desirable growth and reproductive goals. Phenotypic plasticity requires decisions to be made concerning the diversion of scarce growth resources to one facet of development rather than another; for example, to height or leaf area rather than thickness; or, between tissues, stem rather than leaves. Growth substances are coupled to these individual facets of development. They represent a simple way in which the extent of resource diversion can be controlled.

Cells in specific tissues acquire sensitivity to particular growth substances at a stage in their development when environmental variability often necessitates choices to be made. This acquisition of ontogenetic sensitivity may be all or none. It may reflect acquisition of receptor proteins coupled to specific metabolic events. However in well-nourished plants these phases of development are relatively insensitive to changes in the level of the growth substance/receptor complex. Cells become more sensitive under certain well-defined but specific circumstances, characterized by the general term, poor growth conditions. These are produced by imbalances in one or more of the major environmental (nutritional) requirements for growth, light, nitrogen, water and oxygen. Imbalance in one or more of these produces characteristic and far-reaching metabolic and protein synthesis changes which normally constrain the synthetic processes for growth but amplify metabolic events coupled to growth substances. It is the function of growth substances to circumvent some of these metabolically constraining steps and by applying a constant stimulus to one specific aspect of growth or metabolism permit continued development. The additional input of growth substances into particular facets of development ensures the better maintenance (protection) of that character when competition for resources inside the plant is severe. However competition for scarce resources ensures that continuation of one growth aspect generally leads to relative depletion of others. Thus there are two categories to growth-substance sensitivity; an ontogenetic sensitivity defined by the state of development and the tissue; and a metabolic sensitivity, defined in part by the environment and the cellular metabolic capability responding to that environment.

It may be possible to associate particular growth substances with specific environmental imbalances and thus particular characteristic metabolic states. For example, auxin with starvation in etiolated plants, ethylene with oxygen depletion, abscisic acid with water depletion, cytokinin with nitrogen imbalance.

The above proposal is argued both from the features of developmental plasticity, systems and metabolic control properties, and unbalanced growth and provides an acceptable theoretical framework to assess the contribution of growth substances to development.

I. Development and internal plant communication

Animal and plant development and the evolution of developmental plasticity

Essential differences between animal and plant development have been commented on for some time. 'In the animal body with its parts thus arranged in an ordered hierarchy, there is no such thing as an indefinite succession of limbs, and branches of limbs, numerically unfixed and liable to impede one another; but this is what we find among plants in which the urge to self-maintenance leads to the production of an indefinite number of growing points.' 'The individuality of the mammalian body is of a much more fixed character; that body consists of a limited number of members and organs which were already, once and for all, marked out in the embryo and which have no power of subsequent self-multiplication.' Arber, 1950 (see older but similar quotes from Erasmus Darwin in White, 1978). Arber's statement illustrates two facets of plastic development.

A plant can consist of one meristem or thousands; it can bear one leaf (stipule, bract etc.) or thousands; it can produce one seed or millions. This iterative character to both plant structure and development is a critical difference between all sessile and non-sessile organisms whether they be animal or plant. All angiosperms consist of repetitions of the same module structure; above ground the module is the bud plus subtended leaf, below ground repetitions of root meristems (Harper, 1977). In its extreme, angiosperm, form the modules separate physically (as in *Lemna*) and live an independent existence. This raises interesting questions concerning plant communication. If the various meristems (or other organs) do chemically communicate with each other, angiosperms must have the capability for adjustment to a huge concentration range of such information coincident with variation in module number. Or does *Lemna* indicate that such communication, if it exists at all, is only short range, i.e. within the module?

The second of Arber's points is that a pronounced embryonic phase is much less characteristic of plants. Plant development continues throughout the life of the organism and in an environment which fluctuates and which in turn induces compositional variation in the plant. Every mature plant body represents a history of the environmental variation it has encountered and its response to that if we could interpret it. Plasticity in development is caused by variable interference in the expression of the full genetic potential of which a plant is capable but coupled with that plasticity is evident stability in many other aspects of development. How can this apparent conflict be reconciled? If compositional variation induces plasticity, stable aspects must have control systems resistant to such variation. Animals by limiting their critical phases of development to an egg or other protected state in which environmental variation is severely constrained sacrifice plasticity for reproducibility. The sheer complexity of tissue differentiation and function requires the latter. The reasons for this difference originated with the evolutionary split between animals and plants.

Origin of specific aspects to plant development

Plant and animal cells separated in evolutionary terms between 1–2 × 10^9 years ago when both were single cells. The original eucaryotic cell was believed to be photosynthetic and to be surrounded by a cell wall (no doubt initially acting as an excess photosynthate store). The loss of chloroplasts and cell walls by some cells which then proceeded to predate the others marked the plant/animal divide.

Since light, theoretically, was ubiquitously distributed there has never been strong selection pressure to develop organs of movement (motile plants are confined to the algae). Higher plants are sessile organisms but sessility carries with it certain biological hazards to which solutions must be sought. Overgrowing was solved by erect tip growth and eventually the evolutionary conversion of this to a meristem. Competition for resources necessitated an effective mechanism for maximizing the occupation of space. Multicellularity may have evolved from advantage inherent in the convoy principle; it is more difficult for a predator to find cells grouped together in one place than if they are uniformly distributed in space. The necessity for a holdfast initiated tissue specialization. The evolution of the meristem capable of producing others was a critical step forward. It ensured a containment of predation and environmental damage; growth could be simply continued at other undamaged meristems. Branching is also a very effective means of exploiting local spatial resources.

Plant tissue and cell specialization was kept to the minimum compatible with the multicellular state. Specialized organisms are extremely vulnerable to even limited predator damage since vital functions can be quickly lost. Plants are weakly hierarchical systems with no obvious central controlling tissue. Throughout the life cycle of a higher plant at most some 20 cell types can be recognized. There is little or no cytoplasmic differentiation and these cell types can usually only be recognized by their anatomical context or by their cell wall structure. Thus some 70–80% cells in a higher plant seem unspecialized and indeed remain capable of cell division (and subsequent regeneration and reorganization) upon receipt of appropriate signals such as wounding. There is great overlap in function between many vegetative tissues. The lack of specialization is not the characteristic of an unevolved simple organism but an obvious positive evolutionary decision for a sessile organism which must tolerate predation.

Consequences for plant development from lack of specialization

Plant tissues are less integrated than animal tissues

The lack of tissue and thus metabolic specialization, the continued presence of a cell wall (which inhibits cell-to-cell integration), the easy resumption of cell division, the regenerative prowess of many tissues and well-established cell totipotency argue for the continued, relative, isolation and even considerable independence of plant cells in angiosperms. Organization is a labile phenomenon. The lengthy survival of tissue pieces (leaves, roots, stem) after excision argues for a paucity of integration at the tissue level which is reflected by a similar lack of integration at the cellular level; it suggests that most cells retain most (but not all) metabolic functions during development and thus are partly autonomous. Plants are weakly hierarchical at the whole plant, the tissue and even the cellular level. There may be less cell-to-cell communication during plant development than is commonly assumed. Paucity of integration means however paucity of interaction; the processes of plant development are therefore best viewed as pre-eminent at the cellular level.

Clonal concepts of development would support this cellular semi-autonomy. These would argue that meristems are composed of mother cells which simply clone themselves during development. Cells acquire a programme of instructions in the meristem which is then sequentially accomplished during later development, a programme which results in spatially visible changes but which has a strongly curtailing temporal aspect as well. In a recent study of cell development in pea roots the apparent semiautonomy of developmental behaviour of individual cells was strikingly observed (Allan & Trewavas, 1985). The data were interpreted to indicate that cells acquired their individual programme of instructions within the meristem and these instructions were then sequentially but independently expressed in development. A simple analogy is that of forest succession. The colonization of bare land is dominated successively by a variety of species each with different life cycles and each of which is then subsequently submerged as successive types rise to domination. Forest succession is a phenomenon of recognizable reproducibility but which requires only limited interaction between the component species involved. In the same way individual plant cell types or developmental programmes may be analogous and like forest species with the proviso that they are physically joined together.

In animals the requirement for food necessitated the development of tissues specialized to sense and to move. Cells were integrated into complex, coherently behaving organs each with discrete functions. With the evolutionary appearance of animals predating each other the consequences required the further refinement of these functions. The integration of such functions together to improve co-ordination necessitated the development of a nervous system which rapidly became the dominant control tissue. Animal development is strikingly hierarchical. The continued, back and forth, refinement of sensory and movement systems in alternately predator and then prey may well account for the explosive evolution of animals in the last 5×10^8 years.

Because of the pronounced appearance of tissue-specific proteins during animal development, theories ascribing pre-eminence to gene expression hold sway. For plants these theories, while of relevance, are of less obvious

Table 1. *Suggested degree of stability or plasticity of individual characters of development within single plants or between individuals of the same species*

	Extreme stability ←	— Moderate plasticity —	→ Extreme plasticity
1.	Seed and fruit anatomical structure	seed and fruit weight	seed and fruit numbers
2.	flower structure	induction of flower formation	flower numbers
3.	leaf induction (phyllotaxy)		
4.	leaf shape	leaf size	leaf numbers
5.	specification of cell division	size of dividing area	rates of division
6.	specification of cell expansion	initiation of cell division size of expanding area	rates of expansion
7.	shoot, root or bud meristem specification	factors inducing meristem reorganisation	meristem numbers
8.	vascular cell types	numbers of vascular bundles	wound vessel numbers
9.		vascular patterns	
10.	Internode shape	internode length internode thickness	internode number
11.		root/shoot ratio	
12.			plant volume
13.		chemical composition	

The table attempts to summarize the degree of plasticity in individual developmental characters. For example the anatomical structure shows little variation between seeds of the same plant, the weight may however vary up to twofold but the number between different plants of the same species commonly by two to three orders of magnitude. Where such comparisons cannot be made the stability/plasticity position has been determined by a number of factors so far known to be involved in induction, i.e. ease with which the process may be altered experimentally. Thus the anatomical structure of a flower is highly specified but in some species a variety of ways are known to induce flower formation.

value and a molecular (electrical) basis for developmental plasticity has been proposed (Trewavas, Sexton & Kelly, 1984).

Factors inducing developmental plasticity and the role of competition

Stable and plastic characters in plant development

Table 1 summarizes some of the plasticity easily recognizable in plants and enables perhaps a convenient division into two broad categories, iterative plasticity and physiological/morphological plasticity.

The most plastic of plant characters is that of iterative plasticity; the numbers of seeds, buds, leaves, meristems on an individual plant. The variations can be enormous (up to five orders of magnitude) and are detailed by White (1978). They reflect in part the stage of growth and also an adjustment of the plant body to prevailing resources by means of abscission. The means whereby this is accomplished seem to be simply those of competition for available resources, light or water, where the disadvantaged lose out (Addicott, 1982). Individual seeds, leaves, etc. show much less variation in size and this argues for a remarkable sensitivity in the processes initiating abscission. The abscission zone seems able to sense the rate of transport of materials in and out of the appropriate organ thus indicating its degree of functioning (Trewavas *et al.* 1984).

Since seeds, leaves, buds and other organs are often considered rich sources of growth substances, iterative plasticity poses difficult problems for the supposed control of whole plant growth substance levels particularly bearing in mind the associated plasticity of plant volume (size).

Physiological plasticity is exemplified by a number of characteristics. Flexibility in vascular tissue quantities (but not in cell types), ease of meristem reorganization both from intact, wounded tissue or even by subsection of pre-existing meristems, flexibility in signals, initiating or inhibiting meristem activity, ease of reinitiation of cell division (Trewavas, 1981), 1985*a*). Even specific cell types can have indeterminate futures, a phenomenon well demonstrated by Tranh Thanh Van (1981).

However what is most revealing about Table 1 is that it shows that stable and plastic characters exist side by side. Indeed many of the physiologically plastic characters, leaf or internode size for example are ones associated both with resource availability and growth substances. They presumably originate from the compositional variation which accompanies variability in basic resources. However if the plastic characters are determined in this way then the stable characters of plant development must be controlled by entirely novel mechanisms resistant to such compositional fluctuation.

Thus if it is proposed that the levels of auxin contribute to the numbers of vascular cells it is difficult to see how auxin concentrations can be used to specify the direction of vascular channels from stem to leaf which are extremely stable characteristics.

Factors responsible for iterative plasticity and opportunistic growth

Because of their sessile characteristics, seedlings cannot choose the site in which they grow. The microclimate of such sites can be extremely variable (Harper, 1977) and provision of considerable genetic variability in growth and development characteristics would help optimize exploitation and survival by each succeeding generation (Levins, 1969). Considerable differences in many morphological features (e.g. internode length, leaf area, stolon length, flower numbers) which are heritable have been noted between even adjacent plants of the same species collected from the same environmental niche (Burdon, 1980).

Environmental conditions which give rise to plasticity are those involving day-to-day variations in available light, fluctuations of 20° or more (even in tropical forests) and the variable provision of water and minerals. These variations as pointed out give rise to compositional variation but these are additional important factors. Patterns of growth of modular organisms can be considered as ways in which local space is captured since this in turn determines the provision of resources. Available space is altered not only by herbivory and predation *but crucially by other plants.*

Plants in the wild do not grow as isolated individuals but amongst a complex mixture of species all of which by competition or interference alter the availability of local space for capture (Newman, 1982). The 17 or so minerals needed for plant growth are unevenly distributed in the soil and Tilman (1982) has suggested that such uneven distribution with competition may be the major factor in Angiosperm speciation. Root systems are able by branching to opportunistically exploit local areas of soil rich in nitrate, phosphate, water or soil structure but the branching is limited solely to the appropriate stratum of soil (Drew, Saker & Ashley, 1973).

While this opportunistic character may be less obvious in shoots, no doubt because of greater daily resource variation, it becomes apparent when looked for. Harper (1977) has pointed out how the branching patterns of interfering adjacent trees adjust to space limitation as do interfering branches on the same tree. For crop plants and other plants growing in the wild, the canopy structure ensures a range of temperature, humidity, light and wind speed conditions from the top down to soil level and the plant structure compensates plastically and locally by changes in apical dominance and abscission of organs. Laboratory studies on apical dominance may bear little relevance to the reality of branch induction under crowded wild conditions (Harper, 1977). Shoots can grow through light gaps promoting the growth of themselves and others carried on them (White, 1978). Light is a major factor in pronounced phenotypic variation in seedling structure (Grime & Jeffrey, 1965). In different species phenotypic variations in the structure of hypocotyls, cotyledons, internodes, petioles and laminae were observed when seedlings were shaded. Similar local environmental constraints selectively modify the growth of shoots and branches in woody angiosperms optimizing the exploitation of the local environment and shedding the branches, shoots, leaves and buds which are no longer able to compete for the limited carbon and other resources. Denny & Stanton (1928) many years ago demonstrated the remarkable extent to which meristems can grow independently of each other.

In addition to these, predation, (herbivory) and environmental damage can be intensely local and the response, compensatory growth, breakage of dominance and physiological regeneration equally local in its appearance. Watson & Caspar (1984) introducing the concepts of 'integrated physiological units' as a semi-autonomous structural and physiological unit summarize a wealth of evidence showing developmental decisions concerning meristems to be made locally. The characteristics of opportunistic growth described by Tomlinson (1982) emphasize the probabilistic nature of much plant construction. There is a capability for response to chance elements in the plant environment but expression of this response only occurs when the original genetic potential is in some way frustrated. There is not one fixed genomic plan of higher plant construction but only a series of futures each with a differing degree of probability of expression. Such considerations apply equally to branch length, leaf size, root numbers and so on. Such features are less obvious in agricultural and laboratory-grown plants and this may have led to their relative discounting in physiological research interest. But the concept of a plant as a population of growing, competing and self-interfering tissues and meristems is as valid for many crop plants as is the concept of competition for limited resources between different plants.

The ecologists have emphasized for many years how misleading laboratory-grown plants may be when trying to understand aspects of developmental regulation. A process which has evolved to adjust leaf area (within limits) to prevailing environmental circumstances may, if experimental studies are carried out only on laboratory plants, assume a much greater conceptual significance in leaf development than warranted.

Competition is an internal factor in communication and a basic determinant of developmental plasticity

In the absence of a central controlling tissue in plants there must be considerable independence in the behaviour of the individual growing areas subject to competition for internal resources and with assessment of the external enviromental constraints. The plant body is finely adjusted to exploit its local enviroment. Indeed if it is optimally capturing resources then each growing area, each leaf should deprive others of some of the available light, minerals or water.

Plants in many ecosystems are known to grow more slowly than crop plants, seedling establishment is much slower and hazardous and growth responds in many ecosystems to application of minerals (Rorison, 1969). Many experiments even on crop plants have shown that there is competition for available internal resources with those best placed acquiring the most. The shoot more successfully competes for carbohydrate; the root, water and minerals. Loomis (1953) showed that tomatoes deprived of water, minerals or both showed only reduced shoot growth with the root/shoot ratio increasing threefold. The root/shoot ratio of individual tillers on rhizomes of Carex was found to be determined by the local mineral status in which each grew. From high-to-low fertility soils the root/shoot ratio of the individual but joined tillers varied tenfold (Harper, 1977) and there was little evidence for communication of altered ratios to other adjacent tillers. Davidson (1969) reported that temperature could modify the root/shoot ratio up to eightfold, and Chapin (1980) reported variations of 19-fold. Removal of flowers or fruits permits increased vegetative shoot growth (Loomis, 1953). Excision of one shoot tissue permits compensatory growth by others. Goebel (1900) reported many examples of competition between seeds, leaves, stipules, stolons and fruits. Competition for water determines spine formation in *Ulex*, for example. Removal of early potato shoots causes stolons to become erect and become shoots; removal of early stolons the converse.

The critical feature is that individual growing parts suffer a paucity of resources and thus the genetic potential for growth can rarely if ever be fulfilled. What one growing part removes from the resources in circulation is not available to another. With differing resource requirements for growth of specific tissues, this can lead, in turn, to very specific alterations in what is left, which could then act as inductive developmental signals. This is a form of communication, termed negative control, which can be quite specific (Trewavas, 1983*a*, 1985*b*). It is sometimes called nutrient diversion but this term omits its essential competitive nature. However negative communication has been proposed as the mechanism to explain the induction of flowering, tuberization, dormancy, leaf senescence, apical dominance, the switch between leaf and rhizome formation and abscission of fruits and leaves (Sachs, 1977; Addicott, 1982; Trewavas, 1983*b*, 1985*b*). If competition for circulating nitrogen between the young growing leaves, and shoot or stolon apex, putative dormant bud and other leaves, is reduced by application of nitrate to the plant, then flowering, tuberization, dormancy and senescence can all be inhibited. As regards circulating growth substances an excess of binding proteins in one tissue would competitively sequester more growth substance from the circulating level thus denying it to others.

If the levels of nitrogen available to the shoot are low but light is freely available then the shoot tissue very adequately competes for the photosynthate it produces. But the shoot becomes more highly differentiated, cell walls and cuticle are thicker, there is greater lignification and earlier and greater formation of vascular tissue (Loomis, 1953); the processes of secondary development are advanced. Thus even at the metabolic level there may be simple competition between the primary and secondary processes of development with a degree of flexibility built in but with an obvious overall genetic limitation. In the same way it has been suggested that the processes of division and cell expansion undergo internal competition for limiting microtubule resources (Lloyd, 1979; Trewavas, 1982*a*).

Physiological aspects of development are also demonstrably plastic in character

Cell development rates are plastic

Cell development has two important characteristics. Firstly it has a progressive, historical character through programmes of division, expansion/differentiation and maturation and additional longer term changes such as loss of capability for reinitiation of cell division, accumulation of secondary products, lignification etc. These stages are not mutually exclusive and certainly cells in the concomitant act of division, expansion and differentiation have been observed in root development (Allan & Trewavas, 1985) but this historical programme represents a very stable aspect to development. Acquisition and loss of sensitivity to growth substances appear to be additional, progressive, continually changing characters which act to link different stages of development (Trewavas, 1982*b*). The processes of cell development are not understood but no doubt it requires the complex interplay of the whole metabolic system reacting to changes in gene expression.

Secondly, there is quite critically, a certain time period within which these successive changes occur. There may be some linking between the historical and temporal character but selfevidently the linkage is not direct. Every phase in plant development seems to have a limited time available but the concomitant rates or extent of cell division, expansion and maturation are flexible within this time period thus giving rise to plasticity in, for example, internode length, leaf area or fruit volume. Determinate organs in well-nourished plants have more cells which are larger (Sinnott, 1960) but there are obvious genetic limitations to this flexibility.

Attempts to understand the nature of developmental timing seem non-existent. The data of Barlow & Hancock (1959) on coleoptile extension show that the visible events of growth are partly independent of the timing; coleoptile sections growing in the presence or absence of auxin cease growing at the same time. However the timing process is definitely temperature dependent and thus probably metabolic in character.

Plasticity in the molecular and physiological events accompanying growth

In leaves, petioles, coleoptiles, hypocotyls and stems the two gross parameters of size, length/surface area *versus* thickness can vary with relative independence (Grime & Jeffrey, 1965). Leaves of many plants grown in shade have a bigger surface area than those in sunlight but are distinctly thinner and internodes of such plants are frequently longer but thinner (Blackman, 1956; Friend, 1966); rice coleoptiles anaerobically grown submerged are longer but thinner than the aerobically grown counterparts (Alpi & Beevers, 1983), likewise submerged petioles of some water plants (Ridge, 1985). Hypocotyls of etiolated melon and bean seeds from which varying quantities of seed reserve have been removed are longer but thinner (on an initial seed weight basis) than their unmanipulated counterparts (Gould, Pearl, Edwards & Miner, 1934; Shear, 1931); cytokinin treatment of *Lemna* increases the surface area of fronds as does lower available nitrate but with a thinning of the frond; whilst abscisic acid (ABA) induces a corresponding thickening compared to untreated fronds (Smart & Trewavas, 1983; Trewavas, 1972; White, 1937). These data suggest a possible competition between the processes of area/length and thickness; if thickness processes are inhibited the resources are available for elongation or expansion. In all the above examples the plasticity in area or height (length) represents a significant ecological advantage in either light collection or growth of tissue to more favourable circumstances (Grime & Jeffrey, 1965).

Other data show that molecular events of growth are often flexibly associated with each other. Cell extension can take place in the absence of wall deposition leading to thinning of the cell wall (Setterfield & Bailey, 1961); excised tissue sections can grow in the absence of accumulations of RNA and protein observed in intact tissue (Hanson & Trewavas, 1982) and in the immediate absence of changes of turgor pressure or ion flux (Taiz, 1984); *Lemna* can maintain a uniform rate of growth with a three- or fourfold variation in protein content (White, 1937).

The sensing and induction of developmental change can be very plastic

The necessity for plants to accommodate their continuing development to a constantly variable environment has resulted in a multiplicity of responses to different environmental parameters which are best illustrated by example. Mansfield & Davies (1983) comment that stomatal aperture is sensitive to a wider range of stimuli than any known animal sensory tissue; Hillman (1984) lists 14 different ways in which apical dominance can be broken; turions (resting buds) of *Spirodela* can be induced to form by short days, high-light intensity, low temperature, low nitrogen or low phosphate, high sugar levels, overcrowding, pH changes and abscisic acid (Trewavas & Allan, 1985).

The phenomenon is exemplified in other ways. Roberts (1972) lists some 30 different chemicals which can be used to break seed dormancy usually in the same species; substances such as nitrate, ethanol, cyanide, azide, chloroform, CO_2, phenols, thiourea, methylene blue, growth substances as well as light and temperature treatments. Similar lists of chemicals or physical treatments of equal or greater complexity have been produced for the promotion of leaf senescence, adventitious root formation, cell division in shoot buds, abscission, regeneration from callus or epidermal explants, bud dormancy breakage and polarity in *Fucus* egg (Trewavas, 1982*a,b*, 1983*a,b*, 1985*a*; Trewavas *et al.* 1984; Trewavas & Allan, 1985). A variety of chemical factors and other environmental treatments have been shown to modify sex expression, subvert flower induction by photoperiod, cell extension and cambial development (references in Trewavas & Allan, 1985). No doubt if examined many other characters of plant development will be shown to be similarly responsive. The rate of growth of *Lemna* for example has been shown to be promoted by oxalate, glutamine, asparagine, allantoin, salicylic acid, arginine, 6-mercaptopurine, penicillin, tetracycline, benzimidazole, kinetin, p-aminobenzoic acid and gibberellic acid, benzyladenine auxin and ethylene (Nickell, 1955; Hillman, 1961). Such a variety of chemicals suggests either a non-specific effect on the outer membrane or that in cells committed to a particular developmental pathway, effects at a variety of places in the metabolic network are sufficient to promote or initiate the process.

The richness of effects of environmental treatments can be illustrated by temperature. Low-temperature treatments can be used to subvert a photoperiodic control of flowering and tuberization (Evans, 1969) break seed and bud dormancy, alter the balance of male to female flowers (Heslop-Harrison, 1957) break apical dominance in pea (McComb, 1973) induce male sterility (Kaur-Sawhney, 1984) subvert gibberellin insensitivity of dwarf wheat aleurone cells (Singh & Paleg, 1984) induce turion formation and leaf abscission, enhance stomatal opening by abscisic acid (Mansfield & Davies, 1983) and vernalize winter cereals and other plants. High temperature can induce or break seed or bud dormancy (Perry, 1971) obviate a cytokinin requirement for habituation (Meins, 1982) subvert gibberellin control of aleurone amylase (Nicholls, 1982) induce root hair formation in epidermal explants (Tranh Than Van, 1982) overcome a drying requirement for aleurone amylase formation (Norman, Black & Chapman, 1983) and specifically modify leaf area (Milthorpe 1956). No doubt if examined in detail virtually all stages of plant development will be shown to be specifically modifiable by appropriate temperature treatments. Many plants grow unsatisfactorily if grown at constant temperature. Similar conclusions probably apply to light, minerals and water (Sinnott, 1960), (in particular, see for example, specific developmental changes induced by nitrate Trewavas, 1983*b*).

Wild plants live in a constantly variable environment. The factors modifying development must vary too and as is known induce compositional changes. However one would expect the whole metabolic system of the cell to change as environmental conditions alter. How likely is it that variation in water availability or light or changes in temperature or oxygen availability will lead only to the selective synthesis of one or two growth substances? Given the diversity of treatments capable of promoting or inducing development the commonly expressed view that development is regulated by changing the biosynthesis of one or two growth substances is seen to be a gross oversimplification; a confusion between what may be a contributing substance under some circumstances for the only controlling factor. In the case of the previously mentioned induction of turion formation in *Spirodela* abscisic acid may be ‘a’ factor in the promotion of developmental change but it is unlikely to be ‘the’ factor. A variety of factors controlling development would certainly lead to a much greater reliability in the processes involved and this may be essential for organisms so constrained by a variable environment (Trewavas & Allan, 1985).

Any of the factors necessary for development can theoretically be made limiting and adequate dose responses produced by adding them back. However many thousands of small and large molecules are used for each stage of development. It seems to be a matter of finding the experimental conditions to demonstrate the effect.

The plasticity in development expressed at this level is a novel plant characteristic. A necessary adjunct to the sessile mode of life in which the environment must be tolerated rather than avoided. This flexibility in development must surely reflect novel metabolic capabilities which ought to heighten the excitement of molecular biologists anxious to probe these phenomena (Trewavas, 1982*a*).

Physiological plasticity is best exemplified by regeneration and plasticity in polarity

In numerous plants, root meristems can be regenerated from root, shoot, leaf, bud and leaf buds and bulb scales, pollen, epidermal explants, cells in culture and cotyledons. Shoot meristems can be regenerated from an equivalent number of tissues but in fewer species. Callus can be generated from virtually all plant tissues examined and in numerous species. Regeneration is induced by wounding or excision and a possible sequence of metabolic changes has been outlined to explain this organizational lability (Trewavas *et al.* 1984).

Although polarity is generally thought to be a process fixed by early development there are numerous reports in the literature of the regeneration of upside-down plants (Massart, 1916; Neilson-Jones, 1925). Some plants, e.g. bramble, do this naturally, rooting where the stem touches the ground. Others, e.g. *Aloe frutescens* seem to have an inherently weak polarity, but the most recent example is that described by Sheldrake (1974) who regenerated upside-down tomatoes but demonstrated that the polarity of auxin movement remained in the original, rightside-up direction. Such observations, as Sheldrake concludes, raise significant doubts concerning the importance of polar auxin movement to plant development.

An overview of developmental plasticity

Early animal development takes place in a protected, constant environment (e.g. the egg) in which the initial specification, the number of and demarcation of tissues is accomplished in a very short time period. The specified cells are quickly canalized and their development is then irreversible. Resources are distributed throughout the growing organs whose volume is carefully specified. Animals rapidly become strongly hierarchical with a 'unitary' controlling nervous system which adaptively specifies behaviour by coordinating to differing degrees the activities of the various tissues. The nervous system acts autocratically and, in a bureaucratic type of organization, receives and monitors information via hormones and nerves and reissues instructions in the same way. The adaptiveness of the animal lies in the brain. Development is controlled almost solely by internal factors and environmental influences are minimal.

From the seedling onwards the majority of plants continue development in an indeterminate, modular fashion fashioning the body to best exploit the local space and maximize resource capture. There is no central controlling tissue, the organization is basically democratic and the growing parts are left with a high degree of autonomy and flexibility in response after a summation of the availability of both internal and external factors. The numbers of major organs and the size of the plant body (volume) are highly plastic. Development as a process is qualitatively and quantitatively fashioned by a variable environment in ways that have little parallel in animal studies. The organizational structure of plants suggests that interaction is minimal and that development is emphatically at the cellular rather than the tissue level. The democratic, modular nature of plant growth and overlap of many tissue functions enables the plant to resist predation, tolerate damage and optimize local resource exploitation.

II. The role of growth substances in development. Resource allocation under poor growth conditions

Current theory of growth substance action

The current theory emphasizes that plant growth substances have a hormonal function.

Thus 'Movement is indubitably tied to the definition of hormones; hormones are substances active in minute amounts produced in one location and active in another. In angiosperms this movement co-ordinates development' (Jacobs, 1979). 'A small number of organic compounds have now been shown to act as co-ordinators of the growth and development of the plant and to be active in minute amounts. Such compounds are termed plant hormones. Phytohormones move from a site of production to a site of action to evoke characteristic responses' (Letham, Higgins, Goodwin & Jacobsen, 1978).

This theory has within it certain predictions which can be tested against the observations we have previously discussed.

1. Hormones would impede semiautonomy in developmental decisions and thus inhibit local resource exploitation

It is the function of hormones to coordinate the growth and development of different tissues towards specific goals. On a whole plant basis hormones would interfere with localized plasticity in growth and development and act instead to provide a uniform growth behaviour throughout the whole organism. Thus it could be argued that perennial plants become dormant because of high circulating levels of abscisic acid. Data obtained by Denny & Stanton (1928) show on the contrary that bud dormancy is the property of individual meristems and not the result of some circulating inhibitory material. The dormancy of individual buds could be broken in winter and the growing leafy shoot failed to elicit subsequent breakage of others nearby.

If one part of a plant is growing under poor conditions, on a hormonal theory this would act to inhibit the exploitation of good conditions experienced by other parts. The data of Harper (1977) are quite clear. The successive tillers on rhizomes of *Carex* rooted in soils of different mineral status responded plastically to the local conditions. The root/shoot ratio varied up to tenfold and there was little evidence of transmission of this ratio outside the treated tiller.

A back and forth communication of specific growth factors between root and shoot would prevent plasticity in the root/shoot ratio. Since such plasticity is frequently observed the assumption that the root and shoot growth reflects the extent of competition for limited resources seems more justifiable.

2. Negative communication contradicts hormonal controls

The known interactions which occur by negative means (by competition) stands in clear contrast to putative positive hormonal controls. Allometric growth is often used as arguments for hormonal control but is explicable as the result of competition between growing parts for limited resources (Von Bertallanfy, 1968). Historical aspects to development (one group of cells develops into another) can account for much of the supposed allometric relationships particularly if decisions concerning the extent of growth are taken in the meristem.

3. Hormone signals would be destroyed by environmental noise

If tissues are to communicate by single chemicals then it is difficult to see how this would survive the rigours of local compositional and environmental variation. Without monitoring of signals there could be no guarantee that the responding tissue actually responded given the great variety of factors that modify development in plants. The signal would, in information theory parlance, be simply destroyed by noise.

4. *Meaningful communication or distribution of labour*

Perhaps the greatest difficulty with the hormonal theory is the basic experimental structure used to support it. Tissue pieces are excised and attempts made by adding back plant growth substances to recover some of the functional development of either the excised tissue or the remaining plant portion. If a response is detected it is assumed that the excised tissue (or remaining tissue) acts as the source of growth substance and that communication is accomplished by this means. This approach is an obvious attempt to mimic the endocrinologist but it suffers two flaws. Firstly, it fails to take account of pharmacological or artefactual effects of growth substances. Second, so far as is known there are no cells which just perform the function of synthesizing growth substances. Excision of any tissue piece perturbs a whole series of interplant interactions by removing one of the participating components which undeniably perform more functions than synthesis of growth substances. Three examples illustrate the difficulties.

(A) Based on excision experiments, roots are often suggested to communicate with leaves via root-produced cytokinins retarding senescence. But the root also acts as a sink for carbohydrate, other chemicals, and vitamins; as a recirculation point for shoot materials and as a source of water, minerals and reduced nitrogen. Loss of root sink function leading to accumulation of leaf photosynthate has been reported as inducing leaf senescence. Lack of reduced nitrogen invariably leads to senescence (Thomas & Stoddart, 1980; Salama & Wareing, 1978). There is also strong evidence that both shoots and seeds can synthesize cytokinins.

(B) The barley embryo is believed to communicate its growing activity to the cereal aleurone by mean of gibberellin, where it induces amylase formation. However the sink activity of the embryo is critical to the response (Trewavas, 1982*b*) and with the evidence that the barley embryo can produce up to 50 % of the amylase of the cereal seed and that gibberellin may be synthesized in the aleurone (Gibbons, 1979; Atzhorn & Weiler, 1983) the initial simple theory is hardly tenable. Aleurone amylase production may perhaps be more to do with poising the water content of the growing embryo than reserve mobilization.

(C) It is thought that the specification of the vascular channel connecting the stem to the growing leaf may be the result of auxin synthesized by the leaf blade moving in a polar direction downwards. However anatomical data suggests that vascular tissue may develop in an upwards and downwards direction (Esau, 1965; Larson, 1983). The growing leaf blade is a sink which acquires its materials (including auxin) from the pre-existing vascular tissue and grows directionally outwards from the stem. The leaf blade may therefore also acquire auxin in an upward direction. Many factors are known to influence vascular tissue formation not only auxin. Careful studies by Larson (1983) and many others have indicated that apparent acropetal and basipetal development of vascular tissue can occur. The situation is perhaps reminiscent of the direction of renewal of cambial cell division activity in springtime in trees; in some trees the renewed activity direction is apparently downwards but in others apparently upwards (Trewavas, 1985*a*). A more circumspect conclusion might be that the formation of vascular tissue is one of very considerable complexity and attempts to relate it to the movement of one molecule or another will inevitably produce conflicting data when different species and conditions are examined. The renewal of cambial activity may result from a developmentally controlled annual cycle in activity coupled with a sensing of movement of materials in adjacent vascular tissue. No doubt the movements of molecules in both directions are critical.

A further problem issues from the notion that the apparent direction of vascular strand appearance can be easily equated with the direction of a supposed morphogen. It is very difficult to synchronize a response from a group of cells to a uniform signal appearing at one discrete time. The experience of those in the cell cycle field is that response is sporadic and stochastic in character. Even if a vascular strand appeared to develop downwards (thus leading to suppositions of polar movement of the stimulus) this would depend on assumptions of uniform sensitivity to the morphogen by the responding cells for which there is no evidence. Given that one is always dealing with cells of different historical ages is this assumption warranted? The conclusion of Esau (1965) that in leaf vascular development one is simply dealing with a set of relatively, concurrent phenomena in which cause and effect are difficult to distinguish is reasonable. The assumption that leaf removal only leads to auxin depletion ignores other obvious leaf functions and oversimplifies the complexity inherent in such a situation. Auxin may be 'a' factor in vascular development but it is not 'the' factor. Exogenous auxin has effects on many aspects of shoot development and may be better seen as some generalized stimulus, able to maintain cells in a state of relative metabolic activity under certain conditions but with the decision concerning the direction of development already predetermined. In this respect, for immature cortical cells in intact plants, the only possibilities seem to be vascular tissue or cortex.

Other problems with the hormonal theory

These have been dealt with in more detail elsewhere (Trewavas, 1981), 1982*b*, 1983*a*; Trewavas & Allan, 1985) and need not be reiterated here. The hormonal theory seeks to explain what are evidently complicated phenomena by very simple means. How can meaningful communication be distinguished from simple distribution of labour? If labelled sucrose is applied to one leaf some of it can be detected in adjacent leaves. Is this communication? On the other hand much of the sucrose can end up in the root where it can induce lateral root formation. Is this communication? All multicellular organisms distribute their metabolic labour but does this necessarily mean direct communication of that distributed function. Even if most cytokinin is synthesized in plant roots does that justify the assumption that it has a communicative role? The consistent position is either to view all specific metabolic functions (e.g. photosynthesis) as communication or none of them, but at the minimum, meaningful communication should carry with it some mechanisms of monitoring to ensure that the issued signal has been received and correctly interpreted.

The hormonal theory of growth substances is tenable only if the metabolic control of growth is arranged with the pronounced hierarchical structure shown in Figure 1. In that case all other factors which are known to modify development would have to alter the biosynthesis of the growth substance in the appropriate way. Looking at the variety of chemicals modifying development this is hardly a tenable hypothesis. Indeed the very rigidity of the structure shown in Fig. 1A would argue against such a model for metabolic control of plant cell growth. Plant cells have to act flexibly with a variety of resources appearing in unbalanced proportions. The hierarchical structure shown in Fig. 1 is the epitomy of inflexibility. Fig. 1B is a more flexible arrangement and perhaps nearer the truth.

The hormonal theory of growth substances is an unsatisfactory model which has been grafted onto plant studies from the mistaken terminology

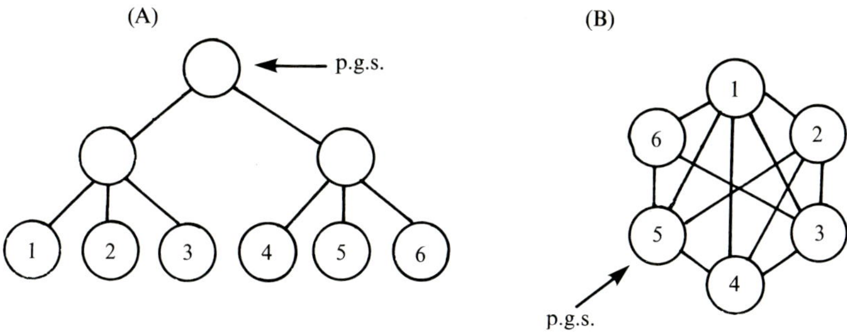

1 cell wall synthesis
2 membrane synthesis
3 protein synthesis
4 turgor generation
5 H^+ ion flux
6 secretion

Fig. 1. Two suggested arrangements for the control of some of the subsystems involved in growth and development.

(A) Hierarchical arrangement implied by classical theory of growth substance action. Ultimate control of growth and development by plant growth substances (p.g.s.) necessitates the inflexible arrangement shown here. Other substances affecting growth have to alter plant growth substance synthesis.

(B) Suggested 'democratic' arrangement of metabolic subsystems in growth. This diagram suggests growth substances may affect only one metabolic area; linkage amongst the subsystems ensures the effects become widespread throughout metabolism.

of plant hormones. By way of conclusion 'Despite a considerable amount of work which has led to the general concept that phytohormones coordinate plant growth there are few systems in which we can state unequivocally that a particular hormone is the coordinating agent' (Letham *et al.* 1978). Even animal embryologists now consider that complex specification needs no more than communication between adjacent cells (Bryant, French & Bryant, 1981). As will be seen later there is adequate reason for growth substances to function in the cells in which they are synthesized. Communication in plants is far more complex than the conveyance of one or two chemicals.

How do growth substances work? Clues from system thinking

Linkages provide systems with novel properties

Growth substances are obviously elements in the metabolic control systems of plant cells. To understand their function we must enquire what is understood concerning metabolic control and this leads directly to systems approaches which are beginning to dominate this area of work.

Systems consist of elements which are linked together. In the cell the elements are the enzymes and proteins; these are linked, via substrates and products in metabolic pathways, enzymes which modify, synthesize other enzyme/proteins or synthesize cofactors, enzymes which transport ions affecting other enzymes, or which modify or induce aggregation/polymerization or enzymes synthesizing molecules which allosterically alter the activities of others and so on. The metabolic system is an extremely complicated but integrated network of linked reactions. It is the linkages which are crucial since they ensure that properties, perturbations and control are shared throughout a substantial if not the whole of cell metabolism. The term metabolic fabric perhaps best characterizes this network concept. At a higher level, cells are interlinked by a variety of chemical, electrical, structural and osmotic interactions as indeed are the tissues in the intact plant.

It is part of the theoretical framework of general system theory to point to essentially similar properties of all systems whether they be political, economic, social or psychological. These similarities result from the structure of the system, i.e. a set of elements which are interlinked.

Metabolic control system theory is in its infancy but sufficient is known to suggest two things. *Many system properties are counter intuitive; quite simply, the complexities of interaction defy easy conceptualization.* And secondly, the properties of even simple systems, e.g. a metabolic network are in general shared by much more complicated ones such as those represented by developing systems. In the latter case changes in gene expression alter the basic elements of the system and thus break or form novel metabolic relationships. This gives rise to a continual shaping or folding of the fabric perhaps best exemplified by Waddington (1957) in his drawings of the epigenetic landscape.

Experimental approaches to defining metabolic system properties are at an early stage and are confined usually to examinations of control of flux through metabolic pathways in simple anabolic systems or photosynthesis. However as Kacser & Burns (1981) point out, the flux rate of some small molecules, e.g. anthocyanins, may be considered to be a genetic character. The important properties of metabolic systems are listed below and the application of these to the growth substance problem follows afterwards. Growth itself is a flux although of a more complex kind involving at least flux of carbohydrate into cell wall and water and ions into vacuoles.

Properties of systems which are important to understanding metabolic control

(1) Within certain limits metabolic systems will buffer against (or absorb) changes in their constituents in terms of flux through the system. If the change is large a threshold is crossed and the flux rapidly alters. Linkages between the enzyme components means that all parts of the system

experience variation in external stimuli even though it may be sensed in only a few places. The degree of buffering is determined by the numbers of interrelations within the system. With a large number of relationships high degrees of variation can be tolerated with little overall change in flux.
(2) The linking of enzyme components means that the control of flux is shared by many metabolic steps. The notions of rate-limiting steps, metabolic master switches (or limiting factors) are derived from very simple models of unlinked systems. These are an incorrect representation of metabolic systems and control and are misleading (see critique in Davies, 1977). Molecular control is democratic and many areas of metabolism and other factors contribute as indeed observations on plant development have amply shown.
(3) The sensitivity of any metabolic step to control (measured as sensitivity or control strength = small change in flux of step/overall change in system flux) is itself determined by the flux through the system. At low fluxes one step may be very sensitive to control but this sensitivity can be rapidly lost as the flux rate increases. The sensitivity of any step to control in a metabolic pathway is determined by the state of the rest of the system; as the state of whole metabolic network changes, so does the sensitivity. One part of a system is sensitive to control under one set of circumstances, i.e. one set of flux rates, but insensitive under others. This property has direct relevance to understanding control by growth substance.
(4) When the flux rate is changed it is unlikely that many individual components will show meaningful parallel variation. System flux rates are determined by many components with many operating controls. Only between adjacent metabolic steps might some sort of meaningful (correlative) relationship be likely to emerge.
(5) System fluxes can only be controlled satisfactorily by changes at many different steps. Attempts to optimize just one part of the system usually act to the detriment of the whole.
(6) Systems which deal with variable external resource inputs usually possess sufficient internal components to cater for the maximal not the average rate of supply over the short term.

Application of metabolic system properties to growth and growth substances

Properties 1 and 6 provide the formal reason for supposing that the two- to threefold variations in growth substance levels commonly observed are unlikely to be sufficiently large for significant control. The level of growth substance may be in effective excess for the short-term variation of environmental conditions experienced by plants. Although environmental conditions fluctuate in the short term one would expect that the synthesized level will slowly change to attempt to anticipate the magnitude of environmental resource fluctuation. This is perhaps why stomata open even with high level of abscisic acid in the leaf after severe water stress (Beardsell & Cohen, 1975). The capability for opening suggests short-term changes in sensitivity to be the operating control factor.

Effect of any one factor on growth is dependent on levels of all other contributing materials

Perhaps the critical property for understanding growth substances is property 3. This implies that the effect of any one contributing factor on the process of growth is dependent upon the state of the metabolic network and thus the levels of all other contributing factors. Alternatively, there will be one set of conditions under which the metabolic fabric operates with maximum responsiveness to changes in the level of growth substance/receptor complex.

This discussion will have to rely on studies involving externally added factors affecting growth but it should be appreciated that since internal growth substance (and receptor) biosynthesis will take place in a metabolic network the properties and conclusions may well be very different.

Growth and development is dependent upon the provision of external factors (CO_2, light, some 17 different minerals, water etc.) and a largely unknown member of internal factors but including growth substances, amino acids, vitamins, sugars, historical metabolic state of the cell, electrical constraints from other cells and so on. For a crop physiologist, optimal growth (and thus yield) is all that is of interest. This leads deceptively to the notion that there is one absolute set of environmental conditions which are needed for growth. It unfortunately disguises the fact that growth occurs under other conditions and that the response curve to any single factor is different under these different conditions. For growth in general there is a whole family of response curves, as many curves as there are significant setting changes of the various raw resources for growth.

In many cases (but not all) when an externally added factor is added to a sensitive tissue the growth response is of the form shown in Fig. 2. A good example is that for K^+ (Leigh & Wyn Jones, 1984). The absolute values of response to K^+ will depend upon the levels of available nitrate, sulphate, average temperature, internal factors etc. While for crop plants there may be one crucial curve, for plants in the wild with variable resource availability, other growth conditions assume much greater relevance.

The only sensible approach to dealing with such a complex problem is a sensitivity analysis. That is, keeping all other factors constant each factor in turn is altered by a tiny amount and the overall effect on growth measured. It is effectively equivalent to determining the slope of line B on the response curve in Fig. 2. One can then determine under that set of conditions the factors to which growth responds with most sensitivity. It should be clear from Fig. 2 that for a factor on its own to significantly regulate growth or development, it should be operating in region A rather than region C. However just as with K^+, we can expect the effects of added exogenous growth substances to be dependent on the availability of all other resources, both internal and external, and the metabolic and developmental status of the cell. While the experimenter has the flexibility of adding and manipulating one exogenous factor at will to obtain a response is that same flexibility available internally to the cell?

The metabolic system is a network and environmental conditions which might alter the biosynthesis of a growth substance would inevitably alter many of the other cellular constituents; enzymes as well as small molecules. The whole metabolic fabric will be altered by environmental and experimental changes and thus the base line of sensitivity to growth substances altered. Wound ethylene biosynthesis and ABA accumulation after water stress both involve changes in protein synthesis (Yang *et al.* 1982; Quarrie & Lister, 1984). But both these stress conditions involve changes in many other enzymes.

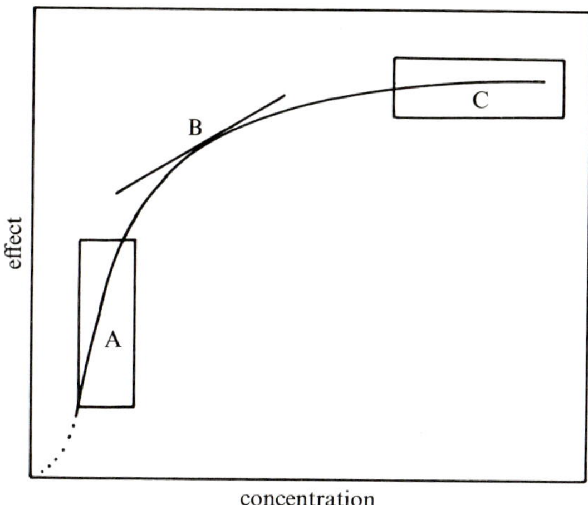

Fig. 2. Variation of growth (or growth rate) with the concentration of an exogenously added promoting substance. Regions A (high sensitivity of response), B (moderate sensitivity) and C (insensitive) are referred to in the script.

The classical hormonal interpretation is that in growth, growth substances are always somewhere in region A of Fig. 2; the notion of 'limiting factors' is often referred to in this respect. This notion is only applicable to added exogenous materials (in an effective unlinked fashion) and like anything else is only determined with respect to the setting of all other exogenous materials and internal status. Thus in the case of mineral deficiency (where perhaps the concept is best supported) it would be better termed mineral imbalance rather than specifying one mineral as 'limiting'. What is 'limiting' at one setting of other factors is no longer so when even other single constituents are altered (Hewitt, 1963) or the means of application changed. Thus we would expect growth substances to operate with maximum sensitivity in only one set of metabolic circumstances.

However in a network while a metabolic area under one set of circumstances might represent the area most sensitive to regulation, this control will inevitably be shared by many other factors, through linked components of the metabolic network. Effective control by individual molecules envisaged by the term 'limiting' is thus simply not possible.

This will not preclude experimental effects of added growth substances being observed under many circumstances but such manipulation will always require addition of growth substance levels greatly in excess of endogenous to counteract the metabolic insensitivity resulting from inappropriate environmental or cellular conditions, i.e. the plant is in region C of Fig. 2. The issue which has so befogged the whole growth substance field is that experimentalists have interpreted effects produced by excessive growth substance concentrations as indicating likely endogenous cellular control under many different metabolic circumstances. If discussion was limited to experiments using endogenous levels of growth substance there would be very little to say.

The growth substance situation can be clarified by the use of a simple system analogy.

In manipulating an economic system, there are occasions when changing the rate of interest of money is a sensitive regulator. Changing the rate of interest will have an effect on economic growth, under certain discrete circumstances, but only when the economic state changes to make that a sensitive economic control. The borrowing of money at a defined rate of interest is normal economic activity. However there is no doubt that under any economic circumstance abolishing the rate of interest would have a dramatic effect on economic growth. While initially the effect might be positive and dramatic it would lead to eventual stagnation as the available money dried up. In the same way applying a dramatically large dose of growth substance (or eliminating the endogenous level) would have an effect under many metabolic circumstances. The effects obtained with larger than endogenous concentrations may therefore be very misleading.

Can the conditions be deduced where growth substances contribute to development with greatest sensitivity i.e. where they operate in region A of Fig. 2. The growth and development of healthy, growing tissues on intact plants is usually very insensitive to added growth substances. This has been shown for intact coleoptiles and auxin (Went, 1935), intact abscission zones, ethylene (Beyer, 1975), intact leaves, cytokinin (Goodwin & Erwee, 1983) and intact stems, gibberellin (McComb, 1977). The simplest way to make these more sensitive to added growth substances is to excise or wound the tissue (Hanson & Trewavas, 1982). Excision generally reduces growth rates, dramatically and specifically modifies protein synthesis, reduces water availability, impairs membrane stability, inhibits phloem function and permits wound-related phenomena to develop in cells near the wound. Thus much of the metabolic fabric is greatly altered increasing the sensitivity of the metabolic system to applied growth substance control. In part excision may mimic poor conditions for growth and suggests that growth substances have their prime action under such circumstances.

The concepts of balanced and unbalanced growth

In 1937, White introduced the important concept of balanced growth. White had been studying the effect of environmental parameters on the growth of *Lemna*. He came to the conclusion: (1) that by varying one constituent, e.g. nitrate, variable rates of growth could be obtained; (2) that at each nitrate concentration there was in addition a separate optimal setting of all other environmental parameters which produced balanced growth at this particular rate. The criterion for balanced growth were 'greatest depth of frond colour, highest protein content, largest frond (leaf) area and optimal rate of increase of frond number' and (3) that variable rates of growth could also be produced by unbalancing the available environmental parameters (e.g. high light with low nitrate) and that unbalanced growth was frequently accompanied by massive starch accumulation, anthocyanin accumulation, loss of depth in frond colour and so on. For a balanced but low rate of growth, low nitrate concentration should be accompanied by low light. White emphasizes *that balance in growth is more important than rate* and intuitively we might expect that plants in balanced growth would be more stress and disease resistant than those which are not even though they may grow more slowly. In *Spirodela*, conditions which 'unbalance growth' are frequently those that lead to turion or dormant bud formation and in others might lead to flower and tuber induction, and leaf senescence (Trewevas, 1983*a*,*b*, 1985*b*) i.e. development change is initiated.

Several important consequences follow from these observations. In the wild it is likely that the 20 or so environmental parameters that affect growth will frequently be presented in an unbalanced condition. Well-balanced growth will probably be the exception rather than the rule with the very extreme exemplified by mineral deficiencies (i.e. imbalances). Balanced growth is obviously a system property (number 5 in the list). Simply optimizing, for example, photosynthetic rates by light intensity and then using that light intensity regardless of other conditions acts to the detriment of the whole except for the one unique setting of parameters. Obtaining balanced growth requires manipulation of the levels of all the other parameters. Balanced growth is thus produced by changing the contributions to the metabolic fabric at many places; not just one or two. It is to be expected that similar conclusions will apply to endogenous control of growth and development as well.

Balanced growth may occur when the flux of materials through the main metabolic pathways is in approximate balance. When for example the flux rate of the main catabolic pathways approximately equals the flux rates of the main anabolic pathways. If the rate of photosynthesis is much higher than the available nitrogen for growth, then the excess will be fed into starch, the cell wall (which may be stiffened), lignin, fatty acids, lipids and other secondary products. Many of these will have deleterious effects on respiration and there will be problems of storage and pH adjustment. The balance of amino acids synthesized will be altered (Hewitt, 1963) favouring the synthesis of some enzymes rather than others and increased protein and enzyme turnover will result (Trewavas, 1972). The rates of many vital processes will be impaired. Likewise for temperature. The temperature optimum of the major metabolic subsystems is unlikely to be identical. Thus low or high temperatures may well mismatch the main metabolic flux rates and in appropriate cases initiate changes in development as previously described.

One strategic response of plants to unbalanced growth conditions is plasticity in development. Some tissues will be abscissed, but, while the growth of some will be impaired, attempts to mitigate unbalanced growth conditions will surely require the redirection of resources to promote others. However there is an evident problem here; all tissues will experience the unbalancing condition to varying degrees. An unbalanced metabolic fabric is not in an ideal condition to put resources into anabolic pathways leading to growth. It is surely here that a function for growth substances emerges; a function which requires a circumventing of the normal metabolic constraints imposed by unbalanced growth conditions; an ability to put selectively into growth and development what must be an increased portion of the diminished essential resources.

Sensitivity of individual metabolic steps to control is dependent upon flux rate. A solution of the dose–response conundrum

Metabolic system measurements have shown that the metabolic processes most sensitive to control, change according to flux rate through the system. Groen *et al.* (1982) measured the sensitivity to control of each of four metabolic steps in respiration at different respiratory flux rates using isolated mitochondria. Their results are shown diagrammatically in Fig. 3. Critically at different flux rates the step most sensitive to control varies. At the lowest flux rates it is H^+ ion permeability. Factors controlling H^+ ion flux, will operate most sensitively only in this lowest respiratory flux range. At higher flux rates, control of respiratory flux is relatively insensitive to changing H^+ ion permeability although slight effects are still observed.

The simplest way to make plant tissue sensitive to added growth substances is to excise the tissue *and reduce the growth (or metabolic flux) rate.* In one well-authenticated case the growth rate can be recovered by adding

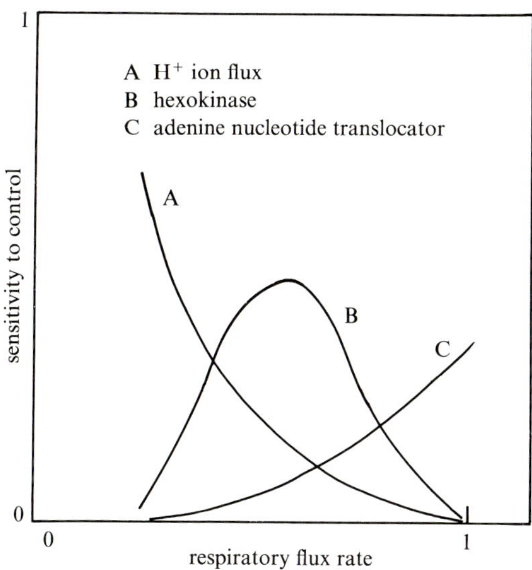

Fig. 3. Variation of sensitivity to control of three metabolic steps in respiration with respiratory flux rate. The data are drawn diagrammatically from Groen *et al.* (1982) and were determined using isolated mitochondria. (A) H^+ ion flux through mitochondrial membrane. (B) Hexokinase. (C) Adenine nucleotide translocator.

auxin thus increasing the H^+ ion permeability of the outer membrane (Taiz, 1984). Clearly H^+ ion flux may be the area of metabolism most sensitive to control under this set of conditions.

The responses of plant tissues to added growth substances may be very insensitive. Usually dose–response curves operate over three to four orders of magnitude or more (Trewavas, 1981). Nissen (personal communication) has analysed hundreds of dose–response curves in the literature and found most to be much wider than the order and a half magnitude expected for the interaction of a growth substance with its receptor. Fig. 4 illustrates the response of growth of *Lemna* to added abscisic acid (ABA) and compares it with responses to isoleucine or nitrate. Changes in growth are very sensitive to changes in concentration of the latter two compounds. A two- to threefold change in isoleucine level totally inhibits growth as does an order of magnitude change in nitrate concentration. Growth is very sensitive to both of these because changes in either affect the synthesis of many if not all cellular enzymes and thus affect all the metabolic subsystems controlling growth. Why then is growth insensitive to changes in the concentration of ABA? One explanation is that ABA regulates only one area of metabolism; possibly believed to be K^+/H^+ flux or cell wall plasticity. It is in the nature of the metabolic system that it will constrain or buffer against change in just one metabolic area. The more ABA that is added, the greater becomes the constraint on the growth response exerted by other metabolic areas not directly responsive to ABA. A network becomes increasingly resistant to distortion in just one part of it.

Fig. 5 shows a similar interpretation of these ideas for the extension growth of coleoptile sections to auxin. Fig. 5A shows the suggested

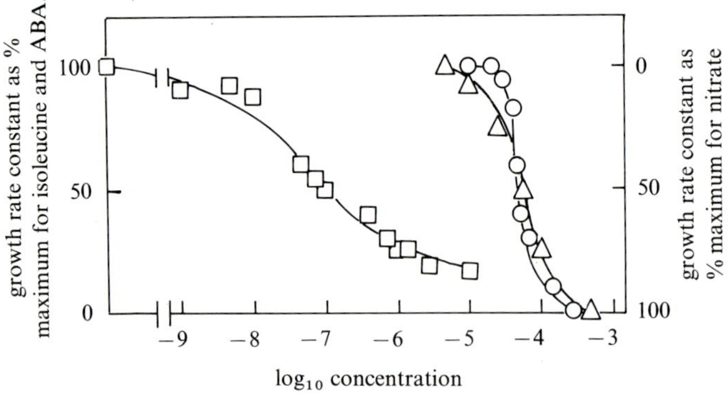

Fig. 4. Variation of growth rate of *Spirodela* or *Lemna* with concentration of added abscisic acid, nitrate or isoleucine. Data is calculated from Smart & Trewavas (1983) and Borstlap (1979). ABA □, nitrate △, isoleucine ○. Note insensitivity of growth to changes in concentration of ABA compared to very sensitive change of growth rate with isoleucine or nitrate.

sensitivity of extension growth to auxin plotted against growth; as greater growth is achieved the change in growth becomes less and less sensitive to added increments of auxin, thus again leading to a wide dose–response curve. Fig. 5B suggests why this might happen. By parallel with Fig. 3 it is proposed that the area of metabolism most sensitive to control, changes as

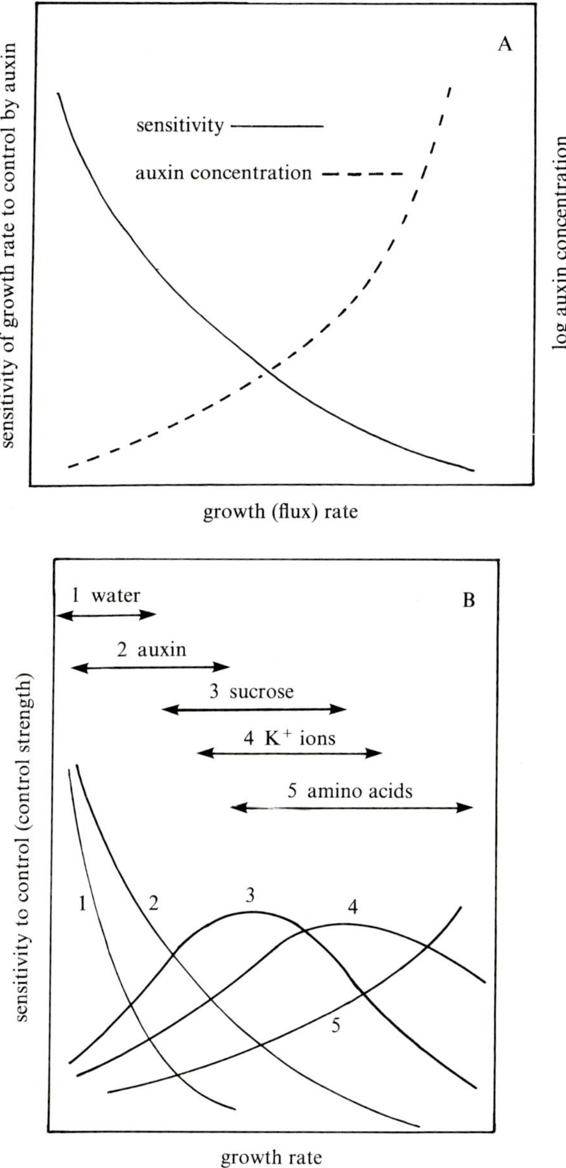

the flux of material into growth changes. At low growth rates, H^+ ion permeability and probably other membrane functions may be the step most sensitive to control; at higher rates, growth is most sensitive to other added substances such as sucrose which it could be anticipated alter the functioning of other metabolic subsystems, i.e. cell wall synthesis or turgor.

The various added factors known to alter growth rates can be deduced to be placed in the order shown in Fig. 5B. Thus the effect of sucrose on extension growth is much greater in the presence of auxin than in its absence suggesting that for higher growth rates the metabolic area most sensitive to control requires the provision of sucrose, probably for cell wall synthesis (Nitsch & Nitsch, 1956). The order of the others can be deduced in the same way (e.g. potassium). Amino acids, required for protein synthesis, have been placed at the highest rates because extension in excised sections can occur in the absence of net protein synthesis.

A critical deduction from Fig. 5B is that auxin will only be the major influence on growth when the growth rate itself is low. The high rates of growth which can be achieved in coleoptile sections by adding higher than endogenous auxin concentration result from the experimental facility of adding auxin levels greatly beyond their endogenous levels without corresponding osmotic side effects. Thus the declining but residual sensitivity to H^+ ion flux control permits the system to be driven into extension growth but in an unbalanced state. An experimentally high level will be necessary to counteract the progressive decline of other necessary resources and the increasing insensitivity of the metabolic network. In the equivalent tissue in an intact plant, because of the adequate provision of lipids, amino acids, minerals, and an absence of growth-inhibiting wound responses, an endogenous level of auxin suffices. The assumption that auxin alone is responsible for high coleoptile growth rates is an experimental artefact and entirely misleading. Much the same conclusions are applicable to other growth

---

Fig. 5. Proposed variation in sensitivity of growth to added external factors as growth rate varies.

(A) Proposed variation in sensitivity of growth rate of coleoptile sections to auxin as growth rate varies. Sensitivity of growth rate to auxin = (solid line). Incremental change in growth rate induced by incremental change in applied auxin. For comparison, exogenous auxin concentration (broken line) is plotted against growth rate.

(B) Proposed variation in sensitivity to control of growth rate of coleoptile sections by added factors. Growth subsystems being controlled may be identified with: (1) Uptake of water for growth. (2) H^+ ion flux controlled by auxin. (3) Cell wall synthesis dependent upon sucrose provision. (4) Turgor generation (or membrane potential) dependent upon added K^+ ions. (5) Protein synthesis dependent upon provision of amino acids.

Arrows above curves suggest the range of growth rates showing maximum sensitivity to control by the added factor, suggesting that different growth rates are differentially sensitive to manipulation of specific growth subsystems. See text for implications.

substance systems. The experimental facility for easily adding large quantities of growth substances to plant parts produces an entirely false perspective as regards the way such systems would be endogenously controlled. Proper control of systems requires manipulation of many areas not just one or two.

Resource allocation under poor growth conditions. The function of growth substances and differential tissue sensitivity

We are now in a position to draw together the threads of argument. It has been argued that each growth substance is likely to act when the metabolic system is in one state. The system is most sensitive to growth substance control under these conditions and these represent particular conditions of unbalanced or poor growth. The change in environmental circumstances (or internally produced unbalanced conditions) institutes the change in sensitivity. The metabolic fabric is folded and gene expression changed, exposing the metabolic aspects coupled to growth substance action.

Higher plant cells are probably more complicated than mammalian cells. The latter by virtue of specialization have simplified their control circuits. However not only does the average plant cell possess and control enzymes for dealing with inorganic materials but for processing secondary products, numerous sugars and polysaccharides. Counting membranes as a compartment, the average plant cell contains at least 24 compartments. To get coordinate metabolic changes amongst these (and surely changes in growth rate would involve coordinate activity amongst many of them) would require a molecule partitioning readily in all relevant cell compartments, membranes as well as soluble fraction. Growth substances by virtue of their chemical structure fit this requirement extremely well. Additionally it could be expected that receptors would be found in many cell compartments.

To institute plasticity in development it is necessary that some tissues be sensitive to growth substances and others not. This is well supported by the literature. Thus, in general, leaves are associated with cytokinin control; petioles and stems with ethylene; abscisic acid, shoots rather than roots; gibberellin, green stems or leaves and auxin, etiolated shoot tissue. Under the appropriate unbalanced growth conditions cells of tissues which incorporate a growth substance will have metabolically constraining steps partly circumvented thus permitting continued growth, within the limitations of other available growth materials. However in plants growing in balanced conditions the growth substance-coupled reactions will still be present but their effects masked; growth will seem to be relatively insensitive to their operation (the difference between being in region C to region A in Fig. 2).

The fact that one can observe effects of added exogenous (albeit excessive) growth substance concentrations under a variety of conditions suggests this to be the case.

The hypothesis proposed here emphasizes that there is always a paucity, a scarcity of resources in plants, and that growth substances evolved to mitigate such conditions and improve survival in the wild. It is the effective reallocation of resources which is the function of growth substances, adjusting the plant body to maximize resource capture or achieve desirable growth or reproductive goals. Since tissues compete for resources, growth substances improve the competitive ability of the sensitive tissues; they provide an additional spur to the growth process and thus deprive insensitive ones. If competition is severe, competitive exclusion (complete inhibition) could result.

As resources vary from a balanced to an unbalanced condition, the reduction in growth of insensitive tissues will release internal growth materials. It could be expected under some circumstances that gross promotion of growth of sensitive tissues could occur. The growth of leaves, for example, is heavily dependent on nitrogen and compositionally leaves are three- to fourfold richer in nitrogen than stems, petioles or roots. Even slight reductions in leaf growth could release sufficient material for a much greater promotion of stem or petiole growth.

The proposal that growth substances act intracellularly obviates many of the difficulties with the hormonal theory. The volume of any plant cell is internally monitored, composition much more easily controlled; previous ontogenetic history predetermined. It would make biological sense to synthesize the growth substance in the same cells which contain receptive proteins.

What are the environmental conditions modifying the metabolic sensitivity to growth substances?

There are two obvious components to sensitivity to growth substances. Firstly, there is an obvious ontogenetic sensitivity. That is, tissues at a certain stage of development acquire the capability to respond – numerous examples of this have been detailed (Trewavas, 1982*b*). Secondly, there is metabolic component which in turn modifies the response qualitatively and quantitatively. This is shown, for example, by the different responses of many intact tissues to added growth substances compared to their equivalent excised ones, as listed earlier; the different responses to ethylene of aerobically grown to immersed coleoptiles or stems (Ku, Suge, Rappaport & Prat, 1970; Raskin & Kende, 1984; Metraux & Kende, 1984; Alpi

& Beevers, 1983; Rose-John & Kende, 1985); the qualitatively different response (division as against expansion) of tuber cells to auxin determined by minerals (Setterfield, 1963); the smaller growth response to cytokinin of *Lemna* growing on full mineral medium to growth on water (Trewavas, 1972); the modification of ABA effects on stomatal aperture by K^+ ions (Snaith & Mansfield, 1983); numerous alterations in regenerative capability determined by medium composition (Trewavas, 1985*a*). There are many others in the literature. Each of these conditions, intact as against excised, aerobic as against immersed, presence or absence of minerals, starvation as against well-nourished, produce metabolically different cells and the alterations in metabolism are known to involve specific changes in enzyme profiles; the metabolic fabric is changed (Mocquot, Prat, Mouches & Pradel, 1981; Macnicol, 1976; Melanson & Trewavas, 1982). The metabolic context of the response, the tissue sensitivity, is altered as a consequence. Under what specific metabolic conditions do growth substances operate with maximum sensitivity? The previous sections have suggested there may be only one.

Ethylene-sensitive metabolic areas function under conditions of oxygen deprivation or partial membrane malfunction

The poor growth conditions which require ethylene as an appropriate response involve a deprivation of oxygen (and concomitant CO_2 accumulation) and, or, a weakly functional membrane system. Thus immersion of plants in water as by flooding (or naturally as in water plants) or in ripening fruit where size and diffusion barriers cause a decline in oxygen are all environmental circumstances in which ethylene-sensitive events can be demonstrated to be involved.

The relationship with oxygen is strikingly shown by the apparent parallels between the effects of ethylene and cyanide, a cytochrome oxidase inhibitor. Both ethylene and cyanide induce cyanide-resistant respiration in storage tissue discs; induce a climacteric in fruit (Laties, 1982); promote adventitious root formation (Fernqvist, 1966); break seed dormancy (Roberts, 1972). The standard method of measuring adventitious root formation stands excised hypocotyls in stagnant water; buried dormant seeds in soil could be expected to experience some anoxia.

The phenomenon of flower fading (Kende & Hanson, 1977) and abscission (Sexton, Lewis, Trewavas & Kelly, 1985) both involve ethylene and seem to be events associated with deteriorating membrane functions. Since deprivation of oxygen will lead to serious declines in ATP production and membrane potential and thus, in turn, to deteriorating membrane function it seems likely that the basic alteration in the metabolic network which elicits ethylene-related responses with maximum sensitivity is the requirement for the cell to continue to function with malfunctioning membranes. The synthesis of wound ethylene is also induced by a process of tissue excision or damage; an event now known to lead to severe disruption of membrane function and breakdown of lipids and other extensive metabolic changes (Laties, 1982).

In different water plants the growth of either the petiole, the stem or the coleoptile may be shown to be positively sensitive to ethylene (Raskin & Kende, 1984; Ridge, 1985; Alpi & Beevers, 1983) and to specifically continue after immersion. The particular processes coupled to ethylene lead to a longer but thinner tissue suggesting the role of ethylene is to maintain length at the expense of thickness under these poor growth conditions. The leaf lamina and roots are insensitive to ethylene and grow slowly if at all under these conditions. However the tissues which continue growth do so after a period of metabolic adaptation (i.e. sensitivity change) (Rose-John & Kende, 1982; Ridge, 1985) involving extensive selective changes in gene expression and protein synthesis (Mocquot, *et al.* 1979); out of these only one or two enzymes, whose synthesis is altered, result in a four- to fivefold increase in ethylene synthesis.

Cytokinin-sensitive metabolic areas may act to maintain leaf lamina expansion under conditions of diminished available nitrogen

Treatment of growing *Lemna* with cytokinins can lead to a considerable increase in leaf area but with little or no additional protein or chlorophyll formation and with a slightly thinner leaf. This suggests that cytokinins may be coupled to reactions allowing flexibility in the extent of lateral expansion of the lamina. This relation is strikingly shown in two ways.

Firstly, as Fig. 6 shows, under various nitrate regimes both the rate of frond (leaf) production and the frond area are maintained to a much greater degree than protein (and indeed chlorophyll) content. This suggests that allocation of resources is maintained to lamina growth under conditions of increasing nitrogen impoverishment. Effective nitrogen starvation leads to substantial and specific decline and change in protein synthesis which then enhance the sensitivity of metabolic areas coupled to cytokinin.

The second originates again from plasticity in leaf area development as a necessary ecological adjustment to shading. Shading of growing leaves of many plants can lead to an *increase* in leaf area, a *thinning* of the leaf, a lower area density of chloroplasts and a very much lower soluble protein content (Blackman, 1956; Boardman, 1977). From the above, the effect on

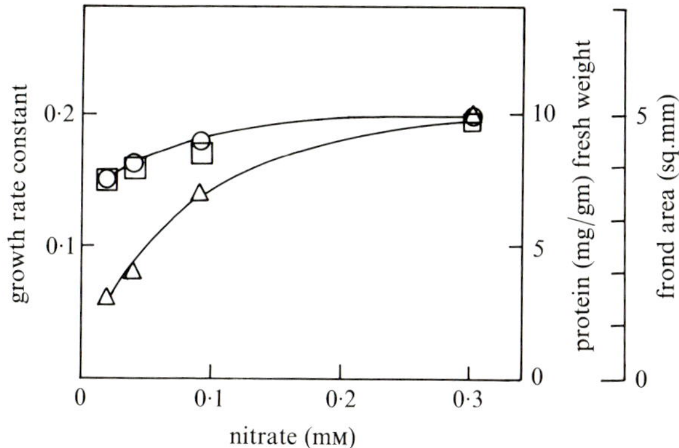

Fig. 6. Variation of growth rate constant frond area and protein concentration with nitrate content of medium for growth of *Lemna*. Note apparent stabilization of the two growth parameters compared to protein content as nitrate diminishes; an effect which may be attributable to cytokinins input into lamina expansion. ○, growth rate constant; □, frond area; △, protein content.

lamina area expansion itself could result from a light-induced alteration in cytokinin sensitivity. Competition for resources between reactions promoting leaf thickness and area could lead to an increase in area if the thickness reactions are diminished by low light intensities; the additional input of cytokinin into area-producing reactions maintaining this process better under such poor growth conditions. The metabolic state which promotes this change in cytokinin sensitivity could again be an alteration in availability of organic nitrogen. Nitrate reductase is located mainly in the leaves. Shading will lower the reducing potential available for nitrate reduction. Declines in nitrate reductase itself may, in addition, lower the level of protein some sevenfold as observed in shade leaves. Specific declines in protein synthesis may be the appropriate metabolic change emphasizing cytokinin-dependent events.

Such observations may also help explain the retarding of senescence in excised leaves by cytokinins; the process of excision mimics a condition of low organic nitrogen and loss of protein-synthesizing capacity, the necessary metabolic fabric changes for sensitive cytokinin control.

Changes in available water institute the necessary metabolic changes sensitive to abscisic acid

Abscisic acid works in a metabolic framework produced by adequate minerals and light but unbalanced by paucity of water. Lack of water is known to institute specific alterations in protein and enzyme synthesis (including the enzymes for ABA synthesis (Quarrie & Lister, 1984)) and it is in this different metabolic framework that ABA will operate with maximum sensitivity.

The particular events associated with abscisic acid seem to devolve from turgor changes and osmoadaptation which accompany water depletion. To avoid serious disturbance to growing tissues some additional constraint on growth is essential and in general the leaf (transpirational) area is reduced. Exogenous abscisic acid stiffens the cell wall of growing leaf tissue (perhaps explaining why exogenous ABA closes stomata), increases the thickness of the leaf and reduces aerenchyma formation (Smart & Trewavas, 1983). Carbon resources are accumulated as starch, a thicker cell wall and the excess allocated for maintaining the growth of stem and roots neither of which are as sensitive as the leaf to abscisic acid.

The effect of ABA on cell wall rigidity may help explain the presence of viviparous seeds in ABA-deficient mutants (Koorneef, 1982). The processes of radical extension of the imbibed seed require a loosening of the cell wall structure which has been previously rigidified during embryogenesis (Schopfer & Plachy, 1985). This rigidification is associated with abscisic acid and helps retard precocious germination of immature developing acids until the decline in available water accompanying natural seed drying eliminates the possibility.

The metabolic areas most sensitive to auxin manipulation are induced in wounded and etiolated plants

The physiological effects of auxin seem to be widespread but this may be because of its putative role in wound healing. The metabolic effects of wounding have been extensively characterized and extend some considerable distance from the wound (Walker-Simmons, Hollander-Czytko, Andersen & Ryan, 1984). There is a rapid breakdown of phospholipid and lipid and production of free fatty acids impairing respiration (Laties, 1982) accompanied by very specific changes in gene expression (Kahl, 1981). Cells near the wound must suffer considerable water deficit and permeability dysfunction. Auxin seems to be functional under this discrete set of metabolic circumstances, acting to help draw in resources from surrounding cells for the purposes of suberization and limited cell division. It thus helps to maintain a functioning membrane system (Hanson & Trewavas, 1982). The formation of callus requires the prior production of the metabolic stance directly associated with wound damage, an induction of auxin sensitivity.

Other conditions experienced by plants may mimic the metabolic stance of wounding. Sudden temperature changes or water deficits may be two such events. Both are likely to be more frequently experienced and to be more damaging for seedlings than older plants and this may help explain why auxin effects often seem limited to these younger plants. The promotive effects of auxin seem to be largely limited to etiolated tissue and to shoots rather than roots. Etiolation is an unusual metabolic condition, a developmental step which seems to be irreversibly lost after exposure to light and is characterized by a paucity of resources. De-etiolation frequently leads to a marked decline in auxin sensitivity. The germinating cereal seedling is one of evident competition between shoot and root for the same available resources from the endosperm. However the root is advantageously placed to obtain water and without some additional growth stimulus shoot growth could be very slow. Once again resource allocation under poor growth conditions becomes critical.

Under conditions of continued starvation however resources are directed into elongation rather than thickening (Gould *et al.* 1934); the resultant shoot is thinner but achieves the greater stabilization of height necessary for a plant searching for light beneath a dense canopy (Fig. 7). This suggests that auxin is coupled only to reactions leading to length rather than thickness. Starvation will induce many profound metabolic changes but only under conditions of starvation are auxin-coupled reactions expressed with

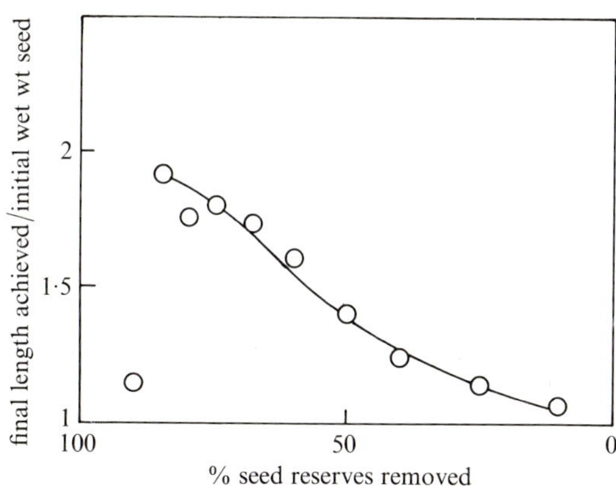

Fig. 7. Variation of final height of etiolated melon seedlings/initial wet weight of seed with percentage of seed reserves removed. Melon seeds were clipped to remove a known portion of the seed reserves and then grown in total darkness until growth ceased. The height was measured and expressed as a ratio to initial wet weight of the seed. Note how with increasing starvation (less seed reserves) there is a greater allocation of the reduced resources to length (height). The hypocotyls are considerably thinner as a consequence and this effect may be attributable to auxin acting solely as an input to elongation. Data calculated from Gould *et al.* (1934).

maximum sensitivity. With a varying environment and an indeterminate phase of imbibed dormancy the level of reserves available for growth of the seedling may be quite variable in the wild. Indeed seedling growth under starvation conditions in the wild may be the rule rather than the exception. It could be anticipated that excision and incubation of stem sections on water mimic starvation conditions. After several hours such tissues may adapt and reinitiate high rates of growth, the result of increased sensitivity to auxin (Hanson & Trewavas, 1982).

Gibberellin-coupled responses operate with maximum sensitivity in green plants subjected to light imbalance

The effects of gibberellin are associated with length (height) both in cereal stem and leaves and in the pea internode. The metabolic conditions under which this is emphasized are those of low light but adequacy in other resources; the reduction in light intensity selfevidently initiates changes in sensitivity with extensive compositional alterations.

In cereals the effect of low light is a pronounced inhibition of branching but with a relatively greater allocation of resources to the growth of the stem (Friend, 1966). The leaf shape changes. It becomes longer but with reduced breadth; thinner but with greater area. Since gibberellins can be shown by bioassay to promote length, the effects of competition can again be seen to be crucial. In the poor growth conditions of low light (generally some 5–10% full sunlight) length, with its additional gibberellin component more than adequately competes for the reduced growth resources maintaining itself. Indeed with the release of resources from the other components of leaf growth it shows enhancement. Low light also leads to a remarkable increase in stem growth (Friend, 1966).

Much the same is true for pea. Under low light conditions a greater relative share of the reduced resources finds its way to internode length which is thus maintained although the internode becomes thinner (McComb, 1977). There is, in addition, a stricter apical dominance and reduced allocation to the leaves.

It is noticeable that both these plants are those which will grow up through a canopy and will, in the wild, experience frequent overgrowing with the necessity for physiological adjustment. Gross stem elongation in grasses is surely an essential feature for wind pollination. Allocation of resources specifically to stem height will be advantageous if they are in short supply. The gibberellin/receptor complex will provide the necessary spur when resources are scarce. If resources are abundant then the effective function of gibberellin will be masked even though the gibberellin-dependent metabolic processes may still be coupled to growth.

III. Summary and conclusions

The view emphasized in this article is different to that of the classical model. Growth substances evolved in wild plants for certain ecological reasons. Being sessile, plants have to tolerate a wide range of environmental conditions and variation and one of their strategies to mitigate these is phenotypic plasticity; a response which results in a reallocation of resources to certain processes (e.g. length rather than thickness), in an attempt to counterblance and to continue growth for eventual reproduction. However all of the environmental modifications discussed above are wide ranging in their metabolic effects involving substantial changes in the metabolic fabric; one is simply not dealing with changes just in growth substance level but with very different metabolic situations, i.e. complex changes in sensitivity. The problems with the hormonal theory are well known but the fact that it always stopped short of specifying how levels of growth substances could be changed, leaving this question conveniently unanswered, has always been its weakest point. So far as is known controlled changes in gene expression, e.g. the synthesis of more or less of appropriate enzymes, are the only way known for the levels to be changed. But these changes occur as part of a substantial set of enzyme changes involving many other metabolic constituents. In other words metabolic situations between good or poor growth conditions are not meaningfully comparable with respect to growth substance action.

I have emphasized here that growth substances probably function best under poor growth conditions. This emphasizes the contribution resources make to growth regulation. The overall growth of the plant will be diminished, indeed it is this that may unmask growth-substance-related growth. The plant cannot outgrow its available resources; if these are low then overall growth is low whatever the eventual internal reallocations. Under such a situation however, competition for resources is enhanced and the additional spur to growth (provided by growth substances) in tissues which are sensitive to them is a component which will help resource reallocation. Growth substances seem to be coupled to one aspect only of the growth process so that if increased elongation occurs under poor conditions, the sensitive tissue is finally thinner, as are the cell walls in the direction of length.

Phenotypic variation indicates the extent to which modification of the process of growth can be achieved by the intact plant. It is not leaf (stem, coleoptile etc.) growth *per se* which is growth-substance dependent but part of leaf growth; a portion reserved for flexible environmental responses within strictly defined developmental boundaries. A further consequence is

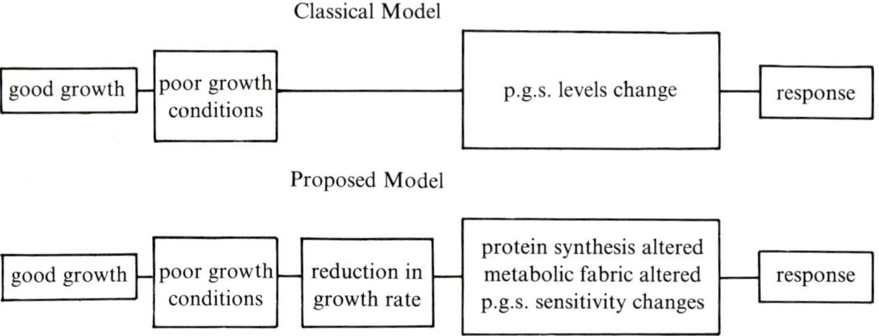

Fig. 8. Summary of classical view of proposed sequence of metabolic changes to environmental change with the sequence of changes proposed here.

that the assumption that growth substances are hormones, having their effects at a distance (in the plant) from sites of production, is unnecessary. Plant cells are complicated enough on their own to merit internal regulation by growth substances without the added complication of specifying concentration at a distance in a plant body whose volume is plastic. Tissue and cell communication are quite evidently far more complex than the conveyance of one or two simple chemicals. The classical theory confuses playing 'a' role with playing 'the' role, an easy conceptual slip made by those who favour the notion that botanical development is a simple process rather than a very complicated one.

We may finally compare the classical theory of growth substances with that argued here. The classical view is active (changes in development occur by changing concentration), hierarchical (the metabolic developmental structure is seen as a sort of pyramid with the growth substance on top) and communication-oriented (tissue and cell growth coordinated by this means). In contrast the view expressed here is passive (changes in the system, sensitivity, predominate) non-hierarchical (development is viewed as democratically organized, many molecules contribute) and considers communication by growth substances to be unlikely (communication involves many molecules and in plants is primarily negative). Fig. 8 summarizes this situation.

The ideas in this article come from many sources and many people. I must thank Martin Canny specifically for enlightening discussion on information and systems theory.

References

ADDICOTT, F. T. (1982). *Abscission*. Berkeley, University of California Press.

ALLAN, E. & TREWAVAS, A. J. (1985). Heterogeneity of tissue dependent cell growth in the root apex of *Pisum sativum*. *Bot. Gaz.* (in press).

Alpi, A. & Beevers, H. (1983). Effects of O_2 concentration on rice seedlings. *Pl. Physiol.* **71**, 30–34.

Arber, A. R. (1950). *Natural Philosophy of Plant Form.* Cambridge: Cambridge University Press.

Atzhorn, R. & Weiler, E. W. (1983). The role of endogenous gibberellins in the formation of amylase by aleurone layers of germinating barley caryopsis. *Planta* **157**, 289–299.

Barlow, H. W. B. & Hancock, C. R. (1959). Studies on extension growth in coleoptile sections. III The interaction of temperature and indolylacetic acid on section growth. *J. exp. Bot.* **10**, 157–168.

Beardsell, M. F. & Cohen, D. (1975). Relationships between leaf water status, abscisic acid levels and stomatal resistance in *Maize* and *Sorghum. Pl. Physiol.* **56**, 207–212.

Beyer, E. M. (1975). Abscission. The initial effect of ethylene is in the leaf blade. *Pl. Physiol.* **55**, 322–327.

Blackman, G. E. (1956). Influence of light and temperature on leaf growth. In *The Growth of Leaves* (ed. F. L. Milthorpe), pp. 151–170. London: Butterworths.

Boardman, N. K. (1977). Comparative photosynthesis of sun and shade leaves. *A. Rev. Pl. Physiol.* **28**, 355–377.

Borstlap, A. C. (1979). Antagonistic effects of branched chain amino acids on the growth of Spirodela. *Acta. bot. neerl.* **19**, 211–215.

Bryant, S. V., French, V. & Bryant, P. J. (1981). Distal regeneration and symmetry. *Science* **212**, 993–1002.

Burdon, J. J. (1980). Intraspecific diversity in a natural population of *Trifolium repens. J. Ecol.* **68**, 717–735.

Chapin, F. S. (1980). The mineral nutrition of wild plants. *A. Rev. Ecol. System.* **11**, 233–261.

Davidson, R. C. (1969). Effect of root/leaf temperature differentials on root/shoot ratios in some pasture grasses and clover. *Ann. Bot.* **33**, 561–569.

Davies, D. D. (1977). Regulation of enzyme levels and activity. In *The Molecular Biology of Plant Cells* (ed. H. Smith), pp. 306–329.Oxford: Blackwells Scientific Publications.

Denny, F. E. & Stanton, E. N. (1928). Localisation of response of woody tissues to chemical treatments that break the rest period. *Am. J. Bot.* **15**, 337–344.

Drew, M. C., Saker, R. & Ashley, T. W. (1973). Nutrient supply and the growth of the seminal root system in barley. *J. exp. Bot.* **24**, 1189–1202.

Esau, K. (1965). *Vascular Differentiation in Plants.* New York: Holt, Reinhart and Winston.

Evans, L. T. (1969). The nature of flower induction. In *The Induction of Flowering. Some Case Histories* (ed. L. T. Evans), pp. 437–465. Melbourne, McMillan.

Fernqvist, I. (1966). Studies on factors in adventitious root formation. *LantbrHögsk. Annlr.* **32**, 109–244.

Friend, D. J. C. (1966). The effects of light and temperature on the growth of cereals. In *The Growth of Cereals and Grasses* (ed. F. L. Milthorpe & J. D. Ivins), pp. 181–199. London: Butterworths.

Gibbons, G. C. (1979). On the localisation and transport of amylase during germination and early seedling growth of *Hordeum vulgare. Carlsberg res. Commun.* **44**, 353–366.

Goebel, L. (1900). *Organography of Plants*, vol. 1. Reprint 1969. New York: Hafner Publishing Co.

Goodwin, P. B. & Erwee, M. G. (1983). Hormonal influences on leaf growth. In *The Growth and Functioning of Leaves* (ed. J. E. Dale & F. L. Milthorpe), pp. 207–233. Cambridge: Cambridge University Press.

Gould, G. A., Pearl, R., Edwards, T. I. & Miner, J. R. (1934). On the effects of partial removal of the cotyledons upon the growth and duration of life of Canteloup seedlings without exogenous food. *Ann. Bot.* **48**, 575–599.

Grime, J. P. & Jeffrey, D. W. (1965). Seedling establishment in vertical gradients of sunlight. *J. Ecol.* **53**, 621–642.

GROEN, A. K., WANDERS, R. J. A., WESTERHOFF, H. V., VAN DEN MEER, R. & TAGER, J. M. (1982). Quantification of the contribution of various steps to the control of mitochondrial respiration. *J. biol. Chem.* **257**, 2754–2758.

HANSON, J. & TREWAVAS, A. J. (1982). Regulation of plant cell growth; the changing perspective. *New Phytol.* **90**, 1–21.

HARPER, J. L. (1977). *Population Biology of Plants.* London, Academic Press.

HESLOP-HARRISON, J. (1957). The experimental modification of sex expression in flowering plants. *Biol. Rev.* **32**, 38–90.

HEWITT, E. J. (1963). The essential nutrient elements; requirements and interactions in plants. In *Plant Physiology* vol. 3 (ed. F. C. Steward), pp. 137–361. New York: Academic Press.

HILLMAN, J. (1984). Apical dominance. In *Advanced Plant Physiology* (ed. M. B. Wilkins), pp. 127–149. London: Pitman.

HILLMAN, W. (1961). The Lemnaceae or duckweeds. A review of the descriptive and experimental literature. *Bot. Rev.* **27**, 221–287.

JACOBS, W. P. (1979). *Plant Hormones and Plant Development.* Cambridge: Cambridge University Press.

KACSER, H. & BURNS, J. A. (1981). The molecular basis of dominance. *Genetics* **97**, 639–666.

KAHL, G. (1981). *The Biochemistry of Wounded Plant Tissue.* Berlin: Springer-Verlag.

KAUR-SAWHNEY, V. (1983). The role of temperature and its relationship with gibberellic acid in the development of floral organs in tomato. *Can. J. Bot.* **61**, 1258–1265.

KENDE, H. & HANSON, A. D. (1977). On the role of ethylene in ageing. In *Plant Growth Regulation* (ed. P. E. Pilet), pp. 172–181. Berlin: Springer-Verlag.

KOORNNEEF, M. (1982). *The Genetics of Some Plant Hormones and Photoreceptors.* Wageningen, PUDOC.

KU, H. S., SUGE, H., RAPPAPORT, L. & PRATT, H. K. (1970). Stimulation of rice coleoptile growth by ethylene. *Planta* **90**, 333–339.

LARSON, P. R. (1983). Primary vascularisation and the siting of primordia. In *The Growth of Leaves (ed. J. E. Dale & F. L. Milthorpe), pp. 25–53. Cambridge: Cambridge University Press.*

LATIES, G. G. (1982). The cyanide resistant alternative path in higher plant respiration. *A. Rev. Pl. Physiol.* **33**, 519–557.

LEIGH, R. A. & WYN JONES, R. G. (1984). A hypothesis relating critical potassium concentrations for growth to the distribution and functions of this ion in the plant cell. *New Phytol.* **97**, 1–13.

LETHAM, D. G., HIGGINS, T. J. V., GOODWIN, P. B. & JACOBSEN, J. V. (1978). Phytohormones in retrospect. In *Phytohormones and Related Compounds – A Comprehensive Treatise*, vol. 1 (ed. D. S. Letham, P. B. Goodwin & T. J. V. Higgins), pp. 1–27. Elsevier: Amsterdam.

LEVINS, R. (1969). Dormancy as an adaptive strategy. In *Dormancy and Survival. Symp. Soc. expl biol.* XXIII (ed. H. W. Woolhouse), pp. 1–20. Cambridge: Cambridge University Press.

LLOYD, C. (1979). The shapely cells cycle. *Trends. biochem. Sci.* **4**, 187–189.

LOOMIS, W. E. (1953). *Growth and Differentiation in Plants.* Ames: Iowa State College Press.

MCCOMB, A. J. (1977). Control of root and shoot development. In *The Physiology of the Garden Pea* (ed. J. F. Sutcliffe & J. S. Pate), pp. 235–263. London: Academic Press.

MACNICOL, P. K. (1976). Rapid metabolic changes in the wounding response of leaf cells following excision. *Pl. Physiol.* **57**, 80–84.

MANSFIELD, T. A. & DAVIES, W. T. (1983). Abscisic acid and water stress. *Biochem. Soc. Trans.* **11**, 557–560.

MASSART, J. (1922). Sur la polarite des organes vegetaux. *Recueil de l'Instit. bot. Leo Errera* **10**, 107–118.

MEINS, F. (1982). Heritable variation in plant cell culture. *A. Rev. Pl. Physiol.* **34**, 327–346.

MELANSON, D. & TREWAVAS, A. J. (1982). Changes in tissue protein pattern in relation to auxin induction of DNA synthesis. *Pl. Cell Environ.* **5**, 53–64.

METRAUX, J. D. & KENDE, H. (1984). The cellular basis of the elongation response in submerged deep water rice. *Planta* **160**, 73–77.

MILTHORPE, F. L. (1956). The relative importance of the different stages of leaf growth in determining the resultant area. In *The Growth of Leaves* (ed. F. L. Milthorpe), pp. 141–151. London: Butterworths.

MOCQUOT, B., PRAT, C., MOUCHES, C. & PRADET, A. (1981). Effect of anoxia on energy charge and protein synthesis in rice embryo. *Pl. Physiol.* **68**, 636–640.

NEILSON-JONES, W. (1925). Polarity phenomena in seakale roots. *Ann. Bot.* **39**, 359–372.

NEWMAN, E. I. (1982). Niche separation and species diversity in terrestrial vegetation. In *The Plant Community as a Working Mechanism* (ed. E. I. Newman), pp. 61–78. Oxford: Blackwells Scientific Publications.

NICHOLLS, P. B. (1982). Influence of temperature during grain growth and ripening of barley on the subsequent response to gibberellic acid. *Aust. J. Pl. Physiol.* **9**, 373–383.

NICKELL, L. G. (1955). Effects of antigrowth substances in normal and atypical plant growth. In *Antimetabolites and Cancer* (ed. C. P. Rhoads), pp. 129–150. Washington: American Association for the Advancement of Science.

NITSCH, J. P. & NITSCH, C. (1956). Studies on the growth of coleoptile and first internode sections. *Pl. Physiol* **31**, 94–111.

NORMAN, H. A., BLACK, M. & CHAPMAN, J. M. (1982). The induction of sensitivity to gibberellin in aleurone tissue of developing wheat grains. *Planta* **154**, 578–587.

PERRY, T. O. (1971). Dormancy of trees in winter. *Science* **171**, 29–36.

QUARRIE, S. A. & LISTER, P. G. (1984). Effects of inhibitors of protein synthesis on abscisic acid accumulation in wheat. *Z. Pflanzenphysiol.* **114**, 309–314.

RASKIN, I. & KENDE, H. (1984). Regulation of growth in stem sections of deep water rice. *Planta* **160**, 66–72.

RIDGE, I. (1985). Ethylene and petiole development in amphibious plants. In *Ethylene and Plant Development* (ed. J. A. Roberts & G. A. Tucker), pp. 267–277. London: Butterworths.

ROBERTS, E. H. (1972). Oxidative processes and the control of seed germination. In *Seed Ecology* (ed. W. Heydecker), pp. 189–213. London: Butterworths.

RORISON, I. H. (1969). Ecological inferences from laboratory experiments on mineral nutrition. In *Ecological Aspects of the Mineral Nutrition of Plants. Symp. Br. ecol. Soc.* (ed. I. H. Rorison), pp. 155–177. Oxford: Blackwells Scientific Publications.

ROSE-JOHN, S. & KENDE, H. (1985). Short term growth response of deep water rice to submergence and ethylene. *Pl. sci. Lett.* **38**, 129–134.

SACHS, R. M. (1977). Nutrient diversion; an hypothesis to explain the chemical control of flowering. *Hort. Sci.* **12**, 220–222.

SALAMA, A. M. & WAREING, P. F. (1979). Effects of mineral nutrition on endogenous cytokinin in plants of sunflower. *J. exp. Bot.* **30**, 971–981.

SCHOPFER, P. & PLACHY, C. (1985). Control of seed germination by abscisic acid. *Pl. Physiol.* **77**, 676–686.

SETTERFIELD, G. (1963). Growth regulation in excised slices of Jerusalem artichoke tuber tissue. In *Cell Differentiation. Symp. Soc. exp. Biol.* XVII (ed. G. E. Fogg), pp. 98–126. Cambridge: Cambridge University Press.

SETTERFIELD, G. & BAYLEY, S. T. (1961). Structure and physiology of cell walls. *A. Rev. Pl. Physiol.* **12**, 35–63.

SEXTON, R., LEWIS, L. N., TREWAVAS, A. J. & KELLY, P. (1985). Ethylene and abscission. In *Ethylene and Plant Development* (ed. J. A. Roberts & G. A. Tucker), pp. 173–196. London: Butterworths.

SHEAR, G. M. (1931). Studies on inanition in *Arachis* and *Phaseolus*. *Pl. Physiol.* **6**, 277–294.

SHELDRAKE, A. R. (1974). The polarity of auxin transport in inverted cuttings. *New Phytol.* **73**, 637–642.

SINGH, S. P. & PALEG, L. G. (1984). Low temperature induction of hormonal sensitivity in genotypically gibberellic acid insensitive aleurone tissue. *Pl. Physiol.* **74**, 437–438.

SINNOTT, E. W. (1960). *Plant Morphogenesis*. New York: McGraw Hill Book Co. Ltd.

SMART, C. C. & TREWAVAS, A. J. (1983). Abscisic acid induced turion formation in *Spirodela polyrrhiza*. *Pl. Cell Environ.* **6**, 507–514.

SNAITH, P. J. & MANSFIELD, T. A. (1982). Stomatal sensitivity to abscisic acid; can it be defined? *Pl. Cell Environ.* **5**, 309–311.

TAIZ, L. (1984). Cell extension. *A. Rev. Pl. Physiol.* **35**, 585–656.

THOMAS, H. & STODDART, J. L. (1980). Leaf senescence. *A. Rev. Pl. Physiol.* **31**, 83–111.

TILMAN, D. (1982). *Resource Competition and Community Structure*. Princeton, Princeton University Press.

TOMLINSON, P. B. (1982). A morphogenetic basis for plant morphology. In *Axioms and Principles of Plant Construction* (ed. R. Sattler), pp. 162–183. The Hague: Martinus Nijhoff.

TRAN THANH VAN, K. M. (1981). Control of morphogenesis in *in vitro* cultures. *A. Rev. Pl. Physiol.* **32**, 291–313.

TREWAVAS, A. J. (1972). Control of the protein turnover rates in *Lemna* minor. *Pl. Physiol.* **49**, 47–51.

TREWAVAS, A. J. (1981). How do plant growth substances work? *Pl. Cell Environ.* **4**, 203–228.

TREWAVAS, A. J. (1982*a*). Possible control points in plant development. In *The Molecular Biology of Plant Development* (ed. H. Smith & D. Grierson), pp. 7–27. Oxford: Blackwells Scientific Publications.

TREWAVAS, A. J. (1982*b*). Growth substance sensitivity: the limiting factor in plant development. *Physiol. Pl.* **35**, 60–72.

TREWAVAS, A. J. (1983*a*). Plant growth substances; metabolic fly wheels for plant development. *Cell Biol. int. Rep.* **7**, 569–575.

TREWAVAS, A. J. (1983*b*). Nitrate as a plant hormone. In *Interactions between Nitrogen and Growth Regulators in the Control of Plant Development* (ed. M. B. Jackson), pp. 97–110. Wantage: British Plant Growth Regulator Group.

TREWAVAS, A. J. (1985*a*). Growth substances, calcium and cell division. In *The Cell Division Cycle in Plants* (ed. J. A. Bryant & D. Francis), pp. 133–157. Cambridge: Cambridge University Press.

TREWAVAS, A. J. (1985*b*). A pivotal role for nitrate and leaf growth in plant development. In *Control of Leaf Growth* (ed. N. Baker, C. Ong & W. Davies), pp. 77–91. Cambridge: Cambridge University Press.

TREWAVAS, A. J. & ALLAN, E. (1985). An assessment of the contribution of growth substances to development. In *Plant Growth Modelling for Resource Management* (ed. K. Wisiol). Boca Raton: CRC Press Inc. (in press).

TREWAVAS, A. J., SEXTON, R. & KELLY, P. (1984). Polarity, calcium and abscission; molecular bases for developmental plasticity in plants. *J. Embryol. exp. Morph.* **83 Supplement**, 179–195.

VON BERTALLANFY, L. (1968). *General System Theory*. London: Allen Lane, The Penguin Press.

WADDINGTON, C. H. (1957). *The Strategy of the Genes*. London: Allen and Unwin Ltd.

WALKER-SIMMONS, M., HOLLANDER-CZYTKO, H., ANDERSEN, J. K. & RYAN, C. A. (1984). Wound signals in plants. *Proc. natn. Acad. Sci. U.S.A.* **81**, 3737–3741.

WATSON, M. A. & CASPAR, B. B. (1984). Morphogenetic constraints on patterns of carbon distribution in plants. *A. Rev. Ecol. Syst.* **15**, 233–258.

WENT, F. W. (1935). Coleoptile growth as affected by auxin, ageing and food. *Proc. Kned. Akad. Wet.* **38**, 752–767.

WHITE, H. L. (1937). The interaction of factors in the growth of *Lemna*. *Ann. Bot.* **1** 623–647.

WHITE, J. (1978). The plant as a metapopulation. *A. Rev. Ecol. System.* **10**, 109–145.

YANG, S. F., HOFFMAN, N. E., MCKEON, T., RIOV, J., KAO, C. H. & YUNG, K. H. (1982). Mechanism and regulation of ethylene biosynthesis. In *Plant Growth Substances 1982* (ed. P. F. Wareing), pp. 239–248. London: Academic Press.

UNSTABLE GENES IN PLANTS

*C. A. CULLIS**

John Innes Institute, Colney Lane, Norwich, NR4 7UH, UK

Summary

The fluidity of the plant genome during development and reproduction has been considered. Although some cases of differential replication have been described there is little evidence for this process playing a large part in development. However the genome flexibility in response to 'shocks' to the genome observed in flax and maize suggest that this process may be important in the generation of rapid changes in genome. These rapid changes appear to occur in particular subsets of the genome which may allow a radical but limited reorganization of the genome in response to genomic challenge.

Introduction

A fundamental tenet of modern genetics is that the germline and the soma have distinct destinies. The somatic cells form the body of the organism and support and nourish the reproductive cells. Any changes which occur in the somatic cells cannot, therefore, be transmitted to subsequent generations. The separation of these two cell lineages means that Lamarkian evolution, in which useful acquired characteristics are transmitted via the germline to the offspring is all but impossible. This was first expounded by August Weismann in the 1890s and is often referred to as Weismann's rule. A corollary of this rule is that the somatic cells may be free to acquire mutations and changes which would be unacceptable in the germline insofar as the integrity of the genome is concerned.

Weismann's rule appears applicable to higher animals where there is a clear, early separation of the germline and soma. This presence of a germline allows irreversible somatic differentiation in some animal tissues, such as the loss of the nucleus (erythropoiesis in mammals), the loss of chromatin (in *Ascaris* embryos) or non-conservative genomic rearrangements (ontogeny of the antibody-producing lineages).

* Present Address: Department of Biology, Case Western Reserve University, Cleveland, Ohio 44106, USA.

On the other hand, plants have no formal germline but their life cycle has two distinct phases, the haploid gametophyte which produces the gametes and the diploid sporophyte which contains cells capable of undergoing meiosis. After fertilization the embryonic development establishes the basic body plan of the root shoot axis and the first adult tissue and organ systems soon differentiate. The plant embryo contains only a fraction of the components of the final adult body. It subsequently grows by the division and expansion of the preexisting cells and subsequently initiates organ proliferation by setting up a series of stem cell populations, the apical meristems. These meristems further proliferate until a trigger switches all, or some, of them to reproductive development. Thus the cells which ultimately form the gametes have already been involved in the organization of the somatic body of the plant with the opportunity to accumulate genetic changes which can be subsequently transmitted to their progeny.

The flexibility afforded to the higher plants by this somatic testing will be considered here, along with the known examples of variation, at the genomic level in terminally differentiated tissues. For the differentiated tissues those of the seed, namely maize endosperm, pea cotyledon and melon fruit have been most extensively studied. The flexibility of the genome during the growth of the plant will be considered from three perspectives. These are:

(i) The appearance of bud sports
(ii) The environmentally induced changes in flax
(iii) The appearance of somaclonal variation.

Developmental variation

The occurrence of genomic variation during development has been well documented in a number of studies.

Chromosome rearrangements have been shown to occur in the phase variation in *Salmonella* (Silverman & Simon, 1983) and the mating type switch in yeast (Haber, 1983). This type of chromosomal rearrangement during development has not been demonstrated in higher plants.

Gene amplification and loss is now known to occur in many species. Amplification of the ribosomal genes has been demonstrated in protists, invertebrates, vertebrates and plants (Long & Dawid, 1980). In plants the evidence comes from changes in the proportion of rDNA in maize endosperm (Phillips, Wang & Knowles, 1983), pea cotyledons (Cullis & Davies, 1975) and pea roots (van't Hoff, Bjirkenes & Delihas, 1983). Change in other plant DNA sequences has also been shown; for example, the proportion of melon satellite sequence in fruit compared to seed and leaves

(Pearson, Timmis & Ingle, 1974). However, the amplification of specific protein-encoding genes, such as that observed for dihydrofolate reductase in methotrexate-resistant mammalian cells (Schimke, Kaufman, Alt & Kellems, 1978) or the chorion genes in *Drosophila* (Spradling & Mahowald, 1980) during follicular development in *Drosophila*, has not been demonstrated in higher plants.

Transposable elements were first recognized in maize by their effect at particular developmental stages. The biology and molecular biology of these elements have been reviewed recently in great depth (Bregliano & Kidwell, 1983; Federoff, 1983; Freeling, 1984). Although these elements provide regulated disruption of the cells in which they are active, and their activity appears to have a developmental component, their role in developing *per se* is unknown. Their possible role in evolution will be returned to later.

The fluidity of the nuclear genome

The lack of a separate germline in higher plants and presence of multiple meristems means that the plant can be considered as an assemblage of multiple repeating units. Each of these is capable of reproduction and they compete with one another. Control over which of the units currently dominates the development form is exercised through apical dominance. However, the release of alternative units usually follows biological or physical damage of the dominant meristems. Additionally, in long-lived plants the growth of new sectors each year allows the propagation of new somatic variants. These variants then have the opportunity to differentiate into reproductive structures and so become incorporated into the gene pool.

These somatic mutations, known as bud sports, have been widely observed and utilized in the horticultural industry. The world's entire crop of pink grapefruit owes its existence to a sport branch from a normal grapefruit tree.

The appearance of sports is not incompatible with notions of Darwinian evolution since it is clear that mutations can arise and provided the rate of appearance of sports is not greatly in excess of the prevailing mutation rate then no paradox arises. However, if the rate of appearance of new forms is greatly in excess of the mutation rate then this is paradoxical. One such case, the environmental induction of heritable changes in flax, *Linum usitatissimum* has been extensively described (Durrant, 1962, 1971; Cullis, 1977, 1983).

Environmentally induced heritable changes in flax

Heritable changes have been found in some flax varieties after they have been grown in different, characterized environments for a single generation (Durrant, 1962, 1971; Cullis & Charlton, 1981). The stable lines produced (termed genotrophs) differed from one another and the original variety from which they were derived (Stormont Cirrus, termed P1) in a number of characters. These include plant weight and height (Durrant, 1962); nuclear DNA content (Evans, 1968); the number of genes coding for the 25S, 18S and 5S ribosomal RNAs (Cullis, 1976; Goldsbrough, Ellis & Cullis, 1981) and for a number of other cloned repetitive sequences (Cullis, 1985).

Flax contains about 1·5 pg DNA per 2C nucleus and some 50 % of this comprises repeated sequences. Members of all the highly repetitive sequences in the flax genome have been cloned (Cullis & Cleary, 1986).

These cloned sequences have subsequently been used as probes to compare the nuclear DNAs from a number of genotrophs as well as related wild *Linum bienne* species. It was found that all the families except one, could vary quantitatively, and a number also vary qualitatively (Cullis & Cleary, 1985). One of these, the 5S DNA shows the variation clearly and is described further.

5S DNA variation

The 5S DNA of flax is arranged in tandem arrays of a 350- to 370-base pair repeating sequence (Goldsbrough, Ellis & Cullis, 1981). There is both length and sequence heterogeneity and the number of copies can vary more than twofold. In the genotrophs with the highest number of copies this sequence can comprise 3 % of the total DNA. It has been possible to distinguish a subset of the 5S genes which appear to be differentially affected. This subset is preferentially deleted when the 5S genes are reduced during the environmental induction of heritable changes (Cullis & Cleary, 1986; Fig. 1). This subset can be characterized since a site for the restriction endonuclease, TaqI is missing from the repeat unit so the subset is not cut by TaqI. Thus genotrophs with high 5S gene numbers show a large proportion of their 5S DNA lacking a TaqI site while genotrophs with a low 5S gene number show very little of this subset (Fig. 1). Thus within the 5S genes there is differentiation into two recognizable subsets, one of which is hypervariable when compared to the other.

There is also evidence that for a number of the repeated sequence families a hypervariable fraction and a much more stable fraction (Cullis, 1985) can be distinguished. This apparent compartmentalization of the genome into

Fig. 1. Hybridization of cloned 5S DNA to TaqI digests of a high 5S DNA line (A) and a low 5S DNA line (B). The arrow indicates the spared DNA which is uncut by the enzyme. The two lanes were not loaded with equal amounts of DNA.

a highly variable fraction and approximately constant fraction will be returned to later.

Somaclonal variation

Variants and mutant lines have often been found in plant tissue cultures and in plants regenerated from these cultures (Larkin & Scowcroft, 1983).

Gross karyotypic changes have also frequently been observed in tissue-cultured plant cells and these undoubtedly account for some of the variability. However, in a number of cases phenotypic variation has been found in regenerated plants in the absence of karyotypic changes (Edallo, Zucchinali, Perezin & Salamini 1981; Shepard, Bidney & Shahin, 1980). This mutational variation has been analysed at the molecular level for some microspore-derived doubled haploids from *Nicotiana* species (de Paepe, Prat & Huguet, 1982; Dhillon, Wernsman & Miksche, 1983) where it was suggested that specific DNA amplification and modification can occur during the culture process.

A study of DNA variation during culture has been carried out in flax. DNAs from leaf and callus tissue have been compared using the cloned probes representing all the highly repeated sequence families previously generated to compare the DNAs from the genotrophs (Cullis, 1985). The data showed that differences could be observed between leaf and callus DNA and those differences were very similar to the differences found when the DNAs from the genotrophs were compared. In particular the same subset of 5S genes which was found to be hypervariable in the generation of the genotrophs was also found to be hypervariable in callus tissue. However, there is no evidence yet available to demonstrate a causal relationship between this DNA variation and any phenotypic changes observed in regenerated plants.

Conclusion

There is mounting evidence that the plant genome is dynamic and changes occurring by amplification, deletion and transposition events can be found at a high frequency. However evidence, in particular with the induction of heritable changes in flax and with the activation of transposable elements in maize, indicates that the frequency can be modulated by the external environment. In most cases described, the frequency of change increases when the external environment can be considered stressful, in that it is not conducive to optimal growth. As well as the external environment, the internal nuclear environment may also have an effect as maize transposable elements can also be activated by wide crosses (McClintock, 1978, 1984).

The discussion so far has focused on variation. However it is clear that a large proportion of the genome remains aloof from all the chopping and changing. The sequences coding for structural genes, for example, would be expected to be in this relatively constant fraction of the genome. This has, in fact, been confirmed for the tubulin genes in flax (Cullis, unpublished).

Thus the plant genome may comprise 'islands' of instability in that the majority of rapid changes occur in the sequences found in these 'islands'. Certainly there appears to be particularly highly variable sequences in the flax genome and perhaps the families of transposable elements in maize also make up variable subsets. Variation in these 'islands' may then be triggered by 'shocks' or 'stresses' applied to the genome. Does this response to 'stress' have any specific function? One possibility is that the genomic rearrangements provide a new set of novel variants which can overcome the threat to survival generated by the stress (McClintock, 1984). In order for this to be true these genomic rearrangements must generate a phenotype which is at an advantage in that stress environment. This connection has yet to be shown for any of the rapid genomic changes thus far described.

References

BREGLIANO, J-C. & KIDWELL, M. G. (1983). Hybrid dysgenesis determinants. In *Mobile Genetic Elements* (ed. J. A. Shapiro), pp. 363–410. New York: Academic Press.

CULLIS, C. A. (1976). Environmentally induced changes in ribosomal RNA cistron number in flax. *Heredity* **36**, 73–79.

CULLIS, C. A. (1977). Molecular aspects of the environmental induction of heritable changes in flax. *Heredity* **38**, 129–154.

CULLIS, C. A. (1983). Environmentally induced DNA changes in plants. *CRC crit. Rev. pl. Sciences* **1**, 117–131.

CULLIS, C. A. (1985). Plant DNA variation and stress. *Stadler Sympos.* **15** (in press).

CULLIS, C. A. & CHARLTON, L. M. (1981). The induction of ribosomal DNA changes in flax. *Pl. Sci. Lett.* **20**, 213–217.

CULLIS, C. A. & CLEARY, W. (1986). Rapidly varying DNA sequences in flax. *Can. J. Genet. Cytol*, **28** (*in press*).

CULLIS, C. A. & DAVIES, D. R. (1975). rDNA amounts in *Pisum sativum*. *Genetics* **81**, 485–492.

DE PAEPE, R., PRAT, D. & HUGUET, T. (1982). Heritable nuclear DNA changes in doubled haploid (D.H.) plants obtained by pollen culture of *Nicotiana sylvestris*. *Pl. Sci. Lett.* **28**, 11–28.

DHILLON, S. S., WERNSMAN, E. A. & MICKSCHE, J. P. (1983). Evaluation of nuclear DNA content and heterochromatin changes in anther-derived dihaploids of tobacco (*Nicotiana tabacum*) C.V. Coker 139. *Can. J. Genet. Cytol* **25**, 169–173.

DURRANT, A. (1962). The environmental induction of heritable changes in *Linum*. *Heredity* **17**, 27–61.

DURRANT, A. (1971). Induction and growth of flax genotrophs. *Heredity* **27**, 277–298.

EDALLO, S., ZUCCHINALI, C., PEREZIN, M. & SALAMINI, F. (1981). Chromosomal variation and frequency of spontaneous mutation associated with *in vitro* culture and plant regeneration in maize. *Maydica* **26**, 39–56.

EVANS, G. M. (1968). Nuclear changes in flax. *Heredity* **23**, 25–38.

FEDEROFF, N. V. (1983). Controlling elements in maize. In *Mobile Genetic Elements* (ed. J. A. Shapiro), pp. 1–63. New York: Academic Press.

FREELING, M. (1984). Plant transposable elements and insertion sequences. *A. Rev. pl. Physiol* **35**, 277–298.

GOLDSBROUGH, P. B., ELLIS, T. H. N. & CULLIS, C. A. (1981). Organisation of the 5S RNA genes in flax. *Nucl. Acid Res.* **9**, 5895–5904.

HABER, J. E. (1983). Mating-type genes of *Saccharomyces cerevisiae*. In *Mobile Genetic Elements* (ed. J. A. Shapiro), pp. 559–619. New York: Academic Press.

LARKIN, P. J. & SCOWCROFT, W. R. (1983). Somaclonal variation and crop improvement. In *Genetic Engineering in Plants* (ed. T. Kosuge, C. P. Meredith and A. Hollander), pp. 289–314. New York: Plenum Press.

LONG, E. O. & DAWID, I. B. (1980). Repeated genes in eukaryotes. *A. Rev. Biochem.* **49**, 727–764.

MCCLINTOCK, B. (1978). Mechanisms that rapidly reorganise the genome. *Stadler Symp.* **10**, 25–47.

MCCLINTOCK, B. (1984). The significance of responses of the genome to challenge. *Science* **226**, 792–801.

PEARSON, G. G., TIMMIS, J. N. & INGLE, J. (1974). The differential replication of DNA during plant development. *Chromosoma* **45**, 281–294.

PHILLIPS, R. L., WANG, A. S. & KNOWLES, R. V. (1983). Molecular and developmental cytogenetics of gene multiplicity in maize. *Stadler Symp.* **15**, 105–118.

SCHIMKE, R. T., KAUFMAN, R. J., ALT, F. W. & KELLEMS, R. F. (1978). Gene amplification and drug resistance in cultured murine cells. *Science* **202**, 1051–1055.

SHEPARD, J. F., BIDNEY, D. & SHAHIN, E. (1980). Potato protoplasts in crop improvement. *Science* **208**, 17–24.

SILVERMAN, M. & SIMON, M. (1983). Phase variation and related systems. In *Mobile Genetic Elements* (ed. J. A. Shapiro), pp. 537–557. New York: Academic Press.

SPRADLING, A. C. & MAHOWALD, A. P. (1980). Amplification of the genes for chorion proteins during oogenesis in *Drosophila melanogaster*. *Proc. natn. Acad. Sci., USA* **77**, 1096–2002.

VAN'T HOF, J., BJIRKENES, C. A. & DELIHAS, N. R. (1983). Excision and replication of extrachromosomal DNA of pea (*Pisum sativum*) *Molec. Cell Biol.* **3**, 172–181.

Printed in Great Britain © Society for Experimental Biology 1986

TRANSFORMATION OF THE GENOMIC EXPRESSION OF PLANT CELLS

M. R. DAVEY, K. M. A. GARTLAND AND B. J. MULLIGAN

Plant Genetic Manipulation Group, Department of Botany, University of Nottingham, University Park, Nottingham, NG7 2RD, UK

Summary

Agrobacterium-induced transformation of plant cells results from integration of T-DNA of the Ti or Ri plasmids into the genome of susceptible plants. Expression of T-DNA genes induces physiological changes in transformed cells which modify normal plant development to produce proliferations characteristic of crown gall and hairy root diseases. Understanding of the molecular basis of the transformation events associated with these examples of naturally occurring genetic engineering of plant cells, has stimulated efforts to construct vectors for transferring specific genes into plants. Vector construction has progressed from the use of wild-type Ti plasmids, giving phenotypically abnormal regenerated plants, to non-oncogenic plasmids. The range of vectors now available should enable useful foreign genes to be inserted into a range of dicotyledons and monocotyledons without impairing normal plant development.

Introduction

During the last fifteen years, considerable effort has been expended in developing the methodology for transferring useful genes into plants. Much of the stimulus for this work is based on the fact that the Gram negative soil bacteria *Agrobacterium tumefaciens* and *A. rhizogenes* have already evolved a mechanism of genetically engineering plant cells; the transfer, integration into the plant genome and expression of prokaryotic genes from the respective micro-organisms being manifest morphologically as crown galls and hairy roots in a range of susceptible Dicotyledons. In both cases, relatively small alterations to the plant genome following transformation by *Agrobacterium* elicit dramatic changes in the physiology and phenotype of recipient cells, reflecting the plasticity of the plant body as a whole. Undoubtedly, some of these novel effects will further our knowledge of the control of gene expression in plants; others may be useful in modifying the development of crop plants in a specific way. There is now a very considerable literature describing crown gall, with an expanding interest in hairy root disease. Indeed, understanding of the molecular basis of tumorigenesis has already been exploited to construct gene vectors. Since the impact of genetic engineering will arise from subtle changes rather than gross modifications to existing crop plants, this is reflected in the development of vectors from oncogenic agents to those which cause the minimum of disturbance to the genome, physiology, and phenotype of recipient plants.

Characteristics of *Agrobacterium* plasmids

Virulence in *Agrobacterium* is conferred by large Ti (tumour-inducing) or Ri (root-inducing) plasmids, according to their morphological effects on susceptible plant hosts. Transformation of plant cells involves the transfer of a specific DNA segment of the Ti or Ri plasmids, the T-DNA, from the bacteria, followed by its genomic incorporation and expression in recipient plant cells. The Ti plasmid of oncogenic strains of *A. tumefaciens* is a single copy molecule approx. 90–115 $\times$ 10^6 daltons (180–220 kb) in size. All strains of *A. rhizogenes* have at least one plasmid of a size comparable to that of the Ti plasmid (Costantino *et al.* 1981), with some strains harbouring three plasmids, e.g. strain 15843 carries plasmids a (107 $\times$ 10^6 daltons), b (154 $\times$ 10^6 daltons) and c (258 $\times$ 10^6 daltons). Virulence is carried on plasmid b; plasmid c is a cointegrate of a and b. T-DNA genes determine the morphological and physiological characteristics of transformed cells. A specific feature of T-DNA genes is that they govern the synthesis in transformed plant cells of unusual amino acids (opines). Other genes outside the T-DNA catabolize opines, enabling the latter to serve as carbon and nitrogen sources for the inciting bacteria. On this basis Ti and Ri plasmids, *Agrobacterium* strains, crown gall tumours and hairy roots can be conveniently classified according to the opines produced in transformed cells and degraded by the bacteria. The major classes are octopine, nopaline, and agropine Ti plasmids, and agropine and mannopine Ri plasmids.

Both Ti and Ri plasmids have a common virulence (*vir*) region which is implicated in the transformation process, but which is itself not transferred. Indeed, Ri *vir* regions can effect transfer of Ti plasmid segments to plant cells (Hoekema, Hooykaas & Schilperoort, 1984*a*). Restriction enzyme mapping and molecular hybridization have indicated homology of about 160 kb between the 250 kb pRiA4b, the octopine pTiA6 and the nopaline pTiT37, this homology being mainly in the *vir* and the plasmid replication (*ori*) regions (Huffmann, White, Gordon & Nester, 1984). Similar homology has been reported between other Ri and Ti plasmids (Jouanin, 1984). Although Ti T-DNA from octopine plasmids and Ri T-DNA from agropine plasmids are divided into two regions, TL (left) and TR (right), only localized regions of the pRiA4 T-DNA are partially homologous with pTiA6 T-DNA in regions governing tumour morphology. A structural feature implicated in T-DNA transfer are common 25 bp imperfect direct repeat sequences at the boundaries of nopaline T-DNA (separated by 22 kb and octopine TL-DNA (separated by 13 kb) (Gielen *et al.* 1984) and TR-DNA (separated by 8 kb). More recently, nucleotide sequencing has revealed similar 25 bp sequences located at the borders of the TL-DNA of pRiA4 (Slightom *et al.* 1985). The right 25 bp repeat is essential for T-DNA transfer during crown gall tumorigenesis (Caplan, Van Montagu & Schell, 1985), and is probably involved in the formation of circular intermediates within the bacterium during the early stages of the transfer process (Koukolíková-Nicola *et al.* 1985).

The high degree of sequence homology between Ri and Ti plasmids in the region concerned with oncogenicity may indicate that Ri and Ti plasmids have evolved from a common ancestral plasmid. Perhaps Ri plasmids should be regarded as a special group of Ti plasmids, possibly derived by recombination from the latter (Willmitzer, Sanchez-Serrano, Buschfield & Schell, 1982*a*). Ti and Ri plasmids can be transferred between *Agrobacterium* species, transconjugants resulting from transfer of specific plasmid to a cured (plasmidless) strain inciting a transformation response characteristic of the plasmid type.

Transformation of plant cells by wild-type *Agrobacteria*

The ability of *Agrobacterium* to direct abnormal development of plant cells is reflected both morphologically and biochemically.

Morphological plasticity

Both crown gall and hairy root diseases are characterized by unlimited and rapid host cell proliferation following invasion of wound sites by the inciting micro-organisms. In nature, infection frequently occurs at ground level, which, in the case of invasion by *A. tumefaciens* may result in tumours in the crown of the stem. These significantly reduce plant growth and often result in host death. In hairy root disease, considered to be a special type of tumour response (White & Nester, 1980), proliferation of adventitious roots may produce a secondary rhizosphere near the soil surface. Roots induced on more aerial parts of the plant, as in the case of experimental inoculations of tobacco plants with *A. rhizogenes*, often remain short and cone-like with tumorous tissue at the point of emergence of the roots from the host (Akermann, 1977). Whilst *A. tumefaciens* is a natural pathogen, the benign response and additional root system induced by *A. rhizogenes* could be of benefit under some conditions (Tepfer, 1984), and has been reported to enhance the drought tolerance of apple seedlings (Moore, Warren & Strobel, 1979).

In the laboratory, axenic stems and leaves provide suitable explants for inoculation, the bacterium being applied with an inoculating loop to cut surfaces, or introduced into wounds using a sharp instrument. In culture, the hairy root character of *A. rhizogenes* induced proliferations is strikingly apparent, since the humidity of the culture vessels encourages maximal root hair development. Such roots are plagiotropic or negatively geotropic, have reduced apical dominance, and are much branched. They grow more rapidly than non-transformed adventitious roots. In some cases, as in *Nicotiana tabacum* cv Xanthi, roots emerge from the inoculation site with the minimum of callus, but on pea, root development is preceded by growth of undifferentiated tissue (Spano, Wullems, Schilperoort & Costantino, 1981).

Although these general host responses of tumour or hairy root production typically distinguish *A. tumefaciens* from *A. rhizogenes*, the assumption that tumorigenic activity is restricted to *A. tumefaciens* and rhizogenic activity to *A. rhizogenes* is not as precise as the definition implies, since the response is related to the genetic constitution and regenerative capacity of the host plant as well as to the bacterial strain. Thus, the octopine *A. tumefaciens* strain B6 induced growths which produced roots on *Kalanchoë diagremontiana*, while several strains of *A. rhizogenes* induced neoplasms lacking roots on *Vicia faba* and *Phaseolus vulgaris* (De Cleene & De Ley, 1981). Similarly, *A. rhizogenes* strains LBA9402 and LBA9422 incited only overgrowths on tomato. LBA9402 tumours remained small, but those induced by LBA9422 made prolific growth (Hoekema *et al.* 1984*a*). The plant genotype plays a rôle in determining the response to *Agrobacterium*. In soybean, three genotypes were highly susceptible, ten genotypes moderately susceptible, eleven weakly susceptible and two gave no tumorous response to infection by *A. tumefaciens*. Of twenty-six genotypes inoculated with *A. rhizogenes*, only seven formed hairy roots (Owens & Cress, 1985). Differences in bacterial virulence on specific hosts can be overcome by mixed infections, the octopine strain B653 increasing the virulence of the nopaline strain C58 on *Kalanchoë* by a 'helper-effect' (Otten *et al.* 1985).

The site of inoculation and physiological status of the host plant can affect the response. Using the nopaline strain T37 of *A. tumefaciens*, Braun (1953) reported that decapitated tobacco plants responded to infection either with teratomatous (tumours which spontaneously produce phenotypically abnormal shoots) growth, but intact plants gave unorganized tumours. Ryder, Tate & Kerr (1985) showed that some strains of *A. rhizogenes* were virulent on the basal and apical surfaces of parsnip root discs, but others were more virulent on the apical surface. This response is related to auxin deficiency in the basal tissues and unidirectional auxin transport to the apical surface. Inoculation of tobacco stems with *A. rhizogenes* A4 gave hairy roots, but wounded leaves only occasionally formed roots. Instead, plantlets developed at wound sites, again indicating that the target tissues influence T-DNA expression (Tepfer, 1984).

Intact plants and organ explants have been used extensively as recipient systems for bacterial inoculation, but cultured cells, have, in the last few years been favoured by a number of workers studying crown gall tumorigenesis because they facilitate the production of clonal transformants. Such systems include (i) chemically stimulated uptake of isolated plasmids into freshly isolated protoplasts, (ii) fusion of *Agrobacterium* spheroplasts with isolated plant protoplasts, (iii) interaction (uptake and, or, fusion of liposomes carrying DNA with isolated protoplasts (Freeman *et al.* 1984), and (iv) infection (cocultivation) of protoplasts regenerating new cell walls with intact Agrobacteria (Fraley *et al.* 1984). Interestingly, transformants selected by their growth hormone autotrophy following the infection of *N. tabacum* cv Xanthi mesophyll protoplasts with wild-type strains (T37, Ach5) of *A. tumefaciens* exhibited morphological variation ranging from non-differentiated compact growth or friable tissues, to those showing spontaneous shoot regeneration (Davey, Freeman, Draper & Cocking, 1982).

Whilst the effects of *Agrobacterium* on higher plants are well documented, there are reports that *Agrobacterium* can influence the morphology of lower plants, buds and gametophores being induced on the moss *Pylaisiella selwynii* by *A. tumefaciens* (Spiess, Lippincott & Lippincott, 1984). However, it remains to be established as to whether moss cells become transformed.

Biochemical plasticity

Crown gall tumours and hairy roots can be freed of inciting bacteria by suitable antibiotic treatment (e.g. carbenicillin, cefotaxime) for periods of a few days or weeks, and subsequently maintained indefinitely in culture with routine transfer every 2 to 6 weeks depending on the rapidity of tissue growth. Transfer to *in vitro* conditions is facilitated by the recipient material being in an axenic condition prior to inoculation.

Nutrient requirements of transformed cells

Characteristically, transformed tissues have less-exacting nutrient requirements than non-transformed tissues. White & Braun (1942) reported that axenic crown galls could be cultured in a simple medium containing sucrose, salts and vitamins, whereas we now know that non-transformed tobacco pith tissue required auxins and cytokinins for proliferation. Thus, Braun (1956) concluded that transformation must result in the activation of biosynthetic systems that produce auxin and cytokinin. Likewise, hairy roots can be maintained either in liquid or on semisolid medium in the absence of growth substances. However, in this case the transformed roots resemble their non-transformed counterparts, since, in cases where excised non-transformed roots can be cultured, this is usually achieved in the absence of auxins and cytokinins.

Although there are no reports, to date, which quantify the endogenous levels of auxins and cytokinins in hairy roots, analysis of crown galls has shown that they contain auxins and cytokinins at levels sufficient to support continuous growth and cell division. IAA levels range from 10^{-6} to 10^{-7} moles kg^{-1} fresh weight, with an increase during the initial stages of culture. In reviewing the data of a number of workers, Kado (1984) concluded that the level of IAA in crown galls was 2- to 500-fold higher than in non-transformed cells. Friable unorganized tobacco tumours contained about ten-fold more IAA than compact unorganized tissues, and about 20- to 30-fold greater auxin concentrations than teratoma tissues. Both Binns (1984) and Kado (1984) reviewed the evidence for cytokinins in crown galls. Although some tumours did not contain cytokinins at levels significantly higher than control tissues, the majority analysed contained N^6-substituted adenyl derivatives (e.g. trans-zeatin riboside and isopentenyl adenosine) and glycosylated derivatives of these compounds at physiological levels sufficient to stimulate cell division (10^{-6} to 10^{-8} moles kg^{-1} fresh weight). Indeed, the levels of trans-zeatin riboside may be 1620-fold higher in some tobacco crown galls compared to levels in non-transformed tissues. Variation within specific tissues may be a reflection of the age and physiological state of transformed cells. Crown galls may contain 'cytokinesins' (compounds with a hypoxanthine base), but further characterization of these compounds is required. Interestingly, the growth of crown gall cells is not enhanced by exogenous auxin or cytokinin in the culture medium.

In general, not all cells within uncloned tumours are transformed, estimates indicating that 1 transformed cell in 200–1000 can crossfeed the non-transformed population to give an overall tumorous response. Although the autonomous nature of crown gall tumours may result from abnormal regulation of auxin and cytokin synthesis, other physiological characters may also contribute to the autonomous growth of transformed tissues. *Vinca* crown galls accumulated radiolabelled potassium and orthophosphate more rapidly than non-transformed tissues (Wood & Braun, 1965), while octopine tumours can utilize lactose in contrast to non-transformed cells which require sucrose as carbon source (Li & Schieder, 1981). Such evidence suggests that tumorigenesis may affect the permeability and uptake capacity of cells as well as the endogenous hormone levels.

Opine synthesis

Opines are unusual amino acid derivatives whose synthesis in transformed cells is determined by T-DNA genes. Such compounds may be metabolized specifically by *Agrobacterium* strains carrying a Ti or Ri plasmid of the type responsible for transformation. Thus, by inciting opine synthesis in its host, the bacterium creates a chemical environment favourable for its own growth and multiplication. In addition, some opines also induce conjugal transfer of virulence plasmids between *Agrobacterium* species.

Three distinct classes of opines have been reported in crown galls. Specifically, (i) the octopine family, which are N^2-(D-1-carboxyethyl) derivatives of L-arginine (octopine), L-ornithine (octopinic acid), L-lysine (lysopine) and L-histidine (histopine), induced by strains such as Ach5, B6, (ii) the nopaline family, N^2-(1,3-dicarboxypropyl) derivatives of L-arginine (nopaline) and L-ornithine (nopalinic acid) incited by T37 and C58, and (iii) the agropine family which includes derivatives of L-glutamine such as agropine itself, mannopine, mannopinic acid and agropinic acid in B0542- and A281-derived tumours. Crown galls incited by strains AT181, EU6 and T10/73 synthesize succinamopine with a structure analagous to nopaline, but with asparagine replacing arginine (Chilton, Tempé, Matzke & Chilton, 1984). Some octopine tumours also synthesize agropine and related compounds. In addition to the three families of opines whose structures have been chemically defined, a further group, the agrocinopines, are known to exist, and are phosphorylated sugars of unknown structure. Agrocinopines A and B have been identified in some nopaline tumours, while agrocinopines C and D are present in agropine tumours (Petit *et al.*

1983). Recently, Messens, Lenaerts, Hedges & Van Montagu (1985) have shown that the phosphorylated organic compound agrocinopine A is secreted into the surrounding medium from nopaline-type tobacco tumours. Agropine may account for as much as 7% of the dry weight of tumours, and is readily visualized using the silver-nitrate-based Sakagyuchi reagent. Phenanthrenequinone is a sensitive reagent normally used to detect octopine and nopaline present in tumours. Lysopine dehydrogenase (LpDH), the enzyme involved in opine synthesis, may be detected in transformed cells as early as 36 h after infection (Otten, 1982).

In a detailed study of the opines of hairy roots induced by a number of *A. rhizogenes* strains and their transconjugants, Petit *et al.* (1983) detected four silver-nitrate-positive compounds, enabling the inciting bacteria to be classified into two types, namely agropine type (e.g. strains A4, 15843 and HRI) and mannopine type (8196, TR7, Tr101). Hairy roots of the former group synthesize agropine, mannopinic acid and agrocinopine A; those of the mannopine group contain mannopine, mannopinic acid, agropinic acid, and agrocinopine C. The concentration of mannopine in both types of roots was about tenfold higher than that of mannopinic acid, while agropinic acid levels were dependent on the age of the tissue, extraction procedure, and conditions of storage of the product. Mannopine and agropine undergo chemical rearrangement to agropinic acid in aqueous solution, and this probably also occurs in living material. In old hairy root cultures, agropinic acid accounted for up to 50% of the silver-nitrate-positive compounds, while mannopine constituted 0·2–1·0% of the fresh weight of roots incited by strain 8196. Although all mannopine type roots synthesized silver-nitrate-positive compounds, opines were absent in some roots induced by agropine strains of *A. rhizogenes*, despite their hairy root appearance. Agrocinopines have been identified in hairy roots using phosphomolybdate staining.

Pigmentation of transformed cells

Crown gall tumours vary in their pigmentation, which is related to the host and the inciting bacterial strain. Whilst many lack chlorophyll and are creamy coloured, others, such as tissues derived from *Petunia* protoplasts transformed by isolated octopine (Ach5) Ti plasmid, are intensely green compared to the non-transformed tissues used for protoplast isolation (Davey *et al.* 1980). In such *Petunia* transformants, chlorophyll synthesis appears stable over many subcultures when tissues are maintained under low-intensity illumination (700 lux). In other cases, tissue pigmentation may vary with the period following excision from the host, and the time after subculture. The pigment complement and ultrastructure of chloroplasts within transformed tissues have not been analysed in detail.

Protein patterns of transformed cells

A necessary prerequisite for the high growth rate of tumours is an adequate supply of structural and enzymatic proteins which are synthesized *de novo*. These, in turn, require the synthesis of various mRNAs, tRNAs and rRNAs. Polyadenylated mRNAs coding a variety of proteins and the crown-gall-specific opine synthases, are produced by tumour cells, together with tRNAs and rRNAs. Synthesis of all these compounds culminates in the most vigorously proliferating tumours and declines as tumours age. In a detailed study of the protein changes that occur during tumour induction by *A. tumefaciens* C58 on potato tuber discs, Kahl & Schäfer (1984) confirmed that dramatic increases in RNA synthesis were parallelled by increase in chromatin-bound DNA-dependent polymerases I and II. Tumours had a characteristic protein pattern compared to non-transformed tissues, although this pattern remained unchanged throughout tumour growth and senescence. The phosphorylation pattern of proteins increased during tumour development and was stage specific, with phosphorylation of low molecular weight proteins (presumably specific histone phosphorylation) being observed in older tumours where mitotic activity had ceased. This intensified histone phosphorylation may account for chromosome condensation and cessation of mitosis.

Characterization of bacterial DNA in crown gall tumours

DNA transferred from *Agrobacterium* to recipient cells is covalently joined to plant DNA. Although the T-DNA of octopine tumours is shorter than the 23 kb length found in nopaline tumours, it can be more complex since it may occur as separate left (TL) and right (TR) portions (Fig. 1). TL is usually present in low copy number; TR may be amplified considerably (Thomashow *et al.* 1980). Frequently, TR is absent. Whilst this variation exists, the T-DNA of tumours contains a 9 kb region that is highly conserved between various octopine and nopaline tumours, and which corresponds to the TL of octopine tumours.

Transcription analysis of tumours has shown that the TL-DNA codes for seven polyadenylated transcripts (Willmitzer, Simons & Schell, 1982*b*) ranging from 670 to 2700 bases in length, while up to 13 transcripts of 900 to 2700 bases are encoded by the T-DNA of nopaline tumours (Willmitzer *et al.* 1983). The 5′–3′ orientation of most of the transcripts has been

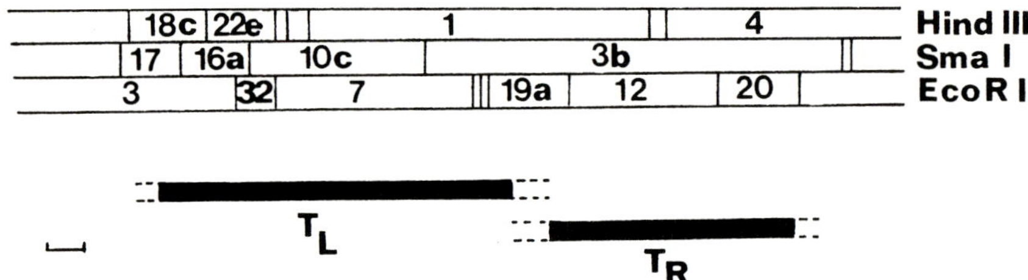

Fig. 1. Restriction endonuclease maps of the T-region of the octopine plasmid pTi Ach5 showing the TL (left) and TR (right) portions. Bar = 1 kb.

determined by hybridizing labelled RNA to separated complementary strands of the T-DNA. At least five, and probably six, crosshybridizing transcripts of the same size, location, polarity and function, are common to octopine and nopaline tumours (Fig. 2).

The functional organization of the T-DNA has also been established by site-directed mutagenesis involving insertion of transposons into the T-DNA or deletion of parts of the T-DNA, and subsequent analysis of the morphology of tumours incited by such mutant bacterial strains. Using *Agrobacterium* mutants with Tn5 or Tn3 insertions, Garfinkel *et al.* (1981) identified three loci on the T-DNA of the octopine plasmid pTiA6NC:
(1) a 3·1 kb *tms* ('shooty') locus,
(2) a 1·0 kb *tmr* ('rooty') locus, and
(3) a 1·25 kb *tml* ('large tumour') locus.
Agrobacterium mutants with mutations in loci (1) and (2) exhibited prolific shoot or root formation respectively. Inserts into the *tml* locus produced tumours two or three times larger than those of the wild-type strain on tobacco. In subsequent analysis of these regions, Ream, Gordon & Nester (1983) obtained evidence suggesting that the *tms* and *tmr* regions controlled auxin and cytokinin synthesis respectively in crown galls. Mutants in *tms* block endogenous auxin synthesis, leading to over-production of cytokinins and shoot development. Mutants in *tmr* block cytokinin synthesis and the resulting high auxin to cytokinin balance in the tissues stimulates rooting. In confirmation of this hypothesis, *tms* mutants of tomato treated with exogenous auxin and *tmr* mutants of the same host treated with exogenous cytokinins both form undifferentiated tumours. More recently, Barry, Rogers, Fraley & Brand (1984) x confirmed that the *tmr* region from the nopaline plasmid pTiT37 encodes isopentenyl transferase, an enzyme that catalyses the first step in cytokinin biosynthesis.

Collectively, the transcription and mutagenesis experiments indicate that genes 1 and 2 are involved in auxin production, and gene 4 in cytokinin synthesis. More detailed genetic analysis has confirmed that exogenous

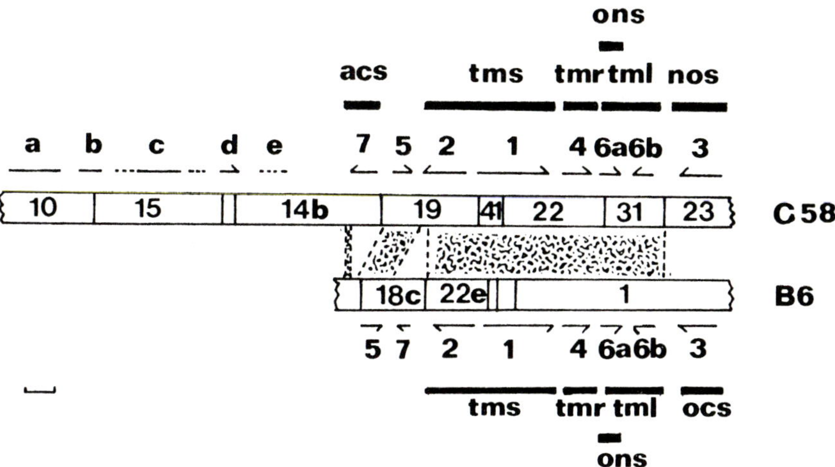

Fig. 2. Restriction endonuclease Hind III map of the nopaline plasmid C58 and the octopine plasmid B6 showing the location of transcripts and the direction of transcription. acs, nos, ocs – loci for agrocinopine, nopaline and octopine synthesis respectively. ons – octopine and nopaline secretion by tumours. tms, tmr, tml – loci for 'shooty', 'rooty' and 'large' tumour morphologies respectively. Regions of homology are indicated by stippled areas between the two maps. Bar = 1 kb.

auxin can restore to wild type the phenotype of tumours induced by mutations in genes 1 or 2, that gene 1 codes for an enzyme involved in the synthesis of an indole-3-acetyl derivative (Inzé *et al* 1984), and that gene 2 probably codes for indoleaceticamide hydrolase which participates in auxin biosynthesis (Thomashow, Reeves & Thomashow, 1984).

Although Ream *et al.* (1983) suggested that genes 6a and 6b might enhance cytokinin activity or inhibit auxin activity since some mutants in the *tml* locus affect transcript 6a and others transcript 6b, Messens *et al.* (1985) have now assigned a definite function to gene 6a, that of octopine or nopaline secretion from crown galls. Transcript 3 encodes either octopine or nopaline synthase in tumours and is, perhaps, the most studied of the T-DNA transcripts. Bevan, Barnes & Chilton (1983*a*) have sequenced the entire nopaline synthesase gene, and found its transcription signals to be typically eukaryotic. Three AT-rich polyadenylation sites, one major and two minor, were found to be connected by a mRNA 1460 nucleotides in length. However, unlike many eukaryotic genes this one has no introns. Shaw, Carter, Watson & Shaw (1984) produced a functional map of the nopaline synthase promoter by constructing a series of overlapping deletion mutants, within the region upstream of the coding region, and comparing enzyme activities. It was found that 88 bp upstream of the transcription initiation site were essential for wild-type expression levels.

This region contains a 'CAAT' box, deletion of which results in a reduction in activity of at least 80 %. Replacement of the 'CAAT' box with an intact, or partial 'TATA' box gave only barely detectable nopaline synthase levels. Transcript 7 of nopaline plasmids governs agrocinopine synthesis. Overall, at least four transcripts of the 13 kb TL-DNA of octopine tumours are involved in control of the tumour phenotype. Although auxin-locus and cytokinin-locus mutants of *A. tumefaciens* have reduced oncogenicity, full tumour induction can be restored using mixtures of the mutants. Inzé *et al.* (1984) found that whereas transcripts 1, 2 and 4 can be expressed independently of other T-DNA genes, only transcript 4 (*tmr*) can induce tumours by itself. Likewise, strains with mutations in the auxin transcripts 1 and 2 can complement each other (Van Slogteren, Hooykaas & Schilperoort, 1984*a,b*). Interestingly, the cytokinin gene determines the host range of *A. tumefaciens* (Hoekema *et al.* 1984*b*).

Unlike genes of the TL-DNA, the TR genes of octopine plasmids are not necessary for tumour induction and maintenance. Salomon *et al.* (1984) have shown that mannopine and agropine production are TR-linked traits, agropine production involving three T-DNA genes in contrast to the biosynthesis of octopine and nopaline where single T-DNA genes are involved (Ellis, Ryder & Tate, 1984). Karcher, Di Rita & Gelvin (1984) have identified TR transcripts of 780, 1050, 1450 bases and two of 1600 bases in size (Fig. 3). Their observations, combined with those of Komro, Di Rita, Gelvin & Kemp (1984) indicate that a precursor to mannopine is formed under the control of the translation product of the 1450 base transcript. Conversion of the mannopine precursor to mannopine, and the latter to agropine, is controlled by proteins encoded by two 1600 base transcripts.

DNA–DNA hybridization has revealed the T-DNA insertion pattern within crown gall transformants. As uncloned tumours are a mixture of cells, often with different inserts, single cell cloning techniques are essential to separate the individual transformants prior to analysis of their T-DNA. The size of the T-DNA insert depends, to a certain extent, on the bacterial

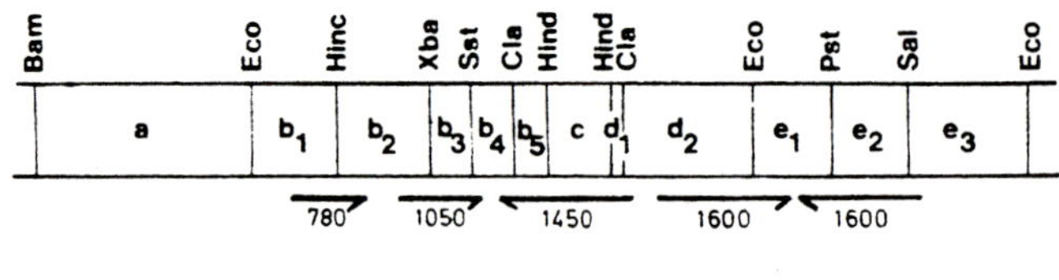

Fig. 3. Restriction endonuclease map of the TR of the octopine tobacco crown gall tumor E9 showing location of transcripts and the direction of transcription (Karcher, Di Rita & Gelvin, 1984). Bar = 1 kb.

strain and the recipient plant. Even cloned transformants selected following the cocultivation of protoplasts regenerating new cell walls with a specific bacterial strain e.g. *Nicotiana tabacum* cv Xanthi mesophyll protoplasts with Ach5 or T37, display a range of T-DNA inserts (Davey *et al.* 1982).

Whilst many transformants have been produced in several laboratories, the number of crown galls analysed remains relatively small. Draper, Freeman, Davey & Scott (1986) have summarized the T-DNA patterns reported in a number of crown galls and transformants arising from the cocultivation of protoplasts with intact Agrobacteria, enabling some generalizations to be made.

Most octopine tumours growing as unorganized callus contained core TL-DNA with little overall variation between tumours induced on different host plants or varieties of the same species with Agrobacteria harbouring various wild-type or mutant Ti plasmids, although there was a higher incidence of altered T-DNAs in transformants derived by cocultivation. The main deviation from the 'core' DNA was loss of the right-hand end of the insert, resulting in lack of opine synthesis by transformed cells. Ooms *et al.* (1982) reported an extension of the left border of the TL-DNA; Ursic, Slightom & Kemp (1983) described a right extension of the TL-DNA. The number of T-DNA inserts is usually between one and five, although Kwok, Nester & Gordon (1985) have reported ten copies in a cloned tobacco crown gall tumour. Another of the tobacco clones contained two copies of TL-DNA inverted in orientation with respect to one another.

Several polyadenylation sites have been found for nopaline synthase (Depicker *et al.* 1982) and octopine synthase (De Greve *et al.* 1982). Both of these genes had the sequence AATAAA $\pm$ one nucleotide preceding within 50 bp of the polyA site. Genes for leghaemoglobin, zein and legumin all have the same feature. The alcohol dehydrogenase gene (Gerlack *et al.* 1982) sequence AATGAG was somewhat different to this. The small subunit of RUBP carboxylase was found not to have any similar sequence upstream of its polyA site. These results suggest that the plant polyA addition mechanism tolerates greater variety in recognition site structure compared to animal genes, where only one or two nucleotides variation is found.

T-DNA methylation may also influence expression following integration into the plant genome. High methylation levels are thought to result in reduced levels of transcription. Hepburn, Clarke, Pearson & White (1983) found that all 24 copies of T-DNA in flax tumours were methylated to some extent, but that the degree of methylation varied, and did not reflect methylation of flanking plant DNA. Interestingly, demethylation by 5-azacytidine resulted in increased transcription levels, correlating with at least one extra DNA copy being demethylated per cell. This suggests that cytosine methylation is capable of suppressing plant gene expression *in vivo*.

Draper *et al.* (1986) reported that, on average, only 31% of octopine crown galls contained TR-DNA. In rare cases e.g. *Petunia parodii* – Ach5 tumours, the TR was fused to TL. TR appeared to be more frequent in tumours incited by 'shooty' mutants.

In nopaline tumours the number of insertions ranged from one to eight, with the majority of cells having less than three inserts. Of crown galls induced by T37 or C58 86% had a normal nopaline type T-DNA pattern, the morphology of tumours ranging from unorganized callus to those producing teratomas. As in octopine tumours, those nopaline tumours lacking the right portion of the T-DNA failed to synthesize opine.

In cases where the normal right border of the T-DNA of nopaline tumours and the TL of octopine tumours, and hence the 25 bp repeat, was missing, the right end of the T-DNA may terminate in DNA sequences with greater than 50% homology to the 25 bp repeat. Alternatively, the right-hand T-DNA may be deleted after DNA integration into the plant cell. In general, the presence of more than one copy of an insert was rare in transformants derived by cocultivation. Those transformants with a copy number greater than 1 had an abnormal integration pattern with deletions and rearrangements, probably as a result of postintegration modification. Deletions of the left part of the T-DNA, corresponding to transcripts 1 and 2, normally resulted in spontaneous shoot formation in both octopine and nopaline tumours. Multiple T-DNA copies were integrated in tandem or some other repeated pattern. Probably the greatest variation in T-DNA insertion pattern occurred in clones derived from protoplasts transformed by isolated Ti plasmids, *Petunia* transformants containing grossly reduced T-DNAs (Draper *et al.* 1982), while those of tobacco showed enlarged T-DNAs (Krens, Molendijk, Wullems & Schilperoort, 1982).

The variation observed from DNA hybridization indicates considerable plasticity at the level of DNA integration into plant cells. Interaction between the relative expression levels of T-DNA genes, endogenous growth regulators, and morphogenetic potential of individual transformants contributes to the plasticity observed at the cell, tissue and whole plant level.

Regeneration of plants from crown gall tumours

There has been considerable interest over the years, in the characteristics of plants regenerated from crown galls and hairy roots. Since the ability to recover plants is fundamental to present day genetic manipulation programmes, this basic knowledge has been essential in developing the strategy for vector construction to be discussed later.

The spontaneous production of morphologically abnormal shoots, particularly those incited by the nopaline strain T37, has been recognized for many years. In detailed studies of such structures, Braun & Wood (1976) reported that tobacco teratomas failed to develop roots, but would undergo phenotypic reversion giving fertile shoots following grafting to healthy vigorous tobacco stocks. These shoots synthesized nopaline, and were resistant to superinfection by *Agrobacterium*. Thus, at the whole plant level, the neoplastic state was suppressed, and all of the specialized cell types constituting the organs of the phenotypic revertants were histologically and functionally indistinguishable from those in non-transformed tobacco shoots of comparable age.

An intriguing observation was that leaf explants derived from phenotypic revertants resumed teratomatous growth when placed on hormone-free medium, demonstrating reinitiation of the tumorous phenotype. In contrast, stem pith, cortex and epidermal tissues did not show the same response on hormone-free medium, but required auxin for growth. However, once stimulated by auxin, these tissues also grew as teratomas after transfer to hormone-free medium, indicating a positive feedback of the hormone autonomy system.

Turgeon (1982) reviewed the characteristics of the T37 revertants documented in subsequent work by Braun and colleagues. Grafted plants retained tumour markers and T-DNA. In studies of the inheritance of crown gall characters, Yang *et al.* (1980) reported that grafted T37 plants gave offspring in which all the tumour markers, as well as the T-DNA, were lost. Subsequently, normal-appearing shoots derived from T37 crown galls by cytokinin treatment, produced F_1 seedlings which were able to form roots and had lost all tumorous traits. These seedlings contained only T-DNA sequences homologous to the ends of the T-DNA (Yang & Simpson, 1981). Thus, from these results, it was doubtful whether the complete T-DNA would go through meiosis.

Although much of the earlier work suggested that spontaneous shoot regeneration was restricted to nopaline crown galls, more extensive investigation of octopine tumours, especially of transformants derived from the cocultivation of protoplasts regenerating new cell walls with several strains of *A. tumefaciens*, indicated that plants could also be recovered from octopine transformants. Following cocultivation of 3-day-old tobacco protoplasts with octopine or nopaline strains of *A. tumefaciens*, Wullems, Molendijk, Ooms & Schilperoort (1981*a*) selected a number of clones by their hormone autotrophy, some of which synthesized octopine, while others did not express this ability. One octopine-positive line later required exogenous auxin and cytokinin, but retained opine synthesis. Similarly, hormone autotrophic nopaline-positive and nopaline-negative phenotypes were recovered. The phenotypes of the various transformants remained stable during long periods of culture. An interesting observation was that 50 % of the octopine transformants spontaneously formed shoots, in contrast to crown gall tumours incited by the same bacterial strains. These shoots, like those from nopaline crown galls, underwent phenotypic reversion following grafting to stock plants.

Evidence for the presence of T-DNA within regenerants has also been presented. In a subsequent study of regenerated shoots from *in vitro* transformants, Wullems, Molendijk, Ooms & Schilperoort (1981*b*) reported the heterostylous nature (stigma above the anthers) of flowers of tumorous plants. The plants were also male sterile as a result of defective pollen, rather than aberrant flower morphology, as artificial selfpollination of the plants failed to result in fertilization, and pollen from transformants was unable to fertilize non-transformed plants. Seeds could only be obtained when the stamens of grafted plants were crosspollinated by pollen from normal plants. Seeds of the octopine and nopaline transformants showed 90 % germination in soil. Although these seedlings developed their own roots, they retained characteristics of their transformed parents, including heterostylous flowers, the need to be crosspollinated by non-transformed pollen, and resistance to tumour induction by virulent Agrobacteria. However, only one seedling synthesized nopaline, this individual being distinguished from the rest of the seedlings by its slower growth. Growth of this plant was, in fact, promoted by grafting. The retention of nopaline synthesis ability suggested that T-DNA was retained through meiosis and differentially expressed in the F_1 progeny.

More detailed examination of larger seedling populations (241 F_1 plants) arising from cross pollination of nopaline transformants with pollen of non-transformed tobacco plants, showed that 56·5 % of the F_1 seedlings appeared normal, whereas 43·5 % contained the T-DNA-specific enzyme nopaline dehydrogenase, and exhibited the teratoma phenotype. This result confirmed that the T-DNA marker was transmitted to the F_1 progeny with Mendelian segregation ratios (Memelink, Wullems & Schilperoort, 1983). In these experiments, seeds were sown onto culture medium rather than soil to ensure that any transformed seedlings lacking a functional root system would still be recovered. Backcrossing of the grafted nopaline-positive F_1 seedlings recovered by Wullems *et al.* (1981*b*) with the non-transformed parent produced 55·4 % morphologically normal and 44·6 %

phenotypically transformed seedlings. Two nopaline-positive F_1 seedlings analysed by the Southern blot hybridization procedure contained a T-DNA insert similar to that in the primary transformed callus and the parental plants. The absence of the left portion of the T-DNA, but the presence of T-DNA coding for transcript 4, the cytokinin gene, would account for spontaneous shoot formation by the original crown gall tumour. These results confirmed that the inserted T-DNA remained stably integrated during plant regeneration, and was transmitted unchanged to the sexually produced offspring (Memelink *et al.* 1983).

More recent work (Wöstemeyer, Otten & Schell, 1984) involving *in vitro* infection of protoplasts of the same streptomycin-resistant line of tobacco (*N. tabacum* cv Petit Havana SRI) employed by Wullems *et al.* (1981*a*) with nopaline (C58) and octopine (LBA4013) strains of *A. tumefaciens*, resulted in transformants which spontaneously produced shoots in culture on hormone-free medium. In contrast to the results of Wullems *et al.* (1981*b*), male sterility was related to the nature of the tobacco line, rather than being a tumour-specific trait. Selfing or crossing of grafted shoots with normal SRI plants gave two types of seedlings. Those with thick stems, dark-green leaves, and poorly developed roots, which were opine positive, and others which appeared normal, with long roots, slender stems and light-green leaves. The latter were opine negative. The phenotypically abnormal plantlets developed roots in response to treatment with a commercial rooting preparation, but only survived for about 4 months in soil. However, in culture they showed vigorous growth, and leaf explants developed teratoma tissue on hormone-free medium. Segregation of the two types of seedlings following crossing of a transformed plant with normal tobacco were near to the expected ratio of 1 : 1. In selfings of tumorous shoots, and crosses between tumorous shoots, 75 % of the F_1 were expected to express tumorous characters. This was the case for a selfed octopine regenerant, but was somewhat lower (64 %) for a nopaline regenerant. Reciprocal crosses between fertile octopine and nopaline shoots yielded the expected ratios. 25 % of the F_1 progeny contained T-DNAs of both parents. However, such seedlings grew less well in culture than those with only one T-DNA marker. Overall, these observations led Wöstemeyer *et al.* (1984) to conclude that suppression of root formation and opine production were linked, and that transformed shoots were hemizygous for the T-DNA linked genes which were expressed as a dominant locus. In agreement with the results of Memelink *et al.* (1983), those of Wöstemeyer *et al.* (1984) established that some tumour-controlling genes can be sexually transmitted and do not interfere directly with seed development, germination, and early shoot formation. However, the formation of roots by transformed seedlings is suppressed.

Ooms, Karp & Roberts (1983) described the morphology and cytology of potato regenerants. Tumours from the tetraploid potato cultivar 'Maris Bard' produced both transformed and non-transformed shoots. The former, like transformed tobacco shoots, required grafting for maintenance. However, axillary buds of the grafted shoots produced stolons which developed into tubers. Non-transformed shoots, lacking opines, developed a functional root system and could be selected from transformed shoots by this character. Significantly, non-transformed shoots had a normal chromosome complement (48). They were morphologically identical to the parent plant, in contrast to protoplast-derived non-transformed plants which exhibited morphological and cytological variation.

The difficulty, particularly in earlier work, in regenerating whole plants containing T-DNA prompted several workers to use Agrobacteria containing mutated Ti plasmids. As previously discussed, bacterial strains with insertions into the *tms* locus have been useful not only in determining the functions of transcripts 1 and 2, but also in stimulating shoot production from several crown galls (Ooms, Klapwijk, Poulis & Schilperoort, 1980, Ooms, Hooykaas, Moolenaar & Schilperoort, 1981; Otten *et al.* 1981; Binns, Sciaky & Wood, 1982). However, maintenance of such regenerants still necessitated grafting. Thus, some effort has been directed towards regenerating transformants which produce a functional root system.

In studies involving tumour formation on tobacco with a mutated bacterial strain containing a Tn7 insertion into an octopine plasmid (pGV2100), Otten *et al.* (1981) noted that a regenerated shoot (rGV1) contained the T-DNA specific enzyme lysopine dehydrogenase (LpDH) and formed roots. After transfer to soil, the regenerant developed into a morphologically normal tobacco plant. Cells of the regenerant contained T-DNA, but this T-DNA had an internal deletion, eliminating the Tn7 insertion. Vegetatively produced offspring also contained the deleted T-DNA and retained LpDH activity. Both selfpollination of the regenerant and crosses between the regenerant and normal tobacco, showed that opine synthesis was transmitted through the pollen and eggs of the regenerant as a single dominant factor with Mendelian segregation ratios typical for monohybrid crosses. Repeated selfing produced homozygous plants which bred true with respect to LpDH. In later analysis of the regenerant rGV1, De Greve *et al.* (1982) established that the plant expressed only TL-DNA transcript 3, specifying octopine synthase, the remainder of the T-DNA being absent. In addition to forming a normal root system, the regenerant, and other similar plants, did not spontaneously form tumours, their cells required exogenous hormones for division in culture, and the plants were susceptible to infection by other *Agrobacterium* strains. These results established that morphologically normal plants could be regenerated from crown gall tumours provided those regions of the T-DNA encoding tumour functions were eliminated.

Because the major obstacle to whole plant recovery appears to be the inability of transformed shoots to form roots, Barton, Binns, Matzke & Chilton (1983) proposed that mutants in the 'rooty' locus of the nopaline Ti plasmid pTiT37 might 'disarm' the plasmid, permitting root formation by transformed shoots. Following insertion of cloned DNA sequences encoding yeast alcohol dehydrogenase or a bacterial neomycin phosphotransferase into the 'rooty' locus, transformation of tobacco stem segments produced tumours which, on transfer to medium with $0{\cdot}3\,\mathrm{mg\,l^{-1}}$ kinetin, gave rise to nopaline-positive, T-DNA-containing shoots. The latter rooted on transfer to hormone-free medium. The plants were fertile, and seedlings resulting from the selfpollination of regenerated plants also contained intact copies of the engineered T-DNA, again providing evidence of stable T-DNA transfer through meiosis.

Phenotypic variation of tumours can result from suppression of the expression of T-DNA oncogenes, rather than T-DNA loss or mutation. Amasino, Powell & Gordon (1984) described an octopine tumour which produced normal-appearing, rooted plants. Tissues from such plants required exogenous phytohormones for growth in culture, indicating that T-DNA expression in the plants was suppressed. Progeny from self-fertilization of regenerated plants also lacked T-DNA expression, although their tissues contained T-DNA. However, tissues of the regenerated plants treated with 5-azacytidine, an inhibitor of DNA methylation, resumed phytohormone-independent growth. These observations provided the first report of the regeneration from tumour cells of normal-appearing, rooted plants containing the auxin and cytokinin loci of the T-DNA. In tobacco octopine tumours induced by 'shooty' mutants of *A. tumefaciens*, Van Slogteren, Hooykaas & Schilperoort (1984*b*) reported activation of T-DNA genes involved in octopine, agropine, and mannopine synthesis in one particular line following treatment with 5-azacytidine. The genes also became active following grafting of regenerated shoots, and after an unusual form of differentiation in which shoots developed from the upper surface of abnormal, differentiated leaves.

Although studies of the expression of T-DNA genes in regenerated plants have been largely confined to members of the Solanaceae, Norton & Towers (1983) reported interesting results using the wild-type pTiT37 on a member of the Compositae, *Bidens alba*. Significantly, transformed shoots arising on tumours incited by the unmodified plasmid developed roots, eliminating the need for grafting. Although such transformed plants exhibited several morphological traits which distinguished them from normal plants, including their smaller size, reduced apical dominance, hypertrophy of the hypocotyl, lower nodes and petiole bases, and often an extra spur of tissue in ray florets, T-DNA traits were transmitted through subsequent sexual generations. One of these, nopaline synthesis, was transmitted to the fourth generation, although there was progressive decrease in the level of expression. Octopine-type tumours could be induced on nopaline plants, to yield double transformants. DNA analysis should confirm the sexual transmission of T-DNA in this plant.

Collectively, analysis of the characters of plants regenerated from crown galls indicate that although T-DNA can be transmitted sexually, its modification by deletion, mutation, or methylation facilitates the regeneration of morphologically normal plants capable of developing a functional root system. The fact that plants of *Bidens alba* transformed by pTiT37 can exist on their own roots, would suggest that analysis of the expression of unmodified T-DNA in a wider range of hosts warrants consideration in the future.

Regeneration of plants from hairy roots

Ackermann (1977) observed that *Nicotiana tabacum* cv White Burley plants infected with *A. rhizogenes* produced tumours with short cone-like roots. Occasionally, teratomas developed at the inoculation sites, and these structures could be propagated as cuttings. Roots from such cuttings formed shoots following transfer to culture. Both cuttings and regenerants were fertile, but exhibited crowded, wrinkled leaves compared to control plants, these features being carried through to the first and second daughter generations. Spontaneous development of cone-like roots occurred on transformed plants in the absence of the inciting bacterium.

Other workers have since reported that plants can be regenerated with comparative ease from hairy roots of tobacco, either directly (Ooms, White, Antoniw & Gibson, 1984), or via a callus stage. In this respect, the Ri plasmid may represent a naturally disarmed version of the Ti plasmid

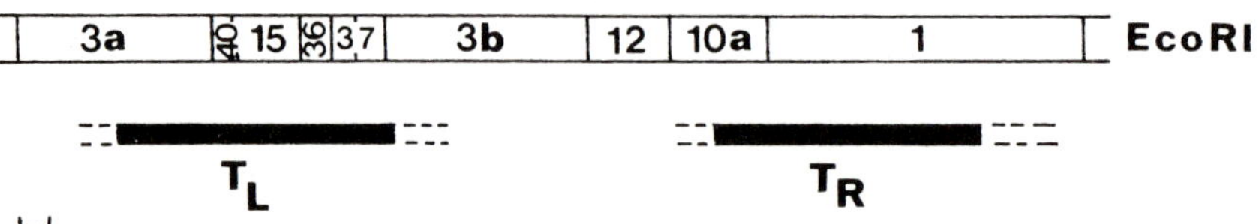

Fig. 4. Restriction endonuclease EcoR1 map of the T-DNA region of the Ri plasmid of *A. rhizogenes* strain A4. Bar = 2 kb.

(Byrne *et al.* 1983). Hairy roots of a streptomycin-resistant line of *Nicotiana tabacum* cv Petite Havana multiplied on hormone-free medium or on medium containing 0·2 mg l^{-1} kinetin, but formed callus in the presence of NAA (2·0 mg l^{-1}) and kinetin (0·2 mg l^{-1}). Shoots were produced following transfer of callus to hormone-free medium (Spano *et al.* 1981).

In a subsequent study of regenerants from hairy roots incited on the same host by *A. rhizogenes* strain 1855, the regenerants exhibited the same morphological characters as normal plants and were susceptible to infection by both *A. rhizogenes* and *A. tumefaciens* (Spano & Costantino, 1982). However, unlike the flowers of non-transformed tobacco plants in which the stamens and stigma are of equal length, those of the regenerants were heterostylous (pistil longer than the stamens) and selfsterile. Such modified flowers exhibited pollen sterility ranging from 50–100 %. Selfing fertile plants and crosspollinating sterile plants with pollen from streptomycin-resistant *N. tabacum* cv Petite Havana or *N. tabacum* cv Bright Virginia, gave some abnormally shaped fruits containing a limited number of seeds.

In comparing the differentiation response of hairy root regenerants and non-transformed plants, Benvenuto, Ancora, Spano & Costantino (1983) reported that leaf explants of transformants exhibited profuse root formation in the presence of 0·17 mg l^{-1} IAA and 1·0 mg l^{-1} kinetin, whereas explants of non-transformed streptomycin-resistant Petite Havana tobacco plants differentiated shoots. Such hairy-root-producing explants only later formed shoots. Explants from the latter exhibited a similar pattern of root production. Only at high concentration (2·0 mg l^{-1}) of kinetin was hairy root production suppressed and shoot formation promoted. However, even on a high kinetin medium roots reappeared after prolonged culture (45 days). From these results Benvenuto *et al.* (1983) concluded that transformation permanently modifies the hormonal equilibrium of plant cells and results in an altered programme of differentiation. Examination of the four major peroxidase groups (G_I,G_{II},G_{III},G_{IV}), which are known to play an important rôle in plant cell differentiation and organogenesis, indicated that those present in roots of hairy root regenerants were the same as those in roots of non-transformed plants (G_{II},G_{III},G_{IV}). Leaves of non-transformed plants contained peroxidases G_I and G_{III}, but leaves of hairy root regenerants exhibited all the four major peroxidases. These findings constitute evidence for the effects of Ri T-DNA on the regulation of endogenous plant genes, and provide another example of biochemical plasticity. Other analytical studies of *N. tabacum* hairy root regenerants has shown that the levels of pathogenesis-related (PR) proteins were similar to those of non-transformed plants. No significant difference was observed between normal and transformed plants in the number of lesions per leaf following inoculation with TMV (Ooms *et al.* 1984). Interestingly, transformants displayed the wrinkled leaf character described by Ackermann (1977).

Carrot has been used as a model system for somatic embryogenesis, and this developmental sequence has been employed to recover plants from hairy roots. Hairy roots, induced on carrot discs by strain 8196, produced callus on medium containing 2,4-D and kinetin. Cell suspensions initiated from this callus developed into somatic embryoids following omission of growth regulators from the medium. The 20 plantlets produced from such embryoids contained mannopine (Chilton *et al.* 1982). In an extension of this work, using cloned hairy roots incited by strain 8196 and its transconjugant 8196TC, Byrne *et al.* (1983) showed that the 8196 clone contained five non-identical copies of T-DNA, which together comprised a T-DNA complement of 34–42 kb of the Ri plasmid, three possible arrangements of the T-DNA within the transformed cells being presented. However, only two of these copies covered the core region (Bam H1 fragments 10a, 6, 19 and 14a) of the T-DNA. In contrast, the T-DNA in the 8196TC-derived line contained shorter lengths of DNA covering only the core T-DNA, root cells having four identical T-DNA copies 17–18 kb long, and one truncated T-DNA copy. Each copy resulted from an independent transformation event, since each exhibited different plant DNA/T-DNA border sequences. There was no evidence for tandem integration of multiple copies. From analysis of hairy roots incited on carrot and potato by strain 815834 Willmitzer *et al.* (1982*a*) concluded that the T-DNA was about 40–50 kb in size and double the molecular weight of the T-region of nopaline Ti plasmids. Subsequently, David, Chilton & Tepfer (1984) examined the plants regenerated from the hairy root clones described by Byrne *et al.* (1983), 50 regenerants being obtained from the 8196 clone and 20 from the 8196TC line. The 8196 T1 (1st generation of genetically transformed) plants produced abundant, negatively geotropic roots, 20 of the plants containing mannopine in their leaves and roots. The 8196TC regenerants all contained mannopine, and produced an extensive root system *in vitro*, but few leaves. T-DNA analysis of three 8196 regenerants and one 8196TC regenerant showed the T-DNA pattern to be identical to that in the parental root cultures (Byrne *et al.* 1983). 8196TC regenerants did not survive transfer from culture to the greenhouse, indicating that the four copies of the core DNA present in regenerants may exceed the tolerance of carrot plants to the presence of foreign DNA. Opine synthesis segregated in T2 plants obtained by selfing an 8196T1 regenerant, nine plants being mannopine positive and eight mannopine negative. The mannopine-negative T2 plants lost their hairy root characters. However, the

T-DNA of two opine-positive T2 plants was identical to that of the T1 parent. These results established that plants containing full length copies of Ri T-DNA could be regenerated without the need to modify the T-DNA.

To date, the most comprehensive analysis of Ri regenerants has come from the work of Tepfer (1983, 1984), following inoculation of *A. rhizogenes* strain A4 on stem explants of *N. tabacum* cv Xanthi and *Convolvulus arvensis*, and carrot root discs. Spontaneous plant regeneration occurred from hairy roots of tobacco and *Convolvulus*. Carrot plants were regenerated by somatic embryogenesis after callus induction. In all cases, hairy root regenerants were strikingly different from those regenerated from control roots. In a detailed examination of the transformed phenotype, Tepfer (1984) recognized characters which were common to all three plants. Other characters varied according to the host, the clone, or the individual. Non-variable traits were a high growth rate in culture, increased leaf width to length ratio, and the wrinkled leaf characteristics first reported by Ackermann (1977). Traits characteristic of particular species included reduced internode distance producing dwarfism, increased adventitious root production together with spontaneous plant regeneration from roots, and flowering with reduced flower size, heterostyly, and reduced seed production in tobacco. Carrot showed increased growth of aerial parts, reduced seed production, and a switch from biennial to annual habit. Clonal variation included pollen viability in tobacco, germination being 1%, 65% and 85% in the three clones examined compared to 90% for non-transformed material. However, pollen of all four types was morphologically similar following acetocarmine staining, in contrast to the results of Spano & Costantino (1982) who showed non-viable pollen to have morphological defects. Opine synthesis was a trait which may vary from individual to individual, being repressed in some seed progeny of *Convolvulus*, possibly as a result of hypermethylation of T-DNA. Interestingly, opine synthesis in *Convolvulus* showed seasonal variation, ceasing when plants became dormant.

Ri transformants produce more ethylene than normal plants, and transformed plants grow more vigorously in sealed Petri dishes (Tepfer 1984). The latter characteristic was used to assess inheritance of the transformed phenotype which was found to be Mendelian and dominant. Selfing of tobacco transformants produced some progeny that were probably homozygous for T-DNA as judged by their ratio of production and their growth in sealed containers. Such progeny had an exaggerated transformed phenotype, T*. Progeny produced from self-fertilization of one particular clone also displayed a super transformed (T′) phenotype, with marked dwarfism and profuse leaf crinkling. Some of the lateral branches on the T′

plant exhibited the simple transformed (T) phenotype, but this was the only case of phenotypic reversion in a total of 200 tobacco, 40 *Convolvulus* and 40 carrot plants observed by Tepfer (1984) over a 4-year period.

Using an A4 hairy root clone of *Convolvulus*, Slightom *et al.* (1985) analysed the nucleotide sequence of the TL-DNA/plant DNA junctions and confirmed that the 25 bp known to be important in the transfer and, or, integration of pTi-T-DNAs, is also a structural feature of the Ri plasmid. Thus, while the informational contents of the pRi and pTi T-DNAs are quite different, the mechanisms for their transfer and integration are probably similar. In subsequent work with material generated by Tepfer (1984), Durand-Tardif, Broglie, Slightom & Tepfer (1985) compared the T-DNA boundaries in hairy root clones of tobacco with those of *Convolvulus*, and found a reduced TL-DNA in tobacco. In *Convolvulus*, carrot and *Nicotiana plumbaginifolia* the boundary of the TL-DNA was within the BamH1 fragment 32, but in two clones of *N. tabacum* cv Xanthi, it was within or to the left of EcoR1 fragment 40. However, the right border of the TL-DNA is similar in all species so far examined. The only function tentatively assigned to the missing area in tobacco T-DNA, by homology to Ti T-DNA, is agrocinopine synthesis.

Durand-Tardif *et al.* (1985) found that the right-hand portion of the TL-DNA was actively transcribed in tobacco, but their inability to detect transcription from the TR-DNA indicated that the TR was probably not responsible for the transformed phenotype. Moreover, since regions of the TR-DNA are not homologous to the *tms* genes found in the TL-DNA of pTi, the transformed phenotype is probably not due to T-DNA encoded auxin synthesis. In general, transcripts encoded by TL-DNA were more abundant in roots than in leaves of plants regenerated from hairy roots. T-DNA structure was similar in the transformed (T) and supertransformed (T′) tobacco regenerants, and it was concluded that the T′ phenotype was not due to large-scale deletion or insertion, or to transposition of the T-DNA itself, as the border fragments were the same in plants of both phenotypes. Instead the T′ phenotype was correlated with the appearance of a leaf-specific 850-base transcript homologous to EcoR1 fragment 15. Thus, the T′ phenotype is caused by heritable changes in T-DNA expression, but the cellular mechanisms altered by this information remain to be defined.

Recently, more attention has been focused on the way Ri T-DNA genes can be used to modify the development of important crop plants such as oilseed rape and potato. Ri (strain LBA9402) regenerants of *Brassica napus* and *Solanum tuberosum* cv Desiree had distinct phenotypes, with abundant roots exhibiting reduced geotropism, and crinkled leaves.

Tubers of transformed potato plants were larger with more frequent, prominent eyes than those of non-transformed plants. Ten of 42 transformants had either 47 or 49 chromosomes instead of the normal 48 (Ooms *et al.* 1985*b*). In contrast, oilseed rape regenerants had a normal chromosome complement (38). However, these plants failed to set seed (Ooms *et al.* 1985*a*). The fact that T-DNA genes modify potato development, should be useful in future studies of the complex process of tuberization.

Transformation of monocotyledons by *Agrobacterium*

Although *Agrobacterium* induces a transformation response on a wide range of dicotyledons (De Cleene & De Ley, 1981), it is only recently that confirmation has been obtained for its ability to transform monocotyledons.

Hernalsteens, Thia-Toong, Schell & Van Montagu (1984) reported that cultured stem explants of *Asparagus officinalis* developed tumours following inoculation with the nopaline strain C58 of *A. tumefaciens*. Such tumours could be propagated *in vitro* on hormone-free medium, and synthesized nopaline and agrocinopine, providing evidence for stable T-DNA transfer and expression. Other workers (Hooykaas-Van Slogteren, Hooykaas & Schilperoort, 1984) inoculated plants of *Chlorophytum capenese* (Liliaceae) and *Narcissus* (Amaryllidaceae) with octopine and nopaline strains of *A. tumefaciens*. In these cases, swellings, rather than tumours developed at the inoculation sites. However, the tissue enlargements synthesized opines. These two significant reports will, undoubtedly, form the basis of more extensive studies on expression of T-DNA genes in a range of monocotyledons, especially crops such as cereals. The fact that T-DNA transfer to *Chlorophytum* and *Narcissus* is not accompanied by the induction of large tumours, suggests that cells of these monocotyledons, and probably cells of most other monocotyledons, do not respond to the products derived from oncogenicity genes encoded by T-DNA in the same way as those of susceptible Dicotyledons, perhaps because of peculiarities in their endogenous hormone metabolism.

Vectors for plant transformation

The last five years has witnessed rapid progress in the transfer and expression of foreign genes in plants, and the strategy in vector construction has been influenced, to a considerable extent, by knowledge of the effects of T-DNA genes on plant development. Although detailed discussion of vector construction and the genes so far transferred to plant cells is beyond the scope of this article, it is useful to consider the major events which have resulted in those vectors currently available.

The stimulus for using the Ti plasmid in this way must be attributed to Hernalsteens *et al.* (1980), who, after inserting Tn7 into the nopaline synthase gene of pTiT37, demonstrated the presence of the transposon within the T-DNA of tobacco tumours incited by the engineered *Agrobacterium* strain. Although Tn7, coding for resistance to streptomycin, spectinomycin and trimethoprim, failed to express in transformed cells, the report confirmed that foreign genes could be transferred with the T-DNA and maintained in plant cells.

Cloning of T-DNA in *E. coli* has enabled foreign genes to be inserted into specific sites in the T-DNA, and the latter to be transferred into *Agrobacterium* by recombination. Whilst this approach has been used to introduce a number of genes into plant cells, including those coding for zein, the small subunit of ribulose bisphosphate carboxylase, soybean leghaemoglobin, yeast alcohol dehydrogenase, rabbit β-globin, human interferon and phaseolin (see Shaw, 1984, for references), only phaseolin was expressed correctly at low level (Murai *et al.* 1983).

Success in foreign gene expression has been achieved by employing Ti plasmids not only as gene vectors, but also as donors of expression sequences. Thus, several groups of workers have constructed chimaeric genes which combine the upstream promoter sequences of the nopaline synthase gene (*nos*) with the coding sequences of bacterial antibiotic-resistance genes, and demonstrated the expression of such chimaeric genes in plant cells. Examples of such bacterial antibiotic resistance genes include aminoglycoside phosphotransferase (APH(3′)II; Herrera-Estrella *et al.* 1983*a*; Bevan, Flavell & Chilton, 1983; Fraley *et al.* 1983), dihydrofolate reductase (DHFR; Herrera-Estrella *et al.* 1983*a*), and chloramphenicol acetyltransferase (CAT; Herrera-Estrella, Depicker, Van Montagu & Schell, 1983*b*), which confer resistance to kanamycin (also neomycin and G418), methotrexate, and chloramphenicol respectively. The chimaeric genes were delivered to plant cells by inoculating explants with the engineered Agrobacteria, or by infection of protoplast-derived cells with the micro-organisms. Transformed cells were both growth-substance independent, because of their tumorous nature, and antibiotic resistant. Those of *N. tabacum* cv Wisconsin 38 were resistant to $100\,\mu g\,ml^{-1}$ of kanamycin compared to $16\,\mu g\,ml^{-1}$ for C58 tumour tissues (Herrera-Estrella *et al.* 1983*a*), while 'Mitchell' *Petunia* protoplast-derived cells survived 20-fold higher levels of kanamycin ($50\,\mu g\,ml^{-1}$) than protoplasts transformed by the corresponding wild-type Ti plasmid (Fraley *et al.* 1983). A significant observation was that antibiotic resistance could be employed as a dominant selectable marker, the transformation frequency in cocultivation being comparable to that obtained using hormone-independent selection.

Although Barton *et al.* (1983) showed that intact plants containing full-length T-DNA could be regenerated following tumour induction on tobacco with *Agrobacterium* mutants carrying foreign DNA inserted into the 'rooty' locus of the Ti plasmid, it was not known why this particular T-DNA did not interfere with regeneration, and whether or not its non-oncogenic phenotype in infected plant cells would be reproducible in all conditions of plant cell growth (Zambryski *et al.* 1983). The requirement for a non-oncogenic vector which would guarantee regeneration of normal plants prompted the latter workers to construct a Ti plasmid mutant (pGV3850) in which all the oncogenic functions of the T-DNA were deleted and replaced by pBR322. Such a vector, which still contains T-DNA borders, is extremely versatile, since any cloned DNA of interest contained in a pBR-like plasmid, can be introduced into the vector by a single recombination event.

Using the disarmed vector pGV3850 to transform tobacco protoplasts at frequencies up to 8·7% by cocultivation, De Block *et al.* (1984) selected tissues resistant to kanamycin, methotrexate and chloramphenicol. Phenotypically normal, fertile plants were regenerated from these antibiotic-resistant clones, and the chimaeric genes were transmitted to seed progeny in a typical Mendelian manner. Similar results have been reported for *N. plumbaginifolia* protoplasts cocultivated with *Agrobacterium tumefaciens* carrying a disarmed Ti vector with a chimaeric gene for kanamycin resistance (Horsch *et al.* 1984). Interestingly, these authors utilized split-end vectors in which the T-DNA borders were on separate vectors before recombination. Herrera-Estrella *et al.* (1984) have demonstrated light-inducible expression of the CAT gene in tobacco using the promoter of the gene coding for the small subunit of RUBP carboxylase of pea. Recently, the disarmed vector described by Horsch *et al.* (1984) has been used to introduce a wheat gene encoding the major chlorophyll a/b-binding protein (Cab) of the light-harvesting complex into the genomes of tobacco and *Petunia*, with demonstration of light-regulated organ-specific expression of this monocotyledonous gene in the transformed dicotyledonous regenerated plants (Lamppa, Nagy & Chua, 1985). Improvements to the transformation system described by Horsch *et al.* (1984) have included the construction of a vector delivered by *A. tumefaciens* which was non-oncogenic and lacking the left T-DNA border and which was used to produce kanamycin-resistant plants of *Petunia*, tobacco, and tomato by direct shoot regeneration (Horsch *et al.* 1985).

Other chimaeric genes have been constructed for use in plant cell transformation, including one in which the *N*-terminal coding region of nopaline synthase was fused to the *E. coli* β-galactosidase gene. Using this gene, Helmer *et al.* (1984) demonstrated lac$^+$ expression in sunflower and streptomycin-resistant tobacco tissues using ONPG and X-gal selection. Organelle-associated transformation has also been reported, De Block, Schell & Van Montagu (1985) employing a cointegrate-type vector containing the *nos* promoter, the CAT gene of Tn9 and the *nos* polyA signals to obtain chloroplast-associated transformation in tobacco. Similarly, a cointegrate plasmid was used by De Blaere *et al.* (1985) to obtain kanamycin-resistant colonies from tobacco protoplasts. However, this vector utilized the octopine, rather than the nopaline, T-DNA borders.

The Ri plasmid has also been used in gene transfer. Comai *et al.* (1985) have recently demonstrated that an important plant metabolic enzyme may be complemented with its bacterial counterpart. Using cointegrate vectors containing mutant *aroA* genes from *Salmonella typhimurium* inserted into pRiA4 TL-DNA, tobacco leaf discs were transformed to agropine production or kanamycin resistance. Regenerated plants had between three and seven times the normal resistance to glyphosate, a result which has application in genetically engineering crop plants to herbicide resistance.

An interesting concept is that of binary vectors based on separation of the T-DNA and *vir*-regions of the Ti plasmid. Hoekema, Hirsch, Hooykaas & Schilperoort (1983) showed that a strain of *A. tumefaciens* harbouring two compatible plasmids, one containing the *vir*-region and the other carrying the T-DNA, still induced tumours synthesizing octopine on tomato, *Kalanchoë*, tobacco, and pea. However, a strain of *Agrobacterium* with only the T-DNA-containing plasmid was non-oncogenic. The advantage of such a system is that the plasmid carrying the T-DNA can replicate autonomously in *E. coli*, facilitating handling and insertion of foreign genes into the T-DNA. A similar approach, but based on the nopaline Ti plasmid T37 has also been reported (De Framond, Barton & Chilton, 1983).

Recently, An *et al.* (1985) constructed a set of small vectors based on the Ti plasmid which contains a chimaeric *nos*-neomycin phosphotransferase gene, the ColE1 replicon, the cos site of bacteriophage λ, T-DNA border sequences and a wide host range replicon. The unique restriction sites between the T-DNA borders permit easy insertion of foreign DNA up to 35 kbp in size. These small vectors can be stably introduced into both *E. coli* and *A. tumefaciens*. An *et al.* (1985) have shown that it is unnecessary to clone the T-DNA on a small replicon, since, when introduced into wild-type strains of *A. tumefaciens*, such small vectors act in *trans* with the intact wild-type Ti plasmid which donates the functions necessary for DNA transfer and integration. Using the 15·6 kbp pGA471, An *et al.* (1985) showed that tumours incited on axenic shoots or leaves of *N. glauca* were resistant to kanamycin at 500 μg mg^{-1}, whereas tumours lacking the chimaeric gene were sensitive to 20 μg mg^{-1}. Similarly, mesophyll protoplasts of *N. tabacum* cv Xanthi were transformed to kanamycin resistance (200 μg mg^{-1}) at 10 % transformation efficiency. The pTiA6 *tmr* gene responsible for shoot proliferation was also expressed in *N. glauca* tumours following transfer to plant cells by vector pGA437 (18·3 kbp). Since cotransformation of the phytohormone-independent trait in tissues selected for kanamycin resistance was approximately 10–20 %, An *et al.* (1985) suggested that most drug-resistant transformants should be able to regenerate into whole plants by adjustment of the phytohormone levels of the culture medium, and that it was unnecessary to employ T-DNA deleted Ti plasmid as 'helpers' to assist the shuttle vectors.

A logical extension of the binary vector concept, and which, in fact, preceded the report of An *et al.* (1985), was the construction of a non-oncogenic binary system (Bin 6) reported by Bevan (1984), which was used to transform stem explants of *N. plumbaginifolia* to kanamycin resistance.

Although several workers have based their constructs on the Ti plasmid, others have investigated the use of non-Ti vectors. CaMV is attractive in this respect because the double-stranded genome can be manipulated *in vitro*; the viral DNA is infectious when rubbed onto healthy leaves, and the virus spreads through the host plant. By replacing the CaMV open reading frame II, which is not essential for infection, with a bacterial dihydrofolate reductase gene, Brisson *et al.* (1984) demonstrated expression of the foreign DNA in CaMV-infected turnip plants. Simple vectors can also be used to transform plant cells. Thus, Paszkowski *et al.* (1984) transformed tobacco protoplasts to kanamycin resistance following polyethylene-glycol-stimulated uptake of an *E. coli* plasmid carrying the aminoglycoside phosphotransferase gene under the control of the CaMV gene VI promoter. Plants regenerated from transformed protoplasts were phenotypically normal and fertile. Subsequent, detailed analysis (Potrykus *et al.* 1985*a*) confirmed that one functional copy of the hybrid gene was stably integrated into the chromosomal DNA of the original tobacco transformants, that the gene was stably maintained during clonal propagation, and inherited as a dominant trait. However, some exceptions were found which did not follow the expected inheritance patterns, with deletions of some of the integrated DNA both in regenerated plants and their progeny.

Undoubtedly, the most significant advance in recent years has been the demonstration that simple vectors can be used to transform Monocotyledons. Potrykus *et al.* (1985*b*) used the vector constructed by

Paszkowski *et al.* (1984) to transform protoplasts of *Lolium multiflorum* to kanamycin resistance, while Lörz, Baker & Schell (1985) also used a pBR322-derived plasmid carrying a chimaeric gene comprising the protein-coding region of the Tn5 aminoglycoside phosphotransferase gene, the *nos* promoter and the polyadenylation signal of the octopine synthase gene, to transform protoplasts isolated from suspension cultured cells of *Triticum monococcum* to resistance to the same antibiotic. These two reports confirm that, in principle, members of the Gramineae can be transformed by isolated DNA. At present, the main limitation in extending this approach to many of the important Monocotyledonous crops lies, not with the vectors available, but in the inability to regenerate plants from isolated protoplasts.

Conclusion

Studies of crown gall and hairy root reflect plasticity at various levels during transformation. The plant genome itself is plastic enough to accommodate Ti and Ri plasmid DNA, although studies with Ri plasmids indicate a limit as to the number of T-DNA copies that can be introduced into the genome of a recipient cell. Various factors, including the nature of the DNA itself, the plant genotype and the age and physiology of the plant, interact to determine the phenotypic response and the biochemical characteristics of transformed cells. Tumours may be deleterious to long-term survival of the host, but hairy roots may be advantageous under some conditions. Expression of the auxin and cytokinin loci common to the T-DNA of both octopine and nopaline Ti plasmids interferes with plant development; elimination of these loci by deletion or mutation, or their inactivation by methylation, being a prerequisite for the regeneration of phenotypically normal plants from transformed tissues.

Although functions have been assigned to several Ti T-DNA transcripts, further investigation is required to determine the functions of the remaining transcripts. Likewise, considerable effort is needed to elucidate the effect of Ri T-DNA transcripts at the plant level. Identification of the transcript responsible for the supertransformed phenotype represents the initial stage in this direction.

Understanding of the molecular basis of crown gall tumorigenesis has enabled rapid progress to be achieved during the last few years in the construction of non-oncogenic plant vectors, and the latter will be used increasingly in the immediate future for the genetic engineering of a range of Dicotyledonous and Monocotyledonous crop plants.

References

ACKERMANN, C. (1977). Pflanzen aus *Agrobacterium rhizogenes*-tumoren an *Nicotiana tabacum*. *Pl. sci. Lett.* **8**, 23–30.

AMASINO, R. M., POWELL, A. T. & GORDON, M. P. (1984). Changes in T-DNA methylation and expression are associated with phenotypic variation and plant regeneration in a crown gall tumor line. *Mol. gen. Genet.* **197**, 437–446.

AN, G., WATSON, B. D., STACHEL, S., GORDON, M. P. & NESTER, E. W. (1985). New cloning vehicles for transformation of higher plants. *EMBO J.* **4**, 277–284.

BARRY, G. F., ROGERS, S. G., FRALEY, R. T. & BRAND, L. (1984). Identification of a cloned cytokinin biosynthetic gene. *Proc. natn. Acad. Sci. U.S.A.* **81**, 4776–4780.

BARTON, K. A., BINNS, A. N., MATZKE, A. J. M. & CHILTON, M-D. (1983). Regeneration of intact tobacco plants containing full length copies of genetically engineered T-DNA, and transmission of T-DNA to R1 progeny. *Cell* **32**, 1033–1043.

BENVENUTO, E., ANCORA, G., SPANO, L. & COSTANTINO, P. (1983). Morphogenesis and isoperoxidase characterization in tobacco 'Hairy root' regenerants. *Z. Pflanzenphysiol.* **110**, 239–245.

BEVAN, M. (1984). Binary *Agrobacterium* vectors for plant transformation. *Nucl. Acid. Res.* **12**, 8711–8721.

BEVAN, M., BARNES, W. M. AND CHILTON, M-D. (1983*a*). Structure and transmission of the nopaline synthase gene region of T-DNA. *Nucl. Acid. Res.* **11**, 369–385.

BEVAN, M. W., FLAVELL, R. B. & CHILTON, M-D. (1983*b*). A chimaeric antibiotic resistance gene as a selectable marker for plant cell transformation. *Nature* **304**, 184–187.

BINNS, A. N. (1984). The biology and molecular biology of plant cells infected by *Agrobacterium tumefaciens*. In *Oxford Surveys of Plant Molecular and Cell Biology*, vol. 1 (ed. B. J. M. Flin), pp. 133–160. Oxford: Clarendon Press.

BINNS, A. N., SCIAKY, D. & WOOD, H. W. (1982). Variation in hormone autonomy and regenerative potential of cells transformed by strain A66 of *Agrobacterium tumefaciens*. *Cell* **31**, 605–612.

BRAUN, A. C. (1953). Bacterial and host factors concerned in determining tumor morphology in crown gall. *Bot. Gaz.* **114**, 363–371.

BRAUN, A. C. (1956). The activation of two growth-substance systems accompanying the conversion of normal to tumor cells in crown gall. *Cancer Res.* **16**, 53–56.

BRAUN, A. C. & WOOD, H. N. (1976). Suppression of the neoplastic state with the acquisition of specialised functions in cells, tissues, and organs of crown gall teratomas of tobacco. *Proc. natn. Acad. Sci. U.S.A.* **73**, 496–500.

BRISSON, N., PASZKOWSKI, J., PENSWICK, J. R., GRONENBORN, B., POTRYKUS, I. & HOHN, T. (1984). Expression of a bacterial gene in plants using a viral vector. *Nature* **310**, 511–514.

BYRNE, M. C., KOPLOW, J., DAVID, C., TEMPÉ, J. & CHILTON, M-D. (1983). Structure of T-DNA in roots transformed by *Agrobacterium rhizogenes*. *J. molec. appl. Genet.* **2**, 201–209.

CAPLAN, A. B., VAN MONTAGU, M. & SCHELL, J. (1985). Genetic analysis of integration mediated by single T-DNA borders. *J. Bact.* **161**, 655–664.

CHILTON, W. S., TEMPÉ, J., MATZKE, M. & CHILTON, M-D. (1984). Succinamopine: a new crown gall opine. *J. Bact.* **157**, 357–362.

CHILTON, M-D., TEPFER, D., PETIT, A., DAVID, C., CASSE-DELBART, F. & TEMPÉ, J. (1982). *Agrobacterium rhizogenes* inserts T-DNA into the genomes of host plant root cells. *Nature* **295**, 432–434.

COMAI, L., FACCIOTTI, D., HIATT, W. R., THOMPOL, G., ROZE, R. E. & STALKER, D. M. (1985). Expression in plants of a mutant *aroA* gene from *Salmonella typhimurium* confers tolerance to glyphosphate. *Nature* **317**, 714–744.

COSTANTINO, P., MAURO, M. L., MICHELI, G., RISULEO, G., HOOYKAAS, P. J. J. & SCHILPEROORT, R. A. (1981). Fingerprinting and sequence homology of plasmids of from different virulent strains of *Agrobacterium rhizogenes*. *Plasmid* **5**, 170–182.

DAVEY, M. R., COCKING, E. C., FREEMAN, J. P., PEARCE, N. & TUDOR, I. (1980). Transformation of *Petunia* protoplasts by isolated *Agrobacterium* plasmids. *Pl. sci. Lett.* **18**, 307–313.

DAVEY, M. R., FREEMAN, J. P., DRAPER, J. & COCKING, E. C. (1982). Transformation of protoplasts by *Agrobacterium* and isolated Ti plasmid. In *Plant Tissue Culture, 1982. Proceedings 5th International Congress of Plant Tissue and Cell Culture* (ed. A. Fujiwara), pp. 515–516. Tokyo: Abe Photo Printing Co. Ltd.

DAVID, C., CHILTON, M-D. & TEPFER, D. (1984). Conservation of T-DNA in plants regenerated from hairy root cultures. *Biotechnol.* **2**, 73–76.

DEBLAERE, R., BYTEBIER, B., DEGREVE, H., DEBOECK, F., SCHELL, J., VAN MONTAGU, M. & LEEMANS, J. (1985). Efficient octopine Ti plasmid-derived vectors for *Agrobacterium*-mediated gene transfer to plants. *Nucl. acid. Res.* **13**, 4777–4788.

DE BLOCK, M., HERRERA-ESTRELLA, L., VAN MONTAGU, M., SCHELL, J. & ZAMBRYSKI, P. (1984). Expression of foreign genes in regenerated plants and in their progeny. *EMBO J.* **3**, 1681–1689.

DE BLOCK, M., SCHELL, J. & VAN MONTAGU, M. (1985). Chloroplast transformation by *Agrobacterium tumefaciens. EMBO J.* **4**, 1367–1372.

DE CLEENE, M. & DE LEY, J. (1976). The host range of crown gall. *Bot. Rev.* **42**, 389–466.

DE FRAMOND, A. J., BARTON, K. A. & CHILTON, M-D. (1983). Mini-Ti: A new vector strategy for plant genetic engineering. *Biotechnol.* **1**, 262–269.

DE GREVE, H., LEEMANS, J., HERNALSTEENS, J-P., THIA-TOONG, L., DE BEUCKELEER, M., WILLMITZER, L., OTTEN, L., VAN MONTAGU, M. & SCHELL, J. (1982). Regeneration of normal and fertile plants that express octopine synthase from tobacco crown galls after deletion of tumour-controlling functions. *Nature* **300**, 752–755.

DEPICKER, A., STACHEL, S., DHAESE, P., ZAMBRYSKI, P. & GOODMAN, H. M. (1982). Nopaline synthase: Transcript mapping and DNA sequence. *J. molec. appl. Genet* **1**, 561–574.

DRAPER, J., DAVEY, M. R., FREEMAN, J. P., COCKING, E. C. & COX, B. J. (1982). Ti plasmid homologous sequences present in tissues from *Agrobacterium* plasmid-transformed *Petunia* protoplasts. *Pl. Cell Physiol.* **23**, 451–458.

DRAPER, J., FREEMAN, J. P., DAVEY, M. R., SCOTT, R. J. & COCKING, E. C. (1986). Increased T-DNA copy number in transformed plant cells is often associated with aberrant integrations when using oncogenic Ti plasmid vectors with *cis*-acting *vir* genes. *Cell* (submitted).

DURAND-TARDIF, M., BROGLIE, R., SLIGHTOM, J. & TEPFER, D. (1985). Structure and expression of Ri T-DNA from *Agrobacterium rhizogenes* in *Nicotiana tabacum.* Organ and phenotypic specificity. *J. molec. Biol.* **186**, 557–564.

ELLIS, J. G., RYDER, M. H. & TATE, M. E. (1984). *Agrobacterium tumefaciens* Ti-DNA encodes a pathway for agropine biosynthesis. *Mol. gen. Genet.* **195**, 466–473.

FRALEY, R. T., HORSCH, R. B., MATZKE, A., CHILTON, M-D., CHILTON, W. S. & SANDERS, P. R. (1984). *In vitro* transformation of *Petunia* cells by an improved method of co-cultivation with *A. tumefaciens* strains. *Pl. molec. Biol.* **3**, 371–378.

FRALEY, R. T., ROGERS, S. G., HORSCH, R. B., SANDERS, P. S., FLICK, J. S., ADAMS, S. P., BITTNER, M. L., BRAND, L. A., FINK, C. L., FRY, J. S., GALLUPPI, G. R., GOLDBERG, S. B., HOFFMANN, N. L. & WOO, S. C. (1983). Expression of bacterial genes in plant cells. *Proc. natn. Acad. Sci. U.S.A.* **80**, 4807–4807.

FREEMAN, J. P., DRAPER, J., DAVEY, M. R., COCKING, E. C., GARTLAND, K. M. A., HARDING, K. & PENTAL, D. (1984). A comparison of methods for plasmid delivery into plant protoplasts. *Pl. Cell Physiol.* **25**, 1353–1365.

GARFINKEL, D. J., SIMPSON, R. B., REAM, L. W., WHITE, F. F., GORDON, M. P. & NESTER, E. W. (1981). Genetic analysis of crown gall: fine structure map of the T-DNA by site directed mutagenesis. *Cell* **27**, 143–153.

GERLACH, W. L., PRYOR, A. J., DENNIS, E. S., FERL, R. J., SACHS, M. M. & PEACOCK, W. J. (1982). cDNA cloning and introduction of the alcohol dehydrogenase gene (Adhl) of maize. *Proc. natn. Acad. Sci. U.S.A.* **79**, 2981–2985.

GIELEN, J., DE BEUCKELEER, M., SEURICK, J., DEBOECK, F., DE GREVE, H., LEMMERS, M., VAN MONTAGU, M. & SCHELL, J. (1984). The complete nucleotide sequence of the T-DNA of the *Agrobacterium tumefaciens* plasmid pTiACH5. *EMBO J.* **3**, 835–846.

HELMER, G., CASADABAN, M., BEVAN, M., KAYES, L. & CHILTON, M-D. (1984). A new chimeric gene as a marker for plant transformation: the expression of *Escherichia coli* β-galactosidase in sunflower and tobacco cells. *Biotechnol.* **2**, 520–527.

HEPBURN, A. G., CLARKE, L. E., PEARSON, L. & WHITE, J. (1983). The rôle of cytosine methylation in the control of nopaline synthase gene expression in a plant tumor. *J. molec. appl. Genet.* **2**, 315–329.

HERNALSTEENS, J-P., THIA-TOONG, L., SCHELL, J. & VAN MONTAGU, M. (1984). An *Agrobacterium*-transformed cell culture from the monot *Asparagus officinalis. EMBO J.* **3**, 3039–3041.

HERNALSTEENS, J-P., VAN VLIET, F. DE BEUCKELEER, M., DEPICKER, A., ENGLER, G., LEMMERS, M., HOLSTERS, M., VAN MONTAGU, M. & SCHELL, J. (1980). The *Agrobacterium tumefaciens*, Ti plasmid as a host vector for introducing DNA in plant cells. *Nature* **287**, 654–656.

HERRERA-ESTRELLA, L., DE BLOCK, M., MESSENS, E., HERNALSTEENS, J-P., VAN MONTAGU, M. & SCHELL, J. (1983*a*). Chimeric genes as dominant selectable markers in plant cells. *EMBO J.* **2**, 987–995.

HERRERA-ESTRELLA, L., DEPICKER, A., VAN MONTAGU, M. & SCHELL, J. (1983*b*). Expression of chimeric genes transferred into plant cells using a Ti plasmid-derived vector. *Nature* **303**, 209–213.

HERRERA-ESTRELLA, L., VAN DEN BROECK, G., MAENHAUT, R., VAN MONTAGU, M., SCHELL, J., TIMKO, M. & CASHMORE A. (1984). Light-inducible and chloroplast associated expression of a chimaeric gene introduced into *Nicotiana tabacum* using a Ti plasmid vector. *Nature* **310**, 115–120.

HOEKEMA, A., HIRSCH, P. R., HOOYKAAS, P. J. J. & SCHILPEROORT, R. A. (1983). A binary plant vector strategy based on separation of *vir*- and T-region of the *Agrobacterium tumefaciens* Ti plasmid. *Nature* **303**, 179–180.

HOEKEMA, A., HOOYKAAS, P. J. & SCHILPEROORT, R. A. (1984*a*). Transfer of octopine T-DNA segment to plant cells mediated by different types of *Agrobacterium* tumor- or root-inducing plasmids: generality of virulence systems. *J. Bact.* **158**, 383–385.

HOEKEMA, A., DE PATER, B. S., FELLINGER, A. J., HOOYKAAS, P. J. J. & SCHILPEROORT, R. A. (1984*b*). The limited host range of an *Agrobacterium* strain extended by a cytokinin gene from a wide host range T-region. *EMBO J.* **3**, 3043–3047.

HOOYKAAS-VAN SLOGTEREN, G. M. S., HOOYKAAS, P. J. J. & SCHILPEROORT, R. A. (1984). Expression of Ti plasmid genes in monocotyledonous plants infected with *Agrobacterium tumefaciens. Nature* **311**, 763–764.

HORSCH, R. B., FRALEY, R. T., ROGERS, S. G., SANDERS, P. R., LLOYD, A. & HOFFMANN, N. (1984). Inheritance of functional foreign genes in plants. *Science* **223**, 496–498.

HORSCH, R. B., FRY, J. B., HOFFMANN, N. L., EICHHOLTZ, D., ROGERS, S. G. & FRALEY, R. T. (1985). A simple and general method for transferring genes into plants. *Science* **227**, 1229–1231.

HUFFMANN, G. A., WHITE, F. F., GORDON, M. P. & NESTER, E. W. (1984). Hairy-root-inducing plasmid: physical map and homology to tumor-inducing plasmids. *J. Bact.* **157**, 269–276.

INZÉ, D., FOLLIN, A., VAN LIJSEBETTENS, M., SIMOENS, C., GENETELLO, C., VAN MONTAGU, M. & SCHELL, J. (1984). Genetic analysis of the individual T-DNA genes of *Agrobacterium tumefaciens*; further evidence that two genes are involved in indole-3-acetic acid synthesis. *Mol. gen. Genet.* **194**, 265–274.

JOUANIN, L. (1984). Restriction map of an agropine-type Ri plasmid and its homologies with Ti plasmids. *Plasmid* **12**, 91–102.

KADO, C. I. (1984). Phytohormone-mediated tumorigenesis by plant pathogenic bacteria. In *Plant Gene Research. Genes Involved in Microbe-Plant Interactions* (ed. D. P. S. Verma and T. Hohn), pp. 311–336. Vienna, New York: Springer-Verlag.

KAHL, G. & SCHÄFER, W. (1984). Phosphorylation of chromosomal proteins changes during the development of crown gall tumors. *Pl. Cell Physiol.* **25**, 1187–1196.

KARCHER, S. J., DI RITA, V. J. & GELVIN, S. B. (1984). Transcript analysis of TR DNA in octopine-type crown gall tumors. *Mol. gen. Genet.* **194**, 159–165.

KOMRO, C. T., DI RITA, V. J., GELVIN, S. B. & KEMP, J. D. (1985). Site-specific mutagenesis in the TR-DNA region of octopine-type Ti plasmids. *Plant molec. Biol.* **4**, 253–263.

KOUKOLÍKOVÁ-NICOLA, Z., SHILLITO, R. D., HOHN, B., WANG, K., VAN MONTAGU, M. & ZAMBRYSKI, P. (1985). Involvement of circular intermediates in the transfer of T-DNA from *Agrobacterium tumefaciens* to plant cells. *Nature* **313**, 191–196.

KRENS, F. A., MOLENDIJK, L., WULLEMS, G. J. & SCHILPEROORT, R. A. (1982). *In vitro* transformation of plant protoplasts with Ti plasmid DNA. *Nature* **296**, 72–74.

KWOK, W. W., NESTER, E. W. & GORDON, M. P. (1985). Unusual plasmid DNA organization in an octopine crown gall tumor. *Nucl. acid. Res.* **13**, 459–471.

LAMPPA, G., NAGY, F. & CHUA, N-H. (1985). Light-regulated and organ-specific expression of a wheat Cat gene in transgenic tobacco. *Nature* **316**, 750–752.

LI, X. & SCHIEDER, O. (1981). Utilization *in vitro* of D-lactose by B653 tumor cells of tobacco. *Pl. sci. Lett.* **21**, 209–214.

LÖRZ, H., BAKER, B. & SCHELL, J. (1985). Gene transfer to cereal cells mediated by protoplast transformation. *Mol. gen. Genet.* **199**, 178–182.

MEMELINK, J., WULLEMS, G. J. & SCHILPEROORT, R. A. (1983). Nopaline T-DNA is maintained during regeneration and generative propagation of transformed tobacco plants. *Mol. gen. Genet.* **190**, 516–522.

MESSENS, E., LENAERTS, A., HEDGES, R. W. & VAN MONTAGU, M. (1985). Agrocinopine A, a phosphorylated opine is secreted from crown gall cells. *EMBO J.* **4**, 571–577.

MOORE, L., WARREN, G. & STROBEL, G. (1979). Involvement of a plasmid in the hairy root disease of plants caused by *Agrobacterium rhizogenes. Plasmid* **2**, 617–662.

MURAI, N., SUTTON, D. W., MURRAY, M. G., SLIGHTOM, J. L., MERLO, C. A., BARKER, R. F., KEMP, J. D. & HALL, T. C. (1983). Phaseolin gene from bean is expressed after transfer to sunflower via tumor-inducing plasmid vectors. *Science* **222**, 476–482.

NORTON, R. A. & TOWERS, G. H. N. (1983). Transmission of nopaline crown gall tumour markers through meiosis in regenerated whole plants of *Bidens alba. Can. J. Bot.* **62**, 408–413.

OOMS, G., BAINS, A., BURRELL, M., KARP, A., TWELL, D. & WILCOX, E. (1985*a*). Genetic manipulation in cultivars of oilseed rape (*Brassica napus*) using *Agrobacterium. Theor. appl. Genet.* **71**, 325–329.

OÓMS, G., BAKKER, A., MOLENDIJK, L., WULLEMS, G. J., GORDON, M. P., NESTER, E. W. & SCHILPEROORT, R. A. (1982). T-DNA organization in homogeneous and heterogeneous octopine-type crown gall tissues of *Nicotiana tabacum. Cell* **30**, 589–597.

OOMS, G., HOOYKAAS, P. J. J., MOOLENAAR, G. & SCHILPEROORT, R. A. (1981). Crown gall plant tumors of abnormal morphology, induced by *Agrobacterium tumefaciens* carrying mutated octopine Ti-plasmid; analysis of T-DNA functions. *Gene* **14**, 33–50.

OOMS, G., KARP, A., BURRELL, H. M., TWELL, D. & ROBERTS, J. (1985*b*). Genetic modification of potato development using Ri T-DNA. *Theor. appl. Genet.* **70**, 440–446.

OOMS, G., KARP, A. & ROBERTS, J. (1983). From tumour to tuber; tumour cell characteristics and chromosome numbers of crown gall-derived tetraploid potato plants (*Solanum tuberosum* cv 'Maris Bard'). *Theor. appl. Genet.* **66**, 169–172.

OOMS, G., KLAPWIJK, P. M., POULIS, J. A. & SCHILPEROORT, R. A. (1980). Characterization of Tn904 insertions in octopine Ti plasmid mutants of *Agrobacterium tumefaciens. J. Bact.* **144**, 82–91.

OOMS, G., WHITE, R. F., ANTONIW, J. F. & GIBSON, R. W. (1984). *Agrobacterium rhizogenes*-transformed and untransformed tobacco plants have similar pathogenesis related protein concentrations and similar susceptibility to virus infection. *Pl. sci. Lett.* **35**, 169–173.

OTTEN, L. A. B. M. (1982). Lysopine dihydrogenase activity as an early maker in crown gall transformation. *Pl. sci. Lett.* **25**, 15–27.

OTTEN, L. A. B. M., DE GREVE, H., HERNALSTEENS, J-P., VAN MONTAGU, M., SCHIEDER, O., STRAUB, J. & SCHELL, J. S. (1981). Mendelian transmission of genes introduced into plants by the Ti plasmids of *Agrobacterium tumefaciens*. *Mol. gen. Genet.* **183**, 209–213.

OTTEN, L., PIOTROWIAK, G., HOOYKAAS, P., DUBOIS, M., SZEGEDI, E. & SCHELL, J. (1985). Identification of an *Agrobacterium tumefaciens* pTiB653 vir region fragment that enhances the virulence of pTiC58. *Mol. gen. Genet.* **199**, 189–193.

OWENS, L. D. & CRESS, D. E. (1985). Genotypic variability of soybean response to *Agrobacterium* strains harboring the Ti or Ri plasmids. *Pl. Physiol.* **77**, 87–94.

PASZKOWSKI, J., SHILLITO, R. D., SAUL, M. W., MANDÁK, V., HOHN, T., HOHN, B. & POTRYKUS, I. (1984). Direct gene transfer to plants. *EMBO J.* **3**, 2717–2722.

PETIT, A., DAVID, C., DAHL, G. A., ELLIS, J. G., GUYON, P. CASSE-DELBART, F. & TEMPÉ, J. (1983). Further extension of the opine concept: plasmids in *Agrobacterium rhizogenes* co-operate for opine degradation. *Mol. gen. Genet.* **190**, 204–214.

POTRYKUS, I., PASZKOWSKI, J., SAUL, M. W., PETRUSKA, J. & SHILLITO, R. D. (1985*a*). Molecular and general genetics of a hybrid foreign gene introduced into tobacco by direct gene transfer. *Mol. gen. Genet.* **199**, 169–177.

POTRYKUS, I., SAUL, M. W., PETRUSKA, J., PASZKOWSKI, J. & SHILLITO, R. D. (1985*b*). Direct gene transfer to cells of a gramineous monocot. *Mol. gen. Genet.* **199**, 183–188.

REAM, L. W., GORDON, M. P. & NESTER, E. W. (1983). Multiple mutations in the T region of the *Agrobacterium tumefaciens* tumor-inducing plasmid. *Proc. natn. Acad. Sci. U.S.A.* **80**, 1660–1664.

RYDER, M. H., TATE, M. E. & KERR, A. (1985). Virulence properties of strains of *Agrobacterium* on the apical and based surfaces of carrot root discs. *Pl. Physiol.* **77**, 215–221.

SALOMON, F., DEBLAERE, R., LEEMANS, J., HERNALSTEEMS, J-P., VAN MONTAGU, M. & SCHELL, J. (1984). Genetic identification of functions of TR-DNA transcripts in octopine crown galls. *EMBO J.* **3**, 141–146.

SHAW, C. H. (1984). Ti plasmid-derived plant gene vectors. In *Oxford Surveys of Plant Molecular and Cell Biology*, vol. 1 (ed. B. J. Miflin), pp. 211–216. Oxford: Clarendon Press.

SHAW, C. H., CARTER, G. H., WATSON, M. D. & SHAW, C. H. (1984). A functional map of the nopaline synthase promoter. *Nucl. acid. Res.* **12**, 7831–7846.

SLIGHTOM, J. L., JOUANIN, L., LEACH, F., DRONG, R. & TEPFER, D. (1985). Isolation and identification of TL-DNA/plant junctions in *Convolvulus arvensis* transformed by *Agrobacterium rhizogenes* strain A4. *EMBO J.* **4**, 3069–3077.

SPANO, L. & COSTANTINO, P. (1982). Regeneration of plants from callus cultures of roots induced by *Agrobacterium rhizogenes* on tobacco. *Z. Pflanzenphysiol.* **106**, 87–92.

SPANO, L., WULLEMS, G. J., SCHILPEROORT, R. A. & COSTANTINO, P. (1981). Hairy root: *in vitro* growth properties of tissues induced by *Agrobacterium rhizogenes* on tobacco. *Pl. sci. Lett.* **23**, 299–305.

SPIESS, L. D., LIPPINCOTT, B. B. & LIPPINCOTT, J. A. (1984). Rôle of the moss cell wall in gametophore formation induced by *Agrobacterium tumefaciens*. *Bot. Gaz.* **145**, 302–307.

TEPFER, D. (1983). The potential uses of *Agrobacterium rhizogenes* in the genetic engineering of higher plants: Nature got there first. In *Genetic Engineering in Eukaryotes*, (NATO AS1 Series. Series A. Life Sciences) vol. 61 (ed. P. F. Lurquin & A. Kleinhofs), pp. 153–164. New York: Plenum.

TEPFER, D. (1984). Transformation of several species of higher plants by *Agrobacterium rhizogenes*: sexual transmission of the transformed genotype and phenotype. *Cell* **37**, 959–967.

THOMASHOW, M. F., NUTTER, R., MONTOYA, A. L., GORDON, M. P. & NESTER, E. W. (1980). Integration and organization of Ti plasmid sequences in crown gall tumors. *Cell* **19**, 729–739.

THOMASHOW, L. S., REEVES, S. & THOMASHOW, M. F. (1984). Crown gall oncogenesis: evidence that a T-DNA gene from the *Agrobacterium* Ti plasmid pTiA6 encodes an enzyme that catalyses the synthesis of indoleacetic acid. *Proc. natn. Acad. Sci. U.S.A.* **81**, 5071–5075.

TURGEON, R. (1982). Teratomas and secondary tumors. In *Molecular Biology of Plant Tumors* (ed. G. Kahl & J. Schell), pp. 391–414. New York: Academic Press.

URSIC, D., SLIGHTOM, J. L. & KEMP, J. D. (1983). *Agrobacterium tumefaciens* T-DNA integrates into multiple sites of the sunflower crown gall genome. *Mol. gen. Genet.* **190**, 494–503.

VAN SLOGTEREN, G. M. S., HOOYKAAS, P. J. J. & SCHILPEROORT, R. A. (1984*a*). Tumor formation on plants by mixtures of attenuated *Agrobacterium tumefaciens* T-DNA mutants. *Pl. molec. Biol.* **3**, 337–344.

VAN SLOGTEREN, G. M. S., HOOYKAAS, P. J. J. & SCHILPEROORT, R. A. (1984*b*). Silent T-DNA genes in plant lines transformed by *Agrobacterium tumefaciens* are activated by grafting and 5-azacytidine treatment. *Pl. molec. Biol.* **3**, 333–336.

WHITE, P. R. & BRAUN, A. C. (1942). A cancerous neoplasm of plants. Autonomous bacteria-free crown gall tissue. *Cancer Res.* **2**, 597–617.

WHITE, F. F. & NESTER, E. W. (1980). Hairy root: plasmid encodes virulence traits in *Agrobacterium rhizogenes. J. Bact.* **141**, 1134–1141.

WILLMITZER, L., DEHAESE, P., SCHREIER, P. H., SCHMALENBACH, W., VAN MONTAGU, M. & SCHELL, J. (1983). Size, location and polarity of T-DNA-encoded transcripts in nopaline crown gall tumors; common transcripts in octopine and nopaline tumors. *Cell* **32**, 1045–1056.

WILLMITZER, L., SANCHEZ-SERRANO, J., BUSCHFELD, E. & SCHELL, J. (1982*a*). DNA from *Agrobacterium rhizogenes* is transferred to and expressed in axenic hairy root plant tissues. *Molec. gen. Genet.* **186**, 16–22.

WILLMITZER, L., SIMONS, G. & SCHELL, J. (1982*b*). The TL-DNA in octopine crown gall tumours codes for seven well defined polyadenylated transcripts. *EMBO J.* **2**, 139–146.

WOOD, H. N. & BRAUN, A. C. (1965). Studies on the net uptake of solutes by normal and crown gall tumor cells. *Proc. natn. Acad. Sci. U.S.A.* **54**, 1532–1538.

WÖSTEMEYER, A., OTTEN, L. A. B. M. AND SCHELL, J. S. (1984). Sexual transmission of T-DNA in abnormal tobacco regenerants transformed by octopine and nopaline strains of *Agrobacterium tumefaciens. Molec. gen. Genet.* **194**, 500–507.

WULLEMS, G. J., MOLDENDIJK, L., OOMS, G. & SCHILPEROORT, R. A. (1981*a*). Differential expression of crown gall tumor markers in transformants obtained after *in vitro Agrobacterium tumefaciens*-induced transformation of cell wall regenerating protoplasts derived from *Nicotiana tabacum. Proc. natn. Acad. Sci. U.S.A.* **78**, 4344–4348.

WULLEMS, G. J., MOLENDIJK, L., OOMS, G. & SCHILPEROORT, R. A. (1981*b*). Retention of tumor markers in F1 progeny plants from *in vitro* induced octopine and nopaline tumor tissue. *Cell* **24**, 719–727.

YANG, F., MONTOYA, A. L., MERLO, D. J., DRUMMOND, M. H., CHILTON, M-D., NESTER, E. W. & GORDON, M. P. (1980). Foreign DNA sequences in crown gall teratomas and their fate during the loss of the tumorous traits. *Molec. gen. Genet.* **177**, 707–714.

YANG, F. & SIMPSON, R. B. (1981). Revertant seedlings from crown gall tumors retain a portion of bacterial Ti plasmid DNA sequences. *Proc. natn. Acad. Sci. U.S.A.* **78**, 4151–4155.

ZAMBRYSKI, P., JOOS, H., GENETELLO, C., LEEMANS, J., VAN MONTAGU, M. & SCHELL, J. (1983). Ti plasmid vector for the introduction of DNA into plant cells without alteration of their normal regeneration capacity. *EMBO J.* **2**, 2143–2150.

Note added in proof: Detailed restriction maps of Ri, TL and TR-DNA have now been published. See WHITE, F. F., TAYLOR, B. H., HUFFMAN, G. A., GORDON, M. P. & NESTER, E. W. (1985). Molecular and genetic analysis of the transferred DNA regions of the root-inducing plasmid of *Agrobacterium rhizogenes. J. Bact.* **164**, 33–44.

STABILITY AND PLASTICITY DURING CHLOROPLAST DEVELOPMENT

RACHEL M. LEECH

Department of Biology, University of York, Heslington, York YO1 5DD UK

Summary

Chloroplast development occurs during cellular development. In non-limiting conditions chloroplast development is a highly conserved process, it is also complex and involves the continuous interaction of both chloroplast and nuclear genomes.

In the first part of the paper the sequential and structural changes characteristic of chloroplast division and development in angiosperms are described. The synthesis of the major chloroplast components including chlorophylls a and b, lipids, nucleic acids and the major soluble and membrane proteins are then described. Chloroplast development in biochemical terms is a quantitative accretion of additional functional units. In development from proplastid to fully mature chloroplast the molecular changes are almost exclusively quantitative and the youngest plastids that can be analysed are already photochemically fully competent.

In the second part of the paper the dominant role of the nuclear genome in chloroplast development is discussed. Recent work in the author's laboratory on the synthesis and accumulation of ribulose bisphosphate carboxylase–oxygenase in the developing chloroplasts of young wheat leaves is cited to illustrate the stable genomic and genotypic differences that can be recognized. In comparisons of wheat species of differing ploidy, in hexaploid cultivars and in artificially processed genetic lines, several genomic and genotypic effects have been detected.

The possibilities for future investigation are discussed.

Introduction

Leaf development and chloroplast development are processes remarkable for their consistency and reproducibility. The sequence of changes responsible for the expansion of a leaf primordium into a mature leaf is repeated many times during the growth of a plant and normally the development of the leaf is so tightly controlled that 'the product' is immediately recognizable as belonging to the parental plant. This consistency in the pattern of leaf development is parallelled by analogous tightly controlled patterns of change during chloroplast development: and there is little doubt that the higher plant chloroplast is a remarkably conserved organelle.

Comparative ultrastructural studies in several widely differing species of higher plant have revealed a striking similarity in the basic construction of their photosynthesizing chloroplasts (Leech, 1984). Higher plant chloroplasts all have several distinctive features in common. They are between 5 μm and 10 μm in diameter, resemble oblate or prolate ellipsoids in form and are bounded by a double envelope of two membranes. The outer envelope membrane is freely permeable and separates the organelle from the cytosol but the inner envelope membrane is selectively permeable and specific translocases within the membrane control the influx and efflux of metabolites. The matrix or stroma of the chloroplast contains up to a thousand enzymes and the biochemical elements of the chloroplast genetic system, including 70S ribosomes and chloroplast (cp) DNA. A predominant soluble protein of the stroma in C3-type chloroplasts is ribulose bisphosphate carboxylase–oxygenase (RuBPCase or Fraction I protein). This protein accounts for 60% of leaf protein in wheat and at maturity each chloroplast contains between 10 and 15 pg of the enzyme. Chloroplasts may also contain a variety of temporary inclusions in their stroma, for example starch, lipidic plastoglobuli and crystals of salts, particularly oxalate. Centrally within the stromal compartment of every chloroplast lies the fretwork of pigmented membranes containing chlorophyll and is responsible for the photon harvesting and energy transduction phases of photosynthesis. The photosynthetic membranes are in the form of flattened vesicles which may be appressed and stacked to form grana in some regions of the chloroplast. In one type of chloroplast there are few or no appressed regions and these are generally referred to as 'agranal' or 'lamellate' chloroplasts. A more common arrangement of the photosynthetic membranes is one in which regions of appressed vesicles are interconnected by regions where there is no appression: these are 'granal' chloroplasts. No exceptions to the granal or lamellate chloroplast forms have yet been discovered in angiosperms. Although we are far from understanding the significance of the special characteristics and form of the higher plant chloroplast, it might be suggested that this high degree of conservation in such a complex organelle could be explained if the chloroplast is near-perfectly engineered for its major photosynthetic role in land plants.

One definition of plasticity is 'the capacity to respond to change resulting in *permanent* new form or function'. 'Stability', the converse of 'plasticity', is therefore the capacity to resist change. On this definition the development of photosynthetically competent leaf chloroplasts is a particularly stable process.

In this chapter the remarkable stability and some of the underlying mechanisms responsible for the control of the development of leaf chloroplasts will be discussed. The literature is particularly rich in reports describing the visually dramatic episodic and non-permanent changes which may be induced in chloroplast structure by violent changes in environment during development. The magnitude and variety of the changes which developing chloroplasts are able to tolerate is certainly impressive but the majority of these effects should be properly regarded merely as manifestations of temporary responses to severe stress. For example the distinct differences between 'sun' and 'shade' leaves and changes in membrane lipid composition associated with temperature variation are acclimations of the fully developed leaf and have not so far been linked with alterations in the pattern of chloroplast development. The underlying patterns of cellular and chloroplast development in leaves are extremely reproducible if the plants are allowed to develop normally in non-limiting environments, as might be anticipated in a situation which is under tight genetic control. The chemical composition of mature chloroplasts has been analysed in considerable detail and it is quite possible to describe the biochemistry of a 'typical higher plant chloroplast' by referring, for example, to the ratio of the number of individual carrier molecules or the ratio of molecules of different lipid molecular species in the photosynthetic membranes. Such consistencies in the quantitative accumulation of components during chloroplast development must certainly reflect a close interrelation in the rates of synthesis of its individual components and also a very tight integration of the separate syntheses over the timescale of chloroplast biogenesis.

Few studies have been dedicated to providing a structural and functional description of the usual development of chloroplasts. Present evidence suggests that consistency in chloroplast development is genotypically controlled and related genotypes of the same species show distinct variants which are repeated recognizably in each leaf of that particular genotype. However, such 'small characteristic' and reproducible differences in development prove elusive to the investigator unless the plants used for comparative purposes are relatively homogeneous genetically and are grown in controlled non-limiting environment conditions. The consistencies and variations in chloroplast development are best revealed if the process is studied in depth in a single species or genus. In this way changes in developmental pattern can be effectively distinguished from changes in the rates of individual phases of the process.

In this chapter I will describe the pattern of development of chloroplasts in the first leaves of young wheat plants grown under a normal diurnal light regime in a precisely controlled environment. Most of the work was carried out in my laboratory in the Department of Biology, University of York, England, in association with my colleagues over a period of years. Several postdoctoral and predoctoral students and visiting colleagues have made their own special contributions to the programme and their ideas and contributions are contained, and as far as possible identified, in the account which follows. Complementary studies on the development of photochemical capacity in similar leaves grown from the same genetical stocks have been pioneered by Dr Neil Baker in the Department of Biology, University of Essex. His results are also included in the text.

The growth of uniform wheat plants suitable for developmental studies

Wheat was chosen as our experimental plant because of its importance as a world crop, because its leaves develop uniformly from a basal intercalary meristem and because actively photosynthesizing chloroplasts with high rates of photoreduction can be isolated easily from young wheat leaves. In addition the genetics of the wheat genus (*Triticum*) is particularly well documented and large numbers of cultivated species and cultivars of known genetic origin are available for detailed analysis. Wheat is also one of the few plant species chosen by plant molecular biologists for intensive analysis with a view to its future genetic manipulation. In addition, the special genetic lines which have been artificially produced cytogenetically for use in wheat breeding programmes provide an especially valuable source of experimental material since the effects of small changes in genetic background can be detected by comparative biochemical examinations. This rich array of plant material includes thousands of genetically distinct modern hexaploid cultivars, many tetraploids and diploid species of both wild and cultivated lineage, artificially produced autotetraploids and plants whose chromosome complements have been altered by additions, deletions and, or, substitutions. Comparisons of aspects of chloroplast development in wheat plants of different nuclear and cytoplasmic genetic backgrounds thus afford an opportunity to recognize and characterize different aspects of chloroplast development and to relate them to nuclear and plastid genomic differences.

Plant growth conditions

A supply of normal plants which show consistency in the details of their development is a prerequisite for the competent analysis of the invariable characteristics of chloroplast development. In our early experiments we soon discovered that because the growth of the young wheat plants we were using was so rapid, the details of time of sowing and the time of growth and harvesting of plants relative to the timing of the light period were particularly critical. For example, plants developing from grains sown 2 h earlier or 2 h later than in the standard procedure could be recognized immediately as differing morphologically and biochemically from the standards. Since the growing conditions are particularly critical in the assessment and recognition of genomic and genotypic influences on leaf and chloroplast development a full description of the planting and growing regime is included below.

We are fortunate in York in having the services of two excellent plant growth technologists, Colin Abbott and Keith Partridge, and freely acknowledge that many of our discoveries would not have been possible without their skill in culturing the plants. They are able to provide batches of plants grown in constant environment cabinets which are uniformly consistent in their development. The procedure used is as follows. Grains are soaked in running tap water at 20° from 16.00 until 10.00 and planted at a depth of 1 cm in Levington Universal compost (Fisons UK). The seedlings are grown at 70% relative humidity using a photoperiod of 16 h at 20° with a 5° night depression. The light intensity at the level of the seedlings measured with a solarimeter (Kipps and Zonen) is 60 W m^{-2}. The plants are harvested at 10.00, i.e. 2 h after the onset of the light period after 6, 7, 8 and 9 days growth respectively. Before analysis the leaves are cut at their bases, washed and their coleoptiles gently removed. Small variations in time of planting (1–2 h), humidity ($\pm$10%) or light intensity ($\pm$5%) can be detected because the *rate* of leaf development is affected but not the *pattern* of leaf development. Under uniform environmental conditions the rate of growth of comparable individual leaves on different wheat plants shows very little variation. The means and standard error of the growth rates of 20 seedlings of *Triticum aestivum* cv. Maris Dove are shown in Fig. 1 and illustrate the general finding for more than 20 different genotypes we examined.

Chloroplast development in wheat leaves

The growth characteristics of strap-shaped grass leaves such as wheat which provide an ideal system for the study of cell development, also facilitate a study of the development of their chloroplasts. The growth of these leaves has been described in detail elsewhere (Boffey, Sellden & Leech, 1980; Leech, 1984). The young leaf consists of a linear gradient of

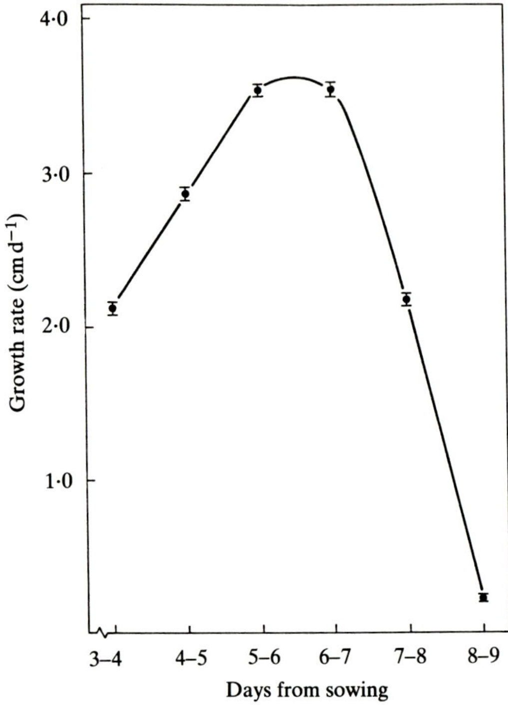

Fig. 1. The growth rates of the first leaves of 20 seedlings of *Triticum aestivum* cv. Maris Dove. The height of the lamina was measured each day at 10 a.m. The graph shows the means and standard errors. The seedlings were grown in the standardized environmental conditions described in the text (Dean, 1982).

sequentially older cells, with the oldest cells near the tip of the leaf and the youngest nearest its base. Within the developing mesophyll cells the plastids are developing, so successively older cells also possess successively more highly differentiated chloroplasts. Several species of Gramineae (including wheat) have now been examined and the sequential series of changes during chloroplast development appear to be very similar in all cases. The youngest, smallest proplastids, less than 1 μm in diameter in the meristematic cells, develop to mature chloroplasts about 10 μm in diameter. In the young wheat leaf this process of chloroplast development is completed in 6 h and as the chloroplast increases five-to tenfold in diameter, extensive internal membrane proliferation and very rapid pigment, lipid, nucleic acid and protein synthesis is also occurring (Dean & Leech, 1982*c*). The youngest organelle recognizable as a plastid is seen in meristematic cells of the basal intercalary meristem and is a generally spherical but also pleomorphic organelle bounded by a double envelope of two membranes, the inner of which often appears more electron opaque and broader than the outer. The internal non-envelope membranes of the proplastid contain small amounts of chlorophyll and serial sectioning of the membranes in proplastids of rye grass (*Lolium perenne*) has shown they are perforated plates folded and occasionally fused so as to appear vesiculate in cross section (Brangeon & Mustardy, 1979). In the meristematic mesophyll cells proplastids continue to divide and the postmitotic cell in hexaploid wheat contains about 50 plastids. All the major structural changes in developing chloroplasts are observed in plastids of postmitotic cells. As the chloroplast continues to increase in size there is a brief obligatory phase during which starch accumulates followed by a short amoeboid stage. Plastids isolated at the amoeboid stage in their differentiation show frequent rapid changes in shape and this characteristic behaviour can be observed clearly under Nomarski interference optics. At the end of the amoeboid phase proliferation of the internal membranes of the young chloroplast continues by the folding back and appression of some of these membranes to produce the characteristic regions of appressed membranes in 'granal' stacks interspersed with membrane-bound non-appressed 'agranal' regions. In the later

Table 1. *Cellular and chloroplast components in a 7-day-old wheat leaf of* Triticum aestivum *cv. Maris Dove.*

	Distance from leaf base (cm)			
	2	4	6	8
Chloroplasts (mesophyll cell^{-1})	69	90	109	133
Cytoplasmic rRNA (pg cell^{-1}) 25S	51	62	64	55
18S	28	36	36	31
Chloroplast rRNA (pg mesophyll cell^{-1}) 23S	24	54	69	79
16S	18	36	45	48
RuPBCase (pg mesophyll cell^{-1})	146	324	821	1691
RuBPCase (pg plastid^{-1})	2·1	3·6	7.5	12·7
Chlorophyll (pg plastid^{-1})	0·1	0·4	0·7	0·9

	Age of cell (days from final mitosis)				
	1	1·5	2·0	2·5	3·0
Protein (pg cell^{-1})	340	520	950	1500	2050
RNA (pg cell^{-1})	82	120	177	180	165
DNA (pg cell^{-1})	50	43	55	60	60

Data from Leech, Dean, Boffey and Sellden (unpublished).

stages of its development the plastid increases greatly in volume. In all the monocotyledons so far examined (Leech, 1984; Whatley, 1977) this sequence of phases appears to be similar and Whatley has also described a similar sequence in the dicotyledon *Phaseolus vulgaris* (Whatley, 1979).

In wheat, chloroplast development is typically completed in six hours and during the development from the proplastid to the mature chloroplast very large changes occur, particularly in the quantitative characteristics of the plastid (Fig. 2). The major membrane lipids increase three- to fourfold (Leese & Leech, 1976), proteins and chloroplast ribosomal RNA increase fivefold (Dean & Leech, 1982*c*), and chlorophyll about tenfold (Boffey *et al.* 1980). The major soluble chloroplast protein RuBPCase increases six-fold per plastid (Table 1). The maximum period of accumulation of plastid protein and rRNA in the population of developing leaf chloroplasts is in the period 36 to 48 h after cell division ceases. Maximal cellular rates of accumulation of RuBPCase of 80 pg h^{-1}, chlorophyll accumulation at the

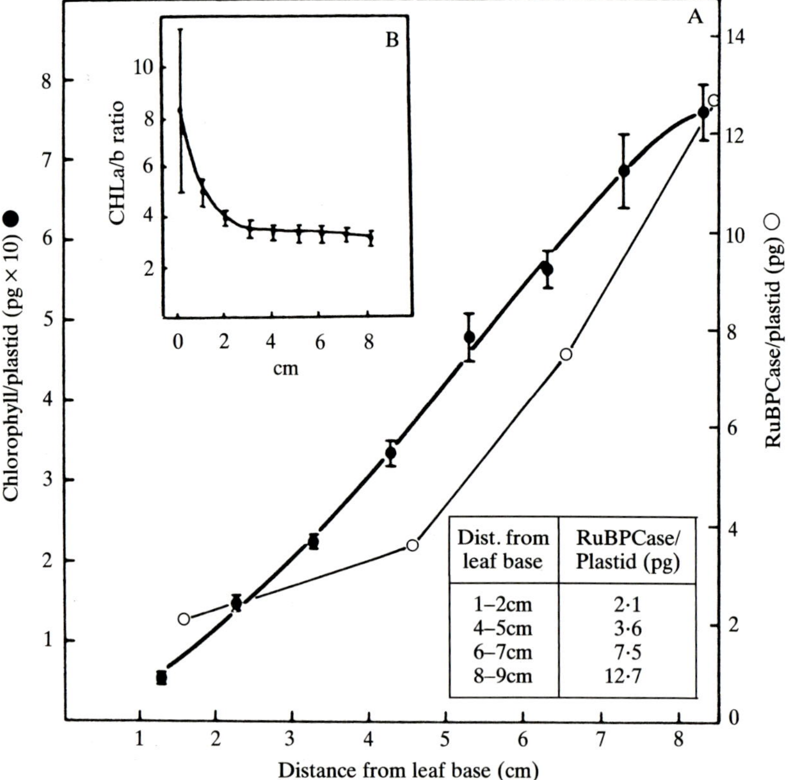

Fig. 2. The changing amount of molecular components in the chloroplasts of developing wheat leaves (*Triticum aestivum* cv. Maris Dove).

rate of 9 pg h^{-1} and 70S ribosomes at the rate of $19 \times 10^5 h^{-1}$ are observed in this period of 12 h.

Chloroplast division during chloroplast differentiation

The cellular rates of accumulation of chloroplast components reflect not merely the activity of individual differentiating plastids but also the increases related to the division of the young chloroplasts. This division occurs in all leaf mesophyll cells after cell division and nuclear DNA synthesis have ceased (Boffey & Leech, 1982; Ellis, Jellings & Leech, 1983). The division takes place along the shorter axis of the chloroplast and appears to be more or less synchronous in the plastids of the same cell, and in wheat the process is generally completed in less than an hour (Leech, Thomson & Platt-Aloia, 1981). The grana and the cpDNA appear to be partitioned more or less equally into the daughter plastids (Sellden & Leech, 1981; Dyer *et al.* 1983). The nature of the mechanisms which initiate and terminate chloroplast division are unknown (for a review see Possingham, 1980) but some form of physical initiation induced by changes in the chloroplast itself is consistent with the observations of the changes in the ultrastructural appearance of dividing young chloroplasts. It is possible that termination of the continuing cycles of division is actually the regulatory mode. Certainly the mean chloroplast number per cell appears to be strictly species specific and the control of chloroplast number per cell is predominantly nucleotypic (the chloroplast complement of a hexaploid wheat mesophyll cell is shown in Fig. 3). Tetraploid species of wheat, for example, have c. 80 % more plastids than diploids and hexaploid species have 80 % more plastids than tetraploids (Dean & Leech, 1982*d*; Pyke & Leech, 1985*b*). Isogenic lines of diploid, tetraploid, hexaploid and octoploid Alfalfa show a similar increasing cellular chloroplast number with increasing ploidy (Meyers *et al.* 1982). A dramatic demonstration of the nucleotypic control of chloroplast number can be found by the observation of wheat hybrids in which an alien nucleus has been introduced into a cytoplasm of differing ploidy. In three different genetic crosses of this type the chloroplast number of the resultant hybrid reflects the ploidy level of the alien nucleus introduced into the cell and not the typical chloroplast number of the recipient female line (Leech, unpublished).

Chloroplast DNA synthesis is probably complete before the young chloroplast begins to divide and chloroplast DNA synthesis itself occurs quite independently of nuclear DNA synthesis (Scott & Possingham, 1980; Boffey & Leech, 1982). The grana in young dividing chloroplasts have stacks with several appressed membranes yet prior to chloroplast division

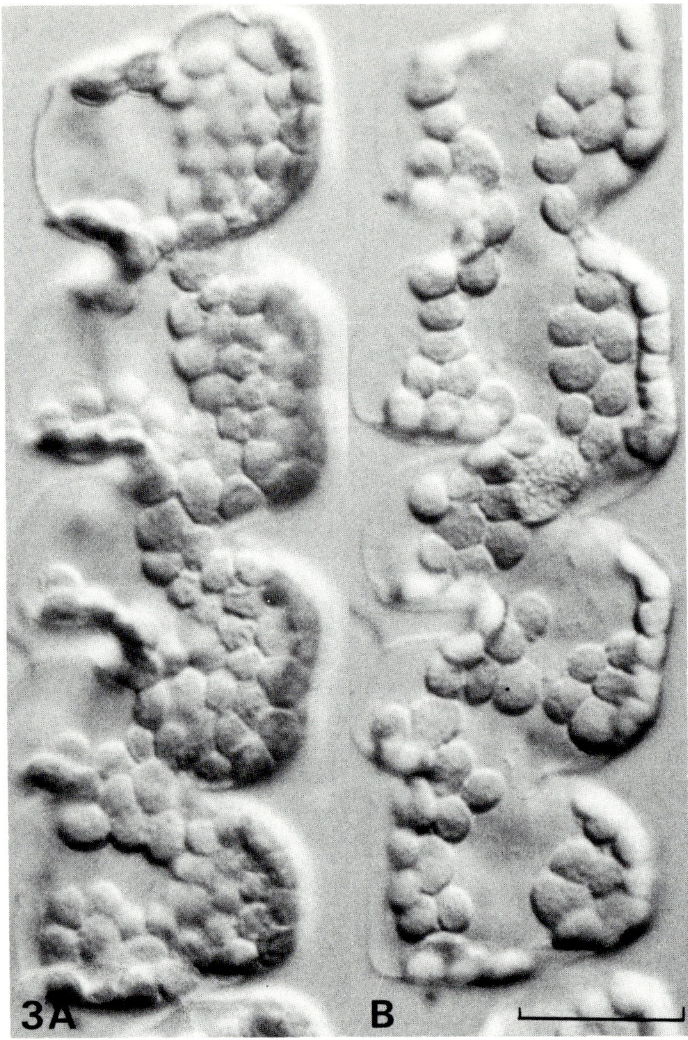

Fig. 3. The chloroplasts of a mesophyll leaf cell of *Triticum aestivum* cv. Maris Dove. A and B are two views of the same cell viewed by Nomarski Interference optics. (Photos by A. J. Jellings.) The cell samples were prepared following the procedure of Boffey, Ellis, Sellden & Leech (1979). Scale bar, 30 μm.

the number of copies of plastome DNA can rise to over a thousand per plastid but is dramatically lowered after chloroplast division ceases (to 200 or 300). In spinach leaves c. 200 copies of cpDNA are present per plastid, i.e. 5000 plastome copies per cell. In hexaploid wheat cells there are over 40 000 plastome copies therefore per cell, i.e. c. 300 copies per mature chloroplast. The significance of this massive synthesis of plastid DNA is not known but clearly the amount of chloroplast DNA is unlikely to be a major limiting factor in the continuing development of the chloroplasts.

Cells with larger nuclear genomes are also usually larger in volume, and at least in plants grown in non-limiting environmental conditions, the cessation of cell volume increase seems to exert a controlling influence on the cessation of chloroplast division and to act as a major control of the final chloroplast number. In an individual leaf larger cells have more chloroplasts than do smaller cells (Ellis & Leech, 1985; Pyke & Leech, 1985*b*). When leaves of several species of different ploidy are compared, then it is seen that although the measured cell volumes differ considerably between the species the differences in chloroplast number directly reflect the differences in size of the individual mesophyll cells. Fig. 4 shows a plot of mesophyll cell plan area against number of chloroplasts per cell for diploid, tetraploid and hexaploid genotypes of the *Triticum* genus. Each point represents the characteristic chloroplast number of a single cell. There is clearly a consistent relationship between cell size and chloroplast number across a wide range of cell size and this suggests that in the genus

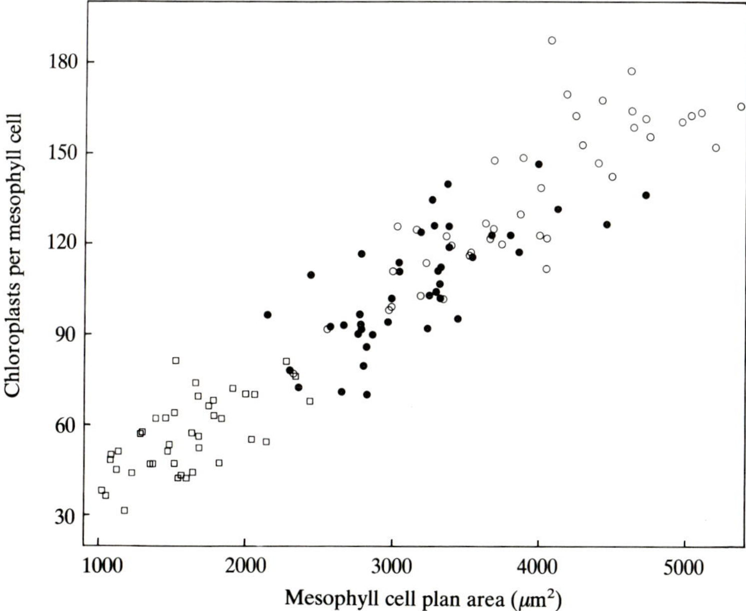

Fig. 4. The chloroplast number and mesophyll cell plan area in mature wheat mesophyll cells in the first leaves of 9-day-old wheat seedlings. (K. Pyke, unpublished data.) The chloroplast number was determined in leaves of *Triticum* species of different ploidies. Mesophyll cell plan area measured according to Pyke & Leech (1985*b*). □ Diploid species; *T. monococcum*, *T. tauschii*. ● Tetraploid species; *T. timopheevii*, *T. durum*. ○ Hexaploid species; *T. aestivum*, cvs. Hobbit and Maris Ranger $r^2 = 0{\cdot}88$, $P < 0{\cdot}001$.

Triticum specifically and perhaps more generally this relationship may be fundamental to the competent functioning of the cell.

In addition to the large incremental increase in chloroplast number associated with increase in nuclear genome size, cell size is also a dominant factor in determining absolute chloroplast number in the individual cells of each leaf. The smaller mesophyll cells of a leaf consistently have fewer chloroplasts than the larger ones and the 'fingerprint' mean chloroplast number which identifies a particular genotype also directly reflects the size distribution of the mesophyll cells.

The differentiation of individual chloroplasts in developing mesophyll cells is apparently always accompanied by two or three division cycles of these differentiating plastids. Indeed the replication of young green differentiating chloroplasts with extensively proliferated membranes and some membrane appression has been observed in young leaves of all the species so far examined. It appears to be an essential stage for the continuing normal development of the cell and the plastids. Certainly chloroplast division leads to large increases in chloroplast number per cell in the mature leaf and therefore concomitant increases in the potential photosynthetic capacity of the cell.

Closely integrated with mesophyll cellular development is the development of the chloroplasts. Chloroplast development cannot occur in the absence of cellular development since both chloroplast and nuclear genomes are involved in and essential for the synthesis of the majority of chloroplast proteins. Cellular and chloroplast development occur simultaneously and are continuously interdependent. The sequence of events leading to the maturation of young plastids into chloroplasts is tightly regulated and appears to be relatively immutable in non-limiting environments. The relative timescale of the individual phases of chloroplast development may be modified to some extent by environmental factors, particularly modulations in temperature, light intensity or quality or by nutrient status, but the underlying sequence itself is not altered but merely retimed. Even in conditions of extreme stress such as complete light deprivation (as in the standard conditions for etiolation), the plastid is not permanently altered and indeed when normal light conditions are restored apparently normal chloroplasts are eventually formed. In situations of severe nitrogen deprivation (for example in the poor soils on subAntarctic islands) chloroplasts of grass leaves develop normally but are smaller and have fewer grana (Jellings, Usher & Leech, 1983). Non-limiting nutrient levels restore the chloroplasts to their normal size.

Protein synthesis during chloroplast differentiation

The collaborative function of the nuclear and chloroplast genomes in the control of the synthesis of chloroplast components is epitomized in the synthesis of the chloroplast proteins. Fig. 5 illustrates some of the feed-back systems known to be involved in the process. Most, but not all, chloroplast polypeptides are encoded in the nuclear genome and synthesized, frequently as precursors, on free cytoplasmic 70S ribosomes. The proteins then move into the chloroplasts, generally losing transit peptides in the process. For example the small subunit of RuBPCase protein is formed as a higher molecular weight precursor (M_r = 20K) possessing a transit peptide (M_r = 5–6K, c. 60 amino acids) on cytoplasmic ribosomes and transported into the chloroplast. Inside the chloroplast, the assembly of the holoenzyme appears to involve an additional protein, the large subunit-binding protein. The suggestion has been made that the large subunit, synthesized in the chloroplast stroma, is solubilized by binding to the large subunit-binding protein and this complex then reacts with the small subunit to produce the holoenzyme. The holoenzyme consists of eight large and eight small subunits: the catalytic site is associated with the large subunits and the small subunits exert a controlling role, not yet precisely specified.

Concurrent with the synthesis of RuBPCase the two major membrane proteins of the chloroplast light-harvesting complex (LHCP) are also

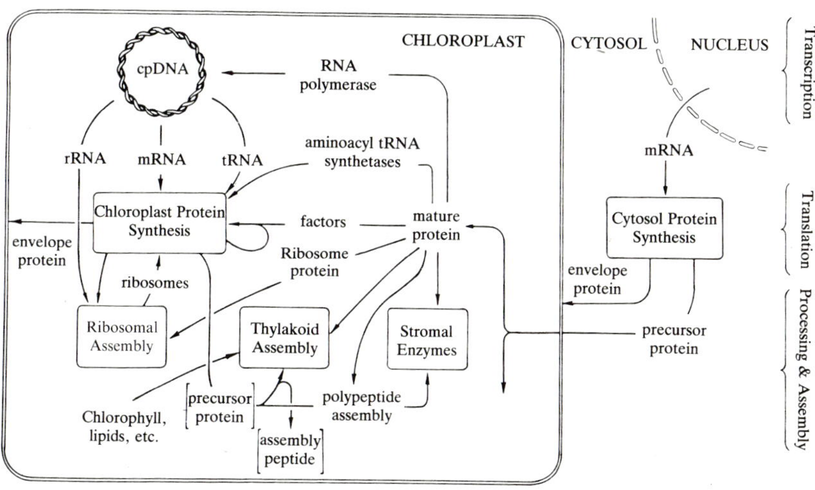

Fig. 5. Diagram showing the interaction of the chloroplast and nuclear genomes in the synthesis of chloroplast proteins (from Dyer, 1984).

rapidly synthesized. The two major polypeptides of the complex are chlorophyll a/b binding proteins (also recently named Cab proteins). These polypeptides are encoded in the nucleus and synthesized as precursors on cytoplasmic ribosomes. After movement into the chloroplast the proteins assemble with the chlorophylls synthesized inside the chloroplast and are incorporated as a complex into the developing photosynthetic membranes. The complex also contains several quantitatively minor polypeptides about whose synthesis and accumulation there has not as yet been any extensive investigation. Another membrane multisubunit protein complex which has been examined recently is the ATP synthase complex, some of whose subunits are encoded and synthesized in the cytosol and others encoded and synthesized within the chloroplast. Assembly occurs within the chloroplast, apparently within the membranes.

The development of the structurally and functionally competent chloroplast therefore clearly depends on continuing close co-ordination of the syntheses of the individual subunits of the multisubunit proteins and superco-ordination of the patterns of synthesis of all the individual proteins which are required in a photosynthetically competent chloroplast. A description of the qualitative and quantitative changes in leaf polypeptides which occur during chloroplast differentiation is a prerequisite to studies in which the integrative processes are studied. Until recently, no such description was available but young graminaceous leaves are also extremely good systems in which to study protein synthesis during cellular and chloroplast development. Qualitative and quantitative changes in leaf and chloroplast polypeptides can be followed after separation using polyacrylamide gel electrophoresis (PAGE). Polypeptides can be identified by their specific staining, by partial proteolytic digest and by immunoblotting techniques and quantified by densitometric measurements. Synthesis

---

Fig. 6. (A) Autoradiograph of an SDS-polyacrylamide gel showing *in vivo* labelled polypeptides isolated from 5 mm leaf sections of the first leaf of *Triticum aestivum*. The leaves were labelled for 3 h with [^{35}S]methionine and the gels loaded so that each track contained equal cts min^{-1}. The *in vivo* synthesized LSU, SSU, light-harvesting chlorophyll–protein complex (LHCP) and the α and β subunits of CF_1 are identified. The two nuclear polypeptides are marked with *.

(B) Autoradiograph of an SDS-polyacrylamide gel showing the translation products of a reticulocyte lysate cell-free protein-synthesizing extract stimulated with RNA isolated from 5 mm leaf sections taken at positions in the leaf as indicated on the figure.

One μg RNA was used to stimulate each translation. The products of endogenous protein synthesis are shown on the right-hand track in the water control. The *in vitro* synthesized LSU and the precursors pSSU and pLHCP are identified.

Molecular weight markers are, from top to bottom in 6A and 6B: bovine serum albumin (68,000), ovalbumin (43 000), chymotrypsin (25 000), trypsin (23 000), myoglobin (17 000) and haemoglobin (15 500) (Dean & Leech, unpublished).

can be quantified from changes in specific radioactivity following feeding of the leaves with radioactive amino acids: [^{35}S]methionine and [^{14}C]leucine are particularly useful for this purpose. After radioactive labelling intact chloroplasts can be isolated from the leaf tissue and their components analysed. In Fig. 6A is shown an autoradiographic electrophoretogram in each track of which the prelabelled polypeptides have been run out from

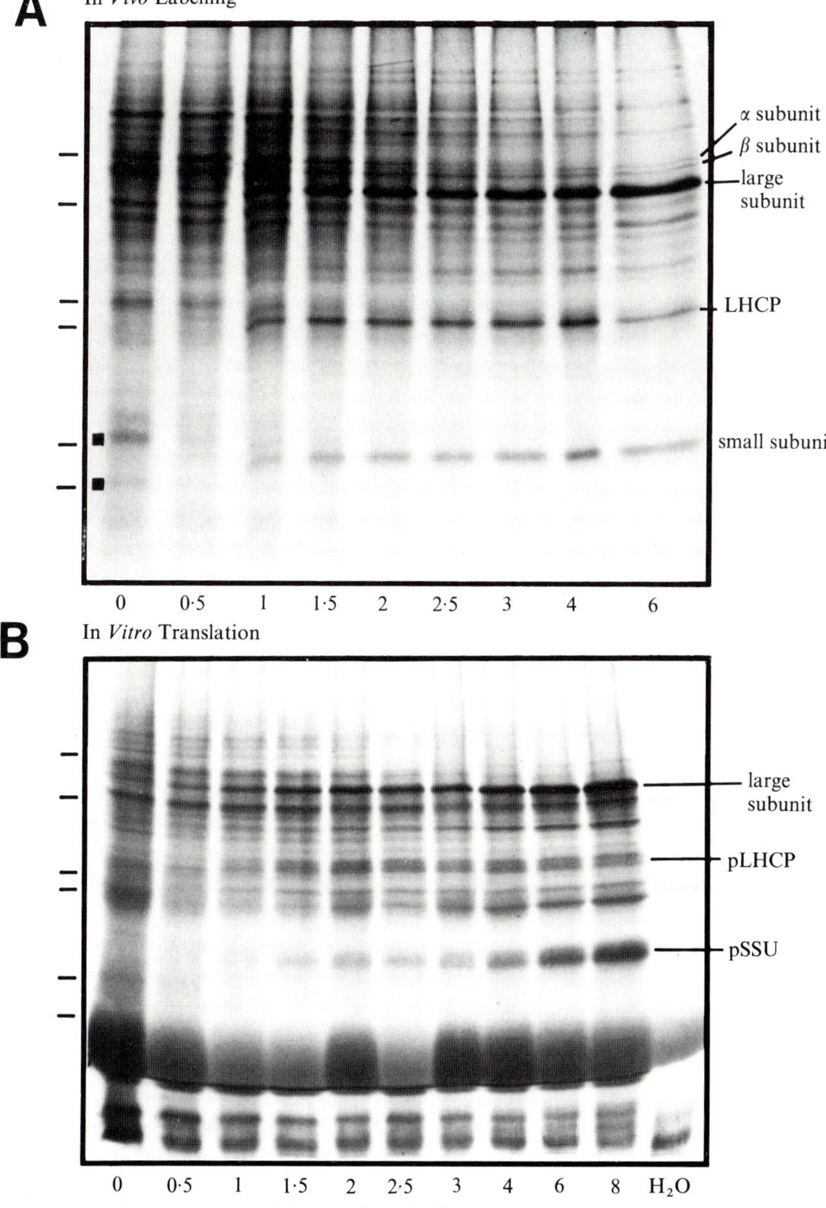

samples which contain identical counts isolated from leaf cells of different ages. The intensity of blackening of the autoradiogram gives a semiquantitative measurement of the *relative* rates of incorporation of [^{35}S]methionine into chloroplast polypeptides at different stages during chloroplast development. It can be seen immediately that the changes are predominantly quantitative. The pattern of polypeptides which have become labelled with [^{35}S]methionine also closely resemble the spectrum of the polypeptides which accumulate in these leaves during development.

The synthesis of RuBPCase in developing wheat leaves

A most striking observation from the polypeptide analysis is the continuous close co-ordination in the biosynthesis of the constituent subunits within an individual protein throughout chloroplast development and this is particularly clear when the parallel increases in labelling of the constituent subunits are studied in detail. The co-ordinated syntheses of the subunits of RuBPCase have been analysed by two different groups; in wheat (Dean & Leech, 1982*a*) and in barley (Nivison & Stocking, 1983). In the youngest cells which have been analysed in which the plastids are less than 1 μm in diameter, the small (SSU) nuclear-encoded and the large (LSU) chloroplast-encoded subunits of the holoenzyme are both present and the subsequent rates of synthesis of the two subunits are closely synchronized throughout chloroplast development. The co-ordinated synthesis is extremely rapid and in the first leaf of wheat the cellular content of the holoenzyme increases 20-fold over 36 h and rates of synthesis of 80 pg cell^{-1} h^{-1} have been recorded in actively growing tissue (Dean & Leech, 1982*d*). The closely co-ordinated synthesis of the large and small subunits of RuBPCase has been demonstrated in several other species using different methods of analysis. Nivison & Stocking (1983) have given a particularly clear example in barley using [^{14}C]leucine where parallel rapid rates of synthesis during development are followed by parallel slower rates of synthesis of the two subunits during maturation and senescence of the leaf cells (Fig. 7). The tightly linked synthesis is difficult to dislocate in normally developing leaves. This is particularly clearly exemplified in the study of a genetic line of wheat in which a nucleus has been introduced into an alien plastid and cytoplasmic background (Dean & Leech, 1982*b*). The chosen wheat line had the nuclear genetic component from the hexaploid wheat *Triticum aestivum* cv. Chinese Spring and the cytoplasm from a diploid wheat *Aegilops umbellulata* (there is no transfer of plastids or cytoplasms from the male gamete during fertilization in wheat and the genetic line had been back crossed through nine generations to ensure a pure nuclear background). The first leaves of the artificial genetic line are much paler green than in the euploid, suggesting some dislocation in

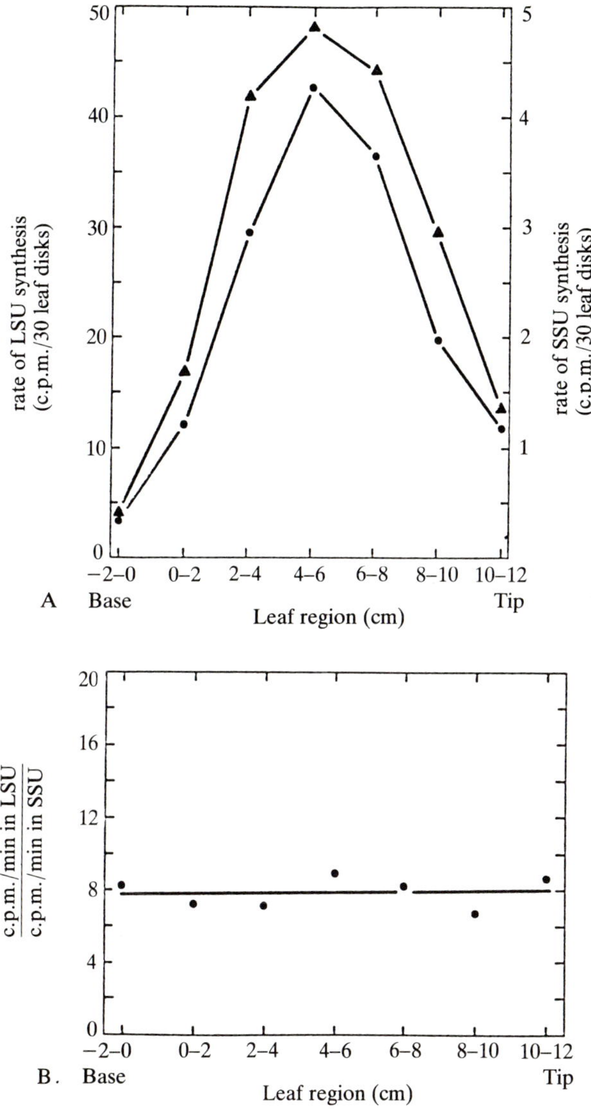

Fig. 7. Rates of synthesis of RuBPCase subunits in each successively older leaf region of 7-day-old barley seedlings (*Hordeum vulgare* L. var UC566).

Samples of 30 leaf discs were incubated for c. 160 min in 0·48 mM-leucine (104 μCi [^{14}C] leucine μmol^{-1}). The subunits were resolved on two-dimensional gel electrophoresis.

(A) Rates of large (LS) (—●) and small (SS) (—▲) subunit synthesis.

(B) Ratio of the rate of large subunit synthesis to the rate of small subunit synthesis (from Nivison & Stocking, 1983).

chloroplast development, yet the very tight co-ordination between the biosynthesis of the large and small subunits of RuBPCase can still be observed throughout chloroplast development in the hybrid leaf. So even when nuclei and cytoplasm of different genetic lineages of differing ploidy are combined, relatively normal leaf growth occurs and the co-ordination of subunit synthesis for RuBPCase protein is not affected.

In general the co-ordinated synthesis of polypeptides reflects parallel and co-ordinated synthesis of messenger RNAs. This has been clearly demonstrated for the RuBPCase subunits by studying the translatable mRNA populations *in vitro*. The activity of translatable mRNA populations for the polypeptides which are synthesized extensively during chloroplast development can be investigated using the rabbit reticulocyte lysate system. This is a good choice for the study of leaf mRNAs since it allows translation of both 70S and 80S type mRNAs, i.e. both chloroplast- and nuclear-encoded messages. Fig. 6B shows the polypeptide products of the *in vitro* translation of wheat leaf RNA extracted from cells of different ontogenetic age. Each track contains the labelled translation products produced by the activity of mRNA from increasingly older wheat leaf cells (from left to right = from young to old). Partial proteolytic digest positively identified the large subunit and the small subunit precursor of RuBPCase and densitometric tracings of the autoradiograph showed that the translatable mRNAs from the LSU and the small subunit precursor (pSSU) continue to increase throughout the first 65 h period after cell development begins. These changes are entirely consistent with the changes which are found in the labelling of the two subunits *in vivo* (Fig. 6A) and clearly indicate that the control of the rates of synthesis of the polypeptides is controlled by the rates of synthesis of their mRNAs.

The synthesis of the RuBPCase subunits is co-ordinated at the transcriptional level, but the specific genetic mechanisms which ensure both the co-ordination of subunit synthesis and the maintenance of the co-ordination throughout leaf mesophyll cell development are not known. However, there are many indications that the nuclear genome is the controlling partner and that the rate of synthesis of the small subunit precursor in the cytoplasm controls the synthesis of the large subunit in the chloroplast. In any case, in general, nuclear transcription must dictate the rates of chloroplast transcription since the polymerases for chloroplast mRNA (and for other cpRNAs) are encoded in the nucleus (Dyer, 1984 and Fig. 5). As previously mentioned the multiple copies of cpDNA and the composition of the chloroplast genome suggest that it is unlikely that the number or rate of synthesis of chloroplast transcripts could limit genome expression in the chloroplast; the vast excessive coding capacity in the chloroplast genes compared with the nuclear genes would appear to preclude such limitations. Other key factors are the location in the chloroplast genome of multiple copies of chloroplast ribosomal genes and the rapid and massive synthesis of chloroplast ribosomes which occurs early in mesophyll development. Calculations for the first leaf of wheat show that the synthesis of chloroplast 70S ribosomes continues for 18 h at the rate of 2 million ribosomes h^{-1} before and during the period of maximum protein accumulation in the leaf mesophyll cells.

Equal accumulation of the two subunits and their combination as the holoenzyme in the chloroplast will be a consequence of the tight co-ordination of the rates of synthesis of the two subunits of RuBPCase (and also of any degradative processes) throughout chloroplast development. Certainly pools of large subunits or small subunits or the small subunit precursor

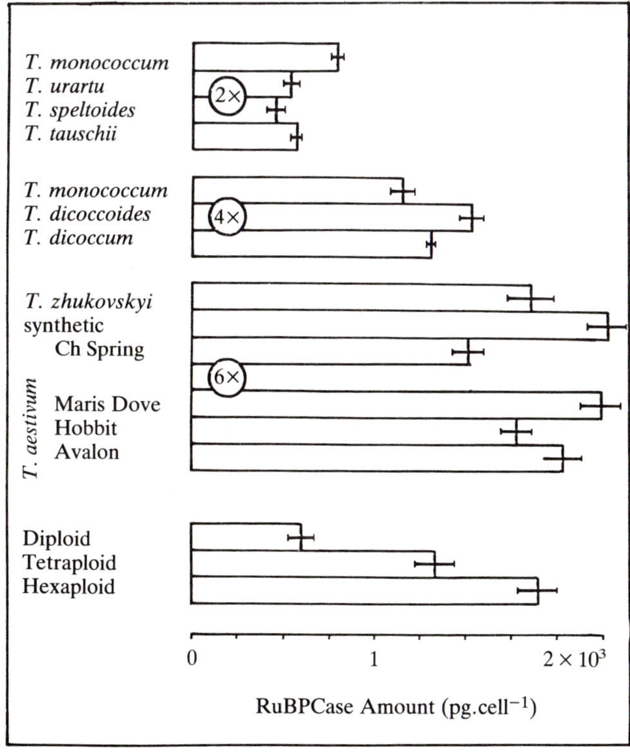

Fig. 8. RuBPCase per cell (pg) in diploid, tetraploid and hexaploid *Triticum* genotypes. The diploid genotypes are *T. monococcum*, *T. urartu*, *T. speltoides* and *T. tauschii*; the tetraploids are *T. monococcum*, *T. dicoccoides* and *T. dicoccum*; and the hexaploids are *T. zhukovskyi*, the synthetic *T. dicoccoides* × *T. tauschii*, and the cultivars of *T. aestivum*, Chinese (Ch) Spring, Holfast, Maris Dove, Hobbit and Avalon. The bars indicate S.E.S. (Modified from Leech *et al.* 1985*b*.)

have never been found in actively developing leaf tissue. Of particular significance in this regard is our recent discovery that the level of accumulation of RuBPCase, i.e. the amount of protein per cell, is also under nucleotypic control (Dean & Leech, 1982*d*; Leech, Leese & Jellings, 1985). The discovery was made initially during a comparative study in which the cellular levels of RuBPCase in diploid, tetraploid and hexaploid wheat species were compared. Subsequently similar nucleotypic control has been confirmed to exist in an isogenic series of Alfalfa (Meyers *et al.* 1982) and also in diploid and polyploid *Festuca* species (Joseph, Randall & Nelson, 1981, Byrne, Nelson & Randall, 1981). In initial investigations in wheat, the cellular ratio of RuBPCase amount : nuclear DNA amount in mature leaf cells was constant at 65 for *Triticum monococcum* (2x), *Triticum dicoccum* (4x) and *Triticum aestivum* (6x) showing a quantitative gene dosage effect on RuBPCase accumulation in the mature wheat leaf cell. Similar analyses have now been extended (Fig. 8) to include additional wheat genotypes and the relationship between ploidy and RuBPCase level per cell in wheat has been confirmed (Leech *et al.* 1985). The quantitative gene dosage effect shown in comparisons between diploid species and their artificially produced isogenic autotetraploids is particularly interesting.

Further dissection of the physical basis for the nucleotypic control of the cellular accumulation of RuBPCase is possible because of the availability of a monosomic series in the cultivar Chinese Spring of *T. aestivum* (6x). Each of these 21 different aneuploids lacks one chromosome of the euploid complement of 42. In comparisons with the euploid (42 chromosomes) aneuploids lacking either a group 4A or a group 4B chromosome showed a one-sixth reduction in the cellular accumulation of RuBPCase (Jellings, Leese & Leech, 1983). This is a clear demonstration that a major influence of the nuclear genotypic control of the RuBPCase amount resides in the group 4A and the group 4B chromosomes. In addition, when accumulation of RuBPCase is examined, in cells of nullitetrasomics and in tetrasomics for 4A, the expected increases in RuBPCase are demonstrated (Leech & Pyke, unpublished). From an examination of deletion lines in which either the long arm or the short arm of chromosome 4A has been lost, it can be shown that the control resides on the short arm.

In modern hexaploid cultivars of *T. aestivum* statistically highly significant consistent intergenotypic differences exist in the accumulation of RuBPCase per cell (Fig. 9). These genotypic differences are manifest in each individual leaf and after an initial analysis we are now able to predict the leaf cell content of RuBPCase for each of the wild and cultivated genotypes we have examined. Consideration of this relationship reveals a truly remarkable state of affairs in which the rates of synthesis of the two

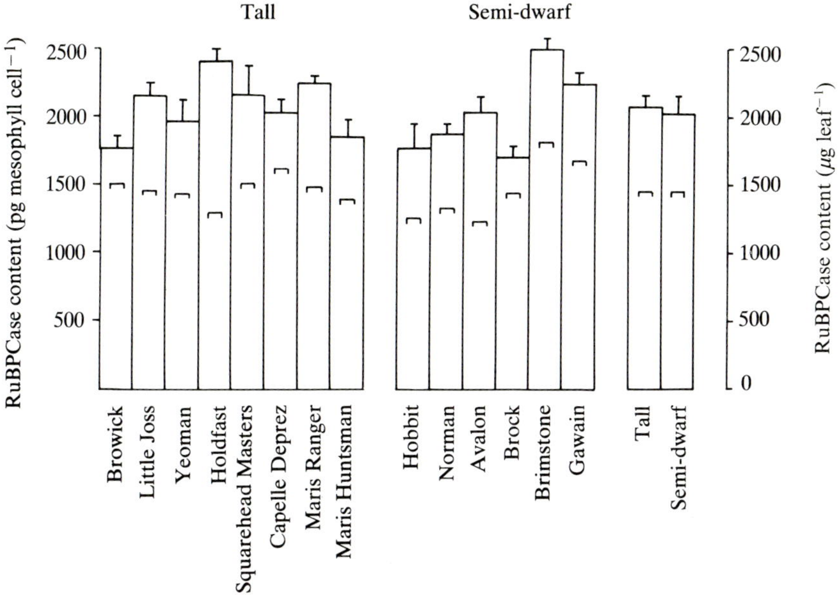

Fig. 9. Level of RuBPCase per mesophyll cell and per leaf in 14 genotypes of *Triticum aestivum*.

Standard error bars are shown for cellular values and inserts (⌐⌐) indicate RuBPCase content per leaf (right-hand scale).

subunits of the major chloroplast protein, one encoded in the nucleus and synthesized in the cytosol and the other encoded and synthesized in the chloroplasts are so subtly co-ordinated in space and time throughout the complex sequence of chloroplast and cellular development as to ensure an exact quantitative accumulation of a major photosynthetic enzyme in the photosynthesizing cell. Each genotype is fingerprinted for a particular cellular amount of carboxylase (Pyke & Leech, 1985*a*) and it is hard to imagine a clearer indication of the intense stability of the development of chloroplastic function. The major control is genotypic and the finer controls are exerted by genomic differences and by genic differences.

It is interesting to speculate about the generality of this kind of relationship. How many syntheses of key enzymes of chloroplast metabolism are controlled in this type of way? We have preliminary evidence that a key enzyme in lipid metabolism is also influenced by gene dosage effects in a similar manner. Dr. Hawke in my laboratory has recently been studying the amount of the enzyme acetyl CoA carboxylase in wheat leaves and has shown a consistent 80 % increase per cell between diploids and tetraploids. The linking of increases in enzyme activity with increases in protein amount are particularly interesting because so far activities rather than amounts have been the primary concern of the biochemist interested in rates of synthesis. It is possible that in chloroplasts the majority of the molecules of their major enzymes are functional. Successful land plants clearly reflect success in conserving and utilizing available energy and this may be one manifestation of the general situation.

The development of photosynthetic membranes in differentiating chloroplasts

For many years the study of the etioplast to chloroplast transition was used as a model for normal chloroplast development in the belief – now revealed as mistaken (see Leech & Baker, 1983; Leech, 1984; Treffry, 1978 for reviews) – that changes during recovery from etiolation reflected changes during normal leaf development. There is now abundant evidence that normal chloroplast differentiation differs in several fundamental features (Leech, 1985) from the recovery of etioplasts from light deprivation and the etioplast models can no longer be used (Baker & Barber, 1984). When recovery from etiolation and normal chloroplast development are compared the rates of chlorophyll synthesis, changes in the chlorophyll a/b ratio during development (Boffey *et al.* 1980), the products of protein synthesis (Grebanier, Steinbeck & Bogorad, 1979), the number of plastids per cell (Possingham, 1980), and most important the relative rates of development of the two photosystems (Baker, 1984) and of photochemical competence (Baker *et al.* 1984) all differ markedly. The description which follows therefore relates entirely to the development of photosynthetic membranes and the acquisition of photosynthetic competence in normally grown grass species.

Several membrane chloroplast polypeptides are synthesized during chloroplast development and the labelling patterns for a differentiating leaf are seen in Fig. 6. There are five major protein complexes in the photosynthetic membrane. They are the light-harvesting complex (LHCP), the photosystem I (PSI) complex, the photosystem II (PSII) complex, the cytochrome b–cytochrome f complex, and the ATP–synthase (coupling factor) complex containing CF_0 and CF_1 groups of subunit polypeptides. All these complexes are nuclear-chloroplast encoded hybrids. In photosystem II it has recently been shown that at least three of the proteins are chloroplast encoded.

The synthesis of the light-harvesting complex

The quantitatively dominant membrane proteins in chloroplasts are the two major polypeptides of the light-harvesting complex (Thornber & Markwell, 1981) (recently renamed the two Cab proteins by molecular biologists) and the accumulation of these two membrane polypeptides closely follows the accumulation of the subunits of RuBPCase (Fig. 6A). This parallel accumulation continues over the first 50 h of chloroplast development, but subsequently the accumulation of the first two Cab proteins slows down relative to the accumulation of RuBPCase. The two Cab proteins are phosphoproteins (Bennett, 1979), encoded in the nucleus and synthesized as high molecular weight precursors on free cytoplasmic ribosomes and transported to the chloroplast where they are processed and assembled as smaller polypeptides (25K and 26K M_r) into the developing membranes in association with chlorophyll a and chlorophyll b. In the dark, in the absence of chlorophyll biosynthesis, the proteins of the light-harvesting complex disintegrate (Bennett, 1981). During normal development however, chlorophyll biosynthesis occurs rapidly throughout chloroplast differentiation and appears to continue during the chloroplast division phase. In mature chloroplasts all the chlorophyll is complexed to proteins (Thornber & Markwell, 1981) and the assembly of pigment–protein complexes into developing membranes is of critical importance in the acquisition of photosynthetic competence since the light-harvesting complex operates both as a light-harvesting system and also in the transfer of excitation energy to the reaction centres of PSI and PSII during photosynthesis. The physical structure of the complex is not understood in detail, but it contains nearly all the chlorophyll b and at least 50% of the chlorophyll a of the photosynthetic membrane.

The synthesis of the cytochrome b–cytochrome f complex and the ATP-synthase complex

The light-harvesting complex is present in the membranes of the plastids in the youngest cells which can be examined, i.e. in the cells which are just postmitotic, and the synthesis of the complex continues without interruption throughout chloroplast development. The same pattern of synthesis and assembly is apparently the norm for the other membrane protein complexes which are present in about a tenth molar concentration compared to the light-harvesting complex. Cytochrome f polypeptides and the α and β subunits of the CF_1 component of the ATP synthase complex can be seen in the autoradiogram in Fig. 6A. ATP synthase complex is a multi-subunit protein whose synthesis is co-ordinated in a rapid accumulation phase (first 50 h) in the developing plastid membranes but prior to the period of extensive membrane appression and granal formation. This is in line with extensive evidence that the synthase complex is confined to the exposed surfaces of non-appressed membranes and to the upper and lower surfaces of the grana. In contrast, the synthesis of the cytochrome f complex continues considerably longer than either the synthesis and assembly

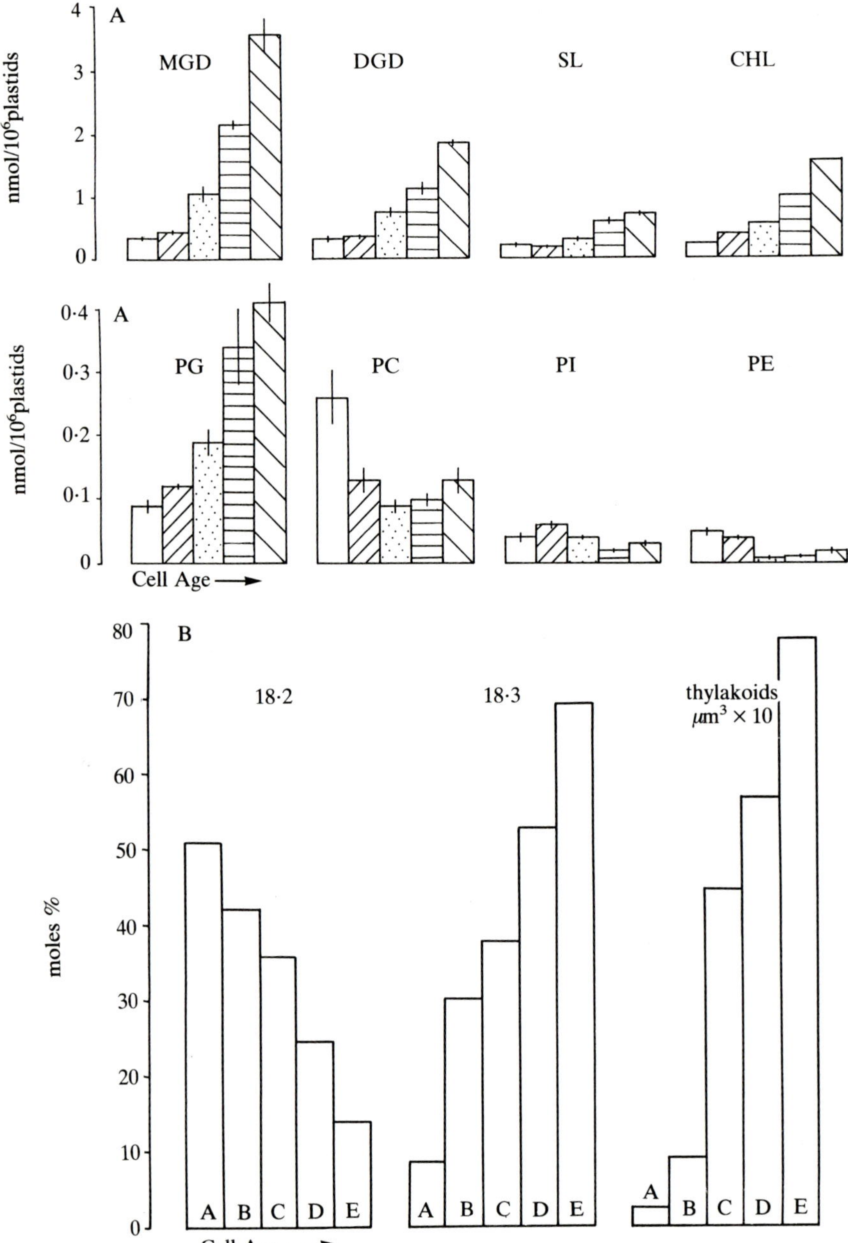

of CF_1 or the synthesis and assembly of RuBPCase, but cytochrome f is present in both appressed and non-appressed regions of the photosynthetic membranes. The continued synthesis of cytochrome f during the period of extensive increase in granal formation is therefore also in line with its known position in the chloroplast membrane (Dean, 1982).

The synthesis of chloroplast membrane lipids

The photosynthetic membranes are lipid protein membranes of a fluid mosaic type of construction. The lipids apparently maintain membrane stability and also contribute to creating a suitable environment for photochemical function. The photosynthetic membrane has a unique acyl lipid complement in which highly polyunsaturated glycerol lipids are the main components (for review see Leech & Walton, 1983). The lipids of the mature photosynthetic membrane (accounting for 75% by weight) are the neutral galactolipids, monogalactosyl diacyl glycerol (MGD) and digalactosyl diacyl glycerol (DGD). An additional 10% by dry weight is contributed by each of two neutral lipids, sulphoquinovosyl diacyl glycerol (SQDG) and phosphatidyl glycerol (PG). At maturity the acyl moiety of the acyl galactolipids are almost exclusively α-linolenyl residues (18 : 3).

The quantitative and qualitative changes in the molecular species of the plastid lipids which occur during chloroplast development have been analysed in some detail (Leech, Rumsby & Thomson, 1973; Leese & Leech, 1976) with a view to identifying the molecules and assemblies of molecules which are specifically required for the efficient development of light absorption and energy transduction functions in the photosynthetic membrane. Massive lipid biosynthesis occurs during chloroplast differentiation (Leech *et al.* 1973) and the largest increases are in the acyl lipids, e.g. MGD shows a sixfold increase and DGD a fourfold increase per plastid respectively (Fig. 10A). All the chloroplast membrane lipids become progressively more unsaturated during chloroplast biogenesis, and the changing fatty acid spectrum of the chloroplast lipids during the development of barley leaves

---

Fig. 10 (A) The amounts of lipid in plastids isolated from green developing maize (*Zea mays*) leaves. Methods described by Leese & Leech (1976). Cell age increases from left to right in each set of histograms.

MGD, monoglactosyl diacyl glycerol; DGD, digalactosyl diacyl glycerol; SL, sulphoquinososyl diacyl glycerol; CHL, chlorophyll; PG, phosphatidyl glycerol; PC, phosphatidyl choline; PI, phosphatidyl inositol; PE, phosphatidyl ethanolamine.

(B) The changing moles % content of linoleic (18 : 2) and linolenic (18 : 3) acids in successively older (A to E) sections of a 7-day-old barley leaf (*Hordeum vulgare* cv. Sundance). The third histogram shows the increases in photosynthetic (thylakoid) membrane extension in plastids of the same leaf tissue (from Walton, 1985).

is shown in Fig. 10B. The synthesis of phosphatidyl glycerol during chloroplast biogenesis is particularly interesting since its synthesis closely follows the synthesis of chlorophyll and at maturity there is a stoichiometric ratio of chlorophyll to phosphatidyl glycerol molecules of 3 : 1.

Although the increase in the degree of polyunsaturation of the membrane lipids is occurring at the same time as the chloroplast membranes are rapidly proliferating and extensive appression is occurring, there is no evidence for a causal relationship between the two processes. It has recently been shown categorically that a high content of 18 : 3 residues is not an essential requirement for rapid and extensive appression of membranes (Leech, Walton & Baker, 1985) and also that the increasing polyunsaturation of the membranes occurs in several cellular components during leaf development and is not merely restricted to the chloroplast.

The development of photochemical competence in developing chloroplasts

Recently the development of photochemical competence in normally grown green wheat leaves has been measured by Neil Baker's group, using non-destructive fluorescent monitoring techniques (Baker *et al.* 1984). Using such techniques, the group are able to analyse the qualitative and quantitative changes in photochemical competence in developing chloroplasts as judged by the primary photochemical ability of PSII, by the transfer of excitation energy from PSII to PSI and by the photo-oxidation of water. All these processes take place very efficiently even in the youngest leaf cells that can be analysed and whose proplastids have only sparse single perforated membranes and in which membrane appression is at a minimum, i.e. only a few scattered bithylakoid assemblies are present (Webber, Baker, Platt-Aloia & Thomson, 1984). Most significantly, the photochemical competence and efficiency do not change significantly during the subsequent phases of chloroplast differentiation. The older chloroplasts differ from the young undifferentiated plastids only in one respect, that is in their ability to metabolically regulate excitation energy distribution between PSI and PSII (the ability to mediate the State I–State II transition). It is abundantly clear that normal chloroplast development is characterized by an increase in the absolute concentration of photochemically competent units in the photosynthetic membranes and not by a step-wise accretion of functional competence. These normal changes are in no way parallelled in the etioplast to chloroplast transition: plastids recovering from etiolation do so in very slow, jerky steps, and the different aspects of their photochemical activity recover at different rates.

A nice example of the remarkable stability of photosynthetic membrane biogenesis is illustrated by the normal development of the chloroplast structure in leaves in barley plants whose 18 : 3/18 : 2 ratio has been changed from c. 60 % to c. 20 % by feeding the seedlings with the herbicide San 9785 (St. John & Christiansen, 1976). In these treated plants all the chloroplasts are ultrastructurally normal and contain normal amounts of chlorophyll and lipids but the ratio of appressed : non-appressed membranes increases from a ratio of 2·5 in the control plants to a ratio of 3·4 in the treated ones (Walton, 1979; Leech & Walton, 1983). This enormous change in degree of unsaturation has not affected the primary photochemical activity of PSII and the excitation energy transfer from PSII to PSI actually increases in the treated plants (Leech *et al.* 1985). This phenomenon can be explained in terms of the predicted lateral heterogeneity (Anderson, 1981, 1982; Anderson & Melis, 1983) of photosynthetic membranes because the number of end granal membranes is increased in the treated plants allowing relatively more excitation transfer from PSII to PSI.

Conclusions

The emphasis throughout this paper has been on the stability of the integrated process of chloroplast development. Such a high degree of conservation of an organelle which is primarily dedicated to photosynthesis and on whose continuing function the survival of the parent plant depends is perhaps not unexpected. The requirement for co-ordinated synthesis of well over a thousand biochemical components and for their appropriate incorporation into the chloroplast during its development is required to yield a competently functioning chloroplast. Such a complex process, which is completed over a period of hours allows for little flexibility. A higher plant lacking competent chloroplasts is soon a dead plant and few developmental ‘mistakes’ in plastid development are to be tolerated. Indeed as I have shown, when chloroplast development is analysed under suitable conditions, very few degrees of freedom in the pattern of plastid ontogeny can be demonstrated. In non-limiting environmental conditions, the dominant controls lie in the nuclear genome but the chloroplast genome is also an essential partner since the biosynthesis of all the major classes of chloroplast proteins depends on the effective functioning of the chloroplast genetic system. Chloroplast development is a cellular process and the integrated development of the cell and the chloroplast cannot be divorced from each other.

Many of the examples used in this paper have been taken from detailed studies of the development of chloroplasts in a single species of hexaploid wheat (*Triticum aestivum*) and in particular a single cultivar Maris Dove. When a single species is studied in detail in this way it is possible to distinguish the genetically determined pattern of development from environmentally and intergenotypically induced modifications. At the current level of sophistication of chemical analysis of DNA, RNA and proteins, we have the tools for recognizing and analysing genic and specific differences in genotypic expression and also for distinguishing genotypic from environmental responses. Normal chloroplast development in a non-limiting environment is a remarkably non-plastic process and appears to be largely a quantitative accretion of additional molecules and their assembly into increasingly larger numbers of functional units. The smallest organelles recognized are proplastids with small bithylakoid assemblies which are already fully functional photochemically so already at this early stage in chloroplast development a relatively immutable developmental pattern has been determined. Any endogenous or external factors which could permanently affect the development of leaf chloroplasts i.e. increase 'plasticity' as manifested by an increase in the variety of form or function of the developed chloroplasts might be expected to operate before this period in their development. The subsequent development of chloroplasts involving further biosynthesis of these numerous components, membrane assembly, increases in chloroplast number, and a large increase in size, continues until the cell is replete.

The finite limits of the cell volume appear to be the major constraints on increases in chloroplast size and number during development. Within an individual wheat leaf the mesophyll cells are not identical in size and the larger cells at maturity always have more chloroplasts than the smaller ones. There is scope for small variations in chloroplast number (c. 5%) between cells but within a cell the individual chloroplasts are remarkably uniform in shape and size and in the synchrony of their development and division. It remains for future investigation to determine if changes in mature cell size can be influenced by environmental factors and whether cell size changes are reflected in changes in chloroplast number or size.

The reproducibility of the pattern of chloroplast development in genetically similar individuals is anticipated by the experienced physiologist or biochemist who expects to find reproducibility from day to day in the activities of enzymes and in the physiological responses in the samples of leaf tissue which are examined. Experience has shown that not only molecular ratios of constituent chloroplast components but also the levels of enzyme activities have a reliable consistency in successive samples of leaves and plants of the same genotype. One of the long-term objectives of future studies of chloroplast development will be to describe and explain such specific and genic differences in genetic terms.

The concept of plasticity seems to have very limited value when applied to the process of chloroplast development as it is presently understood. The descriptive phase in understanding the molecular biology of this process is only in its infancy but there is no doubt that future research into the subtleties of the chemical controls which integrate the developmental processes in chloroplasts will gain immeasurably as the development of techniques and understanding of molecular biology progresses. Some examples of differences in nucleic acid and in protein structure which provide diagnostic distinctions have already been described. For example, chloroplast DNA structure differs markedly in pea, spinach and wheat (Dyer, 1984) and the number of amino acids in the transit peptide of pSSU of the RuBPCase differs in pea and wheat. Again, the Q_b polypeptide (a component of LHC) has a single amino acid change in plants which have become resistant to atrazine herbicides as compared with atrazine-sensitive individuals. All these modifications are found in chloroplasts which have developed perfectly normally. It can be expected that many other modifications may be detected, particularly if non-intrusive methods allowing *in vivo* analysis become more widely used. Nuclear magnetic resonance and fluorescence monitoring techniques are expected to be particularly valuable. These methods can be effectively deployed if they are used to quantify changes in chloroplast function which in turn might help to identify the basis for changes in leaf tissue function (some of the approaches which can be used effectively in this type of study have been described elsewhere – Jellings & Leech, 1982, 1984; Holbrook, Keys & Leech, 1984). In addition the increasing availability of specific DNA and RNA probes and monoclonal antibodies can be expected to greatly expand the possibilities for the analysis of the inductive and control processes that are operational during chloroplast development. Again once these processes have been described it will be possible to look for any modulations leading to *permanent* changes in the chloroplast effected by endogenous or exogenous factors and quantify the amount of change effected. A permanent change of this type would indicate a degree of plasticity in the system. On present evidence plasticity is most likely to be effected at the post-translational stage and by modification of the already formed chloroplast.

A discussion of the effects of environmental modulation on mature chloroplasts is outside the scope of this article. General observation shows us that normal chloroplasts develop in species growing in a myriad of environmental conditions from deepest shade in the rain forest to exposed arid conditions of a desert environment. All these chloroplasts apparently serve their parent plants effectively and the major control systems are genetic. Haberlandt (1926) discussed the role of light as the major environmental factor in leaf development and came to the conclusion that its role may be described as 'purely quantitative'. Almost sixty years later it is concluded in a recent paper that in the maize leaf the initial synthesis of the mRNAs for the major chloroplast proteins pSSU and LSU of RuBPCase and LHCP is light independent and that light only influences the levels to which each mRNA accumulates (Nelson, Harpster, Mayfield & Taylor, 1984). Current indications suggest that in molecular biological terms chloroplast development is affected quantitatively not qualitatively by environmental influences. In the few cases so far investigated external influences have been shown to affect the *pace* but not the *pattern* of chloroplast development. Changes in pace can only be detected if appropriate base lines are used and parameters such as 'light-hours' or 'temperature-days' may perhaps have considerable value. The development of chloroplasts involves a continuously changing pattern of interactions and it should be possible as suitable probes become available to determine the phases when transcription and translation of specific gene products is occurring. The analysis of the role of individual gene families in development for such proteins as pSSU (a multigene family of 20 to 30 in hexaploid wheat) is a particularly exciting challenge for the future. So far RuBPCase and LHCP have become the paradigms for the study of chloroplast molecular biology. Investigations will certainly also be extended in the future to the quantitatively less-dominant chloroplast components as in the recent paper by Mayfield & Taylor (1984). It is already clear that the expression of many nuclear genes involved in the coding of chloroplast polypeptides is normally tissue specific. It will also be intriguing to see if the cell-specific expression of RuBPCase in the bundle sheath cells but not the mesophyll cells of C4-plants such as maize is only the first example of cell-specific expression which has many parallels in the development of other chloroplast enzymes. In these and many other ways we can anticipate that the further study of integration of chloroplast development at the molecular, organelle and cellular level will provide exciting challenges far into the future.

I particularly wish to acknowledge the many helpful discussions and valuable advice received from Dr. Kevin Pyke during the preparation of this manuscript. He has generously allowed me to quote extensively from his unpublished work and has also prepared many of the diagrams in the paper.

References

ANDERSON, J. M. (1981). Consequences of spatial separation of photosystem 1 and 2 in thylakoid membranes of higher plant chloroplasts. *FEBS Lett.* **124**, 1–10.

ANDERSON, J. M. (1982). The significance of grana stacking in chlorophyll b-containing chloroplasts. *Photochem. Photobiol.* **3**, 225–241.

ANDERSON, J. M. & MELIS, A. (1983). Localisation of different photosystems in separate regions of chloroplast membranes. *Proc. natn. Acad. Sci. U.S.A.* **80**, 745–749.

BAKER, N. R. (1984). Development of chloroplast photochemical function. In *Chloroplast Biogenesis* (ed. N. R. Baker & J. Barber), ch. 5, pp. 207–253. Amsterdam: Elsevier.

BAKER, N. R. AND BARBER, J. (1984). *Chloroplast Biogenesis.* Amsterdam: Elsevier.

BAKER, N. R., WEBBER, A. N., BRADBURY, M., MARKWELL, J. P., BAKER, M. G. & THORNBER, J. P. (1984). Development of photochemical competence during growth of the wheat leaf. In *UCLA symposium on Molecular and Cellular biology*, new series, vol. 14, *Biosynthesis of the Photosynthetic Apparatus: Molecular Biology, Development, and Regulation* (ed. J. P. Thornber, L. A. Staehelin and R. B. Hallick), pp. 237–255. New York: Alan Rhiss Inc.

BENNETT, J. (1979). Chloroplast phosphoproteins. Phosphorylation of polypeptides of the light-harvesting chlorophyll protein complex. *Eur. J. Biochem.* **99**, 133–137.

BENNETT, J. (1981). Biosynthesis of the light-harvesting chlorophyll a/b protein. Polypeptide turnover in darkness. *Eur. J. Biochem.* **118**, 61–70.

BOFFEY, S. A., ELLIS, J. R., SELLDEN, G. & LEECH, R. M. (1979). Chloroplast division and DNA synthesis in light-grown wheat leaves. *Pl. Physiol.* **64**, 503–505.

BOFFEY, S. A., SELLDEN, G. & LEECH, R. M. (1980). The influence of cell age on chlorophyll formation in light-grown and etiolated wheat seedlings. *Pl. Physiol.* **65**, 680–684.

BOFFEY, S. A. & LEECH, R. M. (1982). Chloroplast DNA levels and the control of chloroplast division in light-grown wheat leaves. *Pl. Physiol.* **69**, 1387–1391.

BRANGEON, J. & MUSTARDY, L. (1979). The autogenetic assembly of intrachloroplastic lamellae viewed in 3-dimension. *Biologie Cellulaire* **36**, 71–80.

BYRNE, M. C., NELSON, C. J. & RANDALL, D. D. (1981). Ploidy effects on anatomy and gas exchange of tall fescue leaves. *Pl. Physiol.* **68**, 891–893.

DEAN, C. (1982). Investigations of genome expression in young wheat leaves. D.Phil. Thesis, University of York, UK.

DEAN, C. & LEECH, R. M. (1982*a*). The co-ordinated synthesis of the large and small subunits of ribulose biphosphate carboxylase during early cellular development within a seven day wheat leaf. *FEBS Lett.* **140**, 113–116.

DEAN, C. & LEECH, R. M. (1982*b*). The co-ordinated synthesis of the subunits of ribulose biphosphate carboxylase in a wheat line with alien cytoplasm. *FEBS Lett.* **144**, 154–156.

DEAN, C. & LEECH, R. M. (1982*c*). Cellular and chloroplast numbers and DNA, RNA and protein levels in tissues of different ages within a seven day old wheat leaf. *Pl. Physiol..* **69**, 904–910.

DEAN, C. & LEECH, R. M. (1982*d*). Genome expression during normal leaf development. 2. The direct correlation between ribulose biphosphate carboxylase content and nuclear ploidy in a polyploid series of wheat. *Pl. Physiol.* **70**, 1605–1608.

DYER, T. A. (1984). The chloroplast genome: its nature and role in development. In *Chloroplast Biogenesis* (ed. N. R. Baker and J. Barber), pp. 23–71. Amsterdam: Elsevier.

DYER, T., BOWMAN, C., KOLLER, B., DELIUS, H., GRAY, J., DOHERTY, A., HOWE, C., LEECH, R. & SELLDEN, G. (1983). The chloroplast genome of wheat. In *Kew Chromosome Conference 11.* (ed. P. E. Brandham & M. D. Bennett), pp. 91–96. London: George Allen and Unwin.

ELLIS, J. R., JELLINGS, A. J. & LEECH, R. M. (1983). Nuclear DNA content and the control of chloroplast replication in wheat leaves. *Planta* **157**, 376–380.

ELLIS, J. R. & LEECH, R. M. (1985). Cell size and chloroplast size in relation to chloroplast replication in light-grown wheat leaves. *Planta* **165**, 120–125.

GREBANIER, A. E., STEINBECK, K. E. & BOGORAD, L. (1979). Comparison of the molecular weights of proteins synthesized by isolated chloroplasts with those which appear during greening in *Zea mays*. *Pl. Physiol.* **63**, 436–439.

HABERLANDT, G. (1926). In *Physiological Plant Anatomy*, ch. 6. *The Photosynthetic System*, IV, *Influence of Light upon the Distribution and Organization of the Photosynthetic System*, pp. 296. London: Macmillan and Co., Ltd.

HOLBROOK, G. P., KEYS, A. J. & LEECH, R. M. (1984). Biochemistry of photosynthesis in Species of *Triticum* of differing ploidy. *Pl. Physiol.* **74**, 12–15.

JELLINGS, A. J. & LEECH, R. M. (1982). The importance of quantitative anatomy in the interpretation of whole leaf biochemistry in species of *Triticum*, *Hordeum* and *Avena*. *New Phytol.* **92**, 39–48.

JELLINGS, A. J. & LEECH, R. M. (1984). Anatomical variation in first leaves of nine *Triticum* genotypes, and its relationship to photosynthetic capacity. *New Phytol.* **96**, 371–382.

JELLINGS, A. J., LEESE, B. M. & LEECH, R. M. (1983). Location of chromosomal control of ribulose biphosphate carboxylase amounts in wheat. *Mol. gen. Genet.* **192**, 272–274.

JELLINGS, A. J., USHER, M. B. & LEECH, R. M. (1983). Chloroplast size in tall and short phenotypes of *Poa flabellata* on South Georgia. *Br. Antarct. Surv. Bull.* **59**, 41–46.

JOSEPH, M. C., RANDALL, D. D. & NELSON, C. J. (1981). Photosynthesis in polyploid tall fescue. II. Photosynthesis and ribulose 1,5-bisphosphate carboxylase of polyploid tall fescue. *Pl. Physiol.* **68**, 890–894.

LEECH, R. M. (1984). Chloroplast development in angiosperms: current knowledge and future prospects. In *Chloroplast Biogenesis* (ed. N. R. Baker & J. Barber), ch. 1, pp. 1–21. Amsterdam: Elsevier.

LEECH, R. M. (1985). The synthesis of cellular components in leaves. In *Control of Leaf Growth*, S.E.B. Seminar Series Volume **27** (ed. N. R. Baker, W. D. Davies & C. Ong). Cambridge: Cambridge University Press.

LEECH, R. M. & BAKER, N. R. (1983). The development of photosynthetic capacity in leaves. In *The Growth and Functioning of Leaves* (ed. J. E. Dale & F. L. Milthorpe). Cambridge: Cambridge University Press.

LEECH, R. M., LEESE, B. M. & JELLINGS, A. J. (1985*a*). Variation in cellular ribulose bisphosphate carboxylase content in leaves of *Triticum* genotypes at three levels of ploidy. *Planta* **166**, 259–263.

LEECH, R. M., RUMSBY, M. G. & THOMSON, W. W. (1973). Plastid differentiation, acyl lipid and fatty acid changes in developing green maize leaves. *Pl. Physiol.* **52**, 240–245.

LEECH, R. M., THOMSON, W. W. & PLATT-ALOIA, K. A. (1981). Observations on the mechanism of chloroplast division in higher plants. *New Phytol.* **87**, 1–9.

LEECH, R. M. & WALTON, C. A. (1983). Modification of fatty acid composition during chloroplast ontogeny and the effects on thylakoid appression and primary photochemistry. In *Biosynthesis and Function of Plant Lipids* (ed. W. W. Thomson, J. B. Mudd & M. Gibbs), pp. 56–80. Rockville, Maryland: American Society of Plant Physiologists.

LEECH, R. M., WALTON, C. A. & BAKER, N. R. (1985*b*). Some effects of San 9785 on the development of chloroplast thylakoid membranes in *Hordeum vulgare*. *Planta* **165**, 277–283.

LEESE, B. M. & LEECH, R. M. (1976). Sequential changes in the lipids of developing proplastids isolated from green maize leaves. *Pl. Physiol.* **57**, 789–794.

MAYFIELD, S. P. & TAYLOR, W. C. (1984). The appearance of photosynthetic proteins in developing maize leaves. *Planta* **161**, 481–486.

MEYERS, S. P., NICHOLS, S. L., BAER, G. R., MOLIN, W. T. & SCHRADER, L. E. (1982). Ploidy effects in isogenic populations of alfalfa. I. Ribulose-1,5-bisphosphate carboxylase, soluble protein, chlorophyll, and DNA in leaves. *Pl. Physiol.* **70**, 1704–1709.

NELSON, T., HARPSTER, M. H., MAYFIELD, S. P. & TAYLOR, W. C. (1984). Light-regulated gene expression during maize leaf development. *J. Cell Biol.* **98**, 558–564.

NIVISON, H. T. & STOCKING, C. R. (1983). Ribulose bisphosphate carboxylase synthesis in barley leaves: a developmental approach to the question of co-ordinated subunit synthesis. *Pl. Physiol.* **73**, 906–911.

POSSINGHAM, J. V. (1980). Plastid replication and development in the life cycle of higher plants. *A. Rev. Pl. Physiol.* **31**, 113–129.

PYKE, K. A. & LEECH, R. M. (1985*a*). Variation in ribulose 1,5 bisphosphate carboxylase content in a range of winter wheat genotypes. *J. exp. Bot.* **36**, 1523–1529.

PYKE, K. A. & LEECH, R. M. (1985*b*). Chloroplast number in wheat mesophyll cells. *Planta* (in press).

SCOTT, N. S. & POSSINGHAM, J. V. (1980). Chloroplast DNA in expanding spinach leaves. *J. exp. Bot.* **31**, 1081–1092.

ST. JOHN, J. B. & CHRISTIANSEN, M. N. (1976). Inhibition of linolenic acid synthesis and modification of chilling resistance in cotton seedlings. *Pl. Physiol.* **57**, 257–259.

SELLDEN, G. & LEECH, R. M. (1981). Localisation of DNA in mature and young wheat chloroplasts using the fluorescent probe 4′-6-diamidino-2-phenylindole. *Pl. Physiol.* **68**, 731–734.

THORNBER, J. P. & MARKWELL, J. P. (1981). Photosynthetic pigment protein complexes in plant and bacterial membranes. *Trends Biochem. Sci.* **6**, 122–125.

TREFFRY, T. (1978). Biogenesis of the photochemical apparatus. *Int. Rev. Cytol.* **52**, 159–196.

WALTON, C. A. (1979). Some effects of 4-chloro-5-(dimethylamino)-2-phenyl-3(2H)-pyridazilone on the development of the chloroplast thylakoid membrane of *Hordeum vulgare*. D.Phil., Thesis, University of York.

WEBBER, A. N., BAKER, N. R., PLATT-ALOIA, K. A. & THOMSON, W. W. (1984). Appearance of a State I-state 2 transition during chloroplast development in the wheat leaf: Energetic and structural considerations. *Physiol. Plant.* **60**, 171–179.

WHATLEY, J. M. (1977). Variations in the basic pathway of chloroplast development. *New Phytol.* **78**, 407–420.

WHATLEY, J. M. (1979). Plastid development in the primary leaf of *Phaselus vulgaris*: variations between different types of cell. *New Phytol.* **82**, 1–10.

STABILITY OF THE DETERMINED STATE

FREDERICK MEINS, JR. and HERMAN WENZLER
Friedrich Miescher-Institut, P.O. Box 2543, CH-4002 Basel, Switzerland

Summary

During development parts of plants become determined for specific fates which can persist in populations of dividing cells. Students of plant development have tended to favour the view that the determined state is stabilized at the supracellular level. We provide evidence for the alternative view that determination can be inherited at the cellular level. This conclusion is based on the observation that cultured cells derived from the leaf lamina and cortex of the stem of tobacco plants inherit different states of cytokinin requirement. Plant regeneration experiments show that the cytokinin-requiring (C^-) state characteristic of leaf cells and the cytokinin autotrophic (C^+) state characteristic of cortex cells are stable but not permanent. Progeny of both cell types can give rise to complete plants with tissues exhibiting the cytokinin requirement of comparable tissues of seed grown plants. Pith cells can shift from the C^- to the C^+ state by a process known as habituation. Evidence is presented that this epigenetic change is stabilized by a positive-feedback mechanism in which cytokinins appear to promote their own biosynthesis. A single dominant, Mendelian gene, *H1–2*, controls expression of the C^- and C^+ phenotypes. There are hints that this gene changes state in cultured cells at rates expected for epigenetic modifications. This suggests that the C^- and C^+ state can also be stabilized by genetic mechanisms.

Introduction

'The shop seemed to be full of all manner of curious things – but the oddest part of it all was that, whenever she looked hard at any shelf, to make out exactly what it had on it, that particular shelf was always quite empty, though the others round it were crowded as full as they could hold.' Lewis Carroll, *Through the Looking-Glass and What Alice Found There.*

Determination is an elusive concept. Just as one aspect of the problem seems within reason it appears to vanish into thin air. Some of the difficulties are semantic. Determination is a portmanteau term, often poorly defined and used in different ways by different authors. A more fundamental difficulty is that determination, unlike cell specialization and morphogenesis, is an invisible process that is only discernible when cells, tissues and organs are subjected to experimental manipulation.

The concept has its origin in animal embryology. If, for example, tissue from the presumptive eye region of an early-gastrula-stage newt embryo is transplanted to the trunk region of another embryo of the same stage, it forms trunk structures (Spemann, 1938). On the other hand, presumptive eye tissue from the later, neurula-stage embryo eventually forms an eye when transplanted to the trunk region. Apparently, between the early-gastrula and neurula the 'eyeness' of the tissue, although still unexpressed, has become fixed. Thus, determination is the process whereby part of an organism becomes progressively restricted in developmental potency (e.g. Balinsky, 1965).

Implicit in this definition are two important concepts. First, determination results from stable changes in phenotype that persist in the absence of the agent that originally induced the change. This stability is a fundamental property of developing systems. Parts of an organism can 'remember' their past and this, in turn, leads to progressive new formation, i.e. epigenesis. Second, determination is relative. It depends on the properties of cells, tissues, or organs as well as the conditions of the experiment (Meins, 1985*a*). Developmental states stable in one environment are not necessarily stable in some other environment. Stability does not imply permanence.

Determination in plants

There is compelling evidence that plant tissues and organs become determined during ontogeny (Heslop-Harrison, 1967; Wareing, 1978; Meins & Binns, 1979; Henshaw, O'Hara & Webb, 1982). For example, depending upon the relative concentrations of auxin and cytokinin in the culture medium, explants of tobacco stem form roots, form shoots, or form unorganized callus (Skoog & Miller, 1957). Substantially the same results can be obtained with cloned lines of tobacco tissues derived from single cells (Vasil & Hildebrandt, 1965). This shows that the progeny of cells with the potential to form both roots and shoots become determined to express just one of these potentialities.

The time in development and where in the plant determination occurs depends on the particular organ and the plant species (Meins, 1985*a*). There are even gradients of determination within individual organs (Oehlkers, 1955, 1956; Chailakhyan, Aksenova, Konstantinova & Bavrina, 1975; McDaniel, 1978; Wernicke & Brettell, 1980). A good illustration of discontinuous gradients comes from studies of culture initiation with tissues explanted from different parts of the maize leaf.

When small transverse segments of leaf from young, axenically grown maize plants are cultured on a standard, auxin-containing medium, most of

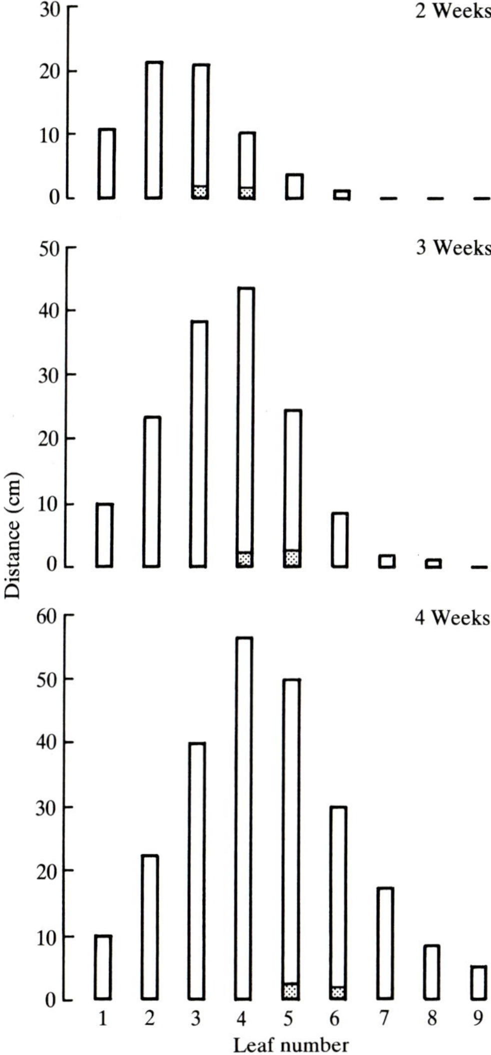

Fig. 1. Regions of young maize leaves capable of proliferation in culture. Transverse sections of leaf cultured by the method of Wernicke & Brettell (1980) on Green & Phillips (1975) medium supplemented with $2{\cdot}0\,\mathrm{mg\,l^{-1}}$ of 2,4-dichlorophenoxyacetic acid. Stippled areas represent the regions of leaves from five to eight replicate 'Seneca 60' maize plants forming proliferating cultures. Leaves were harvested, as indicated, 2-, 3-, and 4-weeks postgermination. Leaf 1 is the developmentally oldest leaf. Distances are measured from the base to the tip of the leaves.

the explants do not grow. A few of the explants from regions near the base of the leaf consistently form proliferating cultures. The presence of this responsive zone, which extends less than 40 mm from the leaf base, depends on the developmental age of the leaf and the age of the plant (Fig. 1). Apparently, during development stable changes occur in specific regions of the leaf which can be detected as differences in the proliferative capacity of the tissues in culture.

The responsive regions have sharp, definite boundaries. This was established by plotting the cumulative incidence of responding explants obtained with replicate plants as a function of distance from the leaf base. Representative plots obtained with leaf 4 from 2-, 3- and 4-week-old plants are shown in Fig. 2. If the probability of response is constant, then the plot should be linear with positive slope (Parzen, 1960). If, on the other hand, no segments respond, then the slope within the region should be zero. The results show that the response is constant within the zone extending ca. 20 mm from the leaf base. The probability of response depends on the developmental age of the plant. The response reaches a maximum at 3

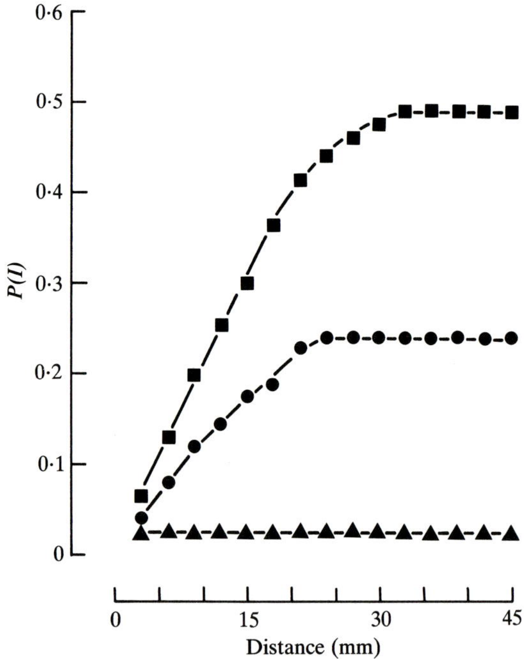

Fig. 2. The cumulative incidence of tissue explants that form proliferating cultures, P(I), as a function of distance from the leaf base. Representative results obtained with leaf 4 from plants 2-(●), 3-(■), and 4-(▲) weeks postgermination. P(I) was calculated from the incidence of transverse sections forming proliferating cultures after 4 weeks obtained with five to eight replicate plants.

weeks and is completely lost by 4 weeks. This leads to the conclusion that there is a window of competence for proliferation in culture, which has a width of two adjacent leaves and a length of ca. 20 mm from the base of the responsive leaves. Figure 1 shows that with increasing age of the plant, this window 'moves' toward pairs of developmentally younger leaves.

In this example, stable states were assayed by measuring the proliferative response of tissues in culture. There are other examples in which stable states established in the plant persist when organs and tissues are serially propagated in culture. Using the appropriate medium, cultured root meristems can continue to form roots and cultured shoot meristems form shoots (Reinhard, 1954; Torrey, 1954; Smith & Murashige, 1970). Tissues from different parts of the same plant can give rise to cultures that continue to exhibit different phenotypes when serially subcultured (Meins, 1985*a*). In a few rare cases the cultures even retain differentiated traits characteristic of the tissue from which they were derived (e.g. Boutenko & Volodarsky, 1968; Nagel & Reinhard, 1975; Khavkin, Misharin & Polikarpochkina, 1979; Raff, Hutchinson, Knox & Clarke, 1979; Shimamoto, Ackermann & Dierks-Ventling, 1983). The significance of these observations lies in the fact that the different phenotypes persist in growing tissues and organs cultured in isolation. This leads to the important conclusion that in some cases, at least, the determined state can persist in populations of dividing cells.

Two classes of mechanisms have been proposed to account for the stability of the determined state (Henshaw *et al.* 1982). The first appears to have its origin in Vöchting's classical dictum: 'the fate of a cell is a function of its position' (Lang, 1965). According to this view, stability is a supracellular phenomenon; it depends upon interactions among cells, gradients of morphogens, etc. The alternative hypothesis is that determination is clonal. Individual cells become committed for specific fates and this commitment is transmitted to daughter cells, i.e. determination results in an alteration in cellular heredity.

Students of plant development have tended to favour supracellular mechanisms for determination (Henshaw *et al.* 1982). One reason for this appears to be the misconception that totipotency and cellular commitment are mutually exclusive. Because determination is relative, cells determined under one set of conditions can give rise to complete plants under another set of conditions (Meins & Binns, 1979). Indeed, direct genetic analysis has shown that certain ciliate protozoa and bacteria with the same genotype can inherit different phenotypes (Beale, 1958; Novick & Weiner, 1957). Observations of this type have led to the useful concept of epigenetic (i.e. developmental) inheritance.

Nanney (1958) has proposed that there is an epigenetic system concerned with the somatic inheritance of developmental states. Thus, alterations in cellular heredity that do not result from permanent genetic changes are known as *epigenetic changes* (Harris, 1964). Epigenetic changes are defined operationally (Meins, 1983): (1) The alteration in cellular heredity is directed, i.e. the changes in phenotype occur at high rates under inductive conditions and at low rates otherwise. (2) Because the genome has not been permanently altered, the range of possible phenotypes is limited and the changes are potentially reversible. (3) Finally, by definition epigenetic changes are not transmitted through meiosis.

The specific test for distinguishing between determination at the supracellular level and cellular inheritance of the determined state is to clone the cells (Heslop-Harrison, 1967). If a phenotype is inherited at the cellular level, it should persist when the cells are cloned. In the case of totipotent cells, this test can be extended to distinguish between epigenetic changes and classical genetic mutations (Meins, 1983). Because mutations revert at very low rates, tissues in plants regenerated from the heritably altered cells should exhibit the variant phenotype and this trait should be transmitted in genetic crosses. On the other hand, epigenetic changes should be lost at some stage of plant regeneration or during meiosis.

Cell-heritable states of cytokinin requirement

Epigenetic variation

Direct evidence for cellular inheritance of the determined state comes from studies of the cytokinin requirement of cultured tobacco tissues. Tissues cultured from explants of leaf lamina require both auxin and a cell-division factor such as cytokinin for continuous growth on an otherwise complete culture medium. In contrast, cultures established from the cortex of the stem, while still auxin requiring, are cytokinin autotrophic (Meins & Lutz, 1979). Thus, the cytokinin requirement of cultured tobacco tissues depends upon their origin in the plant; leaf-derived tissues are cytokinin requiring (C^-) and cortex-derived tissues are cytokinin autotrophic (C^+).

The stability of the C^- and C^+ phenotypes has been assayed by isolating single-cell clones from cultured lines of leaf- and cortex-derived tissues (Meins & Lutz, 1979). Of 79 leaf clones isolated, 90–95% exhibited the C^- phenotype characteristic of the parent tissue line. The remaining 5–10% grew very slowly in the absence of added cytokinin. On the other hand, 99% of the 100 clones of cortex origin exhibited the C^+ phenotype.

Although a few clones appeared to lose their tissue-specific phenotype, the great majority did not. The cortex- and leaf-specific states of cytokinin requirement can be inherited by individual cells.

These results show that alterations in cellular heredity occur during the development of the tobacco plant to give cells determined to express different states of cytokinin requirement in culture. To find out whether these heritable changes are potentially reversible, plants were regenerated from cloned lines of C^- leaf cells and C^+ cortex cells (Meins, 1985*b*). Cortex- and leaf-derived tissues from the regenerated plants were assayed for their capacity to grow on culture medium with and without cytokinin added (Table 1). Regardless of the clone used as a source of the regenerated plants, leaf-derived tissues exhibited the C^- phenotype and cortex-derived tissues exhibited the C^+ phenotype expected for comparable tissues of seed-grown plants.

These results, summarized as the plant regeneration cycle in Fig. 3, show that the leaf- and cortex-specific states of cytokinin requirement are 'reset' at some point during plant regeneration. Resetting is a directed process that occurs rapidly relative to classical mutations (Meins & Binns, 1982) and involves stable changes in heritable phenotypes that arise regularly in development. This provides good evidence that the cell heritable changes that generate the cortex- and leaf-specific states and the resetting of these states are potentially reversible and have an epigenetic basis. Totipotent cells can inherit different states of determination.

Competence for habituation

Tobacco cells can shift from the C^- to the C^+ state in culture by a process known as cytokinin habituation (Meins, 1982). Cultured

Table 1. *Cytokinin requirement of leaf and cortex tissues from plants regenerated from leaf and cortex cells.*

Source of plants	Tissue assayed	Number of plants assayed* C^-	C^+
Leaf clones	Leaf	18	0
	Cortex	0	13
Cortex clones	Leaf	15	0
	Cortex	0	3

* Tissues exhibiting the cytokinin-requiring (C^-) or cytokinin-autotrophic (C^+) phenotype after two successive transfers in culture assayed as described by Meins & Lutz (1979). Data from Meins (1985*b*).

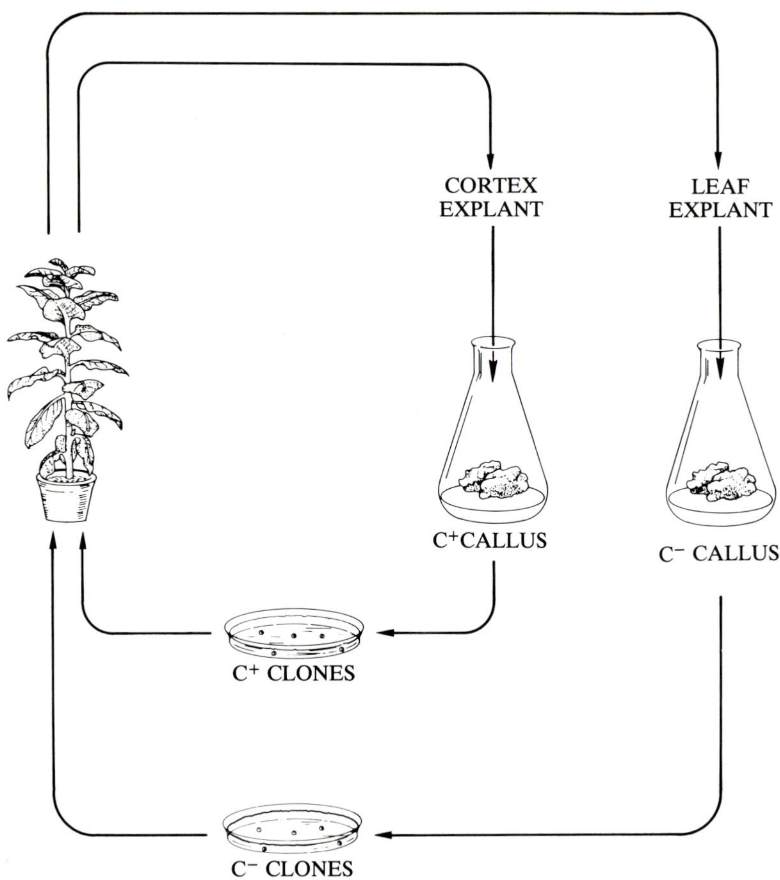

Fig. 3. Summary of plant regeneration experiments with cloned lines of leaf- and cortex-derived tissues. C^-, cytokinin-requiring phenotype; C^+, cytokinin-autotrophic phenotype.

pith-parenchyma tissue, like leaf-derived tissue, exhibits the C^- phenotype. After a variable number of passages in culture, lines of this tissue sometimes become cytokinin habituated. Thereafter, the habituated tissues and clones isolated from these tissues continue to exhibit the C^+ phenotype indicating that the habituated state is inherited by individual cells (Binns & Meins, 1973).

Tobacco cells also vary in their competence for habituation. Primary explants of pith tissue consist of two types of cells: *inducible* C^- cells that habituate at high rates when incubated at 35 °C or in the presence of cytokinins; and *non-inducible* C^- cells which, like C^- cells of leaf origin, do not habituate under inductive conditions (Meins, Lutz & Binns, 1980). Cloning and plant regeneration experiments of the type described in the previous section show that the inducible and non-inducible states, although cell heritable, are not permanent. They are regularly reset during the plant regeneration process to yield cells that exhibit the competence observed with comparable cell types from seed-grown plants (Meins & Lutz, 1980*a*; Meins & Foster, 1985). Therefore, habituation as well as competence for habituation result from epigenetic changes.

Mechanisms for epigenetic changes

Positive feedback circuits

Two types of mechanisms have been proposed to account for inheritance of the C^+ phenotype (Meins, 1982): self-perpetuating regulatory circuits and conservative genetic modifications. The positive-feedback model for habituation, described in detail elsewhere (Meins & Binns, 1978) is based on the notion that certain regulatory circuits can exhibit alternative, self-perpetuating states (Delbrück, 1949). This model specifies that cell-division factors such as the cytokinins induce their own synthesis. Provided there is a mechanism to prevent the intracellular cytokinin concentration from increasing indefinitely, the metabolic pathway can exist in two states, one in which the cytokinin is not produced; the other in which cytokinin is produced and reaches some steady-state concentration. According to this hypothesis, cells competent to habituate are poised to produce cytokinin, but only do so when the cytokinin concentration exceeds a critical threshold. If the kinetic properties of this system do not change when cells divide, the cytokinin-producing state can be transmitted to daughter cells. Thus, two populations of cells with the same genotype could express different cytokinin requirements depending upon their history.

The evidence for the positive-feedback hypothesis is indirect. First, cytokinins induce cytokinin habituation of primary explants of tobacco pith tissue. The dose–response curve for this effect exhibits a sharp threshold as would be expected for an autocatalytic system (Meins & Lutz, 1980*b*). Second, C^+ cells return to the C^- state when incubated under conditions that appear to block cytokinin biosynthesis. Cloned lines of C^+ pith cells exhibit the C^- phenotype when incubated at 16 °C or at the standard temperature, 25 °C, on media containing reduced levels of auxin (Meins & Binns, 1978; Binns, 1979). If cells are incubated under the non-permissive conditions on concentrations of cytokinin above the threshold required for habituation, then the cells exhibit the C^+ phenotype when returned to permissive conditions (Meins & Binns, 1978). On the other hand, cells incubated under non-permissive conditions on concentrations of cytokinin lower than the threshold exhibit the C^- phenotype when returned to permissive conditions. Nevertheless, these cells are still able to habituate when incubated on cytokinin-containing medium. Apparently, interruption of the putative positive-feedback loop is sufficient to induce cells to shift from the C^+ to the C^- state.

Direct physiological evidence for this model is lacking. Studies with labelled precursors show that C^+ tissues of tobacco can produce a variety of cytokinins (Einset & Skoog, 1973; Nishinari & Syono, 1980; Burrows & Fuell, 1981). What is unclear is the relationship between capacity for cytokinin autotrophic growth and cytokinin content. There are reports that cytokinins are present in C^+ but not in C^- tissues (Dyson & Hall, 1972; Einset & Skoog, 1973) and other reports that cytokinins are not detectable in either cell type (Yokota & Takahashi, 1981; Hansen, Meins & Milani, 1985). Interpretation of this data is further complicated by the observation that auxin added in the medium to support growth can also block cytokinin accumulation (Hansen *et al.* 1985). The crucial test of the positive-feedback hypothesis is to demonstrate that exogenous cytokinin induces cells to produce cytokinin. This test is in progress.

Genetic modifications

Feedback models provide a plausible explanation for 'poised' developmental changes such as cytokinin habituation in which the C^- state appears to be metastable. There is, at present, no evidence that this type of mechanism is involved in stabilizing the C^+ cortex and C^- leaf states. Hints that this stabilization has a genetic basis have come from attempts to generate C^+ sublines from cloned lines of C^- leaf and pith cells that do not normally habituate in culture. By subculturing the C^- lines successively on media containing 10% the cytokinin concentration used in the previous transfer, C^+ lines were obtained after only two to three subculture cycles (Meins & Foster, 1985; Meins, 1985*b*). Leaf tissue of plants regenerated from cloned lines of the C^+ cells always exhibited the C^+ phenotype in culture, i.e. the C^+ phenotype was not reset during the plant regeneration process. In the case of leaf-derived C^+ cells, this *habituated leaf* trait, designated Hl–2 to distinguish it from a similar phenotype identified earlier (Meins, Foster & Lutz, 1983), segregated in breeding tests in the manner expected for a single, dominant, Mendelian factor (Meins, 1985*b*).

The discovery of the Hl–2 trait was of particular interest because it showed that there are at least two forms of cytokinin habituation: an epigenetic form, which is reset during plant regeneration; and, a genetic form, which involves alterations of a specific gene. The important question that arises is whether or not genetic habituation is a directed process. The key test is to measure the rate of heritable change on a per cell generation basis. If a change is directed, it should occur at very high rates under inductive conditions and at very low rates otherwise. On the other hand, mutations should occur at very low rates independent of the culture conditions.

Unfortunately, the conversion of individual cells cannot be measured directly because the capacity of tissues for proliferation is the criterion used to distinguish the C^+ and C^- phenotypes. The indirect approach we used, which is described in detail elsewhere (Meins, 1975; Meins, 1985*b*), is borrowed from population biologists. The basic idea is that for an exponentially growing population of cells, the frequency of C^+ cells (q) as a function of time depends on three factors: (1) the doubling constants of C^- and C^+ cells (α and β respectively); (2) the rates of conversion of C^- cells to C^+ cells (μ) and C^+ to C^- cells (v); and (3) the frequency of C^+ cells at the start of the experiment. By growing tissues on a medium that favours the proliferation of C^- cells, the population should eventually reach an equilibrium in which the rates of phenotypic conversion and the rates of proliferation are balanced. At equilibrium, the minimum rate of conversion of C^- cells to C^+, μ_{min}, is related to the equilibrium frequency of C^+ cells, $\hat{q}$, by the expression (Meins, 1985*b*):

$$\mu_{min} = (1 - \frac{\beta}{\alpha})\hat{q}$$

The reason this equation provides a minimum estimate of rate is that it was derived using the simplifying assumption that C^+ cells do not revert to C^- cells, i.e. $v = 0$.

Because the cloning efficiencies of C^+ and C^- cells are similar (Meins & Binns, 1977) it was possible to obtain estimates of q and to verify that population equilibrium is reached. The estimates obtained for the minimum rate of conversion of C^- cells to C^+ cells at equilibrium in three different tissue lines was $5{\cdot}1 \pm 1{\cdot}0 \times 10^{-3}$ conversions per cell generation (Meins, 1985*b*). Although it has yet to be established that every C^+ cell has undergone a genetic alteration at the same gene, the data suggest that the *H1–2* gene can change state at rates that are 100 to 1000 times faster than the rate of somatic mutation (Sand, Sparrow & Smith, 1960; Carlson, 1974). The fact that different states of this gene persist in regenerated plants and are inherited in crosses according to well-established laws of heredity leads to the conclusion that the *H1–2* gene is unstable in cultured cells but fixed in cells of the plant.

Conclusions

The results presented here provide strong evidence that at least some states of determination in plants can be inherited by individual cells. Moreover, these states, although extremely stable for many cell generations, are not permanent; determination of the C^+ and C^- phenotypes is a reversible process. Studies with chimaeric plants have shown that there are cell lineages in ontogeny (Coe & Neuffer, 1978; Stewart, 1978), as predicted by the clonal hypothesis for determination. Nevertheless, this lineage is not as strict as in certain animals where individual differentiated cells always have the same clonal origin (Stent, 1985). Depending upon the organ and plant species, there is some flexibility as to which cell gives rise to a particular structure (Stewart, 1978). Therefore, it appears that both cellular heredity and supracellular mechanisms have a role in stabilizing the determined state in plant development.

There are hints that cellular heredity and supracellular interactions may, in some cases, have the same underlying mechanism. In the case of cytokinin habituation, there is evidence that the C^+ state is maintained by a positive-feedback loop in which cytokinins induce their own synthesis. There is also evidence for autocatalytic production of other plant-growth regulators, *viz.*, auxin (Cheng, 1972; Nishinari & Yamaki, 1976), ethylene (Kende & Baumgartner, 1974), and gibberellins (Atzorn & Weiler, 1983) suggesting that positive-feedback regulation is a general phenomenon.

This regulation may have a causal role in morphogenesis. As pointed out by Lang (1965), several developmental processes in plants have 'infectious' qualities, i.e. cells exhibiting a particular phenotype induce the same phenotype in other cells. Gersani & Sachs (1984) have proposed that the progressive differentiation of vascular tissue has as its basis a positive-feedback relationship in which auxin induces a selfreinforcing polar transport of auxin. Reaction–diffusion models incorporating diffusable morphogens with autocatalytic properties can generate stable, periodic structures reminiscent of those found in plants (Meinhardt, 1976, 1982). Thus, it is plausible to consider that gradients of growth regulators, which are known to act as morphogens, trigger competent cells to produce the regulators. This in turn would perturb the gradient and trigger cell proliferation and differentiation in a specific spatial pattern.

Studies of cytokinin habituation also bear on the fundamental question of whether determination results from genetic changes. Although the reversible nature of epigenetic changes excludes classical somatic mutation, it does not necessarily exclude certain conservative forms of genetic change such as gene amplification and transposition of genetic elements which are known to occur in plants (Buiatti, 1977; Freeling, 1984). Alternatively the genetic material could be chemically modified. It is known that DNA methylation results in reversible, cell-heritable changes in the expression of T-DNA genes by crown-gall transformed cells (Hepburn, Clarke, Pearson & White, 1983; Amasino, Powell & Gordon, 1984). Nevertheless, it has not been demonstrated that these modifications are directed or that they have a causal role in determination.

Tobacco leaf cells bearing the *H1–2* allele mimic cortex cells in their cytokinin phenotype suggesting that epigenetic changes affect expression of the *H1–2* gene or that this gene modifies the resetting of epigenetic states of cytokinin requirement. The evidence presented here suggests that the *H1–2* gene can change state at the same high rates as epigenetic changes such as the resetting of the leaf and cortex states, cytokinin habituation of pith cells, and organ initiation in culture (Meins & Binns, 1982). Our working hypothesis is that variation in the *H1–2* gene involves some type of non-classical genetic modification. One approach for testing this hypothesis is to identify protein markers specific for the C^+ state, which can be used to isolate messenger RNAs and ultimately the genes involved. Because the C^+ phenotype is a selectable marker, we are also exploring the possibility of isolating the *H1–2* gene by methods analogous to those used to isolate mammalian oncogenes (Goldfarb, Shimizu, Perucho & Wigler, 1982).

References

Amasino, R. M., Powell, A. L. G. & Gordon, M. P. (1984). Changes in T-DNA methylation and expression are associated with phenotypic variation and plant regeneration in a crown gall tumor line. *Mol. gen. Genet.* **197**, 437–446.

Atzorn, R. & Weiler, E. W. (1983). The role of endogenous gibberellins in the formation of α-amylase by aleurone layers of germinating barley caryopses. *Planta* **159**, 289–299.

Balinsky, B. I. (1965). *An Introduction to Embryology*, 2nd ed. Philadelphia and London: W. B. Saunders.

Beale, G. H. (1958). The role of the cytoplasm in antigen determination in *Paramecium aurelia*. *Proc. R. Soc.* B. **148**, 308–314.

Binns, A. N. (1979). Habituation of tobacco pith cells for factors promoting cell division. Ph.D. Dissertation, Princeton University, Princeton, NJ. USA.

Binns, A. & Meins, F., Jr. (1973). Habituation of tobacco pith cells for factors promoting cell division is heritable and potentially reversible. *Proc. natn. Acad. Sci. U.S.A.* **70**, 2660–2662.

Boutenko, R. G. & Volodarsky, A. D. (1968). Analyse immunochimique de la differentiation cellulaire dans les cultures de tissues de tabac. *Physiol. Vég.* **6**, 299–309.

Buiatti, M. (1977). DNA amplification and tissue cultures. In *Plant Cell, Tissue, and Organ Culture* (ed. J. Reinert & Y. P. S. Bajaj), pp. 358–372. Berlin–Heidelberg–New York: Springer-Verlag.

Burrows, W. J. & Fuell, K. J. (1981). Cytokinin biosynthesis in cytokinin-autonomous and bacteria-transformed tobacco callus tissue. In *Metabolism and Molecular Activities of Cytokinins* (ed. J. Guern & C. Péaud-Lenoël), pp. 44–55. Berlin: Springer-Verlag.

CARLSON, P. S. (1974). Mitotic crossing-over in a higher plant. *Genet. Res.* **24**, 109–112.

CHAILAKHYAN, M. KH., AKSENOVA, N. P., KONSTANTINOVA, T. N. & T. V. BAVRINA (1975). The callus model of plant flowering. *Proc. R. Soc. Lond.* B. **190**, 333–340.

CHENG, T.-Y. (1972). Induction of indole acetic acid synthetases in tobacco pith explants. *Pl. Physiol.* **50**, 723–727.

COE, E. H., JR. & NEUFFER, M. G. (1978). Embryo cells and their destinies in the corn plant. *Symp. Soc. devl Biol.* **36**, 112–129.

DELBRÜCK, M. (1949). In the discussion following a paper by T. M. Sonneborn & G. H. Beale. *Colloq. Int. C.N.R.S.* **7**, 25.

DYSON, W. H. & HALL, R. H. (1972). N^6-(Δ^2-Isopentenyl) adenosine: its occurrence as a free nucleoside in an autonomous strain of tobacco tissue. *Pl. Physiol.* **59**, 45–47.

EINSET, J. W. & SKOOG, F. (1973). Biosynthesis of cytokinins in cytokinin-autotrophic tobacco callus. *Proc. natn. Acad. Sci. U.S.A.* **70**, 658–660.

FREELING, M. (1984). Plant transposable elements and insertion sequences. *A. Rev. Pl. Physiol.* **35**, 277–298.

GERSANI, M. & SACHS, T. (1984). Polarity reorientation in beans expressed by vascular differentiation and polar auxin transport. *Differentiation* **25**, 205–208.

GOLDFARB, M., SHIMIZU, K., PERUCHO, M. & WIGLER, M. (1982). Isolation and preliminary characterization of a human transforming gene from T44 bladder carcinoma cells. *Nature* **296**, 404–409.

GREEN, C. E. & PHILLIPS, R. L. (1975). Plant regeneration from tissue cultures of maize. *Crop Sci.* **15**, 417–421.

HANSEN, C. E., MEINS, F., JR. & MILANI, A. (1985). Clonal and physiological variation in the cytokinin content of tobacco-cell lines differing in cytokinin requirement and capacity for neoplastic growth. *Differentiation* **29**, 1–6.

HARRIS, M. (1964). *Cell Culture and Somatic Variation.* New York: Holt, Rinehart and Winston.

HENSHAW, G. G., O'HARA, J. F. & WEBB, K. J. (1982). Morphogenetic studies in plant tissue cultures. In *Differentiation In Vitro* (ed. M. M. Yeoman & D. E. S. Truman), pp. 231–251. Cambridge: Cambridge University Press.

HEPBURN, A. G., CLARKE, L. E., PEARSON, L. & WHITE, J. (1983). The role of cytosine methylation in the control of nopaline synthase gene expression in a plant tumor. *J. molec. appl. Genet.* **2**, 315–329.

HESLOP-HARRISON, J. (1967). Differentiation. *A. Rev. Pl. Physiol.* **18**, 325–348.

KENDE, H. & BAUMGARTNER, B. (1974). Regulation of ageing in flowers of *Ipomoea tricolor* by ethylene. *Planta* **116**, 279–289.

KHAVKIN, E. E., MISHARIN, S. I. & POLIKARPOCHKINA, R. T. (1979). Identical embryonal proteins in intact and isolated tissues of maize (*Zea Mays* L.). *Planta* **145**, 245–251.

LANG, A. (1965). Progressiveness and contagiousness in plant differentiation and development. In *Encyclopedia of Plant Physiology* vol. 15, part 1 (ed. W. Ruhland), pp. 409–423. Berlin: Springer-Verlag.

MCDANIEL, C. N. (1978). Determination for growth pattern in axillary buds of *Nicotiana tabacum* L. *Devl Biol.* **66**, 250–255.

MEINHARDT, H. (1976). Morphogenesis of lines and nets. *Differentiation* **6**, 117–123.

MEINHARDT, H. (1982). Generation of structures in a developing organism. *Symp. Soc. devl Biol.* **40**, 439–461.

MEINS, F., JR. (1975). Cell division and the determination phase of cytodifferentiation in plants. In *Cell Cycle and Cell Differentiation* (ed. J. Reinert & H. Holtzer), pp. 151–175. Berlin–Heidelberg–New York: Springer.

MEINS, F., JR. (1982). Habituation of cultured plant cells. In *Molecular Biology of Plant Tumors* (ed. J. Schell & G. Kahl), pp. 3–31. New York: Academic Press.

MEINS, F., JR. (1983). Heritable variation in plant cell culture. *A. Rev. Pl. Physiol.* **34**, 327–346.

MEINS, F., JR. (1985*a*). Determination and morphogenetic competence in plant tissue culture. In *Plant Cell Culture Technology* (ed. M. M. Yeoman). Oxford: Blackwell Scientific Publications. (In press).

MEINS, F., JR. (1985*b*). Cell heritable changes during development. *UCLA Symp. molec. Cell Biol.* **35**, 45–59.

MEINS, F., JR. & BINNS, A. N. (1977). Epigenetic variation of cultured somatic cells: Evidence for gradual changes in the requirement for factors promoting cell division. *Proc. natn. Acad. Sci. U.S.A.* **74**, 2928–2932.

MEINS, F., JR. & BINNS, A. N. (1978). Epigenetic clonal variation in the requirement of plant cells for cytokinins. *Symp. Soc. devl Biol.* **36**, 185–201.

MEINS, F., JR., & BINNS, A. N. (1979). Cell determination in plant development. *Biosci.* **29**, 221–225.

MEINS, F., JR. & BINNS, A. N. (1982). Rapid reversion of cell-division-factor habituated cells in culture. *Differentiation* **23**, 10–12.

MEINS, F., JR. & FOSTER, R. (1985). Reversible, cell-heritable changes during the development of tobacco pith tissues. *Devl Biol.* **108**, 1–5.

MEINS, F., JR., FOSTER, R. & LUTZ, J. D. (1983). Evidence for a Mendelian factor controlling the cytokinin requirement of cultured tobacco cells. *Devl Genet.* **4**, 129–141.

MEINS, F., JR. & LUTZ, J. (1979). Tissue-specific variation in the cytokinin habituation of cultured tobacco cells. *Differentiation* **15**, 1–6.

MEINS, F., JR. & LUTZ, J. (1980*a*). Epigenetic changes in tobacco cell cultures: Studies of cytokinin habituation. In *Genetic Improvement of Crops: Emergent Techniques* (ed. I. Rubenstein, B. Gengenbach, R. L. Phillips & C. E. Green), pp. 220–236. Minneapolis: University of Minnesota Press.

MEINS, F., JR. & LUTZ, J. (1980*b*). The induction of cytokinin habituation in primary pith explants of tobacco. *Planta* **149**, 402–407.

MEINS, F., JR., LUTZ, J. & BINNS, A. N. (1980). Variation in the competence of tobacco pith cells for cytokinin habituation in culture. *Differentiation* **16**, 71–75.

NAGEL, M. & REINHARD, E. (1975). Das ätherische öl der Calluskulturen von *Ruta graveolens* L. I. Die Zusammensetzung des Oeles. *Planta Med.* **27**, 151–158.

NANNEY, D. L. (1958). Epigenetic control systems. *Proc. natn. Acad. Sci. U.S.A.* **44**, 712–717.

NISHINARI, N. & SYONO, K. (1980). Cell-free biosynthesis of cytokinins in cultured tobacco cells. *Z. Pflanzenphysiol.* **99**, 383–392.

NISHINARI, N. & YAMAKI, T. (1976). Relationship between cell division and endogenous auxin in synchronously cultured tobacco cells. *Bot. Mag., Tokyo* **89**, 73–81.

NOVICK, A. & WEINER, M. (1957). Enzyme induction as an all-or-none phenomenon. *Proc. natn. Acad. Sci. U.S.A.* **44**, 712–717.

OEHLKERS, F. (1955). Blattstecklinge als Indikatoren für blütenbildende Substanzen. *Z. Naturforsch.* **10**, 158–160.

OEHLKERS, F. (1956). Veränderungen in der Blühbereitschaft vernalisierter Cotyledonen von *Streptocarpus*, kenntlich gemacht durch Blattstecklinge. *Z. Naturforsch.* **11**, 471–480.

PARZEN, E. (1960). *Modern Probability Theory and its Applications*. New York: John Wiley.

RAFF, J. W., HUTCHINSON, J. F., KNOX, R. B. & CLARKE, A. E. (1979). Cell recognition: antigen determination of plant organs and their cultured callus cells. *Differentiation* **12**, 179–186.

REINHARD, E. (1954). Beobachtungen an *in vitro* kultivierten Geweben aus dem Vegetationskegel der *Pisum*-Wurzel. *Z. Bot.* **42**, 353–376.

SAND, S. A., SPARROW, A. H. & SMITH, H. H. (1960). Chronic gamma irradiation effects on the mutable V and stable R loci in clones of *Nicotiana*. *Genetics* **45**, 289–308.

SHIMAMOTO, K., ACKERMANN, M. & DIERKS-VENTLING, C. (1983). Expression of zein in long term endosperm cultures of maize. *Pl. Physiol.* **73**, 915–920.

SKOOG, F. & MILLER, C. O. (1957). Chemical regulation of growth and organ formation in plant tissues cultivated *in vitro*. In *The Biological Action of Growth Substances* (11th Symposium of the Society for Experimental Biology) (ed. H.K. Porter), pp. 118–131. Cambridge: Cambridge University Press.

SMITH, R. H. & MURASHIGE, T. (1970). *In vitro* development of the isolated shoot apical meristem of angiosperm. *Am. J. Bot.* **57**, 562–568.

SPEMANN, H. (1938). *Embryonic Development and Induction.* New Haven: Yale University.

STENT, G. S. (1985). The role of cell lineage in development. *Phil. Trans. R. Soc.* B. (In press.)

STEWART, R. N. (1978). Ontogeny of the primary body in chimeral forms of higher plants. *Symp. Soc. devl Biol.* **36**, 131–160.

TORREY, J. G. (1954). The role of vitamins and micronutrient elements in the nutrition of the apical meristem of pea roots. *Pl. Physiol.* **29**, 279–287.

VASIL, V. & HILDEBRANDT, A. C. (1965). Differentiation of tobacco plants from single, isolated cells in microculture. *Science* **150**, 889–892.

WAREING, P. F. (1978). Determination and related aspects of plant development. In *The Molecular Biology of Plant Development* (ed. H. Smith & D. Grierson), pp. 517–541. Oxford: Blackwells Scientific Publications.

WERNICKE, W. & BRETTELL, R. (1980). Somatic embryogenesis from *Sorghum bicolor* leaves. *Nature* **287**, 138–139.

YOKOTA, T. & TAKAHASHI, N. (1981). Hormonal autonomy of tobacco cells. *Int. Assoc. Pl. Tissue Cult. Newsletter* **34**, 2–4.

PLASTICITY IN MORPHOGENETIC EXPRESSION IN PLANT

KIEM TRAN THANH VAN

Institut de Physiologie Végétale, C.N.R.S., 91190 Gif sur Yvette, France

Summary

This article discusses the plasticity of morphogenetic programmes in plants. It outlines the numerous ways in which the flowering programme can be accelerated or modified into partial flower formation and describes the differentiation of naked ovules on anthers in intact plants. The generation of embryos and flowers from cultured cells is then described and some of the properties of hypohaploids outlined. It is concluded that *in vitro* culture provides a useful facility for manipulating plant development and that the interaction between the nucleus and the cytoplasm may exemplify and explain the process of developmental plasticity.

Introduction

The plant kingdom as compared to the animal kingdom may be characterized by a greater capacity to survive extreme atmospheric conditions and by a longer life cycle. Lack of mobility coupled with a long life cycle necessitates that poor growth conditions must be tolerated rather than avoided. Both physiological and morphological adaptations occur in response to stressful conditions. The processes of photosynthesis and respiration can adapt, and this is frequently coupled with changes in stem and leaf morphology. In addition most plants can regenerate lost organs (roots, buds or even flowers) and virtually all plant tissues (excepting vascular tissue or hairs) can be induced to divide and subsequently form callus. This apparent physiological, morphological and regenerative plasticity is accompanied by stability in other characters of development. In this short paper some of the plasticity and stability of morphogenetic programmes are described both *in vivo* (or *in situ* on the entire plant) and *in vitro* (on excised organs or cultured tissues).

Herbaceous plants

In vivo

A classical illustration of the plasticity of plant development is its alternative but sequential cycles of development: the juvenile, vegetative and reproductive phases. Such sequential development as well as the characteristic morphology of the species, is normally tightly programmed under precisely specified environmental conditions. However, a shift in light (in some instances, a very brief duration of red and, or, far-red light), temperature and, or, nutritional regime is sufficient to change the developmental programme. In some ornamental species such as *Forsythia* or *Rhododendron*, an exclusive programme of leaf production can be shifted into an exclusive programme of flower production.

Vegetative/reproductive changes

By careful adjustment of temperature and nutritional regimes, several thousand flowers instead of an average of 50 flowers per plant can be produced by *Geum urbanum* (Tran Thanh Van, 1965; Tran Thanh Van, 1980; Tran Thanh Van, 1985). Thus, not only the morphogenetic pattern can be changed but also the amplitude of the response. By changing the mineral nutrients combined with a gibberellic acid supply, the terminal bud of a perennial rosette plant can be induced to elongate and to flower (Tran Thanh Van, 1965; Tran Thanh Van, 1985). Thus a genetically determined polycarpic habit and a rosette structure can be experimentally changed into a monocarpic and elongated plant. Considering the relatively simple nature of the trigger, the response is remarkable.

Miniaturization of floral meristems in Geum urbanum

Classically it was thought that flower induction and formation is a very stable programme which often occurs as soon as plants experience stress conditions. One good example is the limited size of some desert plants which flower very precociously – after prompt germination following sudden rain; the flowers of such plants are frequently normal in size and shape. However the following experiments suggest that the flower programme itself can be altered and reduced to its minimal expression, the male programme, when a threshold of cell number is not reached. Flowers formed on a floral stalk of *Geum urbanum* were removed at early stages. The floral meristems which subsequently developed, after a certain number of flower-pruning cycles, decreased in size and exhibited the following different types of structures:

(a) a flower which developed after the first verticille of petaloid sepals
(b) a highly altered flower reduced to one filament with an anther at the axil of one stipule-like organ
(c) a small, vegetative, juvenile rosette of leaves with a terminal flower
(d) a vegetative rosette with adventitious roots
(e) a plantlet with a cotyledon-like structure.

The results obtained could be interpreted as the redirection of the genetic programme following intensive wounding. What could be the earliest signal released in the cell during and after wounding? According to the literature, there are several candidates; DNA amplification, ionic rearrangement and release of oligosaccharides from cell walls or physicochemical changes in membrane structure and properties. Any of these could account for the changes in the network of correlations previously found in intact plants.

Control of flower morphology and function by nuclear/cytoplasmic interaction: controlled shifts in cell competence

Differentiation of naked ovules on anthers

Several reciprocal backcrosses between *Nicotiana plumbaginifolia* and *N. tabacum* resulted in male-sterile hybrids (Tran Thanh Van & Trinh, 1982). Their flowers had split petals and stigmatoid anthers. If the female partner was *N. plumbaginifolia*, the male-sterile hybrids exhibited a new developmental pattern: naked ovules were formed at the plane of pollen grains on the filament of the stigmatoid anthers (Fig. 1). Callose formation occurring prior to meiotic division and normally observed in ovarian ovules was also detected (Vergne, Trinh & Tran Thanh Van, 1985).

These naked ovules constitute a new genetic expression of this specific hybrid. Since the style and stigma barriers were absent, both *in vitro* and *in vivo* pollinations have been attempted in order to cross with other species, permitting the creation of new genotypes which would otherwise not be possible.

A new potential exhibited by these naked ovules is their ability to form haploid embryos; the intraovarian ovules of the normal flower, do not form embryos when excised and cultured under the same conditions. This ovule differentiation suggests that male and female gamete differentiation can originate from a common base and that sex differentiation is specified at a later, more terminal, stage.

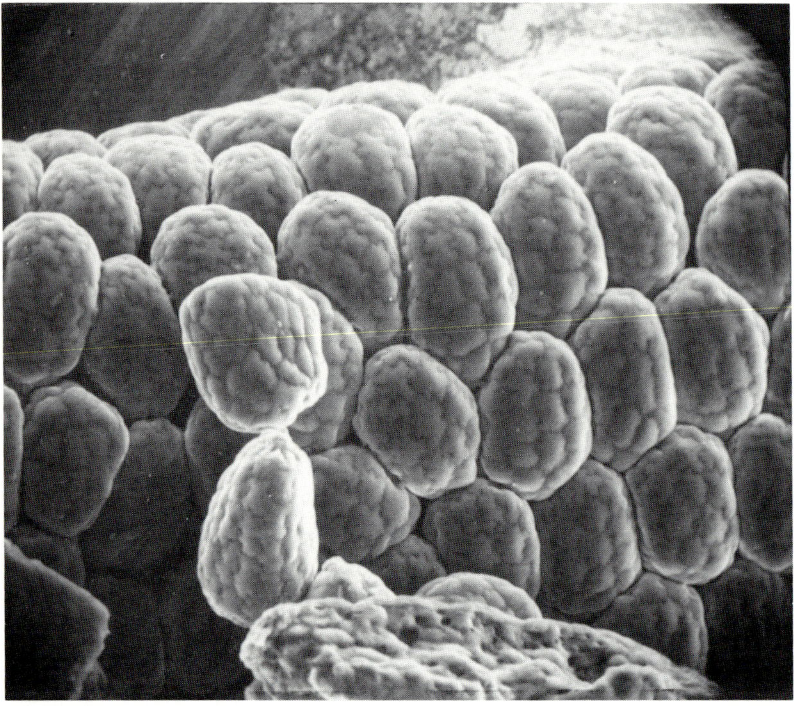

Fig. 1. Naked ovules on the stamen of a backcross *Nicotiana plumbaginifolia* × *Nicotiana tabacum*.

Differentiation of flowers on leaf blades and of anthers on the edge of petals

The seventh backcross between two cultivars of *Nicotiana* (rustica and mammoth) resulted in a hybrid which had lost its ability to form flowers. However, a change in the temperature regime to 22°/17° (day/night alternation) induced flowering in this hybrid; half of a leaf blade was modified into a flower. The leaf, in this case a normal part of the vegetative programme, has now become part of the reproductive programme. In some *Petunia* mutants, anthers containing pollen grains were formed on the petals.

In vitro

In vitro systems exhibit an even greater plasticity in their morphogenetic expression and their metabolic pathways.

Embryo formation from embryogenetic tissue, from somatic cells and from male and female gametophytes

Cells isolated from carrot callus can be induced to form somatic embryos (Steward, 1958). Since this first discovery, which led to the idea of cell totipotency, somatic embryos have been obtained from several sources of plant materials. They have been induced to form on roots, on leaves (Sondalh & Sharp, 1977), or from somatic cells isolated from callus or from protoplasts. In several species, either pollen grains or ovules were induced to form androgenetic or gynogenetic embryos respectively. In *Psophocarpus tetragonolobus* L., cultured anthers and unfertilized ovules grown *in vitro*, developed embryos which were mixoploids, with both haploid and diploid cells (Trinh, Lie-Shrick & Tran Thanh Van, 1985). Embryo formation from gametophytes can sometimes occur *in vivo*, leading to the spontaneous formation of a small percentage of haploid embryos.

In *Brassica napus*, somatic embryos can form a second generation of embryos from the epidermal cells of the original embryo (Loh & Ingram, 1982). In *Oryza sativa*, embryos have been formed from pollen grains after a callus phase. In Palm trees and in other monocotyledons, embryos have been formed directly from the basal part of young leaf primordia (Reynolds & Murashige, 1979). Most workers report that when embryo formation occurs no other morphogenetic programme was obtained except callus. In certain defined families the somatic embryo programme can be expressed either from a previous embryo (reiteration of the same programme) or alternatively from somatic cells. Callus formation and embryo formation seem to have certain parts of a common route and may be considered as relatively simple genetic programmes.

Since an embryo is a potential adult organism, this easy reiteration of the embryo programme recalls the suggested totipotency of plant cells. To be more precise, however, one can state that carrot cells are embryo-potent rather than totipotent. But this may not be strictly applicable to many other plants for two reasons. Firstly, not all plant species have shown the potential to produce all types of morphogenetic patterns *in vitro*. There are genetic and physicochemical barriers which have yet to be removed before competence for a certain number of morphogenetic programmes can be demonstrated. Secondly, once these barriers are overcome, by hybridization or other physiological preparation of the donor plants, not all cells are equally competent for *in vitro* differentiation processes. In the case of *Nicotiana tabacum*, generally the most favourable species for androgenesis, only a certain percentage of the population of pollen grains are competent for embryogenesis, and within a competent pollen only the vegetative cell is embryogenetic. Furthermore, this competence depends upon the environmental conditions applied to the donor plant and upon its genotype.

In *N. plumbaginifolia*, only pollen grains resulting from an *in vitro*-induced meiosis of diploid pollen mother cells can give rise to embryos (30% compared to 1% for *in vivo* meiosis). We have shown that the frequency of chromosome pairing in haploid cells is significantly higher *in vitro* than *in vivo* (Tran Thanh Van & Trinh, 1978). The meiotic events in diploid cells also differ: a greater number of nucleoli are observed *in vitro* indicating a possible derepression in the control of nucleolar organization (El-Antri, Trinh, Tran Thanh Van & Zickler, unpublished results).

Hypohaploidization

One of the important consequences of differences in the embryogenetic potential of *in vitro* pollen grains formed from haploid pollen mother cells is the formation of hypohaploid plants with an aneuploid chromosomal number lower than the haploid number (*N. plumbaginifolia*, N = 10). The plasticity here is expressed in terms of variation in flower shape (absence of petal and of carpel wall, naked ovarian ovules), and of the ability of the naked ovules to form embryos with an even more reduced chromosome number (five chromosomes). Several genotypes of hypohaploids do not synthesize chlorophyll or certain secondary products such as nicotine. In others, nicotine is synthesized in the leaves. Even with such a reduced genome, however, several functions such as flowering, photosynthesis (in certain genotypes), and phytochrome synthesis were all maintained in a certain number of genotypes. In *N. tabacum* the hypohaploids were reminiscent of only one of the parental genotypes, namely *N. sylvestris*. These new genotypes are suitable material for the study of chromosome rearrangements and the regulation and expression of a genome which is reduced to a level lower than the haploid level.

Hypohaploidization, or even simple androgenesis from pollen grains for species reluctant to androgenesis, is possible if the gametophytes are differentiated *in vitro*. For species in which flower differentiation *in vitro* raises problems, we suggest that either flower primordia could be cultured *in vitro* or they can be supplied *in situ* with growth substances. Wheat flower primordia have been successfully cultured *in vitro* and meiosis demonstrated to occur for example (Tran Thanh Van, 1981; Tran Thanh Van & Purushotam, unpublished results).

Differentiation of floral shoots and/or direct differentiation of flowers

These programmes include a very sophisticated one, namely the meiotic process. Generally, vegetative buds which become precociously floral in the culture flask (i.e. *in vitro* floral shoot formation) have been recorded in the literature as *in vitro* flowers. In fact, there are only two cases known of direct flower formation:

(1) from thin layer of epidermal and subepidermal cells of flowering *N. tabacum* plants (Tran Thanh Van, 1973; Tran Thanh Van, 1981).

(2) from cotyledon and from mature leaves of vegetative plant of *Torenia* (Tran Thanh Van, 1980).

In the first case, the donor plant must have reached a precise stage of flowering in order that cultured thin cell layers from the donor can express *in vitro* flower formation. The differentiation of flowers under these conditions could be considered an inevitable response expressed by the 'induced' tissues of the flowering donor. But, from this same 'floral-induced' tissue, other morphological patterns can also be generated; roots, vegetative buds and callus can all be formed. Thus, the same layer of cytologically highly differentiated cells can be 'reprogrammed' into almost all the morphogenetic patterns of an adult plant excepting embryos. This last programme has only been obtained on thin cell layers of specific *Nicotiana* hybrids (Tran Thanh Van, 1981).

In *Torenia*, both vegetative and juvenile tissues can form flowers. This would indicate that the floral message (i.e. florigen), if it exists cannot only be synthesized by flowering tissues. In addition, vegetative buds, roots, callus or unicellular hairs can all be differentiated from cotyledons thus illustrating the multipotentiality of epidermal cells.

Woody plants

The plasticity which is exhibited by herbaceous plants does not seem to be widespread amongst woody species. Successful attempts have been made to regenerate young buds from mature organs of an 85-year-old tree of *Pseudotsuga* (Tran Thanh Van & Trinh, 1979; Tran Thanh Van, Trinh & Yilmaz, 1985). A thin layer of cortical cells excised from the stem, formed actively growing callus from which later organogenetic potentials could be revealed. *In vitro* cone development with fertile male and female gametophytes was obtained from vegetative buds of sprouts developed at the base of the stem of adult *Sequoia sempervirens* (Tran Thanh Van, Trinh & Yilmaz, 1985). Suspension cell cultures were observed to produce embryos in several woody species. These results demonstrate that plasticity can be revealed in some woody species.

Discussion and Conclusion

Plasticity is observed at the cell level when a protoplast rebuilds its cell wall after enzymatic hydrolysis. It also is observed when certain metabolites normally synthesized by the entire plant are also made by isolated cells maintained in suspension culture. The regeneration capacity of plant cells has made them suitable for genetic manipulation as several generations can be obtained rapidly for the screening of the expression of the inserted gene after a genetic transformation. The variability of regenerates may result from plasticity of the cytoplasm/genome interaction. The loss or gain of one selected trait could result from the reorganization of this network of interactions.

Although flexible, plasticity in plants must overcome genetic barriers to be expressed. *In vivo*, the composition and structure of cell wall and of cytoskeleton as well as mitotic and meiotic programmes are very stable. On the other hand, *in vitro* conditions allow, to a certain extent, a degree of flexibility in the expression of the cytoplasm/genome interaction. The effect of wounding coupled with different components of the culture medium enhances certain metabolic pathways. The ability to use certain signals such as carbohydrates, including oligosaccharides (Tran Thanh Van *et al.*, 1985) growth substances or growth retardants, minerals – macro and micro elements, external and cytoplasmic pH, and those occurring from cell-to-cell signals, to generate well-defined morphogenetic pathways makes the *in vitro* system a powerful tool for the study of the control of differentiation processes.

References

LOH, C. S. & INGRAM, D. (1982). Production of haploid plants from anther cultures and secondary embryoids of winter oil seed rape, *Brassica napus* ssp. Oleifere, *New Phytol.* **91**, 507–516.

REYNOLDS, J. F. & MURASHIGE, T. (1979). Asexual embryogenesis in callus cultures of palms. *In Vitro* **15**, 383–387.

SONDAHL, M. R. & SHARP, W. R. (1977). Frequency induction of somatic embryos in cultured leaf explants of *Coffea arabica*. *Z. Pflanzenphysiol.* **81**, 395–408.

STEWARD, F. C. (1958). Growth and organized development of cultured cells. III. Interpretations of growth from free cell to carrot plant. *Am. J. Bot.* **45**, 709–713.

TRAN THANH VAN, K. (1965). La vernalisation du *Geum urbanum*. Etude expérimentale de la mise à fleur chez une plante vivace en rosette exigeant le froid vernalisant pour fleurir. *Annls. Sci. nat. Bot.* **6**, 373–594.

TRAN THANH VAN, K. (1973). *In vitro* control of *de novo* flower, bud, root and callus differentiation from excised epidermal tissue. *Nature* **246**, 44–45.

TRAN THANH VAN, K. (1980). Control of morphogenesis or what shapes a group of cells? In *Advances in Biochemical Engineering* (ed. A. Fiechter), pp. 152–171. Berlin: Springer-Verlag.

TRAN THANH VAN, K. (1981). Control of morphogenesis. *A. Rev. Pl. Physiol.* **32**, 291–311.

TRAN THANH VAN, K. (1985). *Geum urbanum*. In *Handbook of Flowering*, Vol. III (ed. A. Halevy), pp. 53–62. Roca Baton: CRS Press.

TRAN THANH VAN, K., TOUBART, P., COUSSON, A., DARVILL, A. G., GOLLIN, D. J., CHELF, P. & ALBERSHEIM, P. (1985). Manipulation of the morphogenetic pathways of tobacco explants by oligosaccharins. *Nature* **314**, 615–617.

TRAN THANH VAN, K. & TRINH, T. H. (1978). Plant propagation: non identical and identical copies. In *Propagation of Higher Plants Through Tissue Culture* (ed. K. W. Hugues, R. Henke & M. Constantin), pp. 87–101. Springfield: National Technical Information Service.

TRAN THANH VAN, K. & TRINH, T. H. (1979). Micropropagation d'arbres fruitiers. AFOCEL 12–6 cover page.

TRAN THANH VAN, K. & TRINH, T. H. (1982). Cytoplasm genone interaction: its influence on differentiation of reproductive organs. *Proc. 5th int. Cong. Plant Tissue and Cell Culture* pp. 127–128. Tokyo.

TRAN THANH VAN, K., TRINH, T. H. & YILMAZ, D. (1985). How to programme *in vitro* morphogenesis in certain conifers. In *Tissue Culture in Forestry* (ed. J. M. Bonga & D. J. Durzan). The Hague, The Netherlands: Martinus Nyhoff Publishers NY. (In press).

TRINH, T. H., LIE-SHRICK, E. & TRAN THANH VAN, K. (1985). Regeneration des plantes a partir de cultures d'antheres et d'ovules non feconds du Haricot aile (*Psophocarpus tetragonolobus* L.) *Vleme Colloque de la section française de l' IAPTC* 'Obtention d'haploides in vitro: etat actuel et perspectives'.

VERGNE, P., TRINH, T. H. & TRAN THANH VAN, K. (1985). The control of ovule receptivity in the process in vitro pollination. In *Biotechnology and Ecology of Pollen* (ed. D. L. Mulcahy & E. Ottaviano). Berlin: Springer-Verlag. (In press).

CELLULAR INTERACTIONS IN TISSUE AND ORGAN DEVELOPMENT

TSVI SACHS

Department of Botany, The Hebrew University of Jerusalem, Jerusalem 91904, Israel

Summary

Developmental patterns result from combinations of interactions and intracellular programmes. The purpose here is to define the roles of interactions wherever possible and to consider their major parameters, such as the timing of their action, their specificity and the distances over which they occur. The approach is one of a board survey, attempting to outline major interaction systems on the basis of information from different sources. The evidence concerning interactions that control development must come primarily from development itself. Both disturbed, as during regeneration and grafts, and normal development are relevant.

Growing apices interact over relatively long distances. They reduce the development of similar apices and induce the development of axial tissues that connect them to the plant. Young shoot tissues also induce the development of root apices and *vice versa*. These various effects can be understood on the basis of a hormonal feedback involving auxins and cytokinins. Vascular differentiation, furthermore, is a cellular expression of these interactions. It occurs along the flow of auxin from the young tissues of the shoot towards the root apices. This flow is canalized by a positive feedback between cell polarization and the polar flow that both controls and results from this polarization. Structural relations between pholem and xylem, limitations of regeneration and the formation of rays all indicate the existence of additional, radial interactions.

The fate of individual cells in development is varied and often follows no recognizable rules. This indicates interactions that operate on the size of a tissue or organ rather than on its precise cellular development. On the other hand, the continuity of plasmodesmata, wall thickenings and cytoplasmic strands demonstrate local interactions between neighbouring cells.

It is concluded that, though the possibilities of developmental interactions may be bewildering, the list, when known, may not be all that long. The interactions specify orientation and quantity rather than the precise fate of cells. Their effects are gradual and they involve feedback loops.

Growth factors, even known growth factors, play surprisingly large roles in cellular interactions. Such controls whose effect is gradual and general could provide a basis for developmental plasticity.

The developmental role of cellular interactions

The cells of a multicellular organism must interact, for otherwise it would be a colony rather than an organism. The subject here, however, is development, and thus not all cellular interactions need be relevant. The development of organized tissues and organs is largely separate from their mature functions as parts of the plant. Such a separation is obvious in animals, where most aspects of development are restricted to early, embryonic stages or, in insects, to special periods during which most mature functions are suspended. The development of new organized structures in plants, however, is no less separate. It is localized in special meristematic tissues even though it does overlap mature functions in time. Development may thus depend on interactions that precede and are more or less distinct from those of mature tissues, and the differences and degrees of distinction are major questions for discussion.

Cellular interactions are a means by which events in neighbouring cells and tissues can be correlated. They could therefore be a major basis for any organized, or patterned, growth and differentiation. The role of cellular interactions, however, cannot be taken for granted in any specific case, for it is possible for organized development to depend on programmes that do not involve cues external to the developing cells themselves. An extreme example of the operation of such intracellular programmes is the development of nematodes (Kimble, 1981). Such programmes could even play a role in developmental plasticity. This would occur if a choice between internal programmes or the duration and rate of specific processes were dependent directly on environmental cues. The possible roles of intracellular programmes and of cellular interactions in the development of the structure of plant tissues is perhaps best shown by concrete examples. The ones chosen here are concerned with the relation between neighbouring stomata and between a stoma and the cells that adjoin it.

It has long been recognized that the distribution of stomata is not random (Fig. 1). The intuitive impression is that in most plants each stoma is surrounded by a region in which additional stomata do not occur (Bünning, 1953, 1965). This is therefore an example of a spatial pattern of specialized cells in a two-dimensional tissue (Wolpert, 1971). It was suggested that this spacing is due to each stoma inhibiting its immediate surrounding from differentiating additional stomata (Bünning, 1953, 1965).

Fig. 1. Stomata spacing. (A) *Kalanchoe verticillata.* (B) *Zebrina pendula.* The distribution is not random, but it does show local variations in both types of plants.

This suggestion is so reasonable that it has often been cited as an obvious fact. It has also been the basis of mathematical models (Gierer & Meinhardt, 1972).

Following stomatal development, however, suggests a different interpretation. Stomata form following one or more unequal division of the original mother cells (Fig. 2). The typical divisions that are the earliest stage of stomatal differentiation often occur in neighbouring cells. Thus at this stage there is no evidence of cellular interactions. Mature stomata are at various distances from one another. This, however, is because the stoma forms together with some or all of it surrounding cells, as a result of the same intracellular programme (Fig. 2; Sachs, 1978*a*, 1979; Sachs & Benouaiche, 1978). The unit of development is therefore not a stoma but a stoma surrounded by epidermal cells, and these units can be in direct

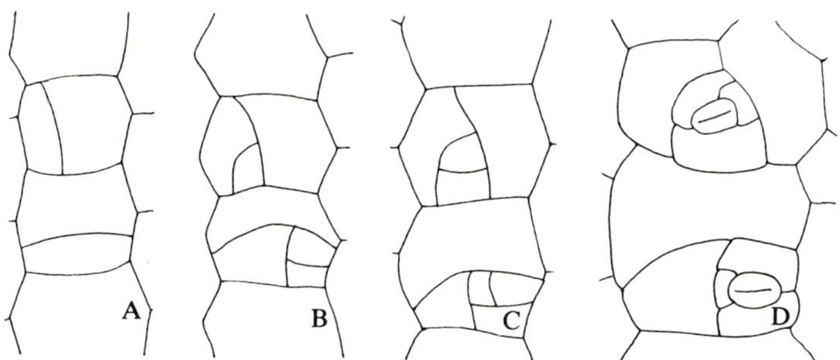

Fig. 2. Reconstruction of stomata development in *Sedum.* (A) First unequal divisions. (B, C) Continued divisions and development. (D) Mature stomata. The drawings are diagramatic, representing an hypothesis, not facts, but they are based on many observations. The large increases in size from A to D were omitted for the sake of clarity.

contact with one another. A simple statistical analysis shows that the intracellular programmes that form such units can account for the only repeated, orderly, aspect of stomatal distribution: the very rare occurrence of stomata that are close together (Sachs, 1978*a*; Marx & Sachs, 1977).

A comparison of stomatal development in various plants, however, provides one of the best indications for an interaction between neighbouring cells. This indication comes from the relations between the stomatal guard cells and the neighbouring subsidiary cells (Fig. 3). As mentioned above, the subsidiary cells, which may not be specialized, are often the product of the same mother cells as the stoma itself. In many monocotyledons, however, the sequence of development is different and cannot be anticipated from mature structures (Stebbins & Shah, 1960). It is easy to follow this development, however, because the various stages are arranged in a row in accordance with their maturity, being sequential products of an intercalary meristem. The subsidiary cells are products of unequal divisions in the cells that neighbour the stomatal mother cells. These unequal divisions appear to be induced by some intercellular influence that coordinates the events in the neighbouring cells (Stebbins & Shah, 1960). The possibility of such an inductive influence is supported by some evidence of abnormal development and the use of inhibitory substances (Stebbins, Shah, Jamin & Jura, 1967). The critical experiments of damaging the appropriate cells at different times during development are feasible but have apparently not been performed.

These examples show that structure can be used as an indication of cellular interactions but that further evidence is required. Though the presence and importance of cellular interactions has been recognized for a long time (Bünning, 1953; Sinnott, 1960; Wardlaw, 1968) the subject appears to lack a theoretical framework and good experimental systems. Thus reviews of cellular recognition or cellular interactions in plants do not

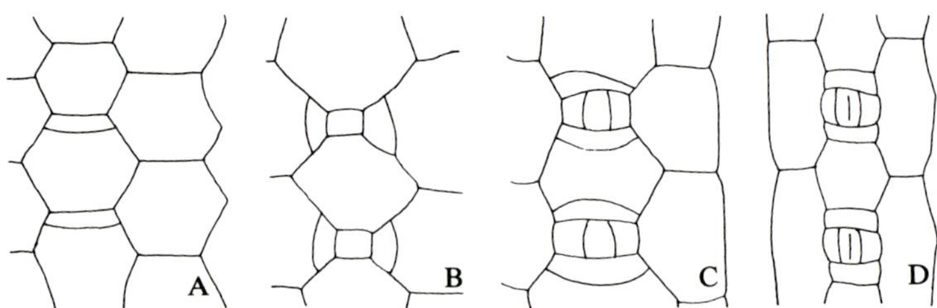

Fig. 3. Reconstruction of stomata development in *Zebrina*. (A) First unequal divisions. (B, C) Unequal divisions in cells neighbouring the stoma mother cell. (D) Two mature stomata.

Drawings of stages that could form a developmental sequence, and one that would not have been expected from mature structure. The large increases in size from A to D were omitted for the sake of clarity.

put great stress on normal development (Clarke & Knox, 1978; Heslop Harrison & Linskens, 1984). A major purpose of this article is therefore to define major cases in which cellular interactions occur. The approach is one of a broad survey, attempting to construct a framework of major types of cellular interactions. No such framework is available at present and the conclusions here will be at best a bold hypothesis. So as to restrict this challenge somewhat, only the vegetative development of seed plants will be considered, ignoring both embryonic and reproductive stages.

It would be desireable to know something about the nature of the signals that pass between cells. These could be diverse: physical stress, electrical currents, small or large molecules or changes, even periodic changes, in any of these factors. The passage of molecules could be through plasmodesmata, and thus restricted to the symplast, or through the non-living cell walls and intercellular spaces of the apoplast. Nevertheless the approach here will not be ambitious concerning these possibilities. Instead, the stress will be on defining the basic parameters of cellular interactions. Such parameters could provide answers for the following questions, all of them important in relation to developmental plasticity.

(i) Over what distances do the different interactions occur? Thus, there could be recognition processes that involve only the surfaces of cells, inductive effects that control one or two neighbouring cells and correlations between organs that pass from cell to cell over distances of centimetres and even metres.

(ii) When do interactions take place? They could be restricted to short periods early or late in the development of a tissue. They could also be gradual and occur during the entire time development takes place, thus permitting a greater plasticity.

(iii) What do the interactions specify? They could control the differentiation of one cell type in one location or influence the state and competence of many different cells.

(iv) Do cellular relations take the form of an induction, where one cell or tissue is dominant, or of complex feedback relations that could themselves be the source of developmental stability?

Finally, the problem of evidence must be mentioned. By its very nature an interaction disappears when its components are isolated. The major evidence must come, therefore from development itself and the various ways it can be perturbed. These include the influence of wounds that lead to regeneration and grafts that bring together tissues that had not been in contact previously. The role of organs and even individual tissues could also be modified by local environmental conditions and by parasites. Knowledge of the transport of substances and other possible signals is also likely to be valuable. Most of the information available concerning transport, however, relates to mature rather than developing tissues (Sachs, 1984).

The correlative relations of apices

It is convenient to start with the relations between the various apices of a plant. These occur over large distances, even entire plants. For this reason they are relatively well known. As will be seen below, these interactions also have consequences at the cellular level.

Correlative relations of apices are suggested by the repeatable form of plants of a given genotype. More direct evidence comes from simple experiments in which an apex is removed. Rather than consider individual experiments, however, a limited number of generalizations will be made, based not only on organ removal but also on a survey of normal development and the addition of organs by grafting. There certainly are exceptions to these generalizations, but it is surprising and significant how broad is their application. Of course, one cannot claim that these generalizations are always apparent. The growth of an organ necessarily depends on many controls and the correlative relations between organs need not be the limiting factor in any given situation.

The presence of a growing organ inhibits the development of similar organs

The most common expression of this principle is the growth of lateral buds when the shoot above them is removed – (apical dominance – Fig. 4, A,B; Thimann, 1977. It is seen, however, in all plant organs and is often expressed by relative growth rate rather than complete inhibition. In other cases the removal of an organ results in a reduction of the abscission of comparable parts of the plant (Jacobs, 1962) or in the initiation of new shoot and especially new root apices (Fig. 4, G).

A growing organ tends to cause other organs to become different from itself

Lateral buds often grow as horizontal branches (Snow, 1945), storage organs (Woolley & Wareing, 1972) or short shoots that may carry thorns or reproductive organs (Umrath, 1948). All these laterals are able to replace a dominant shoot that is removed early enough (Fig. 4, C,D). Though the known repertoire of root development is limited, the phenomena of the induced differentiation of lateral apices can be seen here as well.

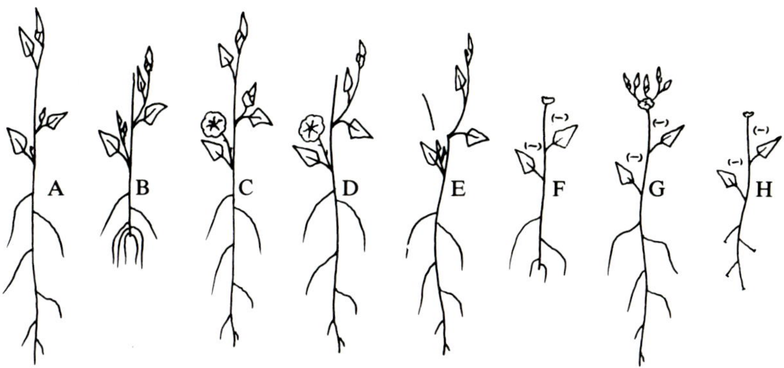

Fig. 4. Effects of the removal of shoot and root apices. (A) intact control. (B) Removed shoot and root tips are replaced by lateral buds and new roots. (C) Inhibited lateral buds develop on an intact plant but form flowers rather than long shoots. (D) Removed shoot tip replaced by a lateral that had not yet been determined as a reproductive apex. (E) Stems above the uppermost growing bud do not develop and they may abscise. (F) Absence of all shoot tips, including buds, reduces new root development (compare with B). (G) Callus and adventitious shoots may develop in the absence of all buds and the presence of the roots. (H) As in G, but with repeated removal of the roots. Callus and bud formation are reduced.

Organ development is correlated with the differentiation and maintenance of its connection with the rest of the plant

This relation is obvious in the development of undisturbed plants. It is confirmed when organs are removed: this leads to the cessation of all aspects of vascular differentiation and, when the removal is early in ontogeny, of parenchyma growth as well. The development of new apices, following adventitious initiation, grafting or release from inhibition, is always associated with the differentiation of vascular tissues that connect them with the complimentary organs – shoots in the case of roots and *vice versa*. Other expressions of the relation of a growing apex to the axis that connects it to the plant are the abscission or degeneration of tissues leading to a damaged organ. Similar abscission occurs when a shoot is in shaded conditions (selfpruning).

Shoot tissues enhance root development and vice versa

This mutual promotion is evident in the general balance of plant development but it is not always evident in experiments and measurement of fresh and dry weights. A reasonable explanation is that there is a mutual promotion, but it is expressed primarily in primordial development, the processes by which new tips are initiated and perpetuated, and not in the elongation that contributes most to the weight of an organ (Keeble, Nelson

& Snow, 1930). The dependence of new initiation on the complementary organs is seen most clearly in cuttings of various types. Young expanding leaves are more effective than photosynthetically active, mature leaves in inducing roots (Smith & Wareing, 1972). Roots promote bud initiation even in conditions in which water and ion absorption could play no part (Harris & Hart, 1964).

It may be concluded that all organs are sources of signals that regulate their relations with the rest of the plant. This conclusion raises the questions of the nature of these signals and how their various effects are related and coordinated. It is not likely that the complex relations of an organ with the plant could depend only on one type of signal and control. In the following, however, there is an emphasis on an hypothesis that a major control is hormonal. This is not because this is likely to be the whole truth but rather because it is one control whose existence is supported by concrete evidence.

Shortly after auxin was discovered as a cell elongation factor it was found to influence numerous other processes. Thimann & Skoog (1933) demonstrated that (i) growing shoots inhibit lateral bud growth, (ii) auxin inhibits lateral bud growth and (iii) growing shoots produce auxin. On the basis of these three facts they concluded that auxin must be one of the signals by which a shoot inhibits lateral buds. This is a logical conclusion, not an hypothesis. It has been contested on various grounds. The effect of auxin is certainly partial (Thimann, 1977), but this only shows that it is not the only factor involved. Auxin does not inhibit bud growth in all plants in all conditions (Jacobs, Danielson, Hurst & Adams, 1959; Thimann, Sachs & Mathur, 1971), but the effect is remarkably general. It is not known whether auxin inhibits buds directly, but the question of the mechanism of action does not enter into the argument. Most commonly, the evidence for the role of auxin has been ignored. The results of numerous observations made since 1933, however, tend to support the generality of facts on the basis of which the original conclusion was made (White, 1976).

Auxin is therefore not only a cell elongation factor. The statement that elongation is its most 'typical' function is at best vague. As is well known, furthermore, many other effects of auxin have been found. It is less commonly recognized that these all mimic the influence of a growing shoot on the rest of the plant (Sachs, 1975). Thus auxin influences not only bud growth but the development of such buds as horizontal branches (Snow, 1945) or storage organs (Woolley & Wareing, 1972). Auxin enhances the initiation of new roots while inhibiting the initiation of shoots (Skoog & Miller, 1957; Thimann, 1977). Auxin, furthermore, induces all types of vascular differentiation (Snow, 1935; Jacobs, 1952; Sachs, 1981*a*). These effects show that auxin can not be characterized by one response it elicits from the various tissues of the plant. Rather, the known facts suggest that the role of auxin in the plant is that of a major hormonal signal specifying the presence of growing shoots (Sachs, 1975, 1981*a*).

This raises the question of the nature of the influence of the roots. One way they could act is as sinks into which auxin is diverted. This could be a factor in root inhibition of the initiation of additional roots, an initiation which occurs where auxin accumulates (Thimann, 1977). As discussed below, such a 'sink' effect could also account for the influence of roots on vascular differentiation. This, however, may not be the only way roots influence the rest of the plant. Cytokinins, discovered as cell division factors in tissue cultures, have been found to be produced by roots (Goodwin, Gollonow & Letham, 1978). Though there may be exceptions in which they are produced by other tissues (Wang & Wareing, 1979), the roots are their major and most common source. Cytokinins, furthermore, replace the roots in inhibiting root initiation while they induce the initiation as well as the maintenance of shoots (Skoog & Miller, 1957; Sachs, 1975). These facts suggest that cytokinins are major hormonal signals of the roots. They would thus resemble auxins in being characterized by their role in the plant rather than by any specific tissue response that they elicit. The evidence for this role of cytokinins, however, is not as clear as the evidence for the role of auxins.

These conclusions suggest a positive feedback relation between shoot and root development and between auxin and cytokinin production. This feedback would depend on quantitative correlations between (i) the production of root-inducing signals, such as auxin, and the volume and rate of developing shoot tissues, and (ii) the production of shoot-inducing signals, such as cytokinins, and the volume and rate of developing primordial root tissues. There is little direct evidence for these relations, but they are supported by whatever evidence is available and by observations of both intact and damaged plants. It is a general rule that rapidly growing apices have large effects on the plant and large vascular supplies. A major control of the various relations of plant organs could be, therefore, a feedback of hormonal signals. These would precede the functional effects of supplies of necessary metabolites and their transport by mature tissues (Sachs, 1975). This hormonal control would act over large distances but, as will be seen below, it could have major consequences at the cell and tissue levels.

Many objections can be found in the literature concerning various parts of this auxin–cytokinin feedback hypothesis. None of these, however, contradict the basic evidence nor the logic of the suggestions. The objections

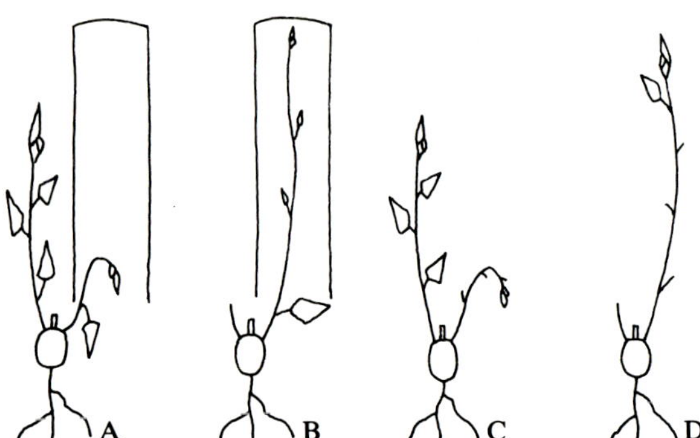

Fig. 5. The experiments of Snow (1931) on the relations between two growing shoots. Seedlings were decapitated and plants with two equal shoots selected. (A) The development of a darkened shoot ceases and it often dies. (B) As in A, but the shoot in the light was removed. The darkened shoot was etiolated, but grew rapidly. (C, D) As in A and B, but the treated shoot had its leaves removed. It developed only when the other shoot was not present.

relate to the fact that the quantitative relations are not fully substantiated (Goodwin *et al.* 1978). It is also true that not all the effects of a removed organ can be replaced by the application of known hormones by methods used at present. For example, there are very rapid correlative effects in plants (e.g. Desbiez, Kergosien, Champagnat & Thellier, 1984) which cannot be accounted for by auxins and cytokinins. Most objections, however, relate to questions of mechanism of action, which do not enter into an hypothesis that specifies only substances that leave an organ as signals, not how they influence the rest of the plant.

The hormonal feedback hypothesis suggests a basis for the plasticity of organ relations. This is not only interesting in itself but might also provide future tests for the hypothesis. It can be suggested that the production and sensitivity to hormones could be a function of the condition an organ is in. An expression of this might be the selfpruning of branches that are in the shade and the dominant growth of those that are in the best conditions. An experimental analysis and demonstration of this phenomenon was attempted by Snow (1931). He shaded or damaged one of two branches of experimental plants and observed its growth in the presence and absence of the correlative effects of the other branch (Fig. 5). This work is being repeated and extended by Novoplansky.

Induction along the longitudinal axis

A major aspect of the organization of plant tissues is the presence of a dominant longitudinal axis. This axis is recognizable not only in the elongation of organs but also in the shape of most cells. It is obvious, furthermore, in the patterns of differentiated cells in rows of similar cells along this axis, as seen most clearly in the vessels and sieve tubes. There must be, therefore, interactions between cells that have a preferred axis or axes and thus do not act equally in all directions. Such an axiality could be specific indication concerning the nature of the interactions (Sachs, 1981*a*; 1984).

A key observation concerning axial differentiation appeared above, in relation to the effects of growing apices. The development of all parts of shoots is closely correlated with the differentiation of the tissues that connect them to the plant. Grafting buds as well as many other results (Sachs, 1981*a*) demonstrate that vascular tissues are actively induced by young leaves. As in the case of bud inhibition, this effect of growing shoots can be replaced, at least partially, by the auxin which these shoots are known to produce (Jacobs, 1952; Sachs 1981*a*). It may be concluded, therefore, that auxin is a natural inducing substance, or evocator, that controls the differentiation of the various types of vascular tissues that form along the plant axis.

This raises the question of the nature of the effect of roots on vascular differentiation. As mentioned above, root development is also associated with the differentiation of vascular tissues. Vascular differentiation in the direction of the roots, however, continues even in the absence of roots (Sachs, 1968). Therefore roots cannot be sources of signals that are immediately necessary for the differentiation of vascular tissues. This suggests that their orienting effect on differentiation when they are present is due to their acting as sinks for auxin, and possibly other differentiation-inducing signals, that originate in the shoots (Sachs, 1968, 1981*a*).

If young shoot tissues are the primary source and root tips major sinks of signals for vascular differentiation, then it can be suggested that vascular differentiation occurs along the channels of the flow of these signals through the plant (Sachs, 1968; 1978*b*; 1981*a*). This central concept is supported by evidence from a variety of sources. The first is the general form of the vascular tissues, which is that of a drainage system. The processes of vascular differentiation also support the concept of control by flow, since this differentiation can occur very rapidly along very large trees (Tepper & Hollis, 1969). Regeneration appears to be related to flow when it occurs around wounds (Fig. 6 A). Finally, differentiation follows tissue polarity in a way that clearly suggests a dependence on the polar transport of auxin (Goldsmith, 1977; Sachs, 1984).

A possible basis for the pattern of vascular differentiation is suggested by the conditions in which vascular differentiation does and does not depend on the original polarity of the differentiating tissue (Sachs, 1981*a, b*). It was

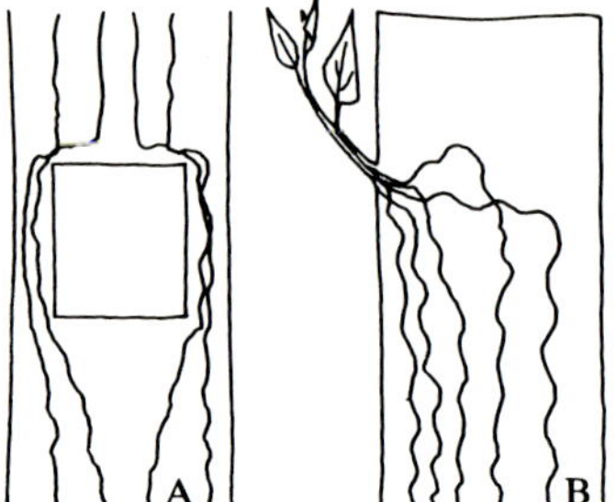

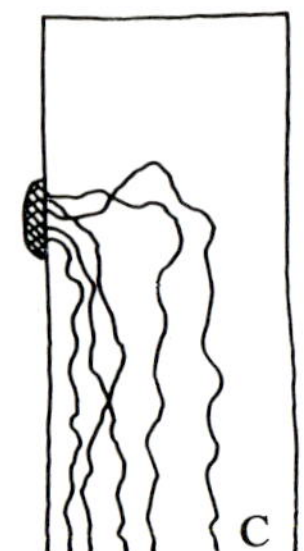

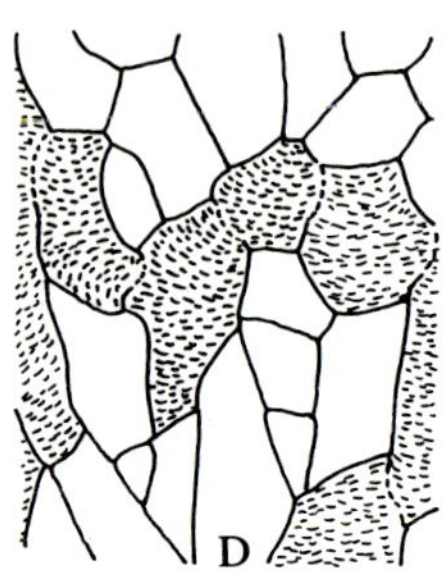

Fig. 6. Regeneration of vascular tissues. New vessels are indicated by wavy lines. (A) Regeneration in the form of a flow around a rectangular wound. (B) New vessels are induced by a growing lateral bud on a decapitated stem. (C) Similar induction by a source of auxin. (D) Vessels induced by auxin in turnip storage roots. The shape of the cells, determined in the intact tissue, does not reflect the same polarity as the differentiation induced by auxin.

found long ago by Vöchting (1892) that, in grafts in which one of the two members was inverted, vascular differentiation is an anatomical expression of the original polarity of the tissues (Fig. 7A, B). This occurs even if it prevents the establishment of new shoot–root connections and thus leads to the death of the grafted plants. The same polarity is seen when auxin is applied (Fig. 6C) and when plants are wounded (Fig. 7C). Under other conditions, however, vascular differentiation occurs readily at all possible angles to the original polarity of the tissue (Fig. 7D–F; Sachs, 1981*a, b*). A survey of all the cases in which polarity is or is not expressed in new differentiation suggests a simple principle (Sachs, 1981*b*). Tissue polarity determines auxin flow, and thus determines the course of differentiation. This occurs even when it is detrimental to the survival of the plants.

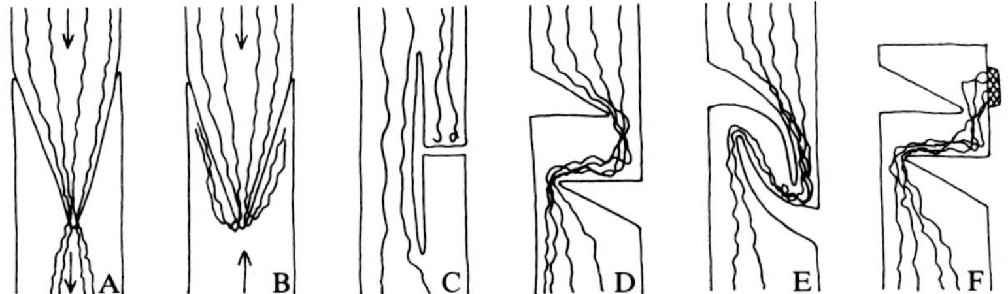

Fig. 7. New vascular differentiation in relation to tissue polarity. Wavy lines indicate only the new vessels. Arrows point in the original direction of the tissue towards the roots. (A) Grafts of tissues whose polarity corresponds. This polarity is expressed by the course of the vessels. (B) Lower grafted tissues were inverted. Vessels follow the original direction towards the roots. (C) Stems cut so that tissue flaps are connected to either the roots or the shoots. Polarity is expressed by differentiation occurring only in the tissue connected directly to the shoot side. (D) Only a transverse bridge connects the shoot with the root. New differentiation occurs readily at right angles to the original axis of the stem. (E) As in D, but cuts more extreme. There is an actual reversal of shoot–root polarity. (F) Differentiation that involves tissue reorientation is induced by a source of auxin.

When wounds prevent auxin flow along tissue polarity, however, auxin accumulates and a new flow is started by diffusion. The critical point is that this new flow induces a new tissue polarity and this leads, eventually, to new vascular differentiation.

It is therefore suggested that there is a feedback relation between tissue polarity and auxin flow. The concept of polarity determining flow is well established (Goldsmith, 1977; Thimann, 1977) but the converse, that flow can determine polarity, requires further evidence. Polarity as it is apparent in vascular differentiation can clearly be changed (Fig. 7D–F). Recent measurements of auxin transport through horizontal tissue bridges, cut as in Fig. 7D, show that a new polarity of auxin transport can also be detected (Gersani & Sachs, 1984). This new transport precedes overt differentiation by over a day, as would be expected if it were an early, determining step (Gersani, 1985). The unique directional effect of auxin on differentiation (Fig. 7F) can thus be understood. This would also account for the directional effect of new shoots that 'take over' the axis that adjoins them (Fig. 6B), a process which is of major importance for the developmental plasticity of plant development.

An important consequence of a positive feedback between polarity and auxin flow is that it could account for the canalization of differentiation to discrete rows of cells (Sachs, 1978*b*, 1981*a*). This would be true if the positive feedback is gradual and continues for some time. It would lead first to a broad front of cells becoming polarized and later to the specialization of some channels as the most effective transport system, draining the signal flow from their neighbours (Sachs, 1978*b*, 1981*a*). This 'canalization hypothesis' would thus account for a major cell pattern on the basis of properties and reactions that are known even if they are not understood. This hypothesis has been a subject of mathematical modelling (Mitchison, 1980) and it is supported by indirect evidence of various types. This evidence has been reviewed (Sachs, 1981*a*) and for reasons of space only its major aspects will be mentioned. The effect of auxin flow on differentiation is, as expected, gradual (Sachs, 1981*b*). The same gradual aspect is also present in the structure of the vascular system. Finally both direct evidence from the transport of radioactive auxin and indirect evidence from the control of the contacts between new and old vascular strands indicate the cells of the vascular system are the preferred pathway of transport for auxin.

The consideration of vascular differentiation has been based on the observation of vessels. The reason for this is the ease with which these vessels form and can be observed. Both young leaves and the auxin they produce, however, induce the oriented growth, cell division and all other aspects of vascular differentiation, including the sieve tubes, the cambium and the parenchyma that surrounds the transporting channels (Sachs, 1981*a*). The one exception is the formation of the procambium (Young 1954), and even here it is not clear that the problem is not one of local application. This is very difficult when the tissues occupy a very small volume and are thus readily flooded with auxin that moves in all directions by diffusion. The canalization hypothesis suggests that the parenchyma could be 'partially induced' tissue, left over when the future vascular tissues become the preferred channels for signal transport (Sachs, 1981*a*). The samc hypothesis does not provide, however, reasons for the different fates of the xylem, the phloem and the cambium between them. This is a major challenge for future research (Sachs, 1981*b*), though one possibility, that of radial interactions, will be considered in the following section.

It is suggested here that the differentiation of the vascular tissues and the parenchyma that surrounds them depends on the flow of auxin and presumably other signals from the shoots to the roots. This means that the formation and differentiation of the plant axis is an expression of the hormonal feedback system considered in the previous section. Thus axial differentiation, and especially that of the vascular system, is a cellular result of the same long-distance signals that control the relations between the various apices of a plant. This is a remarkable economy of controls of development. The positive feedback between tissue polarity and auxin flow, furthermore, could be an important basis for the stability in the relations between organs and, at the same time, the plasticity shown by these relations following severe damage. Finally, the flow hypothesis raises the old 'diversion theory' concerning the relations between apices of the same type (Sachs, 1970). A dominant organ, by virtue of its vascular supply, would receive most if not all of the essential promotive signals coming from the complementary organs (shoots in the case of roots and *vice versa*). This would enable the dominant organ to continue to be the main producer of its own signals and continue to receive the supplies from the rest of the plant. This might not be the only mechanism of apical dominance, but it could well be an important one (Sachs, 1970; 1981*a*).

Finally, it is necessary to consider what the relation of differentiation to flow and to canalization of flow means with respect to the interactions between neighbouring cells. The signals passing from one cell to another would be auxin and possibly other unknown molecules. The passage, as far as is known, is through the apoplast, the cell walls and intercellular spaces, and not the plasmodesmata (Goldsmith, 1977). The information the signals would carry would not be specific for any cell type, but would specify orientation and, through quantity, the intensity of the meristematic activity that is the source or the sink for these signals. The way a cell would influence one neighbour in preference to all others would be by concentrating the exit of auxin on one side. This as far as is known (Goldsmith, 1977; Jacobs & Gilbert, 1983) is due to a localization of channels for the passage of auxin in one part of the plasmalemma. Regardless of whether this is correct, the directional signals that pass from one cell to another are not dependent, as might have been expected, on microtubules (Hardham, 1982). The evidence for this is that colchicine, whose effect on the microtubules can be clearly seen in the distruption of the pattern of cell walls, does not prevent the induction of vessels that consist of rows of specialized cells. It is remarkable that the same process that serves to induce the differentiation of the cells along the future vessel or sieve tube is also part of the interaction between a cell and its other neighbours. This 'lateral inhibition' (Gierer & Meinhardt, 1972) is not due to a special signal but rather to the draining away of auxin towards the canalized flow, the flow that is limited to the cells that continue to differentiate.

Radial interactions

Mature plant structures are necessarily three dimensional, so that they could not be established only by the longitudinal interactions considered above. Additional interactions might occur along other axes or they may be local and more or less specific, involving pairs of cells and tissues. These are two possibilities that may complement rather than exclude one another. A first indication of an additional system of interactions over relatively long distances that have a major role in development would be the repeated occurrence of structural patterns not only in a given species but in most seed plants. According to this criterion the most likely orientation of such additional interactions would be the radius of the stems and roots.

The radius is characterized by repeated changes of tissue and cell types, in contrast with their continuity along the longitudinal axis. A similar change is found along the dorsoventral direction of leaves, except that most leaves may correspond only to half rather than an entire stem (Warren Wilson & Warren Wilson, 1984). There is one exception to this repeated change: the rays, whose cells are oriented along the radius.

One possible interaction might be between the parenchyma and the vascular tissues that are embedded in it. This relation has already been briefly considered above, as an expression of a possible drainage of signals towards the vascular tissues that continue to differentiate as preferred channels of transport. This, however, does not exclude additional radial interactions. There is, furthermore, a close spatial relation of the phloem, cambium and xylem (Sachs, 1981*a*; Warren Wilson & Warren Wilson, 1984). Phloem can occur without xylem, but only in limited quantities, the amount depending on the species. Xylem differentiation over distances of more than a few cells does not occur without recognizable phloem. When the formation of both tissues is extensive they are always connected by rays. The proportion of the tissue occupied by rays is maintained when an organ grows in circumference (Bünning, 1965), indicating active controls. The presence of such controls is confirmed by the large increase in the proportion of rays when the formation of xylem and phloem is specially rapid. This increase occurs even at the expense of space that limits the shoot–root connections of the plant (Carmi, Sachs & Fahn, 1972).

The number of xylem and phloem groups seen in cross sections of roots increases as the diameter of the roots increases (Jost, 1931). This could be another expression of an interdependence of xylem and phloem differentiation. Their relations could limit the absolute size of the mass of each separate tissue, leading to more groups forming when the organs are larger (Sachs, 1981*a*).

The phloem–xylem relations are directional. An experimental expression of this directionality is seen in regeneration following grafting (Warren Wilson & Warren Wilson, 1984). Such regeneration always connects the cut cambium so that the phloem–xylem polarity is maintained. No cases of regeneration in which radial polarity is not maintained have been reported. Another expression of this directionality along the radial axis might be seen in the initiation of new organs, both regular and adventitious (Sinnott, 1960). Though there are some exceptions, it is a general rule that new shoots form on the surface and new roots form internally, generally in direct contact with the xylem.

Concerning the nature of the interactions along the phloem–xylem axis there have been two suggestions. The first is that there are radial gradients that control the differentiation of the tissues (Warren Wilson & Warren Wilson, 1961). Specific suggestions have been made that these are gradients of auxin and sucrose which both depend on and induce the appropriate vascular differentiation (Warren Wilson & Warren Wilson, 1984). The other suggestion is that there is a movement of inductive signals, probably from the phloem to the xylem. This movement would be expressed by the formation and maintenance of the rays, on which this suggestion is largely based (Sachs, 1981*a*). It would also account, however, for other aspects of the phloem–xylem relations.

Controls of size

The discussion above dealt with interactions that specified the fate of individual cells. Development, however, could also depend on interactions of a different type. It is perhaps best to explain this statement by a general example based on zoological work on chalones (Bullough, 1975). Suppose that all cells of a given type produce a controlling substance. The concentration of this substance in the tissue would depend on its synthesis and on its diffusion away to other tissues. As the tissue grows, its surface–volume ratio necessarily changes, and this would lead to changes in the concentration of the controlling substance. At a critical size this concentration could reach a threshold at which the producing tissue would stop growing.

A control of this type would involve the movement of signals between cells, but it would not specify the fate of any given cell. It could be an important basis for the plasticity of plant development, for both the synthesis and sensitivity to the controlling substances could be readily influenced by the environment. A possible example is etiolation: both the cessation of stem elongation and the continuation of leaf development in response to light do not appear to be related to the activity of any special cells and could involve general effects of concentration.

It is therefore necessary to seek evidence for controls that are not expressed at the single cell level. Here the cellular variability of the development of plants (and most other organisms) becomes meaningful. It is often assumed that the only way an organ can develop is as a result of a precise cell lineage. Such lineages have been reconstructed on the basis of sections through comparable organs at different stages of development. For example, a precise course of leaf development (Avery, 1933) has been widely quoted. Individual sections, however, are variable and cannot be readily coerced into logical sequences (Esau, 1965). This variability means that one cannot obtain a true picture of the development by reconstruction, and more direct methods are necessary. These must deal with the changes in a specific, living region. The direct approach has been possible in three cases. (i) Surface tissues can be followed without any necessary damage. This was originally done on small roots (Sinnott & Bloch, 1939) and later on apices (Ball, 1960; Green & Poethig, 1982) and the development of stomata patterns of the leaf epidermis (Sachs, 1978*a*, 1979). (ii) The xylem preserves a record of the cellular pattern of the cambium from which it was formed. Serial sections of the xylem along the plant radius thus reveal cellular changes over periods of very many years (Sachs, 1981*a*). (iii) Cell lineage can be followed in chimaeras. In these a tissue forms from cells of more than one genotype. There are many garden chimaeras in which one of the apical initials cannot form chlorophyll and all its descendant cells can be recognized (Stewart, 1978). Mutations of all types can also be induced at chosen stages of development (Satina, Blakeslee & Avery, 1940; Dulieu, 1970).

Observations of mature structure (Fig. 1) and the results of all these methods of following development show that the developmental course of any given cell is not predictable. There are, of course, exceptions to this rule, and even organs where development is very orderly (Gunning, 1982). These are valuable experimental objects. In most cases, however, individual cells appear to be even competing with one another. The mature multicellular structure, on the other hand, is functional and many of its parameters are quite repeatable. It follows that there must be controls that correct or select developmental variations. These controls must include interactions and they could have a generalized form determining the state of the entire tissue and the time it stops growing, as considered above, though direct evidence for this is needed.

Two examples of hypotheses of controls of the state of a tissue and not its individual cells may be useful here. The first is concerned with stomatal density. This density is an example of developmental plasticity: it varies both in relation to area and to the number of other epidermal cells (Umrath, 1948). It was explained above (Fig. 2; Sachs, 1978*a*) that cell lineage accounts for the minimum distance between neighbouring stomata and that this is the only patterned aspect of their distribution. The minimal distance, however, is not the actual distance, which varies greatly, nor is it the average distance which is directly related to density. There could be, therefore, a control of density that does not influence the location or the occurrence of any given stoma (Marx & Sachs, 1977). The most common way such controls could operate is through the size of epidermal cells, but, as mentioned above, this could not account for all available data. When the stomatal pores are blocked with gelatin as they mature the number of unequal divisions leading to additional stomata formation is greatly increased (Sachs, unpublished). It is therefore possible that the density of stomata is influenced by the concentrations of gasses inside the developing leaf. These undergo rapid diffusion, so their effects would not necessarily be local. Further evidence, however, is clearly needed.

The promeristematic tips of shoot apices may be a second example of controls that operate directly on size and shape. These embryonic regions maintain their traits during developmental cycles and regenerate after severe wounding (Wardlaw, 1968). Yet both sections and chimaeras (Stewart, 1978) show that the fate of their individual cells is variable. It is possible that there are precise lateral interactions between the various cells of the apical dome. It is also possible, however, that development is controlled by the supplies of critical signals from the rest of the plant (Sachs, 1972). One such signal could be cytokinins, known to limit the initiation of new apices (Skoog & Miller, 1957). Whatever their nature, the availability of key signals in the apex could depend on the effects of the meristematic cells on the plant. A large number of apical cells could obtain a larger supply from the rest of the plant than the sum of each individual cell (Sachs, 1972). The cells could thus act in collaboration without necessarily interacting directly with one another.

Interactions of Neighboring Cells

Finally, there is a group of interactions that involve cells that are in actual contact with one another. The passage of signals thus occurs over very short distances or even within the surfaces that are in contact. The following are the major reasons for assuming the existence of such interactions.

(i) A prominent, though not necessarily the most general, expression of the relations between neighbouring cells is the continuity of various wall structures. These include the wall thickenings of both primary and regenerative xylem (Sinnott & Bloch, 1945), the openings between the cells along vessels and sieve tubes and the Casparian strips of the endodermis.

(ii) The position of cross walls in neighbouring cells are not random (Sinnott & Bloch, 1941). For example, the new walls seen in cross sections of the cambium are continuous with one another while in most other tissues continuity is clearly avoided. This means that the location of cell divisions is influenced by conditions at the cell surface.

(iii) The formation of new plasmodesmata could express cellular interactions. The presence of plasmodesmata between plant cells is almost universal (Gunning & Robards, 1976). They are normally formed at the time a cell divides and later growth only reduces their density (Juniper & Barlow, 1969; Gunning, 1978). There are a number of cases, however, where the formation of new plasmodesmata between existing, healthy cells can be shown. These include the union of grafted tissues, across which new sieve tubes can be found. The sieve areas of these develop from plasmodesmata and thus indicate their formation in the graft. Plasmodesmata can also be identified between grafted parenchyma cells (Lindsay, Yeoman & Brown, 1974, Yeoman, 1984), even when the grafted cells belong to very different plants and their joined surfaces can be recognized (Kollmann & Glockman, 1985). Plasmodesmata, furthermore, occur in chimaera plants formed when cells on two sides of a graft collaborate to form new shoot apices (Burgess, 1972).

The most common location of newly formed plasmodesmata through existing walls is probably in the cambium. The contacts between the cells of this meristem change constantly, as a result of intrusive growth (Fig. 8C; Sinnott, 1960). Even after hundreds of years of such changes, as common in many trees, the cambium probably contains a normal distribution of plasmodesmata. This is indicated, at least, by the formation of sieve tubes, since when the cambium is wounded, sieve area formation can occur in all possible locations. It is possible, therefore, that the formation of new plasmodesmata is not an unusual process. It may even be an important component of the plastic capabilities of plant development.

(iv) The capacity of plasmodesmata to transport can be modified in accordance with the state of the cells they connect. The best evidence for this is again the formation of sieve areas as modifications of plasmodesmata. This can occur, as a regenerative process, in a variety of cells (Sachs, 1981*a*). The opposite process, the occlusion of plasmodesmata, occurs in the late stages of stomata differentiation and in the development of some organs (Gunning, 1978). Observations on the activity of plasmodesmata in meristems have been made recently (Goodwin & Lyndon, 1983). Use was made of the spread in tissues of fluorescent molecules of various sizes that do not pass through biological membranes after injection into living cells. The size of the largest molecules that pass through the plasmodesmata decreases when an apex undergoes the transition to reproductive development. This size increases when cells are plasmolysed and then allowed to regenerate their contacts (Erwee & Goodwin, 1984). Measurements of electrical coupling indicate that plasmodesmata might have a polarity, that is a prefered direction of transport (Overall & Gunning, 1982), a possibility that should be further studied. Modifications of plasmodesmata have also been suggested on structural grounds (Overall, Wolfe & Gunning, 1982). There are technical problems to demonstrating and following such modifications in the electron microscope.

(v) Grafted tissues are joined by bonds that are much too strong to be accounted for by plasmodesmata or vascular strands (Yoeman & Brown, 1976). The early stages of this joining are not specific and can occur even with an inanimate object (Moore & Walker, 1981). Later stages, however, depend on the compatability of the grafted tissues and imply some recognition processes (Clarke & Knox, 1978; Yoeman, 1984). Since these recognition processes are expressed only over periods of days, they are difficult to study and little is known about their nature. Their existence has been doubted (Moore, 1984).

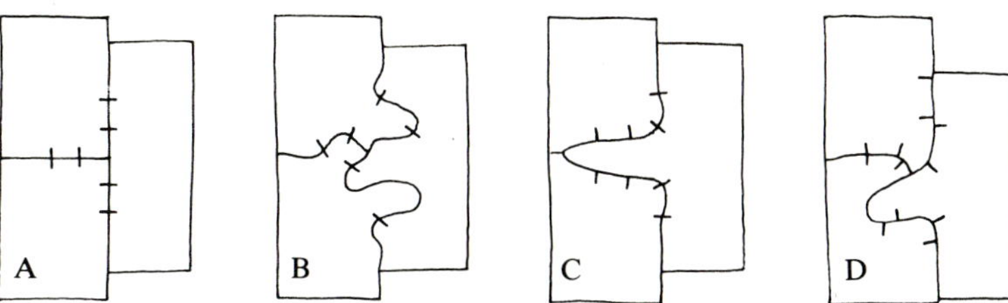

Fig. 8. Possible relations of neighbouring cells during growth. The short lines indicate specific locations of the walls, such as plasmodesmata. (A) Original state, before growth. (B) Symplastic growth. Though different parts of the wall of any given cell grew at different rates, the walls of neighbouring cells always grew together. (C) Intrusive growth. Localized tip growth of the cell on the right separated its two neighbours. New wall contacts were formed, but in no case did one wall slide over another. (D) Sliding growth. Neighbouring wall regions changed their relative locations. There is no good evidence that this kind of cell growth occurs in plants.

(vi) The growth of most neighbouring plant cells is symplastic: regions that are in contact grow together, at the same rate (Fig. 8B). This type of growth may well result from physical adhesion between cells, but regardless of its basis it means the events in neighbouring cells are closely correlated. Following development by all available ways does not yield any evidence for cells sliding over one another (Fig. 8D; Sinnott & Bloch, 1939, Sinnott, 1960). A variety of plant cells, including those of the cambium and differentiating sclerenchyma, do grow in a way that shows a remarkable independence of neighbours. This is intrusive growth (Fig. 8C; Sinnott, 1960) which involves only the tips of cells. These penetrate between neighbouring cells, forming new contacts.

(vii) Strands of cytoplasm generally appear to be continuous from one cell to another, presumably through the plasmodesmata. (Sinnott & Bloch, 1945; Kirschner & Sachs, 1979). Such strands are seen most clearly in the primary meristems of shoots and roots, where vacuoles have already formed but do not fill the entire lumen of the cells. Except for the continuity of the strands in neighbouring cells, the arrangement and orientation of the cytoplasm in undisturbed meristems appears to follow no rules. When cytoplasmic strands are followed in living *Tradescantia* roots, however, they are found to change their entire pattern over periods of an hour or less (Sachs, unpublished). It is therefore possible that the average time that the strands are in contact with any neighbour will be found to be a critical parameter concerning the relations between cells.

These various expressions of relations between neighbouring cells mean that cells must be able to interact. It is now necessary to ask how these interactions depend on the genotype, differentiation and orientation of the cells. Answers can only be obtained by causing drastic changes of tissue configuration, and primarily from grafts in which cells of different types are brought together. As a general rule easy joining is obtained only in grafts of closely related plants: member of the same family or the same genus. There are, however, exceptions to this rule (Brabec, 1965). In some of these exceptions there is true tissue joining (Kollmann & Glockmann, 1985). In others there might be only a coordination of vascular development, which depends on long distance interactions and is discussed above. On the other hand, there are varieties of apples that are not compatible even though this is a species where grafting is a general practice. The joining of tissues from different species and even genera can be complete. This is demonstrated by the 'graft hybrids' mentioned above, in which entire, vigorous plants consist of cells of different genotypes whose development is perfectly co-ordinated (Brabec, 1965).

Different tissues from different locations on the plant can be grafted together readily. The interactions that lead to union are most rapid in young, rapidly growing tissues. The surprising exception is that promeristematic tissues of the extreme tips do not join, not even other cells of the same type (Ball, 1950; Sachs, unpublished). The ready grafting of tissues from different parts of the plant does not lead to any developmental events in the region of the union. This contrasts with the situation in animals, where such experiments reveal the existence of tissue gradients (French, Bryant & Bryant, 1976). The slow tissue union in plants, however, may be associated with 'dedifferentiation' processes so that the original traits of the tissue are not expressed. In most cases it is callus cells that join, though the original cells of the cut tissues can also participate if they are in good contact (Lindsay *et al.* 1974).

It is commonly held that tissues of opposite orientations, or shoot–root polarities, cannot join (Bünning, 1953; Sinnott, 1960). This is not correct. Such grafts join readily, as may be seen even in earliest reports on polarity and grafting in plants (Vöchting 1892). The origin of this mistaken opinion is that, as discussed above, polarity influences not tissue union but vascular differentiation. As a result vascular contacts between the shoot and the root may not form in inverted grafts and the plants eventually die (Fig. 7B; Vöchting, 1892). The possibility of changes in the local relations between cells is also seen in the regenerative processes that follow severe wounds. Vessel pores and sieve areas form readily along all axes of the tissue (Figs 6D; 7D-F; Sachs, 1981*a,b*). Thus the possibility of local interactions between cells is not limited by cell polarity and not, except in extreme cases, by tissue differentiation.

The discussion here brought together a variety of expressions of the local relations between cells. These relations raise a number of general problems. The first is whether all their expressions depend on the same interaction mechanisms. The only answer that can be given at present is that there is no good way by which various possible mechanisms can be separated, so further evidence is required. A second question is how the short-distance interactions relate to the long-distance ones, considered above. It can only be stated that local events such as sieve area formation are part of vascular differentiation along the entire plant. On the other hand, vascular differentiation can be induced without tissue contact (Moore, 1984) and grafts in which the vascular tissues were coordinated have survived for many years without a strong joining of the tissues (Yeoman, 1984). A third and final question regards the molecular basis of short-distance interactions. Again, no firm knowledge is available. Recognition events during fertilization and between plants and microorganisms appear to involve specific carbohydrates (Clarke & Knox, 1978). This could also be true of cells in normal tissues. The continuity of plasmodesmata, cytoplasmic strands and cell wall characteristics, however, might require more elaborate exchange of information. This exchange could take the form of an active feedback and involve the movement of molecules.

Discussion

The list of interaction types given above is remarkably short. One reason for this is that different interactions are taken together. Another related reason is that details of development and of specialized differentiation types are not considered. A third, very obvious, reason is that the list is not complete. Thus there must be signals from leaves that depend on photoperiodic conditions. There must also be rapid signals that indicate touch in tendrils, *Mimosa pudica* and carnivorous plants. These and other examples were not included for lack of space and because there is no evidence that their passage through cells, the actual interaction, influences development. Even in view of these reasons or reservations it is remarkable how many major aspects of development could be based on very few general interaction systems.

Great stress above has been put on the role of growth factors, especially known hormones. This stress may be a bias towards what is already known. It is surprising, however, that one substance, auxin, is an interaction signal in both the relations between organs and between the individual cells of a vascular strand. Support for the 'growth factor hypothesis' of organization may be found in the development of tumours. Unusual synthesis of both auxin and cytokinins in the same tissues is sufficient to account for their abnormal development (Sachs, 1975). The same substances, in different amounts and ratios, can induce the initiation of both shoot and root apices

(Skoog & Miller, 1957). The requirements of normal cells for growth in culture, furthermore, are an indication what stimulatory signals a tissue must get from the rest of the plant. These requirements include salts and sugar, for whose role as signals there is no clear evidence, and an auxin and a cytokinin as the most common necessary additions. It is not likely that organization depends only on these substances. The facts do suggest, however, that the patterned distribution of auxins and cytokinins is very important.

A central question to be discussed here is how the interactions considered above could influence the plasticity of plant development. Plasticity will be used to refer to the ability of plants of a given genotype to develop differently, depending on the conditions in which they are growing. Thus the most extreme expressions of developmental plasticity are the various regeneration processes that are common to most plants (Figs 4, 6). There are also developmental responses to a heterogeneous environment, as when one of a number of shoots or roots is in more or less favourable conditions (Fig. 5). A final general example of developmental plasticity is the dependence of the rate and duration of plant growth on environmental conditions, resulting in the large variation in the mature size of plants of any one genotype. These expressions of plasticity require that the development of the various parts of the plant be coordinated in ways that maintain their relations and at the same time allow extreme changes. This coordination must include the relations between individual cells so as to optimize the function of organs and their contacts with the rest of the plant. The following are four major traits of the coordinating systems that are relevant to the plasticity of plant development and are indicated by the facts reviewed above.

(i) Development is coordinated and controlled by special signals, at least some of them hormonal. The synthesis of and responses to these signals are probably influenced by environmental conditions and they could thus play a major role in developmental plasticity. This, for example, could be the basis of the results illustrated in Fig. 5. Environmental conditions and organ removal must also influence development through changes in the supply of water, ions and essential metabolites. Special developmental signals are advantageous controls, however, because their dependence on the environment can be selected to be of greatest value in predicting future conditions. The signal changes can also be very rapid, since their quantities are small and they are required continuously. A major advantage of signals, furthermore, is that their effects can be specific. This specificity differentiates between the formation of new primordia and the rapid expansion growth during which most of the bulk of the plant is formed. The specificity of hormonal signals is also expressed by their different and even complementary effects on the primordial development of shoots and roots, two types of development that require the same essential metabolites. Control of development by known hormones or by essential metabolites should not, however, be considered as contrasting possibilities. Since signals such as auxin orient vascular differentiation, they must influence the supply of metabolites to the various organs. If, as suggested above, the synthesis of hormones is coupled in some way to growth rate it would, in turn, be influenced by the supply of the very resources whose distribution the hormones may control.

(ii) Though the signals involved in the interactions considered in this review may act differently on shoots and roots, they still have a wide array of effects and are not specific to any one developmental process. Instead, the specificity of the signals is for the type of organ they come from and their quantity could indicate its size and rate of development. This means that the removal of an organ, or its presence in an environment that differs from that of other comparable organs, results in key signal changes to which the rest of the plant responds. Such changes coordinate not only the development of other organs but also the differentiation of the vascular channels leading to the organs in which the signals originate. This general picture contrasts with the expectation, common in the early days of plant hormone research, that separate substances would be found to control every differentiation process. Developmental plasticity requires, however, key coordination systems and it could not depend only on a large number of specific controlling substances.

(iii) Though plasticity has fairly clear selective advantages, various degrees of developmental stability, or determination, are apparent in all living organisms. This stability of developmental relations and processes may be essential for the reliable formation of complex systems and for the optimal functioning of mature tissues. Limitations of developmental plasticity may also be necessary so as to prevent responses to transient environmental changes. The experiments considered above suggest that positive feedback relations involving hormonal and other signals could be important both in maintaining stability and permitting extreme plasticity where these relations are disrupted. Such possible feedback loops include the promotion of root primordial growth by shoots and *vice versa*, relations which appear to be at least partially hormonal. Another example is the differentiation dependence of vascularization on inductive effects of leaves while the continued development of leaves must depend on supplies reaching them through the differentiating vascular tissues. Such feedback relations have a high degree of stability that is not dependent on determination of any genetic systems or even individual cells. When the plant is damaged, and especially when organs are removed, however, new relations can be set up almost immediately. The presence of part of the plant in special conditions can be expected to elicit a slow modification of the feedback relations and lead to an adaptation to a heterogeneous environment. Positive feedback relations between organs and their vascular supplies are, furthermore, stable without limiting the increase in size. The interactions can also separate the plants into shoot–root systems that become more or less independent, as in many grasses, the degree of this independence being a characteristic of the species.

(iv) The final general suggestions concern cell differentiation in plants. Most plant cells do not appear to be highly specialized nor determined in a way that hinders developmental changes, especially during regeneration processes. This limited cell specialization is seen in the absence of any precise cellular origin of the signals that control development. As considered above, furthermore, plant cells also do not react in any significant way when they are grafted away from their original location. This lack of difference between cells contrasts with the situation in animals, where even cells that appear similar might well be unequal (Lewis & Wolpert, 1976) and interactions between cells that are grafted together show the existence of gradients of determined traits (French *et al.* 1976).

Even plant cells that are clearly specialized, such as those of stomata and vascular channels, differentiate gradually. During this differentiation the cells can be much more than passive recipients of instructions from their surroundings. Their very differentiation changes the distribution of the signals that control their continued differentiation, and thus plays a role in the patterning of the mature tissues. An example of such 'differentiation-dependent' pattern formation (Sachs, 1978*b*) is the formation of vascular strands. As discussed above, the early stages of vascular differentiation include an increased transport of the inductive signals. This restricts flow to certain cells, a 'canalization' of signal flow that leads to the differentiation of discrete strands of cells. Such feedback relations, in which the differentiating cells change the pattern of the signals that control the differentiation that they are undergoing, contrasts with the ideas of positional information (Wolpert, 1971), at least as first stated. Feedback rather than uni-directional controls of cell patterns could offer possibilities for plastic development, a topic yet to be studied.

To conclude, it appears that the opportunities for plasticity are influenced by the ways in which development is controlled. It is important that there are special signals that carry information about the presence and growth rate of organs and that the responses of the rest of the plant are gradual and include feedback relations at all levels. What is called for now is a comparative approach to developmental phenomena, to supplement the studies on model systems such as phototropism in coleoptiles and apical dominance in peas. It is thus significant that the best evidence found above for the role of auxin as a correlative signal is not a particular critical experiment but the wide range of cases in which auxin replaces the effects of a growing shoot on the rest of the plant.

References

AVERY, G. S. (1933). Structure and development of the tobacco leaf. *Am. J. Bot.* **20**, 565–592.

BALL, E. (1950). Isolation, removal and attempted transplants of the central portion of the shoot apex of *Lupinus albus L. Am. J. Bot.* **37**, 117–136.

BALL, E. (1960). Cell divisions in living shoot apices. *Phytomorphol.* **10**, 377–396.

BRABEC, R. (1965). Pfropfung und Chimären, unter besonderer Berucksichtigung der entwicklungsphysiologischen Problematik. In *Encyclopedia of Plant Physiology* Vol XV, Part 2. *Differentiation and Development* (ed. W. Ruhland), pp. 388–498. Berlin, Heidelberg, New York: Springer-Verlag.

BULLOUGH. W. S. (1975). Mitotic control in adult mammalian tissues. *Biol. Rev.* **50**, 99–127.

BÜNNING, E. (1953). *Entwicklungs – und Bewegungsphysiologie der Pflanze.* Dritte Auflage. Berlin: Springer-Verlag.

BÜNNING, E. (1965). Die Entstenhung von Mustern in der Entwicklung von Pflanzen. In *Encyclopedia of Plant Physiology* Vol. XV, Part 2. *Differentiation and Development* (ed. W. Ruhland), pp. 388–408. Berlin, Heidelberg. New York: Springer-Verlag.

BURGESS, J. (1972). The occurrence of plasmodesmata-like structures in a non-division wall. *Protoplasma* **74**, 449–458.

CARMI, A., SACHS, T. & FAHN, A. (1972). The relation of ray spacing to cambial growth. *New Phytol.* **71**, 349–353.

CLARKE, A. E. & KNOX, R. B. (1978). Cell recognition in flowering plants. *Q. Rev. Biol.* **53**, 3–28.

DESBIEZ, M. O., KERGOSIEN, Y., CHAMPAGNAT, P. & THELLIER, M. (1984). Memorization and delayed expression of regulatory messages in plants. *Planta* **160**, 392–399.

DULIEU, H. (1970). Les mutations somatique induites et l'ontogenie de la pusse feuillée. *Ann. Amèl. Plantes* **20**, 27–44.

ERWEE, M. G. & GOODWIN, P. B. (1984) Characterization of *Egeria densa* leaf symplast: response to plasmolysis, deplasmolysis and to aromatic amino acids. *Protoplasma* **122**, 162–168.

ESAU, K. (1965). *Plant Anatomy*. Second Edition. New York: John Wiley & Sons.

FRENCH, V., BRYANT, P. J. & BRYANT, S. V. (1976). Pattern regulation in epimorphic fields. *Science* **193**, 969–981.

GERSANI, M. (1985). Appearance of transport capacity in wounded plants. *J. exp. Bot.* **36**, 1809–1816.

GERSANI, M. & SACHS, T. (1984). Polarity reorientation in beans expressed by vascular differentation and polar auxin transport. *Differentiation* **25**, 205–208.

GIERER, A. & MEINHARDT, H. (1972). A theory of biological pattern formation. *Kybernetik* **12**, 30–39.

GOLDSMITH, M. H. M. (1977). The polar transport of auxin. *A. Rev. Pl. Physiol.* **28**, 439–478.

GOODWIN, P. B., GOLLONOW, B. I. & LETHAM, D. S. (1978). Phytohormones and growth correlations. In *Phytohormones and Related Compounds: A Comprehensive Treatise*, vol 2 (ed. D. S. Letham, P. B. Goodwin & T. J. V. Higgins), pp. 215–250. Amsterdam: Elsevier/ North Holland.

GOODWIN, P. B. & LYNDON, R. F. (1983). Synchronization of cell division during transition of flowering in *Silene* apices not due to increased symplast permeability. *Protoplasma* **116**, 219–222.

GREEN, P. B. & POETHIG, R. S. (1982). Biophysics of the extension and initiation of plant organs. In *Developmental Order: Its Origin and Regulation* (ed. S. Subtelny & P. B. Green), pp. 495–509. New York: Alan Liss.

GUNNING, B. E. S. (1978). Age related and origin control of the numbers of plasmodesmata in cell wall of developing *Azolla* roots. *Planta* **143**, 181–190.

GUNNING, B. E. S. (1982). The root of the water fern *Azolla*: Cellular basis of development and multiple roles for cortical microtubules. In *Developmental Order: Its Origin and Regulation* (ed. S. Subtelny & P. B. Greek), pp. 651–658, New York: Alan Liss.

GUNNING, B. E. S. & ROBARDS, A. W. (1976). *Intercellular Communication in Plants: Studies on Plasmodesmata*. Berlin: Springer-Verlag.

HARDHAM, A. R. (1982). Regulation of polarity in tissues and organs. In *The Cytoskeleton in Plant Growth and Development* (ed. C. W. Lloyd), pp. 377–403, London: Academic Press.

HARRIS, G. P. & HART, E. M. H. (1964). Regeneration from leaf squares of *Peperomia sandersi* A.D.C.: A relationship between rooting and budding. *Ann. Bot.* **20**, 509–526.

HESLOP-HARRISON, J. & LINSKENS, H. F. (1984). Cellular interactions: A brief conspectus. In *Encyclopedia of Plant Physiology* Vol. 17 *Cellular Interactions* (ed. H. F. Linskens & J. Heslop-Harrison), pp. 2–16. Berlin, Heidelberg, New York: Springer-Verlag.

JACOBS, M. & GILBERT, S. F. (1983). Basal localization of the presumptive auxin carrier in pea stem cells. *Science* **220**, 1297–1300.

JACOBS, W. P. (1952). The role of auxin in differentiation of xylem around a wound. *Am. J. Bot.* **39**, 301–309.

JACOBS, W. P. (1962). Longevity of plant organs: internal factors controlling abscission. *A. Rev. Pl. Physiol.* **13**, 403–436.

JACOBS, W. P., DANIELSON, J., HURST, V. & ADAMS, P. (1959). What substances normally control a biological process? II The relation of auxin to apical dominance. *Devl Biol.* **1**, 534–554.

JOST, L. (1931). Die Determinierung der Wurzelstruktur. *Z. Bot.* **25**, 481–522.

JUNIPER, B. E. & BARLOW, P. B. (1969). The distribution of Plasmodesmata in the root of maize. *Planta* **89**, 352–360.

KEEBLE, F., NELSON, M. G. & SNOW, R. (1930). The integration of plant behavior. II The influence of the shoot on the growth of roots in seedlings. *Proc. R. Soc.* B **160**, 182–188.

KIMBLE, J. E. (1981). Strategies for control of pattern formation in *Caenorhabditis elegans*. *Phil. Trans. R. Soc.* B **295**, 539–551.

KIRSCHNER, H. & SACHS, T. (1979). Cytoplasmic reorientation, an early stage of vascular differentiation. *Israel J. Bot.* **27**, 131–137.

KOLLMANN, R. & GLOCKMANN, C. (1985). Studies on graft union. I. Plasmodesmata between cells of plants belonging to different unrelated taxa. *Protoplasma* **124**, 224–235.

LEWIS, J. H. & WOLPERT, L. (1976). The principle of non-equivalence in development. *J. theor. Biol.* **62**, 479–490.

LINDSAY, D. W., YEOMAN, M. M. & BROWN, R. (1974). An analysis of the development of graft union in *Lycopersicon esculantum*. *Ann. Bot.* **38**, 639–646.

MARX, A. & SACHS, T. (1977). The determination of stomata pattern and frequency in *Anagallis*. *Bot. Gaz.* **138**, 385–392.

MITCHISON, G. J. (1980). A model for vein formation in higher plants. *Proc. R. Soc.* B **207**, 79–109.

MOORE, R. (1984). The role of direct cellular contacts in the formation of competent autographs in *Sedum telephoides*. *Ann. Bot.* **54**, 127–133.

MOORE, R. & WALKER, D. B. (1981). Studies of graft compatability – incompatability in higher plants. *Am. J. Bot.* **68**, 820–830.

OVERALL, R. L. & GUNNING, B. E. S. (1982). Intercellular communication in *Azolla* roots. II Electrical coupling. *Protoplasma* **111**, 151–160.

OVERALL, R. L., WOLFE, J. & GUNNING, B. E. S. (1982). Intercellular communication in Azolla roots. I Ultrastructure of plasmodesmata. *Planta* **41**, 134–150.

SACHS, T. (1968). The role of the root in the induction of xylem differentiation in peas. *Ann. Bot.* **32**, 391–399.

SACHS, T. (1970). A control of bud growth by vascular tissue differentiation. *Israel J. Bot.* **19**, 484–498.

SACHS, T. (1972). A possible basis for apical organization in plants. *J. theor. Biol.* **7**, 353–361.

SACHS, T. (1975). Plants tumours resulting from unregulated hormone synthesis. *J. theor. Biol.* **55**, 445–453.

SACHS, T. (1978a). The development of spacing patterns in the leaf epidermis. In *The Clonal Basis of Development* (ed. S. Subtelny & I. M. Sussex), pp. 161–183. New York: Academic Press.

SACHS, T. (1978b). Patterned differentiation in plants. *Differentiation* **11**, 65–73.

SACHS, T. (1979). Cellular interactions in the development of stomata patterns in *Vinca*. *Ann. Bot.* **43**, 693–700.

SACHS, T. (1981a). The control of the patterned differentiation of vascular tissues. *Adv. bot. Res.* **9**, 151–262.

SACHS, T. (1981b). Polarity changes and tissue organization in plants. In *Cell Biology 1980–1981* (ed. H. G. Schweiger) pp. 489–496. Berlin: Springer-Verlag.

SACHS, T. (1984). Axiality and polarity. In *Positional Controls in Plant Development* (ed. P. W. Barlow & D. J. Carr), pp. 193–224. Cambridge: University Press.

SACHS, T. & BENOUAICHE, P. (1978). A control of stomata maturation in *Aeonium*. *Israel J. Bot.* **27**, 47–53.

SATINA, S., BLAKESLEE, A. F. & AVERY, A. G. (1940). Demonstration of the three germ layers in the shoot apex of *Datura* by means of induced polypoloidy in periclinal clineras. *Am. J. Bot.* **27**, 895–905.

SINNOTT, E. W. (1960). *Plant Morphogenesis*. New York: McGraw-Hill.

SINNOTT, E. W. & BLOCH, R. (1939). Changes in intracellular relationships during the growth and differentiation of living plant cells. *Am. J. Bot.* **26**, 625–634.

SINNOTT, E. W. & BLOCH, R. (1941). The relative positions of cell walls in developing plant tissues. *Am. J. Bot.* **28**, 607–617.

SINNOTT, E. W. & BLOCH, R. (1945). The cytoplasmic basis of intercellular patterns in vascular differentiation. *Am. J. Bot.* **32**, 151–156.

SKOOG, M. & MILLER, C. O. (1957). Chemical regulation of growth and organ formation in plant tissues. *Symp. Soc. exp. Biol.* **11**, 118–131.

SMITH, N. G. & WAREING, P. F. (1972). The rooting activity of growing and dormant leafy cuttings in relation to endogenous hormone levels and photoperiod. *New Phytol.* **71**, 483–500.

SNOW, R. (1931). Experiments on growth and inhibition. II New phenomena of inhibition. *Proc. R. Soc.* B **108**, 305–316.

SNOW, R. (1935). Activation of cambial growth by pure hormones. *New Phytol.* **34**, 347–360.

SNOW, R. (1945). Plagiotropism and correlative inhibition. *New Phytol.* **44**, 110–117.

STEBBINS, G. L. & SHAH, S. S. (1960). Developmental studies of cell differentiation in the epidermis of monocotyledons. II Cytological feature of stomatal development in the Gramineae. *Devl Biol.* **2**, 477–500.

STEBBINS, G. L., SHAH, S. S., JAMIN, D. & JURA, P. (1967). Changed orientation of the mitotic spindle of stomatal guard cell divisions in *Hordeum vulgare*. *Am. J. Bot.* **54**, 71–80.

STEWART, R. N. (1978). Ontogeny of the primary body in chimeral forms of higher plants. In *The Clonal Basis of Development*. (ed. S. Subtelny & I. M. Sussex), pp. 131–160. New York: Academic Press.

TEPPER, H. B. & HOLLIS, C. A. (1967). Mitotic reactivation of the terminal bud and cambium of white ash. *Science* **156**, 1635–1636.

THIMANN, K. V. (1977). *Hormone Action in the Whole Life of Plants*. Amherst: The University of Massachusetts Press.

THIMANN, K. V. & SKOOG, F. (1933). Studies on the growth hormone of plants. III The inhibiting action of growth substance on plant development. *Proc. natn. Acad. Sci. U.S.A.* **19**, 714–716.

THIMANN, K. V., SACHS, T. & MATHUR, K. N. (1971). The mechanism of apical dominance in *Coleus*. *Physiolog. Pl.* **24**, 68–72.

UMRATH, K. (1948). Dornenbildung, Blattform und Blutenbildung in abhängigkeit von Wuchsstoff und Korrelativer Hemmung. *Planta* **36**, 262–297.

VÖCHTING, H. (1892). *Über, Transplantation am Pflanzenkorper*. Tübingen: Verlag H. Laupp'schen Buchhandlung.

WANG, T. L. & WAREING, P. F. (1979). Cytokinins and apical dominance in *Solanum andigena*: lateral shoot growth and endogenous cytokinin levels in the absence of roots. *New Phytol.* **82**, 19–28.

WARDLAW, C. W. (1968). *Morphogenesis in Plants*. London: Methuen.

WARREN WILSON, J. & WARREN WILSON, P. M. (1961). The position of regenerating cambia – a new hypothesis. *New Phytol.* **60**, 63–73.

WARREN WILSON, J. & WARREN WILSON, P. M. (1984). Control of tissue patterns in normal development and in regeneration. In *Positional Controls in Plant Development* (ed. P. W. Barlow & D. J. Carr), pp. 225–280. Cambridge: University Press.

WHITE, J. C. (1976). Correlative inhibition of lateral bud growth in *Phaseolus vulgaris* L. Effect of application of IAA to decapitated plants. *Ann. Bot.* **40**, 521–529.

WOLPERT, L. (1971). Positional information and pattern formation. *Curr. Top. devl Biol.* **6**, 183–224.

WOOLLEY, D. J. & WAREING, P. F. (1972). The role of roots, cytokinins and apical dominance in the control of lateral shoot form in *Solanum andigena*. *Planta* **105**, 33–42.

YEOMAN, M. M. (1984). Cellular recognition systems in grafting. In *Encyclopedia of Plant Physiology* New Series Vol. 17, *Cellular Interactions* (ed. H. F. Linskens & J. Heslop-Harrison), pp. 453–472. Berlin, Heidelberg, New York: Springer-Verlag.

YEOMAN, M. M. & BROWN, R. (1976). Implications of the formations of graft union for organization of the intact plant. *Ann. Bot.* **40**, 1265–1276.

YOUNG, B. S. (1954). The effect of leaf formation on differentiation in the stem. *New Phytol.* **53**, 445–460.

PLASTICITY IN SHOOT DEVELOPMENT: A BIOPHYSICAL VIEW

PAUL B. GREEN

Department of Biological Sciences, Stanford University, CA 94305, U.S.A.

Summary

The construction and spacing of leaves can be analysed in terms of the direction of reinforcement in the walls of the organ surface. In general, growth is at right angles to the reinforcement. When, however, tissues are actively stretched by adjacent organs they apparently take on, by cell activity, reinforcement which lies in the direction of stretch. Thus reinforcement can dictate extension direction; extension direction, when imposed on a tissue, may dictate reinforcement direction. This proposed two-way relationship has been used to model the activity of shoot meristems. It produces biophysically plausible schemes for the progressive development of various leaf structures and for the cyclical revision of apical structure seen in various types of phyllotaxis.

Introduction

Plasticity of any sort offers the challenge of trying to explain it in terms of variation on a theme. For this article, the plasticity will be of two kinds: leaf structure and phyllotactic pattern. The theme, or frame of reference, with which to try to explain this variation is that of growth biophysics.

The basic biophysical tenet is that plant growth tends to occur at right angles to the direction in which the cell, or tissue, is reinforced. Thus *Nitella* cells, or young coleoptiles, elongate because their primary walls are transversely reinforced by cellulose microfibrils (see Green, 1980). The 'hoop' reinforcement overcomes the tendency of the stresses in a cylinder to cause it to swell in girth (Fig. 1A). This basic idea for plant growth is traceable to Frey-Wyssling (1935) who called hoop reinforcement 'tube texture'.

A group of contiguous cells sharing the same reinforcement direction will be called a reinforcement field. It will be seen that a young plant organ consists of only a small number of such fields, and these fields combine to give an elongating organ an overall hoop reinforcement. Under usual conditions, a field elongates normal to its reinforcement. Under special

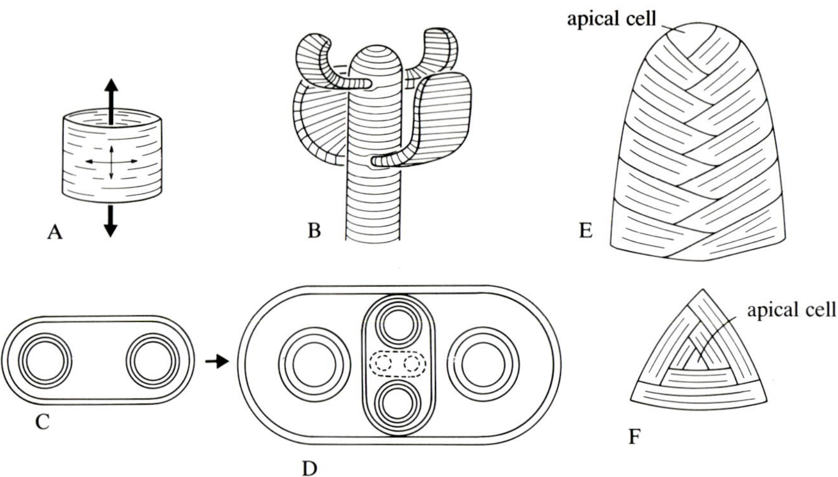

Fig. 1. Hoop-reinforcement. (A) Transverse reinforcement by cellulose gives vertical cell growth despite predominant transverse stress (cross). (B) A stylized shoot shows surface hoop reinforcement on leaf and stem. (C) Top view of an apex shows the primary outer hoops for stem, smaller secondary hoops for leaves. (D) Phyllotaxis in a decussate shoot becomes a problem of generating nesting patterns of hoop reinforcement. (E) In the fern *Onoclea* two reinforcement fields, left and right, are generated by alternate division of the leaf apical cell. This pattern approximates hoop reinforcement for the whole structure. (F) Schematic top view of the *Onoclea* shoot. Consecutive divisions of the apical cell give rise to disjointed hoop reinforcement for the shoot. Alignment of cellulose in the derivative cells parallels the recent wall and the cell's long axis. Alignment is conserved through subsequent division of the derivatives.

circumstances, however, a field may be pulled, by tissue tensions. This appears to bring on cellular responses which shift the reinforcement direction. This offers attractive possibilities for cause and effect sequences in morphogenesis. Shoot development will now be interpreted in terms of the initiation and subsequent behaviour of these fields.

For the present analysis, emphasis is placed on the reinforcement fields at the plant surface, fields comprising epidermal cell walls. The reinforcement direction on the organ surface is likely to be especially important physically because the growth of interior tissues generates very strong tangential tensions which concentrate at the surface. The interaction between these tensions and the reinforcement direction at the surface probably predominates in the control of the rate and direction of growth (see Green & Poethig, 1982).

This simplification has the advantage that analysis is mainly in a plane, albeit curved, and that this plane encompasses the entire organ. Further, this surface plane is the frame of reference used for almost all theories of phyllotaxis. By the same token it is at right angles to the usual histological plane, the longitudinal section. Traditional studies have emphasized events in the 'core' of the forming organ; this article will add information, and concepts, that place at least equal weight on events at the surface, the 'tunica'.

The major biophysical theme is that reinforcement fields combine to give the surface of the shoot and its appendages hoop-reinforcement (Fig. 1B). The variations on this broad theme fall into a hierarchy. The primary variation simply distinguishes leaves from stem. In terms of reinforcement patterns, the hoop reinforcement for internode tissue is on a larger scale than that for leaves. At the stem apex, the large hoops for the internodes encompass the smaller hoops for the leaves, as shown in Fig. 1C. Thus the first variation on the theme of hoop reinforcement is that stem tissue arises from 'first order' hoops, leaves come from the 'second order'. This matter is described in Green (1985*a*) and needs little elaboration.

A second, or deeper, level of variation will concern the origin and character of the reinforcement within leaves. Here striking differences between a fern (*Onoclea*) and angiosperms can be found. This fern leaf's hoop reinforcement consists simply of two fields generated by a single apical cell; angiosperm leaves appear to consist of three surface fields generated by a multicellular process: a single pre-existing field is split by a new field, to give the total of three. There is still finer variation, within angiosperms, in how the tripartite structure is attained.

An issue closely related to how leaves are made is that of leaf placement or phyllotaxis. Clearly, the reinforcement pattern of the apical dome must be readily convertible into that for leaf generation, but only at locations suitable for the phyllotaxis observed. At the same time, the appropriate reinforcement pattern for internodes must be generated. A simple phyllotactic sequence is portrayed in these terms in Fig. 1C, D. Proposals to meet these requirements will be made for distichous, whorled, and spiral phyllotaxis, the three major categories of leaf placement. The concept of reinforcement fields will thus be applied to issues of plasticity, or variation, ranging from the stem vs. leaf distinction to the subtleties of phyllotaxis.

Detection of fields

The major technique used to determine a field's reinforcement direction is polarized light microscopy. It is applied to thin paradermal (hand) sections of the organ surface. These sheets of contiguous outer epidermal walls, often containing whole epidermal cells, are cleared and examined in a polarized light microscope. With a 1/20 wavelength compensator slightly rotated, the birefringence of the aligned cellulose in the walls leads to diagnostic brightness variation in the image. Regions brighter than background have over-all alignment roughly (within 45°) along a given line. Regions darker than the background have alignment roughly at right angles to that line. Regions with intensity equal to the background either have no alignment (unusual) or will display their alignment prominently when the preparation is rotated by 45° (the usual case). Figure legends explain the correlation. The method is indirect but is by far the fastest one that allows one to assess the directionality of cellulose in a field of many cells.

Reinforcement fields in ferns

A striking illustration of reinforcement fields comes from the leaf of the fern *Onoclea*, as shown in Fig. 2A. This is a whole mount but, since the outer walls are both thick and highly birefringent, one sees mainly the surface. There are obviously two opposing fields on the young leaf. The fields abut along the zig-zag line down the centre. When the alignment of cellulose is diagrammed, as in Fig. 1E, it is seen that the young organ has an approximate hoop reinforcement, disjointed at the line of field contact. Using the major biophysical tenet, this hoop reinforcement explains both the form and the elongation of the young leaf primordium.

From the figure it is clear that the apical cell of the leaf divides alternately, to the left and right, each new derivative cell having cellulose alignment parallel to its long axis (Lintilhac & Green, 1976). Thus, in this fern at least,

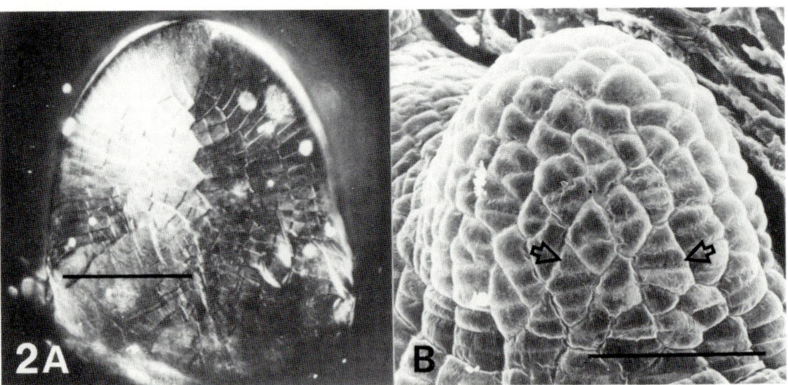

Fig. 2. Leaf primordia. Bars show 0·1 mm. (A) Whole mount of the fern *Onoclea* primordium in polarized light. Viewing the image as a map, bright regions have alignment roughly NW–SE, dark regions are SW–NE. Note two reinforcement fields (light, dark) which contrast at the zig-zag line at the centre (from Lintilhac & Green, 1976). (B) Primordium of the succulent *Graptopetalum*. Blending of histological fields is seen where diamond-shaped cells subdivide to give new files which soon align with older files at left and right to give homogeneous structure around the leaf. There is no reinforcement discontinuity as in the fern.

each field is contributed to by the division of the apical cell. Each field also extends itself by subsequent internal division of the derivatives, the cellulose alignment being maintained through these divisions. Remarkably similar behaviour is seen in the shoot of the same fern. Here the 'three-sided' apical cell produces derivatives in spiral succession. The reinforcement direction in the derived cells produces a rough hoop reinforcement pattern for the stem shoot (Fig. 1F). Thus the morphogenesis of the two fern organs can be directly analysed in terms of the origin and subsequent behaviour of a small number of fields.

From these observations, several generalizations about the fields can be put forward.

(1) Reinforcement fields are structural units intermediate between cells and tissues (e.g. two fields exist in the epidermis of *Onoclea* leaves).

(2) The decision regarding the alignment of cellulose in a cell is made, or is apparent, just after the division which formed the cell. In general, the new cellulose alignment follows the direction of both the recent cross wall and, or, the long axis of the newly formed cell.

(3) For the period when a field is self-extending through cell division, it can be compared to a clone generated by somatic crossing over (Poethig, 1984).

(4) Because of the connection between growth direction and cellulose alignment, an established field will tend to consist of parallel cell files. Conversely, parallel files are likely to share a common reinforcement directions.

This article will now analyse angiosperm shoot variation in terms of such fields.

Reinforcement fields in angiosperm leaves

As we have shown in *Onoclea*, there is a prominent apical cell in the leaf and the surface of the leaf consists of two reinforcement fields. Angiosperm leaf primordia have no specialized apical cells, however, and typically soon cease development at the tip (Esau, 1953). Thus a major departure from the *Onoclea* leaf pattern is expected.

At first glance, many angiosperm leaves appear to consist of a single reinforcement field on the surface. A blade of grass comprises essentially parallel cell files. In a young *Vinca* leaf, natural clones of pigment-producing cells reveal parallel cell files (Fig. 3A). The files, including those on the rim (Fig. 3B), are initially transversely reinforced. Previous studies on the leaf of the succulent *Graptopetalum* (Green & Brooks, 1978) also indicated uniform transverse hoop reinforcement around the young leaf. It is thus

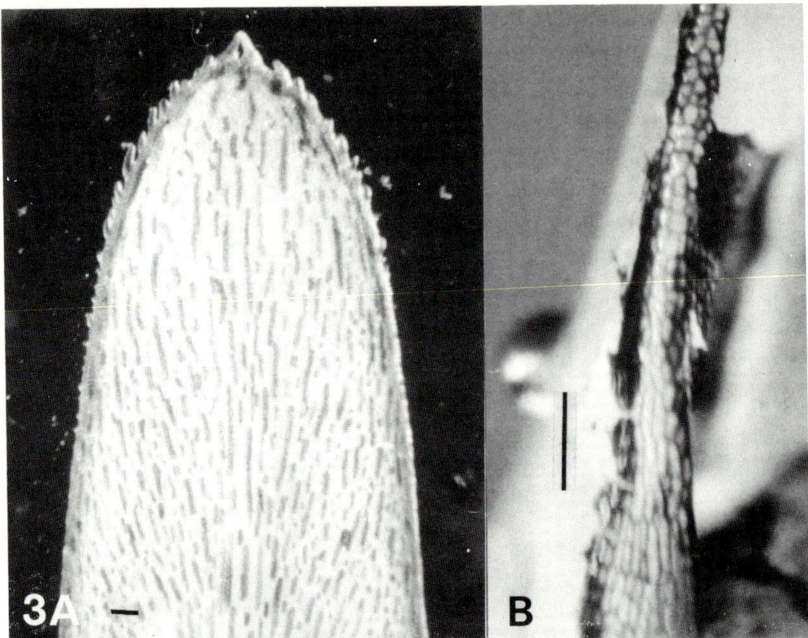

Fig. 3. Leaf cell patterns on *Vinca major*. Bars show 0·1 mm. (A) Young leaf showing natural pigment cell clones. Pigmented cell lineages show no tendency to pass over the leaf margin. Clones are subepidermal but are physically coupled to surface cells. (B) Surface cells on the leaf rim; the negative stain is aqueous nigrosin. Files do not cross over the margin.

natural to imagine that the biophysics of angiosperm leaf development could involve simply the extension, or folding, of a single field on the stem out into the apparent single field covering the surface of the leaf. The following sections show, however, that this simple suggestion is impossible, *a priori*, and that the harmonious reinforcement seen on leaves is apparently derived from a fusion, or blending, of three separate fields formed during development.

The *a priori* argument against simple outfolding is that the extension of a single field on the stem cannot yield a leaf with parallel cell files and harmonious hoop reinforcement. The stem field can indeed be 'pulled' out into a cuff, as in Fig. 4A, but note that the files pass over the rim or margin of the leaf. If the collar is further moulded into the shape of a leaf, with smooth intercalation of new cells with the same reinforcement direction, the resulting structure does not have the basic coherence of the typical leaf. In this 'moulded' leaf, the cell files pass *over* the margin; not parallel to it (Fig. 4B). The reinforcement there would be *parallel* to the margin, not perpendicular to it. More than a simple protrusion must be involved. The simplest remaining possibility is that the leaf surface originally has three

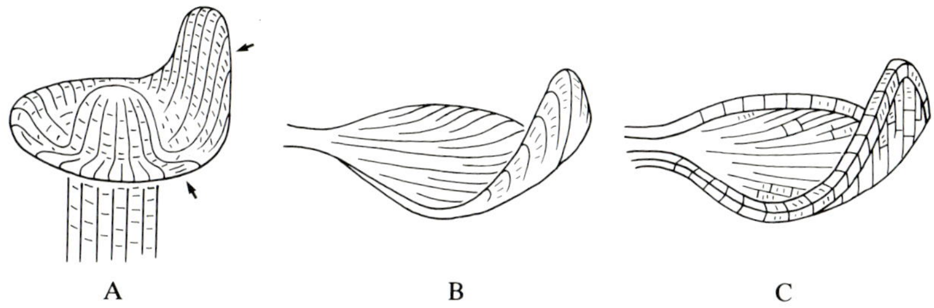

Fig. 4. Leaf surface histology. (A) A model stem with uniform cell files and reinforcement is pulled out into a collar and leaf-like structure. There is no shift in cell axiality or reinforcement. Files pass over the margin; reinforcement parallels it. (B) Detail of a model leaf formed in this way. (C) Structure of a typical young leaf (e.g. *Vinca*) with a distinctive margin roughly parallel to most files of the blade but contrasting with them at the leaf tip. Reinforcement is normal to the margin, but may change later.

fields and that these fields later coalesce to give the largely harmonious pattern (Fig. 4C). This sequence appears to be correct. Thus there is noteworthy variation, or plasticity, in leaf formation between *Onoclea* and certain angiosperms.

A lasting structural indication of a tripartite character to the leaf is sometimes seen at the tip where a distinct file, or group of files, passes over the apex of the leaf (Fig. 3A, 5D, 7D). The right-angle juxtaposition of files on the rim, relative to files of the blade, suggests three fields for the leaf surface: upper surface, rim, and lower surface. In regions other than the tip, these fields may become relatively parallel and coalesce. Blending is often complete in the petiole and in succulent leaves.

Examination of the early stages of leaf formation indicates that the tripartite surface pattern can arise by a relatively simple scheme where a single field, with transverse alignment on the stem, is split by a new field with longitudinal alignment. The idea is that the top of the original field becomes the upper leaf surface, the new field becomes the leaf rim, and the bottom of the old field becomes the lower leaf surface. Within this theme, however, there appears to be plasticity with regard to whether the new rim field is established before, or after, the leaf has protruded as a bulge or ridge. The cellular behaviour leading to the critical shift appears to be different in the two cases. Of the two generative schemes, the apparently rarer one as exemplified in the aquatic plant *Anacharis sp.* is simpler and will be presented first.

Three fields in the leaf of Anacharis

In this monocotyledon the shoot meristem is long and fingerlike above the region of leaf initiation. The stem reinforcement field is thus relatively

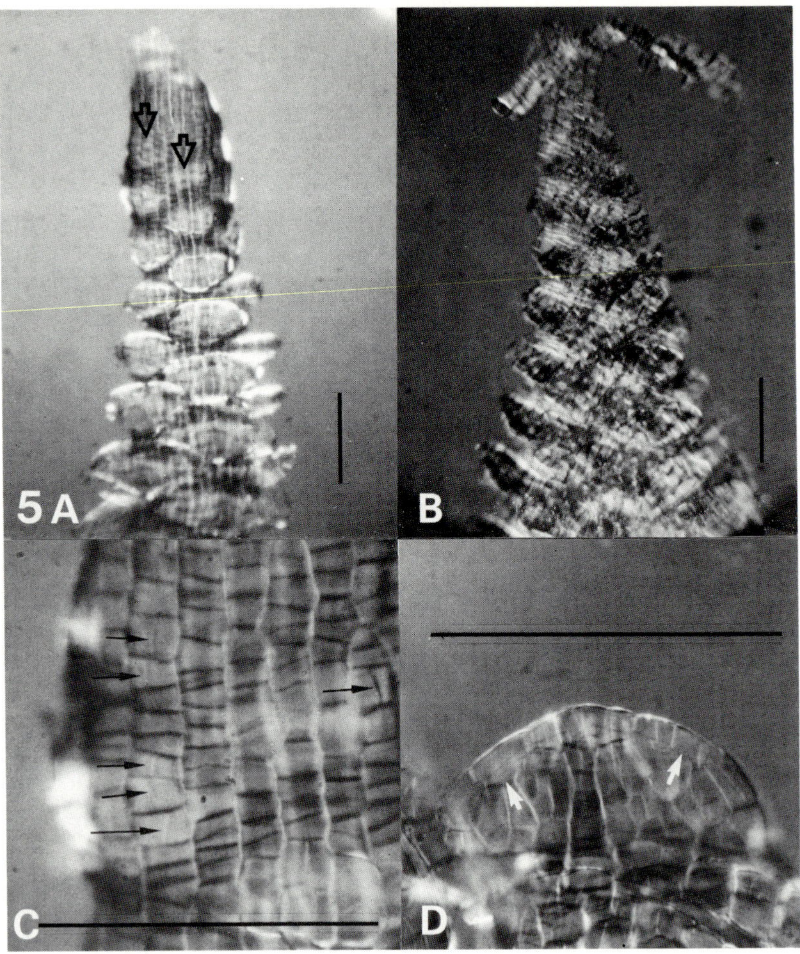

Fig. 5. Stem of *Anacharis* (*Elodea*) in polarized light. Bars show 0·1 mm. (A) Paradermal section showing regular placement of new leaves (arrows) in whorled phyllotaxis. Light areas have reinforcement mainly longitudinal (N–S on the page), while dark areas are tranversely reinforced. (B) Similar preparation but with light areas showing alignment NW–SE, dark areas run SW–NE. This shows much oblique reinforcement in the surface, hence the 'woven' pattern diagrammed in Fig. 6A. (C) Correlation between longitudinal divisions and longitudinal reinforcement at the leaf sites in (A). (D) Young leaf showing distinctive rim files (arrow) and uniseriate midrib. Dark areas are transversely reinforced (E–W), light areas have (N–S) reinforcement.

well established at the site of the leaf formation. In this plant the leaves occur in whorls of four, staggered by 45°, so it is easy to extrapolate from recently formed leaves to the site of leaf origin (Fig. 5A).

Thin paradermal sections, examined in polarized light, show that the stem has overall transverse reinforcement. There is a strong 'woven' character to the cellulose as seen when contrast is adjusted to emphasize obliqueness, alignment $\pm 45°$ to the plant axis (Fig. 5B). The first sign of a new leaf is a weakening of the transverse order, presumably due to the deposition of cellulose in the longitudinal direction. These special regions of lowered, or reversed, contrast contain several recent longitudinal divisions and thus conform to the principle that new reinforcement fields are associated with a change in division direction (Fig. 5C). Curiously, some of the low-contrast cells do not appear to be recent products of a longitudinal division. Such cells are, however, usually neighbours of cells which have had such an origin. Perhaps cells with new alignment can influence alignment in neighbouring cells, after the latter divide.

At any event, several transverse rows of cells with longitudinal reinforcement arise and constitute a new (longitudinally aligned) reinforcement field which cuts across the previous (transverse) stem field. This gives rise to a tripartite field suitable for an angiosperm leaf. The new leaf soon bulges out of the plane of the surface, taking with it the transverse fields from above and below to generate a roughly hoop-reinforced leaf (Fig. 6C, 9A, H). Unfortunately, the birefringence in *Anacharis* is not strong and the

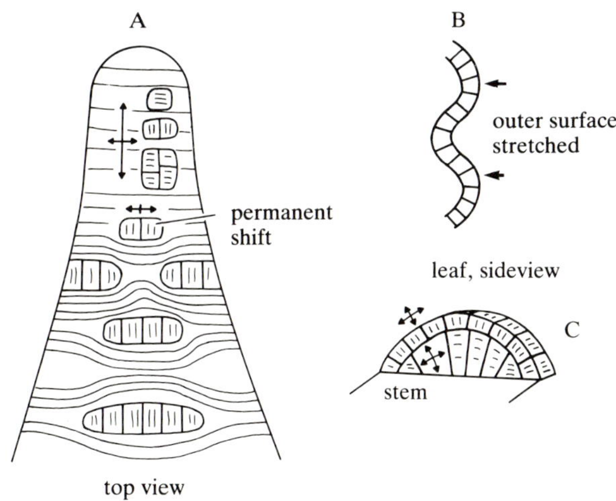

Fig. 6. Diagram of shoot tip of *Anacharis*, interpreting Fig. 5. (A) The finger-like apex is transversely reinforced and presumably shows longitudinal extension (cross). At the leaf initiation site longitudinal divisions occur and shift the reinforcement direction by 90°. These regions show transverse growth as they bulge out of the surface. Growth of leaf base modifies the stem reinforcement to give the woven structure. (B) Accordion-like behaviour of the epidermis. Longitudinal stretch in certain outer epidermal walls may bring on the longitudinal divisions. (C) A young leaf with distinct rim and blade reinforcement. Growth rate maximum in the rim field has the same value as the rate minimum in the blade. Thus fields contrasting in growth maximum and reinforcement can adjoin without tearing.

reinforcement fields become less evident as the leaf develops, even though the rim remains histologically distinct from the blade (Fig. 5D).

In summary, the key manoeuvre appears to be the early splitting of the original stem field to make three fields. The necessary reinforcement shift is associated with longitudinal divisions which give longitudinal reinforcement in the progeny cells. One should recall that in fern apical cell activity, the new reinforcement direction also followed the direction of the new cross-wall.

Three fields in other angiosperm leaves

In other angiosperms the sequence leading to the tripartite character of leaves appears to be different. This may relate to the fact that leaf formation in *Anacharis* occurs on the side of a cylindrical meristem which already has transverse reinforcement. In other forms the leaf is formed atop a dome-shaped structure where stem is also initiated. The main developmental difference is that, on the dome, the leaf first appears as a curved ridge-like bulge, before a reinforcement shift can be detected. This ridge structure has reinforcement in the form of arcs, the arcs running parallel to the curved ridge. Such reinforcement has been described for *Vinca* and *Ribes* (Green, 1985*a*). It is shown here for *Tradescantia* (Fig. 7C), and it is thus seen in both monocotyledons and dicotyledons.

At a later stage the reinforcement at the crest of the ridge undergoes a 90° shift, as shown in Fig. 7D for *Tradescantia.* Such shifts are technically in axiality, or bipolarity, but may be called polarity shifts for convenience. After this shift the surface of the leaf has the three fields and is considered established, biophysically. All but the tip of the leaf thus has 'hoop' reinforcement. Secondary wall thickening may of course alter reinforcement patterns in later stages.

Reinforcement fields on active apical domes

Reinforcement patterns were studied in apices where stem and leaf tissue are initiated in close proximity to each other on the apical dome. Genera were chosen to represent the three major types of phyllotaxis (alternate, whorled, and spiral). In the plants selected, cell division activity throughout the dome was indicated by the presence of thin (recent) anticlinal walls. This was not a universal condition. Other domes, such as that of *Lilium rubrum*, produced leaves at the base of the dome while the tip of the dome appeared inactive by the criterion used. Apices of interest were taken from potted plants or outdoor plantings during the growing season. All genera appeared to have leaves with the three-field composition described above (upper blade, rim, lower blade). The questions are: how does this three-fold arrangement arise at the leaf site, and how do pre-existing leaves determine future leaf sites?

Distichous phyllotaxis: Tradescantia

The apex of this plant is a round to oval dome which is all but engulfed by a single leaf primordium (Fig. 7A). A primordium arises at one end of

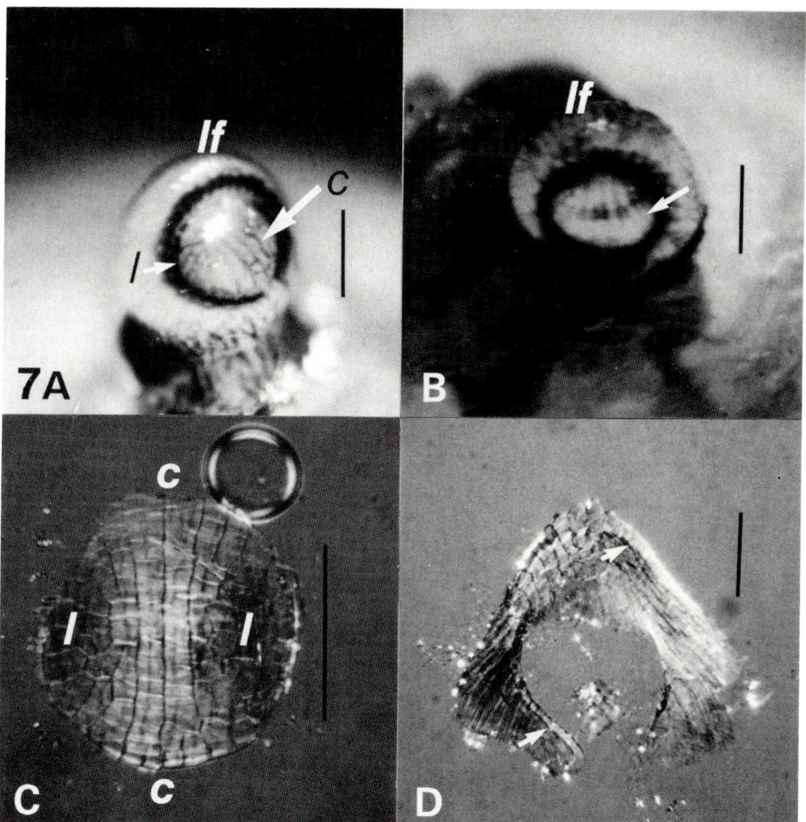

Fig. 7. Apex of *Tradescantia* with distichous (alternate) phyllotaxis. Bars show 0·1 mm. (A) Intact dome, stained to show cell pattern. Dome is almost engulfed by a clasping leaf (*lf*). Big arrow shows corridor (*c*) files, little arrow, files in the lentoid region (*l*). (B) Apex showing flaring cell file pattern at the site where the crescent-shaped new leaf starts (arrow). (C) Surface cells of the dome in polarized light. Light areas are reinforced E–W; dark, N–S. Note continuous files running along the corridor (*c–c*). Leaves form at alternate ends of the corridor. Lentoid regions (*l*) at sides have opposite reinforcement. (D) Established leaf. Arrows point out the distinctive leaf rim which has opposite contrast (light *versus* dark), and hence opposite reinforcement, to adjacent blade tissue. Rim files are interrupted by cutting the specimen.

the dome, as a curved ridge. The tips of the base of this ridge extend around the dome, following the reinforcement lines, and almost touch as they meet at the far end. Their arrival coincides with the start of the next ridge (Fig. 7B) whose tips then extend in the opposite sense. This bilateral symmetry of leaf production correlates strikingly with the reinforcement pattern on the dome (Fig. 7C). The line of symmetry is occupied by remarkably straight cell files that form a 'corridor' where the cells are reinforced at right angles to the corridor axis. On either side of the corridor are flanking regions with reinforcement mostly 90° to that of the corridor. At the margin of the meristem, alignments and files converge to give a hoop-reinforced pattern which is smooth overall (see diagram in Fig. 9B).

A leaf appears to originate, as a ridge, where the files of the corridor and flanks splay, or fan out, as shown in Fig. 7B. This region has reinforcement in the form of arcs. It bulges into a curved ridge which has a shape of a croissant. Only considerably later can one show that the crest of the ridge has undergone an axiality shift to give the leaf the three-field character (Fig. 7D, 9G). In brief, one tripartite pattern on the dome (distinctive files radial), blends to make an arc reinforced area. This area bulges and develops a different tripartite pattern on the leaf (distinctive files circumferential).

It is not clear what causes the 'arc reinforced' dome surface to bulge up into a leaf. One possibility is that local resistance to planar expansion is provided by that reinforcement on the flanks which is at right angles to the arc reinforced area, causing outward growth. At any event, the arching up starts only after the two tips of the previous leaf base have arrived at a region peripheral to the new leaf site.

Whorled phyllotaxis (Vinca, Abelia)

The reinforcement pattern consisting of a central corridor and lateral flanks, seen in *Tradescantia*, is strikingly similar to that shown for *Vinca* (Green, 1985*a*; reproduced in Fig. 8A, B). There are two large flank regions with one reinforcement direction, and a corridor whose central region has a contrasting alignment. Once again leaves appear at sites where the file pattern of the central region of the dome has fanned out into radial files and where arc reinforcement is present. As before, the new leaf starts at about the time of arrival of two growing leaf bases (not shown). In the distichous case the two bases are both from one leaf; in whorled phyllotaxis they are from two different leaves.

A similar description applies to leaf formation in the occasional triradiate apex of the normally decussate shrub *Abelia* (Fig. 8C, D, E). Here

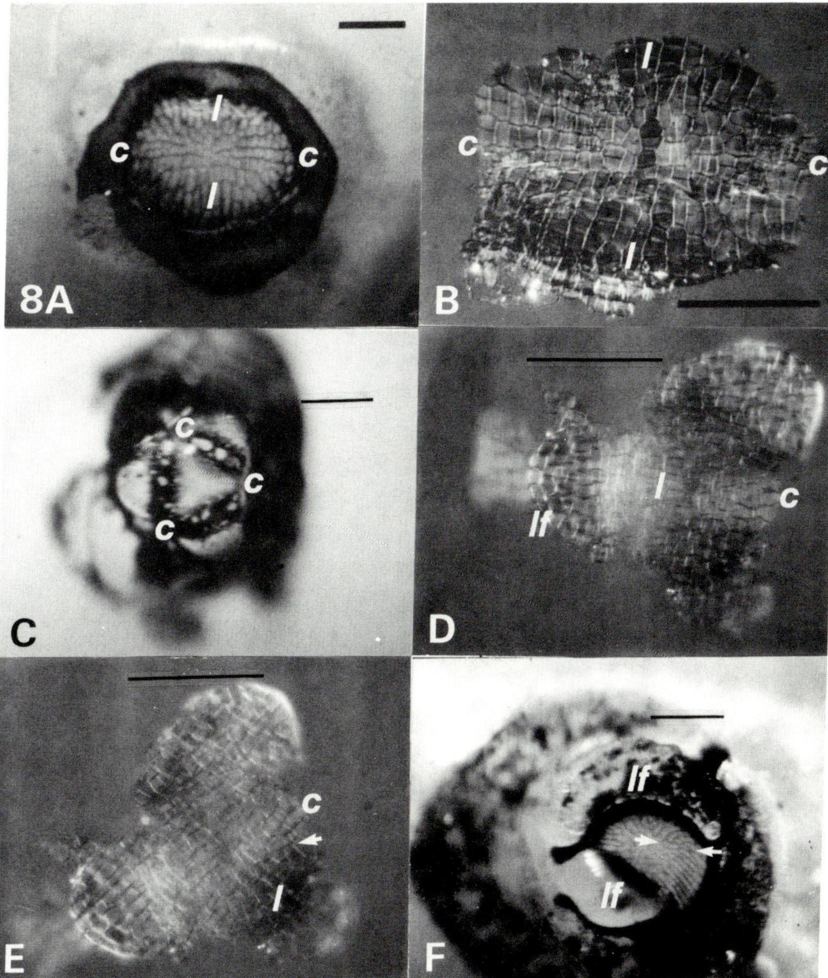

Fig. 8. Whorled and spiral phyllotaxis. Bars show 0·1 mm. (A) Apical dome of decussate *Vinca major*, with files in a corridor (*c*–*c*) and lentoid (*l*) arrangement much like that in Fig. 7C. (B) Paradermal section of the apex showing horizontal, light, corridor with N–S reinforcement. Lentoid regions (*l*) are dark and have reinforcement E–W on the page. The horizontal corridor is interrupted by a single file of cells with reinforcement appropriate for the next corridor. (C) Triradiate apex of *Abelia*. Note that the new primordia subtend large arcs, while future leaf sites at corridors (*c*) are small. (D) Paradermal section of the same apex, in polarized light, in same orientation. Light regions are reinforced N–S; dark, E–W. Out of focus flap at left is outer surface of a hoop reinforced leaf. Light region in centre is leaf inner surface and lentoid region. At right is a short corridor (*c*). (E) Same preparation rotated 45°. Dark regions are reinforced NE–SW; light, NW–SE. Arrow shows contrast between corridor (*c*) and lentoid region (*l*). (F) Apex of *Ribes*, with spiral phyllotaxis. Possible corridor file, between arrows, separates a lower field of parallel files from another field of files which curve toward the designated file. Fig. 7A, B from Green (1985*a*) with permission.

the corridor is triradiate and each of its arms has two flanking regions of opposing reinforcement direction. Thus each leaf site is derived from a local tripartite reinforcement pattern remarkably similar to that seen in the biradiate *Vinca* and in the distichous *Tradescantia* (Fig. 7C). *Abelia* dome structure is diagrammed in Figs 9D and 10. Note that the three-field structure antecedent to the leaf is seen in monocot and dicot species.

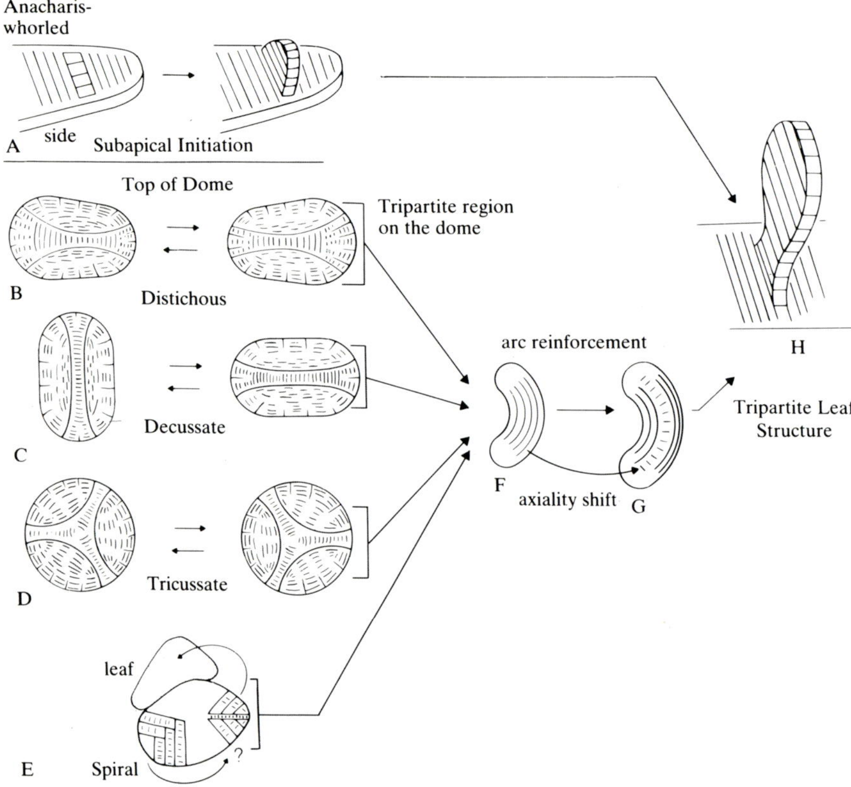

Fig. 9. Interpretation of reinforcement patterns to account for leaf formation and phyllotaxis. The stylized hoop reinforced leaf at right (H) consists of three reinforcement fields. This pattern can arise from a simple band-like axiality shift on established stem tissue, as in *Anacharis* (A). In other shoots where stem and leaf are organized concurrently, the three-field arrangement arises on an arc reinforced area (F, G). Again a band-like axiality shift forms the rim of the leaf. In distichous, decussate, and tricussate phyllotaxis the arc reinforced leaf site arises from a blending of a three-field area on the dome (B, C, D). Note that this dome pattern is different from the later three-field pattern on the leaf. (E) In spiral phyllotaxis (*Ribes*) the leaf site initially has only two fields, of different age. Thus the handedness feature of spiral phyllotaxis is evident locally in biophysical terms. There may be a later transient three-field stage. During a plastochron the apical dome structure must be revised to provide the appropriate new leaf sites (double arrows). A detailed scheme to achieve this for case D is given in Fig. 10.

In whorled forms the structure of the dome must be considerably revised during the plastochron. In decussate apices any given pattern must be recreated at 90 ° to the present orientation, during the next plastochron. In the *Abelia* dome, a new three-fold symmetrical structure must be recreated with an angular shift of 60 °. A scheme to accomplish this is given in the discussion.

Spiral phyllotaxis (Ribes)

With leaves arising just peripheral to a three-component reinforcement pattern in both distichous and whorled phyllotaxis, a corresponding configuration has been sought in spiral forms (Green, 1985*a*). In the case of *Ribes* the site of leaf origin does initially involve discontinuous reinforcement, but of only two fields, rather than the three seen above. Nonetheless, epidermal cell patterns suggest a later transient corridor and flank pattern similar to that of the other forms (Fig. 8F, 9E). If confirmed with polarized light, the local tripartite pattern for a leaf site would be found in all three types. By biophysical criteria, the distichous forms seen to date have far stronger affinity with whorled phyllotaxis than with spiral.

The corridor and flank pattern has shown up in a wide variety of apices. This pattern will serve as the focus of discussion of how new leaves form and then influence the sites for future leaves. That is, how does one corridor and flank pattern, after being converted into leaves at the dome periphery, generate the next corridor and flank pattern at the expected sites?

Discussion

Plasticity in the mode of formation of shoot organs has been analysed in terms of plant biophysics. Models for reinforcement field behaviour, and possible cellular mechanisms for the behaviour, will now be covered. Organogenesis is here viewed as mainly a problem in the manipulation of angular relationships. This stands in contrast to, or at least supplements, more common perspectives which propose chemical activation, or inhibition, to be the primary basis of localization of morphogenetic activity. The nature of leaf hoop reinforcement, and various ways of generating it, will now be discussed.

Leaves

The fern leaf consists of two flanks generated by alternate derivatives of the apical cell. This has long been recognized (Gifford, 1983; Hagemann,

1984). We add that the reinforcement direction for each flank is set at time of division of the apical cell (Lintilhac & Green, 1976), the reinforcement following the direction of the new wall.

The angiosperm leaf appears to consist of three reinforcement fields: upper surface, rim, and lower surface. This configuration can be arrived at directly, as in *Anacharis*, or from a region of arc reinforcement at the periphery of the apical dome (a variety of other angiosperms). This is shown in Fig. 9. The crescent-shaped area of arc reinforcement undergoes a localized axiality shift to give rise to the tripartite reinforcement pattern on the leaf surface. Support for the three-field concept comes from the work of Poethig (1984) on tobacco. He found large somatic clones which spanned one face of the leaf, passed over the rim, and returned down the other face. These are early clones, presumably established before the original stem field had been split by the axiality shift. Smaller, later, clones ran as narrow bands parallel to, and close to, the leaf margin. These would reflect the activity of the rim field, established later. The clones were subepidermal but, in the absence of slippage, should reflect the behaviour of the surface cells as well. Poethig's data, and the present analysis of leaf development, cast doubt on earlier interpretations that much of the leaf blade is generated by a marginal meristem with active initial cells.

The histological development of angiosperm leaves has been reviewed many times (Esau, 1953; Lyndon, 1983) with the proposition that the earliest sign of a new leaf is often a periclinal division in a subepidermal layer. In a study where phenomena in interior and surface cells were followed at the same time, Selker & Green (1984) found that epidermal changes were concurrent with those in the interior, if not somewhat ahead. The spatial frequency of microtubules was higher in the epidermis than in the cortex, suggesting a major role for the former. The association of a new division direction with a new reinforcement direction was found for the interior cells, as well as the epidermis. That is, the well-known periclinal divisions bring on the essential axiality shifts in the interior, just as longitudinal divisions are apparently necessary for the axiality shifts in the epidermis (Green, 1984). It is thus likely that a common set of cell rules will account for the appearance of a new three-dimensional organ. As an expedient, this article deals only with the transformation of the surface reinforcement pattern. To generate the full three-dimensional structure of a leaf at least one more axiality shift is necessary, for the palisade layer. This point was first made by Ziegenspeck (1948).

The issue of the 'first sign' of a new leaf can be rephrased in biophysical terms. The arc reinforced area is derived from a corridor and two flank pattern, in several genera. In distichous phyllotaxis (Fig. 7A, B, C), this three-part pattern is conserved through the plastochron, so the symmetry components of future leaves are apparently always present. Thus in this case there is no obvious 'first sign'. The same can be said for the hoop symmetry of the internodes to come.

On the apical dome a great deal of activity pertinent to the reinforcement pattern of both leaf and internode is carried out before the distinction between the two organs is clear. This contrasts with several other views where leaf initiation is viewed as a discrete event involving activation of apparently totally uncommitted tissue. Thus Holder (1979) postulates that leaf development begins *de novo* where positional information turns on the leaf genes. A similar assumption is made by reaction–diffusion schemes which provide properly positioned sites of activation (Meinhardt, 1982).

Three conclusions on the developmental mechanism emerge from the biophysical perspective. First, there is a commitment to general shoot-forming activity in terms of reinforcement patterns, prior to the distinction between leaf and stem. Second, the cells on the dome take on a significant physical differentiation, their reinforcement direction, at a time when they would be considered undifferentiated by most other criteria. Finally, this differentiation, or commitment, is reversible (Green, 1984). This reversibility is a feature of leaf formation and the cyclic geometrical revision of the apical dome. This leads into the issue of phyllotaxis where revision of the dome is done in a geometrically specific way.

Phyllotaxis

The mathematical description of phyllotaxis has been highly developed (Erickson, 1983; Jean, 1984). The apex surface is the frame of reference, as it is in our structural study. In mathematical models, the leaf is usually portrayed as a simple dot or circle (sometimes a crescent-like folioid). Our studies show that leaf sites have considerable structure in the surface plane. In distichous and whorled phyllotaxis, the leaf is derived from a site consisting of three fields, a corridor with two (lentoid) flanks. This antecedent local pattern has bilateral symmetry. In spiral phyllotaxis (*Ribes*), however, the region giving rise to a leaf consists initially of two fields, of different age.

There are three conclusions pertinent to phyllotaxis from the present work. First, leaf sites are not unstructured points or areas, but arise from specific reinforcement alignments on the dome surface. Second, in spiral phyllotaxis, where handedness is an obvious feature of the whole system, this feature is also detectable locally, at the leaf site itself. Third, distichous and whorled phyllotaxis are biophysically quite similar to each other, and different from spiral. They do not appear to be special cases of spiral phyllotaxis.

In the present treatment, it is assumed that the attainment of the appropriate reinforcement is both necessary and sufficient for leaf formation. Thus the concept of 'first available space' is reinterpreted as 'first appropriately reinforced space'. A special activation of the site may also be involved, but it is not logically required at present.

A key feature of all causal theories of phyllotaxis is to account for the effect of recently formed leaves on future leaf sites. With the basic assumption that a directional response will be related to a directional input, we postulate that the stretching action of the new leaf bases, upon the adjacent dome tissue, is the major influence. As shown in Fig. 10, the arc reinforced area for a new leaf is small. As the leaf base grows, it subtends more arc and presumably stretches adjacent cells circumferentially. There are indications that cells, at division, shift their reinforcement direction when subject to strong pull, so that the reinforcement is parallel to the imposed stretch (Green & Brooks, 1978). The tissue may extend for a while *in* the direction of reinforcement. Later, when the imposed stretch is no longer effective, the same tissue elongates normal to its reinforcement.

A variation on this theme is postulated for the apical dome. The flank and corridor regions just interior to a forming leaf are all caused, by the

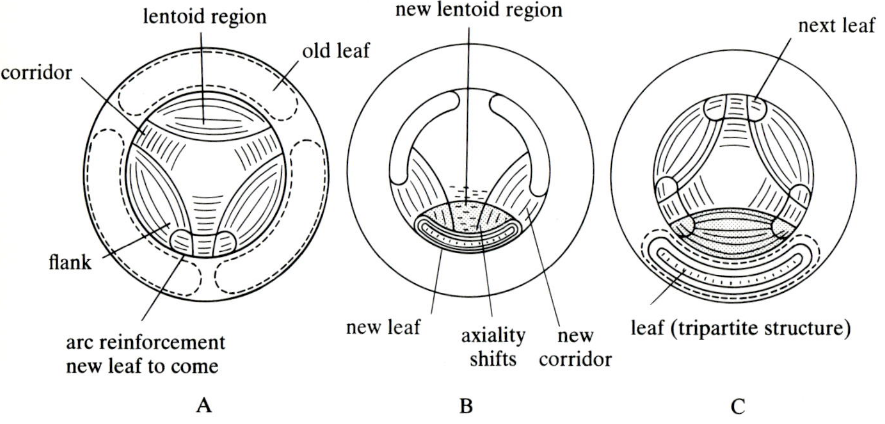

Fig. 10. Proposed mechanism for revision of dome structure in whorled phyllotaxis. (A) The leaf site is where alignment in the corridor blends with that in the adjacent flanks to give arc reinforcement. (B) New leaf bulges and undergoes axiality shift on its crest. As the leaf subtends more arc, it stretches the nearby dome tissue to bring on axiality shifts to yield a new lentoid area (shaded). (C) All three new leaves have each made a new lentoid area. The remaining central regions of the previous lentoid areas become the new corridors. The next internode arises from the large diameter circle just peripheral to the next leaves. The cycle is complete. A closely related scheme appears suitable for spiral phyllotaxis (Green, 1985*a*).

growth of that leaf, to assume a roughly circumferential reinforcement. This activity generates a new lentoid area in front of each new leaf. In the remaining gaps the unmodified previous lentoid areas become the new corridors. This revises apical dome structure. Related arguments can be made for decussate and distichous forms. This process has many features of two-dimensional resonance (Green, 1985*a*) which may explain why phyllotactic systems are relatively stable.

It is remarkable that right-angle alignment 'confrontations' are so prominent on a rounded structure in the distichous and whorled forms. Angular discontinuities are also prominent in the spiral phyllotactic apex of *Ribes* (Green, 1985*a*). In these active apical domes such discontinuities are maintained (distichous) or regenerated (whorled, spiral) at the dome centre while a smoothing off occurs at the periphery of the dome. The sharp angular contrast of 90° may be relatively easily maintained because any angle-smoothing system would be confounded by the issue of which way to turn to bring about a parallel alignment. These confrontations are not universal. Other domes, such as that of *Lilium rubrum* (unpublished) and the floral apices of *Vinca* (Green, 1985*a*) and *Crassula* (Green, 1985*b*), show no such features at the centre. The initiation process is biophysically localized at the periphery.

The surface reinforcement pattern on the floral apex of *Crassula* (Green, 1985*b*) shows hoop reinforcement for forming stamens. The sequence of initiation is similar to that described for whorled phyllotaxis except that no internodes are formed.

With the above indications that surface reinforcement pattern is important in plant development, it is appropriate to consider the cellular basis of reinforcement change.

Cellular basis of axiality shifts

The main suggestion to account for the origin of new reinforcement fields in angiosperms is that excessive stretch in a given direction leads to reinforcement synthesis in that direction. Some non-dividing cells can show a shift in orientation of cellulose synthesis (stomates: Palevitz, 1980; ethylene-treated pea: Lang, Eisinger & Green, 1982). Others, such as elongating *Nitella* internodes, persist in their transversely oriented synthesis despite severe perturbation, including imposed high rates of stretch normal to the cellulose alignment (Gertel & Green, 1977). A study of reinforcement shifts in *Graptopetalum* (Green, 1984; Hardham, 1982) found them associated with shifts in cell division direction. This is likely to be general for meristems.

The suggested mechanism therefore has two consecutive components. First, excessive stretch influences the division direction so that the new wall is parallel to the excessive stretch. Second, the orientation of reinforcement in the side walls of daughter cells becomes parallel to the new wall. These components will be discussed in turn.

Only excessive stretch rate is considered effective because in the typical meristem the stretch direction is at right angles to the reinforcement and no shift in division results. The proposition is that excessive stretch rate, brought on by either mechanical coupling to fast-growing organs (leaf bases) or stress concentration (crest or new leaf primordia), brings on the shift. Unusually rapid extension could be sensed in the cell by an increased sparseness of organelles, including microtubules.

French & Paolillo (1975) showed that alignment of stomates, and hence cell division, was longitudinal in moss capsules that had their calyptra intact. In these plants the stretch of the capsule was strongly longitudinal. With the calyptra removed, capsule growth was much less directed and the stomate orientation was random. Killed calyptra can suffice to maintain alignment, so the effect is physical (see Gunning, 1982). Thus directional stretch has been shown to correlate with division occurring in the direction of the stretch.

As to the subsequent reinforcement direction, Green (1984) found in *Graptopetalum* that new reinforcement typically followed the new cross wall, except in cases where new cell proportions were unusual. When the new wall was at one end of a narrow cell, the synthesis followed the cell's long axis and was normal to the new wall. In the present model, new cells of such configuration are unlikely to arise because the stretch of the mother cell, and the alignment of the new wall, would tend to make the new wall a long side of the new cell. Thus both the tendency for synthesis to follow the new wall, and to follow the new cell's long dimension, would lead to the same, new, alignment.

In a study of stem formation in regenerating *Graptopetalum*, Green & Brooks (1978) showed a polarity shift in the surface cells. The region of the shift had a demonstrable high strain rate normal to the original reinforcement direction. The high rate could be explained by stress concentration because the tissue spanned a broadening linear gap between two non-growing structures. The stress effect was so strong that the tissue continued to expand in the original direction of stretch even after the reinforcement direction had shifted. A day or so later the stress effect diminished; the responding tissue then grew at right angles to its reinforcement direction. In this case the cellular details of the reinforcement shift are not known, but the over-all process is very similar to that being proposed here for leaf primordia and apical domes.

There is good evidence for other influences on division direction. For example, Cooke & Paolillo (1980) present data showing that in fern protonemata the new wall is transverse or longitudinal according to which orientation gives the lesser area for the wall. Systems vary, apparently, with regard to dimensional criteria for division direction. 'Rib' meristem cells which are much broader than long, obviously place the new wall in the direction which gives the greater area for the new wall. Such dimensional criteria could co-exist with the excessive stretch mechanism, being overridden by the latter when stretch was unusually strong.

The present proposal for an effect of stretch assumes that the cell responds to strain (deformation) and not directly to the stresses that cause it. Stress is a force per unit area, acting on a body, and can be calculated in many situations. Stress cannot be transduced or sensed, however, except through its action in deforming something. For this reason it is assumed that stresses act on cells only through the demonstrable strains brought on by stress. Strain is considered a key component in the mechanisms for leaf formation and phyllotactic pattern, processes showing plasticity at the shoot apex.

References

COOKE, T. J. & PAOLILLO, D. J. JR. (1980). The control of the orientation of cell divisions in fern gametophytes. *Am. J. Bot.* **67**, 1320–1333.

ESAU, K. (1953). *Plant Anatomy*. New York: John Wiley & Sons.

ERICKSON, R. O. (1983). The geometry of phyllotaxis. In *The Growth and Functioning of Leaves* (ed. J. E. Dale & F. L. Milthorpe). Cambridge: Cambridge University.

FRENCH, J. C. & PAOLILLO, D. J. JR. (1975). The effect of the calyptra on the plane of guard cell mother cell division in *Funaria* and *Physcomitrium* capsules. *A. Bot.* **39**, 233–236.

FREY-WYSSLING, A. (1935). *Die Stoffausscheidung der Hoheren Pflanzen*. Berlin: Springer-Verlag.

GERTEL, E. T. & GREEN, P. B. (1977). Cell growth pattern and wall microfibrillar arrangement. *Pl. Physiol.* **60**, 247–254.

GIFFORD, E. (1983). Concept of apical cells in bryophytes and pteridophytes. *A. Rev. Pl. Physiol.* **34**, 419–440.

GREEN, P. B. (1980). Organogenesis – a biophysical view. *A. Rev. Pl. Physiol.* **31**, 51–82.

GREEN, P. B. (1984). Shifts in plant cell axiality: histogenetic influences on cellulose orientation in the succulent, *Graptopetalum*. *Devl Biol.* **103**, 18–27.

GREEN, P. B. (1985*a*). Surface of the shoot apex: a reinforcement-field theory for phyllotaxis. *J. Cell Sci.* **Suppl. 2**, 181–201.

GREEN, P. B. (1985*b*). Form and pattern: linkage through cellulose reinforcement as seen in flowering. In *New Discoveries and Technologies in Developmental Biology*. New York: Alan R. Liss (in press).

GREEN, P. B. & BROOKS, K. E. (1978). Stem formation from a succulent leaf: its bearing on theories of axiation. *Am. J. Bot.* **65**, 13–26.

GREEN, P. B. & POETHIG, R. S. (1982). Biophysics of the extension and initiation of plant organs. In *Developmental Order: Its Origin and Regulation* (ed. S. Subtelney & P. B. Green), 40th Symposium of the Society for Developmental Biology, pp. 485–509. New York: Alan R. Liss.

GUNNING, B. E. S. (1982). The cytokinetic apparatus: its development and spatial regulation. In *The Cytoskeleton in Plant Growth and Development* (ed. C. W. Lloyd), pp. 229–292. London: Academic Press.

HAGEMANN, W. (1984). Morphological aspects of leaf development in ferns and angiosperms. In *Contemporary Problems in Plant Anatomy* (ed. R. A. White & W. C. Dickison), pp. 301–349. New York: Academic Press.

HARDHAM, A. R. (1982). Regulation of polarity in tissues and organs. In *The Cytoskeleton in Plant Growth and Development* (ed. C. W. Lloyd), pp. 377–403. London: Academic Press.

HOLDER, N. (1979). Positional information and pattern formation in plant morphogenesis and a mechanism for the involvement of plant hormones. *J. theor. Biol.* **77**, 195–212.

JEAN, R. V. (1984). *Mathematical Approach to Pattern and Form in Plant Growth.* New York: John Wiley & Sons.

LANG, J. M., EISINGER, W. R. & GREEN, P. B. (1982). Effects of ethylene on the orientation of microtubules and cellulose microfibrils of pea epicotyl cells with polylamellate cell walls. *Protoplasma* **110**, 5–14.

LINTILHAC, P. M. & GREEN, P. B. (1976). Patterns of microfibrillar order in a dormant fern apex. *Am. J. Bot.* **63**, 726–728.

LYNDON, R. F. (1983). The mechanism of leaf initiation. In *The Growth and Functioning of Leaves* (ed. J. E. Dale & F. L. Milthorpe), pp. 3–24. Cambridge: Cambridge University.

MEINHARDT, H. (1982). Models of biological pattern formation. London: Academic Press.

PALEVITZ, B. A. (1982). The stomatal complex as a model of cytoskeletal participation in cell differentiation. In *The Cytoskeleton in Plant Growth and Development* (ed. C. W. Lloyd), pp. 345–376. London: Academic Press.

POETHIG, R. S. (1984). Cellular parameters of leaf morphogenesis in maize and tobacco. In *Contemporary Problems in Plant Anatomy* (ed. R. A. White & W. C. Dickison), pp. 235–259. New York: Academic Press.

SELKER, J. M. & GREEN, P. B. (1984). Organogenesis in *Graptopetalum paraguayense* E. Walther: shifts in orientation of cortical microtubule arrays are associated with periclinal divisions. *Planta* **160**, 289–297.

ZIEGENSPECK, H. (1948). Die Bedeutung des Feinbaues der Pflanzlichen Zellwand für die Physiologische Anatomie. *Mikroskopie* **3**, 72–85.

CONTROL OF SHOOT APICAL DEVELOPMENT VIA CELL DIVISION

R. F. LYNDON AND M. E. CUNNINGHAME

Department of Botany, University of Edinburgh, Mayfield Road, Edinburgh EH9 3JH, Scotland, UK

Summary

Cell division in plants not only partitions the protoplast but also provides the architectural framework for plant form. The shape of the shoot apical meristem is produced and maintained by gradients in the rate and plane of cell division, from the summit to the base of the apical dome, which also determine the region in which primordia can be formed. In *Pisum* leaf initiation is mainly the result of changes in the frequency of periclinal divisions at the leaf site whereas in *Silene* an increase in the rate of cell division seems more important since periclinal divisions are always present. Periclinal divisions may be permissive of primordium initiation rather than causal and may define the maximum area over which primordia can form. The occurrence in *Pisum* and *Silene* of periclinal divisions which do not seem to be related to concurrent outward growth suggests that the plane of division and the direction of growth may be controlled separately and in different ways. The control of outward growth during primordium initiation may lie in the epidermis, which necessarily grows faster at the leaf site. The initial orientation of epidermal growth at the primordial site, inferred as being normal to the plane of cell division, is predominantly longitudinal in *Pisum* but transverse in *Silene*. Longitudinal growth becomes dominant later in leaf development in *Silene*, as in *Pisum*. Several lines of evidence suggest a crucial role for the epidermis in the initial stages of primordium formation although the initial orientation of division planes in it may be concerned more with the shape of the young leaf than with initiation itself. In flower initiation primordial size becomes reduced, and in *Silene* there are alternations of higher and lower rates of cell division in successively initiated primordial types. A fuller understanding of the role of cell division in apical growth depends on better knowledge of the functional relationships between the plane of cell division, the orientation of microtubules and wall microfibrils, and the effect that division in one cell has on its neighbours.

Introduction

Cell division and organogenesis are the dominant characteristics of the shoot apical meristem, but it is far from clear to what extent the division of the meristem into cells is basic to organogenesis. Division into cells may permit more efficient expression of genes at a local level than would be the case in large cells where diffusion rates could perhaps become limiting. This compartmentation of the protoplast may be viewed as a way of erecting, between cells, potential barriers in the form of plasmalemmas through which the passage of molecules from cell to cell may be controlled via plasmodesmata (Goodwin & Lyndon, 1983), thus allowing different pathways of development to be followed in parts of the organism only micrometres apart.

In plants, a further consequence of cell division is the formation of new cell walls as part of the architecture of the organism. Since plant cells do not move with respect to each other the pattern and orientation of cell walls, and the way they subsequently develop, determines the form of the mature plant. The plane of cell division is therefore important in plants because it determines the structure of the framework within which the direction of growth of the cells may be controlled by the orientation of the cellulose microfibrils in the wall (Green, 1980; Taiz, 1984). We would therefore expect that in plants the extent and orientation of cell divisions may alter when the pattern of growth changes.

Growth of a plant can occur in two different modes, iterative and sequential. We may broadly equate iterative with indeterminate growth and sequential with determinate growth. A dominant feature of the plant (as opposed to the animal) is that growth continues throughout its life by the production of repeating units, usually fairly simple and each consisting of node, internode, leaf and axillary bud. An implication of such iterative growth is that the growth pattern changes during formation of the unit and then reverts to its original state to produce the next unit, implying some sort of feedback mechanism. Since the generation of the unit involves cell division we may ask whether there is a cyclic aspect to the rates or planes of cell division during iterative growth. If so, then an understanding of the control of cell division should throw light on the control of the generation of form, or morphogenesis.

Sequential growth is particularly characteristic of organs of limited or determinate growth, occurring for instance, in the development of a leaf. The simple leaf is formed by differentiation of the cells in sequence (Dale, 1982), although there is iteration at the meristematic level to generate the leaf blade for example. Sequential growth is also seen at the terminal meristem when the flower or inflorescence is formed. The growth of a flower is a sequence of different organs although there is iteration within each organ type, as in the repeated initiation of stamens in helical sequence in a Ranalean flower. The particular involvement of cell division in sequential growth is that it leads to the formation of groups of cells which differentiate to form organs and tissues.

Cell division in shoot apical growth and initiation of primordia

Rates and planes of cell division in the shoot apical dome

In meristems in which mean cell volume stays approximately constant the rate of cell division and the rate of cell growth parallel each other. Since the cells can be recognized as discrete units it is not only convenient to measure rates of cell division in order to measure growth rates but extremely useful and informative to be able to measure differences in rates of cell division and hence differences in growth rates in different parts of the meristem. The rate of division is typically least at the summit of the shoot apex, increasing down the flanks (Lyndon, 1973; 1983), and is maximal where the primordia are formed (Fig. 1). Although the rate of cell division may be greatest in the region of primordial initiation the growth rate may be as great or greater in the stem internodes below the apex mainly because of cell enlargement with little cell division.

The plane of cell division is not random throughout the apical meristem of the higher plant. The existence of a tunica of one or more cell layers

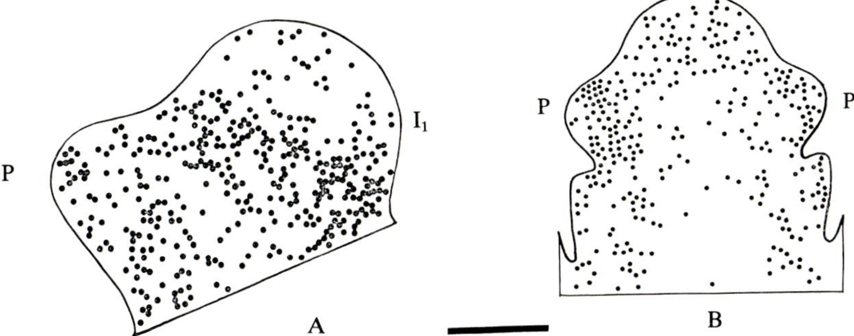

Fig. 1. Distribution of cell division in median longitudinal sections of vegetative shoot apices of (A) *Pisum sativum* and (B) *Silene coeli-rosa*. The points represent colchicine-metaphases, the density of which is proportional to the rate of cell division. The youngest leaf primordia (P) are initiated singly in *Pisum* and in pairs in *Silene*. The next primordium will be formed at I_1 in *Pisum* and at the base of the apical dome but at 90° to the existing pair in *Silene*. Bar = 50 μm. (From Lyndon, 1970*a* and Miller & Lyndon, 1976.)

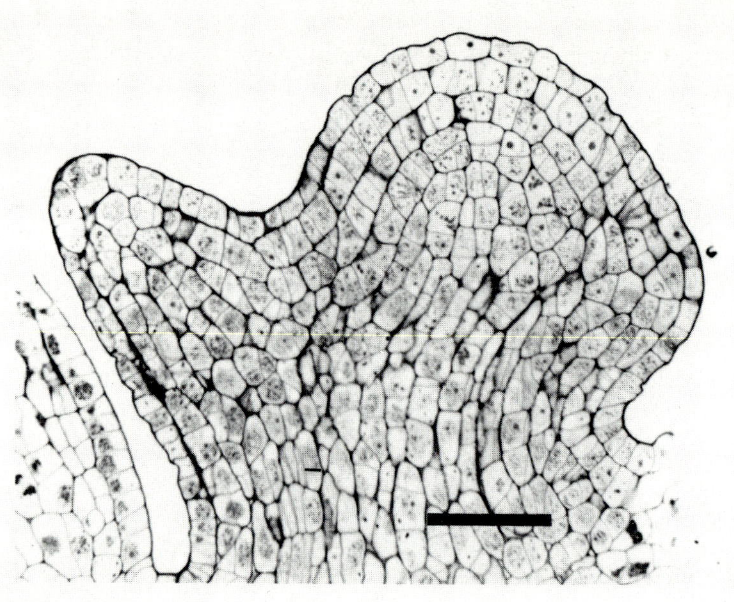

Fig. 2. LS *Pisum* shoot apex showing disruption of layered structure by increasing frequency of periclinal divisions in the young primordium (at the right). Bar = 50 μm.

implies that within it the plane of cell division is predominantly normal to the surface of the apex. When periclinal divisions do occur in the tunica they are obvious because of the layered structure of the apex. When a leaf primordium is formed the layered structure is lost by the occurrence of many periclinal divisions but can still be inferred from the pattern of the older cell walls (Fig. 2).

The occurrence of anticlinal and periclinal cell divisions is useful in distinguishing regions of the apex or cell layers in which the potential direction of growth is, respectively, in the plane of, or normal to, the apical surface. However, the planes of anticlinal divisions can be various. The surface of the shoot apex typically approximates to the form of a hemisphere. Such a domed structure could in theory be maintained by surface growth that is either isotropic, or anisotropic with a strong longitudinal component or anisotropic with a strong transverse component (Green & King, 1966). However, only anisotropic growth with a strong longitudinal component is consistent with a minimum growth rate at the summit of the dome and a maximum on the flanks (Fig. 3) and this corresponds to what is found in the shoot apical dome (Lyndon, 1983). The gradient of basipetally increasing growth rate will tend to be more marked

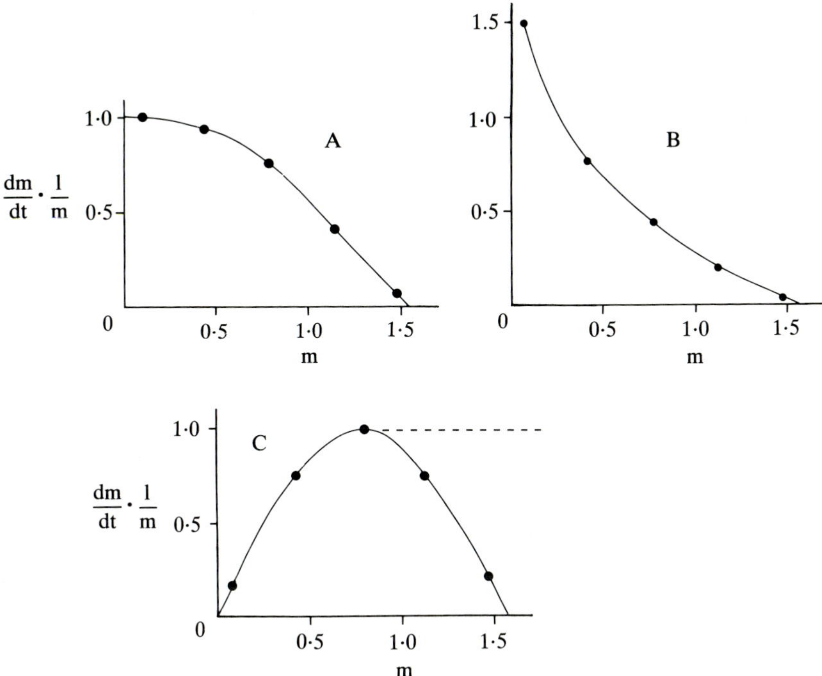

Fig. 3. The elemental rate of meridional extension $[(dm/dt)\cdot(1/m)]$ on the surface of a hemisphere as a function of distance down the meridian (m) from the summit of the hemisphere ($m = 0$) to the base ($m = \pi/2$). (A) Isotropic extension – the growth rate is maximum at the summit falling to zero at the base. (B) Anisotropic extension, rate of transverse twice that of longitudinal extension – growth rate is maximum at the summit falling to zero at the base. (C) Anisotropic extension, rate of longitudinal twice that of transverse extension – growth rate is minimal at summit, maximal on flanks falling to zero at the base. Dashed line – with an increasing longitudinal component, so that transverse extension is zero at the base of the hemisphere, the growth rate can be maintained and persist as longitudinal extension below the apical dome. (After Green & King, 1966.)

in the inner parts of the apex than on its surface because in a domed apex the growth rate of the inner, axial cells near the summit will be much less than the surface cells at the same level (Hejnowicz & Nakielski, 1979). With increasing distance from the summit the difference in growth rates between axial and surface cells will diminish until at the base of the dome the rates will be equal. Since the degree of anisotropy in surface expansion and the form of the growth gradient from the summit to the base of the apical dome are linked, we would expect to find that changes in the shape of the apical dome are accompanied by changes in the elemental growth rate of the surface. Conversely, when growth rates change to different extents in different regions of the apex the directions and planes of cell division may also change.

During growth of the shoot apex, cell size and shape remain roughly constant, so the principal direction of growth will be normal to the principal plane of cell division. The significance of the observed gradients in cell division rate and the distribution of anticlinal and periclinal divisions within the apex can be appreciated by considering the relative importance of changes in growth rates and growth directions during apical growth and the formation of primordia. We may ask to what extent the formation of primordia depends on the existence of a gradient in the rate of cell division from a minimum at the summit of the apex to a maximum on the flanks. If growth is isotropic, then the apex would bulge on its flanks wherever the growth rate (cell division rate) of the underlying tissues is greatest. If the gradient of growth rate were reversed, to be greatest at the summit, it would be the tip which would bulge, giving tip growth.

A gradient in the frequency of periclinal division from summit to flanks would cause the apex to bulge where the frequency of periclinal division was greatest (when growth rate is uniform throughout). If the frequency of periclinal division were greatest at the summit of the apex, tip growth would again result. Clearly, if the maximum in the growth rate gradient coincides with the maximum frequency of periclinal divisions then each would reinforce the other and a bulge would form at the site of the maxima. This corresponds to what occurs in the living plant in which the maximum cell division rate is on the flanks of the apex and periclinal divisions occur mainly on the flanks of the apex at the sites of leaf initiation (Esau, 1965). A primordium might be able to form as a result of either a maximum in the rate of cell division or an increased frequency of periclinal divisions. However just as some growth is essential for a change in form so are some periclinal divisions; without them all divisions would be anticlinal and whatever the rate gradient, growth would simply contribute to the longitudinal elongation of the apex. Periclinal divisions, even if only as part of a random orientation of the plane of cell divisions, are therefore essential for primordium formation if cell size and shape are to remain roughly constant.

The implications are that formation of primordia could result from either a local increase in growth rate (as long as there are periclinal divisions), as seems to be the case in *Silene*, or a local increase in the frequency of periclinal divisions, as occurs in *Pisum*. If there are two such potentially independent systems reinforcing each other then this might help to explain why apical functioning is so stable in a very wide range of environments. It would require an unusual set of environmental conditions to upset both gradients if each were dependent on different cellular and metabolic bases.

The control of the division of individual cells within the meristem is not understood. For instance, if a cell elongates and divides, the adjacent cells must necessarily elongate, but we do not know whether they necessarily divide nor if a cell does divide, whether this affects the probability of division in adjacent cells. The rate and plane of cell division may be altered by mechanical deformation (Yeoman & Brown, 1971; Lintilhac & Vešecky, 1976), but the physiological mechanisms are unknown. If growth and cell division are stimulated at a locus within a tissue, mechanical stress or other effects could perhaps be transmitted to neighbouring cells, so causing them to grow or divide or both. The existence of two populations of cells, slow and fast cycling, in the *Sinapis* apex (Gonthier, Jacqmard & Bernier, 1985) suggests that the shoot meristem may be heterogeneous with respect to cellular growth rates, and this may be possible because of its shape in a way that is not possible in the root, which grows essentially in a single dimension (Green, 1976).

Leaf initiation in Pisum *and* Silene

In the *Pisum* shoot apex periclinal divisions are absent from the summit of the apical dome and also from the side of the apical dome at which the next primordium is about to arise until about 16 h or half a plastochron before the primordium begins to be seen as a bulge, when periclinal divisions suddenly appear in this I_1 region (Fig. 4). Since the rate of cell division does not seem to change appreciably in the apical dome at the site of a potential primordium for almost two plastochrons before it is formed (Lyndon, 1970*a*) the initiation of a primordium in the pea seems to occur mainly as a result of a change in the plane of division at the primordium site (Lyndon, 1983). The position of the primordium in relation to the summit

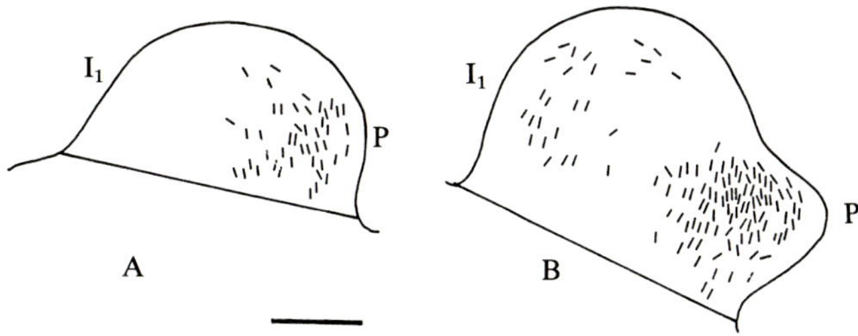

Fig. 4. Distribution of periclinal divisions in median LS *Pisum* apices. (A) When a leaf primordium, P, has just formed there are no periclinal divisions at the site, I_1, of the next leaf. (B) Later in the plastochron, periclinal divisions appear in I_1 before the next primordium is formed there. Bar = 50 μm. (From Cunninghame & Lyndon, 1986.)

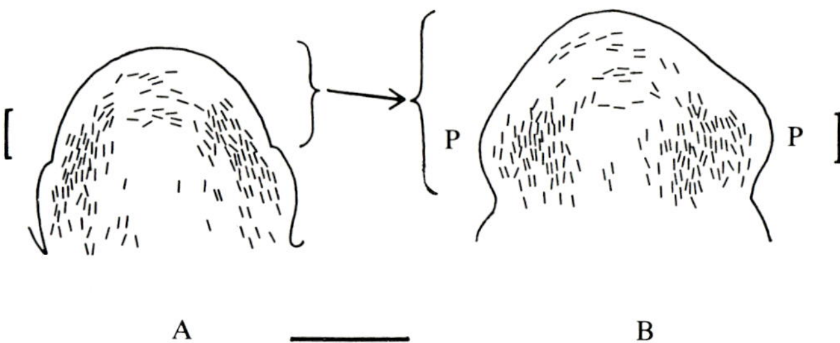

Fig. 5. Distribution of periclinal divisions in median LS *Silene* apices. Periclinal divisions are present in the apical dome and at the potential leaf sites (A) before the leaf primordia are formed, at the level of the vertical line, and also (B) after the primordia, P, have been formed. The apical dome indicated by the bracket in A gives rise to apical dome + primordia in B. Bar = 50 μm. (From Cunninghame & Lyndon, 1986.)

of the apex will, however, still be dependent on the rate of growth and cell division being maximal on the flanks of the apical dome.

In *Silene*, on the other hand, periclinal divisions are present in the apex and the apical dome at all times and there is no abrupt change in their distribution during the plastochron as there is in *Pisum* (Cunninghame & Lyndon, 1986). The distribution of periclinal divisions is not obviously directly related to the occurrence of the bulges which form the paired primordia in *Silene*. Periclinal divisions are present in much of the apical dome (Fig. 5) and in the plastochron before a pair of primordia are formed the distribution of periclinal divisions which is then established does not change appreciably but persists until the primordia are at least a plastochron old (Fig. 5). The position and formation of primordia in *Silene* seem to depend on an increase in the rate of growth and cell division at the primordial sites, which is seen as a high rate of cell division in the young primordia (Fig. 1). The primordia are able to grow out because the occurrence of periclinal divisions allows this. In the apical domes of *Silene* the periclinal divisions may be associated with a less anisotropic and more uniform expansion of the apical dome, since cell division rates seem to be similar throughout the apical dome (Fig. 1).

The position at which primordia arise on the flanks of the apical dome may therefore be fixed in both *Pisum* and *Silene* by a gradient of increasing rate of growth and cell division from the summit to the flanks of the apical dome. However the actual formation of the primordia themselves may depend mainly on a localized increase in the frequency of periclinal divisions in *Pisum* but a localized increase in the rate of growth and cell division in *Silene*. In both, the distribution of periclinal divisions in the apical dome just before primordium formation foreshadows the distribution when the young primordia are forming (Figs 6, 7) (Cunninghame &

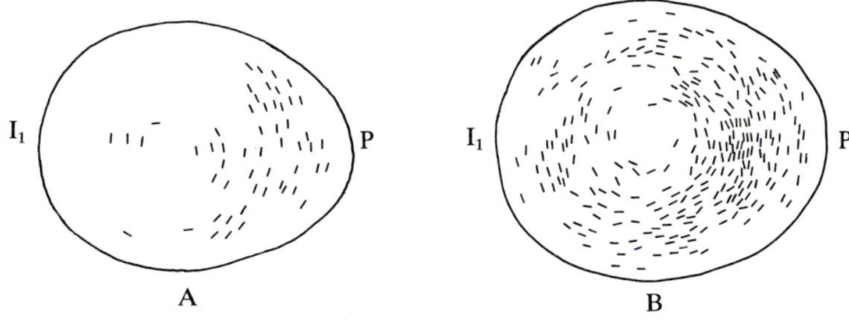

Fig. 6. Distribution of periclinal divisions in TS *Pisum* apical dome. (A) When the primordium, P, is small few periclinal divisions occur in the I_1 region, the site of the next leaf primordium, but occur over the whole of the region forming primordium P. (B) Later in the plastochron, but before the primordium is formed, periclinal divisions appear in I_1 over the whole of the region which forms the next primordium. Bar = 50 μm. (From Cunninghame & Lyndon, 1986.)

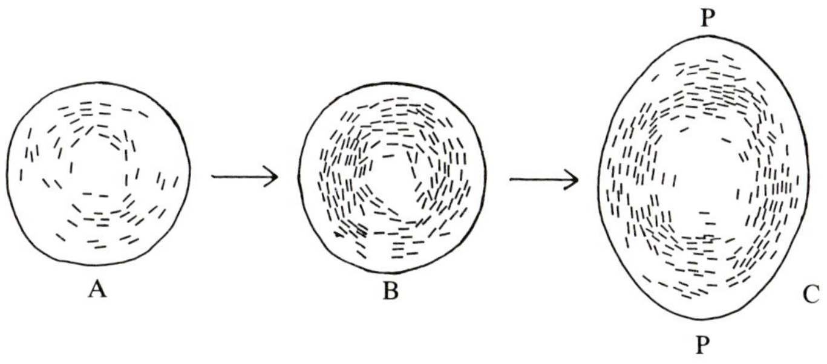

Fig. 7. Distribution of periclinal divisions in TS *Silene* apical dome (A) almost one plastochron and (B) half a plastochron before (C) the formation of the next pair of primordia, P. The distribution of periclinal divisions associated with the young primordia is already present at least half a plastochron before they form. Periclinal divisions seem just as frequent at the left and right sides of the apex which are forming only the collar linking the pair of primordia. Bar = 50 μm. (From Cunninghame & Lyndon, 1986.)

Lyndon, 1986). We may suppose that periclinal divisions, which allow a reorientation of microtubules and cellulose microfibrils (Selker & Green, 1984), also allow the growth direction to change at the site of primordium formation, and may specify the maximum area over which this can occur. The occurrence of periclinal divisions may therefore be permissive of primordium formation which may then depend on other factors for its realization. A more rapid growth rate on the flanks of the apex (when there are already periclinal divisions, as in *Silene*) may also be a permissive rather than a causal factor in primordium formation if there is some overriding structural constraint which does not allow outward growth despite the occurrence of periclinal divisions. Some such overriding constraint is implied by the data for *Silene* since the periclinal divisions seem to be at least as frequent, if not more frequent, at the sides of the apex (Fig. 7) which do not form the main parts of the primordia but only the bases of the primordial pair which meet at the sides of the apex to form a collar (Fig. 8).

Primordium formation may therefore depend on:

(1) the occurrence of periclinal divisions to permit subsequent change in the direction of growth on primordium formation and to specify the maximum area over which this may occur,

(2) a gradient in either the rate of growth and cell division or the frequency of periclinal divisions, or both, from the summit of the apical dome to a maximum on its flanks, and

(3) a change at the time of primordium initiation in the structure(s) in the apex which orientate(s) the direction of growth; presumably this is a change in the plasticity of the walls of those cells in the region which grows out to form the primordium, so that it 'gives' and is able to bulge outwards, accompanied by a reorientation of cellulose microfibrils to provide hoop-reinforcement of the axis of the new organ (Green, 1980) and a local increase in the rate of cell division in the epidermis, as in *Pisum* (Lyndon, 1982).

On this view, one role of periclinal divisions would be to facilitate the

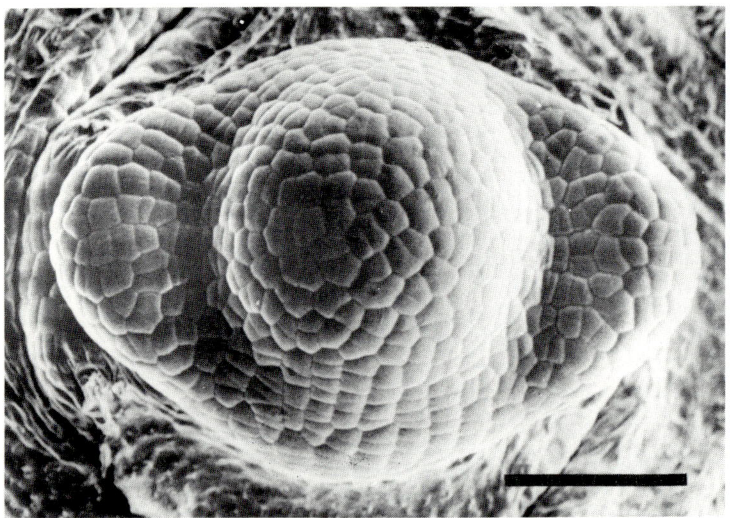

Fig. 8. SEM photograph of a vegetative *Silene* apex. There are vertical cell files at the sides of the apex where the bases of the opposite leaves meet to form a collar, but they are less obvious over the developing leaf primordium. Bar = 50 μm.

reorientation of the microfibrils (Selker & Green, 1984), the orientation of the latter possibly being an important factor in determining the axis of growth of the new primordium. Since the distribution and occurrence of periclinal divisions in *Silene* does not seem to be correlated in space or time with the formation of the primordium, the factors determining the plane of cell division and the outgrowth and axis of growth of the primordium are presumably not the same. The bulging of the surface when a new axis begins to be formed, the reorientation of the wall microfibrils, and the change in the plane of cell division that precedes it may be controlled in different ways. This is perhaps most clearly seen by comparing the formation of a new axis in *Graptopetalum*, in which a periclinal division may be followed by a reorientation of the wall microfibrils, with the continued growth of the root of *Azolla* in which no new axis is formed and a change in division plane is not followed by a change in the orientation of the microfibrils, these remaining transverse to the root axis (Green 1984).

Flower initiation

On initiation of the flower there is a decrease in the size of the primordia relative to the apical dome at the time of their initiation (Table 1) (Lyndon, 1978*b*; Lyndon & Battey, 1985) so that whatever factors control primordium size will also show changes on flowering. Periclinal cell divisions are presumably a prerequisite for the outgrowth of the primordia in the flower as in the vegetative apex. If it were the distribution of periclinal divisions which dictates where the primordia will arise and over what area then we might expect that because sepal primordia are smaller than leaf primordia at initiation the distribution of periclinal divisions may become more restricted to the positions of the incipient sepal primordia. In *Silene* this does not seem to be so (Fig. 9); the occurrence of periclinal divisions seems, as in the vegetative apex, more likely to be permissive of primordium formation than to determine the position and area of the primordia. Periclinal divisions seem to be sometimes more frequent in the developing primordia but this is only to be expected in organs developing a new axis of growth normal to the apical surface.

Together with a reduction in the size of the primordia at initiation when flowers are formed there is also a reduction in the size at initiation of the stem frustum which gives rise to the node and internode (Table 1) (Battey & Lyndon, 1984; Lyndon & Battey, 1985). This implies that fewer cells are assigned to the frustum in the same way as fewer cells are presumably assigned to the primordium. Since the size of the frustum is determined by its vertical height it may be expected that a smaller frustum would be

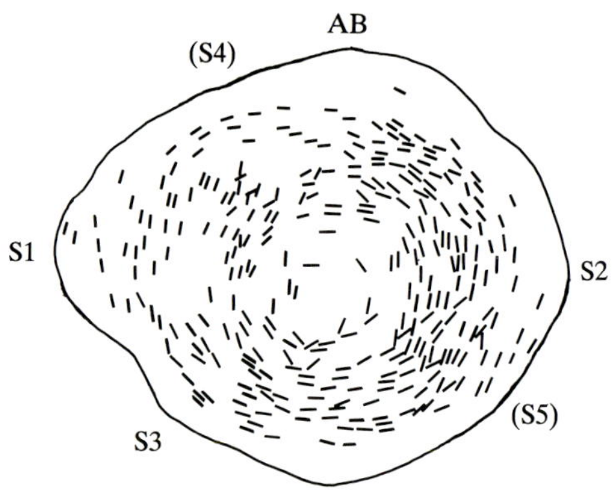

Fig. 9. Distribution of periclinal divisions in TS *Silene* apices at the level of sepal initiation. Sepals 1 and 2 are obvious, sepal 3 is just forming, and the sites of sepals 4 and 5 are shown in parentheses. AB is the axillary bud just below the flower. Periclinal divisions are present all round the apex and are not confined to the sites or potential sites of primordia. Bar = 50 μm.

Table 1. *Sizes of primordia and stem frusta at initiation relative to the generating tissue in vegetative and flower meristems*

	Primordium area	Stem frustum length
Ranunculus		
Leaves	0·71	0·63
Sepals	0·23	0·20
Stamens	0·03	0·02
Impatiens		
Leaves	0·41	0·35
Petals	0·26	0·17
Silene		
Leaves	0·33	–
Sepals	0·07	–
Petals	0·04	–
Stamens	0·08	–

Data from Meicenheimer, 1979 (*Ranunculus*); Battey & Lyndon, 1984 (*Impatiens*); Lyndon, 1978*b* (*Silene*).

associated with fewer transverse cell divisions at or just below the apex.

One of the striking things about the developing flower is that the petals grow more slowly than the sepals or stamens so that in the young flower the petals are less prominent (e.g. see examples in Sattler, 1973; Lyndon,

1978*a*). The relative growth rate of the petals is lower than that of the sepals from their inception (Lyndon, 1978*b*, 1979). This immediately poses the question of how the rate of cell division and growth is controlled locally and precisely in groups of cells on the apex which are only a few cells' width away from other groups with different rates of division. Again it may be that, what is controlled is growth rate and cell division rate is a consequence of growth rate.

The difference in growth rates between petals and other organs is only one facet of differences in growth and cell division rates throughout the developing flower. In the *Silene* flower the growth rate increases distally along the floral axis from the sepal node, in which the rate is lowest (Table 2). However, the floral organ primordia show a different trend. Since the parts of the flower originate in sequence, and the relative growth rates of the organs in the developing flower reflect the relative rates of growth and cell division at initiation of the primordia (Lyndon, 1978*b*, 1979), then the rate of growth and cell division in the apex changes during formation of the flower in *Silene* in the way shown in Table 3. There is an alternation between lower growth rates in the axillary bud, petals, and carpels and higher growth rates in the sepals and stamens. This could possibly represent an oscillation of rates of growth and cell division which is intrinsic to the sequential initiation of the different types of organs and

Table 2. *Volume relative growth rates of successive adjacent portions of the floral axis in* Silene. *(From Lyndon, 1979.)*

	Volume relative growth rate (per day)			
Growth temperature	Pedicel	Sepal node	Petal/stamen node	Floral meristem
13°	0·25	0·09	0·20	0·27
20°	0·29	0·13	0·24	0·37
27°	0·29	0·12	0·20	0·26

Table 3. *Volume relative growth rate of successive primordium types formed in the initiation of* Silene *flowers. (From Lyndon, 1979.)*

	Volume relative growth rate (per day)				
Growth temperature	Axillary bud	Sepals	Petals	Stamens	Carpels (floral meristem)
13°	0·33	0·47	0·39	0·49	0·27
20°	0·36	0·64	0·56	0·66	0·37
27°	0·43	0·57	0·26	0·34	0·26

would correspond to a periodicity of about one day (at 20 °C), about equal to the probable cell cycle time of 1 to 2 days (Lyndon, 1979).

There are clearly gradients of relative growth rate in the axis of the developing flower and possibly an alternation of higher and lower rates of cell division at the initiation of successive types of floral primordia. The growth rate is least in the sepal node, which marks the transition from iterative to sequential growth at the meristem. Whether, in the developing flower, the rate of cell division depends on the rate of growth, or *vice versa*, and whether or how these may be influenced by metabolites or growth substances produced by other floral organs or elsewhere in the plant is at present quite unknown.

The role of the epidermis: rates and planes of cell division

Green (1980) has pointed out that when a new axis is formed on the flanks of an existing one the major change in growth orientation will be found at the sides of the new axis where the major growth direction is reorientated through 90 °. This is indeed what is found in *Graptopetalum* which forms pairs of opposite, decussate leaves which are initially more or less cylindrical (Green & Brooks, 1978; Hardham, Green & Lang, 1980). However, in *Pisum* there did not seem to be an obvious change in the orientation of the plane of cell division in the epidermis at the sides of the emerging leaf primordium (Lyndon, 1982). Cell divisions on the surface of the shoot apical dome of *Pisum* are normal to the main direction of growth and are predominantly transverse (Lyndon, 1976) and remain so during the initiation of the leaf primordium (Lyndon, 1982). This was interpreted as indicating that the *Pisum* leaf was essentially a simple outgrowth of the apical surface, and that the strong dorsiventrality of the leaf meant that relatively few cells constituted the sides or edges of the leaf.

SEM photographs of the epidermis of the *Pisum* apex indicate that the cell divisions in the I_1 region are almost entirely transverse during the first part of the plastochron. During the second part of the plastochron there is apparently an increased proportion of longitudinal divisions which seems to persist during the formation of the young primordium. The ratio of longitudinal/transverse divisions seems to increase at about the same time as periclinal divisions appear in the underlying cells but becomes no greater than about 0·6. This is in accord with the conclusion that the predominantly longitudinal polarity of growth of the epidermis decreases about half a plastochron before primordium formation but is nevertheless maintained throughout primordium initiation (Lyndon, 1982).

Whether, in *Pisum*, the orientation of the microtubules and microfibrils changes in a more marked fashion, as in *Graptopetalum*, is not known. In *Pisum* the longitudinal polarity of growth of the epidermis of the apical dome, which was associated with the transverse orientation of cell division in the epidermis, seemed to become imposed on the underlying cells of the young primordium. In these latter cells the division orientation was random in the half plastochron before the formation of the primordium (Lyndon, 1970*b*; 1982). The axial polarity of the young *Pisum* leaf therefore seems to be derived from the longitudinal polarity (and predominantly transverse division) of the epidermis on the flanks of the apical dome.

In *Silene*, in the area over which a leaf primordium will form, the predominant orientation of the plane of new cell walls is transverse. As the apical surface begins to bulge to form a new primordium the proportion of longitudinal cell walls increases (Fig. 10 and Table 4). The predominant direction of growth will be normal to this and so will have a strong transverse component. The longitudinal direction of growth (as shown by the transverse cell walls) is maintained at the sides of the *Silene* apex where the opposite leaves of a pair meet to form a collar round the stem. These

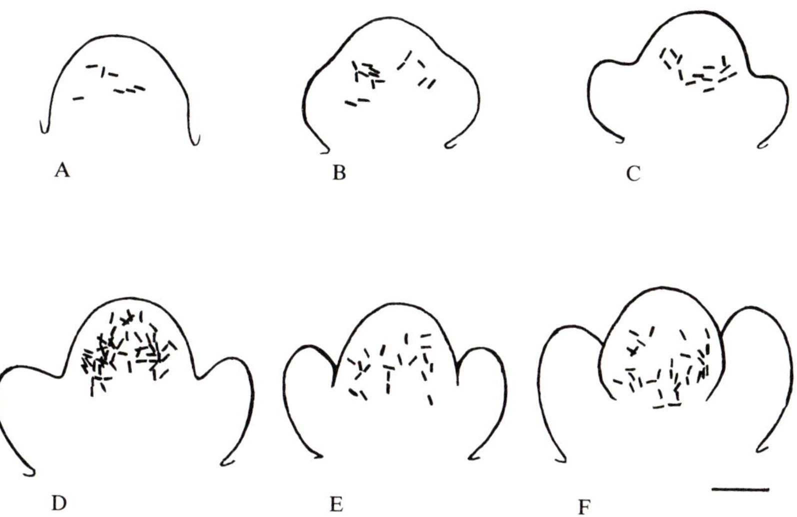

Fig. 10. Distribution and orientation of the most recently formed cell walls in the epidermis of *Silene* at the site of the next leaf primordium. Early in the plastochron (A) the new cell walls are predominantly transverse. In mid- (B) and late- (C) plastochron there are roughly equal numbers of transverse and longitudinal divisions. As the next leaf pair begins to be formed, early in the next plastochron (D) on the sides of the apical dome longitudinal divisions predominate and this is maintained through mid- (E) and late- (F) plastochron as the young primordia begin to bulge out. The preponderance of longitudinal divisions indicates that the leaf of *Silene* begins to form by mainly transverse growth. (Transverse cell walls are those $<45°$ to the horizontal; longitudinal, $<45°$ to the vertical.) Bar = 50 μm. Combined data from 23 apices.

Table 4. *Orientation of cell divisions (as shown in A–F, Fig. 10) on the flanks of the* Silene *shoot apex before (A,B,C) and during (D,E,F) primordium formation.*

		Early	Mid	Late	Early next	Early/Mid	Mid
		A	B	C	D	E	F
Number of divisions	Longitudinal	1	8	6	36	15	21
	Transverse	6	7	8	16	5	8
Ratio: Longitudinal/Transverse		0·2	1·1	0·8	2·3	3·0	2·6

conclusions are consistent with the appearance of the vegetative *Silene* apex, which shows clear vertical cell files at the sides of the apex but less obvious files over the developing primordium (Fig. 8). The *Silene* primordium therefore appears to grow at first by lateral expansion to form the bulge, unlike *Pisum* in which longitudinal expansion predominates (Lyndon, 1982). *Graptopetalum* seems to be intermediate in that the longitudinal direction of growth is conserved over the centre of the putative primordium but transverse growth occurs at the sides (Green & Brooks, 1978). These differences between *Pisum*, *Silene* and *Graptopetalum* in the main direction of growth of the epidermis of the young primordium imply that the initial orientation of growth in the surface cells is not crucial to the actual formation of the primordium. It may be more concerned with the shape of the young primordium, which shows strong dorsiventrality in *Pisum*, which extends round the apex to join with the opposite primordium of the pair in *Silene*, and which is essentially cylindrical in *Graptopetalum*. In the formation of the primordium the orientation of growth, and by implication the orientation of cellulose microfibrils in the wall, may therefore be secondary to the changes in wall plasticity and yield threshold which allow the apical surface to bulge out in a new direction. A change in orientation of the wall microfibrils in the epidermal cells may not be essential for outward growth to occur but only to direct it into the appropriate shape when it does occur.

For a primordium to form at all, the surface of the apex must bulge and the epidermis must therefore grow faster locally (Lyndon, 1983). The crux of the problem is whether the change in shape is controlled by changes in the surface layer, to which the underlying layers accommodate themselves or whether the critical changes are in the inner layers and the epidermis merely acts like a skin, reacting to what is going on underneath (Lyndon, 1971). Since growth of plant cells is driven by turgor, changes in the ability of the cells to expand in a particular direction imply changes in the properties of the cell wall and particularly in its extensibility (Cleland, 1977; Taiz, 1984). The simplest assumption would be that it is the outer wall of the epidermis which is a restraining layer and that it is alterations in the properties of this layer which will determine where the surface bulges.

The control of the shape of the expanding apical surface during organogenesis need not be entirely under the influence of the epidermis. It could perhaps be that the whole meshwork of cell walls, especially in the outer cell layers, provides the restraint on the directions of growth. While the pattern of stresses thus imposed on the cells may be concerned with orientating the new cell walls, which appear to be often in the plane of least shear (Lintilhac, 1974), it would also presumably be possible for stresses to be relieved locally deep within the tissues as long as the surrounding walls were unaffected. If so, the general shape of the apical system need not be altered even though there might be a change in the strain pattern at a particular locus within the tissues. A change of this nature would be consistent with the possibility that, in *Pisum*, cells within the apex may be affected by some metabolite or growth substance so that division planes become random, and so periclinal divisions appear (Lyndon, 1970*a*; Cunninghame & Lyndon, 1986), predominantly in the corpus cells but without a concomitant change in shape of the surface.

During initiation of the flower the arrangement of the primordia changes from that in the vegetative shoot, suggesting that the polarity and surface structure of the apex may also change. In *Clethra* the radial polarity of the epidermal cells in the vegetative apices is lost in the flowering apex (Hara, 1971, 1977). The longitudinal files of cells seen on the flanks of the vegetative *Silene* apex are clearly visible in the flowering apex at the time of sepal initiation. However, this longitudinal polarity of the epidermis is lost once the sepals have been initiated. This may be due to the loss of the predominantly transverse orientation of cell division when the apex expands during flower development. Since stamens are initiated towards the summit of the apical dome rather than on the flanks (Sattler, 1973; Lyndon, 1978*a*; Tucker, 1984) they may therefore be initiated from that part of the apical dome which lacks longitudinal polarity. The appearance of files of cells in young primordia may therefore be partly a consequence only of the position on the apical dome that the primordia arise. However, radial files of cells may later be seen again in young carpels which arise near the summit of the apical dome.

The possible involvement of the epidermis in flowering is evident in a chimaera of *Camellia* where the formation of stamens and carpels is apparently under epidermal control (Stewart, Meyer & Dermen, 1972).

C. japonica has flowers with many petals but no stamens or carpels. *C. sasanqua* has flowers with stamens and carpels as well as petals and sepals. The graft chimaera with a *sasanqua* epidermis and with all underlying cells *japonica* has stamens and carpels. Thus it is the nature and genetic constitution of the epidermis which determines in *Camellia* whether or not stamens and carpels are formed. In this chimaera the degree of epidermal control over primordium initiation apparently alters as the flower develops, suggesting that the initiation of stamens and carpels differs in some way from the initiation of other primordia. If stamens and carpels are formed only from that part of the apex in which the epidermis lacks polarity, then it could perhaps imply that only in the absence of orientation of cell division (absence of polarity) in the epidermis, does the epidermis control whether or not primordia are formed.

The existence of polarity in the growth and cell division planes in the epidermis raises the problems of how the polarity is maintained, and whether it is of importance for primordium formation. The early changes in the *Graptopetalum* epidermis (Hardham *et al.* 1980), the apparent imposition of epidermal polarity on the developing leaf primordium (Lyndon, 1982) and the control of primordium initiation in *Camellia* (Stewart *et al.* 1972) are differing lines of evidence all pointing to an important role for the epidermis in primordium formation. Perhaps the epidermis could be the locus at which the supposed morphogens involved in primordium initiation (Thornley, 1975) might act.

Control of rates and planes of cell division

Because cell size stays roughly constant in apices and, in the eumeristem, cell shape also remains more or less constant, the implication is that cell division and growth go hand in hand. It is therefore difficult to ascribe a special role to cell division other than that of maintaining the cellular structure of the tissue. For short periods at least apical meristems can function without cell division. The protrusion of a leaf primordium can begin in γ-irradiated seedlings in which division has been suppressed (Foard, 1971). The bulging occurs in the epidermal cells, suggesting that the properties of at least the outermost cell walls of these cells become altered to allow the new growth direction. In root apices treated with hydroxyurea cell division is suppressed but growth can continue so that cells become elongated in the direction of growth (Barlow, 1969) and the main orientation of growth in different parts of the apex can thus be observed directly. Furthermore, in root caps treated with colchicine or hydroxyurea to suppress cell division, differentiation of the cells continues showing that cell division is not always an essential precursor of development (Barlow, 1977, 1981). This has also been the conclusion drawn from experiments with stem tissues showing that differentiaton can occur without the cells dividing beforehand (Turgeon, 1975; Hardham & McCully, 1982).

The converse is that not all cell division in apices is necessarily just a consequence of growth in volume. The regions in which procambium developed in the pea apex could first be detected as regions with a higher frequency of cell divisions (Lyndon, 1970*a*). It is not clear whether there is any special significance in the mapping out of the procambium in this way – it may simply be that the first stages of procambium differentiation involve cell division with cells becoming narrower or reduced in volume. If so, then the higher frequency of cell division (perhaps only temporary) may be characteristic of the early stages of many different cell types.

It seems unlikely, however, that cell wall formation is only a response to the direction of growth in the shoot apex. Apart from the formation of the procambium, the occurrence of periclinal divisions with equal frequency all round the *Silene* meristem and perhaps at higher frequency at the sides at 90° to the primordia suggests that there must be some other control on the plane of division. This is also suggested by the pea shoot apex in which periclinal divisions are absent from much of the apical dome until half a plastochron before a leaf primordium is formed, and the appearance of periclinal divisions is marked neither by an increase in the rate of cell division in that part of the apex (Lyndon, 1970*a*) nor by a change in shape of the apex. In the pea, there is a hint that the orientation of division might be associated with a change of metabolism in the apex because at this same time there is a change in the amounts of starch accumulating in the plastids (Lyndon & Robertson, 1976). The mechanism for determining whether or not a primordium forms could perhaps depend on the concentrations of morphogens in the apex (Thornley, 1975). In considering the positioning of primordia in the developing flower (Lyndon, 1978*b*) it seemed necessary to postulate two sets of factors, 'one governing the positions at which primordia will arise and a second set persisting for only two plastochrons, governing the sequence in which primordia are initiated'. Perhaps the first set of factors, governing the positioning of primordia is not chemical but physical in nature and comprises the pattern of wall reinforcement in the apical epidermis recently shown to be associated with primordium arrangement (Green, 1985). Chemical morphogens may perhaps then determine whether or not the surface would bulge to form the primordium at a site predetermined by the structure of the apical surface.

Clearly there are several aspects of cell division in relation to apical growth, and growth in general, which we need to understand (Furuya, 1984). First, we need to understand what controls the plane of cell division especially in circumstances where stress does not seem important, for instance in the formation of stomata (Palevitz & Hepler, 1974) and in the formation of vascular strands, where flow of morphogen through the cells seems important (Sachs, 1975). Mechanical stress is however almost certainly also important (Lintilhac, 1974). This may be another example of the possibility of the plant making use of back-up systems to achieve the same end and thus conferring homeostatic stability on the developing system. Second, we need to understand how the rate of cell division is controlled and how this may affect the plane of cell division. For example if growth is rapid in relation to cell wall synthesis and growth, does this affect the plane of cell division differently from when growth is slower and cell walls perhaps have more rigidity at the time of the next cell division? Third, we need to understand the relationship between the orientation of microtubules and the orientation of the preceding and succeeding cell plates and the relationship between the orientation of microtubules/microfibrils and the direction of growth. It is not clear whether this orientation has to change in order for the direction of growth to change or whether it is a consequence of changes in the plane of cell division and in growth direction. It should be possible for bulging of the surface to occur without a change in orientation of the microfibrils if there is a sufficient increase in extensibility of the walls, which is presumably the determining factor in altering growth direction. It may be in these initial stages of primordium initiation that morphogens are produced which alter the physical properties of the cell walls in specific regions of the apex (Green & Poethig, 1982). If the reorientation of microfibrils follows from, rather than is causal to, initial changes in the direction of growth this would explain why in *Azolla* the orientation of microfibrils does not change when the plane of cell division changes in the root and the direction of growth remains unaltered (Gunning, Hardham & Hughes, 1978; Green, 1984).

We can see that, even if changes occurred in the epidermis but the underlying cells could not grow out (or *vice versa*), then changes in the directions of growth and the formation of primordia would not occur. Clearly the apical system is acting as a whole. There is the danger that, in trying to focus on specific aspects of apical growth or the involvement of cell division in it, we lose sight of the fact that the apex grows as a unitary system. Also there may be several different processes contributing to a given end result so that when the system is perturbed it is not disrupted, because where one aspect of the system may be inactive another may nevertheless achieve the same end though in a different way.

Unpublished work of the authors was supported by SERC Grant GR/C/34199.

References

Barlow, P. W. (1969). Cell growth in the absence of division in a root meristem. *Planta* **88**, 215–223.

Barlow, P. W. (1977). An experimental study of cell and nuclear growth and their relation to a cell diversification within a plant tissue. *Differentiation* **8**, 153–157.

Barlow, P. W. (1981). Division and differentiation during regeneration at the root apex. In *Structure and Function of Plant Roots* (ed. R. Brouwer, O. Gasparikova, J. Koler and B. C. Loughman), pp. 85–87. The Hague: Nijhoff/Junk.

Battey, N. H. & Lyndon, R. F. (1984). Changes in apical growth and phyllotaxis on flowering and reversion in *Impatiens balsamina* L. *Ann. Bot.* **52**, 553–567.

Cunninghame, M. E. & Lyndon, R. F. (1986). The relationship between the distribution of periclinal cell divisions in the shoot apex and leaf initiation. *Ann. Bot.* **57** (in press).

Cleland, R. E. (1977). The control of cell enlargement. In *Integration of Activity in the Higher Plant*, 31st Symposium of the Society for Experimental Biology September 1976 (ed. D. H. Jennings), pp. 101–105. Cambridge: Cambridge University Press.

Dale, J. E. (1982). *The Growth of Leaves.* London: Arnold.

Esau, K. (1965). *Plant Anatomy.* 2nd Edition. New York: Wiley.

Foard, D. E. (1971). The initial protrusion of a leaf primordium can form without concurrent periclinal cell divisions. *Can. J. Bot.* **49**, 1601–1603.

Furuya, M. (1984). Cell division patterns in multicellular plants. *A. Rev. Pl. Physiol.* **35**, 349–373.

Gonthier, R., Jacqmard, A. & Bernier, G. (1985). Occurrence of two cell subpopulations with different cell cycle durations in the central and peripheral zones of the vegetative shoot apex of *Sinapis alba. Planta* **165**, 288–291.

Goodwin, P. B. & Lyndon, R. F. (1983). Synchronisation of cell division during transition to flowering in *Silene* apices not due to increased symplast permeability. *Protoplasma* **116**, 219–222.

Green, P. B. (1976). Growth and cell pattern formation on an axis: critique of concepts, terminology and modes of study. *Bot. Gaz.* **137**, 187–202.

Green, P. B. (1980). Organogenesis – a biophysical view. *A. Rev. Pl. Physiol.* **31**, 51–82.

Green, P. B. (1984). Shifts in plant cell axiality: histogenetic influences on cellulose orientation in the succulent, *Graptopetalum. Devl Biol.* **103**, 18–27.

Green, P. B. (1985). Surface of the shoot apex: a reinforcement – field theory for phyllotaxis. *J. Cell Sci.* Suppl. **2**, 181–201.

Green, P. B. & Brooks, K. E. (1978). Stem formation from a succulent leaf: its bearing on theories of axiation. *Am. J. Bot.* **65**, 13–26.

Green, P. B. & King, A. (1966). A mechanism for the origin of specifically oriented textures in development with special reference to *Nitella* wall texture. *Aust. J. biol. Sci.* **19**, 421–437.

Green, P. B. & Poethig, R. S. (1982). Biophysics of the extension and initiation of plant organs. In *Developmental Order: Its Origin and Regulation* (ed. S. Subtelny & P. B. Green), pp. 485–509. New York: Alan R. Liss, Inc.

Gunning, B. E. S., Hardham, A. R. & Hughes, J. E. (1978). Evidence for initiation of microtubules in discrete regions of the cell cortex in *Azolla* root-tip cells, and an hypothesis on the development of cortical arrays of microtubules. *Planta* **143**, 161–179.

Hara, N. (1971). Structure of the vegetative shoot apex of *Clethra barbinervis*. I. Superficial and transectional views. *Bot. Mag. Tokyo* **84**, 8–17.

Hara, N. (1977). Ontogeny of the reproductive shoot apex of *Clethra barbinervis*, especially on the superficial view. *Bot. Mag. Tokyo* **90**, 89–102.

HARDHAM, A. R., GREEN, P. B. & LANG, J. M. (1980). Reorganization of cortical microtubules and cellulose deposition during leaf formation in *Graptopetalum paraguayense*. *Planta* **149**, 181–195.

HARDHAM, A. R. & MCCULLY, M. E. (1982). Reprogramming of cells following wounding in pea (*Pisum sativum* L.) roots. II. The effects of caffeine and colchicine on the development of new vascular elements. *Protoplasma* **112**, 152–166.

HEJNOWICZ, Z. & NAKIELSKI, J. (1979). Modelling of growth in shoot apical dome. *Acta Soc. Bot. Pol.* **48**, 423–440.

LINTILHAC, P. M. (1974). Differentiation, organogenesis, and the tectonics of cell wall orientation. III. Theoretical considerations of cell wall mechanics. *Am. J. Bot.* **61**, 230–237.

LINTILHAC, P. M. & VESECKY, T. B. (1984). Mechanical stress and cell wall orientation in plants. II. The application of controlled directional stress to growing plants; with a discussion on the nature of the wound reaction. *Am. J. Bot.* **68**, 1222–1230.

LYNDON, R. F. (1970*a*). Rates of cell division in the shoot apical meristem of *Pisum*. *Ann. Bot.* **34**, 1–17.

LYNDON, R. F. (1970*b*). Planes of cell division and growth in the shoot apex of *Pisum*. *Ann. Bot.* **34**, 19–28.

LYNDON, R. F. (1971). Growth of the surface and inner parts of the pea shoot apical meristem during leaf initiation. *Ann. Bot.* **35**, 263–270.

LYNDON, R. F. (1973). The cell cycle in the shoot apex. In *The Cell Cycle in Development and Differentiation* (ed. M. Balls & F. S. Billett), pp. 167–183. Cambridge: Cambridge University Press.

LYNDON, R. F. (1976). The shoot apex. In *Cell Division in Higher Plants* (ed. M. M. Yeoman), pp. 285–314. London: Academic Press.

LYNDON, R. F. (1978*a*). Flower development in *Silene*: morphology and sequence of initiation of primordia. *Ann. Bot.* **42**, 1343–1348.

LYNDON, R. F. (1978*b*). Phyllotaxis and the initiation of primordia during flower development in *Silene*. *Ann. Bot.* **42**, 1349–1360.

LYNDON, R. F. (1979). Rates of growth and primordial initiation during flower development in *Silene* at different temperatures. *Ann. Bot.* **43**, 539 551.

LYNDON, R. F. (1982). Changes in polarity of growth during leaf initiation in the pea, *Pisum sativum* L. *Ann. Bot.* **49**, 281–290.

LYNDON, R. F. (1983). The mechanism of leaf initiation. In *The Growth and Functioning of Leaves* (ed. J. E. Dale & F. L. Milthorpe), pp. 3–24. Cambridge: Cambridge University Press.

LYNDON, R. F. & BATTEY, N. H. (1985). The growth of the shoot apical meristem during flower initiation. *Biol. Plant.* (in press).

LYNDON, R. F. & ROBERTSON, E. S. (1976). The quantitative ultrastructure of the pea shoot apex in relation to leaf initiation. *Protoplasma* **87**, 387–402.

MEICENHEIMER, R. D. (1979). Relationships between shoot growth and changing phyllotaxy of *Ranunculus*. *Am. J. Bot.* **66**, 557–569.

MILLER, M. B. & LYNDON, R. F. (1976). Rates of growth and cell division in the shoot apex of *Silene* during the transition to flowering. *J. exp. Bot.* **27**, 1142–1153.

PALEVITZ, B. A. & HEPLER, P. K. (1974). The control of the plane of division during stomatal differentiation in *Allium*. *Chromosoma* **46**, 297–326.

SACHS, T. (1979). Patterned differentiation in plants. *Differentiation* **11**, 65–73.

SATTLER, R. (1973). *Organogenesis of Flowers. A Photographic Text-Atlas*. Toronto: University of Toronto Press.

SELKER, J. M. L. & GREEN, P. B. (1984). Organogenesis in *Graptopetalum paraguayense* E. Walther: shifts in orientation of cortical microtubule arrays are associated with periclinal divisions. *Planta* **160**, 289–297.

STEWART, R. N., MEYER, F. G. & DERMEN, H. (1972). *Camellia* + 'Daisy Eagleson', a graft chimera of *Camellia sasanqua* and *C. japonica*. *Am. J. Bot.* **59**, 515–524.

Taiz, J. (1984). Plant cell expansion: regulation of cell wall mechanical properties. *A. Rev. Pl. Physiol.* **35**, 585–657.

Thornley, J. H. M. (1975). Phyllotaxis. I. A mechanistic model. *Ann. Bot.* **39**, 491–507.

Tucker, S. C. (1984). Origin of symmetry in flowers. In *Contemporary Problems in Plant Anatomy* (ed. R. A. White & W. C. Dickison), pp. 351–394. New York: Academic Press.

Turgeon, R. (1975). Differentiation of wound vessel members without DNA synthesis, mitosis or cell division. *Nature* **257**, 806–808.

Yeoman, M. M. & Brown, R. (1971). Effects of mechanical stress on the plane of cell division in developing callus cultures. *Ann. Bot.* **35**, 1101–1112.

THE FLOWERING PROCESS AS AN EXAMPLE OF PLASTIC DEVELOPMENT

G. BERNIER

Laboratory of Plant Physiology, Department of Botany, University of Liège, Sart Tilman, 4000 Liège, Belgium

Summary

The field of flowering has been characterized by simplistic ideas, as exemplified by the attempts to classify plants on the basis of the kinds of environmental factors required for their transition to flower initiation and the claims that the process of flower formation in photoperiodic and cold-requiring plants is independent of correlative influences from various organs, e.g. the roots. Other examples of this simplified picture are the concept of a specific leaf-generated floral hormone and floral inhibitor and the search at the level of the meristem of a specific evocational event which would set in motion the whole sequence of other events and commit the meristem to flower initiation. Finally, there is the belief that because flower morphology is basic to species classification the morphogenesis of flowers is a rather invariable process.

All these ideas are essentially erroneous and it is shown that all aspects of the flowering process are much more flexible than is usually believed.

Floral induction may be completed by many, if not all, plants in several alternative sets of environmental factors. At least in some plants, the alternative inductive factors are perceived by different organs, indicating that these factors affect most probably entirely different processes. Thus, at induction, plasticity is extremely large and the fate of any shoot meristem appears to be controlled by a complex and flexible array of promoters and inhibitors arising from all plant parts.

At meristem evocation, there are a number of events which are fundamentally the same in many plants, but so far no single initial critical event has been found. The various evocational changes appear to form sets of interconnected systems and this complex network seems to embody some plasticity since it has been possible to suppress experimentally some of the

Abbreviations: cv.: cultivar; 2,4-D: 2,4-dichlorophenoxyacetic acid; GA: gibberellin; GA_3: gibberellic acid; LD(P): long day (plant); LSDP: long-short-day plant; SD(P): short day (plant).

most universal evocational events or alter their temporal order without impairing evocation itself.

At later stages, it has been observed that all the morphological characters of inflorescences and flowers may be experimentally altered. However, if the occasional and extreme malformations (monstrosities) caused by some growth substances are excluded, morphogenetic processes do not appear flexible to the point that the reproductive structures of one species are transformed into those of a taxonomically unrelated species. Thus, despite the fact that these processes are never absolutely fixed, plasticity at morphogenesis appears less than that at induction.

It is argued that the decreasing plasticity, observed when one scans the whole flowering process from induction to morphogenesis, is related to the progressive increase in the number of levels of organization involved.

Introduction

The physiology of reproductive development in higher plants is a field characterized by more simplistic and dogmatic ideas than any other area of plant physiology. Paradoxically this situation has its roots in a number of important scientific advances made during the first decades of this century. There was first the discoveries of photoperiodism and vernalization and the finding that flowers are initiated in general as an after effect of exposure of plants to a minimal period of favourable daylength or chilling conditions. In other words, the action of daylength or chilling is *inductive*, implying the reaching of *irreversible commitment* to flower by the plant or at least by part of it.

Then, it was found that the sites of perception of daylength and cold are the leaves and shoot apex, respectively. In the case of daylength the sensitive site is clearly distinct from the site of expression of the floral response, i.e. the shoot meristem. This suggested the existence of a translocatable leaf-generated stimulus which in the mood of the 1930s, just after the discovery of circulating sex hormones in animals, was believed to be a *specific floral hormone*. The ability, in grafting experiments, to transmit the floral stimulus from an induced 'donor' plant to a vegetative receptor supported this concept. More recently, it was further demonstrated, using the grafting technique again, that the leaves in some photoperiodic species produce a transmissible *floral inhibitor* when subjected to unfavourable daylengths. Control of flowering in these species could then be ascribed to the balance between the promoting hormone and the inhibitor. In meristems exposed to a favourable balance a highly specific act, now called '*evocation*', is supposed to occur which then sets in motion the inexorable

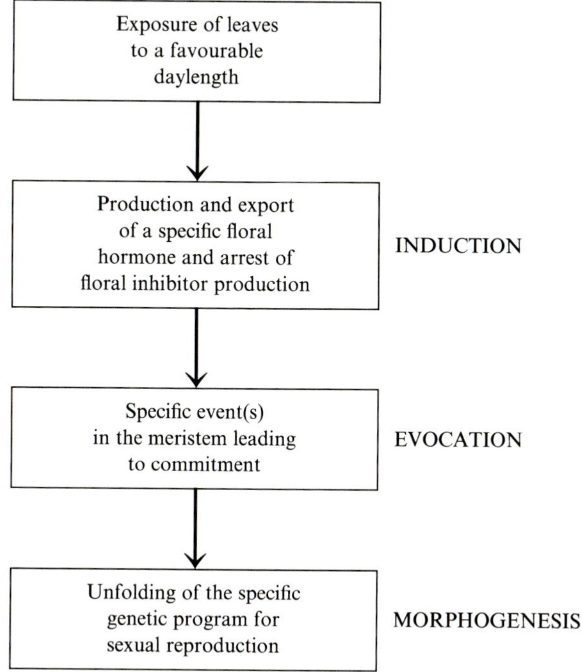

Fig. 1. The classical view of the flowering process in a photoperiodic plant.

sequence of events leading to inflorescence and/or flower formation. The nature of evocation is unknown but, because of the fascination exerted in the last decades by molecular genetics, I believe that a rather common, generally unexpressed, assumption is that evocation consists essentially in the *turning on* of the genetic program concerned with the control of sexual reproduction, i.e. the so-called '*flowering genes*' (Zeevaart, 1962; Wellensiek, 1977).

Finally, because flower morphology is basic to species identification and classification, there was also a tacit feeling that flower morphogenesis by evoked meristems is a rather invariable process.

As illustrated in Fig. 1, using the example of a photoperiodic species, putting all these ideas together results in a very attractive interpretation of the control of reproductive development. The appeal and persistence of such a hypothetical scheme has no doubt been based on its simplicity and coherence, derived respectively from linearity and specificity of all steps throughout. There are many objections to this theory, however, and my aim here will be to pinpoint the experimental data that contradict this rigid scheme and show that most aspects of reproductive development are much less specific and much more flexible than is usually believed.

Induction of flower initiation

Do plants require specific inductive factors?

Investigations in growth cabinets, where the effects of a variety of natural and unnatural combinations of environmental factors can be studied, have revealed that most, if not all, species are able to flower in several different environments. In other words, there are *alternative pathways to induction* of flowering in most plants.

The response of virtually all species sensitive to daylength can be profoundly altered by manipulating the temperature conditions. Thus, plants which are absolute LDP or SDP at temperatures around 20 °C become progressively independent of daylength when the temperature is dropped towards the vernalizing range (Vince-Prue, 1975; Bernier, Kinet & Sachs, 1981*a*; Salisbury, 1982). This behaviour is illustrated in Fig. 2 in the case of the absolute SDP *Perilla*.

Conversely, the natural low temperature requirement (vernalization) of several species, such as *Poa pratensis*, can be bypassed by exposure to SD at normal temperatures (Fig. 3) (Chouard, 1960; Lang, 1965; Vince-Prue,

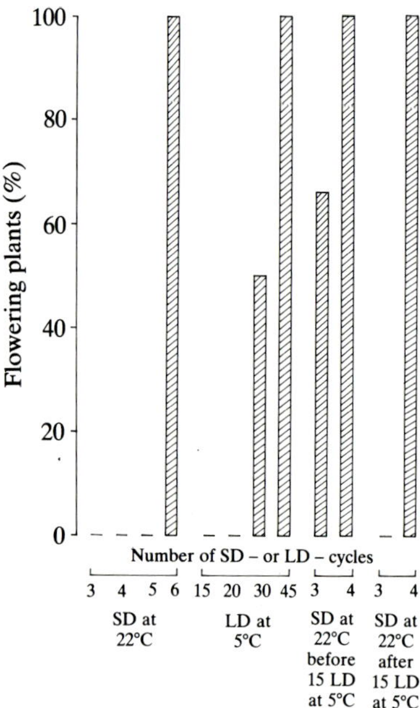

Fig. 2. Flower initiation in the SDP *Perilla ocymoides* as a result of exposure to 9 h SD at 22 °C or to low temperature (5 °C) in LD (continuous light) or a combination of these two inductive treatments given at a subthreshold level and in different orders. Note that this plant never flowers in LD at 22 °C. (Adapted from Deronne & Blondon, 1977.)

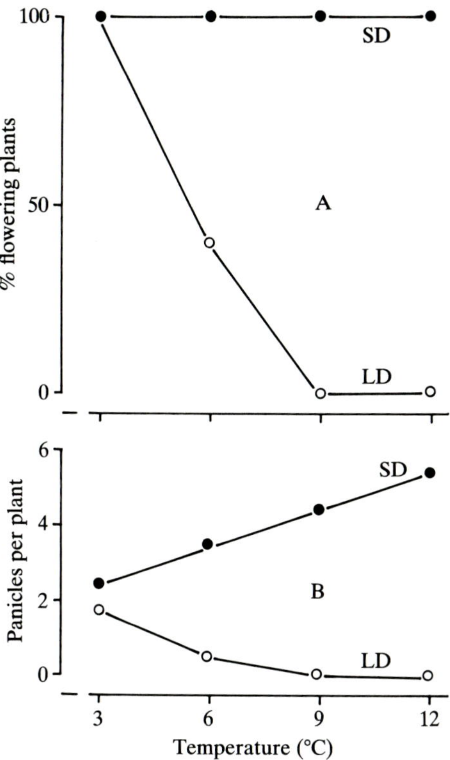

Fig. 3. Interaction of temperature and photoperiod on subsequent flowering in continuous light at 21 °C in a cold-requiring cv. of *Poa pratensis* (cv. Holt). Treatments were applied during 8 weeks. Continuous light at 21 °C is required for inflorescence development and culm elongation. ●—●, 10 h SD; ○—○, 24 h LD. (From Heide, 1980.)

1975). Thus, as noted already by Lang (1965), many plants might be equally classified as SDP or cold-requiring plants since there is no way of deciding which of their alternative requirements is most basic in the conditions of a growth cabinet.

Temperatures around or above 30 °C may also suppress the requirement for LD in various LDP as well as the need of vernalization in few cold-requiring plants (Bernier *et al.* 1981*a*). Other factors that may substitute for the LD requirement of some LDP are high irradiance, increased CO_2 concentration or absence of oxygen in the atmosphere (Bernier *et al.* 1981*a*). High irradiance can also be used to bypass the cold requirement in *Geum urbanum* (Tranh Thanh Van, 1965) and Shuokan *Chrysanthemum* (Blondon, 1976).

Surprisingly, the different environmental factors that promote flower initiation in a given species may be of a *totally opposite* nature. Thus, high temperatures which in a majority of cold-requiring plants are known as 'devernalizing' since they oppose the effect of chilling, may substitute for the required cold treatment in *Festuca arundinacea* and *Scrofularia alata* (Blondon, 1971; Larrieu, 1976).

A similar situation is disclosed in several LDP, such as *Sinapis*, beet, *Rudbeckia*, the ld mutant of *Arabidopsis*, etc., which can initiate their flowers not only in LD, including continuous light, but also in continuous darkness (Bernier *et al.* 1981*a*).

Thus, *the mechanisms controlling floral induction appear extremely flexible*. There are several pathways to induction in a given species and photoperiodism or vernalization is only one of these pathways. Clearly, all environmental factors interact such that each factor changes the threshold values for the effectiveness of the others. *The resulting matrix of controls forms a stunning array.*

Comparative efficiency and summation of different inductive factors

The efficiency of the different factors that cause flower initiation in a single species, estimated from the number of 24 h cycles during which these treatments have to be applied to reach 100 % flowering, varies enormously (Fig. 2). Natural inductive factors are not necessarily more efficient than substitute treatments, as shown by the fact that vernalized sugar beet and the ld mutant of *Arabidopsis*, that are normally absolute LDP, flower more rapidly in total darkness than in LD (Bernier *et al.* 1981*a*). Also, flower formation is obtained in *Scrofularia alata* after a vernalization of 7 weeks (natural induction) or after exposure to the substitute high temperature for only 4 weeks (Larrieu, 1976).

In many of the cases cited above, plants that are exposed successively to two different inductive factors, each at a subthreshold level, will flower indicating summation of whatever changes are caused by each treatment (Fig. 2). In *Silene armeria*, summation occurs irrespective of the kinds of inductive factors combined (LD, low or high temperature) and of their sequences (Wellensiek, 1967). Flexibility in *Silene* is complete, but this is not the general situation. In the SDP *Perilla*, subminimal SD and low-temperature treatments can be summated but, as seen in Fig. 2, summation is more efficient when the SD are given before the low temperature. In the other SDP *Pharbitis*, both high irradiance and low temperature in continuous light may each substitute for photoinduction. These two factors, each given at a subthreshold level, are again summated but *only* when high irradiance is given before the cold (Shinozaki *et al.* 1982). Flexibility is reduced in these cases, and a similar situation was disclosed by Blondon

(1971) in *Festuca* where summation is much easier when the subthreshold cold treatment is given before rather than after the subthreshold treatment by high temperature.

The possibility of summation of subthreshold treatments has been generally taken to suggest that the different inductive factors act through some common mechanism (Blondon, 1971; Wellensiek, 1967; Deronne & Blondon, 1977), but since the flowering response markedly depends in some cases on the sequence of inductive treatments I feel, on the contrary, that the *various factors may initially act on totally different mechanisms*. This view is supported by the observations summarized next.

What plant part perceives the different environmental factors?

Daylength and low temperature, which substitute for each other in many plants, are perceived in general by different plant parts (see Introduction). Since the effects of daylength on mature leaves and those of chilling on the shoot apex are likely to be extremely different there is reason to propose that flower initiation within the same plant may be controlled by very different mechanisms.

Interestingly, the cold treatment substituting for the daylength requirement in the SDP *Perilla* and *Pharbitis* was claimed to be perceived by the leaves, not by the apex (Deronne & Blondon, 1977; Shinozaki & Takimoto, 1982). Such a conclusion can only be tentative, however, when it is based on experiments in which leaves (cotyledons) are removed before or during the cold treatment, e.g. in *Pharbitis* (Shinozaki & Takimoto, 1982). It is known indeed that thermoinduction of apices is almost impossible in the absence of carbohydrates (Lang, 1965), a situation which is likely to occur in defoliated plants.

In the LDP *Silene armeria*, the requirement for LD is suppressed by (a) low temperatures probably perceived by the apex (Wellensiek, personal communication), (b) high temperatures demonstrated to be perceived by the root system (Wellensiek, 1968), and (c) increased CO_2 concentrations in the air (Purohit & Tregunna, 1974), presumably perceived by the leaves.

The situation in cold-requiring plants seems equally complex, as exemplified in the case of cabbage. In this plant the required chilling treatment is known to be perceived by the shoot apex (Lang, 1965) and the effect of cold can be abolished by a subsequent exposure to high temperature, a phenomenon called 'devernalization'. Recently, Pressman & Negbi (1981) have shown that the high temperature is perceived, not by the apex as expected, but by the roots.

A general interpretation of the daylength/temperature interactions, in line with the classical idea (Fig. 1) that flowering in photoperiodic species is controlled by a balance between a promoter and an inhibitor, both of foliar origin, is that the synthesis of the promoter has a different temperature coefficient to that of the inhibitor (Zeevaart, 1979). For example, the production of the inhibitor would be more suppressed at low temperatures than that of the promoter, accounting for the fact that many photoperiodic species will flower in any daylength at low temperatures. The opposite effects of low and high temperatures in cold-requiring plants have received a similar explanation (Lang, 1965). The above observations indicate that these interpretations are too simple, however, and must be expanded in order to include the effects of other environmental factors, like irradiance, atmospheric composition, etc., and also to account for the fact that different environmental factors influencing flowering may not all be perceived by the same plant part.

A more realistic, albeit more complex, hypothesis would imply multiple promotive and inhibitory processes of varied nature occurring concurrently in the various plant parts. These processes are expected to be affected in various ways by different environmental factors and this will explain why the importance of different organs may vary according to the external conditions. This interpretation is also in line with the bewildering variety of exogenous chemicals that can promote or inhibit flower initiation in many intact plants as well as in tissue cultures (Bernier, Kinet & Sachs, 1981*b*; Scorza, 1982).

Independently of the perception of environmental factors, flower formation in a variety of plants has been found to depend strictly on antagonistic interorgan correlations. In *Scrofularia arguta*, for example, axillary flowering is essentially controlled by a balance between the promotive influence of the apical bud and the inhibitory effect of the root system (Miginiac, 1974). In the day-neutral W38 tobacco, the shoot apical meristem normally flowers after production of 30–40 leaves (nodes). McDaniel (1980) succeeded in maintaining it in a perpetually vegetative condition by rooting the upper portion of the shoot each time the plant has developed 6–10 new leaves. Thus, it appears that in this tobacco the roots completely suppress flower formation unless they are separated from the meristem by some minimal node number.

Clearly, *all organs participate in the control of flowering and their participation is modulated by the external conditions*. Such a situation is basic to the successful reproduction of plants in contrasting environments where they have to use *alternative pathways* to induction.

Floral evocation

I shall first describe the changes occurring in apices during the transition to flowering, from the start of exposure of plants to inductive conditions until appearance of the first unquestionable signs of flower initiation. I shall then inquire whether or not there is, among all these changes, a single initial one which would set in motion all the others. Afterwards, I shall try to determine which changes are essential for evocation, which are simply accompanying and thus incidental, and which are consequences of evocation, i.e. occur after irreversible commitment to flower is reached. As will become clear below, work to answer these questions impinges on the problem of evocation plasticity.

What are the changes occurring during the floral transition of meristems?

The nature of the changes occurring in transitional apices was comprehensively reviewed by Bernier *et al.* (1981*b*) and Lyndon & Francis (1984). Fig. 4 illustrates the changes that have been observed in *Sinapis alba*, a LDP requiring a single photoinductive cycle. To summarize briefly the situation, let me say that (a) the changes are extremely varied, (b) they occur at all levels of organization, from the molecular to the morphological, and (c) they each start at a particular time interval after the beginning of induction and, as expected, molecular events occur first, followed by cellular and then morphological (in capital letters in Fig. 4) events.

In *Sinapis*, induction normally requires that the plants are subjected to one 20 h LD with the supplementary hours of this LD given at the same irradiance than the standard SD. The amount of light energy received by the plants is considerably increased by such a treatment and some of the changes observed during the floral transition might thus be related to the increase in photosynthetic input, not to evocation. *Sinapis* can also be induced by what we call a 'displaced SD', i.e. one SD delayed in time by 10 h, and in this case the induced plants receive exactly the same amount of light energy as the vegetative controls kept in standard SD. Examination of the apices of *Sinapis* plants exposed to a displaced SD has revealed that most changes, including the early rise in soluble sugars, are identical to those induced by a LD, and that they occur in a similar sequence (Bernier *et al.* 1974; Bodson, 1977; Pryke & Bernier, 1978; Bodson & Outlaw, 1985; and unpublished data). From this, it was concluded that these changes are unrelated to photosynthetic input and seem thus to be involved in the floral transition itself.

Other species have been less investigated than *Sinapis*, but as far as our

Fig. 4. Sequence of events in the apex of *Sinapis alba* during the floral transition induced by a single LD. The molecular events are on the left side of the time axis. The cellular and morphological events are on the right side. The morphological events are in capital letters. This diagram is built from experimental results discussed in Bernier *et al.* (1981*b*) and unpublished data.

available evidence goes more or less similar changes seem to occur in several species differing widely in the environmental conditions required for induction of flowering and in the kinds of reproductive structures to be constructed. Thus, although numerous changes (perhaps the most important ones) remain to be discovered in *Sinapis* and other plants, many features of the floral transition of meristems seem fairly *universal*. This supports the idea that they are integral parts of evocation, even though other details may vary considerably between different species.

Is there an initial critical event in evocation?

An important finding has been that *part* of the changes that are typical of the floral transition may be produced in apices by treatments that are unable to cause flower initiation when given alone but are known to promote it when given to suboptimally induced plants (Bernier *et al.* 1981*b*). Two such treatments in *Sinapis* are (a) a single SD at high irradiance (Havelange & Bernier, 1983), and (b) a single application of a low dose of a cytokinin in SD (Havelange *et al.*, unpublished data).

Among the changes listed in Fig. 4, the SD at high irradiance produces the increases in soluble sugar and starch levels, in invertase activity, in mitochondrion number, and a change in nucleolus structure (Fig. 5). On the other hand, the exogenous cytokinin produces the rise in starch content, the first wave of cell divisions leading to near synchronization of the cell population in G_1 as well as the splitting of vacuoles and an increased rate of leaf initiation (Fig. 5). These two treatments are thus said to produce '*partial evocation*'. Note that, except for the increased starch content, all changes caused by high irradiance are different from those caused by a cytokinin application and that the meristems stay vegetative, in the sense that they go on initiating new leaves, after each of these two treatments. Refer again to Fig. 4 and note that many changes that are normally observed during the floral transition, e.g. the rises in RNA and DNA synthesis, the second mitotic wave, the precocious initiation of axillary buds and internode elongation, etc. do not occur after these treatments. It is also of interest to mention here that the combination of high irradiance with a cytokinin application does not cause flower formation in *Sinapis* in SD. Thus, there is one or several pieces of evocation lacking and we are still on the track of treatments which are able to cause other parts of evocation.

Partial evocation has also been produced in several other species by a variety of treatments (Bernier *et al.* 1981*b*; Bernier, 1984). In the SDP *Xanthium*, for example, an application of GA_3 in LD increases the mitotic activity, the meristem size, the rate of leaf initiation, the internode growth and alters the phyllotaxis, similarly to photoinduction, but does not cause flower initiation (Maksymowych, Cordero & Erickson, 1976). Yet, GA_3 is known to promote flowering in this plant in suboptimal inductive conditions (Bernier *et al.* 1981*b*).

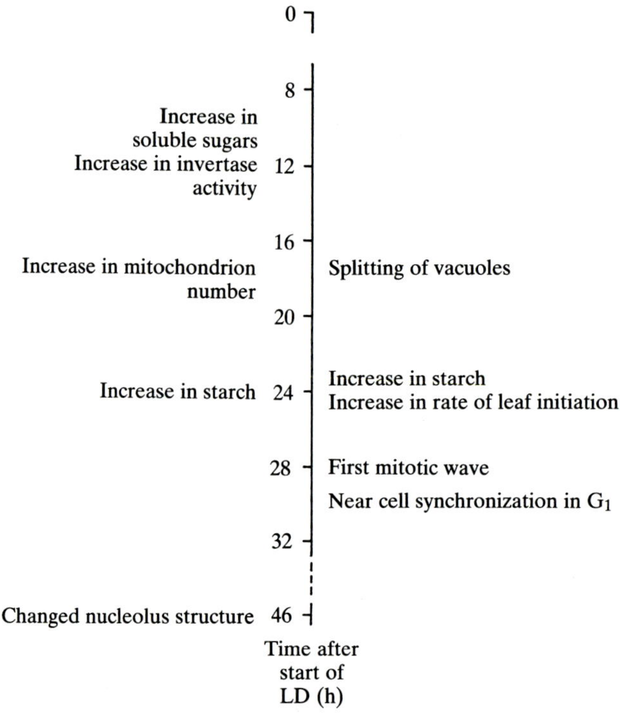

Fig. 5. Partial evocation in *Sinapis alba* produced either by one SD at high irradiance (left side of the time axis) or by one application of a cytokinin in SD (right side). The events caused by either treatment are introduced in this diagram with their timings of occurrence in apices of plants induced by one LD (see Fig. 4). (From Bernier, 1984.)

These observations are the basis for the concept of evocation as a *multi-sequential* process (Fig. 6) in which the multiple changes are seen as forming a limited number of sequences which are controlled independently of each other and thus each can be set in motion by manipulating its particular controlling agent. Full evocation, leading to flower initiation, does not follow automatically the activation of only one of the component sequences but will require the activation of all sequences. If true, this concept implies that there is *no* single initial evocational event which can set in motion all the subsequent changes, and no single controlling agent of evocation as already concluded above.

At present it would appear that the different sequences may be independent initially but they most probably interact (indicated by oblique arrows in Fig. 6) at some later step of the floral transition. In *Sinapis*, for example, the first wave of cell divisions, which results merely from the release into mitosis of G_2 cells, does not seem to depend on an increase in energy metabolism since, when it is caused by a cytokinin application, it is

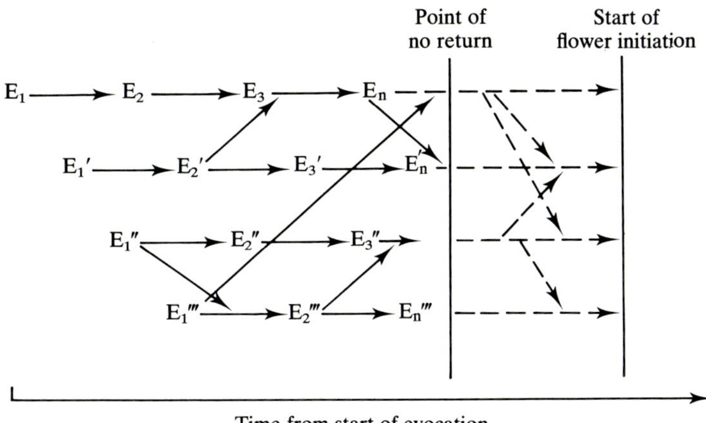

Fig. 6. A model of floral evocation involving several interacting sequences of events. Successive events in each sequence are numbered E_1, E_2, ... E_n. Initial events of the different sequences are represented by E_1, E'_1, E''_1, E'''_1. Note that the different sequences start sequentially. Interactions between sequences are indicated by the oblique arrows. (From Bernier *et al.* 1981*b*.)

unaccompanied by the increases in the level of soluble sugars, in invertase activity and mitochondrion number (Fig. 5). Further changes in cell proliferation, including a sevenfold decrease in the cell-doubling time (Bodson, 1975), will certainly require larger expenditures and turnover of energy-supplying compounds, and thus will depend sooner or later upon an essential interaction with the sequence of events related to energy metabolism.

In a network like that of Fig. 6, the interactions between sequences are presumably multiple and more complex the more advanced is the evocation process. Indeed, any changing element in a sequence is bound to generate signals that will affect the functioning of elements in other sequences. These interactions, at least some of them, may thus be viewed as *essential* for evocation to proceed and reach a point of no return (Bernier *et al* 1981*b*).

In view of all of this, interlocked sequences might be impossible to disentangle completely from each other. The kind of analysis, described above, might thus only give information on the early part of each sequence, i.e. the part preceding interaction with other sequences. Indeed, note that, except for the changed nucleolus structure, all events that are observed so far in partially evoked apices of *Sinapis* (Fig. 5) occur only during the first 30 h following start of the LD (Fig. 4).

Is it possible to alter the temporal order of changes during evocation?

Return to Figs 4 and 5 and note that in *Sinapis* induced by one LD (or by one displaced SD) there is normally a sequential initiation of the different sequences of events which are parts of evocation. Indeed, the changes related to energy metabolism (partial evocation caused by high irradiance) are first detected at 10 h after the start of the LD, 8 h earlier than the earliest changes caused by an application of cytokinin.

What happens now when the normal order is experimentally perturbed? Such a perturbation may be obtained in theory by simply submitting *Sinapis* plants to a treatment which causes partial evocation the day preceding an inductive LD. By doing that we activate one of the sequences 24 h before the others and we may wonder whether this will distort the network of sequences such that evocation will be inhibited. The results of several experiments of this kind indicate that this is not the case, i.e. the per cent of induced plants in response to a single 13 h LD is unaffected when either one SD at high irradiance or one application of cytokinin is given 24 h before exposure to this suboptimal LD (Bernier, Jacqmard & Havelange, unpublished data). Using the model of Fig. 6, this suggests that the order of evocational events can be altered without impairing the whole process, and thus that the network of interactions between the sequences incorporates a certain amount of flexibility.

Although other data, presented below, are in line with this conclusion, the present results are insufficient to rule out the possibility that, whatever happens before, the LD can induce an absolutely normal evocation, i.e. an evocation with the normal order of sequences. Such a situation is by no means excluded as shown by the observation that induction of the first mitotic wave in *Sinapis* the day preceding the LD does not preclude the repetition of this wave, with its normal timing, in response to the LD (Bernier *et al.* 1974).

For further investigation of this question, it could be advantageous to study plants, like LSDP, requiring normally two different inductive factors in an obligate sequence and compare the changes occurring in their meristems when they are submitted to either the required sequence of factors or other sets of environmental conditions.

What are the essential events of evocation?

When confronting the multiplicity of changes in transitional apices, one feels the necessity to determine which events or series of related events are essential for evocation and which are irrelevant.

For such a demonstration two approaches have been explored, one using specific metabolic inhibitors, the other exposing plants to inductive conditions with one of the environmental factors kept at a suboptimal level. The hope in both cases is to suppress one particular event and determine whether or not this results in the inhibition of evocation. In a network of interlocked events, however, suppression of any element will necessarily affect a great number of other elements and make it difficult to relate inhibition of flower initiation to alteration of one particular event. This is illustrated by the following examples.

Application of 5-fluorouracil (FU), an inhibitor of RNA synthesis, to the apex of *Sinapis* plants strongly inhibits flower formation at any time from 8 to 24 h after start of the inductive LD (Kinet, Bodson, Alvinia & Bernier, 1971), suggesting that RNA synthesis during this time interval is essential for evocation. Cell proliferation is one of the numerous cellular processes which are generally perturbed when RNA synthesis is inhibited (Webster & Van't Hof, 1970). Indeed, the mitotic activity of *Sinapis* meristems, treated by FU from 12 to 22 h after start of the LD, is totally arrested but, as seen in Fig. 7, the timing of inhibition of cell divisions is totally different from the timing of FU action. Presumably other processes dependent on RNA synthesis are also altered, each with a different timing of inhibition. In these conditions, how can we decide which essential process (and at which time) is controlled by the RNA molecules made between 8 and 24 h?

Similar difficulties have been encountered in experiments where plants are induced in conditions such that a part of the normal events of the floral transition is inhibited. In *Silene coeli-rosa*, a LDP, the phyllotactic changes associated with the transition from leaf to sepal production require an increase in the size of the shoot meristem relative to the size of its appendages at initiation (Lyndon, 1978). In normal conditions, this increase results from an absolute increase in meristem size together with a reduction in size of nascent appendages. When mineral-starved plants are exposed to LD, flower initiation can occur despite the fact that the size of the shoot meristem is much reduced (Lyndon, personal communication). Obviously, the necessary phyllotactic changes may occur without any gross increase in the absolute size of the meristem. Thus, *there are several ways for an apex to achieve an essential change and the way which is used is in itself unessential.*

This line of reasoning may also very well apply to the observation that, in plants of *Silene* transferred from SD at 20 °C (which keep the plants vegetative) to LD at 13 °C (which induce flowering), there is no increase in the growth rate of the meristem, contrary to what happens when the plants are shifted from SD to LD at either 20 ° or 13 °C (Miller & Lyndon, 1977). What may be essential is perhaps not so much an absolute increase in growth rate of the shoot meristem but an increase relative to that of other plant parts, e.g. young leaves, axillary shoots and, or, roots (Bernier, 1979).

The most general lesson arising from these and other similar observations is that, within some limits, evocation may be successfully completed even when one factor of the environment is unfavourable, and this is possible because the meristem can use alternative sets of events in different conditions to achieve the essential changes. Thus, when one particular sequence of evocational events is blocked experimentally, evocation may nevertheless proceed in some cases and reach completion by a combination of sequences different from that used in normal conditions. Again, we are led to the idea that the network of Fig. 6 is not rigid, and this presumably explains why the same plant may be brought into flowering by alternative environmental factors (see above). But, obviously, there are sets of external factors which totally prevent flowering, indicating that some distortions of

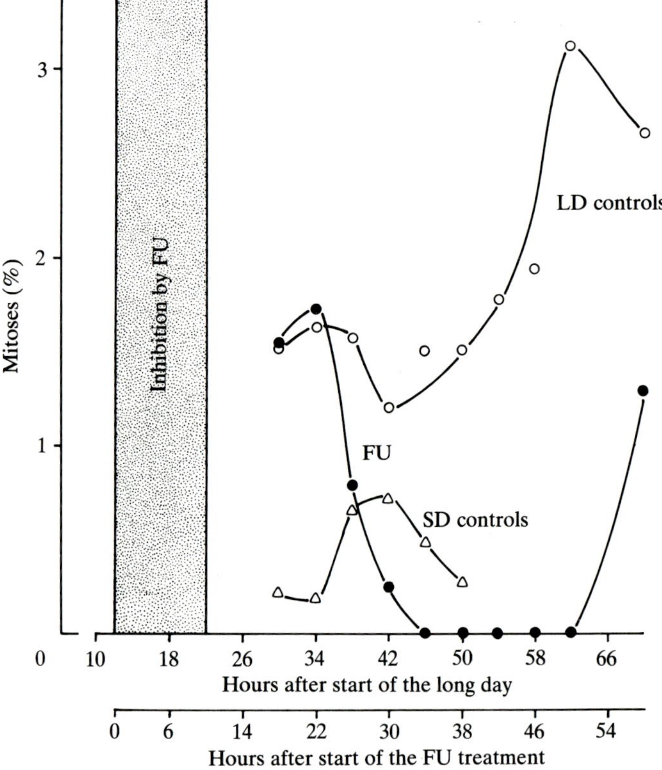

Fig. 7. Effect of 5-fluorouracil (FU) on the mitotic index in the meristem of *Sinapis alba*, as a function of time after start of a single inductive LD. △—△, SD controls; ○—○, LD controls; ●—●, plants treated by 2×10^{-3} M-FU. The FU treatment was begun 12 h after start of the LD and stopped 10 h later by application of $1{\cdot}4 \times 10^{-2}$ M-orotic acid as an antidote. All compounds are directly applied to the apex. Note that the first mitotic wave at 30–34 h is unaffected by FU.

the network are harmful to evocation even though others are not. What is needed now is an exploration of the full extent of flexibility of the apical system, attempting to understand why adaptation is possible in some conditions and impossible in others. This seems the only fruitful way to approach the difficult problem of determining what is essential for evocation.

When is evocation completed?

The point at which commitment of the meristem to produce flower primordia becomes irreversible, or the '*point of no return*', can be determined as the time at which inhibitors applied to the apex during the floral transition can no longer prevent flower initiation. As seen in Table 1, a variety of metabolic or growth inhibitors can inhibit the flowering process in *Sinapis* plants induced by one LD, each compound acting during a particular time interval relative to the start of the inductive LD. Note that the effects of some inhibitors are counteracted after 8 h of treatment by application of an appropriate antidote. For other inhibitory compounds, such as 2,4-DNP, ABA, BAP and NAA, no antidote is available and this may account for their long-lasting effects. No inhibitor is effective however

Table 1. *Chemicals inhibiting the floral transition in* Sinapis *plants induced by a single LD (compiled from Kinet* et al. *1971; Bodson, 1985; and unpublished data).*

Inhibitor applied to the apex	Concentration (M)	Antidote applied 8 h after inhibitor	Time of start and end of inhibitory effect (h after start of the LD)
5-Fluorouracil (FU)	2×10^{-3}	Orotic acid	8 to 24
2-Thiouracil	7×10^{-3}	Orotic acid	0 to 24
Ethionine	1×10^{-2}	Methionine	0 to 28
6-Benzylaminopurine (BAP)[1]	$7{\cdot}5 \times 10^{-4}$	None	−16 to 40
Abscisic acid (ABA)	$9{\cdot}5 \times 10^{-4}$	None	before 0 to 40
2,4-Dinitrophenol (2,4-DNP)	$3{\cdot}5 \times 10^{-4}$	None	8 to 48
5-Fluorodeoxyuridine	5×10^{-5}	Thymidine	20 to 44
α-Naphtaleneacetic acid (NAA)[1]	$5{\cdot}3 \times 10^{-5}$	None	before 0 to 48

[1]BAP and NAA applied at lower concentrations are promotive, instead of inhibitory (Bodson, 1985).

after 40–48 h following start of the LD. On this basis, it has been proposed that the point of no return in *Sinapis* is at 40–48 h, about 10–18 h before the onset of flower initiation. In other species, too, the available evidence suggests that the point of no return is reached some time before the start of flower morphogenesis (Bernier *et al.* 1981*b*).

Inspection of Fig. 4 reveals that the point of no return in *Sinapis* follows a few hours after the appearance of new proteins in the meristem (at 36 h) and the peak of DNA synthesis (at 38 h). Events that start at about the same time as the point of no return are vacuolation and elongation of the cells of the pith-rib meristem, changes in meristem size and shape, decrease of the apical angle, and changes affecting the nucleolus. Some of these events are clearly linked. The pith-rib meristem, with its flattened cells normally resembles a cambium. After vacuolation, it loses its meristematic aspect and is transformed into a core of elongating parenchymatous cells. As a result, the height of the meristem is increased, its shape is changed, and the apical angle decreases. Vacuolation and elongation of the cells of the pith-rib meristem, which is one of the most universal changes at the floral transition (Bernier *et al.* 1981*b*), may thus appear as the turning point in the evocation process or, at least, as one of its most critical components. However, in line with the argument developed above, I feel that the key to commitment might be less in the occurrence of one or several particular events than in appropriate interactions between the different sequences of events. If true, the point of no return would coincide with the occurrence of the last essential interaction between sequences.

Note that most morphological changes (in capital letters in Fig. 4) start at about the time the point of no return is reached or just after. Evocation consists thus essentially of events occurring at levels of organization ranging from the molecular to the histological.

Inflorescence and flower morphogenesis

Botanists have known, since before Linnaeus, that reproductive structures are generally less variable than their vegetative counterparts (Briggs & Walters, 1984). That does not mean, however, that, when an apex is beyond the point of no return, inflorescence and flower morphogenesis will occur in an invariable manner. Indeed, some species are known to have normally more than one type of flowers. Moreover, abnormal structures may arise spontaneously in many species grown in natural conditions, but these deviations are generally so varied and, or, occur so unpredictably that they were often regarded as 'monsters'.

By appropriate manipulations of the environmental factors or applications of growth substances, physiologists are now able to produce *at will* most of these morphological deviations, showing that they reflect an inherent flexibility of reproductive morphogenesis rather than being abnormalities of a monstrous nature. The whole range of aberrant structures obtained experimentally was recently reviewed (Bernier *et al.* 1981*b*; Kinet, Sachs & Bernier, 1985), and I shall thus restrict myself here to a brief survey of a few selected cases.

Position-dependent differences in flower morphology and function within inflorescences

In plants with polymorphic flowers, like diclinous or cleistogamous species, the localization of the different types of flowers on an individual

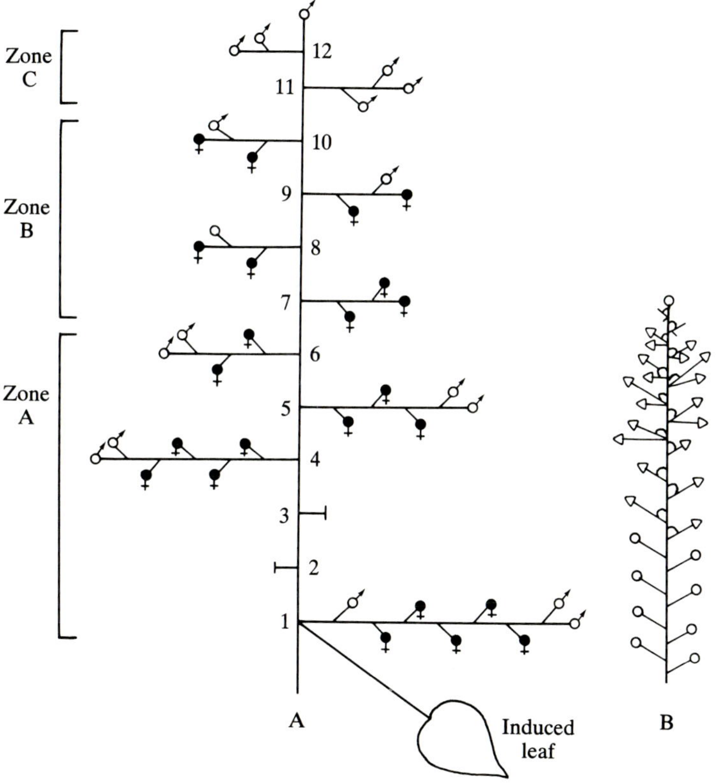

Fig. 8. Schematic representation of the pattern of reproductive morphogenesis in the flowering shoots of (A) *Xanthium strumarium* induced by a single SD cycle (From Léonard *et al.* 1981), and (B) *Chenopodium rubrum* (ecotype 50° 10′N) given three SD cycles (suboptimal induction) ○, reproductive shoot; △ vegetative shoot (From Cook, 1976).

plant may not be random. Thus, along a vine in cucurbits or in the inflorescence in *Begonia*, there is an obligate succession of male and female flowers. In *Xanthium*, the male and female flowers are in separate heads and the distribution of these heads is very complex (Fig. 8A): a flowering shoot can be divided into three zones: the basal zone A in which all terminal heads are male, the intermediate zone B in which they are all female, and the apical zone C, including the apical meristem of the main axis, in which they are all male again (Léonard *et al.* 1981).

In the inflorescence of *Lamium amplexicaule*, there is a progressive shift from cleistogamous to pseudocleistogamous and then chasmogamous flowers (Lord, 1979).

This position-dependent variation in flower form and function, not always fully realized in the past, is viewed by Lord (1979) as being the counterpart of 'heteroblastic' leaf development in maturing vegetative shoot systems.

As evidenced by the case of suboptimally induced *Chenopodium rubrum*, a SDP, a similar situation might exist in plants having only one morphological type of flowers, in the sense that there is a gradient in the flowering potential of axillary meristems within the developing inflorescence (Fig. 8B) (Cook, 1976).

Flowering gradients have been found in a variety of plants and may generally be perturbed by some experimental treatments (Tran Thanh Van, 1965; Goh, 1975; Chailakhyan, 1975), revealing the plasticity of the processes of floral evocation and, or, morphogenesis.

'Vegetative' inflorescences

In some species, such as *Kalanchoe*, *Bryophyllum*, *Dianthus*, branching is typical of the inflorescences (Fig. 9A) whereas the vegetative shoots remain normally unbranched. Branching can be produced, however, in the total

---

Fig. 9. (A) The normal inflorescence of the LSDP *Bryophyllum daigremontianum*. Note the characteristic branching of the dichasial cyme.

(B) 'Vegetative' inflorescence in *Bryophyllum* formed in response to subthreshold inductive conditions. In fact it is a branched vegetative shoot. Note that the vegetative shoot of plants kept in non-inductive conditions remains unbranched. (From Bernier *et al.* 1981*b*.)

(C) The normal unbranched raceme of the LDP *Sinapis alba*.

(D) Inflorescence reversion in a *Sinapis* plant transferred to SD and low irradiance after start of flower initiation in LD. Occurrence of leafy branches indicates the location of reversion. After a period in SD and low irradiance the plants are returned to LD at high irradiance for elongation of axes and macroscopic expression of reversion. This explains the presence of flowers in the last-formed portions of the main inflorescence and its branches. (From Bernier *et al.* 1981*b*.)

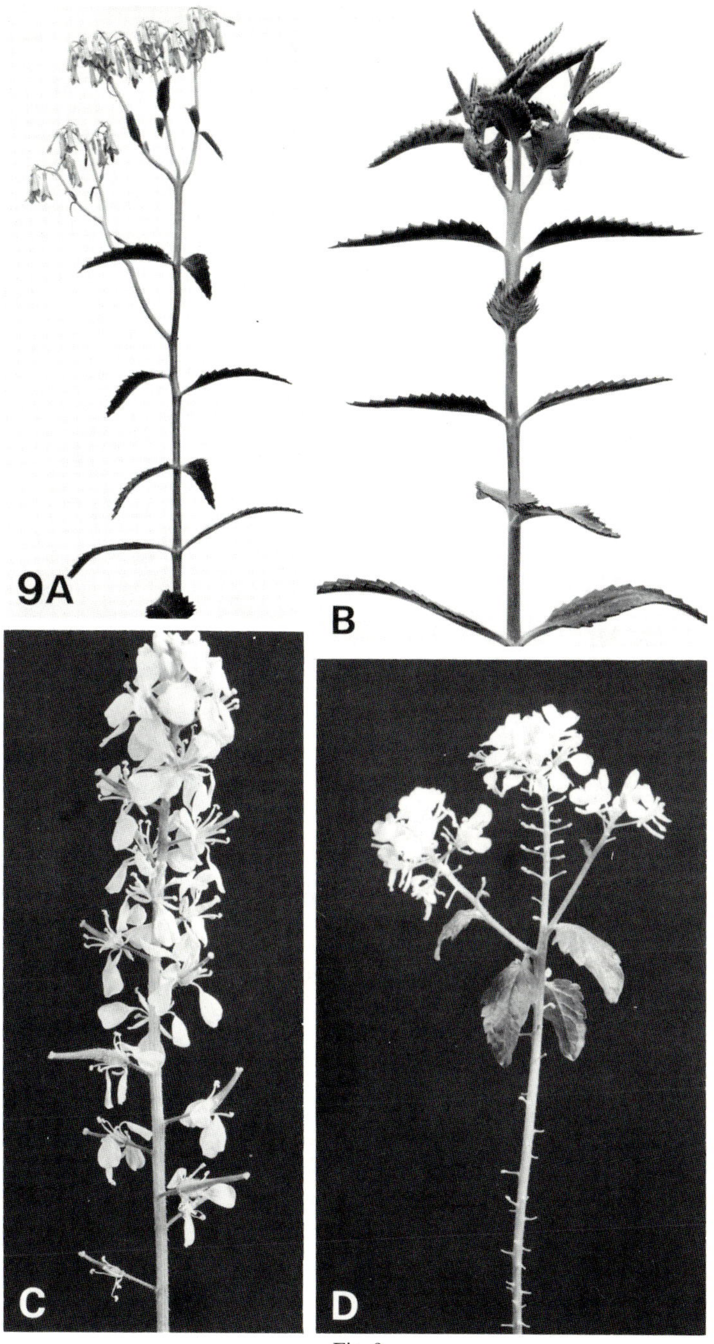

Fig. 9

absence of flowers by exposing these plants to subminimal inductive conditions (Fig. 9B). Since apical branching is apparently inseparable from inflorescence formation in these plants, and is in fact the first step of it, the branched vegetative shoots were called '*vegetative*' inflorescences (Harder, 1948).

Occurrence of such anomalous structures shows that *commitment of the apex to all aspects of reproductive morphogenesis is not reached in one step in these plants, but is a multistep process.*

Reversion of reproductive meristems to vegetative growth

The reproductive condition, once reached, is not necessarily stable as shown by the following examples.

In the cold-requiring plant *Cheiranthus cheiri* and the LDP *Anagallis arvensis*, after transfer from inductive to non-inductive conditions, the inflorescence meristems in *Cheiranthus* or the flower meristems in *Anagallis* are able to return to *all* aspects of vegetative functioning, and this reversion is possible even after more than a year of flower production in *Cheiranthus* or after the gynoecium is formed in *Anagallis* (Diomaiuto-Bonnand, 1984; Brulfert, 1965). Thus, the potential to resume vegetative growth is never lost in these meristems, i.e. *they are never definitively committed to reproductive morphogenesis.*

This situation is exceptional since in most plants only meristems at particular developmental stages are capable of reversion (Bernier *et al.* 1981*b*). In *Sinapis*, for instance, reversions are produced when plants are transferred to SD and, or, low irradiance after start of flower initiation (Bagnard, Bernier & Arnal, 1972; Bagnard, 1983). The flower primordia that have reached the stage of pedicel and sepal initiation at the time of transfer develop until formation of complete flower buds, and then abort. In contrast, flower primordia, that are still at the stage of an undifferentiated hemispherical mass of meristematic cells at the time of transfer, may develop into indeterminate leafy shoots instead of flowers. As a result the inflorescence exhibits an abnormal branched habit (Fig. 9C,D). Interestingly, cytokinin applications during exposure of plants to SD and low irradiance increase the total number of reverted flowers (nodes) in the inflorescence, but the 'vegetative' portion of the inflorescence is now frequently interrupted by normal flowers creating a developmental mosaic (Bagnard, unpublished observations). Thus, *the fate of nascent flower meristems in* Sinapis *is not irreversibly fixed and can be channelled into different morphogenetic pathways depending on the prevailing conditions.* Instability of their physiological state is particularly obvious when cytokinin treatments are combined with poor light conditions. Irrevocable determination of flower morphogenesis only occurs when the stage of sepal and pedicel formation is reached by the primordium.

Aberrant numbers of floral organs and changes in sex expression

The numbers of floral organs may be affected in many species by the growing temperature. In the tulip cv. 'Pride of Haarlem', for example, the total number of floral members, which is 15·02 at 28 °C, a value very close to the normal number of 15 indicated in botany textbooks, rises to 21·38 at 9 °C (Blaauw, Luyten & Hartsema, 1932). In tomato, too, the numbers of all classes of floral organs are increased at low compared to high temperatures but, as seen in Fig. 10, the most conspicuous differences are observed in carpel and locule numbers (Sawhney, 1983). In *Silene*, flowers with an aberrant number of parts are observed at all growing temperatures, but more often at 13 °C and 27 °C than at 20 °C (Lyndon, 1979).

Treatments by exogenous growth substances may also change the numbers of floral members in several species, as for example in carnation after applications of GA_3 or a cytokinin (Garrod & Harris, 1974) and in tomato after GA_3 applications (Sawhney, 1983).

The arrangement of parts in flowers with aberrant numbers of organs is presumably more or less altered. Indeed, extra appendages necessarily arise in unusual places and missing appendages might also conceivably affect the

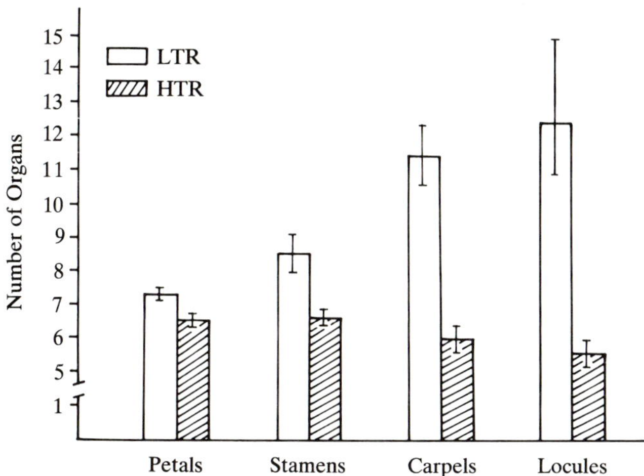

Fig. 10. Effect of the temperature regime on the number of floral organs in tomato (cv. Manitoba). LTR, low temperature regime (18 °C day/15 °C night); HTR, high temperature regime (28 °C day/23 °C night). (From Sawhney, 1983.)

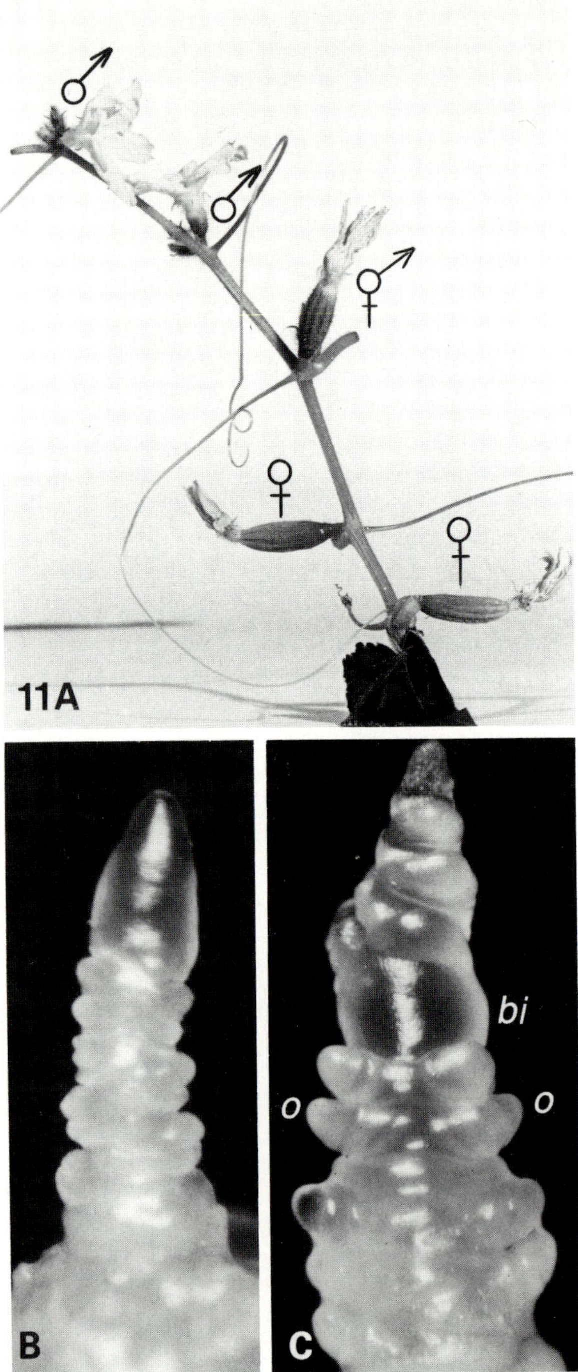

Fig. 11

arrangement of the existing organs. Unfortunately, precise phyllotactic descriptions of abnormal flowers are generally lacking.

Sex expression is another plastic character of many flowers, especially in monoecious and dioecious species (Frankel & Galun, 1977; Kinet *et al.* 1985). In cucumber, in this respect the most extensively investigated monoecious species, the male flowers are restricted to the lower nodes of the stem. Then, the plant passes through a stage in which axillary male and female flowers are formed and, finally, only female flowers develop. Femaleness, as estimated both by the number of nodes to the first female flower and, or, the ratio of male to female flowers, is markedly promoted by SD, high irradiance, low temperature and a high nitrogen supply. The sex of cucumber flowers is also dramatically influenced by growth substances, ethylene being the primary feminizing and GA the masculinizing agent. As expected, then, ethylene inhibitors, such as silver nitrate, increase maleness (Fig. 11A) whereas GA inhibitors (growth retardants) favour femaleness. Auxins and cytokinins are also feminizing factors, but of secondary importance compared to ethylene. Of course, different cucumber genotypes, differing more or less in female or male tendency, may exhibit somewhat different responses to a given treatment and the above statements should be understood as simplified generalizations.

All flowers in cucumber are initially bisexual and very similar in their morphology. Unisexuality results from a secondary unbalanced growth in androecium (stamens) and gynoecium (pistil), one developing to the exclusion of the other which is then represented in mature flowers by rudiments only. The various environmental and chemical factors that can change sex expression in this plant are thus doing it by altering the balance of growth between the androecium and gynoecium.

All these observations make it clear that *the morphogenetic processes during flower ontogeny are not absolutely fixed. Not only the nature of floral*

Fig. 11. (A) Formation of male flowers in a strictly gynoecious cv. of cucumber sprayed by silver nitrate (250 p.p.m.) on two consecutive days. Note that one perfect (hermaphroditic) flower was formed in the transition zone preceding the male flowers. (From Atsmon & Tabback, 1979.)

(B & C) Abnormal morphogenesis at the shoot apex of winter wheat (cv. Capelle Desprez) sprayed by 1–2% 2,4-D at the end of the vegetative phase, at a time the apex is elongating. (From Sharman, 1978.)

(B) A treated apex, growing slowly in length but widening just below the extreme tip, takes the look of a 'scolex'. About seven double ridges are seen below the scolex.

(C) Another treated apex showing a subapical bare interval (*bi*) and spikelets (*o*) in an opposite rather than the normal distichous arrangement. Note that the apex resumes morphogenesis (double ridge initiation) above the bare interval at right angles to the plane of the earlier part below.

organs but also their numbers and presumably their arrangements can be experimentally altered. Thus, it appears that the fate of a primordium inside a developing flower cannot be entirely predicted from its site of initiation.

Extreme aberrations in reproductive structures

The most profound modifications of reproductive structures have in general been obtained by applications of growth substances, either auxins or GA_3. For example, the synthetic auxin 2,4-D produces various abnormalities in wheat, including branched ears, an elongated apex tip without any appendage formed (Fig. 11B), bare intervals in the subapical region of the apex, spikelets in a whorled or opposite arrangement instead of the normal distichous one, divided (twin) spikelets or a 90° shift in the plane of spikelet formation (Fig. 11C) (Sharman, 1978).

The flowers of *Digitalis*, a member of Scrophulariaceae, with normally five free sepals and a corolla tube, may show a partial or complete fusion of sepals and separation of petals after a 2,4-D treatment (Astié, 1962). Also, the normally zygomorphic corolla sometimes becomes actinomorphic. Some of the flowers are so transformed that they resemble flowers of Solanaceae rather than Scrophulariaceae.

In *Saponaria*, a member of the Caryophyllaceae, 2,4-D causes petal or stamen fusion; on rare occasions, nine of the ten stamens fuse producing a structure reminiscent of the staminal tube in Leguminosae (Astié, 1962). On the other hand, the inflorescence which is normally a raceme of cymes (a thyrse) may be transformed into an umbel- or capitulum-like structure. These abnormalities are present in an unpredictable proportion of the treated plants and are very difficult to standardize. In a sense, they may thus be considered as monstrosities, but their interest is that they presumably reveal the maximal extent of plasticity in reproductive morphogenesis. Note finally that the anomalous features in one species may be the normal condition in another.

Conclusions

The three steps of the flowering process that were covered in this paper, namely induction, evocation and morphogenesis, are all undoubtedly flexible, and we have left far behind the rigidity of the classical interpretation of reproductive development depicted in Fig. 1.

As explained above, *induction* may be completed by many, if not all, plants in several alternative sets of environmental factors. At least in some plants, the alternative inductive factors are perceived by different organs, indicating that these factors affect most probably entirely different processes. Thus, as far as induction is concerned, plasticity is very significant.

At first sight, plasticity may seem to be much less at *evocation* since most of the changes observed in transitional meristems are the same in a variety of species. However, as suggested above, these changes should not be considered in isolation. They appear to form sets of interconnected systems and this complex network seems to embody some flexibility. This view is largely speculative but is supported by the observations that, under some particular circumstances, it has been possible to suppress some of the most universal evocational events or alter their temporal order without impairing evocation itself.

We have seen that all morphological characters of inflorescences and flowers may be experimentally altered. However, if occasional and extreme malformations caused by some growth substances are excluded, *morphogenetic* processes do not appear flexible to the point that the reproductive structures of one species will be transformed into those of a taxonomically unrelated species. Thus, the details of the expression of the morphological pattern can be profoundly changed but the pattern itself is, as a rule, maintained. In other words, reproductive morphogenesis can be seen as a process giving, for each species, a statistically predictable pattern with dispersion around the mean.

Plasticity at evocation and morphogenesis thus appears reduced compared to that at induction. This might be explained as follows: induction, as far as I see it, consists essentially in changes in the rates of production of floral promoters and, or, inhibitors in various plant parts; thus it occurs mainly at the molecular level. On the other hand, as discussed above, evocation is an integrated system of changes occurring at several levels of organization, from the molecular to the histological. Morphogenesis is still more complex since it includes events at the morphological (macroscopic shape) level in addition to those occurring at all lower levels of scale. Conceivably, the greater the number of levels involved, the more constrained and less flexible is the system; then plasticity is bound to be maximal at induction and minimal at morphogenesis.

The plasticity found at all steps of the flowering process is evidently related to the adaptation of plants to their changing environments during evolution. However, we still have difficulties when we try to establish precise relationships between plasticity at one step, say induction, and plasticity at a subsequent step like evocation or morphogenesis. This is perhaps due simply to insufficient work on this question. Indeed, when the structure of a flower is changed by an experimental treatment, we do not know in general whether the treatment has affected directly the morphogenetic processes in the flower itself or acted indirectly by influencing some previous step(s). Alternatively, these difficulties might come from the fact that developing plants behave more as probabilistic systems than as deterministic ones (O'Brien, 1982). In developing systems, indeed, the intricacy of interlocked events at all levels of scale might be such that it may well preclude the traditional and simple 'cause and effect' analysis of a response, and this because a large number of responses are occurring simultaneously at different rates and at different levels of organization (O'Brien, 1982). If accepted, this view will imply a major revision of our experimental approach to the flowering process.

I am grateful to Dr D. Atsmon (Rehovot, Israel) and Prof. B. C. Sharman (Calgary, Canada) for supplying photographic materials and to Dr J. M. Kinet for critical reading of the manuscript. Work by my coworkers and myself reviewed here was supported by research grants from the 'Fonds pour la Recherche Fondamentale et Collective' of Belgium (n° 2.4505.78) and from the Belgian government through the programme of 'Action de Recherche Concertée' (n° 80/85-18).

References

Astié, M. (1962). Tératologie spontanée et expérimentale. Exemples. Application à l'étude de quelques problèmes de biologie végétale. *Annls Sci. nat. Bot.* 12e Sér., **3**, 619–844.

Atsmon, D. & Tabbak, C. (1979). Comparative effects of gibberellin, silver nitrate and aminoethoxyvinyl glycine on sexual tendency and ethylene evolution in the cucumber plant (*Cucumis sativus* L.). *Pl. Cell Physiol.* **20**, 1547–1555.

Bagnard, C. (1983). Floraison et réversion chez *Sinapis alba*. III. Effets immédiats et différés de divers régimes d'éclairement appliqués pendant la phase post-inductrice. *Can. J. Bot.* **61**, 3386–3392.

Bagnard, C., Bernier, G. & Arnal, C. (1972). Etude physiologique et histologique de la réversion d'inflorescence chez *Sinapis alba*. *Physiol. Vég.* **10**, 237–254.

Bernier, G. (1979). The sequences of floral evocation. In *La physiologie de la floraison* (ed. P. Champagnat & R. Jacques), pp. 129–168. Paris: C.N.R.S.

Bernier, G. (1984). The factors controlling floral evocation: an overview. In *Light and the Flowering Process* (ed. D. Vince-Prue, B. Thomas & K. E. Cockshull), pp. 277–292. London: Academic Press.

Bernier, G., Kinet, J. M., Bodson, M., Rouma, Y. & Jacqmard, A. (1974). Experimental studies on the mitotic activity of the shoot apical meristem and its relation to floral evocation and morphogenesis in *Sinapis alba*. *Bot. Gaz.* **135**, 345–352.

Bernier, G., Kinet, J. M. & Sachs, R. M (1981*a*). *The Physiology of Flowering*, vol. I. Boca Raton, Florida: C.R.C. Press.

Bernier, G., Kinet, J. M. & Sachs, R. M. (1981*b*). *The Physiology of Flowering*, vol. II. Boca Raton, Florida: C.R.C. Press.

Blaauw, A. H., Luyten, I. & Hartsema, A. M. (1932). Die grundzahl der tulpenblüte in ihrer abhängigkeit von der temperatur. *Proc. K. ned. Akad. Wet.* **35**, 485–497.

Blondon, F. (1971). Action additive de température froide et de température chaude en jours continus sur le processus préparatoire à la floraison chez trois clones de *Festuca arundinacea* Schreb. *C.r. hebd. Séanc. Acad. Sci., Paris* **272**, 2896–2899.

Blondon, F. (1976). Interactions de la lumière et de la température sur la floraison. Les concepts d'induction primaire et d'induction secondaire. In *Etudes de biologie végétale. Hommage au Professeur Pierre Chouard* (ed. R. Jacques), pp. 355–367.

Bodson, M. (1975). Variation in the rate of cell division in the apical meristem of *Sinapis alba* during transition to flowering. *Ann. Bot.* **39**, 547–554.

Bodson, M. (1977). Changes in the carbohydrate content of the leaf and the apical bud of *Sinapis* during transition to flowering. *Planta* **135**, 19–23.

Bodson, M. (1985). *Sinapis alba*. In *Handbook of Flowering*, vol. IV (ed. A. H. Halevy), pp. 336–354. Boca Raton, Florida: C.R.C. Press.

Bodson, M. & Outlaw, W. H., Jr. (1985). Elevation in the sucrose content of the shoot apical meristem of *Sinapis alba* at floral evocation. *Pl. Physiol.* **79**, 420–424.

Briggs, D. & Walters, S. M. (1984). *Plant Variation and Evolution*. Cambridge: Cambridge: Cambridge University Press.

Brulfert, J. (1965). Etude expérimentale du développement végétatif et floral chez *Anagallis arvensis* L., ssp. *phoenicia* Scop. Formation de fleurs prolifères chez cette même espèce. *Rev. gén. Bot.* **72**, 641–694.

Chailakhyan, M. Kh. (1975). Autonomous and induced mechanisms of flowering regulation (in Russian). *Fiziol. Rast.* **22**, 1265–1282.

Chouard, P. (1960). Vernalization and its relations to dormancy. *A. Rev. Pl. Physiol.* **11**, 191–238.

Cook, R. E. (1976). The pattern of reproductive development in *Chenopodium rubrum* L. *J. exp. Bot.* **27**, 541–551.

Deronne, M. & Blondon, F. (1977). Mise en évidence chez le *Perilla ocymoides* L., plante de jours courts typique, d'un autre facteur de l'induction florale: les températures basses. Etudes de l'état induit acquis par la feuille en jours courts ou au froid. *Physiol. Vég.* **15**, 219–237.

Diomaiuto-Bonnand, J. (1984). La floraison et les conditions de son renouvellement périodique chez une espèce vivave polycarpique: la Giroflée Ravenelle (*Cheiranthus cheiri* L.). I. Etudes morphologique et ontogénique. *Rev. Cytol. Biol. Vég.-Bot.* **7**, 119–152.

Frankel, R. & Galun, E. (1977). *Pollination Mechanisms, Reproduction and Plant Breeding*. Berlin: Springer-Verlag.

Garrod, J. F. & Harris, G. P. (1974). Studies on the glasshouse carnation: effects of temperature and growth substances on petal number. *Ann. Bot.* **38**, 1025–1031.

Goh, C. J. (1975). Flowering gradient along the stem axis in an orchid hybrid *Aranda* deborah. *Ann. Bot.* **39**, 931–934.

Harder, R. (1948). Vegetative and reproductive development of *Kalanchoe blossfeldiana*, as influenced by photoperiodism. *Growth. Symp. Soc. exp. Biol.* **2**, 117–137.

Havelange, A. & Bernier, G. (1983). Partial floral evocation by high irradiance in the long-day plant *Sinapis alba*. *Physiol. Plant.* **59**, 545–550.

Heide, O. M. (1980). Studies on flowering in *Poa pratensis* L. ecotypes and cultivars. *Meld. Norg. Landbrukshogsk.* **59**, 1–27.

Kinet, J. M., Bodson, M., Alvinia, A. M. & Bernier, G. (1971). The inhibition of flowering in *Sinapis alba* after the arrival of the floral stimulus at the meristem. *Z. Pflanzenphysiol.* **66**, 49–63.

Kinet, J. M., Sachs, R. M. & Bernier, G. (1985). *The Physiology of Flowering*, vol. III. Boca Raton, Florida: C.R.C. Press.

Lang, A. (1965). Physiology of flower initiation. In *Encyclopedia of Plant Physiology*, vol. 15 (Part 1) (ed. W. Ruhland), pp. 1380–1536. Berlin: Springer-Verlag.

Larrieu, C. (1976). Quelques réflexions sur le déterminisme de l'état vivace et de l'état bisannuel chez deux Scrofulaires (*Scrofularia alata* et *vernalis*). In *Etudes de Biologie végétale. Hommage au Professeur Pierre Chouard* (ed. R. Jacques), pp. 381–389.

Léonard, M., Kinet, J. M., Bodson, M., Havelange, A., Jacqmard, A. & Bernier, G. (1981). Flowering in *Xanthium strumarium*. Initiation and development of female inflorescence and sex expression. *Pl. Physiol.* **67**, 1245–1249.

Lord, E. (1979). The development of cleistogamous and chasmogamous flowers in *Lamium amplexicaule* (Labiatae): an example of heteroblastic inflorescence development. *Bot. Gaz.* **140**, 39–50.

Lyndon, R. F. (1978). Phyllotaxis and the initiation of primordia during flower development in *Silene. Ann. Bot.* **42**, 1349–1360.

Lyndon, R. F. (1979). Aberrations in flower development in *Silene. Can. J. Bot.* **57**, 233–235.

Lyndon, R. F. & Francis, D. (1984). The response of the shoot apex to light-generated signals from the leaves. In *Light and the Flowering Process* (ed. D. Vince-Prue, B. Thomas & K. E. Cockshull), pp. 171–189. London: Academic Press.

Maksymowych, R., Cordero, R. E. & Erickson, R. O. (1976). Long-term developmental changes in *Xanthium* induced by gibberellic acid. *Am. J. Bot.* **63**, 1047–1053.

McDaniel, C. N. (1980). Influence of leaves and roots on meristem development in *Nicotiana tabacum* L. cv. Wisconsin 38. *Planta* **148**, 462–467.

Miginiac, E. (1974). Flowering and correlations between organs in *Scrofularia arguta* Sol. In *Mechanisms of Regulation of Plant Growth* (ed. R. F. Bieleski, A. R. Ferguson & M. M. Cresswell), pp. 539–545. Bull. **12**, Roy. Soc. New Zealand, Wellington.

Miller, M. B. & Lyndon, R. F. (1977). Changes in RNA levels in the shoot apex of *Silene* during the transition to flowering. *Planta* **136**, 167–172.

O'Brien, T. P. (1982). Cell growth and division. In *The Molecular Biology of Plant Development* (ed. H. Smith & D. Grierson), pp. 49–109. Oxford: Blackwell Scientific Publications.

Pressman, E. & Negbi, M. (1981). Bolting and flowering of vernalized *Brassica pekinensis* as affected by root temperature. *J. exp. Bot.* **32**, 821–825.

Pryke, J. A. & Bernier, G. (1978). RNA synthesis in the apex of *Sinapis alba* in transition to flowering. *J. exp. Bot.* **29**, 953–961.

Purohit, A. N. & Tregunna, E. B. (1974). Effects of carbon dioxide on *Pharbitis*, *Xanthium* and *Silene* in short days. *Can. J. Bot.* **52**, 1283–1291.

Salisbury, F. B. (1982). Photoperiodism. *Hort. Rev.* **4**, 66–105.

Sawhney, V. K. (1983). The role of temperature and its relationship with gibberellic acid in the development of floral organs in tomato (*Lycopersicon esculentum*). *Can. J. Bot.* **61**, 1258–1265.

Scorza, R. (1982). *In vitro* flowering. *Hort. Rev.* **4**, 106–127.

Sharman, B. C. (1978). Morphogenesis of 2,4-D induced abnormalities of the inflorescence of bread wheat (*Triticum aestivum* L.). *Ann. Bot.* **42**, 145–153.

Shinozaki, M., Hikichi, M., Yoshida, K., Watanabe, K. & Takimoto, A. (1982). Effect of high-intensity light given prior to low-temperature treatment on the long-day flowering of *Pharbitis nil. Pl. Cell Physiol.* **23**, 473–477.

Shinozaki, M. & Takimoto, A. (1982). The role of cotyledons in flower initiation of *Pharbitis nil* at low temperatures. *Pl. Cell Physiol.* **23**, 403–408.

Tran Thanh Van, M. (1965). La vernalisation du *Geum urbanum* L. Etude expérimentale de la mise à fleur chez une plante vivave en rosette exigeant le froid vernalisant pour fleurir. *Annls Sci. nat. Bot.* **6**, 373–594.

Vince-Prue, D. (1975). *Photoperiodism in Plants.* London: McGraw-Hill Book Company.

Webster, P. L. & Van't Hof, J. (1970). DNA synthesis and mitosis in meristems: requirements for RNA and protein synthesis. *Am. J. Bot.* **57**, 130–139.

Wellensiek, S. J. (1967). The relations between the flower inducing factors in *Silene armeria* L. *Z. Pflanzenphysiol.* **56**, 33–39.

Wellensiek, S. J. (1968). Floral induction through the roots of *Silene armeria* L. *Acta bot. neerl.* **17**, 5–8.

Wellensiek, S. J. (1977). Principles of flower formation. *Acta Hortic.* **68**, 17–27.

Zeevaart, J. A. D. (1962). Physiology of flowering. *Science* **137**, 723–731.

Zeevaart, J. A. D. (1979). Perception, nature and complexity of transmitted signals. In *La Physiologie de la Floraison* (ed. P. Champagnat & R. Jacques), pp. 59–90. Paris: C.N.R.S.

PLASTIC RESPONSES OF LEAVES

J. E. DALE

Botany Department, University of Edinburgh, Mayfield Road, Edinburgh EH9 3JH, UK

Summary

In their development leaves exhibit plastic responses in both shape and size. Variations in shape are often associated with changes in size also but the reverse is not always true. Plastic responses in leaf form resulting from ontogenetic or external influences are initiated very early in primordial development and are brought about by effects on the rate and direction of cell division and expansion in different regions of the primordium. Effects on leaf size are often induced over much longer periods including the phase of lamina expansion.

In *Phaseolus vulgaris* the primary leaves exhibit increases in size when one of the pair is removed or when the stem is decapitated above the primary leaf node. These compensatory growth effects are not the result of a change in cell number but are caused by an increase in mean cell size. Cell wall extensibility is not increased by treatment and the evidence suggests that a small increase in the (turgor – wall yield stress) term may be the cause of the very rapid response to defoliation.

The usefulness of leaf systems for the analysis of plastic responses of shape and size is indicated and the importance of a better understanding of the factors determining the siting and development of the cell wall is stressed.

General considerations

Introduction

The most cursory examination of the species description in any flora will show the importance that the taxonomist attaches to the shape and size of leaves. Because of the apparent stability of these characters it is possible to build up complex classifications of leaf architecture based on such features as shape, veination, marginal details and texture (Hickey, 1973). Yet the impression of stability is illusory for while it is true that differences between species are for the most part greater than those within, significant variation in a range of characters can occur between leaves of the same species and even between leaves on the same plant.

While plant-to-plant variation may be important, for our purpose it is less interesting than that within the plant which indicates genuine development plasticity. In this case, differences are the result of regulated internal control, sometimes modulated by external influences such as nutrition, photoperiod or temperature. Often, such effects are long term and affect several leaves; they are attributable to changes at the stem apex and in the young primordia and may be qualitative, involving form and shape of the leaf, or quantitative involving size, or rate or intensity of some physiological process such as photosynthesis. But there are also short-term plastic responses affecting single leaves or groups of leaves. These are often quantitative and arise during the leaf expansion period; detailed consideration of one such effect is presented in Section II of this article.

Plasticity in the development of form

A clear demonstration that form is highly regulated despite plasticity at the tissue level is often seen in the development of leaves of periclinal chimaeras. Three leaves from successive positions on the stem of a plant of *Ficus elastica* var *variegata* are shown in Fig. 1. The cells of the leaves are derived from three layers of the apex which contribute to the primordium (Neilson-Jones 1969; Kirk & Tylney-Bassett, 1978). The stomata of these leaves contain chloroplasts so the outermost, epidermal layer, L1, is genetically green even though it appears white. Cells in the underlying tissues are derived from the layers L2 and L3 in which chloroplasts are either absent or present. Hence the white regions of the leaf, all located marginally, are composed entirely of cells from L1 and L2, while for the green regions as well as L1, L2 and L3 contribute cells to variable extents along the lamina, identifiable by the degree of green-ness of the leaf. The pattern of variegation is established by the time that leaf unfolding begins and does not change as the blade expands. The photograph shows that while the extent of variegation does not affect leaf shape, the contribution of the layers is extremely plastic, varying between and within leaves in an apparently non-predictable manner with inevitable consequences for the metabolic activities at different parts of the leaf. If there are any rules controlling the pattern and orientation of cell divisions in these leaves, such as have been considered in the case of certain roots (Gunning & Hardham, 1982) and in more theoretical studies (e.g. Lindenmayer, 1984), these do not seem to operate globally over the leaf as a whole although local operation, say within the epidermis, cannot be ruled out. What can be deduced is that developmental plasticity within the tissues is subordinated to an overriding form-controlling mechanism.

Fig. 1. Variegation in three successive leaves of the periclinal chimaera *Ficus elastica var variegata*. The oldest leaf is on the left. Scale bar, 5 cm.

In extreme cases plastic responses may be consolidated into the genotype. An interesting example of this comes from the work of Lewis (1969) who showed substantial differences in the shape and size of leaves of plants of *Geranium sanguineum* (Fig. 2) grown from samples collected at widely differing sites from the Atlantic coast to central European steppes. He concluded that 'the phenotypic expression of leaf dissection is under relatively direct genotypic control' and that the morphological differences seen in the wild are maintained when the lines are cultivated side by side.

Lewis argued that 'two distinct ecoclines involving leaf morphology [operate] in *G. sanguineum* . . . correlated with different ecological gradients . . . [that of] leaf dissection is correlated with the continentality of the original habitat and that of leaf size with the openness of the community'. These genotype–environment interactions are important in conferring plasticity at the species level and can have adaptive significance. For example the differences in leaf shape and size between lines have major effects on the boundary layer characteristics of the leaf and hence on gas and heat transfer; because of this they are of considerable ecophysiological importance (Gates & Papian, 1971; Parkhurst & Loucks, 1972; Grace, 1983).

At the other extreme, where plastic responses can be induced rapidly and where development can be switched reversibly within the same plant, there is the example of heterophylly shown by many aquatic angiosperms. Here, submerged leaves are often highly dissected while aerial leaves have a very different form (see Sculthorpe, 1967). That the effect is genuinely plastic

Fig. 2. Leaf shape in samples of *Geranium sanguineum* taken from plants cultivated from lines collected in limestone-steppe (A), steppe (B) and coastal (C) environments. Data of Lewis (1969).

comes from the fact that it is possible to modify the form of leaf produced by varying the environment (Bostrack & Millington, 1962; Schmidt & Millington, 1968; Cook, 1969; Bodkin, Spence & Weeks, 1979; Kane & Albert, 1982), or interestingly, by application of plant growth regulators (Wallenstein & Albert, 1963; Anderson, 1982; Kane & Albert, 1982; Mohan Ram & Rao, 1982).

To these examples can be added those where ontogenetic drifts in form and size of leaves occur and which are often associated with stem extension and flowering in many species, including a number that are photoperiod-insensitive. In these cases successive primordia, which appear initially similar, develop into leaves of gradually changing form, and often size, frequently culminating in the production of bracts which may be highly reduced. This aspect of heterophylly, or heteroblastic development (Goebel, 1900), is the subject of a voluminous literature which will not be considered further here. What is important to note is that the developmental fate of the primordium is plastic in the sense that it can be changed, but it is also regulated internally so that changes in size and form are, at least in the case of ontogenetic drifts, usually gradual and orderly.

Even more major differences in development can occur. Normally, foliar primordia are committed, by definition, to develop as leaves but in extreme cases primordia may be inhibited or directed into other developmental pathways. For example, it is possible to culture *in vitro*, the primordia of a number of ferns including *Osmunda*, *Matteuccia* and *Acrostichum* and it has been repeatedly found that the youngest primordia tend to give rise to shoots, or to produce anomalous buds, whereas older primordia invariably give rise to leaves in culture (Steeves, 1962; Kuehnert, 1972; Halperin, 1978; von Aderkas & Hicks, 1985). The young primordia demonstrate a plasticity with respect to their development which is lacking in the older ones.

Modification of primordial fate can also be demonstrated in cereals using methods which do less violence to the plant and its parts. In spring barley, more leaves are produced in short photoperiod conditions than in long. However, if young plants are transferred from short to long photoperiods the youngest primordia present will develop to form spikelets – that is to say that their fate has been changed by changing the environment. Since plants grown throughout in long photoperiods produce 6–7 leaves on the mainstem and those in short photoperiods produce 8–12 there are between two and six primordial positions where developmental fate can be switched by photoperiod (Cottrell, 1980). In the case of Petkus winter rye the fate of up to 17 primordia is indeterminate, depending upon whether the plant is vernalized or not (Purves & Gregory, 1937).

The major features of leaf form are established early in primordial development (e.g. Denne, 1966; Fuchs, 1975, 1976; Jeune, 1981) – certainly by the time that the primordium reaches a length of 1 mm and often much earlier still; marginal details and the final features of shape are determined somewhat later but still long before the leaf unfolds and begins rapid expansion. The young primordium shows generalized meristematic activity along its length with higher rates of mitosis in localized areas (Thomasson, 1970; Jeune, 1984; Poethig & Sussex, 1985). It follows that any plastic response which affects form must be generated in the primordial phase. Current thinking on leaf initiation and morphogenesis considers the stem apex and associated young primordia to be subject to the influence of morphogenetic fields, qualitative, quantitative and spatial changes in which will modify development by changing the rate or plane of cell division and the rate and direction of cell enlargement. The nature of the morphogens involved is unknown, but indole acetic acid (IAA) has been shown, using gc-ms methods, to be present in apex and young primordia of *Phaseolus vulgaris* (McDougall & Hillman, 1980) and has long been suggested as a likely compound for this purpose.

The fact that primordial development can be switched experimentally in so many plant species mean that systems are available in which a combination of modern analytical histochemical and radioimmunological techniques linked to examination of cell fine structure at the level of the cytoskeleton, can be expected to give important progress on the question of control of leaf form.

Plasticity and leaf size

Temperature, photoperiod, light quality and quantity, mineral nutrition and water stress can all affect leaf size, without necessarily affecting leaf form. Indeed, it could be argued that in any given situation leaf size reflects the environment and is adapted to it. Defining plasticity, in the limited sense, as the capacity to respond to external influences by changes in size or shape, there is no doubting that the leaf is truly plastic. The response to the environment may be seen at the primordial stage, for instance there is some evidence that nitrogen supply affects primordial size in barley (R. G. Wilson, unpublished data), but environmental factors often operate later, during the period of leaf unfolding and lamina expansion.

An increase in leaf size in response to say, application of nitrogenous fertilizer, could result from an increase in cell number or an increase in mean cell volume or combination of both. It is not infrequently found that mean cell size, at least of the epidermal cells, is smaller in later-formed leaves although these may be larger (Ashby, 1948) because of a higher cell number. Since, for many species, cell division continues over much of the period of leaf expansion (Sunderland, 1960; Dale & Milthorpe, 1983) separation of effects on cell number and size requires measurements on both; it cannot be inferred that because experimental treatments are applied late in leaf expansion, they will necessarily only affect cell size.

Compensatory growth in *Phaseolus vulgaris* – a case history

The response to defoliation

Over 60 years ago, Vyvyan (1924) examined the effect of removing one of the two primary leaves of *Phaseolus vulgaris* on growth of the other. He found, using a novel photographic method which permitted repeated measurements on the same leaf, that the leaf remaining after treatment grew substantially larger in area, by up to 40%, than control leaves. This compensatory growth can be considered to be a plastic response by the plant to a rather drastic treatment. However, analysis of the nature and basis of compensation in this species gives us insight into those mechanisms operating in other plastic responses where size is involved and some results of a series of experiments carried out under controlled environment conditions using the same cultivar as used by Vyvyan (*P. vulgaris* Canadian Wonder) are now reported. A fuller account of the experiments will be published elsewhere.

Confirmation of the magnitude of the compensation effect was found in experiments which also examined the extent to which the response could be affected by nitrogen, supplied every third day at the rates of 20 and 40 mg per plant, and temperatures designed to be slightly above (30 °C day/20 °C night) and slightly below (20 °C day/15 °C night) the optimum for leaf growth in this species (Dale, 1965). When one of the primary leaves was excised from seedlings at the stage when the plumule had emerged and straightened, coinciding with the onset of the phase of rapid area expansion of the primary leaves, the remaining leaf enlarged to give a final area more than 40 % (significant at $P < 0{\cdot}01$) greater than that of leaves where both are present (Table 1). An exception to this was where the higher nitrogen supply was given at the higher temperature and here it may be that the observed value is the maximum possible for expansion of a single leaf in this temperature regime. It was also found that the increase in area was matched by increase in dry weight of the leaves so that treatment did not affect area per unit weight. Thus the plasticity shown in area and weight is regulated so that both are in step.

Table 1. *The effect of temperature, nitrogen supply and removal of one primary leaf on final area (cm^2) and dry weight (mg) of the primary and first trifoliate leaves of plants of* P. vulgaris *cv Canadian Wonder. The extent of compensatory growth, expressed as a percentage, is also shown.*

	Primary leaves				First trifoliate leaf			
	Area		Weight		Area		Weight	
Temperature	30/25°	20/15°	30/25°	20/15°	30/25°	20/15°	30/25°	20/15°
	Control intact plants							
Low nitrogen	108	182	142	445	124	203	180	498
High nitrogen	167	206	244	586	189	229	277	531
	One primary leaf removed							
Low nitrogen	77	142	101	355	105	193	138	476
High nitrogen	100	148	149	399	159	212	219	484
LSD (5 %)	19	36	30	121	24	67	47	70
Compensation*								
Low nitrogen	43	56	42	59				
High nitrogen	19	44	22	36				

* Compensation is expressed as $\frac{\text{control value}}{2 \times \text{defoliated value}} \times 100$

Plants were harvested when total plant dry weight in the high nitrogen control treatment was estimated to have reached 2500 mg; at this stage growth of primary and first trifoliate leaves was complete.

Under these conditions, compensatory growth is restricted to the primary leaf. The first trifoliate leaf is not larger in the defoliated plants; indeed area of this leaf shows a slight reduction in all cases, just reaching significance ($P = 0{\cdot}05$) in the high temperature: high nitrogen treatment where leaf dry weight was also significantly affected. In this situation, the capacity to respond to defoliation is clearly restricted.

Removal of a primary leaf at later stages of development but still before the completion of expansion reduced the compensatory effect and leads eventually to a significant ($P = 0{\cdot}05$) reduction in area of the trifoliate leaf (Table 2). In contrast though, decapitation and disbudding when the primary leaves are fully expanded leads to resumed growth of the latter (see below). The plant responds to treatment in a plastic manner, the effect on an individual leaf depending upon age and the presence of other expanding and competing ones.

Defoliation was performed at a time when cell division in the primary

Table 2. *The effect of time of removal of one primary leaf on final area of the remaining primary and the first trifoliate leaf of* Phaseolus vulgaris. *Values are the means of 10.*

Day of defoliation	Area (cm^2)	
	Primary leaf	1st trifoliate leaf
4	126	66
5	120	75
6	113	71
10	90	60
Never (control)	86*	73
LSD ($P = 0{\cdot}05$)	12·2	8·7

*Value for 1 leaf of the first pair.

leaves was proceeding at its fastest. Nevertheless there was no effect of treatment on cell number in the remaining leaf (Table 3) so that compensatory growth was entirely due to cell enlargement.

In his original studies, Vyvyan (1924) showed that the enhanced growth of the remaining leaf was maintained for many days and detectable as early as one day after defoliation (Fig. 3). His method of measurement did not allow him to show effects on growth earlier than 24 h after treatment, but using conditions under which material grew faster, measurements with a ruler and with a leaf extension meter (Sharp, Osonubi, Wood & Davies, 1979) have shown growth rate of the remaining leaf on a defoliated plant to exceed that of control leaves within 2 h of treatment (Fig. 3, insert).

There was no evidence in our studies that expansion growth of the leaf was less in darkness (Fig. 4). Van Volkenburgh & Cleland (1979) found that light greatly increased growth of material from older leaves of *Phaseolus* where cell divisions had ceased and it is possible that the mechanisms controlling cell expansion change with age over the early unfolding period.

Table 3. *The effect of nitrogen supply and removal of one primary leaf on cell number* ($\times 10^{-6}$) *and mean cell dry weight (ng) of the primary leaves of plants of* P. vulgaris *grown at 20/15 °C**.

	Cell number		Mean cell dry weight	
	Control	Defoliated	Control	Defoliated
Low nitrogen	43·8	42·2	5·07	8·41
High nitrogen	39·6	42·8	7·39	9·32

*Cell counts were not made at the higher temperature.

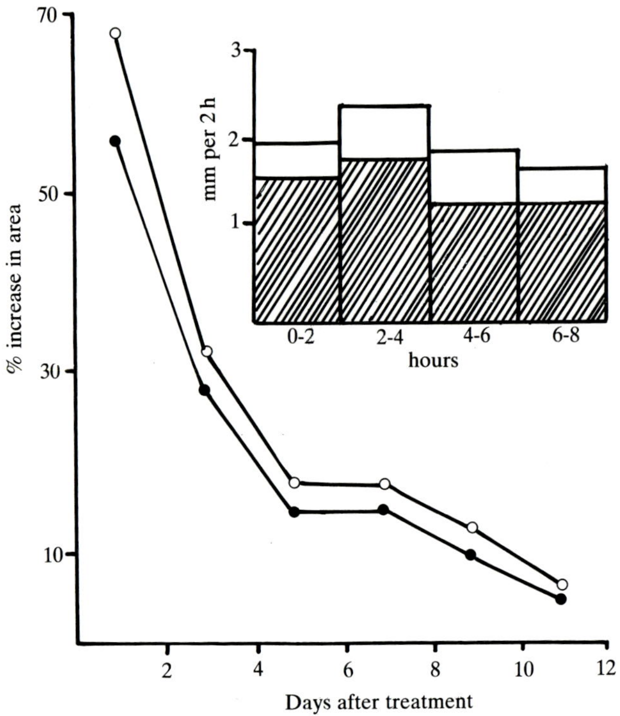

Fig. 3. The time course of increase in area, expressed as a percentage, of primary leaves of intact (●) and defoliated (○) plants of *P. vulgaris*. (Data of Vyvyan, 1924.) The insert shows the increment of length (mm per 3 h) put on by primary leaves immediately after defoliation (complete histogram) or by controls (solid histogram).

The sustained and slightly faster growth rate of the remaining primary leaf resulted in it being 10 % longer and 20 % larger in area after 48 h. The enhancement of dry weight already referred to continued so that by this time the primary leaf on defoliated plants had increased in weight by 146 %. In absolute terms this increase was rather less than that for the two leaves together on the control plants. Because treatment did not affect cell number this resulted in a substantially larger mean cell dry weight (cf. Table 3). In the early part of the postdefoliation period and certainly for the 48 h duration of this experiment, the cotyledons supply material to the developing primary leaves (Dale, 1964, 1976; Dale & Murray, 1969), and the rapid response in dry weight suggests that the remaining leaf benefits from the removal of a competing sink. The vascular anatomy of the cotyledonary and primary leaf nodes is extremely complicated (Biddulph & Cory, 1965; Mullins, 1970) but phloem connections from both cotyledons to both leaves exist so that there is no vascular constraint to movement of material from both cotyledons to one leaf in a defoliated plant.

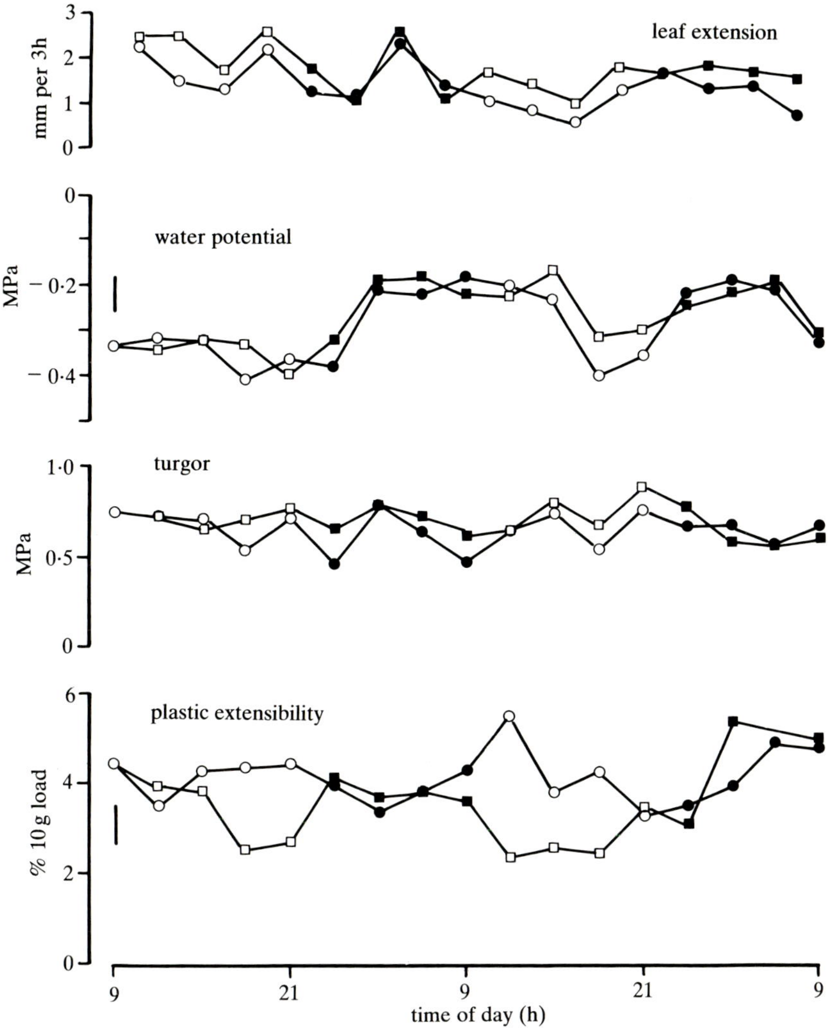

Fig. 4. Changes in length, leaf water potential, turgor and wall extensibility with time for primary leaves of control (○, ●) and defoliated (□, ■) plants of *P. vulgaris*. Defoliation was carried out when the plumular hook had just completed straightening. Plants were grown at 22·5 °C in 12 h photoperiods, darkness being indicated by the filled symbols.

Over recent years the approach of Lockhart (1965) has been extensively used to examine cell expansion in leaf tissue (Van Volkenburgh & Cleland, 1980, 1981; Radin & Boyer, 1984; Matthews, Van Volkenburgh & Boyer, 1984; Van Volkenburgh, Schmidt & Cleland, 1985; see also Tomos, 1985 for review). The simplest form of the Lockhart model (Cosgrove, 1981) relates irreversible volume expansion of a cell or cylinder of tissue to turgor pressure (P), a minimum value of turgor below which growth will not occur, the yield threshold (Y), and irreversible instantaneous wall extension (m):

$$\frac{1}{V} \cdot \frac{dV}{dt} = m\ (P\text{-}Y)$$

Van Volkenburgh & Cleland (1984) have shown how each of the parameters can control leaf growth in various situations and analysis of compensatory growth was undertaken in terms of them (Fig. 4).

Wall extensibility, an estimate of m (see Cleland, 1984), measured by means of an Instron-type stress analyser (Van Volkenburgh, Hunt & Davies, 1984) showed values for control leaves to vary between 3·5 and 5·5%/10 g load; much wider variation was found for the leaf in the defoliated treatment, with an unexpected *decrease* in plastic extensibility occurring during the photoperiod. This is in contrast to the light-induced increase found by Van Volkenburgh & Cleland (1980) using older material, but is consistent with the failure of darkness to reduce expansion. Wall extensibility does not appear to be involved in the compensatory growth response.

Values of turgor (P) were derived from measurement of leaf water potential using a pressure chamber and bulk osmotic potential, using expressed sap and intact leaf disks in a Wescor Osmometer. Treatment had no consistent effect on leaf water potential though the high values in the dark period were significant ($P = 0{\cdot}05$). This trend was closely mirrored by osmotic potential (not shown) with a sharp rise in values in the dark ($P = 0{\cdot}01$). Values for treated material were consistently, but not significantly, higher than the controls. Values of P showed no diurnal fluctuation, varying between 0·45 and 0·80 MPa over all times and treatments. Overall the remaining primary leaves on defoliated plants showed a bulk turgor 0·04 MPa higher, on average, than the controls although the difference just failed to reach significance. All these values are of course bulk estimates. Whether values per cell, particularly values for epidermal cells which are those governing blade expansion, would show greater differences is an open question resolvable only with the use of more refined techniques such as the pressure microprobe (Tomos, 1985; Tomos, Steudle, Zimmerman & Schulze, 1981).

Preliminary estimates on Y, the yield threshold, using the strip extension method (Van Volkenburgh & Cleland, 1981) ranged from 0·47 to 0·52 MPa. These values are rather higher than estimates using the same method but with older material (Van Volkenburgh & Cleland, 1981). Calculating (P–Y) using the lower of our estimates gives an average values for treated leaves which is about 18% higher than the controls. Unfortunately P and Y are not easily determined on the same tissue piece and the exact magnitude of the difference between them is difficult to assess statistically. Nevertheless, it appears that small turgor differences may be the driving force in compensatory growth in these experiments.

The response to decapitation

Other, more drastic treatments, have shown a different type of plastic response by primary leaves of *Phaseolus*. Complete decapitation at the stage when the first trifoliate leaf begins to unfold and when the primary leaves have virtually completed expansion results, after a short lag period, in very large increases in area and thickness of the primary leaves (Van Staden & Carmi, 1982; Carmi & Van Staden, 1983). Treatment caused prolonged increase in length of palisade cells so that 16 days after decapitation they were nearly twice the length of those in control leaves (Table 4). A similar increase in chlorophyll and soluble protein content per unit area was also found suggesting that chloroplast number could well have increased.

In these experiments, the plasticity of leaf development is seen in the continued growth of leaves which would normally have ceased to expand, rather than the accelerated growth of expanding leaves considered previously. Van Volkenburgh *et al.* (1985) have suggested that cessation of expansion in primary leaves of *Phaseolus* is the consequence of a progressive loss of the capacity for acid-induced wall loosening, reflected in a reduction in cell wall extensibility. The continued growth of mature leaves

Table 4. *The effect of decapitation above the primary leaf node on area of the primary leaf, chlorophyll content and length of palisade cells in the primary leaves.*

Days after decapitation	Area cm^2	Chlorophyll mg $leaf^{-1}$	Palisade cell length μm
0 Control	64·6 ± 3·0	2·27	60·4 ± 2·8
2 Control	77·2 ± 5·6	2·44	–
Decapitated	74·6 ± 4·3	2·40	–
8 Control	74·7 ± 5·0	2·39	–
Decapitated	99·4 ± 4·3	4·01	–
16 Control	76·5 ± 5·5	2·10	72·0 ± 2·7
Decapitated	108·2 ± 6·3	7·04	155·1 ± 6·6

Data of Van Staden & Carmi (1982).

on decapitation indicates that in Van Staden's experiments cell wall extensibility cannot be restricting growth of either the epidermal cells, responsible for the area increase, or the palisade cells. Analysis in terms of the cellular parameters relating to the Lockhart model has not been made for these treatments. Such studies could be informative, particularly since it has been shown that cytokinin content, (mainly of zeatin, glucosylzeatin and ribosylzeatin, analysed by bioassay) increases in the enlarging leaves (Van Staden & Carmi, 1982). It has long been argued, on not very strong grounds, that cytokinins are involved in the control of lamina expansion (see Goodwin & Erwee, 1983) although through what mechanism has not been indicated.

The leaf as a plastic system: resumé and prospect

In animals, adult size and form often vary within relatively narrow limits. Growth is highly determinate and the adult condition is usually quickly reached. In contrast indeterminate and prolonged growth is a feature of many plants, having its origin in the organization of meristematic activity into long-lived apices. But even an organ such as a leaf, whose duration is finite and whose growth is, by comparison with that of the plant short-lived, possesses a plasticity far surpassing that possessed by an animal organ.

It is apparent that the bases for this plasticity of development are intimately concerned with cell structure and in particular with the constraining effects of the cell wall. Although the wall effectively prevents the cell movements seen in animal development, as an exoskeleton it confers important properties on the cell in terms of control of the direction and rate of growth. In turn, the cytoskeletal components, microtubules and microfilaments determine the location and deposition of wall material (Gunning & Hardham, 1982), wall rheological properties reflecting chemical organization and the form and extent of linkages within the wall (see Taiz, 1984). All these features are of importance in the developmental changes occurring at the apex which result firstly in the initiation of a primordium and then in the determination of its subsequent developmental fate (see Green, 1980, and this volume). That plastic responses in form occur at all is the consequence of developmental plasticity at the subcellular level controlling and modifying wall growth. Paradoxically it is largely through the wall that developmental flexibility is achieved; the wall does not constrain it. It may be noted in passing that limited positional adjustment of cells during growth can be controlled through the formation of intercellular spaces. These are particularly important in leaves, where up to

50 % of total volume can be accounted for by air spaces. Formation of such spaces involves wall separation and dissolution (Martens, 1937; Roland, 1978) and itself appears to be carefully controlled (Jeffree, Dale & Fry, 1986).

But if the cytoskeleton ultimately controls cell growth and form and hence leaf form, plasticity in size also has its origin in wall properties. Wall extensibility and the sensitivity of this to environmental influences such as light, and wall yield threshold, offers points of control for cell and leaf size, not only in terms of increased cell volume, but in an increase which is vectorial, seen very clearly in growth of the palisade cells during compensatory growth (Table 4). There is an additional element allowing plastic responses in size which comes from the ability of cells to regulate turgor through changes in solute content. Quite apart from any effects of turgor on wall properties, changes in turgor may affect membrane hydraulic conductivity during cell and leaf enlargement although this has not so far been examined for growing leaf cells.

There seems to be no need to invoke specific genetic mechanisms conferring developmental plasticity on leaves. Interplay of factors within the cell will operate to control the formation and positioning of the cytoskeleton and the consequences for cell function and growth, as well as the changes in wall loosening and turgor which ultimately control size. These are the normal mechanisms operating day-to-day to control development and additional genomic regulation of plastic development would appear to be unnecessary. An analogy is that of an architect designing a building to be constructed of brick, dressed stone, or undressed stone. In the first case it is possible to decide exactly how many bricks will be required since these are of standard size; with dressed stone likely to come in various sizes such a prediction is more difficult and is impossible with undressed stone as the building material. Yet the architect's plan can be met without precise knowledge of the numbers and sizes of all the building blocks. The genetic blueprint is activated when the leaf is initiated yet all the indications are that its fulfillment is the result of empirical decision-making during development and not of the operation of tight rules dictating the developmental fate and lineage of any cell or group of cells. As an example of this, differentiation of cells in the expanding leaf varies so that the exact course of development of minor veins is unpredictable (Aloni & Sachs, 1973), yet the proximity of mesophyll cells to the minor veins is assured so that the distance between them is restricted (e.g. Geiger, 1976; Russin & Evert, 1984, 1985).

It would be wrong to give the impression that the many plastic responses shown by leaves are fully understood and can be explained. The previous

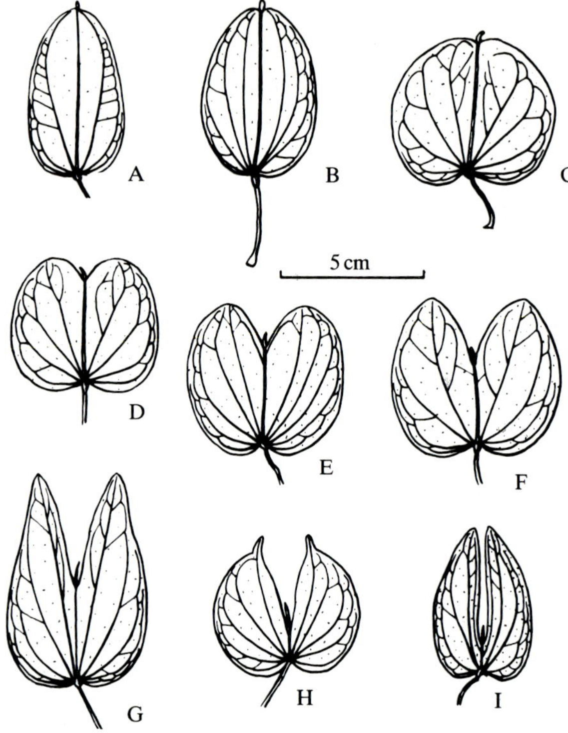

Fig. 5. Trends in leaf shape in nine related species of *Bauhinia*. Drawings of Cusset (1970–71). (A) *B. acuruana*, (B) *B. havilandii*, (C) *B. integrifolia*, (D) *B. tenuiflora*, (E) *B. rufa*, (F) *B. langsdorfiana*, (G) *B. forficata*, (H) *B. rubiginosa*, (I) *B. pennicillilobata*.

paragraphs have served, in effect, to transfer aspects of our ignorance from the leaf as a whole to the cell. The way forward is, on the one hand, to examine and understand the development, control and behaviour of the cytoskeletal components and how wall formation and growth is controlled, and on the other to understand the basis for wall loosening and the rheology of the wall. We urgently need a model, or a series of models, of wall structure in growing cells which takes account of changes in composition, directional growth properties, wall breakdown in space formation, and bond loosening during expansion. The developing leaf, especially that of the grass (cf., this volume), where all cells along the leaf are of known age and developmental status offers convenient easily grown material for such studies. But we must not look only to well-known material. In an intriguing and lengthy study Cusset (1970–1) examined a number of species of *Bauhinia* and showed that a sequence of leaf shapes could be established (Fig. 5), each species in the sequence differing only slightly in leaf shape from those adjacent to it. The basis of this gradation in leaf shape in related species presents an intriguing problem and material such as this would be ideal for examining differences in subcellular morphology and how these are related to subtle differences in form as the leaf primordium develops. Of equal importance but even greater difficulty, would be to discover how the differences can be manipulated experimentally.

References

ALONI, R. & SACHS, T. (1973). The three-dimensional structure of primary phloem systems. *Planta* **113**, 345–353.

ANDERSON, L. W. J. (1982). Effects of abscisic acid on growth and development in American Pondweed (*Potamogeton nodosus* Poin). *Aquatic Bot.* **13**, 29–44.

ASHBY, E. (1948). Studies in the morphogenesis of leaves. II. The area, cell size and cell number of leaves of *Ipomoea* in relation to their position on the shoot. *New Phytol.* **47**, 177–195.

BIDDULPH, O. & CORY, R. (1965). Translocation of ^{14}C-metabolites in the phloem of the bean plant. *Pl. Physiol.* **40**, 119–129.

BODKIN, P. C., SPENCE, D. H. N. & WEEKS, D. C. (1979). Photoreversible control of heterophylly in *Hippurus vulgaris* L. *New Phytol.* **84**, 533–542.

BOSTRACK, J. M. & MILLINGTON, W. F. (1962). On the determination of leaf form in an aquatic heterophyllous species of *Ranunculus*. *Bull. Torrey bot. Club* **89**, 1–20.

CARMI, A. & VAN STADEN, J. (1983). Role of roots in regulating the growth rate and cytokinin content in leaves. *Pl. Physiol.* **73**, 76–78.

CLELAND, R. E. (1984). The Instron technique as a measure of immediate-past wall extensibility. *Planta* **160**, 514–520.

COOK, C. D. K. (1969). On the determination of leaf form in *Ranunculus aquatilis*. *New Phytol.* **68**, 469–480.

COSGROVE, D. J. (1981). Analysis of the dynamic and steady-state responses of growth rate and turgor pressure to changes in cell parameters. *Pl. Physiol.* **68**, 1439–146.

COTTRELL, J. E. (1980). Ph.D. thesis University of Edinburgh.

CUSSET, G. (1970–71). Remarques sur des feuilles de dicotyledones. *Boissiera* **16**, 1–210.

DALE, J. E. (1964). Leaf growth in *Phaseolus vulgaris*. 1. Growth of the first pair of leaves under constant conditions. *Ann. Bot.* **20**, 579–585.

DALE, J. E. (1965). Leaf growth in *Phaseolus vulgaris*. 2. Temperature effects and the light factor. *Ann. Bot.* **29**, 293–308.

DALE, J. E. (1976). Cell division in leaves. In *Cell Division in Higher Plants* (ed. M. M. Yeoman), pp. 315–343. London: Academic Press.

DALE, J. E. & MILTHORPE, F. L. (1983). General features of the production and growth of leaves. In *The Growth and Functioning of Leaves* (ed. J. E. Dale & F. L. Milthorpe), pp. 151–178. Cambridge: Cambridge University Press.

DALE, J. E. & MURRAY, D. (1969). Light and cell division in primary leaves of *Phaseolus*. *Proc. R. Soc.* B, **173**, 541–555.

DENNE, M. P. (1966). Leaf development in *Trifolium repens*. *Bot. Gaz.* **127**, 202–210.

FUCHS, C. (1975). Ontogenèse foliare et acquisition de la forme chez le *Tropaeolum peregrinum* L.1. *Annls Sci. nat. Bot.* **16**, 321–390.

FUCHS, C. (1976). Ontogenèse foliare et acquisition de la forme chez le *Tropaeolum peregrinum* L.2. *Annls Sci. nat. Bot.* **17**, 121–158.

GATES, D. M. & PAPIAN, L. E. (1971). *Atlas of Energy Budgets of Plant Leaves*. New York: Academic Press.

GEIGER, D. R. (1976). Phloem loading in source leaves. In *Transport and Transfer Processes in Plants* (ed. I. F. Wardlaw and J. B. Passioura). New York: Academic Press.

GOEBEL, K. (1900). *Organography of Plants* (tras. I. B. Balfour). Oxford.

GOODWIN, P. B. & ERWEE, M. G. (1983). Hormonal influences on leaf growth. In *The Growth and Functioning of Leaves* (ed. J. E. Dale and F. L. Milthorpe), pp. 207–232. Cambridge: Cambridge University Press.

GRACE, J. (1983). *Plant Atmosphere Relationships*. Chapman & Hall, London.

GREEN, P. B. (1980). Organogenesis – a biophysical view. *A. Rev. Pl. Physiol.* **31**, 51–82.

GUNNING, B. E. S. & HARDHAM, A. R. (1982). Microtubules. *A. Rev. Pl. Physiol.* **33**, 651–698.

HALPERIN, W. (1978). Organogenesis at the shoot apex. *A. Rev. Pl. Physiol.* **29**, 239–262.

HICKEY, L. J. (1973). Classification of the architecture of dicotyledonous leaves. *Am. J. Bot.* **60**, 17–33.

JEFFREE, C. E., DALE, J. E. & FRY, S. C. (1986) The genesis of intercellular spaces in developing leaves of *Phaseolus vulgaris*. *Protoplasma*. (In press).

JEUNE, B. (1981). Modele empirique du developpement des feuilles de Dicotyledones. *Bull. Mus. natn. Hist. nat. Ser.* **3B**, 433–459.

JEUNE, B. (1984). Position et orientation des mitoses dans la zone organogene de jeunes feuilles de *Fraxinus excelsior*, et *Lycopus europaeus*. *Can. J. Bot.* **62**, 2861–2864.

KANE, M. E. & ALBERT, L. S. (1982). Environmental and growth regulator effects on heterophylly and growth in *Proserpinaca intermedia*. *Aquatic Bot.* **13**, 73–85.

KIRK, J. T. O. & TYLNEY-BASSETT, R. A. E. (1978). *The Plastids* (2nd Edition). Amsterdam: Elsevier/North Holland.

KUEHNERT, C. C. (1972). On determination of leaf primordia in *Osmunda cinnamomea* L. *In The Dynamics of Meristem Cell Populations* (ed. M. W. Miller and C. C. Kuehnert), pp. 101–118. New York: Plenum Press.

LEWIS, M. C. (1969). Genecological differentiation of leaf morphology in *Geranium sanguineum*. *New Phytol.* **68**, 481–503.

LINDENMAYER, A. (1984). Models for plant tissue development with cell division orientation regulated by preprophase bands of microtubules. *Differentiation* **26**, 1–10.

LOCKHART, J. A. (1965). An analysis of irreversible plant cell elongation. *J. theor. Biol.* **8**, 264–275.

MARTENS, P. (1937). L'origine des espaces intercellulaires. *Cellule* **46**, 355–388.

MATTHEWS, M. A., VAN VOLKENBURGH, E. & BOYER, J. S. (1984). Acclimation of leaf growth to low water potentials in sunflower. *Pl. Cell Environ.* **7**, 199–206.

McDOUGALL, J. & HILLMAN, J. R. (1980). Distribution of indole-3-acetic acid in shoots of *Phaseolus vulgaris*. *Z. Pflanzenphysiol.* **97**, 367–371.

MOHAN, RAM, H. Y. & RAO, S. (1982). *In vitro* induction of aerial leaves and of precocious flowering in submerged shoots of *Limnophila indica* by abscisic acid. *Planta* **155**, 521–523.

MULLINS, M. G. (1970). Transport of ^{14}C assimilates in seedlings of *Phaseolus vulgaris* L. in relation to vascular anatomy. *Ann. Bot.* **34**, 889–896.

NEILSON-JONES, W. (1969). *Plant Chimeras* (2nd Edition). Methuen, London.

PARKHURST, D. F. & LOUCKS, O. L. (1972). Optimal leaf size in relation to environment. *J. Ecol.* **60**, 505–537.

POETHIG, R. S. & SUSSEX, I. M. (1985). The cellular parameters of leaf development in tobacco: a clonal analysis. *Planta* **165**, 170–184.

PURVES, O. N. & GREGORY, F. G. (1937). Studies in vernalisation of cereals. I. *Ann. Bot.* **1**, 569–592.

RADIN, J. W. & BOYER, J. S. (1982). Control of leaf expansion by nitrogen nutrition in sunflower plants. *Pl. Physiol.* **69**, 771–775.

ROLAND, J. C. (1978). Cell wall differentiation and stages involved with intercellular gas space opening. *J. Cell Sci.* **32**, 325–336.

RUSSIN, W. A. & EVERT, R. F. (1984). Studies on the leaf of *Populus deltoides* (Salicaceae): morphology and anatomy. *Am. J. Bot.* **71**, 1398–1415.

RUSSIN, W. A. & EVERT, R. F. (1985). Studies on the leaf of *Populus deltoides* (Salicaceae): quantitative aspects and solute concentrations of the sieve-tube members. *Am. J. Bot.* **72**, 487–500.

SCHMIDT, B. L. & MILLINGTON, W. F. (1968). Regulation of leaf shape in *Proserpinaca palustris*. *Bull. Torrey bot. Club* **95**, 264–286.

SCULTHORPE, C. D. (1967). *The Biology of Aquatic Plants*. Edward Arnold, London.

SHARP, R. E., OSONUBI, O., WOOD, W. A. & DAVIES, W. J. (1979). A simple instrument for measuring leaf extension in grasses and its application in the study of the effects of water stress on maize and sorghum. *Ann. Bot.* **44**, 35–46.

STEEVES, T. A. (1962). Morphogenesis in isolated fern leaves. In *Regeneration* (ed. D. Rudnick), pp. 117–151. New York: Ronald Press.

SUNDERLAND, N. (1960). Cell division and expansion in the growth of the leaf. *J. exp. Bot.* **11**, 68–80.

TAIZ, L. (1984). Plant cell expansion: regulation of cell wall mechanical properties. *A. Rev. Pl. Physiol.* **35**, 585–657.

THOMASSON, M. (1970). Quelques observations sur la répartition des zones de croissance de la feuille du *Jasminum nudiflorum* Lindley. *Candollea* **25**, 297–340.

TOMOS, D. (1985). The physical limitations of leaf cell expansion. In *Control of Leaf Growth* S.E.B. Seminar Series **27** (ed. N. R. Baker, W. J. Davies and C. Ong). Cambridge: Cambridge University Press.

TOMOS, A. D., STEUDLE, E., ZIMMERMANN, U. & SCHULZE, E.-D. (1981). Water relations of leaf epidermal cells of *Tradescantia virginiana*. *Pl. Physiol.* **68**, 1135–1143.

VAN STADEN, J. & CARMI, A. (1982). The effects of decapitation on the distribution of cytokinins and growth of *Phaseolus vulgaris*. *Physiol. Pl.* **55**, 39–44.

VAN VOLKENBURGH, E. & CLELAND, R. E. (1979). Separation of cell enlargement and division in bean leaves. *Planta* **146**, 245–247.

VAN VOLKENBURGH, E. & CLELAND, R. E. (1980). Proton excretion and cell expansion in bean leaves. *Planta* **148**, 273–278.

VAN VOLKENBURGH, E. & CLELAND, R. E. (1981). Control of light-induced bean leaf expansion: role of osmotic potential, wall yield stress and hydraulic conductivity. *Planta* **153**, 572–577.

VAN VOLKENBURGH, E. & CLELAND, R. E. (1984). Control of leaf growth by changes in cell wall properties. *What's New Pl. Physiol.* **15**, 25–28.

VAN VOLKENBURGH, E., HUNT, S. & DAVIES, W. J. (1983). A simple instrument for measuring cell-wall extensibility. *Ann. Bot.* **51**, 669–672.

VAN VOLKENBURGH, E., SCHMIDT, M. G. & CLELAND, R. E. (1985). Loss of capacity for acid-induced wall loosening as the principal cause of the cessation of cell enlargement in light-grown bean leaves. *Planta* **163**, 500–505.

VON ADERKAS, P. & HICKS, G. (1985). *In vitro* development of isolated leaf primordia of *Matteuccia struthiopteris*. *Can J. Bot.* **63**, 916–919.

VYVYAN, M. C. (1924). Studies of the rate of growth of leaves by a photographic method. 1. The determinants of the rate of growth of first leaves of *Phaseolus vulgaris*. *Ann. Bot. (Old Series)* **38**, 59–103.

WALLENSTEIN, A. & ALBERT, L. S. (1963). Plant morphology: its control in *Proserpinaca* by photoperiod, temperature and gibberellic acid. *Science* **140**, 998–1000.

THE ROLE OF ELECTRICAL PHENOMENA IN TIP GROWTH, WITH SPECIAL REFERENCE TO THE DEVELOPMENTAL PLASTICITY OF FILAMENTOUS FERN GAMETOPHYTES

TODD J. COOKE AND RICHARD H. RACUSEN

Department of Botany, University of Maryland, College Park, MD 20742, USA

Summary

Cell expansion in many plant structures, including algal rhizoids, fungal hyphae, root hairs, and pollen tubes, is restricted to their apical tips. Endogenous electric fields are seen to accompany polarized growth in all tip-growing cells studied to date. The extensive studies on absorptive tip-growing structures have established that positive currents enter their elongating tips, with a portion of the entry current being carried by a localized calcium influx into the extreme tip. The resulting tip-to-base gradient in calcium concentration appears to be responsible for maintaining polarized growth in these systems, although it is uncertain whether this calcium effect is mediated via either electrophoretic or cytoskeletal mechanisms. In contrast, the few electrical measurements made on photosynthetic cells suggest that the orientation of their transcellular fields is transiently or permanently reversed relative to the fields in absorptive structures. In darkness, microelectrode measurements indicate that the apical tip of the fern filament is 5 mV electronegative relative to the base of the apical cell. This cellular dipole is perceived with the vibrating probe as a focused outward current that departs from the tip region and a more diffuse inward current that enters the lateral sides of the apical cell. The tip current is predominantly composed of protons, as can be identified with various cation-selective electrodes. This proton current is thought to help maintain localized wall expansion in the filament tip.

Blue light mediates the major morphogenetic transition in fern gametophytes, i.e. the transition from the tip-growing filament to the planar prothallus. All the above electrical and ionic parameters change in the few minutes of irradiation before the filament tip starts lateral swelling. The plasma membrane at the extreme tip begins to hyperpolarize within 3 s, while the basal region shows a delayed, but greater response. The cellular dipole that had existed in darkness is thus abolished in 10 to 15 min after the start of irradiation. With the vibrating probe a more diffuse pattern of positive currents is observed to emerge from the tip as well as the subapical regions of the apical cell. Simultaneously, proton efflux increases in the subapical region; the resulting decrease in cell wall pH should help plasticize the lateral walls, which may, in turn, facilitate the process of lateral swelling over the next few hours. Other morphological and physiological considerations indicate that the observed change in electrical activity in the filament tip may be necessary, but is insufficient to fully account for the transition from tip growth to the subsequent growth form.

As a general rule, absorptive tip-growing structures tend to show persistent tip growth throughout their existence, whereas photosynthetic ones will often develop into more complex forms. Geometric models were constructed to test whether the relative developmental stability of the different structures can be explained on the basis of the selection pressures to optimize the surface-to-volume relationships for absorption and photoreception.

Introduction

A specialized pattern of cell expansion called tip growth is typically exhibited by the structures which emerge from spores, zygotes, and other single-celled propagules of plants (reviews: Green, 1969; Sievers & Schnepf, 1981). Wall expansion in a tip-growing structure is restricted to the roughly hemispherical dome which is positioned distal to the cylindrical body of the structure. The maximal expansion rate of the dome surface occurs at its extreme tip, while the rate falls to zero at its base. A related feature of polarized growth is the stratified arrangement of cytoplasmic organelles in the apical tip, with the Golgi apparatus and endoplasmic reticulum being concentrated in the apical zone, most other organelles in the subapical zone and a large vacuole in the basal region. Surface expansion in the apical dome is seen to generate a cylindrical surface at its base, and thus, a tip-growing structure appears to grow as an elongating cylinder. Since wall expansion within the dome does not disrupt the cylindrical body, a tip-growing structure can stably propagate its overall form without any change except for an increasing length throughout its life span. However, certain tip-growing forms can be induced to form two- and three-dimensional structures; this transition in growth form is accomplished by disrupting the pre-existing patterns of surface expansion and cytoplasmic zonation in the growing tip.

The overall objective of this paper is to examine the possible developmental mechanisms and evolutionary pressures which might determine the relative stability of various tip-growing forms. The literature on tip growth will be surveyed first to ascertain whether certain physiological features of tip-growing structures are causally related to their developmental stability. We shall also review the extensive investigations of L.F. Jaffe and his collaborators which have established that endogenous electrical fields are intimately involved in the initiation of polarized growth in tip-growing structures. Their discoveries about the electrical phenomena associated with stable patterns of tip growth will then be compared to our findings with the fern gametophyte which changes from a tip-growing filament to a planar prothallus upon exposure to blue light. Finally, we shall explore the possibility that the physiological roles of tip-growing strutures have acted as significant evolutionary constraints on the relative stability of tip growth.

Electrical features of tip growth

Table 1 summarizes the electrical measurements which have been made on a diverse group of tip-growing structures. It is instructive to separate those structures whose primary function is the absorption of nutrients and water from photosynthetic structures. The most studied examples of absorptive tip-growing structures are brown algal rhizoids and angiosperm pollen tubes (reviews: Weisenseel & Kicherer, 1981; Jaffe, 1981, 1982; Nuccitelli, 1984). The behaviour of the algal zygote or pollen grain as an electrical dipole in a conductive medium made it possible for those investigators to monitor the ionic currents in polarized cells with an extracellular vibrating microelectrode (Jaffe & Nuccitelli, 1974; Dorn & Weisenseel, 1982). This research established that the initial cell generates a transcellular electric field, which precedes the initiation of polarized growth. Positive currents in both the algal zygote and the pollen grain enter the precise site from which the tip-growing structure will eventually emerge; moreover, the axis of subsequent growth is observed to parallel the axis of the transcellular field. Although other ions in the surrounding medium seem to act as the prinicipal charge-carrying entities in these endogenous currents, several independent approaches, including $^{45}Ca^{2+}$ autoradiography (Jaffe, Weisenseel, & Jaffe, 1975), chlorotetracycline fluorescence (Reiss & Herth, 1978) and proton-induced X-ray emission (Reiss, Herth & Schnepf, 1983), have demonstrated that the growing tips of pollen tubes accumulate calcuim, which results in an apparent tip-to-base gradient in its concentration. (This gradient may represent the distribution of either cytosolic calcium or sequestered calcium within membrane compartments.) Similarly, the

Table 1. *Morphological and electrical features of various tip-growing structures.*

Tip-growing structure	Organism	Order of emergence from initial cell	Function	Net direction of positive tip currents	Major current carrying ions	Developmentally significant ions	Subsequent growth stage	Reference
Brown algal rhizoid	*Pelvetia, Fucus*	First	Absorption	Inward	K^+, Cl^-	Ca^{2+}	Holdfast	Nuccitelli, 1978, 1984; Jaffe, 1982
Red algal rhizoid	*Griffithsia*	First	Absorption	Inward	?	?	None	Waaland & Lucas, 1984
Fungal hypha	7 genera from 3 divisions	First (only)	Absorption	Inward	H^+	Ca^{2+}?	Reproductive structures	Reiss & Herth, 1979; Armbruster & Weisenseel, 1983; Kropf *et al.* 1983, 1984; Gow, 1984; Horwitz *et al.* 1984
Fungal rhizoid	*Blastocladiella*	First	Absorption	Inward	?	?	None	Stump *et al.* 1980
Angiosperm pollen tube	*Lilium*	First (only)	Absorption	Inward	K^+, H^+	Ca^{2+}	None	Weisenseel & Jaffe, 1976; Jaffe, 1982
Angiosperm root hair	*Hordeum, Lepidium*	First (only)	Absorption	Inward	H^+	Ca^{2+}	None	Weisenseel *et al.* 1979 Reiss & Herth, 1979
Brown algal thallus initial	*Pelvetia, Fucus*	Second	Photosynthesis	Outward	K^+, Cl^-	?	Thallus	Nuccitelli, 1978, 1984
Yellow-green algal filament*	*Vaucheria*	Second	Photosynthesis	Outward, then inward	H^+	H^+, Ca^{2+}?	Reproductive structures	Blatt *et al.* 1981; Weisenseel & Kicherer, 1981
Moss protonema	*Funaria*	Second	Photosynthesis	?	?	Ca^{2+}?	Leafy gametophore	Reiss & Herth, 1979; Saunders & Hepler, 1981
Fern protonema	*Onoclea*	Second	Photosynthesis	Outward	H^+	H^+, Ca^{2+}?	Prothallus	Racusen & Cooke, 1982a,b; Ketchum *et al.* 1984

* No electrical measurements have been made on the germinating zygote of *Vaucheria*, which produces both rhizoids and filaments (Mundie, 1929). The available data came from a study on how blue light induces the initiation of filament branches.

rhizoid pole of fucoid zygotes have been shown to preferentially accumulate calcium before its emergence (Robinson & Jaffe, 1975). These rhizoids are also seen to grow toward the high concentration in a Ca^{2+} gradient, as established by an asymmetric application of the ionophore A23187 (Robinson & Cone, 1980). Given that calcium is intimately involved in secretory processes in many other organisms (Pollard, Creutz, & Pazoles, 1981), it is quite reasonable to speculate that it regulates the localized secretion of wall-precursor vesicles necessary to maintain tip growth.

Other studies on absorptive tip-growing structures, although less exhaustive, suggest that the generalizations from fucoid rhizoids and lily pollen tubes may apply to all such structures, regardless of taxonomic position (see Table 1). Positive currents are consistently seen to enter their growing tips, with calcium component of the entry current apparently being involved in the maintenance of tip growth. It may be significant that these positive currents are often measured to flow into the growing tip as well as the non-growing subapical regions of absorptive structures (Weisenseel & Jaffe, 1976; Kropf, Caldwell, Gow & Harold, 1984). Such generalized current entry should help these tip-growing structures to absorb ion, sugars, and amino acids via various cotransport mechanisms; in particular, Kropf *et al.* (1984) have emphasized that the inward proton currents in the fungus *Achyla* mediate the uptake of methionine and other amino acids.

There have been few electrical measurements of phototsynthetic tip-growing structures (Table 1). Nevertheless, in contrast to the absorptive structures, it appears that the positive tip currents in photosynthetic structures may either initially or permanently be directed outward from the tip. The transcellular currents which enter the young rhizoid of the fucoid zygote depart from the thallus pole (Nuccitelli, 1978), although no measurements have been made on the emerging thallus itself. In the presence of blue irradiation, transitory outward currents are reported to anticipate the formation of side branches in the filamentous yellow-green alga *Vaucheria* (Blatt, Weisenseel & Haupt, 1981; Weisenseel & Kicherer, 1981). This localized current, which is tentatively characterized as a proton efflux, appears to precede the accumulation of chloroplasts at the irradiated region. These organelles are eventually positioned in the extreme tip of the side branch which develops from the irradiated region; interestingly, the current switches its orientation to an inward direction prior to the emergence of the side branch. In darkness, the apical cell of the fern protonema (the filamentous stage of gametophyte development) exhibits a persistent outward tip current (Racusen & Cooke, 1984, unpublished data).

Table 2. *Electrical events associated with the developmental transitions from tip growth to subsequent growth stages.*

Tip-growing structure	Subsequent growth stage	Electrical features of subsequent growth		References
		Current changes	Important ions	
Fungal hypha	Sporangium	Inward to outward to inward	?	Armbruster & Weisenseel, 1983
Moss protonema	Leafy gametophore	?	Ca^{2+}	Saunders & Hepler, 1981, 1983
Fern protonema	Prothallus	Localized outward to diffuse outward	H^{+}	Ketchum *et al.* 1984

Many tip-growing structures, especially those committed to absorptive functions, continue to elongate via tip growth throughout their existence. On the other hand, several tip growing structures do adopt different growth forms at later stages of their development. Table 2 summarizes the limited electrical observations made on tip-growing structures as they are changing into other growth forms. In absorptive structures, the cessation of tip growth occurs in those instances where the structures assume other physiological roles, such as the multicellular holdfasts of intertidal brown algae or the reproductive structures of various fungi. During the formation of the one fungal sporangium studied to date, the current switches its direction several times, with each polarity change corresponding to a specific stage of sporangial development (Armbruster & Weisenseel, 1983). No photosynthetic structure exhibits persistent tip growth. The simplest change occurs in some filamentous algae, which produce spherical reproductive structures at the growing tips of some branches. Other photosynthetic structures, including both algae and land plants, which start their development as tip-growing filaments or protonemata, have the capability to change their growth form under the proper conditions. Thus, these plants provide special opportunities for studying the control mechanisms responsible for tip growth as well as plant morphogenesis in general. For instance, in the mosses, endogenous cytokinins appear to regulate the transition from the tip-growing filamentous form to the typical three-dimensional gametophore (Brandes & Kende, 1968; Brandes, 1973). One of the primary events in this cytokinin effect appears to be a large influx of extracellular calcium and the subsequent activation of calmodulin (Saunders & Hepler, 1981, 1982, 1983). In contrast, the blue-light photoreceptor controls the morphogenetic transition from tip-growing protonema to planar prothallus in fern gametophytes (Miller, 1968. Furuya, 1983). Simultaneously, the outward proton current that was originally localized at the growing tip in darkness becomes a more diffuse outward current which flows from the lateral walls of the apical cell (Racusen & Cooke, 1984, unpublished data).

The topic of how certain evolutionary pressures might select for the developmental stability of absorptive tip-growing structures and the relative plasticity of photosynthetic ones is addressed in a later section.

Cellular mechanisms of tip growth

The persuasive evidence that electric fields are casually related to the induction of cellular polarity, i.e. the initiation of tip growth, is extensively reviewed elsewhere (e.g. Weisenseel, 1979; Weisenseel & Kicherer, 1981; Jaffe, 1981, 1982; Nuccitelli, 1984). Nevertheless, the question of whether electrical fields *per se* are both necessary and sufficient to maintain tip growth in an existing structure remains open.

That electric fields are somehow essential to tip growth has been inferred from experimental studies of localized calcium accumulation into the apical tips (Jaffe *et al.* 1975; Robinson & Jaffe, 1975; Reiss & Herth, 1979; Reiss *et al.* 1983). Given the low mobility of calcium in the cytoplasm, it was hypothesized that standing calcium gradients at the localized site of cation entry should result in an endogenous field of sufficient magnitude to promote 'self-electrophoresis' of cytoplasmic organelles and membrane proteins toward the growing tip (Jaffe, Robinson & Nuccitelli, 1974; Jaffe, 1977). Such transcellular fields are, in theory, aligned to attract cytoplasmic components which would usually bear negative charges at physiological pH values. Aside from the theoretical calculations of the probable electrophoretic mobility of cellular inclusions, it is possible to demonstrate the electrophoretic migration of fluorochrome-tagged membrane proteins in an applied field (e.g. Poo & Robinson, 1977; Poo, 1981). Another suggestive observation is that the carbohydrate fucoidin, which is normally localized in the rhizoid wall of brown algal zygotes, is not incorporated into that wall region unless sulphate groups have been attached to this polymer (Quatrano, 1978). Yet, it is difficult to envisage how negative charges inside membrane vesicles could direct their movement toward a positive pole.

Considerable evidence seems to support the alternative notion that the localized wall expansion in tip-growing cells depends on the biochemical and cellular effects of calcium other than its electrical properties. Treating young algal zygotes with cytochalasin B, which is known to disrupt microfilaments, causes wall materials originally destined for the rhizoid tip to become distributed over the entire cell wall (Quatrano, 1973). Recent experiments have shown that cytochalasin D does significantly reduce the endogenous electrical field around the zygote (Brawley & Robinson, 1985). Since calcium is an important regulator of microfilament activity (Kamiya, 1981; Williamson, 1984), it was proposed that the calcium current directs the orientation and, or, assembly of microfilaments which provide the actual motive force for the movement of wall-precursor vesicles to the growing rhizoid tip. Because this mechanism would require a localized calcium current to initiate, but not neccessarily maintain polarized growth, it provides an explanation for the several instances where tip elongation is not coordinated with the electric field. For instance, Kropf, Lupa, Caldwell & Harold (1983) have noted that direction of current flow, and hence the polarity of the electric field, may transiently reverse in the elongating tips of fungal hyphae with no apparent effect on their growth rate. The current density at the growing tips of red algal rhizoids does not correlate with their elongation rates (Waaland & Lucas, 1984); moreover, dark-adapted rhizoids, which have ceased elongating, can restart tip growth in the absence of any measurable tip currents. Although these observations argue against the putative role of an electrophoretic mechanism in tip growth, it is conceivable that the localized influx of calcium or some other cation could still act as a directional signal to guide microfilament orientation and hence subsequent growth.

Finally, neither the electrophoretic nor the cytoskeletal models consider whether localized ion fluxes across the plasma membrane modulate the mechanical properties of the cell wall in the apical region of tip-growing cells. It is well documented that proton secretion into the cell wall causes increased rates of cell expansion in a wide range of plant tissues (reviews: Rayle & Cleland, 1977; Taiz, 1984); this process of 'wall loosening' is generally hypothesized to involve the breaking of certain acid-labile bonds and, or, the activation of hypothetical wall-bound enzymes. On the other hand, increased levels of wall-associated calcium decreases wall extensibility in most plant systems (e.g. Cooil & Bonner, 1957; Burstom, 1968; Metraux & Taiz, 1977). The wall-hardening effects of calcium are said to involve the imparting of structural rigidity to pectic substances (Burstom 1968; Jarvis, 1984) and, or, the displacement of protons from generalized cation-binding sites (Cleland & Rayle, 1977; Tepfer & Taylor, 1981; Baydoun & Brett, 1984). Thus, localized proton flux into the wall and, or, calcium flux from the wall at the extreme tip of the apical region could help maintain the pattern of wall expansion neccessary to perpetuate tip growth.

Fern gametophyte development

The photosynthetic structure of the typical fern gametophyte, such as those of the fern *Onoclea sensiblis* and *Adiantum capillus-veneris*, will, if kept in continuous darkness, grow into a few-celled filament of several millimetres in length. A new cell wall in the dividing apical cell is positioned perpendicular to the growth axis; thus, cell division in a dark-grown filamentous gametophyte does not disrupt the existing pattern of tip growth. The fern filament exhibits the characteristic features of a tip-growing structure: wall expansion is restricted to the apical tip of the filament (Mohr, 1956; Etzold, 1965), and the apical cell has a polarized arrangement of cytoplasmic organelles, with dictyosomes being concentrated in the distal 10 μm (Wada & O'Brien, 1975). However, an apical-most zone of Golgi vesicles, which is often found in tip-growing cells, cannot be visualized in fern filaments; the apparent lack of this vesicle zone may be attributable to the growth rates of fern gametophytes (ca. 1 $\mu m\ h^{-1}$) which is several orders of magnitude slower than most other tip-growing structures.

An irradiation with blue light induces the morphogenetic transition from the tip-growing filament to the planar prothallus. This transition involves the following sequence of structural events: (1) the apical cell switches from tip growth to isodiametric expansion within 1 to 3 h of irradiation, with a concomitant rearrangement of subcellular organelles so that they become more evenly distributed within the apical cell; (2) the bulbous apical cell undergoes two so-called transverse divisions which are perpendicular to the original filament axis at ca. 16 and 32 h; and (3) the apical daughter cell divides in the longitudinal (i.e. parallel to the axis) plane at ca. 48 h. This last division is seen to commit the gametophyte to the prothallial stage. Subsequent transverse and longitudinal divisions generate the planar form of the mature prothallus, which bears the reproductive organs of the gametophyte generation.

In our opinion, the fern filament is an intriguing system for investigating the role of electric fields in tip growth, because it differs from more studied tip-growing systems, e.g. algal rhizoids, in several significant features. Unlike those structures that are specifically designed for nutrient absorption, the fern filament is a specialized chlorophyllous structure; any electric field measured around the filament is more likely to serve developmental rather than absorptive roles. Indeed, since the protonema is an aerial structure whose external walls are covered by a hydrophobic cutin-like substance (Wada & Staehelin, 1981; Huckaby, Bassel & Miller, 1982), we can determine whether an extracellular field, which requires the presence of a conductive medium like sea water, is an absolute requirement for growth

Table 3. *Electrical measurements of the apical cells of filamentous fern gametophytes**.

Electrophysiological technique	Measured parameter	Darkness		Blue irradiation	
		Tip	Base	Tip	Base
Intracellular microelectrodes†	Membrane potential	$-124·5 \pm 0·6$ mV	$-119·0 \pm 0·3$ mV	$-133·4 \pm 2·0$ mV	$-133·1 \pm 1·6$ mV
Vibrating microelectrode‡	Extracellular currents	$-75·7 \pm 24·2$ nA cm^{-2}	$+17·2 \pm 5·8$ nA cm^{-2}	$-9·3 \pm 2·6$ nA cm^{-2}	$+8·6 \pm 1·1$ nA cm^{-2}
Extracellular ion-selective microelectrodes§	Proton flux	$1·14 \pm 0·12$ mV min^{-1}	$0·04 \pm 0·08$ mV min^{-1}	$0·13 \pm 0·06$ mV min^{-1}	$0·28 \pm 0·11$ mV min^{-1}
	Potassium flux	$-0·78 \pm 0·07$ mV min^{-1}	$-0·67 \pm 0·15$ mV min^{-1}	$-0·38 \pm 0·09$ mV min^{-1}	$-0·16 \pm 0·06$ mV min^{-1}
	Calcium flux	$-0·18 \pm 0·05$ mV min^{-1}	$-0·02 \pm 0·05$ mV min^{-1}	$-0·06 \pm 0·01$ mV min^{-1}	$-0·02 \pm 0·05$ mV min^{-1}

* These data were compiled from Racusen & Cooke (1982a,b, 1984); Cooke *et al.* (1983); Ketchum *et al.* (1984); and unpublished observations from our laboratory.

† The experimental medium used was APW-6 (1 mM-MES (pH 6), 0·5 mM-NaCl, 0·1 mM-$CaCl_2$, 0·1 mM-KCl). A negative sign means that the cell interior is negative relative to the external environment across the plasma membrane.

‡ Same medium as above. The centre of vibration was 25 μm from the cell surface. According to the standard convention, net positive current efflux is represented as a negative value.

§ Same medium as above except that no MES was added. The electrodes were positioned within 2 to 3 μm of the cell surface. A positive sign refers to the efflux of cations from the cytoplasm.

polarity in tip-growing structures. Secondly, absorptive structures emerge from apolar initial cells like algal zygotes and fern spores before the photosynthetic structures do. Thus, we can use the fern filament to test the contention that a tip-growing structure can only arise at the site of positive current entry. Finally, the ability of blue light to alter the growth pattern from tip-growing filament to planar prothallus provides the rather unique opportunity to test whether this change in growth polarity is dependent on a prior change in field orientation.

Electrical measurements of tip growth in fern filaments

Several different electrophysiological techniques have been utilized to measure membrane potentials, endogenous electric fields, and ionic currents in the apical cell of the fern filament (Table 3). These observations have led to the following picture of this photosynthetic tip-growing structure. In darkness, the membrane potential of the apical cell, as measured by a single microelectrode, rests around -120 mV. Simultaneous measurements with two microelectrodes show that the plasma membrane of the extreme tip of this cell is hyperpolarized by 5 mV relative to the basal end (Racusen & Cooke, 1982b). This cellular dipole is expressed in solution as an electric field with positive current exit from the tip (or negative current entry) (Fig. 1). Mapping the current densities around the apical cell with a vibrating probe indicates that the current efflux is focused at the growing apical region (maximum value of ca. 75 nA cm^{-2} opposite the extreme tip), the current polarity reverses within 20 μm of the tip, and more diffuse currents flow into the lateral regions of the cell. The use of external microelectrodes selective for H^+, K^+, and Ca^{2+} confirms that the prominent tip current is mostly composed of protons. An influx of K^+, which is more concentrated in the subapical areas of the cell, appears to counterbalance a portion of the proton efflux. A small, but measurable Ca^{2+} current migrates into the tip region.

The developmental significance of the proton tip current may lie in the apparent correlation between current density and apical cell growth: the extreme tip is the site of the highest values for both electrical activity and wall expansion, with the declining rates being observed toward the base of the apical dome. The currents could help maintain greater acidity in the cell wall at the filament tip, which should, in turn, make this wall region capable of more extension under the force of cell turgor. Thus, this localized proton flow is acting to stablize tip growth. It seems likely that the increased levels of cytoplasmic calcium in the filament tip may serve to mediate various localization phenomena via the same mechanisms thought to operate in

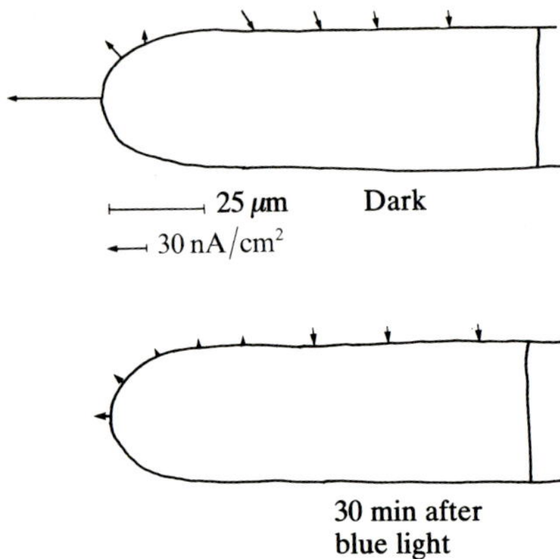

Fig. 1. Electric currents around the apical cell of the fern filament grown in continuous darkness (above) or 30 min after being transferred to blue light (below), as measured with a vibrating microelectrode.

other tip-growing cells. This notion of how calcium might be involved in filamentous growth is supported by some rather peripheral observations from other experiments. Both the calcium chelator EGTA and the calcium ionophore A23187 tend to slow tip elongation of the apical cell in continuous darkness (Cooke & Racusen, 1982). More speculatively, isolated membrane fractions from fern filaments contain extraordinary amounts of endoplasmic reticulum (Racusen, unpublished observations). Since the endoplasmic reticulum is suspected to be a major site of calcium sequestration in eucaryotic cells, this observation makes it plausible that high levels of compartmentalized calcium are required to regulate certain processes in fern development.

The current density around fern filaments is appreciably lower than the values reported for absorptive structures like fucoid rhizoids or lily pollen tubes. Certainly, the extracellular electric field observed in the bathing medium does not account for the 5 mV difference measured with intracellular microelectrodes. Given the presence of a cutin-like substance in the outer region of the cell wall (Wada & Staeheln, 1981; Huckaby *et al.* 1982), one plausible explanation for this apparent discrepancy is that most of the ion traffic outside the plasma membrane may not cross the hydrophobic cuticle. If the space between the plasma membrane and the outer cell wall serves as the major current pathway, then the fern filament can maintain the electrical polarity which is presumably critical for tip growth, even when it is not submerged in an aqueous environment. Because the filament grows in nature as an aerial structure, the maintenance of electrical currents beneath a cuticular insulator may provide the cellular mechanism for directing tip growth in the absence of a supply of media-borne ions.

Our observations provide additional evidence to evaluate the controversy over whether an electrophoretic process or cytoskeletal activity is primarily responsible for maintaining tip growth. The fern filament, whose tip represents the site of positive current efflux and hence the negative pole of the cellular dipole, has the opposite polarity required to attract vesicles and proteins, which are usually carrying a net negative change at cytoplasmic pH, toward the growth zone. It is, however, noteworthy that the calcium current observed in fern filaments has the same direction as those observed in other tip-growing cells, so it remains conceivable that this localized calcium current could direct cytoskeletal activity which might participate in wall formation at the filament tip.

The cytoskeleton can, in principle, regulate two different stages of wall deposition in plant cells: the microfilaments could assist the delivery of new wall materials to the growth zone, and, or, the microtubules could direct the orientation of nascent cellulose microfibrils. Various inhibitors were used to test whether the cytoskeleton played similiar roles in the tip growth of fern filaments. Although several other microtubule antagonists did not affect the tip growth of fern filaments held in darkness, colchicine was observed to induce pronounced lateral swelling of the apical cell (Cooke, unpublished observations). However, lumicolchicine, a photoderivative that does not bind tubulin, caused a similar response; thus, the inhibitory effect of colchicine is apparently unrelated to its ability to promote

Table 4. *Effect of various compounds that affect microfilament activity on tip growth in darkness and on lateral swelling in blue light.*

Chemical treatment	Light treatment	Filament elongation (μm)*	Lateral swelling (μm²)*
Control (1% DMSO)	Darkness	53·1 ± 5·6	101·2 ± 41·3
	Blue light	19·2 ± 6·2	380·7 ± 50·8
2×10^{-5} M-cytochalasin B	Darkness	15·4 ± 8·7	384·3 ± 72·1
2×10^{-5} M-cytochalasin D	Darkness	17·1 ± 7·0	301·9 ± 54·2
5×10^{-4} M-phalloidin	Darkness	41·6 ± 7·3	90·5 ± 31·8
	Blue light	44·1 ± 4·8	129·9 ± 29·5

* Filament elongation and lateral swelling were measured as the change in filament length and cross-sectional area, respectively, during a 24 h exposure to the chemical. The data are represented as the mean of four replicates with a total of 100 filaments ± the standard error of the replicates.

microtubule disassembly. Treating dark-grown filaments with different cytochalasins, which are known to interfere with microfilament activity, disrupts the normal pattern of tip elongation to produce bulbous apical cells (Table 4). Moreover, a pretreatment with phalloidin, which seems to stablize mocrofilaments in position, allows those filaments exposed to blue light to continue tip growth, even though the irradiated controls show considerable lateral expansion. These observations suggest that a particular microfilament alignment in the apical cell is neccessary to maintain tip growth. In conclusion, the current evidence does not contradict the concept that a localized calcium influx guides microfilament-mediated transport of wall materials to the growth zone in fern filaments, in a manner similar to the proposed schemes for fucoid zygotes (Quatrano, 1978; Brawley & Robinson, 1985).

General model for electrical phenomena in tip growth

The electrical measurements on tip-growing cells (Table 1), including fern filaments (Table 3), can be integrated into a general model for the steady ionic currents in tip-growing systems (Fig. 2). An inductive stimulus, e.g. light, gravity, hormones, etc., leads to the establishment of a transcellular electric field across the cell. Proton pumps, which are preferentially distributed at the site of positive current efflux, generate an electrochemical gradient that drives cations in the external medium toward the opposite pole, which represents the principal site of cation entry. Most of the entry current consists of protons and potassium ions, the relative balance being dependent on the particular structure. Smaller calcium currents will passively leak across the plasma membrane at the site of cation influx; the resulting cytosolic calcium gradient appears to govern the orientation and, or, assembly of microfilaments, which direct the transport of Golgi vesicles and other organelles. The accumulation of wall precursors plus the depletion of calcium from the wall permits wall loosening in this localized region, which will then become the growing tip of an absorptive structure.

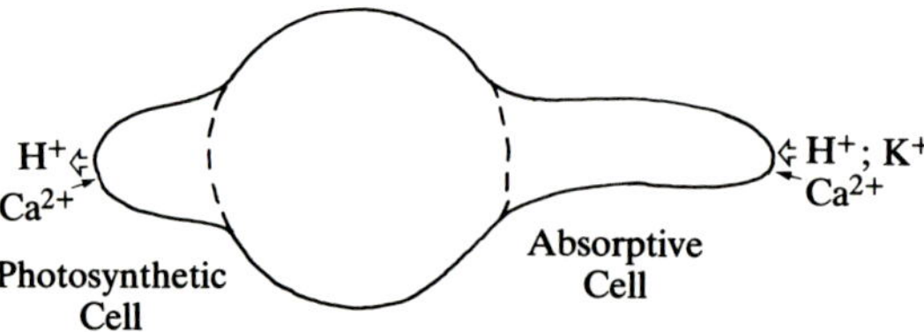

Fig. 2. Summary model for the major ionic currents in both absorptive and photosynthetic tip-growing cells.

In many single-celled systems, no tip-growing structure is destined to form at the other pole of the initial cell, unless it can also produce a photosynthetic structure. There the chloroplasts accumulate near the transient (e.g. *Vaucheria*) or permanent (e.g. *Onoclea*) site of current efflux. We propose that the plasma membranes at these sites are also able to take up calcium by an active H^+/Ca^{2+} antiport mechanism and, or, a passive Ca^{2+} leak. The subsequent transport of wall materials to this wall region is also thought to depend on calcium-directed microfilament activity. The intense, but localized proton current into the adjacent wall loosens acid-labile bonds and, or, activates acid-sensitive hydrolytic enzymes, and thus this portion of the wall becomes the tip region of the emerging photosynthetic cell.

Electric events in the blue light response of fern filaments

As described in a previous section, blue light mediates the major developmental transition in fern gametophytes, namely the transition from tip-growing filament to planar prothallus. Since it is well documented that electrical fields direct the initiation of polarized tip growth in all plant systems studied to date, it seemed worthwhile to test whether a change in field orientation precedes the transition in growth form in fern gametophytes.

Upon blue light irradiation, all the electrical and ionic characteristics of the apical cell are altered within 10 min (Table 3). If one microelectrode is inserted into the tip region, it is possible to discern that the membrane potential at the filament tip begins to hyperpolarize in the first 3 s of the blue light exposure; this potential reaches a new stable level 8 to 10 mV more negative in 5 min (Racusen & Cooke, 1982*b*; Cooke, Racusen & Briggs, 1983). Inserting an additional microelectrode into the basal region shows that this portion of the apical cell remains electrically unresponsive for the first 5 min of blue irradiation, after which the membrane starts to hyperpolarize there (Racusen & Cooke, 1982*a*). The basal hyperpolarization continues over the next 5 min, such that the plasma membrane of the apical cell in blue light becomes nearly equipotential at a voltage that is 10 to 15 mV more negative than was originally measured in the darkened cell. Inhibitor experiments suggest that the hyperpolarization of the apical cell is not attributable to the flow of electrons in the transport chain which is coupled to the putative blue light photoreceptor, but rather depends on the altered activity of the proton-pumping ATPase in the plasma membrane (Cooke *et al.* 1983).

Since this basipetal migration of membrane hyperpolarization has the effect of eliminating the cellular dipole detected with microelectrodes in dark-grown filaments, it was expected that the extracellular electrical field would also decline within several minutes of irradiation. This prediction was confirmed in vibrating-probe experiments which showed that the intense exit current at the filament tip becomes more diffuse, with measurable currents departing from regions beneath the apical tip (Fig. 1). Given these rapid effects of light on cellular electrical parameters, we were not surprised to find that blue light also rapidly affects the rate of acidification in the tip region. There is, however, a noteworthy difference in the electrical and ion responses; proton efflux diminished during the initial 10 min period (Ketchum, Racusen & Cooke, 1984), even though microelectrodes record an increased electronegativity in the tip region. We interpret the apparent lowering of proton flux as a reduction in the density of hydrogen ion transport sites and, or, an increase in the charge-separation capabilities (electrogenicity) of the transport mechanism. For instance, one might imagine a transporter which initially couples the movement of three protons to two charge-balancing monovalent ions (either two inward-moving cations or outward-moving anions). Following irradiation with light, this ratio might be altered to two protons: one balancing ion, with the larger charge separation generating more voltage while moving less total protons. Consistent with this idea is the observation that potassium flux into both the tip and the base is also lower in irradiated cells. Blue light appears to mediate a reduced influx of calcium, which was presumably acting to maintain the cytoskeletal arrangement required for tip elongation in dark-grown filaments. Interestingly, the external acidity of the basal region does not change much for 10 min following irradiation, but then becomes more acid. This delay may somehow be related to the 5 to 10 min lag period that one observes for the hyperpolarization of the basal membrane region.

The most diffuse pattern of proton exit from the apical cell should decrease the wall pH in the subapical region, which should, in turn, facilitate the loosening process required for wall expansion. Thus, the change in ionic current assists the process of lateral swelling which starts around one hour after irradiation. It is, however, apparent that the cytoskeleton must also participate in lateral swelling, as can be demonstrated in our phalloidin experiments described above (Table 4). Since phalloidin acts to specifically inhibit lateral swelling in blue light, this finding suggests that the microfilaments must be repositioned within the apical cell before the lateral walls can expand. These microfilaments could, perhaps, be necessary to move Golgi vesicles with wall material to the expanding walls.

Finally, even though the observed changes in the electrical and ionic activity of the apical cell may favour the process of lateral swelling, it is important to recognize that the lateral swelling by itself does not commit the filament to become a planar prothallus. Despite the profound electrical and morphological changes in the early hours of blue light irradiation, the gametophyte undergoes two more divisions in the transverse direction, which are the same orientation as all divisions in the dark-grown filament, before a longitudinal division of the apicalmost cell marks the commitment to the prothallial growth form. Thus, a simple change in the electric field cannot fully account for the rather complex pattern of cell division that accompanies the transition from tip-growing filament to planar prothallus.

In summary, there is rather cogent evidence that transcellular electric fields mediate the induction of cellular polarity, but other chemical and cellular processes are also necessary to maintain the tip growth that arises in polarized cells. Similarly, a change in electrical activity may be necessary, but is clearly insufficient to mediate the transition from tip growth to the subsequent growth stage.

Adaptive significance of the relative stability of tip growth

Lastly, we want to consider the possibility that the physiological roles of tip-growing structures might act as selective pressures to determine their relative developmental stability. Table 1 documents that tip-growing structures whose primary function is nutrient absorption from the extracellular environment tend to exhibit persistent tip growth for their entire life span, whereas photosynthetic structures will often develop into more complex two- and three-dimensional forms. In the particular instance of the fern gametophyte, if physiological activities do, indeed, represent significant evolutionary constraints on the overall forms of various structures, then one would predict that the developmental change from spherical spore to tip-growing rhizoid should help maximize the process of water and ion absorption, and the corresponding transitions from truncated-spherical initial to tip-growing filament to planar prothallus should similarly promote the process of light absorption. If the optimal form for an absorptive or photoreceptive structure is assumed to be the permissive shape with the highest surface area per unit volume, then these predictions can be tested by calculating the surface-to-volume ratios of geometric models for various actual and hypothetical forms of the two different structures. The following analysis is greatly condensed from another paper which has been submitted for publication elsewhere.

It is possible to envisage unicellular absorptive structures of fern gametophytes which either persist in the initial spherical form of the spore, adopt the cylindrical shape of the typical fern rhizoid, or undergo the hypothetical transition to a planar structure. Since external surface, including cell wall and plasma membrane, offers the greatest resistance to water flow and ion transport in a unicellular structure, this surface serves as the effective surface area for absorptive processes.

A germinated fern spore can be modelled as a perfect sphere. Thus, its surface-to-volume ratio is:

$$\text{Spherical growth} \qquad \frac{S}{V} = \frac{6}{d_s}$$

where d_s is the diameter of the sphere. A tip-growing structure like the fern rhizoid can be represented as a hemisphere with a subtending right cylinder. Thus,

$$\text{Tip growth} \qquad \frac{S}{V} = \frac{4}{d_t} \quad (d_t << h_t)$$

where d_t and h_t are the diameter and the height, respectively, of the tip-growing structure. A hypothetical planar structure can be viewed as a planar solid of uniform thickness, whose four edges consist of half cylinders with quarter spheres at their corners. Thus,

$$\text{Planar growth} \qquad \frac{S}{V} = \frac{2}{t_p} \quad (t_p << L_p, W_p)$$

where t_p, L_p, and W_p are the thickness, length, and width, respectively, of the planar structure.

For any given value assigned to the diameters and the thickness, these equations demonstrate that the spherical spore presents the greatest effective surface area for absorptive processes per unit volume, whereas the tip-growing rhizoid and hypothetical planar structure provide for the intermediate and the lowest absorption efficiencies, respectively. However, the tip-growing rhizoid and the planar structure grow via axis elongation and surface expansion, respectively. Both growth forms are thus able to accommodate an increase in size without any change in their surface-to-volume relations. In contrast, an expanding spore must necessarily exhibit a declining absorption efficiency, because it can only grow by an increase in diameter. This geometric analysis suggests that a tip-growing structure, of the three alternative forms considered above, offers the optimal geometric circumstances for water, ion, and nutrient absorption. Moreover, it seems reasonable to conclude that surface-to-volume relationships have apparently acted as a significant evolutionary constraint that has selected for the developmental stability observed in such absorptive tip-growing structures as the fern rhizoid.

There are three permissible forms for the multicellular photoreceptive forms of fern gametophytes: (1) the truncated-spherical protonemal initial could radially expand into a hypothetical spherical structure whose chloroplasts are restricted to the cells in an outer shell like the large spherical alga *Volvox*; (2) the photoreceptive structure could exhibit stable tip growth as an elongating filament; or (3) the filament could be transformed into a planar prothallus. The models used to characterize the surface-to-volume relations of these structures are similar to those used for absorptive structures, except that they are somewhat arbitrarily divided into isodiametric cells.

Several features of photoreception make it difficult to realistically model the surface-to-volume relations of photoreceptive structures. For instance, the photoreceptive surface is not the cell surface itself but rather the chloroplasts that are positioned near the plasma membrane at the external surface as well as at the internal cell walls. It is therefore necessary to make the reasonable assumption that the chloroplasts occur at equal density along all walls, and it follows that the product of the wall area of an individual cell and the total cell number is proportional to the effective photoreceptive surface.

The geometric models thus constructed have the following effective surface available for photoreception per unit volume:

Spherical growth $$\frac{S}{V} = \frac{6}{t_s} \quad (t_s << R_s)$$

where t_s and R_s are the shell thickness and the sphere radius, respectively.

Tip growth $$\frac{S}{V} = \frac{6}{d_t} \quad (d_t << h_t)$$

Planar growth $$\frac{S}{V} = \frac{6}{t_p} \quad (t_p << L_p, W_p)$$

where all variables represent the same parameters described for absorptive structures

These equations establish the unexpected result that the three forms offer identical surface-to-volume relations for the photoreceptive process. If the geometric models are allowed to mimic the growth of the natural forms, i.e. a constant shell thickness with radial expansion (spherical growth), axis elongation (tip growth) and surface extension (planar growth), then each form approaches the same constant surface-to-volume ratio at high volumes. Apparently, the need to increase photoreceptive efficiency has not acted as a selection factor for a specific photoreceptive structure.

These observations seem to support the general principle that growth form results from the evolutionary compromise among several, often conflicting selection pressures. The fern gametophyte proceeds from the protonemal initial to the mature prothallus without any apparent loss in its photoreception efficiency. However, there are several other aspects of photosynthesis for which the different forms may offer selective advantages independent of surface considerations. The tip-growing filament is best suited to convey the chloroplasts, which are packed in the apical cell, to a region of sufficient light to support net photosynthesis. The more compact form of the mature prothallus results in a much shorter distance for transporting photosynthate to the multicellular sexual organs as well as the young sporophytes inside the archegonia. It seems plausible that the evolutionary pressure, which makes the tip-growing filament a transitory developmental stage in land plant gametophytes, arises from this need to supply the nutritional requirements of those structures.

The research on fern gametophytes in our laboratory was supported by National Science Foundation Grant 81–04085.

References

ARMBRUSTER, B.L., & WEISENSEEL, M.H. (1983) Ionic currents traverse growing hyphae and sporangia of the mycelial mold *Achyla debaryana*. *Protoplasma* **115**, 65–69.

BAYDOUN E.A.-H., and BRETT, C.T. (1984). The effect of pH on the binding of calcium to pea epicotyl cell walls and its implications for the control of cell extension. *J. exp. Bot.* **35**, 1820–1831

BLATT, M., WEISENSEEL, M.H., & HAUPT, W. (1981) A light-dependent current associated with chloroplast aggregation in the alga *Vaucheria sessilis*. *Planta* **152**, 513–526.

BRANDES, H. (1973) Gametophyte development in ferns and bryophytes. *A. Rev. Pl. Physiol.* **24**, 115–128.

BRANDES, H., and KENDE, H. (1968) Studies on cytokinin-controlled bud formation in moss protonemata. *Pl. Physiol.* **43**, 827–837.

BRAWLEY, S.H., and ROBINSON, K.R. (1985) Cytochalasin treatment disrupts the endogenous currents associated with cell polarization in fucoid zygotes: studies of the role of f-actin in embryogenesis. *J. Cell Biol.* **100**, 1173–1184.

BURSTOM, H. (1968) Calcium and plant growth. *Biol. Revs.* **43**, 287–316.

CLELAND, R.E., and RAYLE, D.L. (1977) Reevaluation of the effect of calcium ions on auxin-induced elongation. *Pl. Physiol.* **60**, 709–712.

COOIL, B.J. and BONNER, J. (1957) The nature of growth inhibition by calcium in the *Avena* coleoptile. *Planta* **48**, 696–723.

COOKE, T.J., and RACUSEN, R.H. (1982) Cell expansion in the filamentous gametophytes of the fern *Onoclea sensibilis*. *Planta* **155**, 449–458.

COOKE, T.J., and RACUSEN, R.H., and BRIGGS, W.R.(1983) Initial events in the tip-swelling response of the filamentous gametophyte of *Onoclea sensibilis* L. to blue light. *Planta* **159** 300–307.

DORN, A., & WEISENSEEL, M.H. (1982) Advances in vibrating probe research. *Protoplasma* **113**, 89–96.

ETZOLD, H. (1965) Der Polarotropismus and Phototropismus der Chloronemen von *Dryopteris filix-mas* (L.) Schott. *Planta* **64**, 254–280.

Furuya, M. (1983) Photomorphogenesis in ferns. In *Photomorphogenesis*, Encyclopedia of Plant Physiology, Volume **16B** (ed. W. Shropshire, Jr. and H. Mohr), pp. 569–600. Berlin: Springer-Verlag.

Gow, N.A.R. (1984) Transhyphal electric currents in fungi. *J. gen. Microbiol.* **130**, 3313–3318.

Green, P.B. (1969) Cell morphogenesis. *A. Rev. Pl. Physiol.* **10**, 365–394.

Horwitz, B.A. Weisenseel, M.H., Dorn, A., and Gressel, J. (1984) Electric currents around growing *Trichoderma* hyphae, before and after photoinduction of conidiation. *Pl. Physiol.* **74**, 912–916.

Huckaby, C.S., Bassel, A.R. and Miller, J.H. (1982) Isolation of rhizoid and prothallial protoplasts from gametophytes of the fern, *Onoclea sensibilis. Pl. sci Lett.* **25**, 203–208.

Jaffe, L.A., Weisenseel, M.H., and Jaffe, L.F. (1975) Calcium accumulations within the tips of growing pollen tubes. *J. Cell Biol.* **67**, 488–492.

Jaffe, L.F. (1977) Electrophoresis along cell membranes. *Nature*, **265**, 600–602.

Jaffe, L.F. (1981) The role of ionic currents in establishing developmental pattern. *Phil. Trans. R. Soc.* B. **295**, 553–566.

Jaffe, L.F. (1982) Developmental currents, voltages and gradients. In: *Developmental Order: Its Origin and Regulation*, 40th Symposium of the Society for Developmental Biology (ed. S. Subtelny and P.B. Green), pp. 183–215. New York: Alan R. Liss.

Jaffe, L.F., and Nuccitelli, R. (1974) An ultrasensitive vibrating probe for measuring steady extracellular currents. *J. Cell Biol.* **63**, 614–628.

Jaffe, L.F., Robinson, K.R., and Nuccitelli, R. (1974) Local cation entry and self-electrophoresis as an intracellular localization mechanism. Ann. New York Acad. Sci. **238**, 372–389.

Jarvis, M.C. (1984) Structure and properties of pectin gels in plant cell walls. *Pl. Cell Environ.* **7**, 153–164.

Kamiya, N. (1981) Physical and chemical basis of cytoplasmic streaming. *A. Rev. Pl. Physiol.* **32**, 205–236.

Ketchum, K.A., Racusen, R.H., and Cooke, T.J. (1984) Electrical and ionic manifestations of tip growth in the fern gametophyte. *J. Cell Biol.* **99**, 423a.

Kropf, D.K., Caldwell, J.C., Gow, N.A.R. and Harold, F.M. (1984) Transcellular ion currents in the water mold *Achyla.* Amino acid/proton symport as a mechanism of current entry. *J. Cell Biol.* **99**, 486–496.

Kropf, D.K., Lupa, M.D., Caldwell, J.C., & Harold, F.M. (1983) Cell polarity: endogenous currents precede and predict branching in the water mold *Achyla. Science* **220**, 1385–1387.

Metraux, J.P., & Taiz, L. (1977) Cell wall extension in *Nitella* as influenced by acid and ions. *Proc. natn. Acad. Sci. U.S.A.* **74**, 1565–1569.

Miller, J.H. (1968) Fern gametophytes as experimental material. *Bot. Rev.* **34**, 361–440.

Mohr, H. (1956) Die Abhangigkeit des Protonemawachstums und der Protonemapolaritat bei Farnen vom Licht. *Planta* **47**, 127–158.

Mundrie, J.R. (1929) Cytology and life history of *Vaucheria geminata. Bot. Gaz.* **87**, 397–410.

Nuccitelli, R. (1978) Ooplasmic segregation and secretion in the *Pelvetia* egg is accompanied by a membrane-generated electrical current. *Devl. Biol.* **62**, 13–33.

Nuccitelli, R. (1984) The involvement of transcellular ion currents and electric fields in pattern formation. In *Pattern Formation. A Primer in Developmental Biology* (ed. G. M. Malacinski & S.V. Bryant), pp. 23–46. New York: MacMillan.

Pollard, H.B., Creutz, C.E. & Pazoles, C.J. (1981) Role of ions and intracellular proteins in exocytosis. *Methods Cell Biol.* **23**, 313–334.

Poo, M.M. (1981) In situ electrophoresis of membrane components. *A. Rev. Biophys. Bioeng.* **10**, 245–276.

Poo, M.M. & Robinson, K.R. (1977) Electrophoresis of concanavalin A receptors along embryonic muscle cell membranes. *Nature* **265**, 602–605.

Quatrano, R.S. (1973) Separation of processes associated with differentiation of two-celled *Fucus* embryos. *Devl Biol.* **30**, 209–213.

QUATRANO, R.S. (1978) Development of cell polarity. *A. Rev. Pl. Physiol.* **29**, 487–510.

RACUSEN, R.H. & COOKE, T.J. (1982a) Basipetal migration of electrical activity of fern filaments exposed to blue light. *Pl. Physiol.* **69**, (Suppl.), 85.

RACUSEN, R.H. & COOKE, T.J. (1982a) Electrical changes in the apical cell of the fern gametophyte during irradiation with photo-morphogenetically active light. *Pl. Physiol.* **70**, 331–334.

RACUSEN, R.H. & COOKE, T.J. (1984) Extracellular measurements of an electrical dipole in the apical cell of the fern gametophyte. *Pl. Physiol.* **75**, (Suppl.), 131.

RAYLE, D.L. & CLELAND, R.E. (1977) Control of plant cell enlargement by hydrogen ions. *Curr. Top. devl Biol.* **34**, 187–214.

REISS, H.D. & HERTH, W. (1978) Visualization of the Ca^{2+}-gradient in growing pollen tubes of *Lilium longiflorum* with chlorotetracycline fluorescence. *Protoplasma* **97**, 337–377.

REISS, H.D. & HERTH, W. (1979) Calcium gradients in tip-growing plant cells visualized by chlorotetracycline fluorescence. *Planta* **146**, 615–621.

REISS, H.D., HERTH, W. & SCHNEPF, E. (1983) The tip-to-base calcium gradient in pollen tubes of *Lilium longiflorum* measured by proton-induced x-ray emission (PIXE). *Protoplasma* **115**, 153–159.

ROBINSON, K.R. & CONE, R. (1980) Polarization of fucoid eggs by a calcium ionophore gradient. *Science* **207**, 77–78.

ROBINSON, K.R. & JAFFE, L.F. (1975) Polarizing fucoid eggs drive a calcium current through themselves. *Science* **187**, 70–72.

SAUNDERS, M.J. & HEPLER, P.K. (1981) Localization of membrane-associated calcium following cytokinin treatement in *Funaria* using chlorotetracycline. *Planta* **152**, 272–281.

SAUNDERS, M.J. & HEPLER, P.K. (1982) Calcium ionophore A23187 stimulates cytokinin-like mitosis in *Funaria. Science* **217**, 943–945.

SAUNDERS, M.J. & HEPLER, P.K. (1983) Calcium antagonists and calmodulin inhibitors block cytokinin-induced bud formation in *Funaria. Devl Biol.* **99**, 41–49.

SIEVERS, A. & SCHNEPF, E. (1981) Morphogenesis and polarity of tubular cells with tip growth. In *Cytomorphogenesis in Plants* (ed. O. Kiermayer), pp. 265–299. Wien: Springer-Verlag.

STUMP. R., ROBINSON, K.R., HAROLD, F. & HAROLD, R. (1980) Endogenous electrical currents in the water mold *Blastocladiella emersonii* during growth and sporulation. *Proc. natn. Acad. Sci. U.S.A.* **77**, 6673–6677.

TAIZ, L. (1984) Plant cell extension: regulation of cell wall mechanical properties. *A. Rev. Pl. Physiol.* **35**, 585–657.

TEPFER, M. & TAYLOR, J.E.P. (1981) The interaction of divalent cations with pectic substances and their influence on acid-induced wall loosening. *Can. J. Bot.* **59**, 1522–1525.

WAALAND, S.D. & LUCAS, W.J. (1984) An investigation of the role of transcellular ion currents in morphogenesis of *Griffithsia pacifica* Kylin. *Protoplasma* **123**, 184–191.

WADA, M. & O'BRIEN, T.P. (1975) Observations on the structure of the protonema of *Adiantum capillus-veneris* L. undergoing cell division following white-light irradiation. *Planta* **126**, 213–227.

WADA, M. & STAEHELIN, L.A. (1981) Freeze-fracture observations on the plasma membrane, the cell wall and the cuticle of growing protonemata of *Adiantum capillus-veneris* L. *Planta* **151**, 462–468.

WEISENSEEL, M.H. (1979) Induction of polarity. In *Physiology of Movements*, Encyclopedia of Plant Physiology, Volume 7 (ed. W. Haupt & M.E. Feinleib), pp. 485–505. Berlin: Springer-Verlag.

WEISENSEEL, M.H. & JAFFE, L.F. (1976) The major growth current through lily pollen tubes enters as K^+ and leaves as H^+. *Planta* **133**, 1–7.

WEISENEEL, M.H. & KICHERER. R.M. (1981) Ionic currents as control mechanism in cytomorphogenesis. In *Cytomorphogenesis in Plants* (ed. O. Kiermayer). pp. 379–399. Wien: Springer-Verlag.

WEISENSEEL, M.H., DORN, A. & JAFFE, L.F. (1979) Natural H^+ currents traverse growing roots and root hairs of barley (*Hordeum vulgare*). *Pl. Physiol.* **64**, 512–518.

WILLIAMSON, R.E. (1984) Calcium and the plant cytoskeleton. *Pl. Cell Environ.* **7**, 431–440.

MORPHOLOGICAL PLASTICITY IN FUNGI

D. H. JENNINGS

Botany Department, The University, Liverpool L69 3BX, U.K.

Summary

Fungi grow for the most part as hyphae extending at their tips. Hyphae aggregate into mycelia, the form of which is dependent on many factors but often on the density of tips which is a function of such factors as the degree of hyphal branching, anastomoses and tip and hyphal death. Some possible mechanisms behind these processes are considered. A particularly important element in tip growth and branching is the movement of protons across the plasma membrane. Certain rhythmic growth phenomena are discussed in these terms. Another important element in morphological development is water flow bringing about a redistribution of solutes within a mycelium and probably influencing wall hydration and wall extensibility. Finally, special consideration is given to development of basidiomycete vegetative mycelium where there are indications that cytoplasmic factors can modulate the expressions of the nuclear genome.

Introduction

The focus here is upon filamentous fungi. Though single cell forms are an important element within the fungal kingdom, the filamenous form is the more typical. Nevertheless the ability of some fungi to exhibit a transition from a mycelial (or filamentous) phase to a yeast (or single-cell) phase should be kept in mind, particularly since the transition constitutes a very striking example of phenotypic plasticity (San-Blas & San-Blas, 1984).

Many hyphal filaments grow at their tips but hyphae also branch by the production of a new tip. It is believed that at the point at which a new branch is to be produced, the wall softens and turgor pushes a new hypha forwards. All the evidence that we have is that all structures, whether they be vegetative or reproductive, produced by filamentous fungi can be explained in terms of the degree of aggregation of branching hyphae. The possibility that there can be meristems, similar to those of higher plants, as has been suggested for the growing apex of the root-like structures of rhizomorphs of *Armillaria mellea* (Motta, 1969, 1971) should be discounted (Rayner, Powell, Thompson & Jennings, 1985). Within a mycelium the hyphae may differentiate to a differing degree. Such differentiation can be seen particularly in bulky vegetative structures. In the case of strands, cords and rhizomorphs such differentiation is associated with specialist physiological functioning (Hornung & Jennings, 1981; Brownlee & Jennings, 1982*a,b*; Eamus, Thompson, Cairney & Jennings, 1985).

As yet we have no mechanistic model of branching patterns, although they have been analysed in terms of closed or open branching systems. The patterns of branching exhibited by the former will bear a similarity to river drainage systems which are closed in the sense that they develop or have developed within a more or less fixed boundary, so that the volume of the system has a fixed upper limit. In constrast, open branching systems are capable of indefinite growth. The matter has been most recently reconsidered by Park (1985*a,b*). He has shown that, with respect to branch length, a young fungal colony behaves as an unconstrained system. This is not so when the colony becomes constrained either physically or by conditions in the medium such as nutrient levels. On the other hand, branch number per branch order conformed to what would be expected of a constrained system.

Patterns of hyphal arrangement

It is not the branch pattern *per se* which is of direct concern to us here but the change in pattern generated by environmental change. To date, anatomical evidence has provided little guidance as to how, in all but the simplest structures, individual hyphae are related one with another. This means, for instance, that we have no really clear idea from direct observation about how spreading mycelium of seemingly normal morphology might change into a three-dimensional structure. Nevertheless, a way forward into the matter is suggested by the imaginative model of mycelial growth proposed by Edelstein (1982). This model is based, not on the growth of individual hyphae, but on average properties such as the distribution of hyphal densities. Rightly, I believe, the model focuses on the tip and considers the mycelium in terms of a new variable, tip density. Edelstein points out that, since hyphal length increment occurs only in the presence of a tip, the location and numbers of tips must be of significance in determining whether growth that shapes the tissue takes place. Essentially tips create new hyphal filaments which in turn create new tips. Control of branching rates or viability of tips results in regulated growth.

It is not appropriate to go into the details of the model; they are clearly explained by Edelstein (1982). It is sufficient to say that the model depends on the mathematical versions of several hyphal situations – dichotomous branching, lateral branching, anastomoses (tip–tip and tip–hypha), tip death, tip death due to overcrowding and hyphal death. Given these hyphal situations, the mathematical description of mycelial spread is given in terms of the spread of density distributions which behave like travelling waves.

It is difficult at this stage to know the degree of correctness of the model but it is sufficiently explicit to indicate those matters that must be tested experimentally. The model certainly indicates a number of aspects that have not been at the forefront of the minds of mycologists when considering those internal factors that affect colony growth. Here I am thinking about anastomoses and tip and hyphal death. The ignoring of these factors, certainly in a quantitative way, by most mycologists may be due to the fact that, with respect to the kinetics of growth, the emphasis has been on mould colonies growing in a regular manner in the presence of ample nutrients, when growth takes place in a zone close to the margin, the peripheral growth zone.

I shall only present one situation to which the model has been applied, though it is one which is relevant to a consideration of morphological plasticity within a fungal colony, namely the initiation of a bulky compact three-dimensional structure, such as a fruitbody initial from essentially two-dimensional mycelium. Edelstein noted that, since the initial development of many basidiomycete fruiting bodies can be considered cylindrically symmetric, the one-dimensional model can be applied with the x-axis taking on the role of the axis of symmetry. Such an analysis indicates that the fruiting body initial has abundant free tips throughout the organ with lateral branching and tip–hypha anastomoses. Parenthetically, we would expect anastomoses in a bulky fungal structure, particularly one in which there are specialized conducting structures, to allow nutrient transfer to take place within the structure (Granlund, Jennings & Veltkamp, 1984).

The foregoing will tend to seem obvious to many mycologists but it highlights for the experimentalist some of the phenomena that must be studied to understand how a fungal colony behaves when it exhibits plastic changes. There is a need for mycelial development to be put on a quantitative basis. The model of Edelstein indicates how quantitative information can be given predictive value. The model also indicates the kind of quantitative information which is required. Essentially, I am arguing for an approach to the study of mycelial development similar to that used to study the development of the shoot apex in higher plants (see Lyndon, this volume). Below I consider some of the individual phenomena underlying the model.

However before considering such phenomena, an important *caveat* must be made, namely that there are situations where hyphal growth takes place at locations other than the tip. A striking example is the sporangiophore of *Phycomyces* where at stage 4, extension occurs in the region 1–2 mm behind the swollen sporangium (Castle, 1942). With respect to multihyphal structures, the situation has been highlighted in an elegant electron microscopical study by Read & Beckett (1985) of the mature perithecium of *Sordaria humana*, in which there are what the authors term coherent hyphae-forming tissues which are superficially like parenchymatous tissues of higher plants. For simplicity only, I ignore the development of such tissues that are nevertheless likely to be present in many fungal structures.

Hyphal tip growth

All the information, albeit to a degree circumstantial to date about the growth of fungal hyphae at their tips indicates that much material required for the new wall and membrane comes from some distance away from the tip itself (Grove, 1978; Gooday, 1983). At least some of the material appears from electron microscopy to be carried in vesicles. Apart from one important exception, we know almost nothing of the contents of the vesicles. That exception is the spheroidal 45–65 nm microvesicles, the so-called chitosomes, which have been shown to contain chitin synthetase (Bartnicki-Garcia, Bracker, Reyes & Ruiz-Herrera, 1978; Bartnicki-Garcia, Ruiz-Herrera & Bracker, 1979; Bracker, Ruiz-Herrera & Bartnicki-Garcia, 1976).

While there are large lacunae in our knowledge of the molecular events that occur at the tip during growth, the hypothesis that vesicles are so involved was sufficiently compelling for Prosser & Trinci (1979) to model the process. The model produced was based on the postulate that production takes place throughout the mycelium of vesicles containing small precursors and, or, enzymes required for new wall synthesis. These vesicles travel to the hyphal tip where they fuse, the net result being an increase of the surface area of the hypha and thus elongation. Associated with elongation, there is a duplication cycle which is equivalent to the cell cycle in a unicellular fungus such as yeast (Trinci, 1978). A finite difference model was constructed in which a hypha was divided into equal hypha segments and a tip segment with apical and intercalary compartments bounded by the presence of septa. Tip segments were postulated not to produce vesicles but to absorb them, the rate of absorption of vesicles obeying Michaelis-type kinetics. Septal production was postulated to be related to the duplication cycle. Initially, the apical compartment possesses a stated complement of nuclei. When the cytoplasmic volume : nuclear ratio reaches a critical level the nuclei increase continuously and exponentially to double the initial number. A septum is then formed midway in the apical compartment separating the nuclei into equal numbers. In the model, branching occurs when the flow of vesicles into a segment results in a critical level. In the tip, this will occur when the rate of flow into the segment is greater than the maximum rate of absorption, consequently an apical branch is formed. In a segment behind a septum the initiation of a branch occurs because the flow of vesicles out of the parent compartment is reduced.

There was good agreement between simulated growth of the mycelium and the successive apical compartments and simulated morphology and what was observed in experimental studies for two fungi, *Aspergillus nidulans* and *Geotrichum candidum*. Thus the model indicates that it is appropriate to accept the view that a fundamental process of hyphal extension is the movement of vesicles to the hyphal apex. As for the mechanism of movement, this writer now favours the view that microtubules are involved (Howard & Aist, 1980), particularly since there is impressive evidence from studies on squid axoplasm that microtubules are directly involved in translocation of vesicles in these cells (Gilbert, Allen & Sloboda, 1985).

As far as branch formation is concerned, a correlation has been observed by Mahadevan & Mahadkar (1970) and Fevre (1972) between branching frequency and the activity of lysins capable of degrading wall polymers in respectively *Neurospora crassa* and *Saprolegnia monoica*. The role of such lytic enzymes in wall growth has been discussed by Rosenberger (1979). They appear to be under catabolitic repression. One must presume that their essential role is increasing wall plasticity.

Trinci (1979) has pointed out that branching is an essential prerequisite for the maintenance of exponential growth in moulds. This is a corollary of the fact that individual hyphae eventually attain a linear growth rate yet the colony maintains an exponential growth rate. Thus branch initiation in moulds is an event which can be regarded as physiologically analogous to cell separation in unicellular organisms. This suggests that branch formation is associated with the nuclear cycle and nuclear division. There is certainly an association of branch formation with septation (Trinci, 1979).

Anastomoses, tip and hyphal death

If we turn to anastomoses, tip and hyphal death we move into areas of increasing uncertainty. Anastomoses or hyphal fusion have, of course, been frequently observed in fungal mycelia but we have no idea as to what are the causal factors. Nevertheless for fusion to take place, the growth of a tip must be directed towards another hypha in tip–hyphal anastomoses or two tips to each other in tip–tip anastomoses. This suggests we need to be thinking of receptor sites on at least the growing tip if anastomosis is to occur when there is a significant distance to be traversed. In bulky structures, there will be adpressure of one hyphae against another due to the internal pressure generated by turgor which will aid fusion. There are a number of situations within the fungi that illuminate the whole process of anastomosis from the time when hyphae are separated until the final fusion. These situations are exemplified by the cascade of events leading to sexual fusion in the Mucorales (Bu'Lock, 1976) and the formation of traps by nematophagus fungi in response to the presence of the animals or indeed other fungi (Nordbring-Hertz, 1984).

Tip death is not usually considered as a normal function within a developing mycelium. At a minimum there are two possible ways in which it might occur. First, the tip may stop growing and becomc cssentially non-functional. Perhaps the sequence of events may be very much like those observed by Howard & Aist (1972) when hyphal tips of *Fusarium acuminatum* were perfused with the toxic moiety (methyl benzimidazole-2-ylcarbomate) of the hydrolysis product of the fungi toxin benomyl. These effects included i) displacement of mitochondria from hyphal apices, ii) the disappearance of the Spitzenkorper or collection of vesicles from those apices, iii) metaphase arrest of all mitoses and iv) reduction of the linear growth rate. All these effects could have been mediated through interference with microtubules. Second, tips may become non-functional as a result of bursting due to an unfavourable water potential gradient between the cytoplasm and the external medium (Bartnicki-Garcia & Lippman, 1972), either due to wall weakening or excessive turgor.

Hyphal death has been frequently observed and can be equated in many circumstances with autolysis (Frencl, 1978). The best authenticated example, in terms of possible causes, is in mycelial pellets where autolysis occurs in the interior (Trinci & Rhigelato, 1970; Holligan & Jennings, 1972) and all the indications are that this is due to oxygen limitation (Trinci, 1978). Hyphal death should not be considered as a negative phenomenon. In basidiomycete linear structures such as cords and rhizomorphs, cell death in interconnected longitudinally running hyphae leaves them devoid of cytoplasm and they become the channels for water (Eamus *et al.* 1985).

Integration within the developing vegetative mycelium

I have sketched the processes that are likely to be involved in the development and differentiation of growing mycelium. The plastic response of such mycelium will be dependent on the degree to which the balance between the individual processes can be changed. We know little about how this might occur. There is little evidence to date of hormonal control; only for growth of the stipe of agaric fruit bodies can it be argued that there is an effect of a growth-promoting compound produced at a distance, namely in the pileus (Gruen, 1982). For reasons given below, I shall indicate that such control seems unlikely. Because of the paucity of evidence for growth-regulating compounds within mycelia, I shall focus on the role of water and nutrients in controlling mycelial development.

Before considering the issue of the role of water and nutrients, we must return to the hyphal apex to say something about the physiological processes which appear to be occurring there. First, it is becoming clear that a feature of hyphal tip growth is the presence of an endogenous current travelling through the apex (Gow, 1984; Gow, Kropf & Harold, 1984; Horowitz, Weisenseel, Dorn & Gressel, 1984; Kropf, Caldwell, Gow & Harold, 1984; Kropf, Lupa, Caldwell & Harold, 1983). The function of this current is not at all clear. It was suggested by Jaffe, Robinson & Nuccitelli (1974) that it was responsible for movement of vesicles to the tip by electrophoresis. This now seems very doubtful because of the evidence pointing to the involvement of microtubules as indicated above and because the current into a tip can decline and reverse transiently without any change in growth rate and because electrophoresis does not seem energetically feasible (Kropf *et al.* 1983). The pattern of the current round a hypha of *Achyla* develops in such a way that it is possible to predict where branching might take place (Kropf *et al.* 1983) and, in the same organism, it has been shown by Kropf *et al.* 1984) that protons carry the inward current. These same workers showed that when the organism was growing in media containing amino acids, the inward movement of protons was accompanied by amino acids and the authors also hypothesized that the electrical circuit within the hypha was completed by extrusion of protons via an electrogenic ATPase (Fig. 1). An essentially similar model has been proposed by the marine fungus *Dendryphiella salina* by Jennings (1979) from evidence other than studies of current flow (Fig. 1).

But it is not only current which flows into and longitudinally along a hypha; there can also be a flow of water. Admittedly such a flow of water has only been demonstrated unambiguously for one fungus, *Serpula lacrimans* (Coggins, Jennings & Clarke, 1980; Brownlee & Jennings, 1981; Thompson, Eamus & Jennings, 1985). In this fungus water flow manifests itself as drops when the mycelium grows over a non-absorptive surface. There is now very strong evidence that turgor-driven flow of water is the mechanism by which solutes are translocated through mycelium (Jennings,

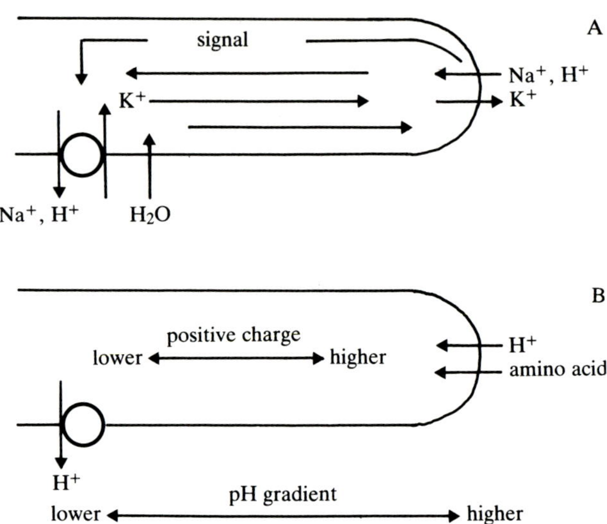

Fig. 1. Diagrams of ion and other flows in the apical portion of hyphae of (A) *Dendryphiella salina*, based on information of Jennings (1979); 'signal' refers to feedback from events at the growing tip to the ATPase in plasma membrane; (B) *Achlya bisexualis*, based on information of Gow *et al.* (1984).

1984; Eamus *et al.* 1985). Translocation has been demonstrated unambiguously in mycelium over non-absorptive, non-nutritive surfaces (Brownlee & Jennings, 1982) but has also been demonstrated in mycelium growing over agar (Wilcoxson & Sudia, 1968). There is no doubt that turgor gradients can exist in mycelium on agar (Eamus & Jennings, 1984).

Let us examine the consequences of the two longitudinal flows, that of ions (= current) and of water, in the development of fungal mycelium, keeping in mind that the two flows will of necessity be coupled in some way. Two comments about this coupling are pertinent. First, the activity of the proton-extrusion pump may generate an electro-osmotic flow of water (Jennings, 1979). Second, it would seem that the flow of water would act against the flow of current. However, the flow of water will generate a streaming potential which will be countered by an electro-osmotic flow due to fixed negative charges in the peripheral cytoplasm. Indeed the observed flows in this region could be brought about by electro-osmosis and not by the mediation of contractile material such as actin (Jennings, 1984).

If the current flow is confined to the peripheral protoplasm, then we have a possible mechanism for tropic movement. The scenario we would be considering would be the release of a compound from another hypha in the vicinity of a growing hyphal tip. Taking into account the observations of

Kropf *et al.* (1984) referred to above, an amino acid could be an appropriate candidate; release of nitrogen compounds has been implicated in the morphogenesis of strands of *S. lacrimans* where hyphae come together to produce aggregated structures (Watkinson, 1984). Let us then consider what might happen if the amino acid is diffusing laterally and can enter the hyphal apex. One consequence might be an increase in current in the peripheral cytoplasm, though it is not easy to see how an increase in current on one side of the hypha will inhibit extension on that side. On the other hand, the current might be reduced through a very local increase in the cytoplasmic concentration of the amino acid in the vicinity of the proton symport and causing inhibition by transinhibition (Pall, 1971). If the latter were to occur and the current moving through those pumps on that side of the hyphae nearest the source of amino acids were to be reduced and, if in some way, activity of the pump governed growth on its longitudinal axis, then it is not difficult to see that the hypha would bend towards the source of amino acid. That is one explanation. Another might be that plasticity of the wall at the tip where growth is occurring is dependent upon a low pH. Removal of hydrogen ions from the wall by the proton symport might increase very locally the wall pH such that there would be decrease in plasticity in that local volume of wall on that side of the apical dome closest to the source of the amino acid. This decrease in plasticity would eventually cause bending towards that source. I shall return to this matter of local plasticity of the wall later; this explanation would demand that proton flow from the symport would be channelled away from it in the peripheral cytoplasm towards the proton extrusion pumps on that side of the hypha closest to the source of the amino acid.

While these hypotheses place a central role on the proton-extrusion pump, it is not at all clear whether or not there is feedback from the tip relating the growth rate to pump activity and if so how feedback occurs. I have suggested (Jennings, 1979) that cyclic AMP may be the regulatory compound. Whatever the signal, one must presume from the above that it is carried in the peripheral cytoplasm by electro-osmosis or by electrophoresis along the surface of the membrane in a manner postulated by Jaffe (1982) or within the membrane itself.

Branch formation

It follows from the above discussion that, if plasticity of the wall is reduced by decreased pH, then the formation of a branch might be initiated by increased extrusion of protons into the wall. This would be contrary to the findings of Kropf *et al.* (1983) that *inwardly* directed endogenous ion currents (carrying protons) precede and predict branching in *Achlya*. Nevertheless, there is certainly good evidence for a hydrogen ion effect in branching. Thus Kropf *et al.* (1984) report that proton-conducting ionophores make *Achlya* branch. Lysek (1984) reporting on a long series of observations on rhythmic growth of the clock mutant of *Podospora anserina* has argued that the increased branching frequency is brought about by increased permeability of the plasma membrane to protons. In view of the foregoing, I would argue that increased branching is driven by the increased activity of proton pumps acting at discrete points in the membrane (but different from those at which a tip will develop) brought about by the increased level of hydrogen ions in the cytoplasm. There is certainly strong evidence from detailed studies on *Neurospora crassa* that decreasing the cytoplasmic pH stimulates pump activity (Sanders & Slayman, 1982). It must follow from these suppositions that there is likely to be some relationship between vesicle density and pump activity, *vide* the consequences of the model of Prosser & Trinci (1979) that branches occur where there is an accumulation of vesicles in the mycelium.

Lysek (1984) has pointed out that rhythmic growth of the kind just mentioned may be a particular example of the widespread ability of filamentous fungi to produce structures of aggregated hyphae, such as basidiomycete fruitbodies. As indicated above, it seems likely that such structures are a product of increased hyphal tip density, lateral branching and tip–hypha anastomoses. The above would suggest that increased permeability of the plasma membrane to protons may well be an important factor in the development of such structures. It may be pertinent that there are very few filamentous members of the Basidiomycotina found in the sea (Kohlmeyer & Kohlmeyer, 1979), which must be considered as an alkaline as well as a saline environment.

Water flow through mycelium

I have discussed at some length on a previous occasion (Jennings, 1984) water flow through mycelium and its role in the translocation of solutes. With respect to the present discussion, I wish to draw attention to the relationship between the accumulation of metabolizable substrate brought by translocation and sporophore formation in mycelium of *Agaricus disporus*. The process has been modelled by Chanter & Thornley (1978) and the model predicts that sporophore initiation will only take place when the required substrate(s) have reached a threshold concentration, the substrate(s) having been brought to the appropriate locale by translocation from other parts of the mycelium. Edelstein & Segel (1983) expanded the model of Edelstein (1982) discussed earlier to take into account not only accumulation of hyphae, but also uptake of nutrient and redistribution by translocation of derived metabolite within the mycelium. The model, consisting of partial differential equations, offered an explanation of concentric mycelial rings, in terms of repeated build-up and depletion of metabolite such that there are different local branching rates and thus distinct bands of differing hyphal densities.

As I have already pointed out, the movement of water along hypha by turgor gradients can result in water being forced out of the hypha at discrete points to form droplets. This will mean that the wall at these points is more hydrated than elsewhere. Such local hydration of the wall could influence the direction of growth. This possibility has been implicated in the avoidance responses of sporangiophores of *Phycomyces*, that is their ability to change direction as they approach another object. Gamow & Bottger (1982) demonstrated that the hypothesis held previously that the sporangiophores respond to a selfemitted gas is correct but that the most likely candidate is water vapour, exerting its effect, as I have indicated, on the hydration of the wall. That hydration of the wall has an influence on its ability to extend has been confirmed by direct determination of mechanical extensibility of sporangiophores in air of different humidities (Chinn & Gamow, 1984).

These observations on the effect of wall hydration and extension have implications for chemotropism and hyphal fusion. If water is ultrafiltered through a tip or a local area of wall and membrane, as has been described above for *Serpula lacrimans*, then a tropism might be generated by an osmotic gradient in the medium, the directed movement of the tip brought about by a change in hydration of the wall. Likewise, if a tip approaching another hypha is exuding water then, as the tip comes close to that other hypha, the water so exuded could increase the hydration of the wall of the approaching hypha, allowing lytic enzymes to be released and thus facilitate anastomosis.

In this section, I have indicated that within a hypha there can be very localized effects on the physiology of that hypha which alter the pattern of water and ion flows through the hypha. How these localized effects, particularly those away from the hyphal tip, are first initiated is not at all clear. But it is not difficult to see that, if the localized effects change in density within the mycelium, there will be a consequent change in mycelial morphology as indicated by the model of Edelstein (1982).

Change in vegetative morphology in the Basidiomycotina

This section is concerned with some thoughts on how an environmental change can bring about a change in the morphology of vegetative mycelium. It is not difficult to see how an environmental change might result in the production of an effector/repressor of some part of the genome leading to morphological change. Photomorphogenesis is an obvious example of such a possibility, where we can hypothesize a cascade of events leading to a response at the level of DNA within the mycelium. One particularly good example is the *Neurospora crassa* clock system that underlies the circadian rhythm of conidiation which is triggered by light. We now have a fairly good indication as to the photoreceptor, with evidence that mitochondrial metabolism may be involved and the density of one genetic locus *frq* playing a kcy role in the organization of the clock (Feldman & Dunlap, 1983). However, environmental change may exert its effect in a somewhat different manner, as may sometimes be the case with respect to morphogenetic change in basidiomycete vegetative mycelium.

The Basidiomycotina are characterized by possessing mycelium that is capable of spreading considerable distances often over non-nutritive surfaces (Jennings, 1982; Rayner *et al.* 1985). When the spread is over long distances, it is by means of so-called 'linear organs' which include all those structures variously described as cords, threads, strands, syrrotia, rhizomorphs and pseudorhiza. They consist of aggregations of predominantly parallel, longitudinally aligned hyphae. Within the structure there can be a wide variety of hyphal types (Hornung & Jennings, 1981; Granlund, Jennings & Veltkamp, 1984), while the structure itself may also differentiate into a distinct outer crust with a core containing many wide vessel hyphae involved in water movement (Eamus *et al.* 1985).

A distinction must be made between truly migratory organs, such as a rhizomorph with its highly organized apical growing point (Granlund, Jennings & Veltkamp, 1984), that are capable of autonomous extension from a food base and the initially diffuse mycelial extension similar in form to other moulds. Nevertheless there is a gradation between the two types even within the same fungus. This variation probably reflects the relative ease of transition between diffuse and aggregated structures. The transitions are likely to depend on the extent of coordination between the faster growing hyphae of the colony margin. Thus we have a spectrum between the highly organized rhizomorph and completely diffuse mycelium in which production of the linear organ is by differentiation *within* the mycelium some distance away from the extending front. The best example of this latter end of the spectrum is *Serpula lacrimans*.

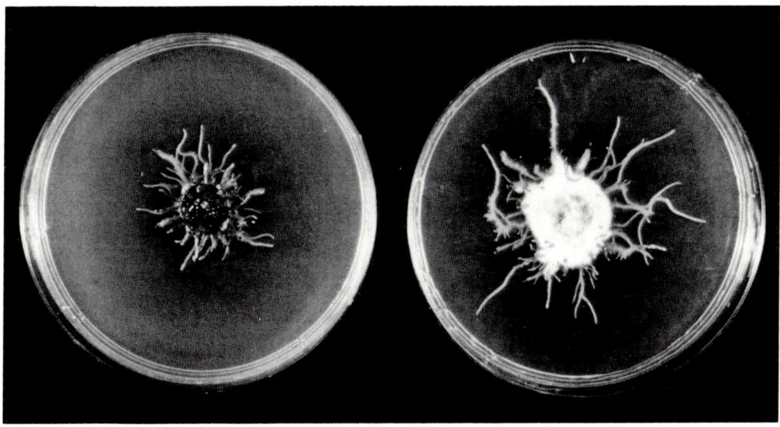

Fig. 2. Rhizomorph production by *Armillaria mellea* on malt (1·5% w/v)–yeast extract (0·5% w/v) agar. Right culture 10 days, left 16 days after inoculation.

The more 'rhizomorphic' a fungus the more readily it will produce linear aggregations even at high nutrient levels on agar media (Fig. 2). However, *Armillaria mellea* produces diffuse mycelium in infected trees (Rayner *et al.* 1985). Fungi at the opposite end of the spectrum do not produce linear organs readily at high nutrient concentrations. On the other hand, the nominally diffuse mycelium of *S. lacrimans* produces under low nutrient conditions forms of fast-growing mycelium, the so-called 'point growth' (Coggins, Hornung, Jennings & Veltkamp, 1980), the fast growth rate of which has been compared on a previous occasion with that of a rhizomorph extending ahead of the front of an undifferentiated colony (Jennings, 1982) (Fig. 3). With respect to point growth, it is important to note that when mycelium from the fast-growing areas is subcultured it appears to maintain its growth rate (Coggins *et al.* 1980).

Perhaps the most illuminating information on the production of faster growing mycelium with a polarized orientation comes from studies on the rhizomorphic organs of *Stereum hirsutum* (Coates & Rayner, 1985). This basidiomycete is normally non-rhizomorphic; however a spontaneous change occurred during storage of a homokaryotic culture which resulted in a transformation of its properties, so that colony growth was no longer slow and dense but much faster and effuse. This culture was able to transform other homokaryons, apparently via a cytoplasmically transmissable factor. Other morphological changes also took place in transferred and reverted strains that are detailed in Coates & Rayner (1985) and Rayner *et al.* (1985). Much more work is needed to elucidate what is happening but what has been described here seems to echo the morphological plasticity in flax described by Cullis (this volume). It is appropriate here to indicate that

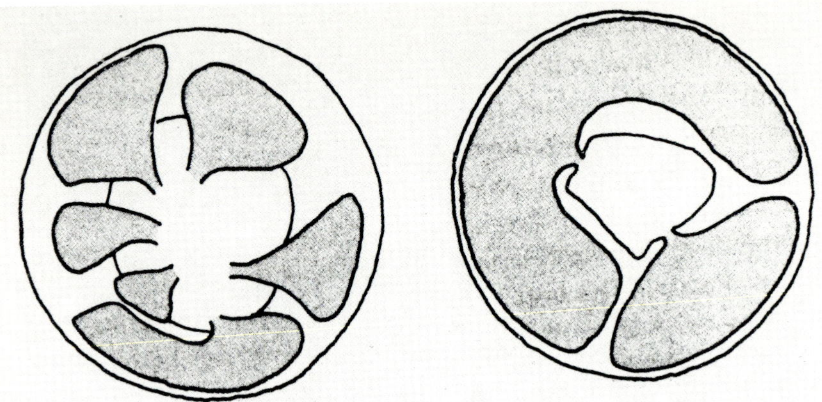

Fig. 3. Drawings from cultures of *Serpula lacrimans* growing on glucose (0·5 % w/v)–tryptone (0·3 % w/v) agar showing the sectoring characteristics of what is termed 'point growth' (Jennings, 1982).

the senescence of mycelium of the ascomycete *Podospora anserina* is now known to be under the control of an extrachromosomal infective principle (Turner, 1978; Esser, Kuck, Stahl & Tudzynski, 1984).

Conclusion

The reader might gain the impression from what I have written that there has been little work on morphological differentiation in the fungi. This is of course not so. But the great majority of studies on fungal development have focused on biochemical changes. There has been insufficient emphasis on the matters raised here, namely those events at the hyphal level which underpin the production of three-dimensional structure. I believe that the information about biochemical changes are more likely to become understandable when anatomical changes such as those referred to in this Chapter have been categorized and described quantitatively. I have implied in making a comparison of this suggested approach with that discussed by Lyndon (in this volume) to describe events at the shoot apex of the higher plant, that there is much to be gained by mycologists concerned with morphological development change in fungi from the ideas and information of botanists concerned with green plants. Certainly, plasticity is not part of the routine vocabulary of mycologists in the way that it is for those concerned with higher plants. Time is now ripe for greater concern by mycologists for the concept of phenotypic plasticity. One hopes that it will not be too long before information about the topic coming from mycology will benefit higher plant studies.

References

Bartnicki-Garcia, S., Bracker, C. E., Reyes, E. & Ruiz-Herrera, J. (1978). Isolation of chitosomes from taxonomically diverse fungi and synthesis of chitin microfibrils *in vitro*. *Expl Mycol.* **2**, 173–192.

Bartnicki-Garcia, S. & Lippman, E. (1972). The bursting tendency of hyphal tips of fungi: presumptive evidence for a delicate balance between wall synthesis and wall lysis in apical growth. *J. gen. Microbiol.* **73**, 487–500.

Bartnicki-Garcia, S., Ruiz-Herrera, J. & Bracker, C. E. (1979). Chitosomes and chitin synthesis. In *Fungal Walls and Hyphal Growth* (ed. J. H. Burnett & A. P. J. Trinci), pp. 149–168. Cambridge: Cambridge University Press.

Bracker, C. E., Ruiz-Herrera, J. & Bartnicki-Garcia, A. (1976). Structure and transformation of chitin synthetase particles (chitosomes) during microfibril synthesis *in vitro*. *Proc. natn. Acad. Sci. U.S.A.* **73**, 4570–4574.

Brownlee, C. & Jennings, D. H. (1981). Further observations on tear or drop formation by mycelium of *Serpula lacrimans*. *Trans. Br. mycol. Soc.* **77**, 33–40.

Brownlee, C. & Jennings, D. H. (1982*a*). Long distance translocation in *Serpula lacrimans*: velocity estimates and the continuous monitoring of induced perturbations. *Trans. Br. mycol. Soc.* **79**, 143–148.

Brownlee, C. & Jennings, D. H. (1982*b*). Pathway of translocation in *Serpula lacrimans*. *Trans. Br. mycol. Soc.* **79**, 401–407.

Bu'Lock, J. D. (1976). Hormones in fungi. In *The Filamentous Fungi. Biosynthesis and Metabolism*, vol. **2** (ed. J. E. Smith & D. R. Berry), pp. 345–368. London: Edward Arnold.

Castle, E. S. (1942). Spiral growth and reversal of spiraling in *Phycomyces* and their bearing on primary wall structure. *Am. J. Bot.* **28**, 664–671.

Chanter, D. O. & Thornley, J. H. M. (1978). Mycelial growth and the initiation and growth of sporophores in the mushroom crop: a mathematical model. *J. gen. Microbial.* **106**, 55–65.

Chinn, J. A. & Gamow, R. I. (1984). *Phycomyces*. An increase in mechanical extensibility after humified wind stimulus. *Pl. Physiology* **76**, 275–277.

Coates, D. & Rayner, A. D. M. (1985). Evidence for a cytoplasmically transmissable factor affecting recognition and somato-sexual differentiation in the basidiomycete *Stereum hirsutum*. *J. gen. Microbiol.* **131**, 207–219.

Coggins, C. R., Hornung, U., Jennings, D. H. & Veltkamp, C. J. (1980). The phenomenon of 'point growth' and its relation to flushing and strand formation in mycelium of *Serpula lacrimans*. *Trans. Br. mycol. Soc.* **75**, 69–76.

Coggins, C. R., Jennings, D. H. & Clarke, R. W. (1980). Tear or drop formation by mycelium of *Serpula lacrimans*. *Trans. Br. mycol. Soc.* **75**, 63–67.

Eamus, D. & Jennings, D. H. (1984). Determination of water, solute and turgor potentials of mycelium of various basidiomycete fungi causing wood decay. *J. exp. Bot.* **35**, 1782–1786.

Eamus, D., Thompson, W., Cairney, J. W. G. & Jennings, D. H. (1985). Internal structure and hydraulic conductivity of basidiomycete translocating organs. *J. exp. Bot.* **36**, 1110–1116.

Edelstein, L. (1982). The propagation of fungal colonies: a model for tissue growth. *J. theor. Biol.* **98**, 679–701.

Edelstein, L. & Segal, L. A. (1983). Growth and metabolism in mycelial fungi. *J. theor. Biol.* **104**, 187–210.

Esser, K., Kuck, U., Stahl, U. & Tudzynski, P. (1984). Senescence in *Podospora anserina* and its implications for genetic engineering. In *The Ecology and Physiology of the Fungal Mycelium* (ed. D. H. Jennings & A. D. M. Rayner), pp. 343–352. Cambridge: Cambridge University Press.

Feldman, J. F. & Dunlap, J. C. (1983). *Neurospora crassa*: a unique system for studying circadian rhythms. In *Photochemical and Photobiological Reviews*, vol. **7** (ed. K. C. Smith), pp. 319–368. New York & London: Plenum Press.

FENCL, Z. (1978). Cell ageing and autolysis. In *The Filamentous Fungi*, vol. **3** (ed. J. E. Smith & D. R. Berry), pp. 389–405. London: Edward Arnold.

FEVRE, M. (1972). Contribution to the study of the determination of mycelium branching of *Saprolegnia monoica*. *Z. Pflanzenphysiol.* **68**, 1–10.

GAMOV, R. I. & BÖTTGER, B. (1982). Avoidance and rheotropic responses in *Phycomyces*. Evidence for an 'avoidance gas' mechanism. *J. gen. Physiol.* **79**, 835–848.

GILBERT, S. P., ALLEN, R. D. & SLOBODA, R. D. (1985). Translocation of vesicles from squid axoplasm on flagellar microtubules. *Nature, Lond.* **315**, 245–248.

GOODAY, G. W. (1983). The hyphal tip. In *Fungal Differentiation* (ed. J. E. Smith), pp. 315–356. New York: Marcel Dakker.

GOW, N. A. R. (1984). Transhyphal electrical currents in fungi. *J. gen. Microbiol.* **130**, 3313–3318.

GOW, N. A. R., KROPF, D. L. & HAROLD, F. M. (1984). Growing hyphae of *Achlya bisexualis* generate a longitudinal pH gradient in the surrounding medium. *J. gen. Microbiol.* **130**, 2967–2974.

GRANLUND, H. I., JENNINGS, D. H. & VELTKAMP, K. (1984). Scanning electron micrope studies of rhizomorphs of *Armillaria mellea*. *Nova Hedwigia* **39**, 85–99.

GROVE, S. N. (1978). The cytology of hyphal tip growth. In *The Filamentous Fungi* vol. **3** (ed. J. E. Smith & D. R. Berry), pp. 28–50. London: Edward Arnold.

GRUEN, H. E. (1982). Control of stipe elongation by the pileus and mycelium in fruit bodies of *Flammulina velutipes* and other Agaricales. In *Basidium and Basidiocarp: Evolution, Cytology, Function and Development* (ed. K. Wells & E. K. Wells), pp. 125–155. New York, Heidelberg, Berlin: Springer-Verlag.

HOLLIGAN, P. M. & JENNINGS, D. H. (1972). Carbohydrate metabolism in the fungus *Dendryphiella salina*. 1. Changes in the levels of soluble carbohydrates during growth. *New Phytol.* **71**, 569–582.

HORNUNG, U. & JENNINGS, D. H. (1981). Light and electron microscopical observations of surface mycelium of *Serpula lacrimans*: stages of growth and hyphal nomenclature. *Nova Hedwigia* **34**, 101–126.

HOROWITZ, B. A., WEISENEEL, M. H., DORN, A. & GRESSEL, J. (1984). Electric currents around growing *Trichoderma* hyphae before and after photoinduction of conidiation. *Pl. Physiol.* **74**, 912–916.

HOWARD, R. J. & AIST, J. R. (1977). Effects of MBC on hyphal tip organisation, growth and mitosis of *Fusarium acuminatum* and their antagonism by D_2O. *Protoplasma* **92**, 195–210.

HOWARD, R. J. & AIST, J. R. (1980). Cytoplasmic microtubules and fungal morphogenesis. Ultrastructural effects of methyl benzimidazole-3-yl carbamate determined by freeze-substitution of hyphal tip cells. *J. Cell Biol.* **87**, 58–64.

JAFFE, L. F. (1982). Developmental currents, voltages and gradients. In *Developmental Order: Its Origin and Regulation* (ed. S. Subtelny), pp. 183. New York: Alan R. Liss.

JAFFE, L. F., ROBINSON, K. R. & NUCCITELLI, R. (1974). Local cation entry and self-electrophoresis as an intracellular localisation mechanism. *Ann. N.Y. Acad. Sci.* **238**, 327–389.

JENNINGS, D. H. (1979). Membrane transport and hyphal growth. In *Fungal Walls and Hyphal Growth* (ed. J. H. Burnett & A. P. J. Trinci), pp. 279–294. Cambridge: Cambridge University Press.

JENNINGS, D. H. (1982). The movement of *Serpula lacrimans* from substrate to substrate over nutritionally inert surfaces. In *Decomposer Basidiomycetes: their Biology and Ecology* (ed. J. C. Frankland, J. N. Hedger & M. J. Swift), pp. 91–108. Cambridge: Cambridge University Press.

JENNINGS, D. H. (1983). Some aspects of the physiology and biochemistry of marine fungi. *Biol. Rev.* **58**, 423–459.

JENNINGS, D. H. (1984). Water flow through mycelia. In *The Ecology and Physiology of the Fungal Mycelium* (ed. D. H. Jennings & A. D. M. Rayner), pp. 143–164. Cambridge: Cambridge University Press.

KOHLMEYER, J. & KOHLMEYER, E. (1979). Marine Mycology: *The Higher Fungi*. New York, San Francisco, London: Academic Press.

KROPF, D. L., CALDWELL, J. H., GOW, N. A. R. & HAROLD, F. M. (1984). Transcellular ion currents in the water mold *Achlya*: amino/proton symport as a mechanism for current entry. *J. Cell Biol.* **99**, 486–496.

KROPF, D. L., LUPA, M. D. A., CALDWELL, J. H. & HAROLD, F. M. (1983). Cell polarity: endogenous ion currents precede and predict branching in the water mold *Achlya*. *Science* **220**, 1385–1387.

LYSEK, G. (1984). Physiology and ecology of rhythmic growth in fungi. In *The Ecology and Physiology of the Fungal Mycelium* (ed. D. H. Jennings & A. D. M. Rayner), pp. 323–342. Cambridge: Cambridge University Press.

MAHADEVAN, P. R. & MAHADKAR, U. R. (1970). Role of enzymes in growth and morphology of *Neurospora crassa*: cell wall bound enzymes. *J. Bact.* **101**, 941–947.

MOTTA, J. M. (1969). Cytology and morphogenesis in the rhizomorph of *Armillaria mellea*. *Am. J. Bot.* **56**, 610–619.

MOTTA, J. M. (1971). Histochemistry of the rhizomorph meristem of *Armillaria mellea*. *Am. J. Bot.* **58**, 80–87.

NORDBRING-HERZ, B. (1984). Mycelial development and lectin-carbohydrate interactions in nematode-trapping fungi. In *The Ecology and Physiology of the Fungal Mycelium* (ed D. H. Jennings & A. D. M. Rayner), pp. 419–432. Cambridge: Cambridge University Press.

PALL, M. L. (1971). Amino acid transport in *Neurospora crassa*. IV Properties and regulation of a methionine transport system. *Biochim. Biophys. Acta* **233**, 201–214.

PARK, D. (1985*a*). Does Horton's law of branch length apply to open branching systems? *J. theor. Biol.* **112**, 299–313.

PARK, D. (1985*b*). Application of Horton's first and second laws of branching to fungi. *Trans Br. mycol. Soc.* **84**, 584–585.

PROSSER, J. I. & TRINCI, A. P. J. (1979). A model of hyphal growth and branching. *J. gen. Microbial.* **111**, 153–164.

RAYNER, A. D. M., POWELL, K. A., THOMPSON, W. & JENNINGS, D. H. (1985). Morphogenesis of vegetative organs. In *Developmental Biology of Higher Fungi* (ed. D. Moore, L. A. Casselton, D. A. Wood & J. Frankland), pp. 249–279. Cambridge: Cambridge University Press.

READ, N. D. & BECKETT, A. (1985). The anatomy of the mature perithecium in *Sordaria humana* and its significance for fungal multicellular development. *Can. J. Bot.* **63**, 281–296.

ROSENBERGER, R. F. (1979). Endogenous lytic enzymes and wall metabolism. In *Fungal Walls and Hyphal Growth* (ed. J. H. Burnett & A. P. J. Trinci), pp. 265–277. Cambridge: Cambridge University Press.

SAN-BLAS, G. & SAN-BLAS, F. (1984). Molecular aspects of fungal dimorphism. *CRC crit. Rev. Microbiol.* **11**, 101–127.

SANDERS, D. & SLAYMAN, C. L. (1982). Control of intracellular pH. Predominant role of oxidative metabolism, not proton transport, in the eukaryotic microorganism *Neurospora*. *J. gen. Physiol.* **80**, 377–402.

THOMPSON, W., EAMUS, D. & JENNINGS, D. H. (1985). Water flux through mycelium of *Serpula lacrimans*. *Trans. Br. mycol. Soc.* **84**, 601–608.

TRINCI, A. P. J. (1978). The duplication cycle and vegetative development in moulds. In *The Filamentous Fungi. Developmental Mycology*, vol. **3** (ed. J. E. Smith & D. R. Berry), pp. 132–163. London: Edward Arnold.

TRINCI, A. P. J. (1979). The duplication cycle and branching in fungi. In *Fungal Walls and Hyphal Growth* (ed. J. H. Burnett & A. P. J. Trinci), pp. 319–358. Cambridge: Cambridge University Press.

TRINCI, A. P. J. & RIGHELATO, R. C. (1970). Changes in constituents and ultrastructure during autolysis of glucose-starved *Penicillium chrysogenum*. *J. gen. Microbiol.* **60**, 239–250.

Turner, G. (1978). Cytoplasmic inheritance and senescence. In *Filamentous Fungi. Developmental Mycology*, vol. **3** (ed. J. E. Smith & D. R. Berry), pp. 406–425. London: Edward Arnold.

Watkinson, S. C. (1984). Morphogenesis of the *Serpula lacrimans* colony in relation to its functions in nature. In *The Ecology and Physiology of the Fungal Mycelium* (ed. D. H. Jennings & A. D. M. Rayner), pp. 164–184. Cambridge University Press.

Wilcoxson, R. D. & Sudia, T. W. (1968). Translocation in fungi. *Bot. Rev.* **34**, 32–50.

PLASTICITY IN ALGAE

J. A. RAVEN

Department of Biological Sciences, University of Dundee, Dundee DD1 4HN, UK

Summary

Unicellular planktonic algae show considerable developmental plasticity in relation to mean cell size and the fraction of the cell volume occupied by various organelles. Changes in cell size and composition in relation to variations in the supply of light and nutrient solutes have been partially characterized with respect to the signals which regulate the changes, and in terms of the possible significance of the changes in maximizing growth rate under different resource-limited conditions. Less is known of the *mechanisms* by which the signals lead to the observed phenotypic effects.

Multicellular attached macroalgae, whether acellular or multicellular, rhizophytic or haptophytic, have greater scope for phenotypic modification of morphology than do microalgae, in addition to the possibility of biochemical (compositional) changes. In addition to biochemical changes in response to variations in the ratio of availability of various resources (photons, N, P) there are also structural changes; significant here is the increased occurrence of (often colourless) hairs in haptophytes and (probably) of enhanced rhizoid development in rhizophytes. Many of the changes in morphology and physiology of macroalgae in response to changes in photon and nutrient supply have analogies in the behaviour of vascular plants (especially of aquatic vascular plants).

Introduction

The algae (construed here as excluding the prokaryotic phototrophs) encompass an enormous range of structural and chemical variation. Algal taxonomy separates Divisions and Classes on the basis of ultrastructural (of plastids, flagella, etc.) and chemical (of pigments, energy/organic C reserves, etc.) differences, thus permitting substantial within-Division and

Abbreviations: PCOC, Photorespiratory Carbon Oxidation Cycle; PCRC, Photosynthetic Carbon Reduction Cycle; P700, Reaction centre redox pigment-protein of photoreaction one; PFD, Photon Flux Density; RUBISCO, Ribulose Bisphosphate Carboxylase–Oxygenase (E.C. 4.1.1.39).

within-Class variations in gross morphology. Similarities in gross morphology between macrophytic members of different Divisions (e.g. Chlorophyta, Phaeophyta and Rhodophyta) or Classes (e.g. Chlorophyceae, Charophyceae, Pleurastrophyceae and Ulvophyceae in the Division Chlorophyta) are, then, attributed to parallel evolution from different unicellular ancestors (see Raven, 1986*a*).

The morphological variations mentioned above in the context of taxonomy and phylogeny are genotypic, i.e. relate to 'life-form' (see Raven, 1986*b*). In the context of phenotypic plasticity ('growth form': Raven, 1986*b*) the algae clearly present a very wide range of structural contexts within which such plasticity can occur (Table 1 indicates, in very broad outlines, some algal life forms).

In unicells, quantitative variations in cell components dominate the possibilities, although qualitative (all or none) changes are possible (flagellate ⇌ non-flagellate; walled ⇌ non-walled; vegetative ⇌ cysts). In macrophytes, we *again* have the cell-level changes, but (in multicells) the additional possibility of 'number of cell' and 'type of cell' differences (sun-shade adaptation; reproduction).

Our discussion of plasticity in algal development will focus mainly on variations of phenotype related to the *acquisition* and *retention* of resources: the observed changes; the signals and mechanisms involved in their production; and their ecological and evolutionary significance. Plant strategies proposed by Grime are considered elsewhere in this volume, and are not explicitly included here; I have considered their application to algae elsewhere (Raven, 1980, 1981, 1984*a*, 1986*b*).

Unicellular algae

The range of unicellular algae

The unicellular algae considered here are the microalgae (as distinct from the acellular macroalgae considered in the next section). We shall deal almost entirely with planktophytes (Table 1). These organisms belong to many algae Divisions and Classes, but it is possible to generalize (*over* generalize?) that cells which can *neither* swim *nor* exhibit buoyancy tend to dominate mixed waters (where vertical water movement velocities can exceed velocities of swimming, or density-difference-induced floating or sinking, by up to 10^3-fold), while 'swimmers' and 'floaters' dominate stratified waters in which the velocity of swimming or upward, buoyancy-related movement can exceed vertical water movements (Raven, 1984*a*; Raven & Richardson, 1986). Examples of 'sinkers' are the diatoms

Table 1. *A classification of life forms of aquatic algae (after Luther, 1949; Den Hartog & Segal, 1964; Raven, 1981, 1984*a*; Raven & Richardson, 1986).*

Category	Definition	Examples
A. PLANOPHYTES	Not attached to the substrate	
A.1. Planktophytes	Microscopic	Many Bacillariophyta, Dinophyta, Prymnesiophyta (formerly Haptophyta); some Chlorophyta (Prasinophyceae, Chlorophyceae); includes unicells, colonies and a few true, multicellular differentiated organisms.
A.2. Pleustophytes	Macroscopic	Some Chlorophyta (Ulvophyceae: *Cladophora aegagropila*; Chlorophyceae: *Hydrodictyon* spp.; Phaeophyta, e.g. *Ascophyllum nodosum* ecad *Mackei*)
B. HAPTOPHYTES	Plants attached to, but not penetrating, a solid substrate whose particle size is large relative to the plant	Most Phaeophyta, Rhodophyta, and benthic Chlorophyta
C. RHIZOPHYTES	Plants with basal parts in a substrate whose particle size is small relative to the plant	Some benthic Chlorophyta (Chlorophyceae: *Protosiphon* spp.; Charophyceae: Characeae; Ulvophyceae: *Caulerpa* spp., *Halimeda* spp., *Penicillus* spp.); some benthic Tribophyta (*Vaucheria* spp., *Botrydium* spp.)

(Bacillariophyta), of 'swimmers' are many dinoflagellates (Dinophyta); and of 'floaters' are some of the Dinophyta and of the prokaryotic blue-green algae (Cyanobacteria) Raven (1984*a*); Raven & Richardson (1986). The Cyanobacteria are not considered in detail in the present paper.

The range of plastic phenomena

Our discussion here relates mainly to responses to environmental changes. These include not only the responses to changed light, nutrient supply and temperature conditions to growth which form the main topic for discussion in this section, but also changes which occur as a result of certain procedures used in producing synchronous cultures of microalgae, and in relation to sexual reproduction and the production of resting stages by sexual (zygospores) or asexual (cysts) means.

Plastic phenomena and the mitotic cell cycle

John *et al.* (1983), working on *Chlamydomonas* and *Chlorella*, showed that very few of the changes in cellular activities and composition found during the synchronous cell growth in light–dark cycles are *directly* and *obligatorily* related to completion of the cell cycle, but are, rather, responses to the conditions imposed to synchronize the cells (light–dark cycles). This was demonstrated by comparing changes during the synchronous cell cycle with light–dark transitions as the synchronizers with those found in synchronous cultures under constant environmental conditions, in which synchrony resulted from size selection of cells to found the culture. This ruled out changes of ratios of respiration/protein; photosynthesis/protein; most changes in enzyme activity/protein and enzyme synthesis/protein; nutrient uptake/protein; total protein synthesis/protein; inner mitochondrial membrane component (succinic dehydrogenase)/inner mitochondrial membrane area; and thylakoid membrane component (light-harvesting pigment-protein complex)/thylakoid membrane area, as obligatory correlates of the cell cycle, since changes in these ratios did not occur during synchronous growth under constant environmental conditions. Using the terminology of John *et al.* (1983), we see that obligatory correlates of the cell cycle are the 'primary controls' (processes directly involved in division, and occurring under all growth conditions) such as the 'initiating control' equivalent to 'commitment' in yeasts, and 'dependent controls' such as DNA synthesis and separation, and cell wall synthesis; in *Chlorella* those 'dependent controls' may also include changes in the activity of α-amylase, oligo-1,6-glucosidase, and DNAase (John *et al.* 1983). 'Secondary controls' (processes directly involved in cell division, but occurring only under some growth conditions, when adequate levels are not already present) are, possibly, tubulin synthesis in light–dark cultures of *Chlamydomonas* and, conceivably, cell wall precursors (depending on C and N supply and metabolism). We shall see (below) that it is difficult to accommodate the 'synchronizing-signal' – dependent influences on relative catalytic activities throughout the cell cycle in a scheme of optimization (maximizing growth rate, and, or, efficiency of resource use, under the prevailing conditions), *via* plasticity, of algal growth under specified culture conditions.

Plastic phenomena and recombination

Sex in *Chlamydomonas* involves a switch (triggered by, e.g. low N) from a mitotic vegetative cycle for the haploid cells to copulation and zygospore production and, ultimately, germination with meiosis, re-establishing the haploid vegetative cycle. This behaviour is 'plastic' to the extent that there is a change from the 'normal' cycle, involving expression of different genes. However, the extent to which 'plasticity' occurs within the sexual cycle (i.e. quantitative changes in behaviour during the sexual cycle) is not clear.

Plastic phenomena and survival

Production of zygospores in *Chlamydomonas* is a part of sexual behaviour. In many algae, no sex has been reported, and such 'resting' stages (e.g. cysts) as occur result from asexual behaviour. In many algae, 'resting' stages are not obviously structurally different from vegetative cells.

Plastic phenomena and cell size

For autospore-producing algae (e.g. many of the Chlorococcales; *Chlamydomonas*) there is the option of producing different numbers of autospores (2^n, where $n = 1$–4 or even 5). The number of autospores produced in synchronous cultures of such algae is nutritionally controlled; better-nourished cells grow faster, and accordingly the mother cell is larger prior to autospore formation. Despite the suggestion of Donnan & John (1983) that sensing of cell-size and of time elapsed since the initiation of the cell cycle are of essentially equal importance in regulating the cell cycle, it would seem that the major determinant of timing and autospore number in the cell cycle is a *sizer* rather than a *timer* (Cavalier-Smith, 1984); better-nourished, faster-growing mother cells grow larger before dividing.

For diatoms, the vegetative cell division process inexorably leads to a decrease in mean cell size; restoration of cell size to the 'original' value involves casting off the silicaceous frustules and producing auxospores/-gametes which subsequently regenerate walls after size restoration (Werner, 1971; Maske, 1982).

In both of these cases the change in cell size under 'constant' environmental conditions is much greater (volume change in 24 h = 16-fold for a 4-sequential mitosis autospore cycle in Chlorococcales; 9-fold in 90 days for growth of *Coscinodiscus*) than for 'normal' binary fission (2-fold volume changes per cell cycle); in both cases there is environmental control of the extent of cell volume decrease or increase before the 'restoring' process occurs.

Independently of these processes, i.e. in cells with binary fission unconstrained by cell wall rigidity, and for autospore size in cells with multiple fission, there are environmentally determined changes in cell size for a given genotype. Cells of a given genotype tend to be *smaller* at lower growth rates (constrained by nutrient supply, light supply and, probably, non-optimal temperature); but this is not always the case (Schlesinger & Shuter, 1981). The *generalized* decrease in cell size with decreasing growth rate for a given genotype contrasts with the *inverse* relation between cell size and *maximum* (resource-saturated) growth rate noted when a range of genotypes of widely varying cell size are compared in the case of the Chlorophyta (Schlesinger & Shuter, 1981; Schlesinger, Molot & Shuter, 1981), Bacillariophyta and Dinophyta (Banse, 1982). We note that the genotypic size dependence of growth rate is relatively weak, requiring at least an order of magnitude variation in cell size to establish the exponent b in an equation such as $\mu_m = a\,V^b + c$ where μ_m = maximum (resource-saturated) specific growth rate (s^{-1}), V is cell volume (m^3), and a, b and c are constants (units: $a = m^{-3}s^{-1}$; b = pure number with a value in the range $-0{\cdot}1$ to $-0{\cdot}2$; $c = s^{-1}$), and would not lead to very significant differences in μ_m between cells where *genotypic* V values only varied as much as is commonly found to occur *phenotypically* in response to environmental influences.

We note that the genotypic *inverse* relationship between cell size and specific growth rate in microalgae is paralleled (but not mechanistically explained) by similar inverse relationships in many other major taxa of chemo-organotrophs and (probably) photolithotrophs (Banse, 1982; Schmidt-Nielsen, 1984; Peters, 1983). Mechanistically, the *phenotypic* decrease in cell size with decreased resource availability can be related to the 'package effect' (for photon capture) and minimum unstirred layer thicknesses and plasmalemma area per unit cell volume (for solute uptake). For a given pigment concentration per unit cell volume, smaller cells (of the same shape) make more efficient use of individual chromophores in light absorption in a given photon field (Kirk, 1983; Raven, 1984*b*), i.e. have a larger value of mol photon absorbed (mol chromophore)$^{-1}$s^{-1}.

For a given bulk-phase nutrient concentration, the *maximum* effective thickness of the unstirred (boundary) layer of a spherical cell is directly proportional to its radius (Pasciak & Gavis, 1974). Assuming that any sinking or swimming of the cell relative to the surrounding water has a negligible effect on unstirred layer thickness, the smaller cell has a greater potential flux of solute (per unit area of surface) from the bulk phase to the surface; this, plus the larger membrane area per unit of cell volume, with its corresponding increased potential for solute flux across the plasmalemma per unit cell volume, should give enhanced nutrient acquisition capacity in smaller cells without the need for any change in porter kinetics or porter density per unit plasmalemma area.

Plastic phenomena and cell composition in relation to resource availability in photolithotrophy

We have just seen that low resource availability tends to phenotypically decrease the size of photolithotrophic microalgal cells. Low resource availability also alters cell composition (see table 1 of Shuter, 1979). A decrease in photon availability (in the presence of adequate chemical resources for growth) generally *increases* the fraction of the cell material devoted to light-harvesting (chromophores; pigment–protein complexes; thylakoid membrane lipids) with generally a *decrease* in the commitment of cell material to catalysts downstream of photon absorption (i.e. catalysts between photon absorption and the production of complete cells). This *antiparallel* relationship is not as trivial as it may seem; while basic structural components of the cell are relatively 'non-negotiable' as a fraction of the biomass, there *is* room for manoeuvre in terms of 'storage' organic carbon compounds (Cohen & Parnas, 1976; Parnas & Cohen, 1976). We note that, although there *is* a reduction in the fraction of biomass devoted to these downstream catalysts, the actual reduction in μ_{max} is sometimes substantially greater than would be predicted from the reduced content (per unit dry biomass) of the catalysts and an assumed equality of catalytic activity per unit catalyst, i.e. the 'low light' cells may have lower achieved *in vivo* specific reaction rates of the downstream catalysts (Raven, 1986*c*; Richardson, Beardall & Raven, 1983). This *could* be due to low *per unit biomass* content (at its typical specific activity) of some 'rate-limiting' catalyst in the low-light cells (Raven, 1986*c*), or to a more general (unspecified) inhibition of catalytic activity (Raven, 1986*c*).

A decrease in N or P (or Fe) availability generally reduces the content of chromophore, pigment–protein complexes, and thylakoid membrane lipids in the biomass; this may be construed as a 'long-term' mechanism of adjusting photon absorption rate to the rate at which the products of photochemistry can be used in growth, granted the limited supply of N, P, Fe (or whatever), and the absence of any well-authenticated mechanism for feedback inhibition of photosynthetic CO_2 fixation. Such a matching of photon absorption rate to the rate of use in growth of the products of photochemical reactions would help to avoid photoinhibition (Raven, 1984*a*,*b*). The finding that the content of stored organic carbon/energy in the biomass is higher in algae grown at low nutrient levels (Shuter, 1979) means that the above-mentioned 'balancing act' is not perfect; some photosynthate is produced in excess of that usable in synthesis of catalytic and structural materials plus the quantity of stored organic carbon/energy produced (per unit biomass) during growth at higher nutrient availability (Shuter, 1979).

At a less gross level of discrimination of cell composition the microalgae show a number of interesting responses to varying nutrient supply. Variations in Cu and Fe availability can, in those algae (many Chlorophyta) which can produce both the Cu-containing plastocyanin and the Fe-containing cytochrome C_{554}, alter the ratio of these catalysts of electron transfer from the (reduced) cytochrome b_6-f-non-haem-Fe complex to (oxidized) P_{700} found in the cells, favouring production of the catalyst which does not use the less-available metal (see Raven, 1984*a*). However, a number of algal Divisions cannot produce plastocyanin and are consequently unable to respond in this way. A somewhat similar situation is found for catalysis of electron transfer from the (reduced) primary acceptor complex of photoreaction one to the (oxidized) $NADP^+$ reductase flavoprotein. The alternatives here are the very widespread, Fe-containing, ferredoxin, and the flavoprotein flavodoxin, which has no known metal requirement, and has (on the basis of perhaps inadequate knowledge) a much more restricted taxonomic distribution. In those (Chlorophytan) algae which can produce both catalysts, it is found that low-Fe-grown cells have more flavodoxin and less ferredoxin. We note that, while plastocyanin and cytochrome C_{554} have very similar specific catalytic activities and M_r values (i.e. have very similar 'non-metal' costs of synthesizing unit catalytic activity), flavodoxin is markedly less catalytically active than is ferredoxin (see Raven, 1984*a*).

For another metal-containing catalyst urease (which needs Ni) which has a non-metal-containing alternate (urea amido-lyase) which catalyses the same overall reaction (albeit with two enzymes rather than one, and with an input of one mol ATP per mol urea hydrolysed), there seems to be no cases of phenotypic switching between catalysts; an algal genotype contains *either* urease *or* urea amido-lyase (Al-Houty & Syrett, 1984; Syrett & Al-Houty, 1984).

A final example of changing patterns of catalysis in response to environmental resource changes is that of CO_2 availability to many microalgae (Raven, 1984*a*, 1985). When grown at high (several times air) CO_2 levels, i.e. under conditions in which diffusive entry of CO_2 effectively saturates the carboxylase activity of RUBISCO and suppresses the oxygenase activity, many microalgae show little PCOC enzyme activity, as befits the negligible production of phosphoglycollate under these conditions. Growth at lower (about air) CO_2 levels derepresses the PCOC enzymes and, in many cases, also derepresses a 'CO_2 concentrating mechanism'. The former derepression permits the organism to metabolize phosphoglycollate to phosphoglycerate (used in biosynthesis) rather than merely excrete the glycollate produced by the action of phosphoglycollate phosphatase. The latter (where it occurs) suppresses phosphoglycollate synthesis by maintaining a high $[CO_2]:[O_2]$ around RUBISCO, substantially reducing carbon flux through the PCOC. The occurrence of the PCOC (without or, more especially, with the 'CO_2 concentrating mechanism') increases the rate of CO_2 conversion to reduced, usable C compounds per unit RUBISCO activity at low ($\sim$air-equilibrium) CO_2 levels in the process of atmospheric O_2 levels. At high external $[O_2]$ levels the repression of PCOC enzymes and the 'CO_2 concentrating mechanisms' economizes on N and energy for biosynthesis. In terms of running costs the energy requirement per net CO_2 fixed and retained by the cells decreases in the order: cell at low external $[CO_2]$ with low PCOC and the presence of 'CO_2 concentrating mechanism' activity (excreting glycollate) > cell at low external $[CO_2]$ with high PCOC $\pm$ 'CO_2 concentrating mechanism' activity > cell at high external $[CO_2]$ with low PCOC and low 'CO_2 concentrating mechanism' activity (Raven & Lucas, 1985).

It is possible that the 'CO_2 concentrating mechanism' increases the 'N use efficiency' of CO_2 fixation (the rate of C fixation per unit cell N) at low external $[CO_2]$, i.e. more net CO_2 fixation occurs per unit N involved in CO_2 transport, PCRC and PCOC when the 'CO_2 concentrating mechanism' is operative than when it is not (Beardall, Griffiths & Raven, 1982). More work is needed to establish the generality of this effect, and to investigate its significance.

Plastic phenomena and cell composition in relation to energy sources for growth in facultatively chemo-organotrophic microalgae

While many microalgae are obligate photolithotrophs, there are a number which are facultative chemo-organotrophs (and, or, photo-organotrophic): see Raven (1976). The presence of an organic substrate which acts as an energy and carbon source for growth derepresses plasmalemma-located porters related to entry of the substrate (in the case of sugars and amino acids but, perhaps, not some fatty acids and hydroxyacids) and the enzymes of its metabolism, and some degree of repression of the photosynthetic apparatus; the repression of the photosynthate apparatus may be greater in the dark. The extent of repression is very variable, being essentially complete on facultatively organotrophic species of *Euglena*, and less complete in such Chlorophyta as *Chlorella*, *Scenedesmus* and *Chlamydomonas* (Raven, 1976). Raven (1976) pointed out that, even in *Euglena* with very substantial repression of the photosynthetic apparatus when growing chemo-organotrophically, the μ_{max} value for chemo-organotrophic growth is no greater than is attained photolithotrophically. In the Chlorophyta, with less complete repression of the photosynthetic apparatus under chemo-organotrophic conditions, the μ_{max} for chemo-organotrophic growth is usually substantially lower than is the case for photolithotrophic growth. These findings are not immediately explained in terms of the model for photolithotrophy presented by Raven (1986*c*) where a lower specific growth rate of photolithotrophs than of otherwise similar chemo-organotrophs (lacking the photosynthetic apparatus, but possessing the less capital-expensive food-acquiring apparatus of chemo-organotrophy) is predicted on the basis of the specific reaction rates of catalysts and their content in the biomass. The need for more catalysts in photolithotrophs than in chemo-organotrophs means that the specific reaction rate of a given catalyst common to both modes of nutrition will be lower in photolithotrophs; this means that μ_{max} will also be lower. We note that phenotypic 'shade' adaptation can also lead to a reduction in μ_{max} in excess of that expected on the basis of increased light-harvesting machinery reducing the fraction of biomass devoted to potentially rate-limiting 'downstream' catalysts (see Raven, 1986*c*; and above).

Mechanisms of plasticity

Transcriptional control appears (as expected) to underpin those phenomena for which data are available and in which there are very large changes in the activity of particular catalysts. The best data are available for derepression of catalysts of chemo-organotrophy or of photolithotrophy respectively in light *minus* organic substrate – dark *plus* organic substrate, and the reverse transition, respectively.

The signals for the changes we have been discussing involve chemical receptors and photoreceptors. The chemical receptor for the derepression of the hexose transport system in *Chlorella* has a different specificity from hexokinase or the transport system (Raven, 1980). The determinants of the 'low CO_2' and 'high CO_2' states in microalgae have been investigated by studying induction (derepression) of the 'CO_2 concentrating mechanism' as a function of [CO_2], [O_2] and pH (Raven, 1985). Photoreceptors involved in the derepression of the photosynthetic apparatus include cryptochrome and (in some cases) porphyrins, including protochlorophyll (Senger, 1980).

Less extreme variations of composition and catalytic activity (i.e. *not* involving a complete switch between photolithotrophy and chemo-organotrophy) are seen during 'sun–shade' adaptation, and 'high CO_2–low CO_2' adaptation. 'Sun–shade' adaptation involves changes in chlorophyll : carbon ratios (using chlorophyll as an indication of light-harvesting capacity, including other chromophores, proteins to which chlorophyll and other chromophores are complexed, and thylakoid polar lipids, and carbon as an indicator of total cell activity in catalysing 'downstream' processes of growth).

R. Geider (personal communication) has produced a 'mechanistic' derivation of the model of Shuter (1979), and has (with T. R. Platt) modelled the interconversion of 'shade' (high chlorophyll : C) and 'sun' (low chlorophyll : C) cells. Much of the data can, apparently, be encompassed by rates of synthesis of the 'rate-limiting' catalysts (chlorophyll for 'shade' cells; C for 'sun' cells) which are similar to those found in steady-state cultures in the appropriate (low light for chlorophyll; high light for C) environment, with decreased rates for the 'non-limiting' catalyst, which establishes the new steady-state cell composition. It thus appears that the rate of adjustment of cell composition can be accounted for in terms of synthetic rates of cell components appropriate to the maximum growth rate (steady-state) under assorted growth conditions. Accordingly, no capacity for synthesis in excess of that needed for steady-state growth is, apparently needed to account for rates of adaptation to 'sun' or 'shade' conditions. Such models of 'adaptation' must, however, take into account the 'special' influence of certain wave lengths of radiation which are not mediated *via* photosynthetic pigments. Especially, we note that blue or blue-green light leads to a more 'shade-adapted' suite of cell characteristics than the same genotype would have under the same photon flux density of light of a wider wavelength range (Senger, 1980; Jeffrey, 1981). This is significant in the context of higher vascular plants where blue light generally signals 'sun' characteristics (Senger, 1980).

Significance of microalgae plasticity

The occurrence of phenotypic changes in microalgae is well established in laboratory cultures (although genotype selection in culture must be borne in mind). Of what significance is this in nature? To what extent does the capacity for phenotypic 'adaptability' contribute to fitness in the natural environment? Whittenbury & Kelly (1977) opined that microbial ecology is largely the province of 'specialist' organisms, with a relatively small number of genotypes able to function at more than one trophic level in laboratory and even these making relatively little use of their adaptability in nature (cf. Vincent, 1980*a,b*). However, it has not proved easy for Whittenbury & Kelly (1977), or subsequent commentators (Raven, 1980, 1984*a*) to quantify even the *potential* advantages of 'specialist' as opposed to 'generalist' organisms, and still less possible to prove that such potentially useful traits do contribute to fitness (Osmond, Bjorkman & Anderson, 1980).

What clues does nature provide as to the extent, and significance, of microalgal plasticity under 'natural' conditions? A general point relates to the 'Paradox of the Plankton' (Hutchinson, 1961), i.e. the diversity of natural phytoplankton assemblages relative to the number of 'perceived' niches. Harris (1983) and Harris, Piccinin & Van Ryn (1983) have recently summarized the evidence as to the status of 'equilibrium' (i.e. having sufficient temporal stability of the environment for competitive exclusion to be a major determinant of species diversity) and 'non-equilibrium' (i.e. having insufficient temporal stability to permit competitive exclusion to be a major determinant of species diversity) models of phytoplankton diversity, and have provided evidence from Hamilton Harbour, Lake Ontario, which is best explained by a 'non-equilibrium' model. Regardless of the validity of 'equilibrium' and 'non-equilibrium' models of phytoplankton diversity, it appears that the 'Paradox of the Plankton' is best explained by *relatively* small plasticity in nature for actively growing populations of microalgae. If a wide range of phenotypes of each genotype were competitive in nature (i.e. the genotype had a large niche width) the number of genotypes which were competitive in nature would be decreased. Evidence consistent with phytoplankton populations in oceanic waters growing at near-maximal rates comes from data on C : N : P ratios (Goldman, McCarthy & Peavey, 1979) which stay close to the values found in laboratory cultures growing rapidly rather than those found in cultures growing less rapidly.

These data relate to niche breadth of photolithotrophic microalgae, and suggest that the niche breadth achieved in nature is more restricted than that exhibited in laboratory cultures. Even fewer data are available for the chemo-organotrophic behaviour in nature of facultatively photolithotrophic microalgae (see Vincent, 1980*a,b*).

Acellular macroalgae

The diversity of acellular macroalgae

Acellular macroalgae include the pleustophyte *Hydrodictyon*, such haptophytes as *Valonia*, *Acetabularia* and *Codium* (with some *Halimeda* species), and rhizophytes such as *Protosiphon*, *Penicillus*, *Caulerpa* and many *Halimeda* species (see Table 1 for categorization of life-forms). With the exception of the undifferentiated colonial *Hydrodictyon* and *Protosiphon* (members of the class Chlorophyceae), the algae mentioned above are in another class (the Ulvophyceae) of the Division Chlorophyta. The only other algae Division with a substantial number of acellular macroalgal representatives is the Tribophyta, with the rhizophytes *Botrydium* and *Vaucheria* (Raven, 1981, 1984*a*).

The range of plastic phenomena

A major feat of many of the acellular macroalgae is the occurrence of substantial differentiation despite the absence of the 'classical' multicellular symplastic organization. Multicellular symplastic organization permits differential gene expression over distances of the order of tens of μm (i.e. in individual cells of radius $\sim$ 10–20 μm), with containment of immediate (RNA) and subsequent 'informational macromolecule' (protein) products of differential gene expression, while permitting the low M_r concomitants of differentiation (hormones, nutrients), and electrical messages, to pass between cells. The ability of many acellular macroalgae (of which *Caulerpa* species are the most striking examples) to show very substantial differentiation recalls the aphonism, attributed to De Bary, that 'organisms make cells, not cells the organism' (see Barlow, 1982). In attempting to account for this paradox, we note that many of the differentiated acellular macroalgae have two mechanisms of intracellular long-distance transport (Raven, 1986*a*). One, based on actomyosin, moves a portion of the cytosol with some entrained organelles; the other, based on microtubules plus an unknown ATP-powered 'motor', moves certain organelles. It remains to be seen how the operation of these two mechanisms is related to differential gene expression *plus* transmission of nutrients and messages over distances of tens of mm or more.

The differentiation mentioned above involves substantial spatial organization of resource acquisition, especially in rhizophytes. We shall examine the possible differential involvement of rhizoids of rhizophytes in N acquisition from sediments of different N availability, as well as the role, in haptophytes, of hairs in nutrient acquisition from the bulk water phase. Furthermore, we shall examine phenotypic 'sun–shade' adaptation in these algae (*Codium* and *Acetabularia*).

Plasticity in nutrient acquisition by rhizophytes

In cinematic terms this heading deals with a 'future attraction' rather than 'tonight's main feature', inasmuch as the field holds prospects rather than hard data. Sediments are commonly substantially enriched in nutrients relative to bulk water phases (Raven, 1981, 1984*a*). Williams (1984) and Williams & Fisher (1985) have shown that *Caulerpa cupressoides* obtains much of its N (as NH_4^+) *via* its rhizoids from the sediment rather than from the bulk water phase, using the photosynthetic 'assimilators'. The sediment is not, however, a significant CO_2 source for photosynthesis of *Penicillus* and *Halimeda* (Table 2). It would be of interest to know how the extent of rhizoid development relates to the nutrient concentration in the sediment and the bulk phase, and to the limitation of growth by nutrients relative to light. Analogies with higher vascular land plants (which have no possibility of nutrient (e.g. N, P) acquisition *via* their photosynthetic shoot system would suggest that (assuming negligible N or P availability from the bulk water phase) for algae the shoot : rhizoid ratio would be high when light, rather than nutrients, limited growth, and *vice versa* (see Thornley, 1972, 1977; Clarkson, 1985).

Plasticity in nutrient acquisition by haptophytes

Raven (1981, 1984*a*) discusses the role of hairs in nutrient acquisition by haptophytes. Among the acellular haptophytes discussed are *Codium* and *Acetabularia*; in both cases the plants have more hairs per unit biomass when grown under conditions of restricted nutrient supply (low bulk phase concentration and, or, little water movement relative to the plant surface). In the case of *Acetabularia* the increased hair density results from delayed abscission of the so-called 'sterile whorls' under nutrient-deprived conditions. The hairs of *Codium* are colourless, while those of *Acetabularia* are chlorophyllous; however, experiments in which the effects of photon

Table 2. *Influence of CO_2 enrichment of medium bathing shoots or rhizoids on photosynthetic and respiratory O_2 exchange in* Halimeda *and* Penicillus.

	Modifications to seawater medium round:		Gas exchange of whole plant at 22 °C nmol O_2 (gdw.s.)$^{-1}$	
	Shoot	Rhizoid	Net photosynthesis at light saturation	Dark respiration
Halimeda sp.	0	0	8·8 ± 0·9	2·9 ± 0·3
	0	equilibrated with 5 %CO_2	8·3 ± 0·9	2·8 ± 0·3
	equilibrated with 5 %CO_2	0	13·2 ± 1·4	3·1 ± 0·3
Penicillus capitatus Lamarc.	0	0	12·2 ± 1·4	3·2 ± 0·4
	0	equilibrated with 5 %CO_2	13·5 ± 1·5	2·9 ± 0·3
	equilibrated with 5 %CO_2	0	18·1 ± 1·9	3·5 ± 0·4

Data given as mean ± standard error of the mean for samples in each case. Shoots and rhizoids of intact plants were incubated in separate bathing media with a water- and gas-impermeable seal around the plant axis; O_2 changes measured by Winkler titration. Unpublished results of Raven & Handley; cf. Table 1 of Raven, Osborne & Johnston (1985).

limitation and inorganic nutrient limitation are compared show that *Acetabularia* hair retention relates to nutrient rather than photon deprivation. The role of hairs in nutrient acquisition from a bulk water phase would benefit from the sorts of analyses used for the role of root hairs and mycorrhizas in nutrient acquisition from soil (Clarkson, 1985).

Plasticity in photon acquisition by acellular macrophytes

In *Acetabularia*, Terborgh & Thimann (1964) showed that growth (length) was a direct function of daily incident photons (mol photon m^{-2}) over a range of photoperiods and photon flux density, while chlorophyll content varied inversely with daily photon dosage. There are also pronounced blue-light-mediated morphogenetic processes in *Acetabularia* (see Lüning, 1981).

Ramus (1978) has reported on the relationship between pigment content and absorptance in *Codium*, and also comments on the role of scattering by air spaces in the thallus in light absorption by certain specimens of *Codium* exposed to high photon flux densities. Ramus, Beale, Mauzerall & Howard (1976*a*) showed, in reciprocal transparent experiments, that 'sun-adapted' plants of *Codium fragile* had less chlorophyll per m^2 of thallus area than did the 'sun-adapted' plants. However, unlike the other multicellular green (*Ulva*) and red (*Chondrus*, *Porphyra*) tested, *Codium* did not have a higher ratio of chlorophyll *a* to 'accessory pigment' when 'sun-adapted'.

Significance of acellular macroalgal plasticity

These relatively slow-growing (generation times of weeks or months rather than the tens of hours of many planktophytes) benthic organisms may, as individuals, be subjected to substantial variations in resource availability on a seasonal basis. Such variations could include photon flux density and daylength at the water surface, variations in turbidity of the water column and of biomass of any canopy-forming plants (e.g. seagrasses), all of which alter the photons incident per day. Further, stratification/destratification phenomena can increase nutrient availability in the winter. The chemical and structural responses outlined above can be construed as potential contributors to fitness in terms of maximizing the rate of resource acquisition (at a cost!) under low light or low bulk phase nutrient concentration conditions. However, it is important to note that these Ulvophycean acellular macrophytes are, at least for the Dasyclydales (e.g. *Acetabularia*) and Caulerpales (e.g. *Caulerpa*), essentially tropical and subtropical organisms, although the Codiales (e.g. *Codium*) have more temperate representatives. Accordingly, seasonality means different resource availability, and other environmental (e.g. temperature) changes than is the case for macroalgae of temperate waters, most of which belong to the 'cellular macrophytes' discussed in the next section.

Multicellular macroalgae

The diversity of multicellular macroalgae

Multicellular macroalgae include a few pleustrophytes (e.g. detached ecads of species *Ascophyllum*, *Sargassum* and *Hormosira* in the Phaeophyta; some *Chara* populations in the Charophyceae (Chlorophyta); a few rhizophytes (e.g. most members of the Characeae in the Charophyceae (Chlorophyta)) and many haptophytes (most Phaeophyta and Rhodophyta; many Chlorophyta, e.g. many Ulvophyceae, non-Characean Charophyceae, and Chlorophyceae): see Table 1.

The range of plastic phenomena

Many of the multicellular macroalgae show considerable differentiation; indeed, it could be argued that a lack of appreciable differentiation between cells defined an organism as 'colonial' rather than 'multicellular' (see Raven, 1984*a*). The explanation *in principal*, of differentiation between parts of the thallus in these multicellular organisms poses fewer problems than does that in the acellular macroalgae considered above. We note that there is a substantial, but incomplete, correlation between differentiation and the occurrence of plasmodesmata (or, in Rhodophyta, 'pit connections'): see Raven (1984*a*).

As with the acellular macroalgae our consideration of plastic phenomena deal mainly with phenomena related to resource acquisition. We accordingly deal with the role of hairs in haptophytes, and of rhizoids in rhizophytes, in nutrient acquisition by multicellular macroalgae under various nutrient supply conditions, and with phenotypic 'sun–shade' adaptation in these algae.

Plasticity in nutrient acquisition by haptophytes

The role of hairs in nutrient acquisition by multicellular algae haptophytes is similar to that outlined earlier for the acellular haptophytes (Raven, 1981, 1984*a*). The frequency of hairs (per unit biomass) on the thalli of many such algae has been shown to increase under conditions which restrict nutrient supply (low bulk phase nutrient concentrations and, or, low water flow velocities over the plant surface)/(Raven, 1981). However, it is only in the case of the rhodophyte *Ceramium rubrum* (de Boer & Whoriskey, 1983) that the presence of hairs has been shown to increase the capacity for nutrient uptake (per unit biomass). The presumed (Raven, 1981) role of the hairs is to increase the surface area of plasmalemma (per unit biomass) which is exposed to the medium. We note (Raven, 1981) that such a membrane amplification could be achieved by *invagination* ('transfer cells') rather than by *evagination* (hairs); however, *invaginations* would not perform the function of placing a part of the plasmalemma outside the macroscopic boundary layer around the main plant surface (Raven, 1981). While invaginations of the outer wall and plasmalemma epidermal (meristodermal) cells occurs in such haptophytes as *Fucus* (McCully, 1968) and *Corallina* (Borowitzka & Vesk, 1978), there are no reports of their correlation with low nutrient availability. It is unlikely that such invaginations would serve functions analogous to those in higher plant 'proteoid roots' (Gardner, Barber & Parbery, 1983).

Plasticity in nutrient acquisition by rhizophytes

Andrews, McInroy & Raven (1980*b*) showed that the extent of rhizoid production in cultures of *Chara hispida* depended on the particle size of the sediment in which the cuttings were 'rooted'; no direct evidence was sought as to the effect on rhizoid development of nutrient availability in the bulk water relative to that in the sediment. However, it was demonstrated (Andrews *et al.* 1984*b*; Box, 1984) that, for plants of *Chara hispida* with only about 1% of their dry weight in the rhizoids, at least 30% of the P uptake from 'natural' inorganic P concentrations (substantially higher in the sediment than in the bulk water: Spence, Barclay & Allen, 1985) could be accounted for by the rhizoids. Box (1984) has produced similar findings for inorganic N (NH_4^+, NO_3^-). Further data are needed on the nutrient acquisition properties of shoots and rhizoids of these plants and of the effect of nutrient availability in bulk phase and in sediment on rhizoid development and functioning.

Certain of these rhizophytes (mainly species of *Nitella*, and ecorticate species of *Chara*) have a mechanism of HCO_3^- 'use' (i.e. a faster rate of photosynthesis than can be accounted for by uncatalysed HCO_3^- to CO_2 conversion at bulk phase pH values with subsequent diffusive CO_2 entry) in photosynthesis which involves acid and alkaline zones, each of several mm^2 in extent, on the plant surface. The zones are based on differentiational occurrence of active ATP-driven H^+ efflux (dominant in acid zones) and of passive (but mediated) H^+ influx or OH^+ efflux (dominant in alkaline zones). The location of the alkaline zones can be 'stabilized' by deposition by $CaCO_3$, but the zones generally show spatial variation with time (Smith, 1985). The occurrence of banding as a function of inorganic C supply (total inorganic C, and pH, in the bulk phase) is not very well defined; nor is the dependence of banding on the occurrence of 'charosomes' (invaginations of a 'transfer cell' type in the plasmalemma) in acid zones. We note that transfer cells are often correlated with the 'acid zones' of freshwater vascular plants with analogous mechanisms of 'HCO_3^--use'. There is also data (not, alas, including data on acid and alkaline zones on 'HCO_3^--use') showing that photosynthesis in a *Nitella* genotype shows a 'C_3-like', i.e. CO_2 compensation concentration, when grown in 'Florida winter' conditions (shorter photoperiod, lower temperature), but 'C_4-like', i.e. low CO_2 compensation concentration, when grown in 'Florida summer' (longer photoperiod, higher temperature) conditions (Salvucci & Bowes, 1981).

Plasticity in photon acquisition in multicellular macroalgae

Much of the work on 'adaptation' to different photon flux availabilities by multicellular macroalgae has been confounded by the use of field samples of a given species growing at different natural photon flux densities (usually achieved by collecting specimens from different depths), with the consequent possibility that different genotypes are being compared from the different light environments. However, such problems are overcome in transplant experiments (Ramus *et al.* 1976*a*; Ramus, Beale & Mauzerall, 1976*b*; Ramus, Lemons & Zimmermann, 1977; Andrews, Box, McInroy & Raven, 1984*a*). In the experiments of Ramus *et al.* (1976*a*,*b*, 1977), a variety of marine multicellular organisms (the Chlorophytan *Ulva*; the Rhodophytans *Chondrus* and *Porphyra*; and the Phaeophytans *Fucus* and *Ascophyllum*) were transplanted (as was the acellular Chlorophytan *Codium* mentioned earlier). In all cases, transplantation to a *lower* photon flux density (i.e. greater depth than the 'normal' growth depth) led to an *increase* in pigment content per unit surface area. This increase is reversed when the original growth conditions are restored; the changes do *not* appear to be dependent on cell division or cell expansion (Ramus *et al.*, 1976*a*). The effect of this increased pigment content is to increase the fraction of incident photons observed by the organism, with the fractional increase being greater in plants which originally had relatively low absorptances (i.e. with low pigment/plant area, and low scattering by the tissues)/(Ramus, 1978).

The increased pigment content, and hence fractional absorption of light in the 'low light' plants leads to increased photosynthesis at rate-limiting incident PFD (Ramus *et al.* 1976*b*, 1977); it appears that the enhanced fractional absorption has little effect on the efficiency of processes downstream of photon absorption, although more data are needed on this point.

Few data are available on the plasticity of the ratio of pigments to other photosynthetic catalysts (broadly 'photosynthetic unit size', although this term is more generally applied to the ratio of pigments to reaction centres or to thylakoid redox intermediates, than to the ratio of pigments to C cycle enzymes such as RUBISCO) as a function of incident PFD in multicellular macroalgae. The relevant measurements have not, in general, been made, although Lapointe & Duke (1984) give values for pigment content and RUBISCO *activity* in *Gracilaria tikvahiae* as a function of changing PFD and N availability. At constant N availability, lower PFD for growth means a lower RUBISCO activity/biomass, but more pigment/biomass. Taking RUBISCO activity as a paradigm of the catalysts downstream of photon absorption, the lower activity of these catalysts per unit biomass would be expected to lead to a reduced capacity for photosynthesis at light saturation in the 'low light' cells. This decreased rate of light-saturated photosynthesis is a general, but not invariable result of 'shade adaptation' in multicellular macroalgae (Ramus *et al.* 1976*b*, 1977).

Two kinds of data can be used to infer whether the 'photosynthetic unit size' (in the broad sense) has increased. One involves a reversal of the argument used at the end of the last paragraph, i.e. equating an increase in light-saturated rate of photosynthesis per unit pigment with a decreased size of the photosynthetic unit, at least insofar as the ratio of pigment to whatever catalyst most limits the light-saturated rate of photosynthesis is concerned. An assumption which is implicit in this argument is that the reaction rate of this catalyst is equal in 'sun' and 'shade' phenotypes; this assumption is not invariably true (see Raven, 1986*c*).

Another approach relates to the ratio of the so-called 'accessory pigments' to chlorophyll a. These 'accessory pigments' are phycobilins in 'phycobiliphytes', chlorophyll(s) c + fucoxanthin in 'chromophytes', and chlorophyll b + siphonein/siphonaxanthin in 'chlorophytes'. These pigments are entirely (phycobilins) or mainly (the rest) confined to the light-harvesting pigment–protein complexes and an increase in their content, relative to that of chlorophyll a, can be taken as an indication of an increase in the ratio of light-harvesting complexes to reaction centre complexes. This ratio does indeed increase in some (*Ulva*; *Chondrus*; *Porphyra*) but not all (*Fucus*, *Ascophyllum*) multicellular macrophytes upon shade adaptation (Ramus *et al.* 1976*a*, 1977), with the acellular *Codium* also showing no change (see previous section).

It is clear that further work is needed to establish whether 'sun–shade' adaptation in macroalgae involves changes in the size of 'photosynthetic units' based on quantitation of pigments *and* of the downstream catalysts, involving measurement of the *amount* of reaction centres, redox and ATP synthesis components, and C cycle enzymes on a biomass basis for comparison with the pigment content. Such work should, preferably, be carried out under controlled conditions, using one of the *relatively* few species of multicellular algal macrophyte which can be maintained in laboratory culture without what many physiologists would regard as excessive effort. An alga which has been used to study interactions of photon and nutrient supply on growth rate, photosynthetic rate, and composition is the haptophyte *Gracilaria tikvahiae* in the Rhodophyta (Lapointe, 1981; Lapointe & Duke, 1984; Lapointe, Tenore & Duke, 1984; cf. Parker, 1982). There are also data on the photosynthetic unit sizes of wild-type *G. tikvahiae* and for some pigment (phycobilin) mutants, although this work has not yet been extended to the comparison of organisms grown under different photon flux densities (Kursar, van der Meer & Alberte, 1983*a*,*b*).

Significance of plasticity in multicellular macroalgae

As with the acellular macroalgae, we are dealing here with organisms which are slow growing (generation times of weeks or months rather than the tens of hours of many planktophytes) and accordingly may, as individuals, be subjected to seasonal variability in resource availability. In contrast to the acellular macroalgae, the multicellular macroalgae are important components of the algal vegetation of temperate (and frigid) as well as tropical waters; indeed, the largest and most highly differentiated examples inhabit cooler waters (e.g. *Macrocystis* spp.). Accordingly, their plasticity may well be of significance in accommodating to seasonal variations in the availability of resources, e.g. the behaviour of temperate- and frigid-zone *Laminaria* spp. in relation to the summer availability of light and the winter availability of nitrate (except when the plants are growing in 'special' environments with a year-round NO_3^- supply): Chapman & Craigie, 1977; Anderson, Cardinal & Larochelle, 1981).

In *Laminaria* spp. from environments with seasonal light and N supply, plant composition changes from a 'high N' condition (NO_3^- and organic N) at the end of winter to a 'high C' (mannitol) condition at the end of summer. However, we note that, at least under 'good' growing conditions there is substantial turnover of biomass (yearly net production exceeds mean biomass) throughout the year, and capitalizing on N and C stores requires translocation from 'storage' to 'growing' regions (Raven, 1984*a*).

Mechanisms of plasticity

Presumably, the signals for the increased capacity for nutrient acquisition per unit biomass (or per unit plant area) at low external nutrient concentrations, and for the morphological (hairs on haptophytes; rhizoids of rhizophytes) changes which also occur in many plants, relate to the photon : nutrient availability ratio (Lapointe & Duke, 1984; De Boer & Whoriskey, 1983). The photoreceptor(s) responsible for the changes in pigment ratios, and contents, which are seen as a result changes in photon flux density are not well characterized. However, it is known that phytochrome is involved in the 'etiolation' phenomena seen in low-light-grown Characeans (Forsberg, 1985; Imahori & Proctor, 1967; Rethy, 1968). We note that 'submersed shade', even in macrophyte stands, can have a component of shading due to absorption by water (far red > red), so that the red : far red ratio incident on the plant may be a less good 'indicator' of shade under water than it is on land. 'Cryptochrome' is the best characterized photoreceptor in marine multicellular macrophytes (Lüning, 1981), although its role in pigment changes is not clear: we have already seen that, while terrestrial plants use blue light as a 'sun' indicator, many planktophytes use it to indicate shade.

General conclusions

Algae show plasticity under laboratory conditions: changing their environment can greatly change their phenotype. We are largely ignorant of the details of how environmental changes can alter the composition and synthetic rates of algae. We are also not very well informed as to the significance of plasticity in nature. We have seen that the 'paradox of the plankton' is exacerbated if individual genotypes are competitive with a wide range of phenotypes, especially if we envisage an 'equilibrium' (competitive) phytoplankton community. For long-lived plants it is likely that we are dealing with a near-equilibrium situation in many cases; the extent of phenotypic plasticity, and hence of niche breadth, is unclear in this habitat too.

Work in my laboratory on resource acquisition by algae has been, and is, supported by N.E.R.C. and S.E.R.C. The work on *Halimeda* and *Penicillus* reported in Table 2 was carried out in the Department of Biological Sciences, Florida International University. Drs M. L. Tracey and J. H. Richards (F.I.U.) kindly provided laboratory space and facilities while Dr H. Griffiths (University of Newcastle-upon-Tyne) kindly loaned the chambers in which the incubations of algae with their rhizoids and shoots in different solutions were conducted. Dr Richard Geider has generously shared his insights, and has pointed me at many useful references on microalgae.

References

Al-Houty, F. A. A. & Syrett, P. J. (1984). The occurrence of urease/urea amido-lyase and glycollate oxidase/dehydrogenase in *Klebsormidium* spp. and members of the Ulotrichales. *Br. phycol. J.* **19**, 1–10.

Anderson, R. M., Cardinal, A. & Larouchelle, J. (1981). An alternate growth pattern for *Laminaria longicruris*. *J. Phycol.* **17**, 405–411.

Andrews, M., Box, R., McInroy, S. & Raven, J. A. (1984*a*). Growth of *Chara hispida* II. Shade adaptation. *J. Ecol.* **72**, 885–895.

Andrews, M., McInroy, S. & Raven, J. A. (1984*b*). Culture of *Chara hispida*. *Br. phycol. J.* **19**, 277–280.

Banse, K. (1982). Cell volumes, maximal growth rates of unicellular algae and ciliates, and the role of ciliates in the marine pelagial. *Limnol. Oceanogr.* **27**, 1059–1071.

Barlow, P. W. (1982). 'The plant forms cells, not cells the plant': the origin of De Bary's aphorism. *Ann. Bot.* **49**, 269–271.

Beardall, J., Griffiths, H. & Raven, J. A. (1982). Carbon isotope discrimination and the CO_2 accumulating mechanism in *Chlorella emersonii*. *J. exp. Bot.* **33**, 729–737.

Borowitzka, M. A. & Vesk, M. (1978). Ultrastructure of the Corallinaceae. I. The vegetative cells of *Corallina officinalis* and *C. civierii*. *Mar. Biol.* **46**, 295–304.

Box, R. (1984). Untersuchungen zur aufnahme von Nahrstoffen durch das Rhizoid der Grunalge *Chara hispida* L. Ph.D. Thesis, Free University of Berlin.

Cavalier-Smith, T. A. (1984). Genetic and epigenetic control of the plant cell cycle. In *The Cell Division Cycle in Plants* (ed. J.A. Bryant & D. Francis), pp. 179–197. Cambridge: University Press.

Chapman, A. R. O. & Craigie, J. S. (1977). Seasonal growth in *Laminaria longicruris*: Relations with dissolved inorganic nutrients and internal reserves of N. *Mar. Biol.* **40**, 197–205.

Clarkson, D. T. (1985). Factors affecting mineral nutrient acquisition by plants. *A. Rev. Pl. Physiol.* **36**, 77–115.

Cohen, D. & Parnas, H. (1976). An optimal policy for the metabolism of storage materials in unicellular algae. *J. theor. Biol.* **56**, 1–18.

De Boer, J. A. & Whoriskey, F. G. (1983). Production and role of hyaline hairs in *Ceramium rubrum*. *Mar. Biol.* **77**, 229–234.

Den Hartog, C. & Segal, C. (1964). A new classification of the waterplant communities. *Acta. bot. neerl.* **13**, 367–393.

Donnan, L. & John, P. C. L. (1983). Cell cycle control by timer and sizer in *Chlamydomonas*. *Nature* **304**, 630–633.

Forsberg, C. (1965). Nutritional studies on *Chara* in axenic cultures. *Physiol. Pl.* **18**, 275–290.

Gardner, W. K., Barber, D. A. & Parbery, D. G. (1983). The acquisition of phosphorus by *Lupinus albus* L. III. The probable mechanism by which phosphorus movement in the soil-root interface is enhanced. *Pl. Soil* **70**, 107–124.

Goldman, J. C., McCarthy, J. J. & Peavey, D. G. (1979). Growth rate influence on the chemical composition of phytoplankton in oceanic waters. *Nature* **279**, 210–215.

Harris, G. P. (1983). Mixed layer physics and phytoplankton populations: studies in equilibrium and non-equilibrium ecology. *Progr. phycol. Res.* **2**, 1–52.

Harris, G. P., Piccinin, B. B. & Van Ryn, J. (1983). Physical variability and phytoplankton communities: V. Cell size, niche diversification and the role of competition. *Arch. Hydrobiol.* **98**, 215–239.

Hutchinson, G. E. (1961). The paradox of the plankton. *Am. Nat.* **95**, 137–145.

Imahori, K. & Proctor, V. W. (1967). An approach to the experimental taxonomy of *Charas* (a freshwater algae). *Science Reports, Osaka* **16**, 25–29.

Jeffrey, S. W. (1981). Responses to light in aquatic plants. In *Encyclopedia of Plant Physiology*, New Series, Vol. 12 Part B *Physiological Plant Ecology* II *Responses to the Physical Environment* (ed. O. Lange, P. S. Nobel, C. B. Osmond & Ziegler), pp. 249–276. Berlin: Springer.

JOHN, P. C. L., DONNAN, L., HARPER, J. D. I., ROLLINS, M. J. & KEENAN, C. A. (1983). Control of cell division in *Chlorella* and *Chlamydomonas*. In *Progress in Cell Cycle Controls* (ed. J. Chaloupka, A. Kotyk & E. Streiblova), pp. 81–95. Prague.

KIRK, J. T. O. (1983). *Light and Photosynthesis in Aquatic Ecosystems*. Cambridge: University Press.

KURSAR, T. A., VAN DER MEER, J. & ALBERTE, R. S. (1983*a*). Light-harvesting system of the red alga *Gracilaria tikvahiae* I. Biochemical analyses of pigment mutations. *Pl. Physiol.* **73**, 353–360.

KURSAR, T. A., VAN DER MEER, J. & ALBERTE, R. S. (1983*b*). Light-harvesting system of the red alga *Gracilaria tikvahiae*. II. Phycobilisome characteristics of pigment mutants. *Pl. Physiol.* **73**, 361–369.

LAPOINTE, B. E. (1981). The effects of light and nitrogen on growth, pigment content, and biochemical composition of *Gracilaria foliifera* v. *angustissima* (Gigartinales, Rhodophyta). *J. Phycol.* **17**, 90–95.

LAPOINTE, B. E. & DUKE, C. S. (1984). Biochemical strategies for growth of *Gracilaria tikvahiae* (Rhodophyta) in relation to light intensity and nitrogen availability. *J. Phycol.* **20**, 488–495.

LAPOINTE, B. E., TENORE, K. R. & DUKE, C. S. (1984). Interactions between light and temperature on the physiological ecology of *Gracilaria tikvahiae* (Gigartinales: Rhodophyta). *Mar. Biol.* **80**, 161–170.

LÜNING, K. (1981). Light. In *The Biology of Seaweeds* (ed. C. S. Lobban & M. J. Wynne), pp. 326–355. Oxford: Blackwell.

LUTHER, H. (1949). Vorschlag zu einer okologischen Grundeinteilung der Hydrophyten. *Act. Bot. Fenn.* **44**, 1–15.

MASKE, H. (1982). Ammonium-limited continuous cultures of *Skeletonema costatum* in steady and transitional state: experimental results and model simulations. *J. mar. biol. Ass. U.K.* **62**, 919–943.

MCCULLY, M. E. (1968). Histological studies of the genus *Fucus*. III. Fine structure and possible functions of the epidermal cells of the vegetative thallus. *J. Cell Sci.* **3**, 1–16.

OSMOND, C. B., BJORKMAN, O. & ANDERSON, D. J. (1980). *Physiological Processes in Plant Ecology: Toward a Synthesis with Atriplex*. Berlin: Springer.

PARKER, H. S. (1982). Effects of simulated current on the growth rate and nitrogen metabolism of *Gracilaria tikvahiae* (Rhodophyta). *Mar. Biol.* **69**, 137–145.

PARNAS, H. & COHEN, D. (1976). The optimal strategy for the metabolism of reserve metabolism of reserve materials in microorganisms. *J. theor. Biol.* **56**, 19–55.

PASCIAK, W. J. & GAVIS, G. (1974). Transport limitation of nutrient uptake in phytoplankton. *Limnol. Oceanogr.* **19**, 881–888.

PETERS, R. H. (1983). *The Ecological Implications of Body Size*. Cambridge: University Press.

RAMUS, J. (1978). Seaweed anatomy and photosynthetic performance: the ecological significance of light guides, heterogeneous absorption and multiple scatter. *J. Phycol.* **14**, 353–362.

RAMUS, J., BEALE, S. I., MAUZERALL, D. & HOWARD, K. L. (1976*a*). Changes in photosynthetic pigment concentration in seaweeds as a function of water depth. *Mar. Biol* **37**, 223–229.

RAMUS, J., BEALE, S. I. & MAUZERALL, D. (1976*b*). Correlation of changes in pigment content with photosynthetic capacity of seaweeds as a function of water depth. *Mar. Biol.* **37**, 231–238.

RAMUS, J., LEMONS, F. & ZIMMERMAN, C. (1977). Adaptation of light-harvesting pigments to downwelling light and consequent photosynthetic performance of the eulittoral rockweeds *Ascophyllum nodosum* and *Fucus vesiculosus*. *Mar. Biol.* **42**, 293–304.

RAVEN, J. A. (1976). Division of labour between chloroplasts and cytoplasm. In *The Intact Chloroplast* (ed. J. Barber), pp. 403–443. Amsterdam: Elsevier.

RAVEN, J. A. (1980). Nutrient transport in micro-algae. *Adv. microb. Physiol.* **21**, 47–226.

RAVEN, J. A. (1981). Nutritional strategies of submerged benthic plants: the acquisition of C, N and P by rhizophytes and haptophytes. *New Phytol.* **88**, 1–30.

RAVEN, J. A. (1984*a*). *Energetics and Transport in Aquatic Plants.* New York: A. R. Liss.

RAVEN, J. A. (1984*b*). A cost-benefit analysis of photon absorption by photosynthetic unicells. *New Phytol.* **98**, 593–625.

RAVEN, J. A. (1985). The CO_2 concentrating mechanism. In *Inorganic Carbon Uptake by Aquatic Photosynthetic Organisms* (ed. W. J. Lucas & J. A. Berry). pp. 67–82. Rockville, Maryland: American Society of Plant Physiologists.

RAVEN, J. A. (1986*a*). Biochemistry biophysics and physiology of chlorophyll b-containing algae: implications for taxonomy and phylogeny. *Progr. Phycol. Res.* **5**. (In press.)

RAVEN, J. A. (1986*b*). Evolution of plant life forms. In *On the Economy of Plant Form and Function* (ed. T. Givnish). pp. 421–492 Cambridge: University Press.

RAVEN, J. A. (1986*c*). Limits to growth. In *Microalgal Biotechnology* (ed. M. A. Borowitzka & L. J. Borowitzka). Cambridge: University Press. (In press.)

RAVEN, J. A. & LUCAS, W. J. (1985). The energetics of carbon acquisition. In *Inorganic Carbon Uptake by Aquatic Photosynthetic Organisms* (ed. W. J. Lucas & J. A. Berry), pp. 305–324. Rockville, Maryland: American Society of Plant Physiologists.

RAVEN, J. A., OSBORNE, B. A. & JOHNSTON, A. M. (1985). Uptake of CO_2 by aquatic vegetation. *Plant, Cell Environ.* **8**, 417–425.

RAVEN, J. A. & RICHARDSON, K. (1986). Photosynthesis in marine environments. In *Photosynthesis in Specific Environments* (ed. N. R. Baker & S. P. Long). Amsterdam: Elsevier. (In press.)

RETHY, R. (1968). Red (R), far-red (FR) photoreversible effects on the growth of *Chara* sporelings. *Z. Pflanzenphysiol.* **59**, 100–102.

RICHARDSON, K., BEARDALL, J. & RAVEN, J. A. (1983). Adaptation of unicellular algae to irradiance: an analysis of strategies. *New Phytol.* **93**, 157–191.

SALVUCCI, M. E. & BOWES, G. (1981). Induction of reduced photorespiratory activity in submersed and amphibious aquatic macrophytes. *Pl. Physiol.* **67**, 335–340.

SCHLESINGER, D. A., MOLOT, L. A. & SHUTER, B. J. (1981). Specific growth rates of freshwater algae in relation to cell size and light intensity. *J. Fish. Res. Bd. Can.* **36**, 1052–1058.

SCHLESINGER, D. A. & SHUTER, B. J. (1981). Patterns of growth and cell composition of freshwater algae in light-limited continuous cultures. *J. Phycol.* **17**, 240–256.

SCHMIDT-NIELSEN, K. (1984). *Scaling: Why is Animal Size so Important?* Cambridge: University Press.

SENGER, H. (1980) (ed.). *The Blue Light Syndrome.* Berlin: Springer.

SHUTER, B. (1979). A model of physiological adaptation in unicellular algae. *J. theor. Biol.* **78**, 519–552.

SMITH, F. A. (1985). Biological occurrence and importance of HCO_3^- utilizing systems: macroalgae (Charophytes). In *Inorganic Carbon Uptake by Aquatic Photosynthetic Organisms* (ed. W. J. Lucas & J. A. Berry). pp. 111–124. Rockville, Maryland: American Society of Plant Physiologists.

SPENCE, D. H. N., BARCLAY, A. M. & ALLEN, E. D. (1985). Limnology and macrophyte vegetation of a deep, clear limestone lake, Loch Borralie. *Bot. Soc. Edinb. Trans.* **44**, 187–204.

SYRETT, P. J. & AL-HOUTY, F. A. A. (1984). The phylogenetic significance of the occurrence of urease/urea amidolyase and glycollate oxidase/dehydrogenase in green algae. *Br. Phycol. J.* **19**, 11–21.

TERBORGH, J. W. & THIMANN, K. V. (1964). Interactions between daylength and light intensity in the growth and light chlorophyll content of *Acetabularia crenata. Planta* **63**, 89–98.

THORNLEY, J. M. M. (1972). A balanced quantitative model for root : shoot ratios in vegetative plants. *Ann. Bot.* **36**, 431–441.

THORNLEY, J. H. M. (1977). Interpretation of shoot : root relations. *Ann. Bot.* **41**, 461–464.

VINCENT, W. F. (1980*a*). The physiological ecology of a *Scenedesmus* population in the hypolimnion of a hypertrophic pond. I. Photoautotrophy. *Br. phycol. J.* **15**, 27–44.

VINCENT, W. F. (1980*b*). The physiological ecology of a *Scenedesmus* population in the hypolimnion of a hypertrophic pond. II. Heterotrophy. *Br. phycol. J.* **15**, 35–41.

WERNER, D. (1971). Der Entwicklungscyclus mit sexualphase ber der marinen Diatomee *Coscinodiscus asteromphalus*. I. Kultur und Synchronisation von Entwicklungsstadien. *Arch. Mikrobiol.* **80**, 43–49.

WHITTENBURY, R. & KELLY, D. P. (1977). Autotrophy: a conceptual phoenix. *Symp. Soc. gen. Microbiol.* **27**, 121–149.

WILLIAMS, S. L. (1984). Uptake of sediment ammonium and translocation in a marine green macroalga *Caulerpa cupressoides*. *Limnol. Oceanogr.* **29**, 374–379.

WILLIAMS, S. L. & FISHER, T. R. (1985). Kinetics of nitrogen-15 labelled ammonium uptake by *Caulerpa cupressoides* (Chlorophyta). *J. Phycol.* **21**, 287–296.

INDEX OF AUTHORS

INDEX OF SUBJECTS